Fourteenth Edition

CULTURAL ANTHROPOLOGY

THE HUMAN CHALLENGE

WILLIAM A. HAVILAND
Professor Emeritus, University of Vermont

HARALD E. L. PRINS
Kansas State University

BUNNY McBRIDE
Kansas State University

DANA WALRATH
University of Vermont

 **WADSWORTH**
CENGAGE Learning·

Australia • Brazil • Japan • Korea • Mexico • Singapore • Spain • United Kingdom • United States

Cultural Anthropology: The Human Challenge,
Fourteenth Edition
**William A. Haviland, Harald E. L. Prins,
Bunny McBride, Dana Walrath**

Publisher: Yolanda Cossio

Senior Acquisitions Editor: Aileen Berg

Senior Developmental Editor: Lin Gaylord

Assistant Editor: Margaux Cameron

Editorial Assistant: Victor Luu

Media Editor: John Chell

Senior Brand Manager: Liz Rhoden

Senior Market Development Manager: Michelle Williams

Senior Content Project Manager: Cheri Palmer

Senior Art Director: Caryl Gorska

Manufacturing Planner: Judy Inouye

Rights Acquisitions Specialist: Don Schlotman

Production Service: Joan Keyes, Dovetail Publishing Services

Photo Researcher: Sarah Evertson

Text Researcher: Sarah D'Stair

Copy Editor: Jennifer Gordon

Text Designer: Lisa Buckley

Cover Designer: Larry Didona

Cover Image: Reclining Buddha, Isunumuni Raja Hama Viharaya, Anuradhapura, Sri Lanka: Keren Su. / Satellite communications disk outside yurt, Mongolia: Bill Bachmann. / Naxi calligrapher and pictogram scholar, The Museum of Naxi Culture, Lijiang: Dave Bartruff. / Globe image: Ocean. / Bull race, West Sumatra Province, Indonesia: Fadil. / !Kung women, Africa: Nigel Pavitt. / Stilt Fishermen, Sri Lanka: Dallas and John Heaton.

Compositor: PreMediaGlobal

For product information and technology assistance, contact us at
Cengage Learning Customer & Sales Support, 1-800-354-9706.
For permission to use material from this text or product,
submit all requests online at **www.cengage.com/permissions.**
Further permissions questions can be e-mailed to
permissionrequest@cengage.com.

Library of Congress Control Number: 2012949884

Student Edition:
ISBN-13: 978-1-133-95742-3
ISBN-10: 1-133-95742-0

Loose-leaf Edition:
ISBN-13: 978-1-133-95597-9
ISBN-10: 1-133-95597-5

Wadsworth
20 Davis Drive
Belmont, CA 94002-3098
USA

Cengage Learning is a leading provider of customized learning solutions with office locations around the globe, including Singapore, the United Kingdom, Australia, Mexico, Brazil, and Japan. Locate your local office at **www.cengage.com/global.**

Cengage Learning products are represented in Canada by Nelson Education, Ltd.

To learn more about Wadsworth, visit **www.cengage.com/wadsworth**
Purchase any of our products at your local college store or at our preferred online store **www.cengagebrain.com.**

Printed in the United States of America
2 3 4 5 6 7 17 16 15 14 13

DEDICATION

To the applied anthropologists of the world, in particular

Ann Dunham (1942–1995), a rural Asia development specialist

who embraced the common humanity in cultural differences. Born in Kansas,

she was a global citizen who committed her scholarship to assisting the

poor in adapting to radical change in the Third World. She was the

mother of the 44th president of the United States.

Putting the World in Perspective

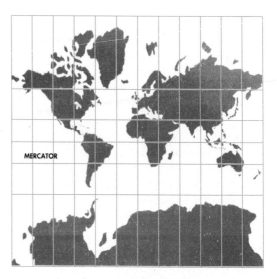

Although all humans we know about are capable of producing accurate sketches of localities and regions with which they are familiar, **cartography** (the craft of mapmaking as we know it today) had its beginnings in 16th-century Europe, and its subsequent development is related to the expansion of Europeans to all parts of the globe. From the beginning, there have been two problems with maps: the technical one of how to depict on a two-dimensional, flat surface a three-dimensional spherical object, and the cultural one of whose worldview they reflect. In fact, the two issues are inseparable, for the particular projection one uses inevitably makes a statement about how one views one's own people and their place in the world. Indeed, maps often shape our perception of reality as much as they reflect it.

In cartography, a **projection** refers to the system of intersecting lines (of longitude and latitude) by which part or all of the globe is represented on a flat surface. There are more than a hundred different projections in use today, ranging from polar perspectives to interrupted "butterflies" to rectangles to heart shapes. Each projection causes distortion in size, shape, or distance in some way or another. A map that correctly shows the shape of a landmass will of necessity misrepresent the size. A map that is accurate along the equator will be deceptive at the poles.

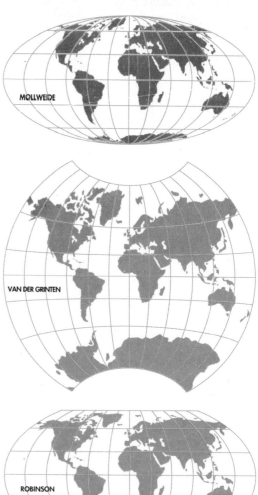

Perhaps no projection has had more influence on the way we see the world than that of Gerhardus Mercator, who devised his map in 1569 as a navigational aid for mariners. So well suited was Mercator's map for this purpose that it continues to be used for navigational charts today. At the same time, the Mercator projection became a standard for depicting landmasses, something for which it was never intended. Although an accurate navigational tool, the Mercator projection greatly exaggerates the size of landmasses in higher latitudes, giving about two-thirds of the map's surface to the northern hemisphere. Thus the lands occupied by Europeans and European descendants appear far larger than those of other people. For example, North America (19 million square kilometers) appears almost twice the size of Africa (30 million square kilometers), whereas Europe is shown as equal in size to South America, which actually has nearly twice the landmass of Europe.

A map developed in 1805 by Karl B. Mollweide was one of the earlier *equal-area projections* of the world. Equal-area projections portray landmasses in correct relative size, but, as a result, distort the shape of continents more than other projections. They most often compress and warp lands in the higher latitudes and vertically stretch landmasses close to the equator. Other equal-area projections include the Lambert Cylindrical Equal-Area Projection (1772), the Hammer Equal-Area Projection (1892), and the Eckert Equal-Area Projection (1906).

The Van der Grinten Projection (1904) was a compromise aimed at minimizing both the distortions of size in the Mercator and the distortion of shape in equal-area maps such as the Mollweide. Although an improvement, the lands of the northern hemisphere are still emphasized at the expense of the southern. For example, in the Van der Grinten, the Commonwealth of Independent States (the former Soviet Union) and Canada are shown at more than twice their relative size.

The Robinson Projection, which was adopted by the National Geographic Society in 1988 to replace the Van der Grinten, is one of the best compromises to date between the distortions of size and shape. Although an improvement over the Van der Grinten, the Robinson Projection still depicts lands in the northern latitudes as proportionally larger at the same time that it depicts lands in the lower latitudes (representing most Third World nations) as proportionally smaller. Like European maps before it, the Robinson Projection places Europe at the center of the map with the Atlantic Ocean and the Americas to the left, emphasizing the cultural connection between Europe and North America, while neglecting the geographic closeness of northwestern North America to northeastern Asia.

The following pages show four maps that each convey quite different cultural messages. Included among them is the Peters Projection, an equal-area map that has been adopted as the official map of UNESCO (the United Nations Educational, Scientific, and Cultural Organization), and a map made in Japan, showing us how the world looks from the other side.

The Robinson Projection

The map below is based on the Robinson Projection, which is used today by the National Geographic Society and Rand McNally. Although the Robinson Projection distorts the relative size of landmasses, it does so much less than most other projections. Still, it places Europe at the center of the map. This particular view of the world has been used to identify the location of many of the cultures discussed in this text.

The Peters Projection

The map below is based on the Peters Projection, which has been adopted as the official map of UNESCO. Although it distorts the shape of continents (countries near the equator are vertically elongated by a ratio of 2 to 1), the Peters Projection does show all continents according to their correct relative size. Though Europe is still at the center, it is not shown as larger and more extensive than the Third World.

Japanese Map

Not all maps place Europe at the center of the world, as this Japanese map illustrates. Besides reflecting the importance the Japanese attach to themselves in the world, this map has the virtue of showing the geographic proximity of North America to Asia, a fact easily overlooked when maps place Europe at their center.

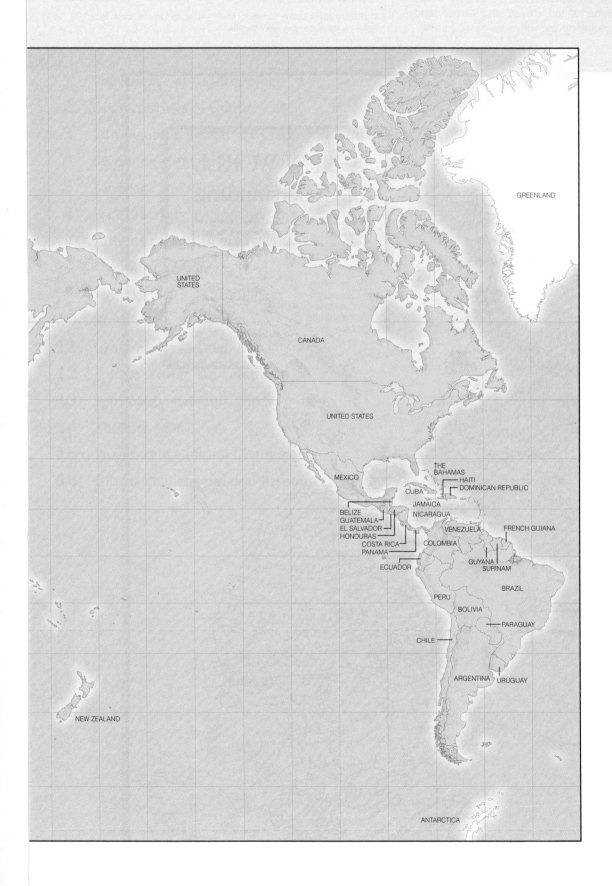

GREENLAND

UNITED STATES

CANADA

UNITED STATES

MEXICO

THE BAHAMAS

HAITI
DOMINICAN REPUBLIC
CUBA
JAMAICA

BELIZE
GUATEMALA
EL SALVADOR
HONDURAS
NICARAGUA

COSTA RICA
PANAMA

VENEZUELA

FRENCH GUIANA

COLOMBIA

GUYANA
SURINAM

ECUADOR

BRAZIL

PERU

BOLIVIA

PARAGUAY

CHILE

ARGENTINA
URUGUAY

NEW ZEALAND

ANTARCTICA

Features Contents

Contents

Veronique de Viguerie/Getty Images

Chapter 4
Becoming Human: The Origin and Diversity of Our Species   72

Chapter 5
Language and Communication   102

Chapter 6
Social Identity, Personality, and Gender   126

Chapter 7
Patterns of Subsistence   150

Chapter 8
Economic Systems   174

© Harald E. L. Prins

Chapter 9
Sex, Marriage, and Family **198**

Chapter 10
Kinship and Descent **224**

Chapter 11
Grouping by Gender, Age, Common Interest, and Social Status **246**

Chapter 12
Politics, Power, War, and Peace 266

Chapter 13
Spirituality, Religion, and Shamanism 296

Preface

There comes a time when we need to clean out the basement—to sort through the piles clear down to the bottom, to determine what should be kept and what should be tossed, to make room for new things that warrant a place in a limited space. That's what has happened with this edition of *Cultural Anthropology: The Human Challenge*—more thoroughly revised than any new edition since Bill Haviland took on coauthors a dozen years ago.

Fueled by our own ongoing research, along with vital feedback from students and anthropology professors who have used and reviewed previous editions, we have scrutinized the archetypal examples of our discipline and weighed them against the latest innovative research methodologies, archaeological discoveries, genetic and other biological findings, linguistic insights, ethnographic descriptions, theoretical revelations, and significant examples of applied anthropology. We believe that these considerations, combined with paying attention to compelling issues in our global theater, have resulted in a lively and relevant textbook that presents both classical and fresh material in ways that stimulate student interest, stir critical reflection, and prompt "ah-ha" moments.

Our Mission

Most students enter an introductory anthropology class intrigued by the general subject but with little more than a vague sense of what it is all about. Thus, the first and most obvious task of our text is to provide a thorough introduction to the discipline—its foundations as a domain of knowledge and its major insights into the rich diversity of humans as a culture-making species. Recognizing the wide spectrum of students enrolled in entry-level anthropology courses, we cover the fundamentals of the discipline in an engaging, illustrative fashion—creating a textbook that establishes a broad platform on which teachers can expand the exploration of concepts and topics in ways that are particularly meaningful to them and their students.

In doing this, we draw from the research and ideas of a number of traditions of anthropological thought, exposing students to a mix of theoretical perspectives and methodologies. Such inclusiveness reflects our conviction that different approaches offer distinctly important insights about human biology, behavior, and beliefs.

If most students start out with only a vague sense of what anthropology is, they often have even less clearly defined—and potentially problematic—views concerning the position of their own species and cultures within the larger world. A second task for this text, then, is to encourage students to appreciate the richness and complexity of human diversity. Along with this goal is the aim of helping them to understand why there are so many differences and similarities in the human condition, past and present.

Debates regarding globalization and notions of progress; the "naturalness" of the mother, father, child(ren) nuclear family; new genetic technologies; and how gender roles relate to biological variation all benefit greatly from the distinct insights gained through anthropology's wide-ranging, holistic perspective. This aspect of the discipline is one of the most valuable gifts we can pass on to those who take our classes. If we as teachers (and textbook authors) do our jobs well, students will gain a wider and more open-minded outlook on the world and a critical but constructive perspective on human origins and on their own biology and culture today. To borrow a favorite line from the famous poet T. S. Eliot, we'll know we've reached the end of our journey when we "arrive where we started/And know the place for the first time" ("Little Gidding" from *The Four Quartets*).

We have written this text, in large part, to help students make sense of our increasingly complex world and to navigate through its interrelated biological and cultural networks with knowledge and skill, whatever professional path they take. We see the book as a guide for people entering the often-bewildering maze of global crossroads in the 21st century.

Organization and Unifying Themes of the Book

In our own teaching, we recognize the value of marking out unifying themes that help students see the big picture as they grapple with the vast array of material involved with the study of human beings. In *Cultural Anthropology: The Human Challenge* we employ three such themes.

1. ***Systemic adaptation.*** We emphasize that every culture, past and present, like the human species itself, is an integrated and dynamic system of adaptation that responds to a combination

of internal and external factors, including influences of the environment.

2. ***Biocultural connection.*** We highlight the integration of human culture and biology in the steps humans take to meet the challenges of survival. The biocultural connection theme is interwoven throughout the text—as a thread in the main narrative and in boxed features that highlight this connection with a topical example for nearly every chapter.

3. ***Globalization.*** We track the emergence of globalization and its disparate impact on various peoples and cultures around the world. European colonization was a global force for centuries, leaving a significant and often devastating footprint on the affected peoples in Asia, Africa, and the Americas. Decolonization began about 200 years ago and became a worldwide wave in the mid-1900s. However, since the 1960s, political and economic hegemony has taken a new and fast-paced form: globalization (in many ways a process that expands or builds on imperialism). Attention to both forms of global domination—colonialism and globalization—runs through *Cultural Anthropology: The Human Challenge,* culminating in the final chapter where we apply the concept of structural power to globalization, discussing it in terms of hard and soft power and linking it to structural violence.

Pedagogy

Cultural Anthropology: The Human Challenge features a range of learning aids, in addition to the three unifying themes described previously. Each pedagogical piece plays an important role in the learning process—from clarifying and enlivening the material to revealing relevancy and aiding recall.

Accessible Language and a Cross-Cultural Voice

In the writing of this text, we consciously cut through unnecessary jargon to speak directly to students. Manuscript reviewers have recognized this, noting that even the most difficult concepts are presented in straightforward and understandable prose for today's first- and second-year college students. Where technical terms are necessary, they appear in bold type with a clear definition in the narrative. The definition appears again in the running glossary at the bottom of our pages, and again in a summary glossary at the end of the book.

To make the narrative more accessible to students, we deliver it in chewable bites—short paragraphs. Numerous subheads provide visual cues to help students track what has been read and what is coming next.

Accessibility involves not only clear writing enhanced by visual cues, but also an engaging voice or style. The voice of *Cultural Anthropology: The Human Challenge* is distinct among introductory texts in the discipline because it has been written from a cross-cultural perspective. We avoid the typical Western "we/they" voice in favor of a more inclusive one to make sure the narrative resonates with both Western and non-Western students and professors. Also, we highlight the theories and work of anthropologists from all over the world. Finally, we have drawn the text's cultural examples from industrial and postindustrial societies as well as nonindustrial ones.

Compelling Visuals

The Haviland et al. texts garner praise from students and faculty for having a rich array of visuals, including maps, photographs, and figures. This is important because humans—like all primates—are visually oriented, and a well-chosen image may serve to "fix" key information in a student's mind. Unlike some competing texts, all of our visuals are in color, enhancing their appeal and impact. Notably, all maps and figures are created with a colorblind-sensitive palette.

Photographs

Our pages feature a hard-sought collection of compelling, content-rich photographs. Large in size, many of them come with substantial captions composed to help students do a "deep read" of the image. Each chapter features more than a dozen pictures, including our popular Visual Counterpoints—side-by-side photos that effectively compare and contrast biological or cultural features.

Maps

Map features include our "Putting the World in Perspective" map series, locator maps, and distribution maps that provide overviews of key issues such as pollution and energy consumption. Of special note are the Globalscape maps and stories, described in the boxed features section a bit farther on.

Challenge Issues

Each chapter opens with a Challenge Issue and accompanying photograph, which together carry forward the book's theme of humankind's responses through time to the fundamental challenges of survival within the context of the particular chapter.

Student Learning Objectives, Knowledge Skills, and Chapter Checklist

New to this edition is the set of learning objectives presented at the start of every chapter just after the Challenge Issue and photograph. These objectives focus students on the main goals, identifying the knowledge skills they are expected to have mastered after studying each chapter. The main goals are incorporated in a closing Chapter Checklist, which is also new to this edition. The Chapter Checklist summarizes the chapter's content in an easy-to-follow format.

Thought-Provoking Questions

Each chapter closes with five Questions for Reflection, including one that relates back to the Challenge Issue introduced in the chapter's opening. Presented right after the Chapter Checklist, these questions ask students to apply the concepts they have learned by analyzing and evaluating situations. They are designed to stimulate and deepen thought, trigger class discussion, and link the material to the students' own lives.

In addition, the Biocultural Connection essay featured in nearly every chapter ends with a probing question designed to help students grapple with and firmly grasp that connection.

Barrel Model of Culture

Past and present, every culture is an integrated and dynamic system of adaptation that responds to a combination of internal and external factors. This is illustrated by a pedagogical device we refer to as the "barrel model" of culture. Depicted in a simple but telling drawing (Figure 2.8), the barrel model shows the interrelatedness of social, ideological, and economic factors within a cultural system along with outside influences of environment, climate, and other societies. Throughout the book examples are linked to this point and this image.

Integrated Gender Coverage

In contrast to many introductory texts, *Cultural Anthropology The Human Challenge* integrates coverage of gender throughout the book. Thus, material on gender-related issues is included in *every* chapter. As a result of this approach, gender-related material in *Cultural Anthropology* far exceeds the single chapter that most books devote to the subject.

We have chosen to integrate this material because concepts and issues surrounding gender are almost always too complicated to remove from their context.

Spreading this material through all of the chapters has a pedagogical purpose because it emphasizes how considerations of gender enter into virtually everything people do. Gender-related material ranges from discussions of gender roles in evolutionary discourse and studies of nonhuman primates to intersexuality, homosexual identity, same-sex marriage, and female genital mutilation. Through a steady drumbeat of such coverage, this edition avoids ghettoizing gender to a single chapter that is preceded and followed by resounding silence.

Glossary as You Go

The running glossary is designed to catch the student's eye, reinforcing the meaning of each newly introduced term. It is also useful for chapter review, enabling students to readily isolate the new terms from those introduced in earlier chapters. A complete glossary is also included at the back of the book. In the glossaries, each term is defined in clear, understandable language. As a result, less class time is required for going over terms, leaving instructors free to pursue other matters of interest.

Special Boxed Features

Our text includes five types of special boxed features. Nearly every chapter contains a Biocultural Connection, along with two of the following three features: an Original Study, Anthropology Applied, and Anthropologist of Note. In addition, about half of the chapters include a Globalscape. These features are carefully placed and introduced within the main narrative to alert students to their importance and relevance. A complete listing of features is presented just before the detailed table of contents.

Biocultural Connection

Appearing in nearly every chapter, this signature feature of the Haviland et al. textbooks illustrates how cultural and biological processes interact to shape human biology, beliefs, and behavior. It reflects the integrated biocultural approach central to the field of anthropology today. All of the Biocultural Connections include a critical thinking question. For a quick peek at titles, see the listing of features on page xiv.

Original Study

Written expressly for this text, or adapted from ethnographies and other original works by anthropologists, these studies present concrete examples that bring specific concepts to life and convey the passion of the authors. Each study sheds additional light on an important anthropological concept or subject area for the chapter in which it appears. Notably, each Original Study is carefully integrated within the flow of the chapter narrative, signaling students that its content is not extraneous or supplemental. Appearing in eleven chapters, Original Studies cover a wide range of topics, evident from their titles (see page xiv).

Anthropology Applied

Featured in eleven chapters, these succinct and fascinating profiles illustrate anthropology's wide-ranging relevance in today's world and give students a glimpse into a variety of the careers anthropologists enjoy (see page xiv for a listing).

Anthropologists of Note

Profiling pioneering and contemporary anthropologists from many corners of the world, this feature puts the work of noted anthropologists in historical perspective and draws attention to the international nature of the discipline in terms of both subject matter and practitioners. This edition highlights fourteen distinct anthropologists from all four fields of the discipline (see page xiv for a list of the profiles).

Globalscape

Appearing in eight chapters, this unique feature charts the global flow of people, goods, and services, as well as pollutants and pathogens. With a map, a story, and a photo highlighting a topic geared toward student interests, every Globalscape shows how the world is interconnected through human activity. Each one ends with a Global Twister—a question that prods students to think critically about globalization. Check out the titles of Globalscapes on page xiv.

Changes and Highlights in the Fourteenth Edition

We have extensively reworked and updated this edition. Definitions of key terms have been honed. Many new visuals and ethnographic examples have been added and others dropped. Every chapter features a new opening photograph and related Challenge Issue that is revised or new. The much-used Questions for Reflection include at least one new question per chapter, plus revisions of effective questions that have been included in previous editions.

As with earlier editions, we further chiseled the writing to make it all the more clear, lively, engaging, and streamlined. On average, chapter narratives have been trimmed by about 10 percent.

New to this edition is the list of student learning objectives at the start of every chapter, tied to the new

Chapter Checklists at the end of every chapter. (Both are described in the pedagogy inventory mentioned earlier.)

In addition to numerous revisions of boxed features, some of these are completely new, including the Biocultural Connection "Modifying the Human Body"; the Original Study "Can Chantek Talk in Codes?" by H. Lyn White Miles; an Anthropology Applied essay, "Anthropologist S. Ann Dunham, Mother to a U.S. President" by Nancy I. Cooper; and Anthropologist of Note profiles on paleogenetics expert Svante Pääbo and shamanic scholar-practitioner Michael Harner.

Finally, we have replaced footnotes with in-text parenthetical citations, making sources and dates more visible and freeing up space for larger visuals. The complete citations appear in the references section at the end of the book.

Beyond these across-the-board changes, significant changes have been made within each chapter.

Chapter 1: The Essence of Anthropology

This chapter gives students a broad-stroke introduction to the holistic discipline of anthropology, the distinct focus of each of its fields, and the common philosophical perspectives and methodological approaches they share. It opens with a new Challenge Issue centered on the mining of coltan—the key component of capacitors in small electronic devices—illustrating our globalized world by revealing the link between the miners and students who use the devices. The lead section on the development of anthropology has been dropped to avoid redundancy with the chapter on ethnographic research. The main narrative now begins with a reworked explanation of the anthropological perspective. As revised, this discussion more carefully contrasts anthropology to other disciplines.

The chapter also offers a brief overview of fieldwork and the comparative method, along with ethical issues and examples of applied anthropology in all four fields, providing a foundation for our two methods chapters—one that explores field methods in cultural anthropology and the other that examines the tools for studying the past shared by archaeology and paleoanthropology. Our presentation of the four fields has been reorganized, starting with cultural anthropology, followed by linguistics, archaeology, and physical or biological anthropology.

This chapter's overview of cultural anthropology has been substantially modified. Changes include a new discussion about how the concept of culture is integral to each of anthropology's four fields. To our narrative on the University of Arizona's modern-day Garbage Project, we added an introductory paragraph about anthropologists studying older garbage dumps, such as shell middens, describing how much these explorations can reveal about everyday life in societies past and present.

The chapter also introduces the concept of ethnocentrism and begins a discussion of globalization that is woven through the text. In addition, this first chapter rejects the characterization of a liberal bias in anthropology, identifying instead the discipline's critical evaluation of the status quo. The ideological diversity among anthropologists is explored while emphasizing their shared methodology that avoids ethnocentrism.

Finally, Chapter 1 introduces the five types of special boxed features that appear in the text, describing the purpose of each, along with an example: a Biocultural Connection on the anthropology of organ transplantation; a Globalscape about the global trafficking of human organs; an Original Study on traditional African healers dealing with HIV/AIDS; an Anthropology Applied about forensic anthropology's role in speaking for the dead; and an Anthropologists of Note profiling two of the discipline's pioneers: Franz Boas and Matilda Coxe Stevenson.

Chapter 2: Characteristics of Culture

This chapter addresses anthropology's core concept of culture, exploring the term and its significance for human individuals and societies. It begins with a new Challenge Issue centered on Kuchi nomads in Afghanistan, easily recognized by their distinctive dress.

As with previous editions, this chapter presents our original "barrel model" illustration, showing the integrative and dynamic nature of culture and introducing the key concepts of the integration of cultural infrastructure, social structure, and superstructure. Subcultures are explored through an ethnographic example of the Amish of North America, and our discussion of ethnicity is illustrated with a map of China's ethnic groups and a photo of the Uyghur. Culture's role in dealing with major issues such as death features a description of cremation rituals in Bali.

As for changes, the section on culture and adaptation has been moved to the beginning of the chapter, setting the foundation for our discussion of culture and its characteristics. As part of the culture and change section, we have added a new discussion distinguishing cultural change from other kinds of change in an individual's life; as well, we have expanded the section on ethnocentrism and reconfigured it into two distinct sections, "Ethnocentrism and Cultural Relativism" and "Evaluation of Cultures." Striking new photographs have been added, along with captions rich with ethnographic detail: a living root bridge in India, a Sri Lankan father teaching his son to stilt fish, Kapauku villagers and their pigs in New Guinea.

Also new is a Biocultural Connection about human body modifications—from tattoos to circumcision, footbinding, and modern cosmetic surgery. George Esber updated the Anthropology Applied feature about his role in helping to design culturally appropriate homes on the Apache Indian reservation. Finally, the Anthropologist of Note profile on Bronislaw Malinowski has been trimmed in half.

Chapter 3: Ethnographic Research: Its History, Methods, and Theories

This chapter takes a unique approach to discussing ethnographic research. It begins with a historical overview on the subject—from the colonial era and salvage ethnography to acculturation studies, advocacy anthropology, and multi-sited ethnography in the era of globalization. We use the work of numerous anthropologists, past and present, to illustrate this historical journey.

The chapter continues with an overview of research methods—marking out what is involved in choosing a research question and site and how one goes about doing preparatory research and participant observation. This section also covers ethnographic tools and aids, data-gathering methods, fieldwork challenges, and the creation of an ethnography in written, film, or digital formats. Readers will also find an overview of anthropology's theoretical perspectives, along with discussions of the comparative method and the Human Relations Area Files, and the moral dilemmas and ethical responsibilities encountered in anthropological research.

Changes in this chapter include new discussions and photos touching on cyberethnography and dangerous anthropology, and a Visual Counterpoint illustrating multi-sited ethnographic research. Annette Weiner's Original Study on fieldwork in the Trobriand Islands has been shortened.

Chapter 4: Becoming Human: The Origin and Diversity of Our Species

This chapter plays a key role in our effort to convey biology's role in culture. It opens with a dramatic new photo of an Australian Aborigine in a cave, touching an ancient image of a hand painted on the rock wall. The accompanying new Challenge Issue raises questions about the origin and evolution of our species, our biological relationship with other primates, as well as our material remains, including fossil bones, tools, and art.

We establish mammalian primate biology as a vital part of being human, bypassing the terms *hominid* and *hominin* to avoid losing students in scientific debates of alternate taxonomies. We provide a brief overview of the evolution and spread of *Homo*, along with a discussion of some of the controversial issues of that development. We note the contrasting roles of primatologists, paleontologists, geneticists, and molecular biologists, in piecing together the complex story of how humans evolved and adapted to radically different natural environments over thousands of generations. In addition to brief mention of the mapping of the *Homo sapiens* genome, the chapter's new Anthropologists of Note profile about paleogeneticist Svante Pääbo touches the Neadertal genome and news of the Neandertal's recently discovered Siberian "cousin," the Denisovan.

We discuss why the concept of race is not useful for studying human biological variation, presenting a historical overview on the creation of false racial categories. We review anthropology's contributions to debunking race as a biological category, starting with the work of Franz Boas and Ashley Montagu and emphasizing the interaction of cultural and biological influences on humans. We also explore race as a social construct and skin color as a biological adaptation.

New visuals for this chapter include a painting depicting the moment when the Laetoli footprints were made; a photo of an artistic reconstruction of Neandertal made from the cast of a skull discovered in Dordogne, France; and a photo of 31,000-year-old cave wall paintings of Ice Age animals. The maps showing Australopithecine and *Homo erectus* fossil sites have been updated.

Special features include a Biocultural Connection, "Paleolithic Prescriptions for Diseases of Today"; Frans de Waal's Original Study, "Reconciliation and Its Cultural Modification in Primates"; and a new Anthropologists of Note box, pairing Jane Goodall, whose work illustrates traditional approaches to primate research, with Svante Pääbo, who epitomizes revolutionary microbiological approaches to the new field of paleogenetics.

Chapter 5: Language and Communication

This chapter investigates the nature of language and the three branches of linguistic anthropology—descriptive linguistics, historical linguistics, and the study of language in its social and cultural settings (sociolinguistics and ethnolinguistics). Also found here are sections on paralanguage and tonal languages, an exploration of talking drums and whistled speech. We have retooled the section on language and gender, and we have revised and retitled the body language section to "Nonverbal Communication" to make it a more fitting header for discussions on proxemics and kinesics.

Our discussion of language loss and revival includes a look at new technology used by linguistic anthropologists collaborating on field research with speakers of endangered Khoisan "click" languages in southern Africa. That section also includes the latest data on the digital divide and its impact on ethnic minority languages, plus an updated chart showing Internet language populations. A historical sketch about writing takes readers from traditional speech performatives and memory devices to Egyptian hieroglyphics to the conception and spread of the alphabet to the 2003 to 2012 Literacy Decade established by the United Nations. A section on literacy and modern telecommunication investigates issues of language in our globalized world.

Boxed features include S. Neyooxet Greymorning's Anthropology Applied essay on language revitalization, a revised Biocultural Connection on the biology of human speech, and a brand-new Original Study and photograph about Lyn Miles's linguistic research with an orangutan.

Chapter 6: Social Identity, Personality, and Gender

Looking at individual identity within a sociocultural context, this chapter surveys the concept of self, enculturation and the behavioral environment, social identity through personal naming, the development of personality, the concepts of group and modal personality, and the idea of national character. It begins with a Challenge Issue about how every society must teach its children the values, social codes, and skills that enable them to become contributing members in the community—illustrated with a new photo of a Khanty mother braiding her daughter's hair inside their tiny wooden home in Siberia.

Our revised investigation of naming practices includes new material on matronyms and teknonyms, the latter illustrated by a striking new photo of a Tuareg naming ceremony. The section on self and the behavioral environment features a new Visual Counterpoint contrasting an Inuit hunter in a sea kayak with an individual navigating cyberspace while waiting to board a plane in a crowded airport.

The heavily reworked discussion of dependence and independence training includes a new narrative and photograph describing interdependence training among the Beng of West Africa. And the section on group personality has a new photo of Yanomami men with a discussion of their masculine ideal of *waiteri*. The sections on alternative gender models and mental disorders across time and cultures have both been significantly revised and resequenced. For example, the former includes new information about five genders acknowledged by Bugis people of Indonesia, a new paragraph and photo about *hijras* in India, and a new photograph of intersexed Olympian track star Caster Semenya from South Africa.

R. K. Williamson's highly personal Original Study about intersexuality has been streamlined by half. Other special features include an Anthropologist of Note on Ruth Fulton Benedict and a Biocultural Connection about cross-cultural perspectives on psychosomatic symptoms and mental health.

Chapter 7: Patterns of Subsistence

Here we investigate the various ways humans meet their basic needs and how societies adapt through culture to the environment. We begin with a discussion of adaptation, followed by profiles on modes of subsistence in which we look at food-foraging and food-producing societies—pastoralism, crop cultivation, and industrialization. In this edition, chapter headings, along with the narratives they introduce, have been significantly revised to provide greater clarity and a consistent focus on how—across time, space, and cultures—food is obtained, produced, and distributed.

The section on adaptation and cultural evolution includes a new subsection recounting the latest ethnohistorical research on ecosystemic collapse on Rapa Nui, commonly known as Easter Island. A discussion of peasantry leads into an extensive narrative about large-scale industrial food production, using chickens as an example.

The chapter's boxed features include a shortened Original Study on slash-and-burn cultivation in the Amazon basin in Brazil and an Anthropology Applied piece about reviving ancient farming practices in Peru. New visuals accompany the Biocultural Connection on high-altitude subsistence in the Andes and the Globalscape on the international poultry industry. Finally, the conclusion summarizes the pros and cons of new subsistence strategies and technological innovations—how they impact different members of a society in the short and long run.

Chapter 8: Economic Systems

Beginning with a bold, ethnographically rich photo of the open market in Keren, Eritrea, this chapter presents a new, broad-stroke introductory discussion on economic anthropology. The chapter delves into the control of resources (natural, technological, labor) and labor division (by gender or age, through cooperation, or by task specialization). The labor division discussion includes compelling new photographs of child labor and women carrying firewood in Vietnam.

A section on distribution and exchange defines various forms of reciprocity (with a detailed and illustrated description of the Kula ring and a revised definition and new discussion of silent trade), along with redistribution and market exchange. The discussion on leveling mechanisms looks at the potlatch.

Our trimmed concluding section on local economies and global capitalism discusses guest laborers, the global tourism industry, the impact of mobile phones on small producers in remote areas, and genetically modified seeds developed and marketed worldwide—all indicating the economic opportunities

and challenges of our era. We also include a new section on the informal economy.

Boxed features in this chapter are a Biocultural Connection on chocolate, Amanda Stronza's Anthropology Applied piece on global ecotourism in Bolivia, and an Anthropologist of Note profile on Rosita Worl, a Tlingit activist.

Chapter 9: Sex, Marriage, and Family

Exploring the inseparable connections among sexual reproductive practices, marriage, family, and household, this chapter opens with a gorgeous new photo of a Muslim bride and her female relatives and friends displaying hands decorated with traditional henna designs. Particulars addressed in this chapter include the incest taboo, endogamy and exogamy, dowry and bridewealth, cousin marriage, same-sex marriage, divorce, residence patterns, and nonfamily households. Up-to-date definitions of *marriage, family, nuclear family*, and *extended family* encompass current real-life situations around the world.

We have reworked and reorganized this chapter's opening paragraphs on marriage and the regulation of sexual relations so they are more logically constructed and easier to follow. A new, recent example of Shariah law as it relates to women and adultery has been added, and the commentary about the relationship between such restrictive rules and the incidence of HIV/AIDS has been nuanced. A short, timely piece on the breakaway Mormon group, the Fundamentalist Church of Jesus of the Latter-Day Saints, has been added to the discussion of polygamy in the United States, along with new data on the decline of polygyny in sub-Saharan Africa.

New visuals include a striking photo of a polyandrous family in Nepal and a vibrant picture of a joyous gay wedding in Connecticut. In the section on residence patterns, we have added brief explanations of ambilocal and avunculocal, and we have fleshed out the section on divorce to clarify its broad impact and the most common reasons for divorce across cultures. Finally, we have revised the chapter's conclusion with new material sketching the impact of global capitalism, electronic communication, and transnationalism on love relations. We have also included new subheads marking the discussions of diversity in families (adoption and new reproductive technologies) and changes in households (migrant workforces).

Boxed features include an Anthropologist of Note box commemorating Claude Lévi-Strauss, Martin Ottenheimer's Biocultural Connection on marriage prohibitions in the United States, a Globalscape chronicling the blessings and issues of transnational adoption, and Serena Nanda's newly illustrated Original Study on arranged marriage in India.

Chapter 10: Kinship and Descent

Beginning with a new photograph showing the opening parade of a clan gathering in Scotland, this chapter marks out the various forms of descent groups and the role descent plays as an integrated feature in a cultural system. We present details and examples concerning lineages, clans, phratries, and moieties (highlighting Hopi Indian matriclans and Scottish highland patriclans, among others), followed by illustrated examples of a representative range of kinship systems and their kinship terminologies. The definition of the term *kinship* itself has been fine-tuned, and the chapter includes an entirely new section on bilateral kinship and the kindred.

This chapter offers ethnographic examples from the Han Chinese, the Maori of New Zealand, and the Canela Indians of Brazil; it also takes a look at diasporic communities in today's globalized world. A section entitled "Making Relatives" explores fictive kin and ritual adoption, illustrating that in cultures everywhere, people have developed ideas about how someone becomes "one of us." Also presented is a discussion of new reproductive technologies, touching on the mind-boggling array of reproductive possibilities and how they are impacting humanity's conceptions of what it means to be biologically related.

Boxed features include an Anthropology Applied piece on resolving Native American tribal membership disputes, a thought-provoking Original Study on honor killings among Turkish immigrants in the Netherlands, and a Biocultural Connection piece about ancient Maori mythical traditions that are now supported by genetic research.

Chapter 11: Grouping by Gender, Age, Common Interest, and Social Status

This much-revised chapter includes discussions of grouping by gender, age, common interest, and social status—starting with a vibrant photograph of Afghan horsemen playing *buzkashi*, their country's fiercely competitive national sport.

The section on age grouping features ethnographic material from the Mundurucu of Brazil and the Tiriki and Maasai of East Africa. Common-interest grouping examples range from the tattooed Yakuzas in Japan to "pink vigilantes" in India and members of the African diaspora in the United States. For the latter, we present new photos and narrative to tell the story of Ashanti migrants, whose locally elected chiefs in major U.S. cities are directly tied to the Ashanti kingdom's confederation in Ghana.

A new subsection titled "Associations in the Digital Age" describes rapid and widespread changes in social networking platforms across the globe. Our reconfigured section on social status indicators has been trimmed in half, and the section on social

mobility has a new paragraph leading into a radically revised Globalscape on sports. Changes in our section about grouping by social status include a new paragraph about ethnic minorities in the United States.

Other boxed features include archaeologist Michael Blakey's Biocultural Connection about the African Burial Ground Project in New York City and Susan Lees's Original Study on the Jewish *eruv*.

Chapter 12: Politics, Power, War, and Violence

Another heavily revised chapter, this one opens with a dramatic image of the Nigerian emir of Kano in a military parade during a festival ending the Muslim holy month of Ramadan. The lead paragraphs in the main narrative have been streamlined, defining power and introducing the concept of political organization. Looking at a range of uncentralized and centralized political systems, the chapter explores the question of power, the intersection of politics and religion, and issues of political leadership and gender.

The sections on bands, tribes, chiefdoms, and states have all been significantly revised—reorganized, tightened, and illustrated with adjusted or new ethnographic examples. For example, the Pashtun are now featured in the section on tribes, and the Kpelle chiefdom narrative carries readers from precolonial to contemporary times. The section on state offers a new definition of the term and updated examples. We also improved significantly our discussions and examples of political systems and authority, politics and religion, and politics and gender.

A new section titled "Cultural Controls in Maintaining Order" streamlines our discussion of cultural control and its two forms (self-control/internalized and social control/externalized), each illustrated with ethnographic examples. In a new subsection on social control through sanctions, we discuss informal and formal sanctions, with a simplified conversation about law as a formal sanction. We have also added another new subsection about witchcraft as a cultural control. In another new section, "Holding Trials, Settling Disputes, and Punishing Crimes," we contrast traditional kin-based approaches to those of politically centralized societies, ending with a discussion of restorative justice.

Also new is a section on the evolution of warfare, which looks at its development in chiefdoms and states, up through World War II, the Chinese civil war, and modern inventions in military technology. It features a new photo and substantive caption about drones. Another new section, "Ideologies of Aggression," discusses how religious motivations and ideological justifications are embedded in a society's worldview. Among the ethnographic examples is fresh material on the militant Christian cult in Uganda that led to Joseph Kony's Lord's Resistance Army.

Sections on genocide and today's armed conflicts have been simplified and trimmed by half, making room for a new section on peace through diplomacy. This addition explores sovereignty and diplomatic protocol across time and cultures, including the example of West Papua's independence struggle led by exiled leader Benny Wenda. In another new section we discuss the politics of nonviolence, offering brief profiles of movements led by Gandhi in India and Aung San Suu Kyi in Myanmar.

Boxed features include an Anthropologist of Note on Laura Nader, an Anthropology Applied piece on William Ury's work with dispute resolution, and a newly illustrated and updated Globalscape chronicling the surprising and complex economics behind piracy off the coast of Somalia.

Chapter 13: Spirituality, Religion, and Shamanism

This entirely revised chapter, rich with new visuals, opens with a Challenge Issue concerning humankind's need to make sense of our place in the universe, illustrated with a new photo showing a crowded pilgrimage to the shrine of the Virgin of Guadalupe, patron saint of Mexico.

The chapter narrative begins with a discussion of superstructure and worldview. Noting the distinction between spirituality and religion, we discuss the roles they play and the anthropological approach to studying them. We introduce myths and their role in mapping cosmology. Then we move on to discuss supernatural beings and spiritual forces—from gods and goddesses to ancestral spirits and the concepts of animism and animatism.

Next we mark out religious specialists. Starting with priests and priestesses, we explore spiritual lineages, describing with ethnographic examples four major ways of legitimizing religious leadership. Examples include the election of the Roman Catholic pope and the reincarnation of Buddhist lamas. Continuing our narrative on religious specialists, we discuss shamans and shamanic healing, introducing a new Anthropologist of Note profile on Michael Harner. Other boxed features include Hillary Crane's Biocultural Connection on masculinization of Taiwanese nuns and Bill Maurer's Original Study on Shariah banking.

In our section on ritual performances, we discuss taboos and cleansing ceremonies (noting the use of water, air, fire, and earth), rites of passage (describing the phases of separation, transition, and incorporation), rites of intensification, magic (imitative and contagious), divination (from geomancy to aeromancy, scapulamancy, chiromancy, and necromancy). A section on witchcraft offers a brief cross-cultural overview, followed by a more detailed description of Navajo skin-walkers. Next we explore sacred sites—from shrines to mountains—and the pilgrimages

(devotions in motion) they inspire. This includes a subsection on female saints, highlighting Marian devotions and Black Madonnas in particular. It also includes a discussion of desecration, past and present.

In the section on cultural dynamics, we explore religious and spiritual change, including revitalization movements and syncretic religions, focusing on Vodou in Haiti. Next we move on to religious pluralism and secularization, providing an overview of spirituality and religious practices today. The chapter concludes by noting that the anthropological study of religion is crucial to gaining an understanding of today's world.

Chapter 14: The Arts

This chapter begins with a Challenge Issue about articulating ideas and emotions through various art forms, illustrated by an arresting new photograph of Kayapo Indians in artful ceremonial paint and dress heading to a political protest aboard a bus. The chapter explores in detail three key categories of art—visual, verbal, and musical—illustrating what art can reveal and how it functions in societies.

We describe the distinctly holistic approach anthropologists bring to the study of art, noting the range of cultural insights art discloses—from kinship structures to social values, religious beliefs, and political ideas. We also explain the various approaches to analyzing art (such as aesthetic and interpretive) as they are applied to rock art in southern Africa. In the verbal arts section, we offer several ethnographic examples including the Abenaki creation myth of Tabaldak, one of many versions of the classic and culturally widespread father/son/donkey tale, and the popular Thanksgiving legend in the United States.

The section on music begins by stepping back in time to flutes made of bones from 42,000 years ago and whistles unearthed by archaeologists. Then we march forward to Abenaki shamans playing cedar flutes to summon game animals, traditional and new age shamans drumming to evoke trances, laborers on the edge of the Sahara working to the beat of a drum, and West African *griots* who recount their people's history through percussion and lyrics. Beyond such examples, this chapter discusses the elements of music, including tonality, rhythm, and melody. The chapter includes a Biocultural Connection about the role of peyote in Huichol art, Margo DeMello's newly illustrated Original Study on the modern tattoo community, and a Globalscape on artful West African coffins that are displayed in museums.

Closing out the chapter is Jennifer Sapiel Neptune's moving Anthropology Applied feature. It describes how endangered indigenous groups use aesthetic traditions as part of their cultural and economic survival strategy.

Chapter 15: Processes of Cultural Change

This chapter starts out with a Challenge Issue calling attention to the many changes people must confront, accompanied by a haunting photograph of Nenet reindeer herders in Siberia facing the undoing of their age-old habitat due to the exploration, extraction, and exportation of natural gas.

The themes and terminology of globalization are woven through this chapter, which includes definitions that distinguish *progress* from *modernization, rebellion* from *revolution,* and *acculturation* from *enculturation.* We discuss mechanisms of change—innovation, diffusion, and cultural loss, as well as repressive change. New paragraphs describe the spear-thrower (atlatl) and briefly mention a half-dozen other familiar primary innovations, followed by descriptions of the evolution of firemaking and wheel-and-axle technology. Also new is a discussion about the dynamics that encourage or discourage innovative tendencies, illustrated with brief accounts of findings by Copernicus and Galileo. The discussion on diffusion includes new mention of bagpipes in Bhutan and two new subsections—one on the spread of maize or corn and the other on the metric system.

Our exploration of cultural change and loss covers acculturation and ethnocide, citing a range of examples of repressive change from around the world—including a revised passage on China and Tibet and a new section about Yąnomami ethnocide, which features a photo of Yąnomami shaman and political leader Davi Kopenawa.

A rewritten section on reactions to change includes a subsection on syncretism, highlighting Trobriand cricket, illustrated with a new photo. We cover revitalization movements, describing cargo cults and presenting a new profile on indigenous revitalization in Bolivia, including a new photo illustrating a return to animism. A discussion on rebellion and revolution adds *insurgency* to our list of defined terms (illustrated by the Zapatista Maya Indian insurgency in southern Mexico) and recounts the Muslim fundamentalist toppling of the imperial regime in Iran in 1979.

The chapter also delves into modernization and the issue of self-determination among indigenous peoples. We highlight two contrasting cases, both greatly revised and updated with new visuals: the Sámi reindeer herders living in the Arctic and sub-Arctic tundra of northwest Russia and Scandinavia and the Shuar Indians of Ecuador.

Boxed features include a Biocultural Connection on the emergence of new diseases, an Anthropologist of Note profile on Eric R. Wolf, and an Anthropology Applied piece on development anthropology and dams, with a fascinating satellite image of China's Three Gorges Dam.

Chapter 16: Global Challenges, Local Responses, and the Role of Anthropology

Our final chapter opens with a photo of an Internet café in China, alongside a Challenge Issue about cultural adaptations that have fueled population growth and placed people in closer proximity in countless ways. A new opening section, "Cultural Revolutions: From *Terra Incognita* to Google Earth," offers a 500-year historical overview of technological inventions that have transformed how humans live and how we perceive our place and destiny in the universe. It ends with the first full-view photograph taken of earth, commentary about our ever-growing interconnectedness, and speculations by some that a homogenous global culture is in the making.

A new section on global integration processes marks out the emergence of international organizations. We then consider pluralistic societies and fragmentation, illustrating the push-and-pull aspects of today's world. A new section on global migrations adds to our understanding of that world, noting the number of internal and external migrants, including transnationals working in one country although remaining citizens of another, plus the millions of refugees forced outside their countries. Marking out challenges migrants face, we introduce two new sections: "Migrants and Xenophobia: Violent Conflict in Assam" and "Migrants, Urbanization, and Slums," reporting on the 1 billion people worldwide now living in slums.

We have retained the vital section "Structural Power in the Age of Globalization," with subsections on hard power (economic and military) and soft power (media). But we have reconfigured the section "Problems of Structural Violence," which now features a new section on poverty that introduces students to the UN's Gini income equality index. We have also entirely reworked the section on hunger, obesity, and malnutrition and the section addressing pollution and global warming.

Special box features include a Biocultural Connection about the threat to Arctic cultures from outside contamination; an updated Globalscape on the practice of dumping toxic waste in the Third World, and a new Anthropology Applied piece on Ann Dunham (President Obama's mother), who was a pioneer in microfinancing. The chapter closes with an uplifting Anthropology of Note profile about Paul Farmer and his global Partners in Health work.

Supplements

Cultural Anthropology: The Human Challenge comes with a comprehensive supplements program to help instructors create an effective learning environment both inside and outside the classroom and to aid students in mastering the material.

Supplements for Instructors

Online Instructor's Manual and Test Bank

The Instructor's Manual offers detailed chapter outlines, lecture suggestions, key terms, and student activities such as video exercises and Internet exercises. In addition, there are over seventy-five chapter test questions including multiple choice, true/false, fill-in-the-blank, short answer, and essay.

PowerLecture™ with ExamView®

This one-stop class preparation tool contains ready-to-use Microsoft® PowerPoint® slides, enabling you to assemble, edit, publish, and present custom lectures with ease. PowerLecture helps you bring together text-specific lecture outlines and art from Haviland et al.'s text along with videos and your own materials—culminating in powerful, personalized, media-enhanced presentations. Featuring automatic grading, ExamView is also available within PowerLecture, allowing you to create, deliver, and customize tests and study guides (both print and online) in minutes. See assessments onscreen exactly as they will print or display online. Build tests of up to 250 questions using up to twelve question types, and enter an unlimited number of new questions or edit existing questions. PowerLecture also includes the text's Instructor's Resource Manual and Test Bank as Word documents.

WebTutor™ on Blackboard® and WebCT™

Jumpstart your course with customizable, rich, text-specific content within your course management system. Whether you want to web-enable your class or put an entire course online, WebTutor delivers. WebTutor offers a wide array of resources including access to the eBook, glossaries, flash cards, quizzes, videos, and more.

Anthropology Coursereader

Anthropology Coursereader allows you to create a fully customized online reader in minutes. Access a rich collection of thousands of primary and secondary sources, readings, and audio and video selections from multiple disciplines. Each selection includes a descriptive introduction that puts it into context, and the selection is further supported by both critical thinking and multiple-choice questions designed to reinforce key points. This easy-to-use solution allows you to select exactly the content you need for your courses and is loaded with convenient pedagogical features like highlighting, printing, note taking, and downloadable MP3 audio files for each reading. You have the freedom to assign and customize individualized content at an affordable price.

The Wadsworth Anthropology Video Library: Volumes I, II, and III

The Wadsworth Anthropology Video Library (featuring BBC Motion Gallery video clips) drives home the relevance of course topics through short, provocative clips of current and historical events. Perfect for enriching lectures and engaging students in discussion, many of the segments in these volumes have been gathered from the BBC Motion Gallery. Ask your Cengage Learning representative for a list of contents.

AIDS in Africa DVD

Southern Africa has been overcome by a pandemic of unparalleled proportions. This documentary series focuses on the democracy of Namibia and the nation's valiant actions to control HIV/AIDS.

Included in this series are four documentary films created by the Periclean Scholars at Elon University: (1) *Young Struggles, Eternal Faith*, which focuses on caregivers in the faith community; (2) *The Shining Lights of Opuwo*, which shows how young people share their messages of hope through song and dance; (3) *A Measure of Our Humanity*, which describes HIV/AIDS as an issue related to gender, poverty, stigma, education, and justice; and (4) *You Wake Me Up*, a story of two HIV-positive women and their acts of courage helping other women learn to survive.

Cengage/Wadsworth is excited to offer these award-winning films to instructors for use in class. When presenting topics such as gender, faith, culture, poverty, and so on, the films will be enlightening for students and will expand their global perspective of HIV/AIDS.

Online Resources for Instructors and Students

CourseMate

Cengage Learning's Anthropology CourseMate brings course concepts to life with interactive learning, study, and exam preparation tools that support the printed textbook. CourseMate includes an integrated eBook, glossaries, flash cards, quizzes, videos, and more—as well as EngagementTracker, an original tool that monitors student engagement in the course. The accompanying instructor website, available through login.cengage.com, offers access to password-protected resources such as an electronic version of the Instructor's Manual, Test Bank files, and PowerPoint® slides. CourseMate can be bundled with the student text. Contact your Cengage sales representative for information on getting access to CourseMate.

Supplements for Students

Telecourse Study Guide

The distance learning course, **Anthropology: The Four Fields**, provides online and print companion study guide options that include study aids, interactive exercises, videos, and more.

Additional Student Resources

Basic Genetics for Anthropology CD-ROM: Principles and Applications (stand-alone version), by Robert Jurmain and Lynn Kilgore

This student CD-ROM expands on such concepts as biological inheritance (genes, DNA sequencing, and so on) and applications of that to modern human populations at the molecular level (human variation and adaptation—to disease, diet, growth, and development). Interactive animations and simulations bring these important concepts to life for students so they can fully understand the essential biological principles required for physical anthropology. Also available are quizzes and interactive flashcards for further study.

Hominid Fossils CD-ROM: An Interactive Atlas, by James Ahern

The interactive atlas CD-ROM includes over seventy-five key fossils important for a clear understanding of human evolution. The QuickTime Virtual Reality (QTVR) "object" movie format for each fossil enables students to have a near-authentic experience of working with these important finds, by allowing them to rotate the fossils 360 degrees.

Unlike some VR media, QTVR objects are made using actual photographs of the real objects and thus better preserve details of color and texture. The fossils used are high-quality research casts as well as actual fossils. Because the atlas is not organized linearly, student are able to access levels and multiple paths, allowing them to see how the fossil fits into the map of human evolution in terms of geography, time, and evolution. The CD-ROM offers students an inviting, authentic learning environment, one that also contains a dynamic quizzing feature that permits students to test their knowledge of fossil and species identification, as well as providing detailed information about the fossil record.

Readings and Case Studies

Classic and Contemporary Readings in Physical Anthropology, edited by M. K. Sandford with Eileen M. Jackson

This highly accessible reader emphasizes science—its principles and methods—as well as the historical development of physical anthropology and the applications of new technology to the discipline. The editors provide an introduction to the reader as well as a brief overview of the article so students know what to look for. Each article also includes discussion questions and Internet resources.

Classic Readings in Cultural Anthropology, 3rd edition, edited by Gary Ferraro

Now in its third edition, this reader includes historical and recent articles that have had a profound effect on the field of anthropology. Organized according to the major topic areas found in most cultural anthropology courses, this reader includes an introduction to the material as well as a brief overview of each article, discussion questions, and InfoTrac College Edition key search terms.

Globalization and Change in Fifteen Cultures: Born in One World, Living in Another, edited by George Spindler and Janice E. Stockard

In this volume, fifteen case study authors write about cultural change in today's diverse settings around the world. Each original article provides insight into the dynamics and meanings of change, as well as the effects of globalization at the local level.

Case Studies in Cultural Anthropology, edited by George Spindler and Janice E. Stockard

Select from more than sixty classic and contemporary ethnographies representing geographic and topical diversity. Newer case studies focus on cultural change and cultural continuity, reflecting the globalization of the world.

Case Studies on Contemporary Social Issues, edited by John A. Young

Framed around social issues, these new contemporary case studies are globally comparative and represent the cutting-edge work of anthropologists today.

Case Studies in Archaeology, edited by Jeffrey Quilter

These engaging accounts of new archaeological techniques, issues, and solutions—as well as studies discussing the collection of material remains—range from site-specific excavations to types of archaeology practiced.

Acknowledgments

In this day and age, no textbook comes to fruition without extensive collaboration. Beyond the shared endeavors of our author team, this book owes its completion to a wide range of individuals, from colleagues in the discipline to those involved in development and production processes. Sincere thanks to colleagues who brought their expertise to bear—as sounding boards and in responding to questions concerning their specializations: Marta P. Alfonso-Durruty, Amber Campbell Hibbs, Frans B. M. de Waal, Jessica Falcone, John Hawks, Heather Loyd, Gillian E. Newell, Martin Ottenheimer, Svante Pääbo, Herbert Prins, and Michael Wesch. We are particularly grateful for the manuscript reviewers listed below, who provided detailed and thoughtful feedback that helped us to hone and re-hone our narrative.

We carefully considered and made use of the wide range of comments provided by these individuals. Our decisions on how to utilize their suggestions were influenced by our own perspectives on anthropology and teaching, combined with the priorities and page limits of this text. Thus, neither our reviewers nor any of the other anthropologists mentioned here should be held responsible for any shortcomings in this book. They should, however, be credited as contributors to many of the book's strengths: Philip Carr, University of South Alabama; Douglas Crews, Ohio State University; William Price, North Country Community College; Frank Salamone, Iona College; David Schwimmer, Columbus State University; and Donna Marshaye White, Webster University.

Thanks, too, go to colleagues who provided material for some of the Original Study, Biocultural Connection, and Anthropology Applied boxes in this text: Michael Blakey, Nancy I. Cooper, Hillary Crane, Margo DeMello, George S. Esber, S. Neyooxet Greymorning, John Hawks, Michael M. Horowitz, Ann Kendall, Suzanne Leclerc-Madlala, Susan Lees, Bill Maurer, H. Lyn White Miles, Serena Nanda, Jennifer Sapiel Neptune, Martin Ottenheimer, Amanda Stronza, William Ury, Clementine van Eck, Annette B. Weiner, Dennis Werner, and R. K. Williamson.

We have debts of gratitude to office workers in our departments for their cheerful help in clerical matters: Karen Rundquist, Patty Redmond, and Tina Griffiths, along with research librarian extraordinaire Nancy Bianchi. Also worthy of note here are the introductory anthropology teaching assistants at Kansas State University and the College of Medicine and Honors College students at the University of Vermont who, through the years, have shed light for us on effective ways to reach new generations of students. And, finally, we recognize the introductory students themselves, who are at the heart of this educational endeavor and who continually provide feedback in formal and informal ways.

Our thanksgiving inventory would be incomplete without mentioning individuals at Wadsworth/ Cengage Learning who helped conceive of this text and bring it to fruition. Of special note is our senior development editor Lin Marshall Gaylord, who has been a shaping force for many generations of the Haviland et al. textbooks. She continues to grace our efforts with vision, resilience, constancy, and anthropological knowledge. We cannot imagine this endeavor without her. Our thanks also go out to Wadsworth's skilled and enthusiastic editorial, marketing, design, and production team: Aileen Berg (senior acquisitions sponsoring editor), Liz Rhoden (senior brand manager), Michelle Williams (senior market development manager), John Chell (media editor), Margaux Cameron (assistant editor), Victor Luu (editorial assistant), as well as Cheri Palmer (content project manager) and Caryl Gorska (art director).

In addition to all of the above, we have had the invaluable aid of several most able freelancers, including veteran photo researcher Sarah Evertson and our alert and artful art team at Graphic World. We are beyond grateful to have once again had the opportunity to work with copy editor Jennifer Gordon and production coordinator Joan Keyes of Dovetail Publishing Services. Consummate professionals and generous souls, both of them keep track of countless details and bring calm efficiency and grace to the demands of meeting difficult deadlines. Their efforts and skills play a major role in making our work doable and pleasurable.

And finally, all of us are indebted to family members and close friends who have not only put up with our textbook preoccupation but cheered us on in the endeavor.

About the Authors

Authors Bunny McBride, Dana Walrath, Harald Prins, and William Haviland

Courtesy of the authors

All four members of this author team share overlapping research interests and a similar vision of what anthropology is (and should be) about. For example, all are true believers in the four-field approach to anthropology and all have some involvement in applied work.

WILLIAM A. HAVILAND is professor emeritus at the University of Vermont, where he founded the Department of Anthropology and taught for thirty-two years. He holds a PhD in anthropology from the University of Pennsylvania.

He has carried out original research in archaeology in Guatemala and Vermont; ethnography in Maine and Vermont; and physical anthropology in Guatemala. This work has been the basis of numerous publications in various national and international books and journals, as well as in media intended for the general public. His books include *The Original Vermonters*, coauthored with Marjorie Power, and a technical monograph on ancient Maya settlement. He also served as consultant for the award-winning telecourse *Faces of Culture*, and he is coeditor of the series *Tikal Reports*, published by the University of Pennsylvania Museum of Archaeology and Anthropology.

Besides his teaching and writing, Dr. Haviland has lectured to numerous professional as well as nonprofessional audiences in Canada, Mexico, Lesotho, South Africa, and Spain, as well as in the United States.

A staunch supporter of indigenous rights, he served as expert witness for the Missisquoi Abenaki of Vermont in an important court case over aboriginal fishing rights.

Awards received by Dr. Haviland include being named University Scholar by the Graduate School of the University of Vermont in 1990; a Certificate of Appreciation from the Sovereign Republic of the Abenaki Nation of Missisquoi, St. Francis/Sokoki Band in 1996; and a Lifetime Achievement Award from the Center for Research on Vermont in 2006. Now retired from teaching, he continues his research, writing, and lecturing from the coast of Maine. He serves as a trustee for the Abbe Museum in Bar Harbor, focused on Maine's Native American history, culture, art, and archaeology. His most recent books are *At the Place of the Lobsters and Crabs* (2009) and *Canoe Indians of Down East Maine* (2012).

HARALD E. L. PRINS is a University Distinguished Professor of cultural anthropology at Kansas State University. Academically trained at half a dozen Dutch and U.S. universities, he previously taught at Radboud University (Netherlands), Bowdoin College and Colby College in Maine, and was a visiting professor at the University of Lund, Sweden. Also named a Distinguished University Teaching Scholar, he received numerous honors for his outstanding academic teaching, including the Presidential Award in 1999, Carnegie Professor of the Year for Kansas in 2006, and the AAA/Oxford University Press Award for Excellence in Undergraduate Teaching of Anthropology in 2010.

His fieldwork focuses on indigenous peoples in the western hemisphere, and he has long served as an advocacy anthropologist on land claims and other Native rights. In that capacity, Dr. Prins has been a key expert witness in both the U.S. Senate and Canadian courts. His numerous academic publications appear in seven languages, and his books include *The Mi'kmaq: Resistance, Accomodation, and Cultural Survival*.

Also trained in filmmaking, he was president of the Society for Visual Anthropology, and coproduced award-winning documentaries. He has been the visual anthropology editor of *American Anthropologist*, coprincipal investigator for the U.S. National Park Service, international observer in Paraguay's presidential elections, and a research associate at the National Museum of Natural History, Smithsonian Institution.

BUNNY MCBRIDE is an award-winning author specializing in cultural anthropology, indigenous peoples, international tourism, and nature conservation issues. Published in dozens of national and international print media, she has reported from Africa, Europe, China, and the Indian Ocean. Holding an MA from Columbia University, she is highly rated as a teacher, and she has served as visiting anthropology faculty at Principia College and the Salt Institute for Documentary Field Studies. Since 1996 she has been an adjunct lecturer of anthropology at Kansas State University.

Among her many publications are books such as *Women of the Dawn*; *Molly Spotted Elk: A Penobscot in Paris*; *Indians in Eden* (with Harald Prins); and *The Audubon Field Guide to African Wildlife*, which she coauthored. McBride has also authored numerous book chapters. Honors include a special commendation from the state legislature of Maine for significant contributions to Native women's history. As an activist and researcher for the Aroostook Band of Micmacs (1981–1991), she assisted this Maine Indian community in its successful efforts to reclaim lands, gain tribal status, and revitalize cultural traditions.

In recent years, she has served as coprincipal investigator for a National Park Service ethnography project and curated several museum exhibits, including "Journeys West: The David & Peggy Rockefeller American Indian Art Collection" for the Abbe Museum in Bar Harbor, Maine. Her latest exhibit, "Indians & Rusticators," received a 2012 Leadership in History Award from the American Association for State and Local History. Currently, she serves as president of the Women's World Summit Foundation, based in Geneva, Switzerland, and is completing a collection of essays.

DANA WALRATH is assistant professor of family medicine at the University of Vermont and an affiliated faculty member for women's and gender studies. After earning her PhD from the University of Pennsylvania, she taught there and at Temple University. Dr. Walrath broke new ground in medical and biological anthropology through her work on biocultural aspects of childbirth. She has also written on a wide range of topics related to gender in paleoanthropology, the social production of sickness and health, sex differences, genetics, and evolutionary medicine. Her work has appeared in edited volumes and in journals such as *Current Anthropology, American Anthropologist, American Journal of Physical Anthropology*, and *Anthropology Now*. She developed a novel curriculum in medical education at the University of Vermont's College of Medicine that brings humanism, anthropological theory and practice, narrative medicine, and professionalism skills to first-year medical students.

Dr. Walrath also has an MFA in creative writing from Vermont College of Fine Arts and has shown her artwork in galleries throughout the country. Her recent work on Alzheimer's disease combines anthropology with memoir and visual art. Spanning a variety of disciplines, her work has been supported by diverse sources such as the National Science Foundation for the Arts, the Centers for Disease Control, the Health Resources and Services Administration, the Vermont Studio Center, the Vermont Arts Council, and the National Endowment for the Arts. She is currently a Fulbright Scholar at the American University of Armenia and the Institute of Ethnography and Archaeology of the National Academy of Sciences of Armenia, where she is completing a project titled "The Narrative Anthropology of Aging in Armenia."

Challenge Issue

It is a challenge to make sense of the world and our place in the universe. Who am I and how am I connected to the person in this picture? Why do I look different from so many other people in the world and why are there so many different languages? Who harvested the cotton for my shirt or felled the tree used to build my house? Why are some people immune from a virus that kills others? How is it that many believe in an afterlife but others do not? When did our ancestors first begin to think? What distinguishes us from other animals? Anthropologists take a holistic, integrated approach to such questions, framing them in a broad context and examining interconnections. Our discipline considers human culture and biology, in all times and places, as inextricably intertwined, each affecting the other. This photograph shows the hands of a miner holding coltan, a tarlike mineral mined in eastern Congo. Refined, coltan turns into a heat-resistant powder capable of storing energy. As the key component of capacitors in small electronic devices, it is highly valued on the global market. Coltan mines, enriching the warring Congolese factions that control them, are hellholes for the thousands of people, including children, who work the mines. Bought, transported, and processed by foreign merchants and corporations, small bits of this mineral eventually end up in mobile phones and laptop computers worldwide. Although the link between you and globalization is complex, no more than "six degrees of separation" exist between your hands and those of the miner in the heart of Africa. Anthropology's holistic and integrative perspective will equip you to explore and negotiate today's interconnected and globalized world.

The Essence of Anthropology

The Anthropological Perspective

Anthropology is the study of humankind in all times and places. Of course, many other disciplines focus on humans in one way or another. For example, anatomy and physiology concentrate on our species as biological organisms. The social sciences examine human relationships, leaving artistic and philosophical aspects of human cultures to the humanities. Anthropology focuses on the interconnections and interdependence of all aspects of the human experience in all places, in the present and deep into the past, well before written history. This unique, broad **holistic perspective** equips anthropologists to address that elusive thing we call *human nature.*

Anthropologists welcome the contributions of researchers from other disciplines, and in return offer their own findings to these other disciplines. An anthropologist may not know as much about the structure of the human eye as an anatomist or as much about the perception of color as a psychologist. As a synthesizer, however, the anthropologist seeks to understand how anatomy and psychology relate to color-naming practices in different societies. Because they look for the broad basis of human ideas and practices without limiting themselves to any single social or biological aspect, anthropologists can acquire an especially expansive and inclusive overview of human biology and culture.

Keeping a holistic perspective allows anthropologists to prevent their own cultural ideas and values from distorting their research. As the old saying goes, people often see what they believe, rather than what appears before their eyes. By maintaining a critical awareness of their own assumptions about human nature—checking and rechecking the ways their beliefs and actions might be shaping their research—anthropologists strive to gain objective knowledge about human beings. With this

anthropology The study of humankind in all times and places.

holistic perspective A fundamental principle of anthropology: The various parts of human culture and biology must be viewed in the broadest possible context in order to understand their interconnections and interdependence.

IN THIS CHAPTER YOU WILL LEARN TO

- Describe the discipline of anthropology and make connections among its four fields.

- Compare anthropology to the sciences and the humanities.

- Identify the characteristics of anthropological field methods and the ethics of anthropological research.

- Explain the usefulness of anthropology in light of globalization.

in mind, anthropologists aim to avoid the pitfalls of **ethnocentrism**, a belief that the ways of one's own culture are the only proper ones.

To some, an inclusive, holistic perspective that emphasizes the diversity within and among human cultures can be mistaken as shorthand for liberal politics among anthropologists. This is not the case. Anthropologists come from many different backgrounds, and individuals practicing the discipline vary in their personal, political, and religious beliefs (**Figure 1.1**). At the same time, they apply a rigorous methodology for researching cultural practices from the perspective of the culture being studied—a methodology that requires them to check for the influences of their own biases. This is as true for an anthropologist analyzing the culture of the global banking industry as it is for one investigating trance dancing among contemporary hunter-gatherers. We might say that anthropology is a discipline concerned with unbiased evaluation of diverse human systems, including one's own. At times this requires challenging the status quo that is maintained and defended by the power elites of the system under study.

While other social sciences have predominantly concentrated on contemporary peoples living in North American and European (Western) societies, anthropologists have traditionally focused on non-Western peoples and cultures. Anthropologists work with the understanding that to fully access the complexities of human ideas, behavior, and biology, *all* humans, wherever and whenever, must be studied. A cross-cultural and long-term evolutionary perspective distinguishes anthropology from other social sciences. This approach guards against theories about the world and reality that are **culture-bound**—based on the assumptions and values that come from the researcher's own culture.

As a case in point, consider the fact that infants in the United States typically sleep apart from their parents. To people accustomed to multibedroom houses, cribs, and car seats, this may seem normal, but cross-cultural research shows that *co-sleeping*, of mother and baby in particular, is the norm (**Figure 1.2**). Further, the practice of sleeping apart favored in the United States dates back only about 200 years.

Recent studies have shown that separation of mother and infant has important biological and cultural consequences. For one thing, it increases the length of the infant's crying bouts. Some mothers incorrectly interpret crying as an indication that the baby is not receiving sufficient breast milk and consequently switch to using bottled formula, which has been shown to be less healthy. In extreme cases, a baby's cries may provoke physical

© Documentary Educational Resources

Figure 1.1 Anthropologist Jayasinhji Jhala Anthropologists come from many corners of the world and carry out research in a huge variety of cultures all around the globe. Dr. Jayasinhji Jhala, pictured here, hails from the old city of Dhrangadhra in Gujarat, northwestern India. A member of the Jhala clan of Rajputs, an aristocratic caste of warriors, he grew up in the royal palace of his father, the maharaja. After earning a bachelor of arts degree in India, he came to the United States and earned a master's in visual studies from MIT, followed by a doctorate in anthropology from Harvard. Currently a professor and director of the programs of Visual Anthropology and the Visual Anthropology Media Laboratory at Temple University, he returns regularly to India with students to film cultural traditions in his own caste-stratified society.

abuse. But the benefits of co-sleeping go beyond significant reductions in crying: Infants who are breastfed receive more stimulation important for brain development, and they are apparently less susceptible to sudden infant death syndrome (SIDS or "crib death"), which occurs at a higher rate in the United States than in any other country. There are benefits to the mother as well: Frequent nursing prevents early ovulation after childbirth, promotes weight

---

ethnocentrism The belief that the ways of one's own culture are the only proper ones.

culture-bound A perspective that produces theories about the world and reality that are based on the assumptions and values from the researcher's own culture.

VISUAL COUNTERPOINT

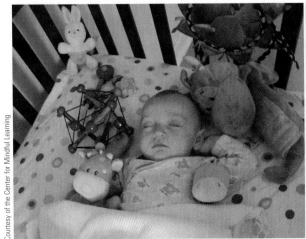
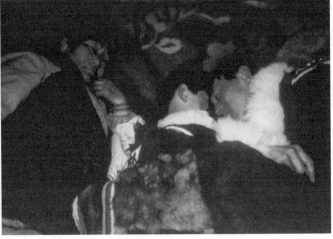

Figure 1.2 **Sleeping Habits across Cultures** Although infants in the United States typically sleep apart from their parents, cross-cultural research shows that co-sleeping, particularly of mother and baby, is the rule. Without the breathing cues provided by someone sleeping nearby, an infant is more susceptible to sudden infant death syndrome (SIDS), a phenomenon in which a 4- to 6-month-old baby stops breathing and dies while asleep. The highest rates of SIDS are found among infants in the United States. The photo on the right shows a Nenet family sleeping together in their *chum* (reindeer-skin tent). Nenet people are Arctic reindeer pastoralists living in Siberia.

loss to shed pregnancy pounds, and allows nursing mothers at least as much sleep as mothers who sleep apart from their infants (McKenna & McDade, 2005).

Why do so many mothers continue to sleep separately from their infants? In the United States, the cultural values of independence and consumerism come into play. To begin building individual identities, babies are provided with rooms (or at least space) of their own. This room also gives parents a place to stow the toys, furniture, and other paraphernalia associated with good and caring childrearing in the United States.

Although the findings of anthropologists have often challenged the conclusions of sociologists, psychologists, and economists, anthropology is absolutely indispensable to those in other disciplines because it is the only consistent check against culture-bound assertions. In a sense, anthropology is to these disciplines what the laboratory is to physics and chemistry: an essential testing ground for their theories.

Anthropology and Its Fields

Individual anthropologists tend to specialize in one of four fields or subdisciplines: cultural anthropology, linguistic anthropology, archaeology, and physical (biological) anthropology (**Figure 1.3**). Some anthropologists consider

archaeology and linguistics to be part of the broader study of human cultures, but archaeology and linguistics also have close ties to physical anthropology. For example, while linguistic anthropology focuses on the social and cultural aspects of language, it has deep connections to the evolution of human language and to the biological basis of speech and language studied within physical anthropology.

Researchers in each of anthropology's fields gather and analyze data to explore similarities and differences among humans, across time and space. Moreover, individuals within

Figure 1.3 **The Four Fields of Anthropology** Note that the divisions among the fields are not sharp, indicating that their boundaries overlap. Note also that all four include the practice of applied anthropology.

The Anthropology of Organ Transplantation

In 1954, the first organ transplant occurred in Boston when surgeons removed a kidney from one identical twin to place it inside his sick brother. Today, transplants between unrelated individuals are common, so much so that organs are trafficked in the black market, often across continents from the poor to the wealthy. Though some transplants rely upon living donors, routine organ transplantation depends largely upon the availability of organs obtained from individuals who have died. To reduce illegal traffic, several European countries have enacted policies that assume that any individual who is "brain dead" is automatically an organ donor unless the person has "opted out" ahead of time.

A practice like organ transplantation can exist only if it fits with cultural beliefs about death and the human body. The North American and European view—that the body is a machine that can be repaired much like a car—makes a practice like organ transplantation acceptable. But this is not the view shared by all societies. Anthropologist Margaret Lock has explored differences between Japanese and North American acceptance of the biological state of brain death and how it affects the practice of organ transplantation.

The diagnosis of brain death relies upon the absence of measurable electrical currents in the brain and the inability to breathe without technological assistance. The brain-dead individual, though attached to machines, still seems alive with a beating heart and normal skin coloring. Part of the reason most North Americans find organ transplantation tolerable with the determination of brain death is that personhood and individuality are culturally ascribed to the mind, and thus located in the brain. North Americans' acceptance of brain death has allowed for the "gift of life" through sometimes anonymous organ donation and subsequent transplantation.

By contrast, in Japan, the concept of brain death is hotly contested, and organ transplants are rarely performed. The Japanese idea of personhood does not incorporate a mind–body split; instead, a person's identity is tied to the entire body rather than solely to the brain. Consequently, the Japanese reject that a warm body is a corpse from which organs can be harvested. Further, organs cannot be transformed into "gifts" because anonymous donation is incompatible with Japanese social patterns of reciprocal exchange.

Organ transplantation involves far greater social meaning than the purely biological movement of an organ from one individual to another. Cultural and biological processes are tightly woven into every aspect of this new social practice.

BIOCULTURAL QUESTION

What criteria do you use for death, and is it compatible with the idea of organ donation? Do you think that donated organs are fairly distributed in your society or throughout the globe?

For more on this subject, see Lock, M. (2001). Twice dead: Organ transplants and the reinvention of death. *Berkeley: University of California Press.*

---

each of the four fields practice **applied anthropology**, which entails the use of anthropological knowledge and methods to solve practical problems. Most applied anthropologists actively collaborate with the communities in which they work—setting goals, solving problems, and conducting research together. In this book, the Anthropology Applied features spotlight how anthropology contributes to solving a wide range of challenges.

applied anthropology The use of anthropological knowledge and methods to solve practical problems, often for a specific client.

medical anthropology A specialization in anthropology that brings theoretical and applied approaches from cultural and biological anthropology to the study of human health and disease.

cultural anthropology The study of patterns in human behavior, thought, and emotions, focusing on humans as culture-producing and culture-reproducing creatures. Also known as *social* or *sociocultural anthropology.*

An early example of the application of anthropological knowledge to a practical problem was the international public health movement that began in the 1920s. This marked the beginning of **medical anthropology**—a specialization that brings theoretical and applied approaches from cultural and biological anthropology to the study of human health and disease. The work of medical anthropologists sheds light on the connections between human health and political and economic forces, both locally and globally. Examples of this specialization appear in some of the Biocultural Connections featured in this text, including the one presented on this page, "The Anthropology of Organ Transplantation."

Cultural Anthropology

Cultural anthropology (also called *social* or *sociocultural anthropology*) is the study of patterns in human behavior, thought, and emotions. It focuses on humans as culture-producing and culture-reproducing creatures. To understand the work of the cultural anthropologist, we must clarify the meaning of **culture**—a society's shared and socially transmitted ideas, values, emotions, and perceptions, which are used to make sense of experience and which generate behavior and are reflected in that behavior. These are the (often unconscious) standards by which societies—structured groups of people—operate. These standards are socially learned, rather than acquired through biological inheritance. The manifestations of culture may vary considerably from place to place, but no individual is "more cultured" in the anthropological sense than any other.

Integral to all the anthropological fields, the concept of culture might be considered anthropology's distinguishing feature. After all, a biological anthropologist is distinct from a biologist *primarily* because he or she takes culture into account. Cultural anthropologists may study the legal, medical, economic, political, or religious system of a given society, knowing that all aspects of the culture interrelate as part of a unified whole. They may focus on divisions in a society—such as by gender, age, or class—factors we will explore in depth later in this text. But it is also worth noting the significance of these same categories to the archaeologist who studies a society through its material remains, to the linguistic anthropologist who examines ancient and modern languages, and to the biological anthropologist who investigates the physical human body.

Cultural anthropology has two main components: ethnography and ethnology. An **ethnography** is a detailed description of a particular culture primarily based on **fieldwork**, which is the term all anthropologists use for on-location research. Because the hallmark of ethnographic fieldwork is a combination of social participation and personal observation within the community being studied and interviews and discussions with individual members of a group, the ethnographic method is commonly referred to as **participant observation** (Figure 1.4). Ethnographies provide the information used to make systematic comparisons among cultures all across the world. Known as **ethnology**, such cross-cultural research allows anthropologists to develop theories that help explain why certain important differences or similarities occur among groups.

Ethnography

Through participant observation—eating a people's food, sleeping under their roof, learning how to speak and behave acceptably, and personally experiencing their habits and customs—the ethnographer seeks to gain the best possible understanding of a particular way of life. Being a participant observer does not mean that the anthropologist must join in battles to study a culture in which warfare is prominent; but by living among a warring people, the ethnographer should be able to understand how warfare fits into the overall cultural framework.

The ethnographer must observe carefully to gain an overview without placing too much emphasis on one

Figure 1.4 Fieldwork in the Arctic British anthropologist Florian Stammler engages in participant observation among Sami reindeer nomads in Siberia. Specializing in Arctic anthropology, particularly in the Russian far north, Stammler coordinates the anthropology research team at the University of Lapland's Arctic Centre. His interests include Arctic economy, human–animal relations, and the anthropology of place and belonging.

cultural feature at the expense of another. Only by discovering how *all* parts of a culture—its social, political, economic, and religious practices and institutions—relate to one another can the ethnographer begin to understand the cultural system. This is the holistic perspective so basic to the discipline.

The popular image of ethnographic fieldwork is that it occurs among hunters, herders, fishers, or farmers who live in far-off, isolated places. To be sure, much ethnographic work has been done in the remote villages of Asia, Africa, or Latin America, islands of the Pacific Ocean, deserts of Australia, and so on. However, as the discipline developed after the mid-1900s with the demise of colonialism, industrialized societies

culture A society's shared and socially transmitted ideas, values, and perceptions, which are used to make sense of experience and which generate behavior and are reflected in that behavior.

ethnography A detailed description of a particular culture primarily based on fieldwork.

fieldwork The term anthropologists use for on-location research.

participant observation In ethnography, the technique of learning a people's culture through social participation and personal observation within the community being studied, as well as interviews and discussion with individual members of the group over an extended period of time.

ethnology The study and analysis of different cultures from a comparative or historical point of view, utilizing ethnographic accounts and developing anthropological theories that help explain why certain important differences or similarities occur among groups.

and genetic relationships, contributes significantly to our understanding of human evolution, adaptation, and diversity. Comparisons among groups separated by time, geography, or the frequency of a particular gene can reveal how humans have adapted and where they have migrated. As experts in the anatomy of human bones and tissues, biological anthropologists lend their knowledge about the body to applied areas such as gross anatomy laboratories, public health, and criminal investigations.

Paleoanthropology

Dealing with much greater time spans than other branches of anthropology, **paleoanthropology** is the study of the origins, predecessors, and early representatives of the present human species. Focusing on long-time biological changes (evolution) paleoanthropologists seek to understand how, when, and why we became the species we are today. In biological terms, we humans are *Homo sapiens,* a species in the larger order of primates, one of the many kinds of mammals. Because we share a common ancestry with other primates (monkeys and apes), paleoanthropologists look back to the earliest primates (about 65 million years ago, abbreviated mya) or even to the earliest mammals (225 mya) to reconstruct the intricate path of human evolution. At times, paleoanthropologists take a **biocultural** approach, focusing on the interaction of biology and culture.

Paleoanthropologists compare fossilized skeletons of our ancestors to other fossils and to the bones of living members of our species. Combining this knowledge with biochemical and genetic evidence, they strive to scientifically reconstruct the complex course of human evolutionary history. With each new fossil discovery, paleoanthropologists have another piece to add to the puzzle still far from fully solved. Further on in this text, we discuss how, genetic evidence establishes the close relationship between humans and ape species—chimpanzees, bonobos, and gorillas. Genetic analyses indicate that the distinctively human line split from the apes sometime between 5 and 8 million years ago.

Primatology

Studying the anatomy and behavior of the other primates helps us understand what we share with our closest living relatives and what makes humans unique. Therefore, **primatology**, or the study of living and fossil primates, is a vital part of physical anthropology. Primates include the

Penelope Breese/Liaison/Getty Images

Figure 1.7 Primatologist Jane Goodall Nearly forty-five years ago Jane Goodall began studying chimpanzees to shed light on the behavior of our distant ancestors. The knowledge she has amassed reveals striking similarities with our species. Goodall has devoted much of her career to championing the rights of our closest living relatives.

Asian and African apes, as well as monkeys, lemurs, lorises, and tarsiers.

Biologically, humans are members of the ape family—large-bodied, broad-shouldered primates with no tail. Detailed studies of ape behavior in the wild indicate that the sharing of learned behavior is a significant part of their social life. Increasingly, primatologists designate the shared, learned behavior of nonhuman apes as *culture.* For example, tool use and communication systems indicate the elementary basis of language in some ape societies.

Primate studies offer scientifically grounded perspectives on the behavior of our ancestors, as well as greater appreciation and respect for the abilities of our closest living relatives. As human activity encroaches on all parts of the world, many primate species are endangered. Primatologists, such as Jane Goodall (**Figure 1.7**), strongly advocate for the preservation of primate habitats so that these remarkable animals will be able to continue to inhabit the earth with us.

Human Growth, Adaptation, and Variation

Some physical anthropologists specialize in the study of human growth and development. They examine biological mechanisms of growth as well as the impact of the environment on the growth process. For example, Franz Boas, a pioneer of American anthropology of the early 20th century (see the Anthropologists of Note feature on the next page) compared the heights of immigrants who spent their

---

paleoanthropology The anthropological study of biological changes through time (evolution) to understand the origins and predecessors of the present human species.

biocultural An approach that focuses on the interaction of biology and culture.

primatology The study of living and fossil primates.

ANTHROPOLOGISTS OF NOTE

Franz Boas (1858–1942) • Matilda Coxe Stevenson (1849–1915)

Franz Boas on a sailing ship, about 1925.

Franz Boas was not the first to teach anthropology in the United States, but it was Boas and his students, with their insistence on scientific rigor, who made anthropology courses common in college and university curricula. Born and raised in Germany where he studied physics, mathematics, and geography, Boas did his first ethnographic research among the Inuit (Eskimos) in Arctic Canada in 1883 and 1884. After a brief academic career in Berlin, he came to the United States where he worked in museums interspersed with ethnographic research among the Kwakiutl (Kwakwaka'wakw) Indians in the Canadian Pacific. In 1896, he became a professor at Columbia University in New York City. He authored an incredible number of publications, founded professional organizations and journals, and taught two generations of great anthropologists, including numerous women and ethnic minorities.

As a Jewish immigrant, Boas recognized the dangers of ethnocentrism and especially racism. Through ethnographic fieldwork and comparative analysis, he demonstrated that white supremacy theories and other schemes ranking non-European peoples and cultures as inferior were biased, ill informed, and unscientific. Throughout his long and illustrious academic career, he promoted anthropology not only as a human science but also as an instrument to combat racism and prejudice in the world.

Among the founders of North American anthropology were a number of women, including **Matilda Coxe Stevenson**, who did fieldwork among the Zuni Indians of Arizona. In 1885, she founded the Women's Anthropological Society in Washington, DC, the first professional association for women scientists. Three years later, hired by the Smithsonian's Bureau of American Ethnology, she became one of the first women in the world to receive a full-time official position in science. Along with several other pioneering female anthropologists in North America, she was highly influential among women's rights advocates in the late 1800s. The tradition of women building careers in anthropology continues. In fact, since World War II more than half the presidents of the now 12,000-member American Anthropological Association have been women.

Matilda Coxe Stevenson in New Mexico, about 1900.

Recording observations on film as well as in notebooks, Stevenson and Boas were also pioneers in visual anthropology. Stevenson used an early box camera to document Pueblo Indian religious ceremonies and material culture, while Boas photographed Inuit and Kwakiutl Indians from the early 1890s for cultural as well as physical anthropological documentation. Today, their early photographs are greatly valued not only by anthropologists and historians, but also by indigenous peoples themselves.

childhood in the "old country" (Europe) to the increased heights reached by their children who grew up in the United States. Today, physical anthropologists study the impact of poverty, pollution, and disease on growth. Comparisons between human and nonhuman primate growth patterns can provide clues to the evolutionary history of humans. Detailed anthropological studies of the hormonal, genetic, and physiological bases of healthy growth in living humans also contribute significantly to the health of children today.

Studies of human adaptation focus on the capacity of humans to adapt or adjust to their material environment—biologically and culturally. This branch of physical anthropology takes a comparative approach to humans living today in a variety of environments. Human beings are the only primates to inhabit the entire earth. Although biological adaptations make it possible for people to live in environmentally extreme regions, cultural adaptations also contribute to our survival in places that are dangerously cold, hot, or of high altitude.

Some of these biological adaptations are built into the genetic makeup of populations. The long period of human growth and development provides ample opportunity for the environment to shape the human body. *Developmental adaptations* are responsible for some features of human variation, such as the enlargement of the right ventricle of the heart to help push blood to the lungs among the Aymara Indians of the Bolivian altiplano—an extensive area of high plateau at the widest part of the Andes. *Physiological adaptations* are short-term changes in response to a particular environmental stimulus. For example, if a woman who normally lives at sea level flies to La Paz, a large Bolivian city in the altiplano at an altitude of 3,660 meters (nearly 12,000 feet), her body will undergo a series of physiological responses, such as increased production of the red blood cells that carry oxygen. These kinds of biological adaptation contribute to present-day human variation.

Genetically based human differences include visible traits such as height, body build, and skin color, as well as biochemical factors such as blood type and susceptibility to certain diseases. Still, we remain members of a single

ANTHROPOLOGY APPLIED

Forensic Anthropology: Voices for the Dead

The work of Clyde C. Snow, Michael Blakey, and Amy Zelson Mundorff

Forensic anthropology is the analysis of skeletal remains for legal purposes. Law enforcement authorities call upon forensic anthropologists to use skeletal remains to identify murder victims, missing persons, or people who have died in disasters, such as plane crashes. Forensic anthropologists have also contributed substantially to the investigation of human rights abuses in all parts of the world by identifying victims and documenting the cause of their death.

Among the best-known forensic anthropologists is Clyde C. Snow. He has been practicing in this field for over forty years, first for the Federal Aviation Administration and more recently as a freelance consultant. In addition to the usual police work, Snow has studied the remains of General George Armstrong Custer and his men from the 1876 battle at Little Big Horn, and in 1985 he went to Brazil, where he identified the remains of the notorious Nazi war criminal Josef Mengele.

Snow was also instrumental in establishing the first forensic team devoted to documenting cases of human rights abuses around the world. This began in 1984 when he went to Argentina at the request of a newly elected civilian government to help with the identification of remains of the *desaparecidos*, or "disappeared ones," the 9,000 or more people who were eliminated by death squads during seven years of military rule. A year later, he returned to give expert testimony at the trial of nine junta members and to teach Argentineans how to recover, clean, repair, preserve, photograph, x-ray, and analyze bones. Besides providing factual accounts of the fate of victims to their surviving kin and refuting the assertions of revisionists that the massacres never happened, the work of Snow and his Argentinean associates was crucial in convicting several military officers of kidnapping, torture, and murder.

Since Snow's pioneering work, forensic anthropologists have become increasingly involved in the investigation of human rights abuses in all parts of the world, from Chile to Guatemala, Haiti, the Philippines, Rwanda, Iraq, Bosnia, and Kosovo. Meanwhile, they continue to do important work for more typical clients. In the United States these clients include the Federal Bureau of Investigation and city, state, and county medical examiners' offices.

Forensic anthropologists specializing in skeletal remains commonly work closely with forensic archaeologists. The relation between them is rather like that between a forensic pathologist, who examines a corpse to establish time and manner of death, and a crime scene investigator, who searches the site for clues. While the forensic anthropologist deals with the human remains—often only bones and teeth— the forensic archaeologist controls the site, recording the position of relevant finds and recovering any clues associated with the remains.

In Rwanda, for example, a team assembled in 1995 to investigate mass murder (genocide) for the United Nations, which included archaeologists from the U.S. National Park Service's Midwest Archaeological Center. They performed the standard archaeological procedures of mapping the site, determining its boundaries, photographing and recording all surface finds, and excavating, photographing, and recording buried skeletons and associated materials in mass graves.[a]

In 1991, in another part of the world, construction workers in New York City discovered an African burial ground from the 17th and 18th centuries.

species. Physical anthropology applies all the techniques of modern biology to achieve fuller understanding of human variation and its relationship to the different environments in which people have lived. Physical anthropologists' research on human variation has debunked false notions of biologically defined races, a belief based on widespread misinterpretation of human variation.

Forensic Anthropology

One of the many practical applications of physical anthropology is **forensic anthropology**—the identification of human skeletal remains for legal purposes. In addition to helping law enforcement authorities identify murder victims, forensic anthropologists investigate human rights abuses such as systematic genocide, terrorism, and war crimes. These specialists use details of skeletal anatomy to establish the age, sex, population affiliation, and stature of the deceased. Forensic anthropologists can also determine whether the person was right- or left-handed, exhibited any physical abnormalities, or had experienced trauma.

While forensics relies upon differing frequencies of certain skeletal characteristics to establish population affiliation, it is nevertheless false to say that all people from a given population have a particular type of skeleton. (See the Anthropology Applied feature to read about the work of several forensic anthropologists and forensic archaeologists.)

forensic anthropology The identification of human skeletal remains for legal purposes.

The excavation of mass graves by the Guatemalan Foundation for Forensic Anthropology (Fernando Moscoso Moller, director) documents the human rights abuses committed during Guatemala's bloody civil war, a conflict that left 200,000 people dead and another 40,000 missing. In 2009, in a mass grave in the Quiche region, Diego Lux Tzunux uses his cell phone to photograph the skeletal remains believed to belong to his brother Manuel who disappeared in 1980. Genetic analyses allow forensic anthropologists to confirm the identity of individuals so that family members can know the fate of their loved ones. The analysis of skeletal remains provides evidence of the torture and massacre sustained by these individuals.

Researchers used a bioarchaeological rather than a strictly forensic approach to examine the complete cultural and historical context and lifeways of the entire population buried there. Directed by Michael Blakey, the African Burial Ground Project provided incontrovertible evidence of the horror of slavery in North America, in the busy northern port of New York City. The more than 400 individuals, many of them children, were worked so far beyond their ability to endure that their spines were fractured.

A decade after construction workers happened upon the African Burial Ground, terrorists attacked the World Trade Center in lower Manhattan. Amy Zelson Mundorff, a forensic anthropologist for New York City's Office of the Chief Medical Examiner, was injured in the September 11 attack. But two days later she returned to work where she supervised and coordinated the management, treatment, and cataloguing of people who lost their lives in the tragedy.

Thus, several kinds of anthropologists analyze human remains for a variety of purposes. Their work contributes to the documentation and correction of violence committed by humans of the past and present.

[a]Haglund, W. D., Conner, M., & Scott, D. D. (2001). The archaeology of contemporary mass graves. *Historical Archaeology* 35 (1), 57–69.

Anthropology, Science, and the Humanities

Anthropology has sometimes been called the most humane of the sciences and the most scientific of the humanities—a designation that most anthropologists accept with pride. Given their intense involvement with people of all times and places, anthropologists have amassed considerable information about human failure and success, weakness and greatness—the real stuff of the humanities.

Anthropologists remain committed to the proposition that one cannot fully understand another culture by simply observing it; as the term *participant observation* implies, one must *experience* it as well. This same commitment to fieldwork and to the systematic collection of data, whether qualitative or quantitative, is also evidence of the scientific side of anthropology. Anthropology is an **empirical** social science based on observations or information taken in through the senses and verified by others rather than on intuition or faith. But anthropology is distinguished from other sciences by the diverse ways in which scientific research is conducted within the discipline.

Science, a carefully honed way of producing knowledge, aims to reveal and explain the underlying logic, the structural processes that make the world tick. The creative scientific endeavor seeks testable explanations for observed phenomena, ideally in terms of the workings of hidden but unchanging principles or laws. Two basic ingredients are essential for this: imagination and skepticism. Imagination, though having the potential to lead us astray, helps us recognize unexpected ways phenomena might be ordered and to think of old things in new ways. Without it, there can be no science. Skepticism allows us to distinguish fact (an observation verified by others) from fancy, to test our speculations, and to prevent our imaginations from running away with us.

In their search for explanations, scientists do not assume that things are always as they appear on the surface. After all, what could be more obvious to the scientifically uninformed observer than the earth staying still while the sun travels around it every day?

Like other scientists, anthropologists often begin their research with a **hypothesis** (a tentative explanation or hunch) about the possible relationships between certain observed facts or events. By gathering various kinds of data that seem to ground such suggested explanations on evidence, anthropologists come up with a **theory**, a coherent statement that provides an explanatory framework for understanding; an explanation or interpretation supported by a reliable body of data. In their effort to demonstrate links between *known* facts or events, anthropologists may discover *unexpected* facts, events, or relationships. An important function of theory is that it guides us in our explorations and may result in new knowledge. Equally important, the newly discovered facts may provide evidence that certain explanations, however popular or firmly believed, are unfounded. When the evidence is lacking or fails to support the suggested explanations, promising hypotheses or attractive hunches must be dropped. In other words, anthropology relies on empirical evidence. Moreover, no scientific theory—no matter how widely accepted by the international community of scholars—is beyond challenge. That includes the findings of some of anthropology's earliest and most respected scholars.

It is important to distinguish between scientific theories—which are always open to challenges born of new evidence or insights—and doctrine. A **doctrine**, or dogma, is an assertion of opinion or belief formally handed down by an authority as true and indisputable. For instance, those who accept a creationist doctrine on the origin of the human species as recounted in sacred texts or myths do so on the basis of religious authority, conceding that such views may be contrary to genetic, geological, biological, or other explanations. Such doctrines cannot be tested or proved one way or another: They are accepted as matters of faith.

Straightforward as the scientific approach may seem, its application is not always easy. For instance, once a hypothesis has been proposed, the person who suggested it is strongly motivated to verify it, and this can cause one to unwittingly overlook negative evidence and unanticipated findings. This is a familiar problem in all science as noted by paleontologist Stephen Jay Gould: "The greatest impediment to scientific innovation is usually a conceptual lock, not a factual lock" (Gould, 1989, p. 226). Because culture provides humans with concepts and shapes our very thoughts, it can be challenging to frame hypotheses or to develop interpretations that are not culture-bound. However, by encompassing both humanism and science, the discipline of anthropology can draw on its internal diversity to overcome conceptual locks.

---

empirical An approach based on observations of the world rather than on intuition or faith.

hypothesis A tentative explanation of the relationships among certain phenomena.

theory A coherent statement that provides an explanatory framework for understanding; an explanation or interpretation supported by a reliable body of data.

doctrine An assertion of opinion or belief formally handed down by an authority as true and indisputable.

culture shock In fieldwork, the anthropologist's personal disorientation and anxiety that may result in depression.

Fieldwork

Anthropologists are keenly aware that their personal identity and cultural background may shape their research questions, bear upon their factual observations, and even influence their interpretations and explanations. To avoid inadvertent bias or distortion, they immerse themselves in the data to the fullest extent possible through on-location research traditionally known as *fieldwork*.

Fieldwork, introduced earlier in this chapter in connection with cultural anthropology, is characteristic of *all* the anthropological subdisciplines. Archaeologists and paleoanthropologists excavate sites in the field, and, as already noted, cultural anthropologists observe human behavior while living and interacting with a group of people wherever the group may reside, work, or travel. Just as an ethnographer will study the culture of a human community by living in it, a primatologist might live among a group of chimpanzees or gorillas in the forest. Likewise, linguistic anthropologists interested in analyzing or comparing words and grammar from undocumented languages must first learn the languages, and they typically do so by living in communities where these are actually spoken. The same is true for colleagues studying how speech is actually "performed" in various social settings. Also, a physical anthropologist interested in the effects of globalization on nutrition and growth may reside in a particular community to research this issue.

Fieldwork requires researchers to step out of their cultural comfort zone into a world that is unfamiliar and sometimes unsettling. Anthropologists in the field are likely to face a host of challenges—physical, social, mental, political, and ethical. They often must deal with the physical challenges of unfamiliar food, climate, and hygiene conditions.

Typically, anthropologists in the field struggle with emotional challenges such as loneliness, feeling like a perpetual outsider, being socially awkward in their new cultural setting, and having to be alert around the clock because anything that is happening or being said may be significant to their research. Political challenges include the possibility of unwittingly letting oneself be used by factions within the community, or being regarded with suspicion by government authorities who may view the anthropologist as a spy. And there are ethical dilemmas: What does the anthropologist do if faced with a troubling cultural practice such as female circumcision? How does the anthropologist deal with demands for food supplies or medicine? Is it acceptable to use deception to gain vital information? Collectively, these multiple challenges may gradually amount to **culture shock**—personal disorientation and anxiety that may result in depression, forcing some anthropologists to abandon their fieldwork and return home for recovery.

More often, however, fieldwork leads to tangible and meaningful personal, professional, and social rewards, ranging from lasting friendships to significant knowledge and insights concerning the human condition. Something of the meaning of anthropological fieldwork—its usefulness and its impact on researcher and subject—is conveyed in the following Original Study by Suzanne Leclerc-Madlala, an anthropologist who left her familiar New England surroundings nearly thirty years ago to do AIDS research among Zulu-speaking people in South Africa. Her research interest has changed the course of her own life, not to mention the lives of many individuals who are dealing with AIDS/HIV.

ORIGINAL STUDY

Fighting HIV/AIDS in Africa: Traditional Healers on the Front Line BY SUZANNE LECLERC-MADLALA

In the 1980s, as an anthropology graduate student at George Washington University, I met and married a Zulu-speaking student from South Africa. It was the height of apartheid (racial segregation), and upon moving to that country I was classified as "honorary black" and forced to live in a segregated township with my husband. The AIDS epidemic was in its infancy, but it was clear from the start that an anthropological understanding of how people perceive and engage with this disease would be crucial for developing interventions. I wanted to learn all that I could to make a difference, and this culminated in earning a doctorate from the University of Natal on the cultural construction of AIDS among the Zulu. The HIV/AIDS pandemic in Africa became my professional passion.

Faced with overwhelming global health-care needs, the World Health Organization passed a series of resolutions in the 1970s promoting collaboration between traditional and modern medicine. Such moves held a special relevance for Africa where traditional healers typically outnumber practitioners of modern medicine by a ratio of 100 to 1 or more. Given Africa's disproportionate burden of disease, supporting partnership efforts with traditional healers makes sense. But what sounds sensible today was once considered absurd, even heretical. For centuries Westerners generally viewed traditional healing as a whole lot of primitive mumbo jumbo practiced by witchdoctors with demonic powers who perpetuated superstition. Yet, its practice survived. Today, as the African continent grapples with an HIV/AIDS epidemic of crisis proportion, millions of sick people who are either too poor or too distant to access modern health care are proving that traditional healers are an invaluable resource in the fight against AIDS.

Of the world's estimated 35 million people currently infected by HIV, nearly 70 percent live in sub-Saharan Africa, and the vast majority of children left orphaned by AIDS are African. From the 1980s onward, as Africa became synonymous with the rapid spread of HIV/AIDS, a number of prevention programs involved traditional healers. My initial research in South Africa's KwaZulu-Natal province—where almost 40 percent of the population is HIV infected—revealed that traditional Zulu healers were regularly consulted for the treatment of sexually transmitted disease (STD). I found that such diseases, along with HIV/AIDS, were usually attributed to transgressions of taboos related to birth, pregnancy, marriage, and death. Moreover, these diseases were often understood within a framework of pollution and contagion, and like most serious illnesses, ultimately believed to have their causal roots in witchcraft.

I investigated a pioneer program in STD and HIV education for traditional healers in the province. It aimed to provide basic biomedical knowledge about the various modes of disease transmission, the means available for prevention, the diagnosing of symptoms, the keeping of records, and the making of patient referrals to local clinics and hospitals.

Interviews with the healers showed that many were deeply suspicious of modern medicine. They perceived AIDS education as a one-way street intended to press them into formal health structures and convince them of the superiority of modern medicine. Yet, today, few of the 6,000-plus KwaZulu-Natal healers who have been trained in AIDS education say they would opt for less collaboration; most want to have more.

Treatments by Zulu healers for HIV/AIDS often take the form of infusions of bitter herbs to "cleanse" the body, strengthen the blood, and remove misfortune and "pollution." Some treatments provide effective relief from common ailments associated with AIDS such as itchy skin rashes, oral thrush, persistent diarrhea, and general debility. Indigenous plants such as *unwele (Sutherlandia frutescens)* and African potato *(Hypoxis hemerocallidea)* are well-known traditional medicines that have proven immuno-boosting properties. Both have recently become available in modern pharmacies packaged in tablet form. With modern anti-retroviral treatments still well beyond the reach of most South Africans, indigenous medicines that can delay or alleviate some of the suffering caused by AIDS are proving to be valuable and popular treatments.

Knowledge about potentially infectious bodily fluids has led healers to change some of their practices. Where porcupine quills were once used to give a type of indigenous injection, patients are now advised to bring their own

sewing needles to consultations. Patients provide their own individual razor blades for making incisions on their skin, where previously healers reused the same razor on many clients. Some healers claim they have given up the practice of biting clients' skin to remove foreign objects from the body. Today, especially in urban centers like Durban, it is not uncommon for healers to proudly display AIDS training certificates in their inner-city "surgeries" where they don white jackets and wear protective latex gloves.

Medical anthropologist Suzanne Leclerc-Madlala visits with "Doctor" Koloko in KwaZulu-Natal, South Africa. This Zulu traditional healer proudly displays her official AIDS training certificate.

Politics and controversy have dogged South Africa's official response to HIV/AIDS. But back home in the waddle-and-daub, animal-skin-draped herbariums and divining huts of traditional healers, the politics of AIDS holds little relevance. Here the sick and dying are coming in droves to be treated by healers who have been part and parcel of community life (and death) since time immemorial. In many cases traditional healers have transformed their homes into hospices for AIDS patients. Because of the strong negative stigma that still plagues the disease, those with AIDS symptoms are often abandoned or sometimes chased away from their homes by family members. They seek refuge with healers who provide them with comfort in their final days. Healers' homes are also becoming orphanages as healers respond to what has been called the "third wave" of AIDS destruction: the growing legions of orphaned children.

Those who are suffering go to traditional healers not only in search of relief for physical symptoms. They go to learn about the ultimate cause of their disease—something other than the immediate cause of a sexually transmitted "germ" or "virus." They go to find answers to the "why me and not him" questions, the "why now" and "why this." As with most traditional healing systems worldwide, healing among the Zulu and most all African ethnic groups cannot be separated from the spiritual concerns of the individual and the cosmological beliefs of the community at large. Traditional healers help to restore a sense of balance between the individual and the community, on one hand, and between the individual and the cosmos, or ancestors, on the other hand. They provide health care that is personalized, culturally appropriate, holistic, and tailored to meet the needs and expectations of the patient. In many ways it is a far more satisfactory form of healing than that offered by modern medicine.

Traditional healing in Africa is flourishing in the era of AIDS, and understanding why this is so requires a shift in the conceptual framework by which we understand, explain, and interpret health. Anthropological methods and its comparative and holistic perspective can facilitate, like no other discipline, the type of understanding that is urgently needed to address the AIDS crisis.

For more details, see Leclerc-Madlala, S. (2002). Bodies and politics: Healing rituals in the democratic South Africa. *In V. Faure (Ed.),* Les cahiers de 'I'IFAS, *no. 2. Johannesburg: The French Institute. Leclerc-Madlala now works for USAID.*

Questions of Ethics

Anthropologists deal with matters that are private and sensitive, including information that individuals would prefer not to have generally known about them. In the early years of the discipline, many anthropologists documented traditional cultures they assumed would disappear due to disease, warfare, or changes imposed by colonialism, growing state power, or international market expansion. Some worked as government administrators or consultants gathering data used to formulate policies concerning indigenous peoples. Others helped predict the behavior of enemies during wartime.

How does one write about important but delicate issues and at the same time protect the privacy of the individuals who have shared their stories? The kinds of research carried out by anthropologists, and the settings within which they work, raise important moral questions about the potential uses and abuses of our knowledge. Who will utilize our findings and for what purposes? Who decides what research questions are asked? Who, if anyone, will benefit from the research? For example, in the case of research on an ethnic or religious minority whose values may be at odds with the dominant society, will government bureaucracies or industrial corporations use anthropological data to suppress that group? And what of traditional communities around the world? Who is to decide what changes should, or should not, be introduced for community development? And who defines "development"—the community, a national government, or an international agency like the World Bank?

After the colonial era ended in the 1960s, and in reaction to controversial research practices by some anthropologists in or near violent conflict areas, anthropologists formulated a code of ethics to ensure that their research would not harm the groups being studied. Formalized in 1971 and revised in 1998 and again in 2009, the American Anthropological Association's (AAA) ethics code outlines a range of moral responsibilities and obligations. It includes this core principle: Anthropological researchers must do everything in their power to ensure that their research does not harm the safety, dignity, or privacy of the people with whom they work, conduct research, or perform other professional activities.

In recent years, some of the debates regarding this code have focused on the potential ethical breaches if anthropologists work for corporations or undertake classified contract work for the military. Although the AAA has no legal authority, it does issue policy statements on research ethics questions as they come up. For example, recently the AAA recommended that research notes from medical settings should be protected and not subject to subpoena in court. This honors the ethical imperative to protect the privacy of individuals who have shared with anthropologists their stories about personal health issues.

Emerging technologies have ethical implications that impact anthropological inquiry. For example, the ability to sequence and patent particular genes has led to debates about who has the right to hold a patent—the individuals from whom the particular genes were obtained or the researcher who studies the genes? Similarly, do ancient remains belong to the scientist, to the people living in the region under scientific investigation, or to whoever happens to have possession of them? Global market forces have converted these remains into expensive collectibles, resulting in a systematic looting of archaeological and fossil sites.

While seeking answers to these questions, anthropologists recognize that they have special obligations to three sets of people: those whom they study, those who fund the research, and those in the profession who rely on published findings to increase our collective knowledge. Because fieldwork requires a relationship of trust between researchers and the community in which they work, the anthropologist's first responsibility clearly is to the people who have shared their stories and their community. Everything possible must be done to protect their physical, social, and psychological welfare and to honor their dignity and privacy. This task is frequently complex. For example, telling the story of a people gives information both to relief agencies who might help them and to others who might take advantage of them.

Maintaining one's own culture is an internationally recognized basic human right, and any connection with

Globalscape

A Global Body Shop?

Lakshmamma, pictured here with her daughter in southern India's rural village of Holalu, near Mandya, has sold one of her kidneys for about 30,000 rupees ($650). This is far below the average going rate of $6,000 per kidney in the global organ transplant business. But the broker took his commission, and corrupt officials needed to be paid as well. Although India passed a law in 1994 prohibiting the buying and selling of human organs, the business is booming. In Europe and North America, kidney transplants can cost over $200,000, plus the waiting list for donor kidneys is long, and dialysis is expensive. Thus "transplant tourism," in India and several other countries, caters to affluent patients in search of "fresh" kidneys to be harvested from poor people like Lakshmamma.[a]

The well-publicized arrest of Brooklyn-based organ broker Levy Izhak Rosenbaum in July 2009—part of an FBI sting operation that also led to the arrest of forty-five other individuals, including several public officials in New Jersey—represents some progress in combatting illegal trafficking of body parts. Charged with brokering illegal kidney transplants—purchasing the organs for $10,000–$25,000 and selling them for as much as $160,000—the Israeli immigrant pleaded guilty to three trafficking counts and agreed to forfeit $420,000 in broker fees. In July 2012, he was sentenced to 2½ years in prison and possible deportation.[b]

Medical anthropologist and activist Nancy Scheper-Hughes has researched the criminal and medical aspects of global organ trafficking for some two decades. Cofounder of Organs Watch in Berkeley, California, an organization working to stop the illegal traffic in organs, she notified the FBI about Rosenbaum in 2002.[c] International crackdowns and changes in local laws are now curbing illegal global networks in human organ trafficking.

Global Twister

Considering that $650 is a fortune in a poor village like Holalu, does medical globalization benefit or exploit people like Lakshmamma, who are looked upon as human commodities? What accounts for the gap between the $650 she received for her kidney and the fees Rosenbaum received for the organ sales he brokered?

[a]Vidya, R. (2002). Karnataka's unabating kidney trade. *Frontline.* www.frontlineonnet.com/fl1907/19070610.htm (retrieved June 10, 2012)

[b]Henry, S., & Porter, D. (2011, October 27). Levy Izhak Rosenbaum pleads guilty to selling black market kidneys. *Huffingtonpost.com.* www.huffingtonpost.com/2011/10/27/levy-izhak-rosenbaum-plea_n_1035624.html (retrieved June 10, 2012)

[c]Glovin, D., & Voreacos, D. (2012, July 12). Kidney broker sentenced to prison. *Bloomberg News.* Retrieved from http://www.businessweek.com/news/2012-07-11/n-dot-y-dot-man-gets-30-month-term-in-first-u-dot-s-dot-organ-case

outsiders can expose and therefore endanger the cultural integrity of the community being studied. To overcome some of these ethical challenges, anthropologists frequently collaborate with and contribute to the communities in which they are working, inviting the people being studied to have some say about if and how their stories are told. In research involving ancient human remains, collaboration with local people not only preserves the remains from market forces but also honors the connections of indigenous people to the places and remains under study.

Anthropology and Globalization

A holistic perspective and a long-term commitment to understanding the human species in all its variety equip anthropologists to grapple with a challenge that has overriding importance for each of us today: **globalization**. This concept refers to worldwide interconnectedness, evidenced in rapid global movement of natural resources, trade goods, human labor, finance capital, information, and infectious diseases. Although worldwide travel, trade relations, and information flow have existed for several centuries, the pace and magnitude of these long-distance exchanges have picked up enormously in recent decades; the Internet, in particular, has greatly expanded information exchange capacities.

The powerful forces driving globalization are technological innovations, cost differences among countries, faster knowledge transfers, and increased trade and financial integration among countries. Touching almost everybody's life on the planet, globalization is about economics as much as politics, and it changes human relations and ideas as well as our natural environments. Even geographically remote communities are quickly becoming interdependent—and often vulnerable—through globalization (see the Globalscape on the opposite page for an example).

Researching in all corners of the world, anthropologists witness the impact of globalization on human communities wherever they are located. They describe and try to explain how individuals and organizations respond to the massive changes confronting them. Dramatically increasing every year, globalization can be a two-edged sword. It may generate economic growth and prosperity, but it also undermines long-established institutions. Generally, globalization has brought significant gains to more-educated groups in wealthier countries, while at the same time contributing to the erosion of traditional cultures. Upheavals due to globalization are key causes for rising levels of ethnic and religious conflict throughout the world.

Because all of us now live in a global village, we can no longer afford the luxury of ignoring our neighbors, no matter how distant they may seem. In this age of globalization, anthropology may not only provide humanity with useful

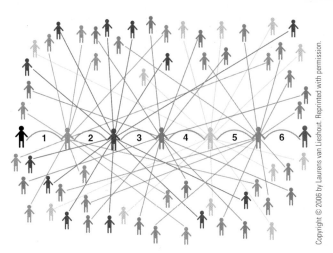

Figure 1.8 **Six Degrees of Separation** The phrase "six degrees of separation," diagrammed here, refers to the idea that everyone is on average approximately six steps away, by way of introduction, from any other person on earth. Thus, a chain of "a friend of a friend" statements can be made to connect any two people in six steps or fewer. Originally coined by Hungarian writer Frigyes Karinthy in his 1929 short story, "Chains," it was popularized by American playwright John Guare's 1993 film, *Six Degrees of Separation*. It became all the more popular after four college students invented the trivia game Six Degrees of Kevin Bacon, in which the goal is to link any actor to film star Kevin Bacon through no more than six performance connections.

insights concerning diversity, but it may also assist us in avoiding or overcoming significant problems born of that diversity. In countless social arenas, from schools to businesses to hospitals to emergency centers, anthropologists have done cross-cultural research that makes it possible for educators, businesspeople, doctors, and humanitarians to do their work more effectively.

As illustrated by many examples in this textbook, ignorance or ethnocentric (mis)information about other societies and their cultural beliefs and practices can cause or fuel serious problems throughout the world. This is especially true in an age when human interactions and interdependence have been transformed by global information exchange and transportation advances. As noted in the Challenge Issue at the start of this chapter, there are only six degrees of separation between each of us and any other person on earth (**Figure 1.8**). Anthropology offers a way of looking at and understanding the world's peoples—insights that are nothing less than basic skills for survival in this age of globalization.

globalization Worldwide interconnectedness, evidenced in rapid global movement of natural resources, trade goods, human labor, finance capital, information, and infectious diseases.

CHAPTER CHECKLIST

What is anthropology?

● Anthropology is the objective and systematic study of humankind in all times and places.

● Anthropology contains four major fields or subdisciplines: cultural anthropology, linguistic anthropology, archaeology, and physical or biological anthropology.

● In each of anthropology's fields some individuals practice applied anthropology, which uses anthropological knowledge to solve practical problems.

What do anthropologists do in each of its four fields?

● Cultural anthropologists study humans in terms of their cultures, the often-unconscious standards by which social groups operate.

● Linguistic anthropologists study human languages and may deal with the description of a language, with the history of languages, or with how languages are used in particular social settings.

● Archaeologists study human cultures through the recovery and analysis of material remains and environmental data.

● Physical anthropologists focus on humans as biological organisms; they particularly emphasize tracing the evolutionary development of the human animal and studying biological variation within the species today.

How is anthropology different from other disciplines?

● Unique among the sciences and humanities, anthropology has long emphasized the study of non-Western societies and a holistic approach, which aims to formulate theoretically valid explanations and interpretations of human diversity based on detailed studies of all aspects of human biology, behavior, and beliefs in all known societies, past and present.

● In anthropology, the humanities, social sciences, and natural sciences come together into a genuinely humanistic science. Anthropology's link with the humanities can be seen in its concern with people's beliefs, values, languages, arts, and literature—oral as well as written—but above all in its attempt to convey the experience of living in different cultures.

How do anthropologists conduct research?

● Fieldwork, characteristic of all the anthropological subdisciplines, includes complete immersion in

research settings ranging from archaeological and paleoanthropological survey and excavation, to living with a group of primates in their natural habitat, to biological data gathered while living with a group. Ethnographic participant observation with a particular culture or subculture is the classic field method of cultural anthropology.

● After the fieldwork of archaeologists and physical anthropologists, researchers conduct laboratory analyses of excavated remains or biological samples collected in the field.

● The comparative method is key to all branches of anthropology. Anthropologists make broad comparisons among peoples and cultures—past and present. They also compare related species and fossil groups. Ethnology, the comparative branch of cultural anthropologists, uses a range of ethnographic accounts to construct theories about cultures from a comparative or historical point of view. Ethnologists often focus on a particular aspect of culture, such as religious or economic practices.

How do anthropologists face the ethical challenges that emerge through conducting anthropological research?

● Anthropologists must stay aware of the potential uses and abuses of anthropological knowledge and the ways that it is obtained.

● The anthropological code of ethics, first formalized in 1971 and continually revised, outlines the moral and ethical responsibilities of anthropologists to the people whom they study, to those who fund the research, and to the profession as a whole.

What can anthropology contribute to the understanding of globalization?

● A long tradition of studying the connections among diverse peoples over time gives anthropology a theoretical framework to study globalization in a world increasingly linked through recent technological advancements.

● Anthropology equips global citizens to challenge ethnocentrism and to understand human diversity.

● Anthropology has essential insights to offer the modern world, particularly today, when understanding our neighbors in the global village has become a matter of survival for all.

QUESTIONS FOR REFLECTION

1. As noted in this chapter's opening Challenge Issue, there are only six degrees of separation between you and the pictured coltan miner working in the heart of Africa. Many miners are poor or orphaned children forced into hard labor and living in squalor, with short life expectancies. When you buy a new electronic device that uses coltan, do you think you contribute to the miserable exploitation of fellow humans?

2. Anthropology embraces a holistic approach to explain all aspects of human beliefs, behavior, and biology. How might anthropology challenge your personal perspective on the question, who am I?

3. From the holistic anthropological perspective, humans have one leg in culture and the other in nature. Are there examples from your life that illustrate the interconnectedness of human biology and culture?

4. Globalization can be described as a two-edged sword. How does it foster growth and destruction simultaneously?

5. The Biocultural Connection in this chapter contrasts different cultural perspectives on brain death, while the Original Study features a discussion about traditional Zulu healers and their role in dealing with AIDS victims. What do these two accounts suggest about the role of applied anthropology in dealing with cross-cultural health issues around the world?

ONLINE STUDY RESOURCES

CourseMate

Access chapter-specific learning tools, including learning objectives, practice quizzes, videos, flash cards, glossaries, and more in your Anthropology CourseMate.

Log into **www.cengagebrain.com** to access the resources your instructor has assigned and to purchase materials.

Challenge Issue

Born naked and speechless, humans are naturally incapable of surviving without culture—a socially learned adaptive system designed to help us meet our challenges of survival. Each culture is distinct, expressing its unique qualities in numerous ways, including the way we speak, what we eat, the clothes we wear, and with whom we live. Although culture goes far beyond what meets the eye, it is inscribed everywhere we look. Here we see a family of Kuchi ("migrant") herders in northeast Afghanistan. Because mobility is a key element in their successful adaptation to an arid environment, nearly everything they own is movable. Coming from different ethnic groups, Kuchi do not all share the same language. The particular fabrics, forms, and colors of their belongings and apparel mark their cultural identity. Many Kuchi have recently settled down, but about 1.5 million are still fully nomadic, with livelihoods dependent upon herds of goats and sheep. Using camels and donkeys to carry their belongings, this family follows age-old migration routes across mountains and valleys. They exchange their surplus animal products—meat, hides, wool, hair, *ghee* (butter), and *quroot* (dried yoghurt)—for wheat, sugar, salt, metal and plastic tools, and other trade goods. Ecological adaptation and symbolic expression of group identity are among the many interrelated functions of culture.

Characteristics of Culture

An introductory anthropology course presents what may seem like an endless variety of human societies, each with its own distinctive way of life, manners, beliefs, arts, and so on. Yet for all this diversity, these societies have one thing in common: Each is a group of human beings cooperating to ensure their collective survival and well-being.

Group living and cooperation are impossible unless individuals know how others are likely to behave in any given situation. Thus, some degree of predictable behavior is required of each person within the society. In humans, it is culture that sets the limits of behavior and guides it along predictable paths that are generally acceptable to those within the culture. The culturally specified ways in which we learn to act so that we conform to the social expectations in our community did not develop randomly. Among the major forces guiding how each culture has developed in its own distinctive way is a process known as adaptation.

Culture and Adaptation

From generation to generation, humans, like all animals, have continuously faced the challenge of adapting to their environment, its conditions and its resources, as well as to changes over time. The term **adaptation** refers to a gradual process by which organisms adjust to the conditions of the locality in which they live. Organisms have generally adapted biologically as the frequency of advantageous anatomical and physiological features increases in a population through the process of natural selection. For example, body hair protects mammals from extremes of temperature, specialized teeth help them to procure the kinds of food they need, and so on. Short-term physiological responses to the environment—along with responses that become incorporated into an organism through interaction with the environment during growth and development—are other kinds of biological adaptations.

adaptation A series of beneficial adjustments to a particular environment.

IN THIS CHAPTER YOU WILL LEARN TO

- Explain culture as a dynamic form of adaptation.

- Distinguish between culture, society, and ethnicity.

- Identify basic characteristics common to all cultures.

- Describe the connection among culture, society, and the individual.

- Define and critique *ethnocentrism*.

Marcus Fornell

Figure 2.1 A Living Bridge This bridge in Meghalaya, India, is made of the roots of living strangler fig trees (*Ficus elastica*). Meghalaya ("Abode of the Clouds") is the wettest place on earth with an average rainfall of some 40 feet a year. Nearly all of the rain is during the summer monsoon season, turning rivers and streams into raging torrents. The tangled roots of strangler figs help keep riverbanks from washing away, and the Khazi people living in this region train the roots into living bridges. Shaping a bridge is an epic project that cannot be accomplished in a single lifetime. From one generation to the next, individuals pass on the knowledge of how to guide and connect the hanging roots so they grow into a strong bridge. Dozens of these bridges form part of an essential and complex network of forest paths connecting the valleys of Meghalaya. Some of them are many centuries old.

Humans, however, have increasingly come to depend on **cultural adaptation**, a complex of ideas, technologies, and activities that enables them to survive and even thrive in their environment. Biology has not provided people with built-in fur coats to protect them in cold climates, but it has given us the ability to make our own coats, build fires, and construct shelters to shield ourselves against the cold. We may not be able to run as fast as a cheetah, but we are able to invent and build vehicles that can carry us faster and farther than any other creature.

Through culture and its many constructions, the human species has secured not just its survival but its expansion as well—at great cost to other species and, increasingly, to the planet at large. And by manipulating environments through cultural means, people have been able to move into a vast range of environments, from the icy Arctic to the searing Sahara Desert to the rainiest place on earth in northeast India (**Figure 2.1**).

This is not to say that everything human beings do is *because* it is adaptive to a particular environment. For one thing, people do not just react to an environment as given; rather, they react to it as they perceive it, and different groups may perceive the same environment in radically different ways. People also react to things other than the environment: their own biological traits, their beliefs and attitudes, and the short- and long-term consequences of their behavior for themselves and other people and life forms that share their habitats.

---

cultural adaptation A complex of ideas, technologies, and activities that enables people to survive and even thrive in their environment.

Figure 2.2 Center-Pivot Irrigation What is adaptive at one time may not be at another. In the Central Plains of North America, irrigation systems and chemical fertilizers have resulted in large but unsustainable crop yields in a principal region of grain cultivation. Here we see crop fields in western Kansas that are watered by a center-pivot irrigation system fed by the Ogallala aquifer. The aquifer, which underlies eight states from southern South Dakota to northwestern Texas, provides about 30 percent of the nation's groundwater used for irrigation, plus drinking water to 82 percent of the people who live within the aquifer boundary. However, over the past five decades, the aquifer's water table has dropped dramatically, and some experts estimate it will dry up in as little as two decades. Moreover, in semi-arid regions steady winds hasten evaporation of surface water. This leads to a buildup of salts in the soil, eventually resulting in toxic levels for plants. Chemical fertilizers also contribute to the pollution problem.

Although people maintain cultures to deal with problems, some cultural practices have proved to be inadequate or ill-fitting, sometimes creating new problems—such as toxic air and water resulting from certain industrial practices and a growing worldwide obesity epidemic spurred on by fast food, spectator sports, motorized transport, electronic media, and other technologies reducing people's physical activity.

A further complication is the relativity of any particular adaptation: What is adaptive in one setting may be seriously maladaptive in another. For example, the hygiene practices of food-foraging peoples—their habits of garbage and human waste disposal—are appropriate to contexts of low population densities, a degree of residential mobility, and organic materials. But these same practices become serious health hazards in large, fully sedentary populations such as urban slums without space to dump (in)disposable waste, including plastic and chemicals. In fact, with almost 4 billion people living in cities, waste management is turning into a huge challenge in many parts of the world.

Similarly, behavior that is adaptive in the short run may be maladaptive over a longer period of time. For instance, the development of irrigation in ancient Mesopotamia (southern Iraq) made it possible for people to increase food production, but it also caused a gradual accumulation of salt in the soil, which contributed to the downfall of that civilization about 4,000 years ago. Similar situations exist in parts of the United States today (**Figure 2.2**).

Today, in many parts of the world the development of prime farmland for purposes other than food production increases dependency on food raised in less than optimal environments. Marginal farmlands can produce high yields with costly technology. However, over time these yields will not be sustainable due to loss of topsoil, increasing salinity of soil, and silting of irrigation works, not to mention the high cost of fresh water and fossil fuel.

All told, for any culture to be successful across generations, it must produce collective human behavior that does not destroy its natural environment. Successful adaptation has been, and continues to be, a major challenge facing every society in its long-term quest for survival. In response to this challenge, our species has developed a great variety of cultures, each with its own unique features befitting the particular needs of societies located in different corners of the globe. So, what do we mean by *culture*?

The Concept of Culture

Anthropologists conceived the modern concept of culture toward the end of the 19th century. The first comprehensive definition came from the British anthropologist Sir Edward Tylor. Writing in 1871, he defined *culture* as "that complex whole which includes knowledge, belief, art, law, morals, custom, and any other capabilities and habits acquired by man as a member of society" (Tylor, 1871, p. 1).

Recent definitions tend to distinguish more clearly between actual behavior and the abstract ideas, values, feelings, and perceptions of the world that inform that behavior. To put it another way, **culture** goes deeper than observable behavior; it is a society's shared and socially transmitted ideas, values, emotions, and perceptions that are used to make sense of experience, generate behavior, and are reflected in that behavior.

Characteristics of Culture

Through the comparative study of many human cultures, past and present, anthropologists have gained an understanding of the basic characteristics evident in all of them: Every culture is socially learned, shared, based on symbols, integrated, and dynamic. A careful study of these characteristics helps us to see the importance and the function of culture itself.

Culture Is Learned

All culture is socially learned rather than biologically inherited. One learns one's culture by growing up with it, and the process whereby culture is passed on from one generation to the next is called **enculturation** (Figure 2.3).

Most animals eat and drink whenever the urge arises. Humans, however, are enculturated to do most of their eating and drinking at certain culturally prescribed times and feel hungry as those times approach. These eating times vary from culture to culture, as does what is eaten, how it is prepared, how it is consumed, and where. To add complexity, food is used to do more than merely satisfy nutritional requirements. When used to celebrate rituals and religious activities, as it often is, food "establishes relationships of give and take, of cooperation, of sharing, of an emotional bond that is universal" (Caroulis, 1996, p. 16).

Through enculturation every person learns socially appropriate ways of satisfying the basic biologically determined needs of all humans: food, sleep, shelter, companionship, self-defense, and sexual gratification. It is important to distinguish between the needs themselves, which are not learned, and the learned ways in which they are satisfied—for each culture determines in its own way how these needs will be met. For instance, a French Canadian fisherman's idea of a great dinner and a comfortable way to sleep may vary greatly from that of a Kazakh nomad in Mongolia.

Most, if not all, mammals exhibit some degree of learned behavior. Several species may even be said to have elementary culture, in that local populations share patterns of behavior that, as among humans, each generation learns from the one before and that differ from one population to another. For example, research shows a distinctive pattern of behavior among lions of southern Africa's Kalahari Desert—behavior that fostered nonaggressive interaction with the region's indigenous hunters and gatherers and that each generation of lions passed on to the next. Moreover, Kalahari lion culture changed over a thirty-year period in response to new circumstances (Thomas, 1994). That said, it is important to note that not all learned behavior is cultural. For instance, a pigeon may learn tricks, but this behavior is reflexive, the result of conditioning by repeated training, not the product of enculturation.

Beyond our species, examples of socially learned behavior are particularly evident among other primates. An example of this is the way a chimpanzee will take a twig, strip it of all leaves, and smooth it down to fashion a tool for extracting termites from their nest. Such toolmaking, which juveniles learn from their elders, is unquestionably a form of cultural behavior once thought to be exclusively human. In Japan, macaque monkeys have learned the advantages of washing sweet potatoes before eating them and passed the practice on to the next generation.

Within any given primate species, one population's way of life often differs from that of others, just as it does among humans. We have discovered both in captivity and in the wild that primates in general and apes in particular "possess a near-human intelligence, generally including the use of sounds in representational ways, a rich awareness of the aims and objectives of others, the ability to engage in tactical deception, and the faculty to use symbols in communication with humans and each other" (Reynolds, 1994, p. 4).

Our increasing awareness of such traits in our primate relatives has spawned numerous movements to extend human rights to apes—rights such as freedom from living in fear, respect for dignity, and not being subjected to incarceration (caging), exploitation (medical experimentation), or other mistreatment. The movement reached a milestone with the Kinshasa Declaration on Great Apes. Signed by over seventy representatives from twenty-four countries and many nongovernmental organizations, convening in the capital of the Democratic Republic of the Congo in 2005, this document affirms a commitment to protect great apes, like chimps, gorillas, and orangutans, and extends some human rights to our closest animal relatives (O'Carroll, 2008).

---

culture A society's shared and socially transmitted ideas, values, emotions, and perceptions, which are used to make sense of experience and generate behavior and are reflected in that behavior.

enculturation The process by which a society's culture is passed on from one generation to the next and individuals become members of their society.

Trent Burkholder Photography

Figure 2.3 Stilt Fishing A father practices the traditional art of stilt fishing with his son in Ahangama, Sri Lanka. It's a tough job, wading through shallow waters before dawn and sitting atop the uncomfortable platform for hours to catch small fish that sell for about 2 cents apiece. The art of stilt fishing has been passed from father to son for generations, but fewer and fewer families are building their lives around this profession today due to low profits, harsh conditions, and tourists who are scaring the fish away.

Culture Is Shared

As a shared set of ideas, values, perceptions, and standards of behavior, culture is the common denominator that makes the actions of individuals intelligible to other members of their society. Culture enables individuals in a society to predict how fellow members are most likely to behave in a given circumstance, and it informs them how to react accordingly. **Society** may be defined as an organized group or groups of interdependent people who generally share a common territory, language, and culture and who act together for collective survival and well-being. The ways in which these people depend upon one another can be seen in such features as their economic, communication, and defense systems. They are also bound together by a general sense of common identity.

Because culture and society are such closely related concepts, anthropologists study both. Obviously, there can be no culture without a society. Conversely, there are no known human societies that do not exhibit culture. Without culture, human society quickly falls apart. This cannot be said for all other animal species. Ants and bees, for example, instinctively cooperate in a manner that clearly indicates a remarkable degree of social organization, yet this instinctual behavior is not a culture.

Although members of a society share a culture, it is important to realize that all is not uniform. For one thing, no two people share the exact same version of their culture. At the very least, there is some distinction between the roles of children and elders, men and women. This stems from the fact that there are obvious differences between infants, fully matured, and highly aged

individuals, as well as between female and male reproductive anatomy and physiology. Every society gives cultural meaning to biological sex differences by explaining them in a particular way and specifying what their significance is in terms of social roles and expected patterns of behavior.

Because each culture does this in its own way, there can be tremendous variation from one society to another. Anthropologists use the term **gender** to refer to the cultural elaborations and meanings assigned to the biological differentiation between the sexes. So, although one's sex is biologically determined, one's gender is socially constructed within the context of one's particular culture (**Figure 2.4** on the next page).

Apart from sexual differences directly related to reproduction, biological underpinnings for contrasting gender roles have largely disappeared in modern industrialized and postindustrial societies. For example, men and women are equally capable of accomplishing tasks requiring muscular strength, such as moving heavy automobile engines, because assembly lines use hydraulic lifts for the job. Nevertheless, all cultures exhibit at least some role differentiation related to biology—some far more so than others.

In addition to cultural variation associated with gender, there is also variation related to age. In any society, children are not expected to behave as adults, and the

society An organized group or groups of interdependent people who generally share a common territory, language, and culture and who act together for collective survival and well-being.

gender The cultural elaborations and meanings assigned to the biological differentiation between the sexes.

Figure 2.4 Gender Identification
In U.S. hospital nurseries, newborn girls are typically wrapped in pink blankets and boys in blue blankets. This is in response to popular expectations in the United States and many other countries that newborn infants be assigned a gender identity of either male or female. Yet significant numbers of infants are born each year whose genitalia do not conform to cultural expectations. Because only two genders are recognized, the usual reaction is to make the young bodies conform to cultural requirements through gender assignment surgery that involves constructing male or female genitalia. This is in contrast to many Native American cultures (among others), which have traditionally recognized more than two genders (Blackless et al., 2000).

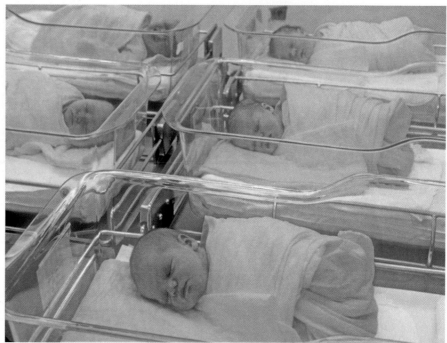

© Randy Duchaine/Alamy

reverse is equally true. But then, who is a child and who is an adult? Again, although age differences are natural, cultures give their own meaning and timetable to the human life cycle. In North America, for example, individuals are generally not regarded as adults until the age of 18; in many other cultures, adulthood begins earlier—often around age 12, an age closer to the biological changes of adolescence.

Subcultures: Groups Within a Larger Society

Besides age and gender differentiation, there may be cultural variation between subgroups in societies that share an overarching culture. These may be occupational groups in societies where there is a complex division of labor, or social classes in a stratified society, or ethnic groups in other societies. When such groups exist within a society—each functioning by its own distinctive set of ideas, values, and behavior patterns while still sharing some common standards—we call them **subcultures**.

Amish communities are one example of a subculture in North America. Specifically, they are an **ethnic group**—people who collectively and publicly identify

themselves as a distinct group based on various cultural features such as shared ancestry and common origin, language, customs, and traditional beliefs. The Amish originated in western Europe during the Protestant revolutions of the 16th century. Today, members of this group number about 100,000 and live mainly in the United States—in Pennsylvania, Ohio, Illinois, and Indiana—as well as in Ontario, Canada (**Figure 2.5**).

These rural pacifists base their lives on their traditional Anabaptist beliefs, which hold that only adult baptism is valid and that "true Christians" (as they define them) should not hold government office, bear arms, or use force. They prohibit marriage outside their faith, which calls for obedience to radical Christian teachings, including social separation from what they see as the wider evil world and rejection of material wealth as vainglorious.

Among themselves, Amish people usually speak a German dialect known as Pennsylvania Dutch (from *Deutsch*, meaning "German"). They use formal German for religious purposes, although children learn English in school. Valuing simplicity, hard work, and a high degree of neighborly cooperation, they dress in a distinctive plain garb and even today rely on the horse for transportation as well as agricultural work (Hostetler & Huntington, 1992). In sum, the Amish share the same **ethnicity**. This term, rooted in the Greek word *ethnikos* ("nation") and related to *ethnos* ("custom"), is the expression for the set of cultural ideas held by an ethnic group.

The goal of Amish education is to teach youngsters reading, writing, and arithmetic, as well as Amish values. Adults in the community reject what they regard

subculture A distinctive set of ideas, values, and behavior patterns by which a group within a larger society operates, while still sharing common standards with that larger society.

ethnic group People who collectively and publicly identify themselves as a distinct group based on shared cultural features such as common origin, language, customs, and traditional beliefs.

ethnicity This term, rooted in the Greek word *ethnikos* ("nation") and related to *ethnos* ("custom"), is the expression for the set of cultural ideas held by an ethnic group.

Figure 2.5 Amish Barn Raising The Amish people have held onto their traditional agrarian way of life in the midst of industrialized North American society. Their strong community spirit—reinforced by close social ties between family and neighbors, common language, traditional customs, and shared religious beliefs that set them apart from non-Amish people—is also expressed in a traditional barn raising, a large collective construction project.

as worldly knowledge and the idea of schools producing good citizens for the state. Resisting all attempts to force their children to attend regular public schools, they insist that education take place near home and that teachers be committed to Amish ideals.

Amish nonconformity to mainstream culture has frequently resulted in conflict with state authorities, as well as personal harassment from people outside their communities. Pressed to compromise, they have introduced vocational training beyond junior high to fulfill state requirements, but they have managed to retain control of their schools and to maintain their way of life.

Confronted with economic challenges that make it impossible for most to subsist solely on farming, some Amish work outside their communities. Many more have established cottage industries and actively market homemade goods to tourists and other outsiders. Yet, although their economic separation from mainstream society has declined somewhat, their cultural separation has not (Kraybill, 2001). They remain a reclusive community, more distrustful than ever of the dominant North American culture surrounding them and mingling as little as possible with non-Amish people.

The Amish are but one example of the way a subculture may develop and be dealt with by the larger culture within which it functions. Different as they are, the Amish actually put into practice many values that other North Americans often respect in the abstract: thrift, hard work, independence, a close family life. The degree of tolerance accorded to them, in contrast to some other ethnic groups, is also due in part to the fact that the Amish are white Europeans; they are defined as being of the same race as those who historically comprise dominant mainstream

society. Notably, as elaborated upon elsewhere in this text, the concept of race has no biological validity when applied to humans, yet it still persists as a powerful social classification. This can be seen in the spatial organization of many U.S. cities in which certain neighborhoods are predominantly Asian, black, white, or Hispanic. This organizational pattern conforms to the racial categories long imposed by U.S. government bureaucracies, which officially reinforce and culturally reproduce a historical race-based ideology in U.S. society.

Implicit in the discussion thus far is that subcultures may develop in different ways. On the one hand, Amish subculture in the United States developed gradually in response to how these members of a strict evangelical Protestant sect have adapted to survive within the wider North American society, while holding tightly to the traditional way of life of their European ancestors. In contrast, North American Indian subcultures are distinctive ways of life rooted in traditions of formerly independent societies. The Native Americans endured invasion of their own territories and colonization by European settlers and were brought under the control of federal governments in the United States, Canada, and Mexico.

Although all American Indian groups have experienced enormous changes due to colonization, many have retained traditions significantly different from those of the dominant Euramerican culture surrounding them. This makes it difficult to determine whether they endure as distinct cultures as opposed to subcultures. In this sense, *culture* and *subculture* represent opposite ends of a continuum, with no clear dividing line between them. The Anthropology Applied feature examines the intersection of culture and subculture with an example concerning Apache Indian housing.

ANTHROPOLOGY APPLIED

New Houses for Apache Indians

By George S. Esber

The United States, in common with other industrialized countries of the world, contains a number of more or less separate subcultures. Those who live by the standards of one particular subculture have their closest relationships with one another, receiving constant reassurance that their perceptions of the world are the only correct ones and coming to take it for granted that the whole culture is as they see it. As a consequence, members of one subculture frequently have trouble understanding the needs and aspirations of other such groups. For this reason anthropologists, with their special understanding of cultural differences, are frequently employed as go-betweens in situations requiring interaction between peoples of differing cultural traditions.

As an example, while I was still a graduate student in anthropology, one of my professors asked me to work with architects and the Tonto Apache Indians in Arizona to research housing needs for a new tribal community. Although the architects knew about cross-cultural differences in the use of space, they had no idea how to get relevant information from the Indian people. For their part, the Apaches had no explicit awareness of their needs, for these were based on unconscious patterns of behavior. For that matter, few people are consciously aware of the space needs for their own social patterns of behavior.

My task was to persuade the architects to hold back on their planning long enough for me to gather, through participant observation and a review of written records, the data from which Apache housing needs could be abstracted. At the same time, I had to overcome Apache anxieties over an outsider coming into their midst to learn about matters as personal as their daily lives as they are acted out, in and around their homes. With these hurdles overcome, I was able to identify and successfully communicate to the architects those features of Apache life having importance for home and community design. At the same time, discussions of my findings with the Apaches enhanced their own awareness of their unique needs.

As a result of my work, the Apaches moved into houses that had been designed with *their* participation, for *their* specific needs. Among my findings was the realization that the Apaches preferred to ease into social interactions rather than to shake hands and begin interacting immediately, as is more typical of the Anglo pattern. Apache etiquette requires that people be in full view of one another so each can assess the behavior of others from a distance prior to engaging in social interaction with them. This requires a large, open living space. At the same time, hosts feel compelled to offer food to guests as a prelude to further social interaction. Thus, cooking and dining areas cannot be separated from living space. Nor is standard middle-class Anglo kitchen equipment suitable because the need for handling large quantities among extended families requires large pots and pans, which in turn calls for extra-large sinks and cupboards. Built with such ideas in mind, the new houses accommodated long-standing native traditions.

On a return visit to the Tonto Apache reservation in 2010, I found that the original houses were fine, but many more units had been squeezed in to accommodate growing needs on a restricted land base. A recent acquisition of new lands, which more than doubled the size of the tiny reservation, offers new possibilities. The Tonto Apache opened a casino in 2007. Its success has resulted in significant changes—from impoverishment to being one of the biggest employers in the area.

Adapted from Esber, G. S. (1987). Designing Apache houses with Apaches. In R. M. Wulff & S. J. Fiske (Eds.), Anthropological praxis: Translating knowledge into action. Boulder, CO: Westview, 2007. Reprinted by permission of George S. Esber.

Pluralism

Our discussion raises the issue of the multi-ethnic or **pluralistic society** in which two or more ethnic groups or nationalities are politically organized into one territorial state but maintain their cultural differences. Pluralistic societies could not have existed before the first politically centralized states arose a mere 5,000 years ago. With the rise of the state, it became possible to bring about the political unification of two or more formerly independent societies, each with its own culture, thereby creating a more complex order that transcends the theoretical one culture–one society linkage.

Anthropology makes an important distinction between state and nation. *States* are politically organized territories that are internationally recognized, whereas

pluralistic society A society in which two or more ethnic groups or nationalities are politically organized into one territorial state but maintain their cultural differences.

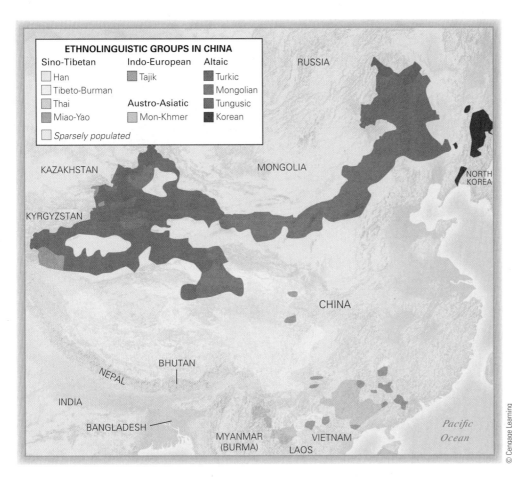

Figure 2.6 Ethnolinguistic Groups in China China is the largest country in the world, with a population of 1.3 billion people. A pluralistic society, it has fifty-five officially recognized nationalities. By far the largest nationality, or ethnic group, is the Han, comprising about 90 percent of the population. However, there are many ethnic minorities speaking radically different languages and having different cultural traditions. For example, the Uyghur (pictured in Figure 2.7), numbering over 8 million, are a Turkic-speaking people in Xinjiang Province in northwestern China. Unlike most Han, who are Buddhists, most Uyghur are Sunni Muslims. Historically dominating the Chinese state, the Han typically see themselves as the "real" Chinese and ignore the ethnic minorities or view them with contempt. This ethnocentrism is also reflected in names historically used for these groups.

nations are socially organized bodies of people who share ethnicity—a common origin, language, and cultural heritage. For example, the Kurds constitute a nation, but their homeland is divided among several states: Iran, Iraq, Turkey, and Syria. The international boundaries among these states were drawn up after World War I (1914–1918), with little regard for the region's indigenous ethnic groups or nations. Similar state formation processes have taken place throughout the world, especially in Asia and Africa, often making political conditions in these countries inherently unstable.

Pluralistic societies, which are common in the world today, all face the same challenge: They are composed of groups that, by virtue of their high degree of cultural variation, are all essentially operating by different sets of rules. Because social living requires predictable behavior, it may be difficult for the members of any one subgroup to accurately interpret and follow the different standards by which the others operate.

Unfortunately, *ethnocentrism*—defined in Chapter 1 as a belief that the ways of one's own culture are the only proper ones—may open the door to cross-cultural misunderstanding and distrust among different subgroups within a pluralistic society. Under stressful circumstances, such as lack of resources due to drought, neighboring ethnic groups may become rivals and intolerance may escalate into violence. There are many examples of troubled pluralistic societies in the world today, including Afghanistan and Nigeria, where central governments face major challenges in maintaining peace and lawful order. In countries where one ethnic group is substantially larger than others, such as the Han in China, greater numbers may be used to political and economic advantage at the expense of minority groups (**Figure 2.6** and **Figure 2.7**). We will return to the topic of ethnocentrism a bit later in this chapter.

Culture Is Based on Symbols

Much of human behavior involves **symbols**—sounds, gestures, marks, and other signs that are linked to something else and represent them in a meaningful way. Because often there is no inherent or necessary relationship between a thing and its representation, symbols are arbitrary, acquiring specific meanings when people agree on usage in their communications.

---

symbol A sound, gesture, mark, or other sign that is arbitrarily linked to something else and represents it in a meaningful way.

© TAO Images Limited/Alamy

Figure 2.7 The Uyghur Minority in China The Uyghur, a Turkic-speaking Muslim ethnic minority in China, live in the country's northwestern province of Xinjiang. Politically dominated by China's Han ethnic majority, who comprise 90 percent of the population, Uyghurs are proud of their cultural identity and hold onto their distinctive traditional heritage—as evident in this photo of a Uyghur family group eating together on carpets woven with traditional Uyghur designs.

In fact, symbols—ranging from national flags to wedding rings to money—enter into every aspect of culture, from social life and religion to politics and economics. We are all familiar with the fervor and devotion that a religious symbol can elicit from a believer. An Islamic crescent, Christian cross, or a Jewish Star of David—as well as the sun among the Inca, a cow among the Hindu, a white buffalo calf among Plains Indians, or any other object of worship—may bring to mind years of struggle and persecution or may stand for a whole philosophy or religion.

The most important symbolic aspect of culture is language—using words to represent objects and ideas. Through language humans are able to transmit culture from one generation to another. In particular, language makes it possible to learn from cumulative, shared experience. Without it, one could not inform others about events, emotions, and other experiences. Language is so important that one of the four main subfields of anthropology is dedicated to its study.

Culture Is Integrated

The breadth and depth of every culture is remarkable. It includes what people do for a living, the tools they use, the ways they work together, how they transform their environments and construct their dwellings, what they eat and drink, how they worship, what they believe is right or wrong, what gifts they exchange and when, who they marry, how they raise their children, how they deal with misfortune, sickness, death, and so on. Because these and all other aspects of a culture must be reasonably well integrated in order to function properly, anthropologists seldom focus on one cultural feature in isolation. Instead, they view each in terms of its larger context and carefully examine its connections to related features.

For purposes of comparison and analysis, anthropologists customarily imagine a culture as a structured system made up of distinctive parts that function together as an organized whole. Although they may sharply identify each part as a clearly defined unit with its own characteristics composed of a collection of ideas, beliefs, and values by which members of a society make sense of the world—its shape, challenges, and opportunities—and understand their place in it. Also known as ideology, this worldview is theoretically arranged in the model's **superstructure**. Including religion and political ideology, superstructure comprises a people's overarching ideas about themselves and the world around them—and it gives meaning and direction to their lives.

Influencing and reinforcing one another—continually adapting to changing demographic, technological, political-economic, and ideological factors—the interconnected features in these three interdependent structures together form part of a cultural system.

Kapauku Culture as an Integrated System

The integration of economic, social, and ideological aspects of a culture can be illustrated by the Kapauku Papuans, a mountain people of Western New Guinea, studied in 1955 by anthropologist Leopold Pospisil (1963). The Kapauku economy relies on plant cultivation, along with pig breeding, hunting, and fishing. Although plant cultivation provides most of the people's food, it is through pig breeding that men achieve political power and positions of legal authority.

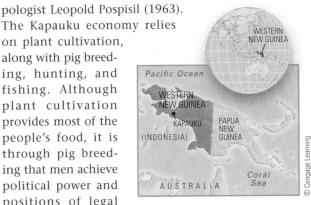

Among the Kapauku, living in an area now claimed by Indonesia, pig breeding is a complex business. Raising a lot of pigs requires a lot of food to feed them. The primary fodder is sweet potatoes, grown in garden plots. According to Kapauku culture, certain garden activities and the tending of pigs are tasks that fall exclusively in the domain of women's work. Thus, to raise many pigs a man needs numerous women in the household. As a result, in Kapauku society multiple wives are not only permitted, they are highly desired. For each

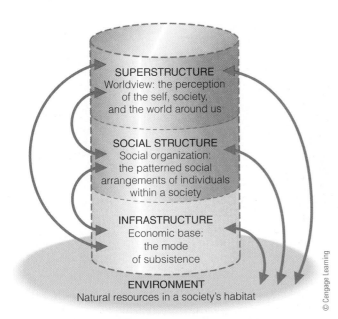

Figure 2.8 The Barrel Model of Culture Every culture is an integrated and dynamic system of adaptation that responds to a combination of internal factors (economic, social, ideological) and external factors (environmental, climatic). Within a cultural system, there are functional relationships among the economic base (infrastructure), the social organization (social structure), and the ideology (superstructure). A change in one leads to a change in the others.

and distinctive place within the larger system, anthropologists recognize that social reality is complex and subject to change and that divisions among cultural units are seldom clear-cut.

Broadly speaking, a society's cultural features fall within three categories: social structure, infrastructure, and superstructure, as depicted in our "barrel model" (**Figure 2.8**).

To ensure a community's biological continuity, a culture must provide a social structure for reproduction and mutual support. **Social structure** concerns rule-governed relationships—with all their rights and obligations—that hold members of a society together. Households, families, associations, and power relations, including politics, are all part of social structure. It establishes group cohesion and enables people to consistently satisfy their basic needs, including food and shelter for themselves and their dependents, by means of work.

There is a direct relationship between a group's social structure and its economic foundation, which includes subsistence practices and the tools and other material equipment used to make a living. Because subsistence practices involve tapping into available resources to satisfy a society's basic needs, this aspect of culture is known as **infrastructure**. It comprises strategies for the production and distribution of goods and services considered necessary for life.

Supported by this economic foundation, a society is held together by a shared sense of identity and worldview

social structure The rule-governed relationships—with all their rights and obligations—that hold members of a society together. This includes households, families, associations, and power relations, including politics.

infrastructure The economic foundation of a society, including its subsistence practices and the tools and other material equipment used to make a living.

superstructure A society's shared sense of identity and worldview. The collective body of ideas, beliefs, and values by which members of a society make sense of the world—its shape, challenges, and opportunities—and understand their place in it. This includes religion and national ideology.

Figure 2.9 Kapauku Papuan Village, Western New Guinea Kapauku economy relies on plant cultivation, hunting, fishing, and especially on the breeding of pigs. Women are responsible for raising the pigs and their main fodder, sweet potatoes. Only men with numerous wives manage to acquire many pigs needed for wealth and prestige. As a result, in Kapauku society multiple wives are not only permitted, they are highly desired.

Courtesy © Jutka Rona

wife, however, a man must pay a bride-price, and this can be expensive. Furthermore, wives have to be compensated for their care of the pigs. Put simply, it takes pigs, by which wealth is measured, to get wives, without whom pigs cannot be raised in the first place. Needless to say, this requires considerable entrepreneurship. It is this ability that produces leaders in Kapauku society (Figure. 2.9).

The interrelatedness of these elements with various other features of Kapauku culture is even more complicated. For example, one condition that encourages men to marry several women is a surplus of adult females, sometimes caused by loss of males through warfare. Among the Kapauku, recurring warfare has long been viewed as a necessary evil. By the rules of war, men may be killed but women may not. This system works to promote the imbalanced sex ratio that fosters the practice of having more than one wife. Having multiple wives tends to work best if all of them come to live in their husband's village, and so it is among the Kapauku. With this arrangement, the men of a village are typically blood relatives of one another, which enhances their ability to cooperate in warfare.

Considering all these factors, it makes sense that Kapauku typically trace descent (ancestry) through men, which, coupled with near-constant warfare, tends to promote male dominance. So it is not surprising to find that only men hold positions of leadership in Kapauku, as they appropriate the products of women's labor in order to enhance their political stature. Such male dominance is by no means characteristic of all human societies. Rather, as with the Kapauku, it arises only under particular sets of circumstances that, if changed, will alter the way in which men and women relate to each other.

Culture Is Dynamic

Cultures are dynamic systems that respond to motions and actions within and around them. When one element within the system shifts or changes, the entire system strives to adjust, just as it does when an outside force applies pressure. To function adequately, a culture must be flexible enough to allow such adjustments in the face of unstable or changing circumstances.

All cultures are, of necessity, dynamic, but some are far less so than others. When a culture is too rigid or static and fails to provide its members with the means required for long-term survival under changing conditions, it is not likely to endure. On the other hand, some cultures are so fluid and open to change that they may lose their distinctive character. The Amish mentioned earlier in this chapter typically resist change as much as possible but are constantly making balanced decisions to adjust when absolutely necessary. North Americans in general, however, have created a culture in which change has become a positive ideal, reflecting the ongoing technological, demographic, and social transformations in their society.

Every culture is dynamically constructed and, not unlike a thermostat regulating room temperature, able to cope with recurrent strains and tensions, even dangerous disruptions and deadly conflicts. Sharing a culture, members of a society are capable of dealing with crises, solving their conflicts, and restoring order. Sometimes, however, the pressures are so great that the cultural features in the system are no longer adequate or acceptable, and the established order is changed.

ANTHROPOLOGIST OF NOTE

Bronislaw Malinowski (1884–1942)

Bronislaw Malinowski in the Trobriand Islands about 1916.

Courtesy Phoebe Apperson Hearst Museum of Anthropology

Bronislaw Malinowski, born in Poland, earned his doctorate in anthropology at the London School of Economics and later, as a professor there, played a vital role in making it an important center of anthropology. Renowned as a pioneer in participant observation, he stated that the ethnographer's goal is "to grasp the native's point of view . . . to realize *his* vision of *his* world."[a]

Writing about culture, Malinowski argued that people everywhere share certain biological and psychological needs and that the ultimate function of all cultural institutions is to fulfill those needs. Everyone, for example, needs to feel secure in relation to the physical universe. Therefore, when science and technology are inadequate to explain certain natural phenomena—such as eclipses or earthquakes—people develop religion and magic to account for those phenomena and to establish a feeling of security.

The quantity and quality of data called for by Malinowski's approach set new scientific standards for anthropological fieldwork. He argued that it was necessary to settle into the community being studied for an extended period of time in order to fully explain its culture. He demonstrated this approach with his research in the Trobriand Islands of the southern Pacific Ocean between 1915 and 1918. Never before had such intensive fieldwork been done nor had such theoretical insights been gained into the functioning of another culture.

[a]Malinowski, B. (1961). *Argonauts of the western Pacific* (p. 25). New York: Dutton.

Functions of Culture

Polish-born British anthropologist Bronislaw Malinowski argued that people everywhere share certain biological and psychological needs and that the ultimate function of all cultural institutions is to fulfill these needs (see Anthropologist of Note). Others have marked out different criteria, but the idea is basically the same: A culture cannot endure if it does not deal effectively with basic challenges. It has to equip members of a society with strategies for the production and distribution of goods and services considered necessary for life. To ensure the biological continuity of the group, it must also offer a social structure for reproduction and mutual support. Further, it has to provide ways and means to pass on knowledge and enculturate new members so they can contribute to their community as well-functioning adults. Moreover, it must facilitate social interaction and provide ways to avoid or resolve conflicts within their group as well as with outsiders.

Because a culture must support all aspects of life, as indicated in our barrel model, it must also meet the psychological and emotional needs of its members. This last function is met, in part, simply by the measure of predictability that each culture, as a shared design for thought and action, brings to everyday life. Of course, it involves much more than that, including a worldview that helps individuals understand their place in the world and face major changes and challenges. For example, every culture provides its members with certain customary ideas and rituals that enable them to think creatively about the meaning of life and death. Many cultures even make it possible for people to imagine an afterlife. Invited to suspend disbelief and engage in such imaginings, people find the means to deal with the grief of losing a loved one and to face their own demise with certain expectations.

In Bali, for instance, Hindu worshipers stage spectacular cremation rituals at special places where they burn the physical remains of their dead. After a colorful procession with musicians, the corpse is carried to a great cremation tower, or *wadah*, representing the three-layered cosmos. It is then transferred into a beautifully decorated sarcophagus, made of wood and cloth artfully shaped in the form of an animal—a bull when the deceased belonged to the island's highest Hindu status group ("caste") of priests and lawgivers (Brahmanas), a winged lion for the second highest status of warriors and administrators (Satrias), and a half-fish/half-elephant for the next status of merchants and traders (Wesias).

After relatives and friends place their offerings atop or inside the sarcophagus, a Hindu priest sets the structure on fire. Soon, the body burns, and according to Balinese Hindu belief, the animal sarcophagus symbolically guides the soul of the deceased to Bali's "mother" mountain Gunung Angung. This is the sacred dwelling place of the island's gods and ancestors, the place to which many Balinese believe they return when they die. Freed from the flesh, the soul may later transmigrate and return in corporeal form. This belief in reincarnation of the soul allows the Balinese to cope with death as a celebration of life.

In sum, for a culture to function properly, its various parts must be consistent with one another. But consistency is not the same as harmony. In fact, there is friction and potential for conflict within every culture—among individuals, factions, and competing institutions. Even on the most basic level of a society, individuals rarely experience the enculturation process in exactly the same way, nor do they perceive their reality in precisely identical fashion. Moreover, conditions may change, brought on by inside or outside forces.

Culture, Society, and the Individual

Ultimately, a society is no more than a union of individuals, all of whom have their own special needs and interests. To survive, it must succeed in balancing the immediate self-interest of its individual members with the needs and demands of the collective well-being of society as a whole. To accomplish this, a society offers rewards for adherence to its culturally prescribed standards. In most cases, these rewards assume the form of social approval. For example, in contemporary North American society a person who holds a good job, takes care of family, pays taxes, and does volunteer work in the neighborhood may be spoken of as a "model citizen" in the community.

To ensure the survival of the group, each person must learn to postpone certain immediate personal satisfactions. Yet the needs of the individual cannot be overlooked entirely or emotional stress and growing resentment may erupt in the form of protest, disruption, and even violence.

Consider, for example, the matter of sexual expression, which, like anything that people do, is shaped by culture. Sexuality is important in every society for it helps to strengthen cooperative bonds among members, ensuring the perpetuation of the social group itself. Yet sex can be disruptive to social living. Without clear rules about who has sexual access to whom, competition for sexual privileges can destroy the cooperative bonds on which human survival depends. In addition, uncontrolled sexual activity can result in reproductive rates that cause a society's population to outstrip its resources. Hence, as it shapes sexual behavior, every culture must balance the needs of society against the individual's sexual needs and desires so that frustration does not build up to the point of being disruptive in itself.

Cultures vary widely in the way they go about this. On one end of the spectrum, societies such as the Amish in North America or the Muslim Brotherhood in Egypt have taken an extremely restrictive approach, specifying no sex outside of marriage. On the other end are societies such as the Norwegians who generally accept premarital sex and often choose to have children outside marriage, or even more extreme, the Canela Indians in Brazil, whose social codes guarantee that, sooner or later, everyone in a given village has had sex with just about everyone of the opposite sex. Yet, even as permissive as the latter situation may sound, there are nonetheless strict rules as to how the system operates (Crocker & Crocker, 2004).

In all life issues, cultures must strike a balance between the needs and desires of individuals and those of society as a whole. When those of society take precedence, people may experience excessive stress. Symptomatic of this are increased levels of social tension, disruptive behavior, emotional depression, even suicide.

Although some societies require a greater degree of cultural uniformity from its members than others, every organized social group imposes pressure on its members to conform to certain cultural models, or standards, of acceptable public behavior, speech, and so on. These standards are commonly accepted and adhered to, and each society has institutions in place with a repertoire of cultural mechanisms to promote or enforce conformity. In many traditional societies, religious institutions play a major role in doing this, whereas a political party may impose conformity in communist state societies. In capitalist societies, business corporations operating on the basis of economic market principles impose conformity in numerous ways, including standards of beauty (see the Biocultural Connection).

Modifying the Human Body

Each healthy human individual, like any other biological organism, is genetically programmed to develop to its full potential. This includes reaching a certain maximum height as a fully mature adult. What that height is, however, varies per population group. Dutch adult males, for example, average well over 1 foot taller than Mbuti men, who do not generally grow taller than 5 feet (150 cm). Whether we actually become as tall as our genes would allow, however, is influenced by multiple factors, including nutrition and disease.

In many cultures, being tall is viewed positively, especially for men. To make up for any perceived flaw in height, there is not much men can do to appear taller beyond wearing shoes with thick soles. But, in other areas, there are many alternatives to increase attraction and improve social status. Playing on this desire, and fueling it, the fashion industry creates and markets ever-changing styles of shoes, dresses, hairstyles, lipstick, perfumes, nail polish, hats, and whatever else to beautify the human body.

For thousands of years, people across the world have also engaged in modifying the human body itself—with tattoos, piercings, circumcision, footbinding, and even altering skull shape. In addition, modern medical technology has provided a whole new range of surgical procedures aimed at this goal.

With medicine as big business, many surgeons have joined forces with the beauty industry in what anthropologist Laura Nader calls "standardizing" bodies. Focusing on women's bodies, she notes "images of the body appear natural within their specific cultural milieus."[a] For example, breast implants are not seen as odd within the cultural milieu of the United States, and female circumcision and infibulation (also known as female genital mutilation or

FGM) are not considered odd among people in several African countries.

Many feminist writers "differentiate [FGM] from breast implantation by arguing that American women *choose* to have breast implants whereas in Africa women are subject to indoctrination"[b] given they experience circumcision as young girls. But is a woman's decision to have breast implants, in fact, the result of indoctrination by the beauty-industrial complex?

This multibillion-dollar industry, notes Nader, "segments the female body and manufactures commodities of and for the body."[c] Among millions of women

PROCEDURE	NUMBER DONE IN 2011
Facial resurfacing and fillers (chemical peel, laser, collagen, etc.)	5,000,000
Brow lift	47,000
Eyelid surgery	196,000
Nose reshaping	244,000
Botox injection	5,700,000
Facelift	119,000
Upper arm lift	15,000
Breast augmentation	307,000
Tummy tuck	116,000
Liposuction	205,000

© Cengage Learning

This figure shows selected cosmetic surgical and nonsurgical procedures in the United States in 2011. In total, there were 1.6 million cosmetic surgeries and 12.2 million nonsurgical procedures (chemical peels, laser treatments, Botox injections, and so on) at a total cost of about $10.4 billion. Ninety-one percent of the total were done on women.

getting "caught in the official beauty ideology" are those in the United States who have breast implantation. On average, they are 36 years old with two children. Designated as the beauty industry's "insecure consumers," these women are "recast as patients" with an illness defined as hypertrophy (small breasts). Psychological health can be restored by cosmetic surgery correcting this so-called deformity in the female body.

The doctors who perform these operations are often regarded as therapists and artists as well as surgeons. One pioneering breast implant surgeon "took as his ideal female figure that of ancient Greek statues, which he carefully measured, noticing the exact size and shape of the breasts, their vertical and horizontal locations."[d] In response to beauty marketing, the business of plastic surgery is now booming, and breast implantation is spreading across the globe.

BIOCULTURAL QUESTION

Have you or anyone close to you made body alterations? If so, were these changes prompted by an "official beauty ideology" or something else?

[a] Nader, L. (1997). Controlling processes: Tracing the dynamics of power. *Current Anthropology* 38, 715–717.

[b] Ibid.

[c] Ibid. See also Coco, L. E. (1994). Silicone breast implants in America: A choice of the official breast? In L. Nader (Ed.), *Essays on controlling processes* (pp. 103–132). *Kroeber Anthropological Society Papers* (no. 77). Berkeley: University of California Press; and Claeson, B. (1994). The privatization of justice: An ethnography of control. In L. Nader (Ed.), *Essays on controlling processes* (pp. 32–64). *Kroeber Anthropological Society Papers* (no. 77). Berkeley: University of California Press.

[d] Nader, 1997.

Culture and Change

Anthropologists today recognize that few peoples still exist in total or near-total isolation; in our current age of globalization, we are witnessing a much accelerated pace of widespread and radical change, discussed in detail in the last chapter of this book. Like our ancestors, all of us experience changes in our lives, but not all change is cultural change.

As living creatures, we humans typically experience multiple changes in the course of a lifetime. Such changes are part of the human life cycle. The average life expectancy for people today is about 64 years (3 years more for women than for men). But in many countries it is at least 20 years less, whereas in others it is a decade or more longer (Japanese may expect to live, on average, 80 years).

No matter how long we live or the changes we experience in our personal lives, few of us have any impact on how our culture is structured or how it operates. For that reason, cultures have been known to remain unchanged for many centuries, sometimes even longer. For anthropologists, an understanding of how cultures change and how people create or respond to change is crucially important—not only for the sake of knowledge itself but also because this knowledge can be applied in preventing or solving problems triggered by change.

Change in a culture may result from one or more factors, such as new technology, foreign invasion, new trade goods, population growth, ecological shifts, and so on. Cultural changes may be generated by forces within a society or may be imposed from the outside. Either way, they lead to a modification of cultural ideas, values, and practices.

Although cultures must have some flexibility to remain adaptive, cultural change can also bring unexpected and sometimes disastrous results. For example, consider the relationship between culture and the droughts that periodically afflict so many people living in African countries just south of the Sahara Desert. The lives of some 14 million nomadic herders native to this region are centered on cattle and other grazing animals. For thousands of years these nomads have migrated seasonally to provide their herds with pasture and water, utilizing vast areas of arid lands in ways that allowed them to survive severe droughts many times in the past.

Today, however, the nomadic way of life is frowned upon by the central governments of modern states in the region. Government officials actively discourage nomadism because it involves moving back and forth across relatively new international boundaries that are often impossible to guard, making it difficult to track the people and their animals for purposes of taxation and other government controls.

Viewing nomads as evading their authority, these governments have tried to stop the migratory herders from ranging through their traditional grazing territories and to convert them into sedentary villagers. Simultaneously, governments have aimed to press pastoralists into a market economy by giving them incentives to raise many more animals than required for their own needs so that the surplus could be sold to augment the tax base. Combined, these policies have led to overgrazing, erosion, and a lack of reserve pasture during recurring droughts. Thus, droughts today are far more disastrous than in the past because when they occur, they jeopardize the nomads' very existence (**Figure 2.10**).

The market economy that led nomads to increase their herds beyond sustainability is a factor in a huge range of cultural changes. Many nomads, including thousands of Kuchi herder families in Afghanistan pictured on the first page of this chapter, settle down as farmers or move to cities for cash-earning work opportunities. Across the globe, swift and often radical cultural change is driven by capitalism and its demand for market growth. Many welcome these changes, but others experience the loss of their traditional way of life as disturbing and feel powerless to stop, let alone reverse, the process.

Figure 2.10
Consequences of Cultural Change Climate and politics have conspired to create serious cultural change among migratory herders. So it is in the arid African grassland regions of Kenya pictured here, where severe drought combined with restrictions on grazing lands have resulted in the death of many animals and turned others into "bones on hoofs." Such catastrophes have forced many herders in Kenya and elsewhere to give up their old lifeways entirely.

Tony Karumba/AFP/Getty Images

VISUAL COUNTERPOINT

Figure 2.11 Perpetrating Ethnocentrism Many people in the world consider their own nation superior to others, framing their nationalist pride by proclaiming to be a "master race," "divine nation," or "chosen people" and viewing their homeland as sacred. Such nationalist ideology is associated with militant ethnocentrism and dislike, fear, or even hatred of foreigners, immigrants, and ethnic minorities. For instance, most Russians now agree with the Nationalist slogan "Russia for the Russians," and almost half believe their nation has a natural right to dominate as an empire. Russian Nationalists (*right*) are right-wing extremists, 10,000 of whom recently marched to St. Petersburg to protest the immigration of Azeri Tajiks, Turks, and other foreigners into Russia. In their extremism, they are matched by the Minutemen Civil Defense Corps in the United States. Active nationwide, Minutemen view whites as the only "true" Americans and are strongly anti-immigrant. The left photo shows the Minutemen in Palominas, Arizona, erecting a U.S.–Mexico border fence on private ranchland.

Ethnocentrism and Cultural Relativism

There are numerous highly diverse cultural solutions to the challenges of human existence. Anthropologists have been intrigued to find that people in most cultures tend to be ethnocentric and see their own way of life as the best of all possible worlds. This is reflected in the way individual societies refer to themselves: Typically, a society's traditional name for itself translates roughly into "true human beings." In contrast, their names for outsiders commonly translate into various versions of "subhumans," including "monkeys," "dogs," "weird-looking people," "funny talkers," and so forth. When it comes to ethnocentrism, it is easy to find examples (**Figure 2.11**).

Anthropologists have been actively engaged in the fight against ethnocentrism ever since they started to study and actually live among traditional peoples with radically different cultures, thus learning by personal experience that these "others" were no less human than anyone else. Resisting the common urge to rank cultures, anthropologists have instead aimed to understand individual cultures and the general concept of culture. To do so, they have examined each culture on its own terms, discerning whether or not the culture satisfies the needs and expectations of the people themselves. If a people practiced human sacrifice or capital punishment, for example, anthropologists asked about the circumstances that made the taking of human life acceptable according to that particular group's values.

This brings us to the concept of **cultural relativism**— the idea that one must suspend judgment of other peoples'

practices in order to understand those practices in their own cultural terms. Only through such an approach can one gain a meaningful view of the values and beliefs that underlie the behaviors and institutions of other peoples and societies as well as clearer insights into the underlying beliefs and practices of one's own society.

Take, for example, the 16th-century Aztec practice of sacrificing humans for religious purposes. Few (if any) North Americans today would condone such practices, but by suspending judgment one can get beneath the surface and discern how it functioned to reassure the populace that the Aztec state was healthy and that the sun would remain in the heavens.

Moreover, an open-minded exploration of Aztec sacrifice rituals may offer a valuable comparative perspective on the death penalty today. Over two-thirds of the countries in the world—141—have now abolished it in law or practice. Among those countries where it continues, China, Iran, Saudi Arabia, the United States, and Yemen are the most frequent executioners (Amnesty International, 2012).

Numerous studies by social scientists have clearly shown that the U.S. death penalty does not deter violent crime, any more than Aztec sacrifice really provided sustenance for the sun. In fact, cross-cultural studies show that homicide rates mostly decline after its abolition (Radelet & Lacock, 2009). Similar to Aztec human sacrifice, capital punishment may be seen as an institutionalized magical

cultural relativism The idea that one must suspend judgment of other people's practices in order to understand them in their own cultural terms.

response to perceived disorder—an act that "reassures many that society is not out of control after all, that the majesty of the law reigns, and that God is indeed in his heaven" (Paredes & Purdum, 1990, p. 9).

Cultural relativism is essential as a research tool. However, employing it for research does not mean suspending judgment forever, nor does it require that anthropologists defend a people's right to engage in any cultural practice, no matter how destructive. All that is necessary is that we avoid *premature* judgments until we have a full understanding of the culture in which we are interested. Only then may anthropologists adopt a critical stance and in an informed way consider the advantages and disadvantages of particular beliefs and behaviors for a society and its members.

Evaluation of Cultures

A valid question to ask is how well does a given culture satisfy the biological, social and psychological needs of those whose behavior it guides (Bodley, 2008). Specific indicators to answer this question are found in the nutritional status and general physical and mental health of its population; the incidence of violence, crime, and delinquency; the demographic structure, stability, and tranquility of domestic life; and the group's relationship to its resource base. The culture of a people who experience high rates of malnutrition (including obesity), violent crime, emotional disorders and despair, and environmental degradation may be said to be operating less well than that of another people who exhibit few such problems (**Figure 2.12**).

In a well-working culture, people "can be proud, jealous, and pugnacious, and live a very satisfactory life without feeling 'angst,' 'alienation,' 'anomie,' 'depression,' or any of the other pervasive ills of our own inhuman and civilized way of living" (Fox, 1968, p. 290). When traditional ways of coping no longer seem to work, and people feel helpless to shape their lives in their own societies, symptoms of cultural breakdown become prominent.

In short, a culture can be understood as a complex maintenance system designed to ensure the continued well-being of a group of people. Therefore, it may be

© Clay McLachlan/Reuters/Corbis

Figure 2.12 Signs of Cultural Dissatisfaction High rates of crime and delinquency are signs that a culture is not adequately satisfying a people's needs and expectations. This San Quentin Prison cellblock in California can be seen as such evidence. It is sobering to note that 25 percent of all imprisoned people in the world are incarcerated in the United States. In the past fifteen years the country's jail and prison population jumped from 1.6 million to 2.3 million. Ironically, people in the United States think of their country as "the land of the free," yet it has the highest incarceration rate in the world (about 750 per 100,000 inhabitants). The median among all countries is about 125 per 100,000 inhabitants.

deemed successful as long as it secures the survival of a society in a way that satisfies its members.

What complicates matters is that any society is made up of groups with different interests, raising the possibility that some people's interests may be better served than those of others. For this reason, anthropologists must always ask *whose* needs and *whose* survival are best served by the culture in question. Only by looking at the overall situation can a reasonably objective judgment be made as to how well a culture is working.

Our species today is challenged by rapid changes all across the globe, much of it triggered by powerful technology and dramatic population growth. In our current age of globalization, we must widen our scope and develop a truly worldwide perspective that enables us to appreciate cultures as increasingly open and interactive systems.

CHAPTER CHECKLIST

What is cultural adaptation?

● Cultural adaptation—a complex of ideas, activities, and technologies that enables people to survive and even thrive in their environment—has enabled humans to survive and expand into a wide variety of environments.

● Cultures have always changed over time, although rarely as rapidly or massively as many are doing today. Sometimes what is adaptive in one set of circumstances or over the short run is maladaptive over time.

What is culture, and what characteristics are common to all cultures?

● Culture is a society's shared and socially transmitted ideas, values, and perceptions that are used to make sense of experience and generate behavior and are reflected in that behavior.

● Although every culture involves a group's shared values, ideas, and behavior, this does not mean that everything within a culture is uniform. For instance, in all cultures people's roles vary according to age and gender, and in some cultures there are other subcultural variations.

● A subculture (for example, the Amish) shares certain overarching assumptions of the larger culture, while observing its own set of distinct rules. Pluralistic societies are those in which two or more ethnic groups or nationalities are politically organized into one territorial state but maintain their cultural differences.

● In addition to being shared, all cultures are learned, with individual members learning the accepted norms of social behavior through the process of enculturation. Also, every culture is based on symbols—transmitted through the communication of ideas, emotions, and desires—especially language. And culture is integrated, so that all aspects function as an integrated whole (albeit not without tension, friction, and even conflict). Finally, all cultures are dynamically designed to adjust to recurrent strains and tensions.

● As illustrated in the barrel model, all aspects of a culture fall into one of three broad, interrelated categories: infrastructure (the subsistence practices or economic system), social structure (the rule-governed relationships), and superstructure (the ideology or worldview).

● Cultural change takes place in response to events such as population growth, technological innovation, environmental crisis, intrusion of outsiders, or modification of values and behavior within the culture. Although cultures must change to adapt to new circumstances, sometimes the unforeseen consequences of change are disastrous for a society.

What is the connection between culture, society, and the individual?

● As a union of individuals, a society must strike a balance between the self-interest of individuals with the needs and demands of the collective well-being of the group. To accomplish this, a society rewards adherence to its culturally prescribed standards in the form of social approval.

● When individual needs and desires are eclipsed by those of society, the result may be stress and mental illness expressed in antisocial behavior such as alienation, substance abuse, or violence.

What are ethnocentrism and cultural relativism, and what is the measure of a society's success?

● Ethnocentrism is the belief that one's own culture is superior to all others. To avoid making ethnocentric judgments, anthropologists adopt the approach of cultural relativism, which requires suspending judgment in order to understand each culture in its own terms.

● One unbiased measure of a culture's success is based on answering this question: How well does a particular culture satisfy the physical and psychological needs of those whose behavior it guides? The following indicators provide answers: the nutritional status and general physical and mental health of the population, the incidence of violence, the stability of domestic life, and the group's relationship to its resource base.

QUESTIONS FOR REFLECTION

1. The barrel model offers a simple framework for imagining what a culture looks like from an analytical point of view. How would you apply that model to your own community and that of the Kuchi herders pictured at the beginning of this chapter?

2. Are you familiar with any subcultures or ethnic minorities in your own society? Could you make friends with or even marry someone from another subculture? What kind of problems would you be likely to encounter?

3. Peoples in all cultures across the world display ethnocentrism, but some more so than others. Considering today's globalization (as described in Chapter 1), do you think ethnocentrism poses more of a problem than in the past?

4. An often overlooked first step for developing an understanding of another culture is having knowledge and respect for one's own cultural traditions. Do you know the origins of the worldview commonly held by most people in your community? How do you think it developed over time, and what makes it so accepted or popular in your group today?

5. Currently, about 57 million humans die every year, and 135 million newborns join the more than 7 billion already crowding our planet. With finite natural resources and escalating piles of waste, do you think that technological inventions alone are sufficient to guarantee an additional 78 million more people annually a long and healthy life in pursuit of happiness?

ONLINE STUDY RESOURCES

CourseMate

Access chapter-specific learning tools, including learning objectives, practice quizzes, videos, flash cards, glossaries, and more in your Anthropology CourseMate.

Log into **www.cengagebrain.com** to access the resources your instructor has assigned and to purchase materials.

Challenge Issue

Anthropologists take on the challenge of studying and describing cultures around the world and finding scientific explanations for their differences and similarities. Why do people think, feel, and act in certain ways—and find it wrong or impossible to do otherwise? Answers must come from fact-based knowledge about cultural diversity—knowledge that is not culture-bound and is widely recognized as significant. Over the years, anthropology has generated such knowledge through various theories and research methods. In particular, anthropologists obtain information through long-term, full-immersion fieldwork based on participant observation. Here we see anthropologist Lucas Bessire enjoying the taste of *ajidabia* (a variety of wild honey) with Ayoreo Indian companions alongside a newly found beehive in the dry forest of the Gran Chaco in Paraguay, South America—one involved moment among many in the all-engaging challenge of anthropological fieldwork.

Ethnographic Research: Its History, Methods, and Theories

3

As briefly discussed in Chapter 1, cultural anthropology has two main scholarly components: *ethnography* and *ethnology*. Ethnography is a detailed description of a particular culture primarily based on firsthand observation and interaction. Ethnology is the study and analysis of different cultures from a comparative or historical point of view, utilizing ethnographic accounts and developing anthropological theories that help explain why certain important differences or similarities occur among groups.

Historically, anthropology focused on non-Western traditional peoples whose languages were not written down—people whose communication was often direct and face-to-face, and whose knowledge about the past was based primarily on oral tradition. Even in societies where writing exists, not much of what is of interest to anthropologists is recorded in writing. Thus, anthropologists have made a point of going to these places in person to observe and experience peoples and their cultures firsthand. This is called *fieldwork*.

Today, anthropological fieldwork takes place not only in small-scale communities in distant corners of the world, but also in modern urban neighborhoods in industrial or postindustrial societies. Anthropologists can be found doing fieldwork in a wide range of places and within a host of diverse groups and institutions, including global corporations, nongovernmental organizations (NGOs), migrant labor communities, and peoples scattered and dispersed because of natural or human-made catastrophes.

In our rapidly changing and increasingly interconnected world, where long-standing cultural boundaries between societies are being erased, new social networks and cultural constructs are emerging, made possible by long-distance mass transportation and communication technologies. To better describe, explain, and understand these complex but fascinating dynamics in a globalizing world, anthropologists today are adjusting their theoretical frameworks and research methods and approaches.

IN THIS CHAPTER YOU WILL LEARN TO

- Explain why fieldwork is essential to ethnography.

- Situate historical changes in research questions and applications within their economic, social, and political contexts.

- Describe ethnographic research—its challenges and methods.

- Discuss the relationship between methods and theory.

- Contrast distinctive key theoretical perspectives in anthropology.

- Recognize the ethical responsibilities of anthropological research.

Our research questions are often influenced or even driven by the environmental, economic, political, military, or ideological concerns of a particular period. What we observe and consider significant is shaped or modified by a worldview, and our explanations or interpretations are framed in theories that gain and lose currency depending on ideological and political-economical forces beyond our individual control.

Taking all of this into consideration, this chapter presents a historical overview of anthropology, its research methods and theories—underscoring the idea that ethnographic research does not happen in a timeless vacuum.

History of Ethnographic Research and Its Uses

Anthropology emerged as a formal discipline during the heyday of colonialism (1870s–1930s) when many European anthropologists focused on the study of traditional peoples and their cultures in the colonies overseas. For instance, French anthropologists did most of their research in North and West Africa and Southeast Asia; British anthropologists in southern and East Africa; Dutch anthropologists in what has become Indonesia, Western New Guinea, and Suriname; and Belgian anthropologists in Congo of Africa. Meanwhile, anthropologists in North America focused primarily on their own countries' Native Indian and Eskimo communities—usually residing on tracts of land known as reservations or in remote Arctic villages.

At one time it was common practice to compare peoples still pursuing traditional lifeways—based on hunting, fishing, gathering, and/or small-scale farming or herding—with the ancient prehistoric ancestors of Europeans and to categorize the cultures of these traditional peoples as "primitive." Although anthropologists have long abandoned such ethnocentric terminology, many others still think and speak of these traditional cultures as underdeveloped or even undeveloped. This misconception helped state societies, commercial enterprises, and other powerful outside groups justify expanding their activities and invading the lands belonging to these peoples, often exerting overwhelming pressure on them to change their ancestral ways.

Salvage Ethnography or Urgent Anthropology

In this disturbing and often violent historical context, the survival of thousands of traditional communities worldwide has been at stake. In fact, many of these threatened

peoples have become physically extinct. Others survived but were forced to surrender their territories and lifeways.

Although anthropologists have seldom been able to prevent such tragic events, they have tried to make a record of these cultural groups. This important early anthropological practice of documenting endangered cultures was initially called *salvage ethnography* and later became known as **urgent anthropology**, and it continues to this day (**Figure 3.1**).

By the late 1800s, many European and North American museums were sponsoring anthropological expeditions to collect cultural artifacts and other material remains (including skulls and bones), as well as vocabularies, myths, and other relevant cultural data. Early anthropologists also began taking ethnographic photographs, and by the 1890s some began shooting documentary films or recording the speech, songs, and music of these so-called vanishing peoples.

The first generation of anthropologists often began their careers working for museums, but those coming later were academically trained in the emerging discipline and became active in newly founded anthropology departments. In North America, most of the latter did their fieldwork on tribal reservations where indigenous communities were falling apart in the face of disease, poverty, and despair brought on by pressures of forced cultural change. These anthropologists interviewed American Indian elders still able to recall the ancestral way of life prior to the disruptions forced upon them. The researchers also collected oral histories, traditions, myths, legends, and other information, as well as old artifacts for research, preservation, and public display.

Beyond documenting social practices, beliefs, artifacts, and other disappearing cultural features, anthropologists also sought to reconstruct abandoned traditional lifeways remembered only by surviving elders. Although anthropological theories have come and gone during the past few hundred years or so, the plight of indigenous peoples struggling for cultural survival endures. Anthropologists can and still do contribute to that effort, assisting in cultural preservation efforts. In that work, utilizing a variety of new methods, they can tap into and continue to build on a professional legacy of salvage ethnography and urgent anthropology.

Acculturation Studies

In the 1930s, anthropologists began researching *culture contact*, studying how traditional cultures change when coming in contact with expanding capitalist societies. For several centuries, such contact primarily took place in the context of European *colonialism*—a system by which a society claims and controls a foreign territory for purposes of economic exploitation.

In contrast to Africa and Asia, where the natives vastly outnumbered the colonists, European settlers in the Americas, Australia, and New Zealand expanded their

---

urgent anthropology Ethnographic research that documents endangered cultures; also known as *salvage ethnography*.

Figure 3.1 Endangered Culture Until recently, Ayoreo Indian bands lived largely isolated in the Gran Chaco, a vast wilderness in South America's heartland. One by one, these migratory foragers have been forced to "come out" due to outside encroachment on their habitat. Today, most dispossessed Ayoreo Indians find themselves in different stages of acculturation. This photo shows Ayoreo women of Zapocó in Bolivia's forest. Dressed in Western hand-me-downs and surrounded by plastic from the modern society that is pressing in on them, they weave natural plant fibers into traditionally patterned bags to sell for cash, while men make money by cutting trees for logging companies.

territories, decimating and overwhelming the indigenous inhabitants. These settler societies became politically independent, turning colonies into new states. Several, such as Canada, Brazil, and the United States, recognized that the indigenous peoples had rights to lands on which they could remain, but not as independent nations. Surviving on reservations surrounded by a dominant mainstream society, these indigenous peoples, or tribal nations, are bureaucratically controlled as *internal colonies*.

Typically, as the dominant (often foreign) power establishes its superiority, local indigenous cultures are made to appear inferior, ridiculous, or otherwise unequal, and ethnic groups or smaller nations are often forced to adopt the ways of the more powerful society pressing in on them. Government-sponsored programs designed to compel tribal communities or ethnic minorities to abandon their ancestral languages and cultural traditions for those of the controlling society have ripped apart the unique cultural fabric of one group after another. These programs left many indigenous families impoverished, demoralized, and desperate.

In the United States, this asymmetrical culture contact became known as *acculturation*. This is the often-disruptive process of cultural change occurring in traditional societies as they come in contact with more powerful state societies—in particular, industrialized or capitalist societies.

One of the first anthropologists to study acculturation was Margaret Mead in her 1932 fieldwork among the Omaha Indians of Nebraska. In that research (one of many projects she undertook), she focused on community breakdown and cultural disintegration of this traditional American Indian tribe. In the course of the 20th century, numerous other anthropologists carried out acculturation studies in Asia, Africa, Australia, Oceania, the Americas, and even in parts of Europe, thereby greatly contributing to our knowledge of complex and often disturbing processes of cultural change.

Applied Anthropology

Anthropologists had a unique perspective on the impact of culture contact, but they were not the only ones interested in acculturation. In fact, business corporations, religious institutions, and government agencies responsible for the administration of colonies or tribal reservations actively promoted cultural change.

The British and Dutch governments, for example, had a vested interest in maintaining order over enormous colonies overseas, ruling foreign populations many times larger than their own. For practical purposes, these governments imposed a colonial system of *indirect rule* in which they depended on tribal chiefs, princes, kings, emirs, sultans, maharajas, or whatever their titles. These indigenous rulers, supported by the colonial regimes, managed the peoples under their authority by means of customary law. In the United States and Canada, a somewhat similar political system of indirect rule was established in which indigenous communities residing on tribal reservations were (and still are) governed by their own leaders largely according to their own rules, albeit under the surveillance of federal authorities.

Whatever the political condition of indigenous peoples—whether they reside on reservations, in colonies, or under some other form of authority exercised by a foreign controlling state—the practical value of anthropology became increasingly evident in the course of time. In identifying the disintegrating effects of asymmetrical culture contact, acculturation studies gave birth to *applied anthropology*—the use of anthropological knowledge and methods to solve practical problems in communities confronting new challenges.

In 1937 the British government set up an anthropological research institute in what is now Zambia to study the impact of international markets on Central Africa's traditional societies. In the next decade, anthropologists worked on a number of problem-oriented studies throughout Africa, including the disruptive effects of the mining industry and labor migration on domestic economies and cultures.

Facing similar issues in North America, the U.S. Bureau of Indian Affairs (BIA), which oversees federally recognized tribes on Indian reservations, established an applied anthropology branch in the mid-1930s. Beyond studying the problems of acculturation, the handful of applied anthropologists hired by the BIA were to identify culturally appropriate ways for the U.S. government to introduce social and economic development programs to reduce poverty, promote literacy, and solve a host of other problems on the reservations.

The international Society for Applied Anthropology, founded in 1941, aimed to promote scientific investigation of the principles controlling human relations and their practical application. Applied anthropology developed into an important part of the discipline and continued to grow even after colonized countries in Asia and Africa became self-governing states in the mid-1900s.

In Mexico—perhaps more than anywhere else in the world—anthropology has gained considerable prestige as a discipline, and its practitioners have been appointed to high political positions. The reasons for this are complex, but one factor stands out: Mexico, a former Spanish colony, is a large multi-ethnic democracy inhabited by millions of indigenous peoples who form the demographic majority in many regions. Converting acculturation theory into state-sponsored policies, influential government officials such as anthropologist Gonzalo Aguirre Beltrán sought to integrate myriad indigenous communities into a Mexican state that embraces ethnic diversity in a national culture (Aguirre Beltrán, 1974; Weaver, 2002) (**Figure 3.2**).

Figure 3.2 Postage stamp honoring Gonzalo Aguirre Beltrán First trained as a medical doctor, Dr. Gonzalo Aguirre Beltrán (1908–1996) became one of Mexico's most important anthropologists. He pioneered research on Afro-Mexicans and studied land tenure conflict among Mexican Indian communities in the 1930s. Theoretically influenced by the acculturation approach developed by Melville Herskovits of Northwestern University and Robert Redfield of the University of Chicago, he headed the Instituto Nacional Indigenista (National Indigenous Institute) in the 1950s and 1960s. As an influential government official, he converted acculturation theory into state-sponsored policies integrating and assimilating millions of indigenous Mexican Indians into a national culture embracing ethnic diversity in a democratic state society.

Voicing the need for an applied anthropology to address the negative effects of culture contact on indigenous peoples, Polish-born British anthropologist Bronislaw Malinowski commented, "The anthropologist who is unable to register the tragic errors committed at times with the best intentions remains an antiquarian covered with academic dust and in fool's paradise" (quoted in Mair, 1957, p. 4; see also Malinowski, 1945). Today, many academically trained anthropologists specialize in applied research, working for a variety of local, regional, national, and international institutions, in particular nongovernmental organizations (NGOs), and are active on numerous fronts in every corner of the world.

Studying Cultures at a Distance

During World War II (1939–1945) and the early years of the Cold War (over forty years of political hostility and conflict in diplomacy, economics, and ideology between blocks of capitalist countries led by the United States and rival blocks of communist countries led by Russia), some anthropologists shifted their attention from small-scale traditional communities to modern state societies.

Aiming to discover basic personality traits, or psychological profiles, shared by the majority of the people in modern state societies, several U.S. and British anthropologists became involved in a wartime government program of "national character" studies. Officials believed such studies would help them to better understand and deal with the newly declared enemy states of Japan and Germany (in World War II) and later Russia and others.

During wartime, on-location ethnographic fieldwork was impossible in enemy societies and challenging at best in most other foreign countries. So, Margaret Mead and her close friend Ruth Benedict (one of her former professors at Columbia University), along with several other anthropologists, developed innovative techniques for studying "culture at a distance." Their methods included the analysis of newspapers, literature, photographs, and popular films. They also collected information through structured interviews with immigrants and refugees from the enemy nations, as well as foreigners from other countries (Mead & Métraux, 1953).

The efforts of these anthropologists to portray the national character of peoples inhabiting distant countries included investigating topics such as childrearing beliefs, attitudes, and practices, in conjunction with examining print or film materials for recurrent cultural themes and values. This cultural knowledge was also used for propaganda and psychological warfare. After the war, some of the information and insight based on such long-distance anthropological studies were found useful in temporarily governing the occupied territories and dealing with newly liberated populations in other parts of the world.

Studying Contemporary State Societies

Although there were theoretical flaws in the national character studies and methodological problems in studying cultures at a distance, research on contemporary state societies was more than just a war-related endeavor. Even when anthropologists devoted themselves primarily to researching non-Western small-scale communities, they recognized that a generalized understanding of human relations, ideas, and behavior depends upon knowledge of *all* cultures and peoples, including those in complex, large-scale industrial societies organized in political states. Already during the years of the Great Depression (1930s) several anthropologists worked in their own countries in settings ranging from factories to farming communities and suburban neighborhoods.

One interesting example of an early anthropologist doing research on the home front is Hortense Powdermaker. Born in Philadelphia, Powdermaker went to London to study anthropology under Malinowski and did her first major ethnographic fieldwork among Melanesians in the southern Pacific. When she returned to the United States, she researched a racially segregated town in Mississippi in the 1930s (Powdermaker, 1939). During the next decade, she focused on combating U.S. dominant society's racism against African Americans and other ethnic minorities.

While in the South, Powdermaker became keenly aware of the importance of the mass media in shaping people's worldviews (Wolf & Trager, 1971). To further explore this ideological force in modern culture, she cast her critical eye on the domestic film industry and did a year of fieldwork in Hollywood (1946–1947).

As Powdermaker was wrapping up her Hollywood research, several other anthropologists were launching other kinds of studies in large-scale societies. Convinced that governments and colonial administrations, as well as new global institutions such as the United Nations (founded in 1945), could and should benefit from anthropological insights, Ruth Benedict and Margaret Mead initiated a team project in comparative research on contemporary cultures based at Columbia University in New York (1947–1952).

In 1950, Swiss anthropologist Alfred Métraux put together an international team of U.S., French, and Brazilian researchers to study contemporary race relations in Brazil. The project, sponsored by UNESCO (the United Nations Education, Science, and Culture Organization), was part of the UN's global campaign against racial prejudice and discrimination. Headquartered in Paris, Métraux selected this South American country as a research site primarily for comparative purposes. Like the United States, Brazil was a former European colony with a large multi-ethnic population and a long history of black slavery. It had abolished slavery twenty-five years later than the United States but had made much more progress in terms of its race relations.

In contrast to the racially segregated United States, Brazil was believed to be an ideal example of harmonious, tolerant, and overall positive cross-racial relations. The research findings yielded unexpected results, showing that dark-skinned Brazilians of African descent did face systemic social and economic discrimination—albeit not in the political and legal form of racial segregation that pervaded the United States at the time (Prins & Krebs, 2006).

In 1956 and 1957, anthropologist Julian Steward left the United States to supervise an anthropological research team in developing countries such as Kenya, Nigeria, Peru, Mexico, Japan, Myanmar (Burma), Malaya, and Indonesia. His goal was to study the comparative impact of industrialization and urbanization upon these different populations. Other anthropologists launched similar projects in other parts of the world.

Peasant Studies

In the 1950s, as anthropologists widened their scope to consider the impact of complex state societies on the traditional indigenous groups central to early anthropological study, some zeroed in on peasant communities. Peasants represent an important social category, standing midway between modern industrial society and traditional subsistence foragers, herders, farmers, and fishers (**Figure 3.3**). Part of larger, more complex societies, peasant communities exist worldwide, and peasants number in the many hundreds of millions.

Peasantry represents the largest social category of our species to date. Because peasant unrest over economic and social problems fuels political instability in many developing countries, anthropological studies of these rural populations in Latin America, Africa, Asia, and elsewhere are considered both significant and practical. In addition to improving policies aimed at social and economic development in rural communities, anthropological peasant studies may offer insights into how to deal with peasants resisting challenges to their traditional way of life. Such anthropological research may be useful in promoting social justice by helping to solve, manage, or avoid social conflicts and political violence, including rebellions and guerrilla warfare or insurgencies.

Advocacy Anthropology

By the 1960s, European colonial powers had relinquished almost all of their overseas domains. Many anthropologists turned their attention to the newly independent countries in Africa and Asia, whereas others focused on South and Central America. However, as anti-Western sentiment and political upheaval seriously complicated fieldwork in many parts of the world, significant numbers of anthropologists investigated important issues of cultural change and conflict inside Europe and North America.

Figure 3.3 A Voice for Peasants Peasant studies came to the fore during the 1950s as anthropologists began investigating rural peoples in state societies and the impact of capitalism on traditional small-scale communities. Here a Guarani-speaking peasant leader addresses a crowd in front of the presidential palace in Paraguay's capital city of Asunción at a massive protest rally against land dispossession.

Many of these issues, which remain focal points to this day, involve immigrants and refugees coming from places where anthropologists have conducted research.

Some anthropologists have gone beyond studying such groups to playing a role in helping them adjust to their new circumstances—an example of applied anthropology. Others have become advocates for peasant communities, ethnic or religious minorities, or indigenous groups struggling to hold onto their ancestral lands, natural resources, and customary ways of life. Both focus on identifying, preventing, or solving problems and challenges in groups that form part of complex societies and whose circumstances and affairs are conditioned or even determined by powerful outside institutions or corporations over which they generally have little or no control.

Although anthropologists have privately long championed the rights of indigenous peoples and other cultural groups under siege, one of the first anthropological research

Figure 3.4 Advocacy anthropologist Rodolfo Stavenhagen, UN Special Rapporteur on the Situation of Human Rights and Fundamental Freedom of Indigenous People. Here he appears with Victoria Tauli-Corpuz, chairperson of the UN Permanent Forum on Indigenous Issues, at a press conference near Manilla in the Phillipines in 2007.

projects explicitly and publicly addressing the quest for social justice and cultural survival took place among the Meskwaki, or Fox Indians, on their reservation in the state of Iowa (1948–1959). Based on long-term fieldwork with this North American Indian community, anthropologist Sol Tax challenged government-sponsored applied anthropological research projects and proposed instead that researchers work directly with "disadvantaged, exploited, and oppressed communities [to help *them*] identify and solve their [*own*] problems" (Field, 2004; see also Lurie, 1973).

Over the past few decades, anthropologists committed to social justice and human rights have become actively and increasingly involved in efforts to assist indigenous groups, peasant communities, and ethnic minorities. Today, most anthropologists committed to community-based and politically involved research refer to their work as **advocacy anthropology**.

Anthropologist Robert Hitchcock has practiced advocacy anthropology for over three decades. Specializing in development issues, he has focused primarily on land rights, as well as the social, economic, and cultural rights, of indigenous peoples in southern Africa—especially Bushmen (San, Basarwa) groups in Botswana. Hitchcock's work has involved helping Bushmen to ensure their rights to land—for foraging, pasturing, farming, and income-generation purposes—in the face of development projects aimed at setting aside land for the ranching, mining, or conservation interests of others. He helped draw up legislation on subsistence hunting in Botswana, making it the only country in Africa that allows broad-based hunting rights for indigenous peoples who forage for part of their livelihood (Hitchcock & Enghoff, 2004).

Today's most wide-ranging advocacy anthropologist is Rodolfo Stavenhagen, the UN's specialist on indigenous rights (**Figure 3.4**). A research professor at the Colegio de Mexico since 1965, he is founder and first president of the Mexican Academy of Human Rights. Stavenhagen leads investigations on the human rights and fundamental freedoms of indigenous peoples throughout the world.

Studying Up

Given anthropology's mission to understand the human condition in its full cross-cultural range and complexity—not just in distant places or at the margins of our own societies—some scholars have urged ethnographic research in the centers of political and economic power in the world's dominant societies. This wide scope is especially important for applied and advocacy anthropologists researching groups or communities embedded in larger and more complex processes of state-level politics and economics or even transnational levels of global institutions and multinational corporations. Of particular note in this effort is anthropologist Laura Nader. Coining the term *studying up*, she has called upon anthropologists to focus on Western elites, government bureaucracies, global corporations, philanthropic foundations, media empires, business clubs, and so on.

Studying up is easier said than done because it is a formidable challenge to do participant observation in such well-guarded circles. And when these elites are confronted

advocacy anthropology Research that is community based and politically involved.

with research projects or findings not to their liking, they have the capacity and political power to stop or seriously obstruct the research or the dissemination of its results.

Globalization and Multi-Sited Ethnography

As noted in Chapter 1, the impact of globalization is everywhere. Distant localities are becoming linked in such a way that forces and activities occurring thousands of miles away are shaping local events and situations, and vice versa. Connected by modern transportation, world trade, finance capital, transnational labor pools, and information superhighways, even the most geographically remote communities have become increasingly interdependent. Indeed, all of humanity now exists in what we refer to in this text as a *globalscape*—a worldwide interconnected landscape with multiple intertwining and overlapping peoples and cultures on the move.

One consequence of globalization is the formation of *diasporic* populations (*diaspora* is a Greek word, originally meaning "scattering"), living and working far from their original homeland. Some diasporic groups feel uprooted and fragmented, but others are able to transcend vast distances and stay in touch with family and friends through communication technologies. With Internet access to blogs and other sources of news, combined with e-mail, text messaging, Twitter, and a variety of social media platforms, geographically dispersed individuals spend more and more of their time in cyberspace (Appadurai, 1996). This electronically mediated environment enables people who are far from home to remain informed, to maintain their social networks, and even to hold onto a historical sense of ethnic identity that culturally distinguishes them from those with whom they share their daily routines in actual geographic space.

Globalization has given rise to a new trend in anthropological research and analysis known as **multi-sited ethnography**—the investigation and documentation of peoples and cultures embedded in the larger structures of a globalizing world, utilizing a range of methods in various locations of time and space. Engaged in such mobile ethnography, researchers seek to capture the emerging global dimension by following individual actors, organizations, objects, images, stories, conflicts, and even pathogens as they move about in various interrelated transnational situations and locations (Marcus, 1995; Robben & Sluka, 2007) Refugee communities around the world also fall into this category (**Figure 3.5**).

Among examples of multi-sited ethnographic research on a diasporic ethnic group is a recent study on transnational Han Chinese identities by Chinese American anthropologist Andrea Louie. Louie's fieldwork carried her to an array of locations in San Francisco, Hong Kong, and southern China—including her ancestral home in the Cantonese village Tiegang in Guangdong Province. Her paternal great-grandfather left the village in the 1840s, crossing the Pacific Ocean to work on railroad construction during the California Gold Rush. But other family members remained in their ancestral homeland. Here, Louie describes her research investigating Chinese identities from different and changing perspectives:

> My fieldwork on Chinese identities employed a type of mobile [ethnography] aimed at examining various parts of a "relationship" being forged anew across national boundaries that draws on metaphors of shared heritage and place. In my investigation of "Chineseness" I conducted participant observation and interviews in San Francisco with Chinese American participants of the In Search of Roots program,[1] as well as later in China when they visited their ancestral villages and participated in government-sponsored Youth Festivals. . . . I interviewed people in their homes, and apartments; in cafes, culture centers, and McDonald's restaurants; and in rural Chinese villages and on jet planes, focusing on various moments and contexts of interaction within which multiple and often discrepant discourses of Chineseness are brought together. (Louie, 2004, pp. 8–9)

Also emerging in multi-sited ethnography are greater interdisciplinary approaches to fieldwork, bringing in theoretical ideas and research methods from cultural studies, media studies, and mass communication. One example is the development of ethnographic studies of social networks, communicative practices, and other cultural expressions in cyberspace by means of digital visual and audio technologies. Known as **digital ethnography**, it is sometimes referred to as *cyberethnography* or *netnography* (Murthy, 2011).

Even in the fast-changing, globalizing world of the 21st century, core ethnographic research methods developed over a century ago continue to be relevant and revealing. New technologies have been added to the anthropologist's toolkit, but the hallmarks of our discipline—holistic research through fieldwork with participant observation—is still a valued and productive tradition. Having presented a sweeping historical overview of shifting anthropological research challenges and strategies, we turn now to the topic of research methods.

---

multi-sited ethnography The investigation and documentation of peoples and cultures embedded in the larger structures of a globalizing world, utilizing a range of methods in various locations of time and space.

digital ethnography An ethnographic study of social networks, communicative practices, and other cultural expressions in cyberspace by means of digital visual and audio technologies; also called *cyberethnography* or *netnography*.

---

[1] This program, run by organizations in Guangzhou and San Francisco, provides an opportunity for young adults (ages 17 to 25) of Cantonese descent to visit their ancestral villages in China.

VISUAL COUNTERPOINT

Figure 3.5 Multi-Sited Ethnography Anthropologist Catherine Besteman began fieldwork with Bantu communities in southern Somalia's Jubba Valley in the late 1980s, just before the outbreak of the civil war that ruined the country and forced many into exile. Since 2003, thousands of Somali Bantu have relocated to Lewiston, Maine, which has become an additional site for Besteman's ongoing research. Some of her undergraduate students at nearby Colby College participate in her work with these refugees. In the photo on the left, Besteman (in orange blouse) is interviewing in the Somalian village of Qardale. In the photo on the right, Besteman's students Elizabeth Powell and Nicole Mitchell are interviewing Iman Osman in his family's Lewiston apartment the year he graduated from high school. He and his family fled the war when he was just 4 years old, living in a refugee camp for a decade before finally coming to the United States.

Doing Ethnography

Every culture comprises underlying rules or standards that are rarely obvious. A major challenge to the anthropologist is to identify and analyze those rules. Fundamental to the effort is **ethnographic fieldwork**—extended on-location research to gather detailed and in-depth information on a society's customary ideas, values, and practices through participation in its collective social life.

Although the scope of cultural anthropology has expanded to include urban life in complex industrial and postindustrial societies, and even virtual communities in cyberspace, ethnographic methods developed for fieldwork in traditional small-scale societies continue to be central to anthropological research in all types of communities. The methodology still includes personal observation of and participation in the everyday activities of the community, along with interviews, mapping, collection of genealogical data, and recording of sounds and visual images. It all begins with selecting a research site and a research problem or question.

Site Selection and Research Question

Anthropologists usually work outside their own culture, society, or ethnic group, most often in a foreign country.

Although it has much to offer, anthropological study within one's own society may present special problems, as described by noted British anthropologist Sir Edmund Leach:

> Surprising though it may seem, fieldwork in a cultural context of which you already have intimate firsthand experience seems to be much more difficult than fieldwork which is approached from the naïve viewpoint of a total stranger. When anthropologists study facets of their own society their vision seems to become distorted by prejudices which derive from private rather than public experience. (Leach, 1982, p. 124)

Anthropologists doing studies in societies to which they belong are likely to be more successful if the researcher has first done work in some other culture. The more one learns of other cultures, the more one gains a fresh and more revealing perspective on one's own.

But wherever the site, research requires advance planning that usually includes obtaining funding and securing permission from the community to be studied

ethnographic fieldwork Extended on-location research to gather detailed and in-depth information on a society's customary ideas, values, and practices through participation in its collective social life.

(and, where mandated, permission from government officials as well). If possible, researchers make a preliminary trip to the site to make arrangements before moving there for more extended research.

After exploring the local conditions and circumstances, ethnographers have the opportunity to better define their specific research question or problem. For instance, what is the psychological impact of a new highway on members of a traditionally isolated farming community? Or how does the introduction of electronic media such as cell phones influence long-established gender relations in cultures with religious restrictions on social contact between men and women?

Preparatory Research

Before heading into the field, anthropologists do preparatory research. This includes delving into any existing written, visual, or sound information available about the people and place one has chosen to study. It may involve contacting and interviewing others who have some knowledge about or experience with the community, region, or country.

Because communication is key in ethnographic research, anthropologists need to learn the language used in the community selected for fieldwork. Many of the more than 6,000 languages currently spoken in the world have been recorded and written down, especially during the past century, so it is possible to learn some foreign languages prior to fieldwork. However, as in the early days of the discipline, some of today's anthropologists do research among peoples whose native languages have not yet been written down. In this case, the researcher may be able to find someone who is minimally bilingual to help him or her gain some proficiency with the language. Another possibility is to first learn an already recorded and closely related language, which provides some elementary communication skills during the early phase of the actual fieldwork.

Finally, anthropologists prepare for fieldwork by studying theoretical, historical, ethnographic, and other literature relevant to the research. For instance, anthropologists interested in understanding violence, both between and within groups, will read studies describing and theoretically explaining conflicts such as wars, insurgencies, raids, feuds, vengeance killings, and so on. Having delved into the existing literature, they may then formulate a theoretical framework and research question to guide them in their fieldwork. Such was the case when anthropologist Napoleon Chagnon applied sociobiological theory to his study of violence within Yanomamö Indian communities in South America's tropical rainforest, suggesting that males with an aggressive reputation as killers are reproductively more successful than those without such a status (Chagnon, 1988a).

Christopher Boehm took a different theoretical approach in his research on blood revenge among Slavic mountain people in Montenegro. He framed his research question in terms of the ecological function of this violent tradition because it regulated relations between groups competing for survival in a harsh environment with scarce natural resources (Boehm, 1987).

Participant Observation: Ethnographic Tools and Aids

Once in the field, anthropologists rely on *participant observation*—a research method in which one learns about a group's behaviors and beliefs through social involvement and personal observation within the community, as well as interviews and discussion with individual members of the group over an extended stay in the community (**Figure 3.6**). This work requires an ability to socially and psychologically adapt to a community with a different way of life. Keen personal observation skills are also essential, employing *all* the senses—sight, touch, smell, taste, and hearing—in order to perceive collective life in the other culture.

When participating in an unfamiliar culture, anthropologists are often helped by one or more generous individuals

Figure 3.6 Participant Observation The hallmark research methodology for anthropologists is participant observation—illustrated by this photo of anthropologist Julia Jean (*center*), who is both observing *and* participating in a Hindu ritual at a temple for the goddess Kamakhya in northeastern India.

in the village or neighborhood. They may also be taken in by a family, and through participation in the daily routine of a household, they will gradually become familiar with the community's basic shared cultural features.

Anthropologists may also formally enlist the assistance of **key consultants**—members of the society being studied who provide information to help researchers understand the meaning of what they observe. (Early anthropologists referred to such individuals as *informants*.) Just as parents guide a child toward proper behavior, so do these insiders help researchers unravel the mysteries of what at first is a strange, puzzling, and unpredictable world. To compensate local individuals for their help, fieldworkers may thank them for their time and expertise with goods, services, or cash.

Beyond the skills and resources noted previously, an anthropologist's most essential ethnographic tools in the field are notebooks, pen/pencil, camera, and sound and video recorders. Nowadays, most also use laptop computers equipped with data processing programs. And some field kits include GPS equipment, smartphones, and other modern handheld devices.

Although researchers may focus on a particular cultural aspect or issue, they will consider the culture as a whole for the sake of context. This holistic and integrative approach, a hallmark of anthropology, requires being tuned in to nearly countless details of daily life, both the ordinary and the extraordinary. By taking part in community life, anthropologists learn why and how events are organized and carried out. Through alert and sustained participation—carefully watching, questioning, listening, and analyzing over a period of time—they can usually identify, explain, and often predict a group's behavior.

Data Gathering: The Ethnographer's Approach

Information collected by ethnographers falls into two main categories: quantitative and qualitative data. **Quantitative data** consist of statistical or measurable information, such as population density, demographic composition of people and animals, and the number and size of houses; the hours worked per day; the types and quantities of crops grown; the amount of carbohydrates or animal protein consumed per individual; the quantity of wood, dung, or other kinds of fuel used to cook food or heat dwellings; the number of children born out of wedlock; the ratio of spouses born and raised within or outside the community; and so on.

Qualitative data include nonstatistical information about features such as settlement patterns, natural resources, social networks of kinship relations, customary beliefs and practices, personal life histories, and so on. Often, these unquantifiable data are the most important part of ethnographic research because they capture the essence of a culture; this information provides us with deeper insights into the unique lives of different peoples, helping us truly understand what, why, and how they feel, think, and act in their own distinctive ways.

Taking Surveys

Unlike many other social scientists, anthropologists do not usually go into the field equipped with predetermined surveys or questionnaires. Those who use surveys usually do so after spending enough time on location to have gained the community's confidence and to know how to compose a questionnaire with categories that are culturally relevant.

Whether studying a community in geographic space or cyberspace, anthropologists who use surveys view them as one small part in a large research strategy that includes a considerable amount of qualitative data (**Figure 3.7**). They recognize that only by keeping an open mind while thoughtfully watching, listening, participating, and asking questions can they discover many aspects of a culture.

As fieldwork proceeds, anthropologists sort their complex impressions and observations into a meaningful whole, sometimes by formulating and testing limited or low-level hypotheses, but just as often by making use of imagination or intuition and following up on hunches. What is important is that the results are constantly checked for accuracy and consistency, for if the parts fail to fit together in a way that is internally coherent, it may be that a mistake has been made and further inquiry is necessary.

Two studies of a village in Peru illustrate the problem of gathering data through surveys alone. A sociologist conducted one study by surveying the villagers with a questionnaire and concluded that people in the village invariably worked together on one another's privately owned plots of land. By contrast, a cultural anthropologist who lived in the village for over a year (including the brief period when the sociologist did his study) witnessed that particular practice only once. The anthropologist's long-term participant observation revealed that although the idea of labor exchange relations was important to the people's sense of themselves, it was not a common economic practice (Chambers, 1995).

---

key consultant A member of the society being studied who provides information that helps researchers understand the meaning of what they observe; early anthropologists referred to such individuals as *informants*.

quantitative data Statistical or measurable information, such as demographic composition, the types and quantities of crops grown, or the ratio of spouses born and raised within or outside the community.

qualitative data Nonstatistical information such as personal life stories and customary beliefs and practices.

Figure 3.7 Surveys in Cyberspace Since spring 2008, anthropologist Jeffrey Snodgrass has been studying videogaming. Conducting participant-observation research in and around the World of Warcraft (WoW), he has gathered information about this virtual community through interviewing and surveying its members. He has been particularly fascinated by players' relationships to their WoW avatars, the in-game graphical representations of their characters. Via avatars, gamers can temporarily separate or even dissociate from their actual-world persons and enter WoW's fantasyscape. Here Snodgrass (the pointy-eared Draenei shaman seated front left) and his virtual research team of graduate and undergraduate collaborators pose beneath WoW's Goblin Messiah.

The point here is that questionnaires all too easily embody the concepts and categories of the researcher, who is an outsider, rather than those of the people being studied. Even where this is not a problem, questionnaires tend to concentrate on what is measurable, answerable, and acceptable as a question, rather than probing the less obvious and more complex qualitative aspects of society or culture.

Moreover, for a host of reasons—fear, ignorance, hostility, hope of reward—people may give false, incomplete, or biased information (Sanjek, 1990). Keeping culture-bound ideas, which are often embedded in standardized questionnaires, out of research methods is an important point in all ethnographic research.

informal interview An unstructured, open-ended conversation in everyday life.
formal interview A structured question/answer session carefully notated as it occurs and based on prepared questions.

Interviewing

Asking questions is fundamental to ethnographic field-work and takes place in **informal interviews** (unstructured, open-ended conversations in everyday life) and **formal interviews** (structured question/answer sessions carefully notated as they occur and based on prepared questions). Informal interviews may be carried out at any time and in any place—on horseback, in a canoe, by a cooking fire, during ritual events, while walking through the community with a local inhabitant, and the list goes on. Such casual exchanges are essential, for it is often in these conversations that people share most freely. Moreover, questions put forth in formal interviews typically grow out of cultural knowledge and insights gained during informal ones.

Getting people to open up is an art born of a genuine interest in both the information and the person who is sharing it. It requires dropping all assumptions and cultivating the ability to *really* listen. It may even require a willingness to be the village idiot by asking simple questions to which the answers may seem obvious. Also, effective interviewers learn early on that numerous follow-up questions are vital given that first answers may mask truth rather than reveal it. Questions generally fall into one of two categories: broad, *open-ended questions* (Can you tell me about your childhood?) and *closed questions* seeking specific pieces of information (Where and when were you born?).

In ethnographic fieldwork, interviews are used to collect a vast range of cultural information: from life histories, genealogies, and myths to craft techniques and midwife practices to beliefs concerning everything from illness to food taboos. Genealogical data can be especially useful because they provide information about a range of social customs (such as cousin marriage), worldviews (such as ancestor worship), political relations (such as alliances), and economic arrangements (such as hunting or harvesting on clan-owned lands).

Researchers employ numerous **eliciting devices**— activities and objects used to draw out individuals and encourage them to recall and share information. There are countless examples of this: taking a walk with a local and asking about songs, legends, and place names linked to geographic features; sharing details about one's own family and neighborhood and inviting a telling in return; joining in a community activity and asking a local to explain the practice and why the participants are doing it; taking and sharing photographs of cultural objects or activities and asking locals to explain what they see in the pictures; presenting research findings to community members and documenting their responses.

Mapping

Many anthropologists have done fieldwork in remote places where there is little geographic documentation. Even if cartographers have mapped the region, standard maps seldom show geographic and spatial features that are culturally significant to the people living there. People inhabiting areas that form part of their ancestral homeland have a particular understanding of the area and their own names for local places. These native names may convey essential geographic information, describing the distinctive features of a locality such as its physical appearance, its specific dangers, or its precious resources.

Place names may derive from certain political realities such as headquarters, territorial boundaries, and so on. Others may make sense only in the cultural context of a local people's worldview as recounted in their myths, legends, songs, or other narrative traditions. Thus, to truly understand a place, some anthropologists make their own detailed geographic maps documenting culturally relevant geographic features in the landscape inhabited by the people they study (**Figure 3.8**).

Especially since the early 1970s, anthropologists have become involved in indigenous land use and occupancy studies for various reasons, including the documentation of traditional land claims. Researchers constructing individual map biographies may gather information from a variety of sources: local oral histories; early written descriptions of explorers, traders, missionaries, and other visitors; and data obtained from archaeological excavations.

One such ethnogeographic research project took place in northwestern Canada, during the planning stage of the building of the Alaska Highway natural gas pipeline. Because the line would cut directly though Native lands, local indigenous community leaders and federal officials insisted that a study be done to determine how the new construction would affect indigenous inhabitants. Canadian anthropologist Hugh Brody, one of the researchers in this ethnogeographic study, explained:

> These maps are the key to the studies and their greatest contribution. Hunters, trappers, fishermen, and berry-pickers mapped out all the land they had ever used in their lifetimes, encircling hunting areas species by species, marking gathering location and camping sites—everything their life on the land had entailed that could be marked on a map. (Brody, 1981, p. 147)

In addition to mapping the local place names and geographic features, anthropologists may also map out information relevant to the local subsistence, such as animal migration routes, favorite fishing areas, places where medicinal plants can be harvested or firewood cut, and so on.

Today, by means of the technology known as global positioning system (GPS), researchers can measure precise distances by triangulating the travel time of radio signals from various orbiting satellites. They can create maps that pinpoint human settlement locations and the layout of dwellings, gardens, public spaces, watering holes, pastures, surrounding mountains, rivers, lakes, seashores, islands, swamps, forests, deserts, and any other relevant feature in the regional environment.

To store, edit, analyze, integrate, and display this geographically referenced spatial information, some anthropologists use cartographic digital technology, known as geographic information systems (GIS). GIS makes it possible to map the geographic features and natural resources in a certain environment—and to link these data to ethnographic information about population density and distribution, social networks of kinship relations, seasonal patterns of land use, private or collective claims of ownership, travel routes, sources of water, and so on. With GIS

---

eliciting devices Activities and objects used to draw out individuals and encourage them to recall and share information.

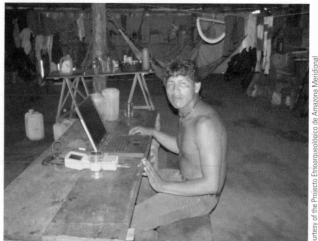

Figure 3.8 Collecting GPS Data For anthropologist Michael Heckenberger, doing fieldwork among the Kuikuro people of the Upper Xingu River in the southern margins of the Amazon rainforest has become a collaborative undertaking. Together with other specialists on his research team, he has trained local tribespeople to help with the research project about their ancestral culture, which includes searching for the remains of ancient earthworks and mapping them. The photos above show trained local assistant Laquai Kuikuro collecting GPS data in a modern field of manioc—a primary dietary staple of indigenous Amazonian communities in Brazil—and later reviewing the downloaded data on a computer. On the right is a map showing GPS-charted indigenous earthworks in the Upper Xingu superimposed over a Landsat satellite image.

researchers can also integrate information about beliefs, myths, legends, songs, and other culturally relevant data associated with distinct locations. Moreover, they can create interactive inquiries for analysis of research data as well as natural and cultural resource management (Schoepfle, 2001).

Photographing and Filming

As noted previously, during fieldwork, most anthropologists use cameras, as well as notepads, computers, or sound recording devices to document their observations. Photography has been instrumental in anthropological research for more than a century. For instance, in the early 1880s, Franz Boas took photographs during his first fieldwork among the Inuit in the Canadian Arctic. And just a few years after the invention of the moving picture camera in 1894, anthropologists began filming people in action—recording traditional dances and other ethnographic subjects of interest.

As film technology developed, anthropologists turned increasingly to visual media for a wide range of cross-cultural research purposes. Some employed still photography in community surveys and elicitation techniques. Others took film cameras into the field to document the disappearing world of traditional foragers, herders, and farmers surviving in remote places. A few focused on

documenting traditional patterns of nonverbal communication such as body language and social space use for research purposes. Soon after the 1960 invention of the portable synchronous-sound camera, ethnographic filmmaking became increasingly important in producing a cross-cultural record of peoples all across the globe.

Since the digital revolution that began in the 1980s, we have been witnessing an explosive growth in visual media all across the world. It is not unusual for anthropologists to arrive in remote villages where at least a few native inhabitants take their own pictures or record their own stories and music. For researchers in the field, native-made audiovisual documents may represent a wealth of precious cultural information. The Anthropologists of Note feature details the long history of such equipment in anthropology.

Margaret Mead (1901–1978) • Gregory Bateson (1904–1980)

From 1936 to 1938 **Margaret Mead** and **Gregory Bateson** did collaborative ethnographic fieldwork in Bali. Bateson, Mead's husband at the time, was a British anthropologist trained by Alfred C. Haddon, who led the 1898 Torres Strait expedition and is credited with making the first ethnographic film in the field. During their stay in Bali, Bateson took about 25,000 photographs and shot 22,000 feet of motion picture

Library of Congress, Prints and Photographs Division

In 1938, after two years of fieldwork in Bali, Margaret Mead and Gregory Bateson began research in Papua New Guinea, where they staged this photograph of themselves to highlight the importance of cameras as part of the ethnographic toolkit. Note the camera on a tripod behind Mead and other cameras atop the desk.

film. Afterward, the couple coauthored the photographic ethnography *Balinese Character: A Photographic Analysis* (1942).

That same year, Bateson worked as an anthropological film analyst studying German motion pictures. Soon Mead and a few other anthropologists became involved in thematic analysis of foreign fictional films. She later compiled a number of such visual anthropology studies in a coedited volume titled *The Study of Culture at a Distance* (1953).

Mead became a tireless promoter of the scholarly use of ethnographic photography and film. In 1960, the year the portable sync-sound film camera was invented, Mead was serving as president of the American Anthropology Association. In her presidential address at the association's annual gathering, she pointed out what she saw as shortcomings in the discipline and urged anthropologists to use cameras more effectively.[a] Chiding her colleagues for not fully utilizing new technological developments, she complained that anthropology had come "to depend on words, and words, and words."

Mead's legacy is commemorated in numerous venues, including the Margaret Mead Film Festival hosted annually since 1977 by the American Museum of Natural History in New York City. Thus, it was fitting that during the Margaret Mead Centennial celebrations in 2001 the American Anthropological Association endorsed a landmark visual media policy statement urging academic committees to consider ethnographic visuals—and not just ethnographic writing—when evaluating scholarly output of academics up for hiring, promotion, and tenure.

[a]Mead, M. (1960). Anthropology among the sciences. *American Anthropologist 63*, 475–482.

Challenges of Ethnographic Fieldwork

Although ethnographic fieldwork offers a range of opportunities to gain better and deeper insight into the community being studied, it comes with a Pandora's box of challenges. At the least, it usually requires researchers to step out of their cultural comfort zone into an unknown world that is sometimes unsettling.

As touched upon in Chapter 1, anthropologists in the field are likely to face a wide array of challenges—physical, social, mental, political, and ethical. While they are handling these challenges, they must be fully engaged

in work and social activities with the community. In addition, they are doing a host of other things, such as interviewing, taking copious notes, and analyzing data. In the following paragraphs we offer details on some of the most common personal struggles anthropologists face in the field.

Social Acceptance

Having decided where to do ethnographic research and what to focus on, anthropologists embark on the journey to their field site. Typically moving into a community with a culture unlike their own, most experience culture shock and loneliness at least during the initial stages of their work—work that requires them to establish social contacts with strangers who have little or no idea who they are, why they have come, or what they want from them. In short, a visiting anthropologist is as much a mystery to those she or he intends to study as the group is to the researcher.

Although there is no sure way of predicting how one will be received, it is certain that success in ethnographic fieldwork depends on mutual goodwill and the ability to develop friendships and other meaningful social relations. As New Zealand anthropologist Jeffrey Sluka notes, "The classic image of successful rapport and good fieldwork relations in cultural anthropology is that of the ethnographer who has been 'adopted' or named by the tribe or people he or she studies" (Sluka, 2007, p. 122).

Anthropologists adopted into networks of kinship relations not only gain social access and certain rights but also assume social obligations associated with their new kinship status. These relationships can be deep and enduring—as illustrated by Smithsonian anthropologist William Crocker's description of his 1991 return to the Canela tribal community after a twelve-year absence. He had lived among these Amazonian Indians in Brazil off and on for a total of sixty-six months from the 1950s through the 1970s (**Figure 3.9**). When he stepped out of the single-motor missionary plane that had brought him back in 1991, he was quickly surrounded by Canela:

> Once on the ground, I groped for names and terms of address while shaking many hands. Soon my Canela mother, Tutkhwey (dove-woman), pulled me over to the shade of a plane's wing and pushed me down to a mat on the ground. She put both hands on my shoulders and, kneeling beside me, her head by mine, cried out words of mourning in a loud yodeling manner. Tears and phlegm dripped onto my shoulder and knees. According to a custom now abandoned by the younger women, she was crying for the loss of a grown daughter, Tsep-khwey (bat-woman), as well as for my return. (Crocker & Crocker, 2004, p. 1)

Since that 1991 reunion, Crocker has visited the Canela community every other year, always receiving a warm welcome and staying with locals. Although many anthropologists are successful in gaining social acceptance and even adoption status in communities where they do participant observation, they rarely go completely native and abandon their own homeland. Even after long stays in a community, and after learning to behave appropriately and communicate well, few become complete insiders.

Distrust and Political Tension

An anthropologist's fieldwork challenges include the possibility of getting caught in political rivalries and unwittingly used by factions within the community or being viewed with suspicion by government authorities who may interpret their systematic inquiries as the work of a spy. Anthropologist June Nash, for instance, has faced serious political and personal challenges doing fieldwork in various Latin American communities experiencing violent changes. As an outsider, she tried to avoid becoming embroiled in local conflicts but could not maintain her position as an impartial observer while researching a tin mining community in the Bolivian highlands. When

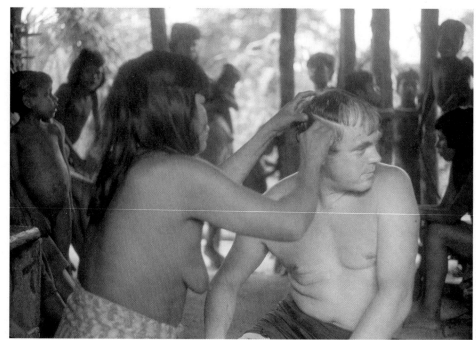

Figure 3.9 Social Acceptance in Fieldwork Anthropologist William Crocker did fieldwork among Canela Indians in Brazil over several decades. He still visits the community regularly. In this 1964 photograph, a Canela woman (M~i~i- kw'ej, or Alligator Woman) gives him a traditional haircut while other members of the community look on. She is the wife of his adoptive Canela "brother" and therefore a "wife" to Crocker in Canela kinship terms. Among the Canela, it is improper for a mother, sister, or daughter to cut a man's hair.

the conflict between local miners and bosses controlling the armed forces became violent, Nash found herself in a revolutionary setting in which miners viewed her tape recorder as an instrument of espionage and suspected her of being a CIA agent (Nash, 1976).

All anthropologists face the overriding challenge of winning the trust that allows people to be themselves and share an unmasked version of their culture with a newcomer. Some do not succeed in meeting this challenge. So it was with anthropologist Lincoln Keiser in his difficult fieldwork in the remote town of Thull, situated in the Hindu Kush Mountains of northwestern Pakistan. Keiser ventured there to explore customary blood feuding among a Kohistani tribal community of 6,000 Muslims making their living by a mix of farming and herding in the rugged region. However, the people he had traveled so far to study did not appreciate his presence. As Keiser recounted, many of the fiercely independent tribesmen in this area, "where the AK-47 symbolizes the violent quality of male social relations," treated him with great disdain and suspicion, as a foreign "infidel":

> Throughout my stay in Thull, many people remained convinced I was a creature sent by the devil to harm the community. . . . [Doing fieldwork there] was a test I failed, for a *jirga* [political council] of my most vocal opponents ultimately forced me to leave Thull three months before I had planned. . . . Obviously, I have difficulty claiming the people of Thull as "my people" because so many of them never ceased to despise me. . . . Still, I learned from being hated. (Keiser, 1991, p. 103)

Gender, Age, Ideology, Ethnicity, and Skin Color

The challenges of Keiser's fieldwork stemmed in part from his non-Muslim religious identity, marking him as an outsider in the local community of the faithful. Gender, age, ethnicity, and skin color can also impact a researcher's access to a community. For instance, male ethnographers may face prohibitions or severe restrictions in interviewing women or observing certain women's activities. Similarly, a female researcher may not find ready reception among males in communities with gender-segregation traditions. With respect to skin color, African American anthropologist Norris Brock-Johnson encountered social obstacles while doing fieldwork in the American Midwest, but his dark skin helped him gain "admission to the world of black Caribbean shipwrights" on the island of Bequia, where he studied traditional boatmaking (Robben, 2007, p. 61; see also Johnson, 1984).

Physical Danger

Ethnographic fieldwork in exotic places can be an adventure, but sometimes it presents physical danger. Although rare, some anthropologists have died in the field due to accident or illness. One dramatic example is that of American anthropologist Michelle Rosaldo. As a 37-year-old mother and university professor who had just published *Knowledge and Passion: Ilongot Notions of Self and Social Life* with Cambridge University Press, she returned to the Philippines for more fieldwork with the Ilongot. Trekking along a mountain trail on Luzon Island with her husband and fellow anthropologist, she slipped and fell to her death.

Another tragic accident involved Richard Condon, part of an American-Russian research team funded by the U.S. National Science Foundation for an anthropological study of health, population growth, and socialization in Alaska and the Russian Far East. In the late summer of 1995, he and three colleagues, along with five Yup'ik Eskimos, were traveling along the Bering Strait when their *umiak* ("skin-boat") flipped. Apparently, their boat had been attacked by a whale, wounded by an earlier party of seafaring Siberian Eskimo hunters. All nine men perished in the ice-cold water (Wenzel & McCartney, 1996).

Swedish anthropologist Anna Hedlund, currently researching non-state-armed groups in the Democratic Republic of Congo (DRC) in Africa, faces physical danger of a different sort. Living among rebels and investigating how they define and legitimize violence, she is surrounded by political tension and conflict (**Figure 3.10**).

Only a handful of anthropologists have been killed in the field. Among them is Raymond Kennedy, a Yale University professor who served as a U.S. military intelligence analyst in World War II. He specialized in Indonesia, a vast archipelago in Southeast Asia, composed of thousands of islands. His life came to an abrupt end in 1950 while he was finishing up a year of acculturation research. Recently independent after a brutal armed struggle that ended three centuries of Dutch colonial rule, the country was not yet stable. Kennedy was in his Jeep, traveling with a *Time Life* magazine photographer through beautiful mountainous terrain on the island of Java, when a band of guerrillas ambushed and executed them for reasons still not known (Embree, 1951; Price, 2011; "Two Americans are found slain," 1950).

Figure 3.10 Dangerous Anthropology Swedish anthropologist Anna Hedlund has done research in a range of politically tense and physically dangerous settings. Currently, she is working on the culture of non-state-armed groups in the DRC, focusing on how combatants define and legitimize violence. The work is based on extensive fieldwork in various military camps in the South Kivu province, eastern Congo. Here, we see her with combatants, pausing during a five-day trek to the rebel camp in the forest. Their faces have been blurred to protect their identities.

Subjectivity and Reflexivity

Whether working near home or abroad, when endeavoring to identify the rules that underlie each culture, ethnographers must grapple with the very real challenge of bias or subjectivity—his or her own and that of members in the community being studied. Researchers are expected to constantly check their own personal or cultural biases and assumptions as they work—and to present these self-reflections along with their observations. This practice of critical self-examination is known as *reflexivity*.

Because perceptions of reality may vary, an anthropologist must be extremely careful in describing a culture. To do so accurately, the researcher needs to seek out and consider three kinds of data:

1. The people's own understanding of their culture and the general rules they share: their ideal sense of the way their own society ought to be.
2. The extent to which people believe they are observing those rules: how they think they really behave.
3. The behavior that can be directly observed: what the anthropologist actually sees happening.

Clearly, the way people think they *should* behave, the way in which they think they *do* behave, and the way in which they *actually* behave may be distinctly different. By carefully examining and comparing these elements, anthropologists can draw up a set of rules that may explain the acceptable range of behavior within a culture.

Beyond the possibility of drawing false conclusions based on a group's ideal sense of itself, anthropologists run the risk of misinterpretation due to personal feelings and biases shaped by their own culture, as well as gender and age. It is important to recognize this challenge and make every effort to overcome it, for otherwise one may seriously misconstrue what one sees.

A case in point is the story of how male bias in the Polish culture in which Malinowski was raised caused him to ignore or miss significant factors in his pioneering study of the Trobrianders. Unlike today, when anthropologists receive special training before going into the field, Malinowski set out to do fieldwork in 1914 with little formal preparation. The following Original Study, written by anthropologist Annette Weiner, who ventured to the same islands almost sixty years later, illustrates how gender can impact one's research findings—both in terms of the bias that may affect a researcher's outlook and in terms of what native consultants may feel comfortable sharing with a particular researcher.

The Importance of Trobriand Women BY ANNETTE B. WEINER

Walking into a village at the beginning of fieldwork is entering a world without cultural guideposts. The task of learning values that others live by is never easy. The rigors of fieldwork involve listening and watching, learning a new language of speech and actions, and most of all, letting go of one's own cultural assumptions in order to understand the meanings others give to work, power, death, family, and friends. During my fieldwork in the Trobriand Islands of Papua New Guinea, I wrestled doggedly with each of these problems—and with the added challenge that I was working in the footsteps of a celebrated anthropological ancestor, Bronislaw Kasper Malinowski. . . .

In 1971, before my first trip to the Trobriands, I thought I understood many things about Trobriand customs and beliefs from having read Malinowski's exhaustive writings. Once there, however, I found that I had much more to discover. Finding significant differences in areas of importance, I gradually came to understand how he reached certain conclusions. . . .

My most significant point of departure from Malinowski's analyses was the attention I gave to women's productive work. In my original research plans, women were not the central focus of study, but on the first day I took up residence in a village I was taken by them to watch a distribution of their own wealth—bundles of banana leaves and banana fiber skirts—which they exchanged with other women in commemoration of someone who had recently died. Watching that event forced me to take women's economic roles more seriously than I would have from reading Malinowski's studies.

Although Malinowski noted the high status of Trobriand women, he attributed their importance to the fact that Trobrianders reckon descent through women. . . . Yet he never considered that this significance was underwritten by women's own wealth because he did not systematically investigate the women's productive activities. . . .

My taking seriously the importance of women's wealth not only brought women as the neglected half of society clearly into the ethnographic picture but also forced me to revise many of Malinowski's assumptions about Trobriand men. . . . For Malinowski, the basic relationships within a Trobriand family were guided by the matrilineal principle of "mother-right" and "father-love." A father was called "stranger" and had little authority over his own children. A woman's brother was the commanding figure and exercised control over his sister's sons. . . .

In my study of Trobriand women and men, a different configuration of reckoning descent through the maternal line emerged. A Trobriand father is not a "stranger" in Malinowski's definition, nor is he a powerless figure. The father is one of the most important persons in his child's life, and remains so even after his child grows up and marries. He gives his child many opportunities to gain things from his matrilineage, thereby adding to the available resources that he or she can draw upon.

At the same time, this giving creates obligations on the part of a man's children toward him that last even beyond his death. Thus, the roles that men and their children play in each other's lives are worked out through extensive cycles of exchanges, which define the strength of their relationships to each other and eventually benefit the other members of both their matrilineages. Central to these exchanges are women and their wealth.

. . . Only recently have anthropologists begun to understand the importance of taking women's work seriously. The "women's point of view" was largely ignored in the study of gender roles because anthropologists generally perceived women as living in the shadows of men—occupying the private rather than the public sectors of society, rearing children rather than engaging in economic or political pursuits.

In the Trobriand Islands, women's wealth consists of banana leaves and banana-fiber skirts, large quantities of which must be given away upon the death of a relative.

Adapted from Weiner, A. B. (1988). The Trobrianders of Papua New Guinea (pp. 4–7). Reprinted by permission of Cengage Learning.

Validation

As the Original Study makes clear, determining the accuracy of anthropological descriptions and conclusions can be difficult. In the natural sciences, one can replicate observations and experiments to try to establish the reliability of a researcher's conclusions. Thus, one can see for oneself if one's colleague has gotten it right. But validating ethnographic research is uniquely challenging because access to sites may be limited or barred altogether, due to a number of factors: insufficient funding, logistical difficulties in reaching the site, problems in obtaining permits, and changing cultural and environmental conditions. These factors mean that what could be observed in a certain context at a certain time cannot be observed at others. As a result, one researcher cannot easily confirm the reliability or completeness of another's account.

For this reason, anthropologists bear a heavy responsibility for factual reporting, including disclosing key issues related to their research: Why was a particular location selected as a research site and for which research objectives? What were the local conditions during fieldwork? Who provided the key information and major insights? How were data collected and recorded? Without such background information, it is difficult to judge the validity of the account and the soundness of the researcher's conclusions.

Putting It All Together: Completing an Ethnography

After collecting ethnographic information, the next challenge is to piece together all that has been gathered into a coherent whole that accurately describes the culture. Traditionally, ethnographies are detailed written descriptions composed of chapters on topics such as the circumstances and place of fieldwork itself; historical background; the community or group today; its natural environment; settlement patterns; subsistence practices; networks of kinship relations and other forms of social organization; marriage and sexuality; economic exchanges; political institutions; myths, sacred beliefs, and ceremonies; and current developments. These may be illustrated with photographs and accompanied by maps, kinship diagrams, and figures showing social and political organizational structures, settlement layout, floor plans of dwellings, seasonal cycles, and so on.

Sometimes ethnographic research is documented not only in writing but also with sound recordings and on film (**Figure 3.11**). Visual records may be used for documentation and illustration as well as for analysis or as a means of gathering additional information in interviews. Moreover, footage shot for the sake

Figure 3.11 Anthropologist-Filmmaker Hu Tai-Li An award-winning pioneer of ethnographic films in Taiwan, Tai-Li is a professor at National Chin-Hua University. She has directed and produced a half-dozen documentaries on a range of topics—including traditional rituals and music, development issues, and national and ethnic identity. Here she is filming Maleveq ("Five-Year Ceremony") rituals in the village of Kulalao, southern Taiwan. During this ceremony, lasting several days, indigenous Paiwan people celebrate their alliance with tribal ancestors and deities. Traditional belief holds that ancestral spirits attend this gathering; villagers beseech their blessings, welcoming them with special songs, dances, and food.

of documentation and research may be edited into a documentary film. Not unlike a written ethnography, such a film is a structured whole composed of numerous selected sequences, visual montage, juxtaposition of sound and visual image, and narrative sequencing, all coherently edited into an accurate visual representation of the ethnographic subject (Collier & Collier, 1986; El Guindi, 2004).

In recent years anthropologists have experimented with various digital media (Ginsburg, Abu-Lughod, & Larkin, 2009). With the emergence of digital technologies, the potential for anthropological research, interpretation, and presentation is greater than ever before. Digital recording devices provide ethnographers with a wealth of material to analyze and utilize toward building hypotheses. They also open the door to sharing findings in new, varied, and interactive ways in the far-reaching digitalized realm of the Internet. Digital ethnographers, having amassed a wealth of digital material while researching, are able to share their findings through a variety of outlets including DVDs, online photo essays, podcasts, and video blogs.

Ethnology: From Description to Interpretation and Theory

Largely descriptive in nature, ethnography provides the basic data needed for *ethnology*—the branch of cultural anthropology that makes cross-cultural comparisons and develops theories that explain why certain important differences or similarities occur between groups. As noted in Chapter 1, the end product of quality anthropological research is a coherent statement about culture or human nature that provides an explanatory framework for understanding the ideas and actions of the people being studied. In short, such an explanation or interpretation supported by a reliable body of data is a **theory**. As discussed in Chapter 1, theory is distinct from doctrine and dogma, which are assertions of opinions or beliefs formally handed down by an authority as indisputably true and accepted as a matter of faith.

Anthropologists do not claim that any one theory about culture is the absolute truth. Rather they judge or measure a theory's validity and soundness by varying degrees of probability; what is considered to be true is what is most probable. But although anthropologists are reluctant to make absolute statements about complex issues such as exactly how cultures function or change, they can and do provide fact-based evidence about whether assumptions have support or are unfounded and thus not true. Therefore, a *theory*, contrary to widespread misuse of the term, is much more than mere speculation; it is a critically examined explanation of observed reality.

Always open to future challenges born of new evidence or insights, scientific theory depends on demonstrable, fact-based evidence and repeated testing. So it is that, as our cross-cultural knowledge expands, the odds favor some anthropological theories over others. Old explanations or interpretations must sometimes be discarded as new theories based on better or more complete evidence are shown to be more effective or probable. Last but not least, theories also guide anthropologists in formulating new research questions and help them decide what data to collect and how to give meaning to their data.

Ethnology and the Comparative Method

A single instance of any phenomenon is generally insufficient for supporting a plausible hypothesis. Without some basis for comparison, the hypothesis grounded in a single case may be no more than a hunch born of a unique happenstance or particular historical coincidence. Theories in anthropology may be generated from worldwide cross-cultural or historical comparisons or even comparisons with other species. For instance, anthropologists may examine a global sample of societies in order to discover whether a hypothesis proposed to explain certain phenomena is supported by fact-based evidence. Of necessity, the cross-cultural researcher depends upon evidence gathered by other scholars as well as his or her own.

A key resource that makes this possible is the **Human Relations Area Files (HRAF)**, which is a vast collection of cross-indexed ethnographic, biocultural, and archaeological data catalogued by cultural characteristics and geographic location. This ever-growing data bank classifies more than 700 cultural characteristics and includes nearly 400 societies, past and present, from all around the world. Archived in about 300 libraries (on microfiche and/or online) and approaching a million pages of information, the HRAF facilitates comparative research on almost any cultural feature imaginable—warfare, subsistence practices, settlement patterns, marriage, rituals, and so on.

Among other things, anthropologists interested in finding explanations for certain social or cultural

---

theory A coherent statement that provides an explanatory framework for understanding; an explanation or interpretation supported by a reliable body of data.

Human Relations Area Files (HRAF) A vast collection of cross-indexed ethnographic, biocultural, and archaeological data catalogued by cultural characteristics and geographic location; archived in about 300 libraries on microfiche and/or online.

© Gunther Deichmann

Challenge Issue

What distinguishes humans from other animals? Why do chimpanzees look so much like us? Where on earth did our earliest ancestors first emerge? What accounts for the biological variation we see among humans across the globe? Challenged by such big questions, anthropologists—aided by a host of other specialists—search for answers, unearth masses of data, and offer theoretical explanations concerning the evolution and distribution of our species. Beyond ancient fossil bones and stone tools, this quest also builds on data revealed through molecular biology and digital technology. Because humans have a distinct capacity for creativity, anthropologists also investigate the art of our early ancestors, dating back tens of thousands of years. Much of it—including music and dance—is lost in time. But some ancient art—carved or painted on skin, hide, wood, bone, ivory, or rock—has been preserved, as seen in the northern Australia cave painting pictured here.

Becoming Human: The Origin and Diversity of Our Species

4

Anthropologists gather information from a variety of sources to piece together an understanding of evolutionary history and humankind's place in the animal kingdom. Studies of living primates (our closest mammal relatives), ancient fossils, and even molecular biology contribute to the story of how humans evolved.

On one level, human evolutionary studies are wholly scientific, formulating and testing hypotheses about biological and behavioral processes in the past. At the same time, like all scientists, anthropologists are influenced by changing cultural values. *Paleoanthropologists*, who study human evolutionary history, and *primatologists*, who study living primates, as well as the physical or biological anthropologists who study contemporary biological diversity, must be critically aware of their personal beliefs and cultural assumptions as they construct their theories.

Evolution Through Adaptation

In a general sense, **evolution** (from the Latin word *evolutio*, literally "rolling forth" or unfolding) refers to change through time. Biologically, it refers to changes in the genetic makeup of a population over generations. Passed from parents to offspring, **genes** are the basic physical units of heredity that specify the biological traits and characteristics of each organism. Although some evolution takes place through a process known as **adaptation**—a series of beneficial adjustments of organisms to their environment—random forces also contribute substantially to evolutionary change.

Adaptation is the cornerstone of the theory of evolution by **natural selection**, originally formulated by English naturalist Charles Darwin.

evolution Changes in the genetic makeup of a population over generations.

genes The basic physical units of heredity that specify the biological traits and characteristics of each organism.

adaptation A series of beneficial adjustments of organisms to their environment.

natural selection The principle or mechanism by which individuals having biological characteristics best suited to a particular environment survive and reproduce with greater frequency than individuals without those characteristics.

Simply put, this theory holds that individuals having biological characteristics best suited to a particular environment survive and reproduce with greater frequency than do individuals without those characteristics.

In this chapter, we will discuss the evolutionary history of our species. Looking at the biology and behavior of our closest living relatives, the other primates, will complement the examination of our past. We will also explore some aspects of human biological variation and the cultural meanings given to this variation.

Distinct among humans is the biological capacity to produce a uniquely rich array of *cultural adaptations*, a complex of ideas, technologies, and activities that enable people to survive and even thrive in their environment. Early humans, like all other creatures, greatly depended on physical attributes for survival. But in the course of time, humans came to rely increasingly on culture as an effective way of adapting to the environment. They figured out how to manufacture and utilize tools; they organized into social units that made food foraging more successful; and they learned to preserve and share their traditions and knowledge through the use of symbols that ultimately included spoken language.

The ability to solve a vast array of challenges through culture has made our species unusual among creatures on this planet. Humans do not merely adapt to the environment through biological change; we shape the environment to suit human needs and desires. Today, computer technology enables us to organize and manipulate an ever-increasing amount of information to keep pace with the environmental changes we have wrought. Space technology may enable us to propagate our species in extraterrestrial environments. If we manage to avoid self-destruction through misuse of our sophisticated tools, biomedical technology may eventually enable us to control genetic inheritance and thus the future course of our biological evolution.

The fundamental elements of human culture came into existence about 2.5 mya. Using scientific know-how to reach far back in time, we can trace the roots of our species and reconstruct the origins of human culture. Before stepping back that far, it is useful to have a glimpse at the work of two 19th-century scholars whose pioneering research and theoretical contributions are important foundation stones in this line of inquiry: Charles Darwin (1809–1882) and Gregor Mendel (1822–1884).

A Brief History of Research on Evolution and Genetics

Charles Darwin came to the idea of natural selection through personal discoveries and observations experienced during a five-year (1831–1836) scientific journey around the world aboard the two-masted British sloop *H.M.S. Beagle*. His findings forced him to radically rethink long-established ideas about the natural order.

Aware that his new theory, which proposed the evolutionary idea of natural selection, would provoke controversy in conservative religious circles, Darwin waited over two decades to publish his research. As expected, his book, *On the Origin of Species by Means of Natural Selection, or the Preservation of Favoured Races in the Struggle for Life*, created a storm upon its release in 1859. Within its pages, Darwin presented this famous passage:

> It may be said that natural selection is daily and hourly scrutinising, throughout the world, every variation, even the slightest; rejecting that which is bad, preserving and adding up all that is good; silently and insensibly working, whenever and wherever opportunity offers, at the improvement of each organic being in relation to its organic and inorganic conditions of life. We see nothing of these slow changes in progress, until the hand of time has marked the long lapses of ages, and then so imperfect is our view into long past geological ages, that we only see that the forms of life are now different from what they formerly were. (Darwin, 2007, p. 53; originally published 1859)

A few years after the publishing of Darwin's landmark book, a Roman Catholic monk named Gregor Mendel presented results from the biological experiments he carried out in the vegetable garden of his monastery in Brno, a city in today's Czech Republic. Raised on a small farm and having studied physics after entering the priesthood, Mendel had a keen and scientific interest in plant variations—so much so that over a seven-year period he cultivated and tested 29,000 pea plants at the monastery. Based on this research, he determined that the inheritance of each biological trait is determined by "units" or "factors" (later called genes) that are passed on to descendents unchanged. Moreover, he found that an individual inherits one such unit from each parent for each trait. And, finally, he demonstrated that a trait may not show up in an individual but can still be passed on to the next generation.

Mendel introduced his findings in an 1865 conference paper "Experiments in Plant Hybridisation." Published the following year, this article was the first to formulate the basic laws of biological inheritance. Although almost completely ignored for nearly four decades, Mendel's findings came to be recognized as a major theoretical contribution, and today, long after his death, the monk is honored as the father of genetics.

Mendel based his laws on statistical frequencies of observed characteristics—the color and surface texture in generations of peas. Later, with the benefit of increasingly precise research instruments (especially more powerful microscopes), his inferences about the mechanisms of inheritance were confirmed through the discovery of the cellular and molecular basis of inheritance.

When chromosomes, the cellular structures containing the genetic information, were discovered at the start of the 20th century, they provided a visible vehicle for transmission of traits proposed in Mendel's laws. In the 1930s and 1940s, combining Mendelian genetics and Darwin's theory of natural selection, a small international group of pioneering zoologists, botanists, and biochemists developed the new field of population genetics, formulating a comprehensive theoretical model.

Known as the *modern evolutionary synthesis*, this neo-Darwinist theory explains that evolution is gradual, based on environmental adaptation and small genetic changes within geographically separated populations after many generations of natural selection. A key building block in this theory is the discovery of DNA (deoxyribonucleic acid) within cells. Microscopic, DNA was first isolated in 1869, but scientists did not discover that these molecules carry genetic information until many decades later. Based on breakthroughs by molecular biologists since the early 1950s, we now understand that the main function of DNA is long-term storage of genetic information used in the development and functioning of all living organisms, including our own species.

Today, having mapped the human **genome** (the genetic design of a species with its complete set of DNA) and those of their closest primate relatives—the chimpanzee, bonobo, gorilla, and orangutan—molecular biologists have determined how much DNA modern *Homo sapiens* have in common with these great apes; our species shares the greatest amount of DNA with the chimpanzee (98.3 percent).

Humans and Other Primates

Humans are one of 10 million species on earth, 4,000 of which are fellow mammals. **Species** are populations or groups of populations having common attributes and the ability to interbreed and produce live, fertile offspring. Different species are reproductively isolated from one another. Biologists organize or classify species into larger groups of biologically related organisms. The human species is one kind of **primate**, a subgroup of mammals that also includes lemurs, lorises, tarsiers, monkeys, and apes. Among fellow primates, humans are most closely related to apes—chimpanzees, bonobos, gorillas, orangutans, and gibbons—all of particular interest to primatologists.

European scientists have argued long and hard over issues of species classification, especially since the start of the age of exploration about 500 years ago that brought them to distant lands inhabited by life forms they had never seen. Most vexing was the question concerning the difference between apes and humans. In 1698, after dissecting a young male chimpanzee captured in West Africa and brought to Europe, an English physician concluded the creature was almost human and classified it as *Homo sylvestris* ("man of the forest").

A few decades later, Swedish naturalist Carolus Linnaeus (1707–1778) published the first edition of his famous *System of Nature* (1735). In it he classified humans with sloths and monkeys in the same order: Anthropomorpha ("human-shaped"). By the time Linnaeus published the tenth edition of his famous book in 1758, he had replaced the name "Anthropomorpha" with "Primate" and included lemurs, monkeys, and humans in that category. Moreover, he now recognized not just one human species but two: *Homo sapiens* or *Homo diurnus* ("active during daylight") and an apelike human he called *Homo nocturnus* ("active during night"). He also referred to the latter as *Homo troglodytes* ("cave-dweller"). Linnaeus's shifting categories typify the struggle of early scientists to classify humans precisely within the natural system.

Perhaps the best illustration of the perplexity involved is a comment made by an 18th-century French bishop upon seeing an orangutan in a menagerie. Uncertain whether the creature before him was human or beast, he proclaimed: "Speak and I shall baptize thee!" (Corbey, 1995, p.1).

In the course of the 18th century, European scientists continued to debate the proper classification of the great apes (as well as human "savages" encountered overseas) and placed chimpanzees and orangutans (gorillas were not recognized as a separate species until 1847) squarely between humans and the other animals. Perhaps going further than any other reputable scholar in Europe at the time, the famous Scottish judge Lord Mondobbo argued in several widely read scholarly publications in the 1770s and 1780s that orangutans should be considered part of the human species. He pointed out that they could walk erect and construct shelters and that they used sticks to defend themselves (**Figure 4.1**). He even suggested that at least in principle these "savages" were

---

genome The genetic design of a species with its complete set of DNA.

species A population or group of populations having common attributes and the ability to interbreed and produce live, fertile offspring. Different species are reproductively isolated from one another.

primate The subgroup of mammals that includes lemurs, lorises, tarsiers, monkeys, apes, and humans.

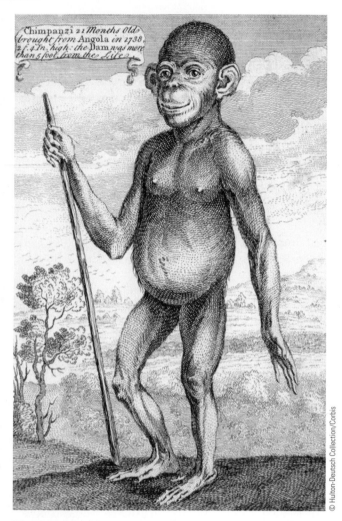

Figure 4.1 **Great Ape or Human?** Early scientific struggles to classify great apes, and to identify and weigh the significance of the similarities and differences between them and humans, are reflected in early European renderings of apes, including this 18th-century image of a chimpanzee portrayed as a biped equipped with a walking stick.

today. By studying our evolutionary history as well as the biology and behavior of our closest living relatives, we gain a better understanding of how and why humans developed as they did.

Evidence from ancient skeletons indicates the first mammals appeared over 200 mya as small nocturnal (night-active) creatures. The earliest primatelike creatures came into being about 65 mya when a new, mild climate favored the spread of dense tropical and subtropical forests over much of the earth. The change in climate and habitat, combined with the sudden extinction of dinosaurs, favored mammal diversification, including the evolutionary development of arboreal (tree-living) mammals from which primates evolved.

The ancestral primates possessed biological characteristics that allowed them to adapt to life in the forests. Their relatively small size enabled them to use tree branches not accessible to larger competitors and predators. Arboreal life opened up an abundant new food supply. The primates were able to gather leaves, flowers, fruits, insects, bird eggs, and even nesting birds, rather than having to wait for them to fall to the ground. Natural selection favored those who judged depth correctly and gripped the branches tightly. Those individuals who survived life in the trees passed on their genes to the succeeding generations.

Although the earliest primates were nocturnal, today most primate species are diurnal (active in the day). The transition to diurnal life in the trees required important biological adjustments that helped shape the biology and behavior of humans today.

Anatomical Adaptation

Ancient and modern primate groups possess a number of anatomical characteristics described next. However, compared to other mammals, primates have only a few anatomical specializations while their behavior patterns are very diverse and flexible.

Primate Dentition

The varied diet available to arboreal primates—shoots, leaves, insects, and fruits—required relatively unspecialized teeth, compared to those found in other mammals. Comparative anatomy and the fossil record reveal that mammals ancestral to primates possessed three incisors, one canine, four premolars, and three molars on each side of the jaw, top and bottom, for a total of forty-four teeth. The incisors (in the front of the mouth) were used for gripping and cutting, canines (behind the incisors) for tearing and shredding, and molars and premolars (the "cheek teeth") for grinding and chewing food.

capable of speech (Barnard in Corbey & Theunissen, 1995, pp. 71, 85).

Still, most Europeans clung to the notion of a marked divide between humans on the one hand and animals on the other. Debates about the exact relationship between humans and other animals continue to this day. These debates include biological data on ancient fossils and genetics, as well as philosophical stances on the "humane" treatment of our closest ape relatives.

One could question the value of including nonhuman primates in this textbook when the distinctive cultural capacities of humans are our major concern. However, humans have a long evolutionary history as mammals and primates that set the stage for the cultural beings we are

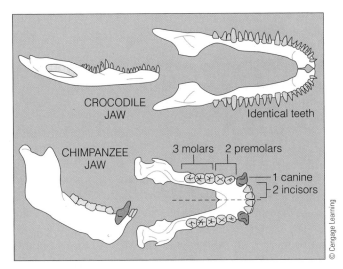

Figure 4.2 Comparing Teeth As seen in all reptiles, the crocodile jaw pictured above contains a series of identically shaped teeth. If a tooth breaks or falls out, a new tooth will emerge in its place. By contrast, primates, like all mammals, have only two sets of teeth: "baby" and adult teeth. Apes and humans possess precise numbers of specialized teeth, each with a particular shape, as indicated on this chimpanzee jaw: Incisors in front are shown in blue, canines behind in red, followed by two premolars and three molars in yellow (the last being the wisdom teeth in humans).

The evolutionary trend for primate dentition has been toward a reduction in the number and size of the teeth (**Figure 4.2**).

Primate Sensory Organs

The primates' adaptation to arboreal life involved changes in the form and function of their sensory organs. The sense of smell was vital for the earliest ground-dwelling, night-active mammals. It enabled them to operate in the dark, to sniff out their food, and to detect hidden predators. However, for active tree life during daylight, good vision is a better guide than smell in judging the location of the next branch or tasty morsel. Accordingly, the sense of smell declined in primates, whereas vision became highly developed.

Traveling through trees demands judgments concerning depth, direction, distance, and the relationships of objects hanging in space, such as vines or branches. Monkeys and apes achieved this through binocular stereoscopic color vision (**Figure 4.3**), the ability to see the world in the three dimensions of height, width, and depth.

Tree-living primates also possess an acute sense of touch. An effective feeling and grasping mechanism helps keep them from falling and tumbling while speeding through the trees. The early mammals from which primates evolved possessed tiny touch-sensitive hairs at the

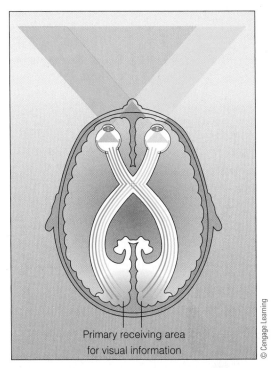

Figure 4.3 Stereoscopic Vision Anthropoid primates possess binocular stereoscopic vision. *Binocular vision* refers to overlapping visual fields due to forward-facing eyes. Three-dimensional or stereoscopic vision comes from binocular vision and the transmission of information from each eye to both sides of the brain.

tips of their hands and feet. In primates, sensitive pads backed up by nails on the tips of the animals' fingers and toes replaced these hairs. In some monkeys from Central and South America, this feeling and grasping ability extends to the tail.

The Primate Brain

An increase in brain size, particularly in the cerebral hemispheres—the areas supporting conscious thought—occurred in the course of primate evolution. In monkeys, apes, and humans the cerebral hemispheres completely cover the cerebellum, the part of the brain that coordinates the muscles and maintains body balance. One of the most significant outcomes of this is the flexibility seen in primate behavior. Rather than relying on reflexes controlled by the cerebellum, primates constantly react to a variety of features in the environment and, of course, to one another.

The Primate Skeleton

The skeleton gives vertebrates—animals with internal backbones—their basic shape or silhouette, supports the soft tissues, and helps protect vital internal organs. Some evolutionary trends are evident in the primate skeleton.

For example, as primates relied increasingly on vision rather than smell, the eyes rotated forward to become enclosed in a protective layer of bone. Simultaneously, the snout reduced in size. The opening at the base of the skull for the spinal cord to pass assumed a more forward position, reflecting some degree of upright posture rather than a constant four-footed stance.

The limbs of the primate skeleton follow the same basic ancestral plan seen in the earliest vertebrates. The upper portion of each arm or leg has a single long bone, the lower portion has two bones, and then hands or feet with five radiating digits. Other animals possess limbs specialized to optimize a particular behavior, such as speed. In nearly all of the primates, the big toe and thumb are *opposable*, making it possible to grasp and manipulate objects such as sticks and stones with their feet as well as their hands. Humans and their direct ancestors are the only exceptions, having lost the opposable big toe. The generalized limb pattern allows for flexible movements by primates.

In the apes, a sturdy collarbone (clavicle) orients the arms at the side rather than at the front of the body, allowing for heightened flexibility. With their broad flexible shoulder joints, apes can hang suspended from tree branches and swing from tree to tree.

The retention of the flexible vertebrate limb pattern in primates was a valuable asset to evolving humans. It was, in part, having hands capable of grasping that enabled our own ancestors to manufacture and use tools and thus alter the course of their evolution.

Behavioral Adaptation

Primates adapt to their environments not only anatomically but also through a wide variety of behaviors. Young apes spend more time reaching adulthood than do most other mammals. During their lengthy growth and development, they learn the behaviors of their social group. Although biological factors play a role in the duration of primate dependency, many of the specific behaviors learned during childhood derive solely from the traditions of the group. The behavior of primates, particularly apes, provides anthropologists with clues about the earliest development of human cultural behavior.

Many studies of the behavior of apes in their natural habitat also provide models for paleoanthropologists interested in reconstructing the behavior of our earliest human ancestors. Although no living primate lives exactly as evolving humans did, these studies have revealed remarkable variation and sophistication in ape behavior. Primatologists increasingly interpret these variations as cultural because they are learned rather than genetically programmed or instinctive. We shall look at the behavior

of two closely related African species of chimpanzee: common chimpanzees and bonobos.

Chimpanzee and Bonobo Behavior

Like nearly all primates, chimpanzees and bonobos are highly social animals. Among chimps, the largest social organizational unit is a group usually composed of fifty or more individuals who collectively inhabit a large geographic area. Rarely, however, are all of these animals together at one time. Instead, they are usually found ranging singly or in small subgroups consisting of adult males, or females with their young, or males and females together with young. In the course of their travels, subgroups may join forces and forage together, but sooner or later these will break up again into smaller units. Typically, when some individuals split off, others join, so the composition of subunits shifts frequently.

Relationships among individuals within the ape communities are relatively harmonious. In the past, primatologists believed that male dominance hierarchies, in which some animals outrank and can dominate others, formed the basis of primate social structures. They noted that physical strength and size play a role in determining an animal's rank. By this measure males generally outrank females. However, with the benefit of detailed field studies over the last fifty years, the nuances of primate social behavior and the importance of female primates have been documented.

High-ranking female chimpanzees may dominate low-ranking males. And among bonobos, female rank determines the social order of the group far more than male rank. Although greater strength and size do contribute to an animal's higher rank, several other factors also come into play in determining its social position. These include the rank of its mother, which is largely determined through her cooperative social behavior and how effective each individual animal is at creating alliances with others.

On the whole, bonobo females form stronger bonds with one another than do chimpanzee females. Moreover, the strength of the bond between mother and son interferes with bonds among males. Not only do bonobo males defer to females in feeding, but *alpha* (high-ranking) females have been observed chasing alpha males; such males may even yield to low-ranking females, particularly when groups of females form alliances (de Waal, Kano, & Parish, 1998).

Widening his gaze beyond social ranking and attack behavior among great apes, Japanese primatologist Kinji Imanishi initiated field studies of bonobos, investigating and demonstrating the importance of social cooperation rather than competition. Likewise, Dutch primatologist Frans de Waal's research, highlighted in the following Original Study, shows that reconciliation after an attack may be even more important from an evolutionary perspective than the actual attack.

Reconciliation and Its Cultural Modification in Primates *BY FRANS B. M. DE WAAL*

Despite the continuing popularity of the struggle-for-life metaphor, it is now recognized that there are drawbacks to open competition, hence that there are sound evolutionary reasons for curbing it. The dependency of social animals on group life and cooperation makes aggression a socially costly strategy. The basic dilemma facing many animals, including humans, is that they sometimes cannot win a fight without losing a friend.

This photo shows what may happen after a conflict—in this case between two female bonobos. About 10 minutes after their fight, the two females approach each other, with one clinging to the other and both rubbing their clitorises and genital swellings together in a pattern known as genito-genital rubbing, or GG-rubbing. This sexual contact, typical of bonobos, constitutes a so-called reconciliation. Chimpanzees, which are closely related to bonobos (and to us: bonobos and chimpanzees are our closest animal relatives), usually reconcile in a less sexual fashion, with an embrace and mouth-to-mouth kiss.

We now possess evidence for reconciliation in more than twenty-five different primate species, not just in apes but also in many monkeys—and in studies conducted on human children in the schoolyard. Researchers have even found reconciliation in dolphins, spotted hyenas, and some other nonprimates. Reconciliation seems widespread: a common mechanism found whenever relationships need to be maintained despite occasional conflict.[a,b]

The definition of *reconciliation* used in animal research is a friendly reunion between former opponents not long after a conflict. This is somewhat different from definitions in the dictionary, primarily because we look for an empirical definition that is useful in observational studies—in our case, the stipulation that the reunion happen not long after the conflict.

Let me describe two interesting elaborations on the mechanism of reconciliation. One is *mediation*. Chimpanzees are the only animals known to use mediators in conflict resolution. To be able to mediate conflict, one needs to understand relationships outside of oneself, which may be the reason why other animals fail to show this aspect of conflict resolution. For example, if two male chimpanzees have been involved in a fight, even on a very large island as where I did my studies, they can easily avoid each other, but instead they will sit opposite from each other, not too far apart, and avoid eye contact. They can sit like this for a long time. In this situation, a third party, such as an older female, may move in and try to solve the issue. The female will approach one of the males and groom him for a brief while. She then gets up and walks slowly to the other male, and the first male walks right behind her.

We have seen situations in which, if the first male failed to follow, the female turned around to grab his arm and make him follow. So the process of getting the two males in proximity seems intentional on the part of the female. She then begins grooming the other male, and the first male grooms her. Before long, the female disappears from the scene, and the males continue grooming: She has in effect brought the two parties together.

There exists a limited anthropological literature on the role of conflict resolution, a process absolutely crucial for the maintenance of the human social fabric in the same way that it is crucial for our primate relatives. In human societies, mediation is often done by high-ranking or senior members of the community, sometimes culminating in feasts in which the restoration of harmony is celebrated.[c]

The second elaboration on the reconciliation concept is that it is not purely instinctive, but a learned social skill subject to what primatologists now increasingly call "culture" (meaning that the animal behavior is subject to learning from others as opposed to genetic transmission).[d] To test the learnability of reconciliation, I conducted an

Two adult female bonobos engage in so-called GG-rubbing, a sexual form of reconciliation typical of the species.

© Amy Parish/Anthro-Photo

experiment with young rhesus and stumptail monkeys. Not nearly as conciliatory as stumptail monkeys, rhesus monkeys have the reputation of being rather aggressive and despotic. Stumptails are considered more laid-back and tolerant. We housed members of the two species together for 5 months. By the end of this period, they were a fully integrated group: They slept, played, and groomed together.

After 5 months, we separated them again, and measured the effect of their time together on conciliatory behavior.

The research controls—rhesus monkeys who had lived with one another, without any stumptails—showed absolutely no change in the tendency to reconcile. Stumptails showed a high rate of reconciliation, which was also expected, because they also do so if living together. The most interesting group was the experimental rhesus monkeys, those who had lived with stumptails. These monkeys started out at the same low level of reconciliation as the rhesus controls, but after they had lived with the stumptails, and after we had segregated them again so that they were now housed only with other rhesus monkeys who had gone through the same experience, these rhesus monkeys reconciled as much as stumptails do. This means that we created a "new and improved" rhesus monkey, one that made up with its opponents far more easily than a regular rhesus monkey.[e]

This was in effect an experiment on monkey culture: We changed the culture of a group of rhesus monkeys and made it more similar to that of stumptail monkeys by exposing them to the practices of this other species. This experiment also shows that there exists a great deal of flexibility in primate behavior. We humans come from a long lineage of primates with great social sophistication and a well-developed potential for behavioral modification and learning from others.

------

[a]de Waal, F. B. M. (2000). Primates—A natural heritage of conflict resolution. *Science 28*, 586–590.

[b]Aureli, F., & de Waal, F. B. M. (2000). *Natural conflict resolution.* Berkeley: University of California Press.

[c]Reviewed by Frye, D. P. (2000). Conflict management in cross-cultural perspective. In F. Aureli & F. B. M. de Waal, *Natural conflict resolution* (pp. 334–351). Berkeley: University of California Press.

[d]For a discussion of the animal culture concept, see de Waal, F. B. M. (2001). *The ape and the sushi master.* New York: Basic.

[e]de Waal, F. B. M., & Johanowicz, D. L. (1993). Modification of reconciliation behavior through social experience: An experiment with two macaque species. *Child Development 64*, 897–908.

Prior to the 1980s primates other than humans were thought to be vegetarians. However, groundbreaking research by Jane Goodall, among others, showed otherwise. This British researcher's fieldwork among chimpanzees in their forest habitat at Gombe, a wildlife reserve on the eastern shores of Lake Tanganyika in Tanzania, revealed that these apes supplement their primary diet of fruits and other plant foods with insects and also meat. Even more surprising, she found that in addition to killing small invertebrate animals for food, they also hunted and ate monkeys, usually flailing them to death (see Anthropologists of Note).

Chimpanzee females sometimes hunt, but males do so far more frequently and may spend hours watching, following, and chasing intended prey. Moreover, in contrast to the usual primate practice of each animal finding its own food, hunting frequently involves teamwork, particularly when the prey is a baboon. Once a potential victim has been isolated from its troop, three or more adult chimps will carefully position themselves so as to block off escape routes while another pursues the prey. Following the kill, most who are present get a share of the meat, either by grabbing a piece as chance affords or by begging for it.

Whatever the nutritional value of meat, hunting is not done purely for dietary purposes but for social and sexual reasons as well. Anthropologist Craig Stanford, who has done fieldwork among the chimpanzees of Gombe in Tanzania since the early 1990s, found that these sizable apes (100-pound males are common) frequently kill animals weighing up to 25 pounds and eat much more meat than previously believed. Although somewhat different chimpanzee hunting practices have been observed elsewhere in Africa, hunts at Gombe usually take place during the dry season when plant foods are less readily available and female chimps display genital swelling, which signals that they are ready to mate. Notably, fertile females are more successful than others at begging for meat, and males often share the meat after copulation (Stanford, 2001) For chimps ready for motherhood, a supply of protein-rich food helps support the increased nutritional requirements of pregnancy and lactation.

Beyond sharing meat to attract sexual partners, males use their catch to reward friends and allies, gaining status in the process. In other words, although Stanford links male hunting and food-sharing behavior with female reproductive biology, these behaviors are part of a complex social system that may be rooted more in the cultural traditions and history of Gombe than in chimpanzee biology.

Among bonobos, hunting is primarily a female activity. Also, female hunters regularly share carcasses with other females but less often with males. Even when the most dominant male throws a tantrum nearby, he may still be denied a share of meat (Ingmanson, 1998). Such discriminatory

ANTHROPOLOGISTS OF NOTE

Jane Goodall (b. 1934) • Svante Pääbo (b. 1955)

Born just twenty years apart, these two anthropologists represent biological anthropology's traditional and modern approaches to research—and illustrate the importance of both.

Jane Goodall observing wild chimpanzees.

In July 1960, **Jane Goodall** arrived with her mother at the Gombe Chimpanzee Reserve on the shores of Lake Tanganyika in Tanzania. Goodall was the first of three women Kenyan anthropologist Louis Leakey sent out to study great apes in the wild (the others were Dian Fossey and Biruté Galdikas, who were to study gorillas and orang-utans, respectively); her task was to begin a long-term study of chimpanzees. Little did she realize that, more than forty years later, she would still be at it.

Born in London, Goodall grew up and was schooled in Bournemouth, England. As a child, she dreamed of going to live in Africa, so when an invitation arrived to visit a friend in Kenya, she jumped at the opportunity. While in Kenya, she met Leakey, who gave her a job as an assistant secretary. Before long, she was on her way to Gombe. Within a year, the outside world began to hear the most extraordinary things about this pioneering woman: tales of toolmaking apes, cooperative hunts by chimpanzees, and what seemed like exotic chimpanzee rain dances. By the mid-1960s, her work had earned her a doctorate from Cambridge University, and Gombe was on its way to becoming one of the most dynamic field stations for the study of animal behavior anywhere in the world.

Although Goodall is still very involved with her chimpanzees and primate conservation, she spends a good deal of time these days lecturing, writing, and overseeing the work of others. Goodall is also passionately dedicated to halting illegal trafficking in chimps and fighting for the humane treatment of captive chimpanzees.

Svante Pääbo, named in 2007 by *Time* magazine as one of the hundred most influential people in the world, has revolutionized our understanding of paleogenetics and human evolution. Born and raised in Sweden, he is the son of an Estonian refugee and a Swedish Nobel Prize winner in biochemistry. As a boy, he was fascinated by Egyptian archaeology. As a young man, he studied Egyptology at Uppsala University before switching to medicine. Pursuing a doctorate in molecular genetics, he applied DNA cloning technologies to ancient human remains and demonstrated DNA survival in a 2,400-year-old Egyptian mummy.

In 1986, after completing his doctorate, Pääbo joined the genetics laboratory at the University of California at Berkeley. Headed by Alan Wilson, who had invented the molecular clock, this lab used the newly invented Polymerase Chain Reaction (PCR) technique. Focusing on evolutionary genetics, Pääbo developed techniques to solve the problem that DNA from ancient remains is often damaged and contaminated.

Pääbo accepted an academic position in Germany in 1990, soon achieving scientific successes: sequencing some Neandertal DNA; determining the small percentage of genetic differences between humans and chimpanzees; and linking the FOXp2 gene to language. In 1997, he became founding director of the Evolutionary Genetics department at the Max Planck Institute for Evolutionary Anthropology. Based on high-throughput DNA sequencing technology, his team then sequenced the draft genome of a Neandertal, based on DNA extracted from 40,000-year-old fossils, and discovered genetic evidence of interbreeding between archaic and anatomically modern humans. News of his scientific overview of the genome (published in 2009 with fifty-three coauthors) created a sensation worldwide.[a]

Svante Pääbo holding a Neandertal skull.

In 2012, Pääbo's team extracted DNA from a small human fossil excavated in a Siberian cave, determined it was almost 80,000 years old, mapped its genome, and discovered it represented an unknown sister group of the Neandertal now named Denisovans. Demonstrating interbreeding between modern *Homo sapiens* ancestors and Neandertals, as well as Denisovans, between 30,000 and 100,000 years ago, Pääbo's pioneering work challenges contemporary evolutionary theory. It reveals that a small percentage of human DNA in living populations is derived from these two archaic humans groups, advances our understanding of prehistoric population movements, and challenges the recent African origins hypothesis. Just as important, it shows that the divisions between human groups are not natural but cultural.

[a]Green, R. E., et al. (2010, May 7). A draft sequence of the Neandertal genome. *Science 328* (5979), 710–722.

sharing among female bonobos is also evident when it comes to other foods such as fruits.

The sexual practices of chimpanzees and bonobos differ as much as their hunting strategies. For chimps, sexual activity—initiated by either the male or the female—occurs only during the periods when females signal their fertility through genital swelling. By most human standards, chimp sexual behavior is promiscuous. A dozen or so males have been observed to have as many as fifty copulations in one day with a single female. Dominant males try to monopolize sexually receptive females, although cooperation from the female is usually required for this to succeed. An individual female and a lower-ranking male sometimes form a temporary bond, leaving the group together for a few private days during the female's fertile period. Thus dominant males do not necessarily father all (or even most) of the offspring in a social group. Social success, achieving alpha male status, does not translate neatly into the evolutionary currency of reproductive success.

Among bonobos (as among humans) sexuality goes far beyond male–female mating for purposes of biological reproduction. Primatologists have observed virtually every possible combination of ages and sexes engaging in a remarkable array of sexual activities, including oral sex, tongue-kissing, and massaging each other's genitals. Male bonobos may mount each other, or one may rub his scrotum against that of the other. Among females, genital rubbing is particularly common. As described in this chapter's Original Study, the primary function of most of this sex, both hetero- and homosexual, is to reduce tensions and resolve social conflicts. Notably, although forced copulation among chimpanzees is known to occur, such rape has never been observed among bonobos (de Waal, 1998).

Chimpanzee and Bonobo Childhood Development

Chimpanzee and bonobo dependence on learned social behavior is related to their extended period of childhood development. Born without built-in responses dictating specific behavior in complex situations, the young chimp or bonobo, like the young human, learns by observation, imitation, and practice how to strategically interact with others and even manipulate them for his or her own benefit. Making mistakes along the way, young primates modify their behavior based on the reactions of other members of the group. They learn to match their interactive behaviors according to each individual's social position and temperament. Anatomical features such as a free upper lip (unlike lemurs or cats, for example) allow monkeys and apes varied facial expression, contributing to greater communication among individuals.

Young chimpanzees and bonobos also learn other functional behaviors from adults, such as how to make and use tools. Beyond deliberately modifying objects to make them suitable for particular purposes, chimps and bonobos can to some extent modify them to regular patterns and may even prepare objects at one location in anticipation of future use at another place. For example, chimps commonly select a long, slender branch, strip off its leaves, and carry it on a "fishing" expedition to a termite nest. Reaching their destination, they insert the stick into the nest, wait a few minutes, and then pull it out to eat the insects clinging to it.

There are numerous examples of chimpanzees using tools: They use leaves as wipes or sponges to get drinking water out of a hollow. Large sticks may serve as clubs or as missiles (as may stones) in aggressive or defensive displays. Recently, a chimp group in Senegal has even been observed fashioning sticks into spears and using them to hunt (Hopkin, 2007; Pruetz & Bertolani, 2007). Stones are used as hammers and anvils to crack open certain kinds of nuts. Twigs are used as toothpicks to clean teeth as well as to extract loose baby teeth (McGrew, 2000).

Bonobos in the wild have not been observed making and using tools to the extent that chimpanzees do. But toolmaking capabilities have been shown by a captive bonobo who independently made stone tools remarkably similar to the earliest tools made by our own ancestors.

Primates have a great range of calls that are often used together with movements of the face or body to convey a message. Observers have not yet established the meaning of all the sounds, but a good number have been distinguished, such as warning calls, threat calls, defense calls, and gathering calls. Experiments with captive apes have revealed even greater communication abilities using American Sign Language and keyboards.

Primatologists are uncovering increasing evidence of the remarkable behavioral sophistication and intelligence of chimpanzees and other apes—including a capacity for conceptual thought previously unsuspected by most scientists. The widespread practice of caging our primate cousins and exploiting them for entertainment or medical experimentation has become increasingly controversial.

Human Ancestors

Figuring out biological links between ancient human fossils and related but long-extinct species within the animal kingdom is as controversial and challenging today as it was in the 18th century when Linnaeus was working on his *System of Nature*. Today, paleoanthropologists developing taxonomic schemes for humans and their ancestors reach beyond Linnaeus's focus on shared physical characteristics to consider genetic makeup. Humans are classified as **hominoids**, the broad-shouldered tailless group of primates that includes all living and extinct apes and humans. Humans and their ancestors are distinct among the hominoids for **bipedalism** ("two-footed")—walking upright on both hind legs.

hominoid The broad-shouldered tailless group of primates that includes all living and extinct apes and humans.

bipedalism "Two-footed"—walking upright on both hind legs—a characteristic of humans and their ancestors.

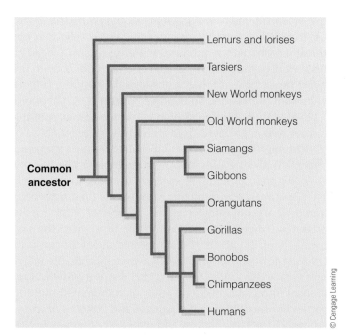

Figure 4.4 Primate Connections The relationship among monkeys, apes, and humans can be established by molecular similarities and differences. Molecular evidence indicates that the split between the human and African ape lines took place between 5 and 8 million years ago. Several important fossil finds dating from 5 to 7 million years ago have been discovered in the last few years.

Over the past few decades, genetic and biochemical studies have confirmed that the African apes—chimpanzees, bonobos, and gorillas—are our closest living relatives (**Figure 4.4**). By comparing genes and proteins among all the apes, scientists have estimated that gibbons, followed by orangutans, were the first to diverge from a very ancient common ancestral line. At some time between 5 and 8 mya, humans, chimpanzees, and gorillas began to follow separate evolutionary courses. Chimpanzees later diverged into two separate species: the common chimpanzee and the bonobo. Early human evolutionary development followed a path that produced, eventually, only one surviving bipedal species: *Homo sapiens*.

Larger brains and bipedal movement constitute the most striking differences between humans and our closest primate relatives. Although we might like to think that it is our larger brains that make us special among fellow primates, it is now clear that bipedalism appeared at the beginning of the ancestral line leading to humans and played a pivotal role in setting us apart from the apes. Brain expansion came later.

The First Bipeds

Between 5 and 15 mya, various kinds of hominoids lived throughout Africa, Asia, and Europe. One of these apes living in Africa between 5 and 8 mya was a direct ancestor to the human line. Each new fossil from this critical time period—such as the 6-million-year-old *Orrorin* fossils discovered in

Kenya in 2001 (Senut, et al., 2001) or the 6- to 7-million-year-old skull discovered in Chad, Central Africa (Brunet, et al., 2002)—is proposed as the latest "missing link" in the evolutionary chain leading to humans.

For a hominoid fossil to be definitively classified as part of the human evolutionary line, evidence of bipedalism is required. However, all early bipeds are not necessarily direct ancestors to the humans. Nevertheless, new discoveries of ancient humanlike fossils, especially in East Africa, repeatedly stir the scientific and popular imagination that a "missing link" has been identified in "the great chain" between the earliest bipeds and the human species today.

Between 4 and 5 mya, the environment of eastern and southern Africa was mostly a mosaic of open country with pockets of woodland. Some early bipeds seem to have lived in such closed wooded areas. One forested pocket existed in what is now the Afar desert of northeastern Ethiopia, where a large number of fossil bone fragments of a very early biped were recently found. Dated to 4.4 mya, they were identified as belonging to a hominoid species called *Ardipithecus ramidus* (in the region's Afar language, *ardi* means "ground" or "floor"; *pithekos* is Greek for "ape"; *ramid* is Afar for "root").

This fossil find included the remains of about thirty-six individuals who hunted small animals and gathered plants and nuts in what was then a humid tropical woodland, especially dense with palm and fig trees. Already very different from chimps, with whom they shared a common ancestor about 2 million years earlier, these ancient hominoids could walk upright. As bipeds, they could carry food in their very long arms as they explored the woodland floor on two short legs. They were also quadrupeds—when climbing and moving about in the trees where they lived.

The most complete skeleton is that of a small-brained 1.22-meter- (4-foot-) tall adult female who weighed about 50 kilograms (120 pounds). Skeletal analysis revealed her bipedalism. First unearthed in 1994, she was named Ardi by the team that found her in the arid floodplain along the middle stretch of the Awash River. Although it is possible that Ardi and the other ardipithecines found in this area represent a species that did not further evolve, many scholars accept them as belonging to the human branch of the primate family tree and, as such, possibly direct ancestors in the evolutionary process that ultimately led to the development of our own species (White, et al., 2009).

Later human ancestors inhabited more open country known as savannah—grasslands with scattered trees and groves—and are assigned to one or another species of the genus **Australopithecus** (from Latin *australis*, meaning "southern," and Greek *pithekos*, meaning "ape"). Opinions vary on just how many species there were in Africa between about 1 and 4 mya. For our purposes and the sake of simplicity, it suffices to refer to them collectively as "australopithecines." The earliest definite australopithecine

Australopithecus The genus including several species of early bipeds from southern, eastern, and Central Africa (Chad) living between about 1.1 and 4.2 million years ago, one of whom was directly ancestral to humans.

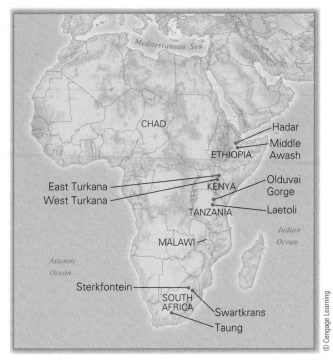

Figure 4.5 Australopithecine Fossil Sites Australopithecine fossils have been found in South Africa, Malawi, Tanzania, Kenya, Ethiopia, and Chad. Among recent important finds is the 3.3-million-year-old skull and partial skeleton of a 3-year-old *Australopithecus afarensis* unearthed by Ethiopian paleoanthropologist Zeresenay Alemseged in his home country. Some experts refer to the young ape as "Lucy's baby" after the famous adult female australopithecine skeleton discovered in 1974 and known as Lucy even though the toddler's fossil is tens of thousands of years older. This fossil provides rare evidence of what young australopithecines were like. Also, unlike Lucy, the child's fossil includes fingers, a foot, a complete torso, and a face.

fossils date back 4.2 million years, (Alemseged, et al., 2006), whereas the most recent ones are only about 1 million years old. They have been found up and down the length of eastern Africa from Ethiopia to South Africa and westward into Chad (**Figure 4.5**) (Wolpoff, 1996).

None of the australopithecines were as large as most modern humans. Whereas all were much more muscular for their size, males were quite a bit larger than females. Australopithecines possessed small brains comparable to those of modern African apes, but the size and structure of their teeth were more like those of contemporary humans (except for the robust australopithecines, who had massive teeth and jaws).

Although first evolving among ardipithecines inhabiting Africa's tropical woodlands, bipedalism is a particularly important adaptive feature in the more open savanna environment (Lewin, 1987). A biped could not run as fast as a quadruped but could travel long distances in search of food and water without tiring. With free hands, a biped could take food to places where it could be eaten in relative safety and could carry infants rather than relying on the babies hang-

ing on for themselves. As bipeds, australopithecines could use their hands to wield sticks or other objects effectively in threat displays and to protect themselves against predators. Also, erect posture exposes a smaller area of the body to the direct heat of the sun than a quadrupedal position, helping to prevent overheating on the open savannah. Furthermore, a biped with its head held high could see farther, spotting food as well as predators from a distance (**Figure 4.6**).

Although adapted fully to bipedalism, curved toe bones and relatively long arms indicate australopithecines had not given up tree climbing altogether. However, to survive in their savannah environment, early bipeds may have been forced to try out supplementary sources of food on the ground, as they likely did around the time when the first members of the genus *Homo* appeared about 2.5 mya. In addition to whatever plant foods were available, the major new source was animal protein. This was not protein from monkey meat obtained as a result of coordinated hunting parties like those of the chimpanzees and bonobos of today, but rather the fatty marrow and whatever other edible leftover flesh remained in and on the bones of dead animals.

Early *Homo*

Increased meat consumption by our early ancestors was important for human evolution. On the savannah, it is hard for a primate with a humanlike digestive system to satisfy its protein requirements from available plant resources.

Figure 4.6 Ancient Ancestral Footprints About 3.6 million years ago in East Africa, early ancestors of *Homo sapiens* walked upright across a field of volcanic ash. Their footprints, preserved in the ash, were discovered in 1976 at Laetoli—about 50 kilometers (31 miles) from Olduvai Gorge, an important paleoanthropological site in northern Tanzania. This 23-meter (75-foot) trail provided early and convincing evidence of bipedalism, based on an analysis of the impressions. Fossil bones and footprints of ancient antelopes, baboons, hyenas, and other mammals (including a gigantic prehistoric relative of modern-day elephants) were found in the same layer of hardened ash.

Figure 4.7 Earliest Fabricated Stone Tools At a remote site known as Gona located in the Afar region of Ethiopia, Ethiopian paleoanthropologist Sileshi Semaw discovered the earliest stone tools made by humans. Dated to the beginning of the Lower Paleolithic or Old Stone Age between 2.5 and 2.6 million years ago, they are part of the Oldowan tool tradition. The 2.6-million-year-old Gona flake on the right is a well-struck cutting tool with sharp edges.

Moreover, failure to do so has serious consequences: stunted growth, malnutrition, starvation, and death. Leaves and legumes (nitrogen-fixing plants, familiar modern examples being beans and peas) provide the most readily accessible plant sources of protein. However, these are hard for primates like us to digest unless they are cooked.

Chimpanzees have a similar problem today when out on the savannah. In such a setting, they spend more than a third of their time going after insects like ants and termites on a year-round basis, while at the same time increasing their search for edible eggs and hunting for small vertebrate animals. Not only are such animal foods easily digestible, but they provide high-quality proteins that contain all the essential amino acids, the building blocks of protein, in just the right proportions.

Our remote ancestors probably solved their dietary problems in much the same way that chimps on the savannah do today (and in some ways, as discussed in this chapter's Biocultural Connection on the next page, their dietary habits and the physical effort it took to secure food made these early human ancestors healthier than many millions of present-day people). However, without the daggerlike teeth for ripping and cutting flesh, they were at a disadvantage. Even chimpanzees, whose canine teeth are far larger and sharper than ours, frequently have trouble tearing through the skin of other animals. It appears then that for more efficient utilization of animal protein, our ancestors needed sharp tools for butchering carcasses.

The earliest *identifiable* stone tools have been found in Africa (in Ethiopia, in northern Kenya near Lake Turkana, and in Tanzania at Olduvai Gorge), often in the same geological strata–distinctive layers of soil, clay, or rock—as the earliest *Homo* fossils. They include flakes and choppers. Flakes were obtained from a "core" stone by striking it with another stone or against a large rock. The flakes that broke off from the core had two sharp edges, effective for cutting meat and scraping hides. Leftover cores were transformed into choppers, used to break open bones.

The appearance of stone flakes and choppers marks the beginning of the **Lower Paleolithic**, the first part of the Old Stone Age, spanning from about 200,000 to 2.6 million years ago. At Olduvai and Lake Turkana, these tools are nearly 2 million years old; those found at the Ethiopian sites are older, at 2.5 to 2.6 million years (**Figure 4.7**). All of these early Lower Paleolithic tools are part of the **Oldowan tool tradition**, a name first given to the tools found at Olduvai Gorge in the 1960s.

Prior to the Lower Paleolithic, australopithecines probably used tools such as heavy sticks to dig up roots or ward off animals, unmodified stones to hurl as weapons or to crack open nuts and bones, and simple carrying devices made of hollow gourds or knotted plant fibers. These tools, however, are not traceable in the long-term archaeological record.

Since the late 1960s, a number of sites in southern and eastern Africa have been discovered with fossil remains of a lightly built biped with a body all but indistinguishable from that of the earlier australopithecines, except that the teeth are smaller and the brain is significantly larger relative to body size (Conroy, 1997). Furthermore, the inside of the skull shows a pattern in the left cerebral hemisphere that, in contemporary people, is associated with language. Although this does not prove that these bipeds could speak, it suggests a marked advance in information-processing capacity over that of australopithecines.

Because major brain-size increase and tooth-size reduction are important trends in the evolution of the genus *Homo*, paleoanthropologists designated these fossils as a new species: ***Homo habilis*** ("handy human").

Lower Paleolithic The first part of the Old Stone Age, spanning from about 200,000 to 2.6 million years ago.

Oldowan tool tradition The first stone tool industry, beginning between 2.5 and 2.6 million years ago at the start of the Lower Paleolithic.

Homo habilis "Handy human." The first fossil members of the genus *Homo* appearing 2.5 million years ago, with larger brains and smaller faces than australopithecines.

BIOCULTURAL CONNECTION

Paleolithic Prescriptions for the Diseases of Civilization

Though increased life expectancy is often hailed as one of modern civilization's greatest accomplishments, in some ways we in the developed world lead far less healthy lifestyles than our ancestors. Throughout most of our evolutionary history, humans led more physically active lives and ate a more varied low-fat diet than we do now. They did not drink or smoke. They spent their days scavenging or hunting for animal protein while gathering vegetable foods with some insects thrown in for good measure. They stayed fit through traveling great distances each day over the savannah and beyond.

Today, we may survive longer, but in old age we are beset by chronic disease. Heart disease, diabetes, high blood pressure, and cancer shape the experience of old age in wealthy indus-

Donna Day/Getty Images/Stone

trialized nations. The prevalence of these "diseases of civilization" has increased rapidly over the past sixty years, fueled by many modern factors including processed foods and physical inactivity. Anthropologists Melvin Konner and Marjorie Shostak and physician Boyd Eaton have suggested that our Paleolithic ancestors have provided a prescription for a cure. They propose that as "stone-agers in a fast lane," people's health will improve by returning to the lifestyle to which their bodies are adapted.[a] Such Paleolithic prescriptions are an example of evolutionary medicine—a branch of medical anthropology that uses evolutionary principles to contribute to human health.

Evolutionary medicine bases its prescriptions on the idea that rates of cultural change exceed the rates of biological change. Our food-forager physiology was shaped over millions of years, whereas the cultural changes leading to contemporary lifestyles have occurred rapidly.

Anthropologists George Armelagos and Mark Nathan Cohen suggest that the downward trajec-

tory for human health began with the earliest human village settlements some 10,000 years ago.[b] When humans began farming rather than gathering, they often switched to single-crop diets. In addition, settlement into villages led directly to the increase in infectious disease. Although the cultural invention of antibiotics has cured many infectious diseases, it also led to the increase in chronic diseases.

Our evolutionary history offers clues about the diet and lifestyle to which our bodies evolved. By returning to our ancient lifeways, we can make the diseases of civilization a thing of the past.

BIOCULTURAL QUESTION

What sort of Paleolithic prescriptions would our evolutionary history contribute toward behaviors such as childrearing practices, sleeping, and work patterns? Are there any ways that your culture or personal lifestyle are well aligned with past lifeways?

[a]Eaton, S. B., Konner, M., & Shostak, M. (1988). Stone-agers in the fast lane: Chronic degenerative diseases in evolutionary perspective. *American Journal of Medicine 84* (4), 739–749.

[b]Cohen, M. N., & Armelagos, G. J. (Eds.). (1984). *Paleopathology at the origins of agriculture.* Orlando: Academic.

Significantly, the earliest fossils to exhibit these trends appeared around 2.5 mya, about the same time as the earliest evidence of stone toolmaking. (Some have argued that *H. habilis* was not the only species of early *Homo.*)

Tools, Food, and Brain Expansion

Evolutionary transformations often occur suddenly as large random mutations produce novel organisms that, by chance, are well adapted to a particular environment. Sometimes natural selection produces change more gradually. This appears to have taken place following the arrival of *Homo habilis*, the first species in the genus *Homo*; with

the demonstrated use of tools, our human ancestors began a course of gradual brain expansion that continued until some 200,000 years ago. By then, brain size had approximately tripled and reached the levels of today's humans.

Many scenarios proposed for the adaptation of early *Homo*—such as the relationship among tools, food, and brain expansion—rely upon a feedback loop between brain size and behavior. The behaviors made possible by larger brains confer advantages to large-brained individuals, contributing to their increased reproductive success. Over time, their genetic variance becomes more common in successive generations, and the population gradually evolves into a larger-brained form.

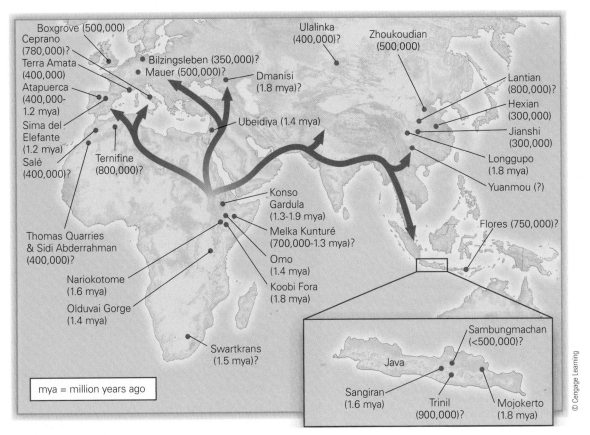

Figure 4.8 *Homo erectus* **Fossil Sites** *Homo erectus* sites are shown here with their dates. The arrows indicate the proposed routes by which *Homo* spread from Africa to Eurasia. The question marks indicate uncertain dating for particular sites.

In the case of toolmaking, the archaeological record provides us with tangible data concerning our ancestors' cultural abilities fitting with the simultaneous biological expansion of the brain. Toolmaking itself puts a premium on manual dexterity as opposed to hand use emphasizing power. In addition, the patterns of stone tools and fossilized animal bones at Oldowan sites in Africa suggest improved organization of the nervous system.

The sources for stone used to make cutting and chopping tools were often far from the sites where tools were used to process parts of animal carcasses. Also, the high density of fossil bones at some Oldowan sites and patterns of seasonal weathering indicate such sites were used repeatedly over a period of years. It appears that the Oldowan sites were places where tools and the raw materials for making them were stockpiled for later use in butchering. This implies advanced preparation for meat processing and thereby attests to the growing importance of foresight and the ability to plan ahead. Beginning with *Homo habilis* in Africa about 2.5 to 2.6 mya, human evolution began a sure course of increasing brain size relative to body size and increasing cultural development, each acting upon and thereby promoting the other.

Homo erectus and Spread of the Genus *Homo*

Shortly after 2 mya, at a time when *Homo habilis* and Oldowan tools had become widespread in Africa, a new species, **Homo erectus** ("upright human"), appeared on that continent. Unlike *H. habilis*, however, *H. erectus* did not remain confined to Africa. In fact, evidence of *H. erectus* fossils almost as old as those discovered in Africa have been found in the Caucasus Mountains of Georgia (between Turkey and Russia), South Asia, China, the island of Java (Indonesia), and western Europe.

Because the fossil evidence also suggests some differences within and among populations of *H. erectus* inhabiting discrete regions of Africa, Asia, and Europe, some paleoanthropologists prefer to split *H. erectus* into several distinct groups. Nonetheless, regardless of species designation, it is clear that beginning 1.8 mya, these larger-brained members of the genus *Homo* lived not only in Africa but also had spread to Eurasia (**Figure 4.8**).

Homo erectus "Upright human." A species within the genus *Homo* first appearing just after 2 million years ago in Africa and ultimately spreading throughout the Old World.

The emergence of *H. erectus* as a new species in the long course of human evolution coincided with the beginning of the Pleistocene epoch or Ice Age, which spanned from about 2 million to 10,000 years ago. During this period of global cooling, Arctic cold conditions and abundant snowfall in the earth's northern hemisphere created vast ice sheets that temporarily covered much of Eurasia and North America. These fluctuating but major glacial periods often lasted tens of thousands of years, separated by intervening warm periods. During interglacial periods the world warmed up to the point that the ice sheets melted and sea levels rose, but during much of this time sea levels were much lower than today, exposing large surfaces of low-lying lands now under water (Fagan, 2000).

Of all the epochs in the earth's 4.6-*billion*-year history, the Pleistocene is particularly significant for our species, for this era of dramatic climate shifts is the period in which humans—from *H. erectus* to *H. sapiens*—evolved and spread all across the globe. Confronted by environmental changes due to climatic fluctuations or movements into different geographic areas, our early human ancestors were constantly challenged to make biological and, especially, cultural adaptations in order to survive and successfully reproduce.

In the course of this long evolutionary process, random mutations introduced new characteristics into evolving populations in different regions of the world. The principle of natural selection was at work on humans as it was on all forms of life, favoring the perpetuation of certain characteristics within particular environmental conditions. At the same time, other characteristics that conferred no particular advantage or disadvantage also appeared by random mutation in geographically removed populations. The end result was a gradually growing physical variation in the human species. In this context, it is not surprising that *H. erectus* fossils found in Africa, Asia, and Europe reveal levels of physical variation not unlike those seen in modern human populations living across the globe today.

Available fossil evidence indicates that *H. erectus* had a body size and proportions similar to modern humans, though with heavier musculature (**Figure 4.9**). Differences in body size between the sexes diminished considerably compared to earlier bipeds, perhaps to facilitate successful childbirth. Based on fossil skull evidence, *H. erectus'* average brain size fell within the higher range of *H. habilis* and within the lower range of modern human brain size. The dentition was fully human, though relatively large by modern standards.

As one might expect, given its larger brain, *H. erectus* outstripped its predecessors in cultural development. In Africa and Eurasia, the Oldowan chopper was replaced by the more sophisticated hand axe. At first, the hand axes—shaped by regular blows giving them a larger and finer cutting edge than chopper tools—were probably all-purpose implements for food procurement and processing, and defense. But *H. erectus* also developed cleavers

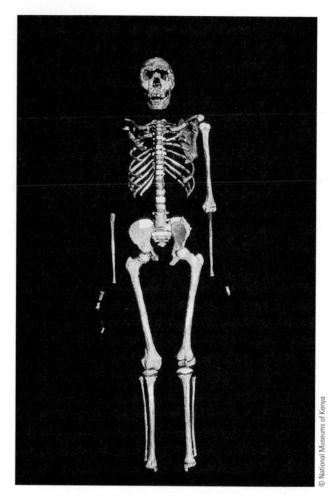

© National Museums of Kenya

Figure 4.9 *Homo erectus* One of the oldest—at 1.6 million years—and most complete fossils of *Homo erectus* is the "strapping youth" found at Nariokotome, West Turkana, Kenya: a tall and muscular boy who was already 5 feet 3 inches tall when he died at about the age of 13.

(like hand axes but without points) and various scrapers to process animal hides for bedding and clothing. In addition, this human ancestor relied on flake tools used "as is" to cut meat and process vegetables, or refined by "retouching" into points and borers for drilling or punching holes in materials.

Improved technological efficiency is also evident in *H. erectus'* use of raw materials. Instead of making a few large tools out of big pieces of stone, these ancestors placed a new emphasis on smaller tools, thus economizing their raw materials.

Firemaking in Early Human Development

Remains found in southern Africa suggest that *H. erectus* may have learned to use fire by 1 mya (Berna et al., 2012). Although there exists considerable variation in physiological conditioning among different human groups and even among individuals within each group, studies of modern humans indicate that most people can remain reasonably comfortable down to 10 degrees Celsius (50 degrees Fahrenheit) with minimal clothing as long as they keep active. Without controlled use of fire, it is unlikely that early humans could have moved successfully into regions where winter temperatures regularly dropped much below that point—as they must have in northern China and most of Europe, where *H. erectus* spread some 800,000 years ago.

Fire gave our human ancestors more control over their environment. It permitted them to continue activities after dark and provided a means to frighten away predators. It supplied them with the warmth and light needed for cave dwelling, and it enabled them to cook food.

The ability to modify food culturally through cooking may have contributed to the eventual reduction in the tooth size and jaws of later fossil groups because cooked food requires less chewing. However, cooking does more than tenderize food. It detoxifies a number of otherwise poisonous plants. In addition, it alters substances in plants, allowing important vitamins, minerals, and proteins to be absorbed by the gut rather than passing unused through the intestines. And, finally, it makes high-energy complex carbohydrates, such as starch, digestible. In short, when our human ancestors learned to employ fire to warm and protect themselves and to cook their food, they dramatically increased their geographic range and nutritional options.

With *H. erectus* we also have evidence of organized hunting as the means for procuring meat, animal hides, horn, bone, and sinew. Early evidence demonstrating the hunting technology of these ancestors includes 400,000-year-old wooden spears discovered in a peat bog (what was originally marsh or swamp land) in northern Germany, although it is likely that evolving humans had begun to hunt before then. Increased organizational ability is also indicated in prehistoric sites such as Ambrona and Torralba in Spain where group hunting techniques were used to drive a variety of large animals (including elephants) into a swamp for killing (Freeman, 1992).

With *H. erectus*, then, we find a clearer manifestation than ever before of the complex interplay among biological, cultural, and ecological factors. Social organization and technology developed along with an increase in brain size and complexity and a reduction in tooth and jaw size. The appearance of cultural adaptations such as controlled use of fire, cooking, and more complex tool kits may have facilitated language development. (See Chapter 5 for more on language origins and the linguistic capacity of our ape cousins.)

Improvements in communication and social organization brought about by language undoubtedly contributed to better methods for food gathering and hunting, to a population increase, and to territorial expansion.

Continuous biological and cultural change through natural selection in the course of hundreds of thousands of years gradually transformed *H. erectus* into the next emerging species: *Homo sapiens*.

Beginnings of *Homo sapiens*

At various Paleolithic sites in Africa, Asia, and Europe, a large number of human fossils have been found that date between roughly 200,000 and 1 million years ago. Among the most notable are those discovered in the mountains of Atapuerca in northern Spain. In another cave in Spain, Gran Dolina, human fossil remains of minimally six individuals were excavated, dating to 800,000 years ago. Further evolving in conditions of geographic and genetic isolation, this variety features a craniofacial architecture more similar to that of *Homo sapiens*, along with a significant increase in cranial capacity. Marking this distinction, researchers named this *Homo erectus* variety *Homo antecessor* ("antecessor" is Latin for "forerunner"). It remains unclear whether this variety became extinct or continued to evolve, with descendants 400,000 years later interbreeding with new waves of African migrants trekking into Europe (Bermúdez de Castro et al., 2004).

Whether one chooses to call these or any other humanlike fossils from that period *H. erectus*, *H. heidelbergensis*, or *H. antecessor* is more than a name game. Fossil names indicate researchers' perspectives about evolutionary relationships among groups. When specimens are given separate species names, it signifies that they form part of a reproductively isolated group.

The most famous site in the Atapuerca Mountains is Sima de los Huesos ("Pit of Bones") at the bottom of a deep chimney in one of the large cave systems (**Figure 4.10**). There, researchers discovered more than 5,000 human bones, including the fossil remains of thirty individuals of both sexes and all ages, up to about forty years. Dated to about 400,000 years ago, these are thought to be early ancestors of the Neandertals, which evolved in Europe in conditions of geographic and genetic isolation in the late Pleistocene (Arsuaga, et al., 2000).

The Neandertal Debate

As we proceed along the human evolutionary trajectory, the fossil record provides us with many more human specimens compared to earlier periods. The record is particularly rich when it comes to the Neandertals, a distinct and certainly controversial ancient member of the genus *Homo*. Typically, they are represented as the classic cavemen, stereotyped in Western popular media and even in natural history museum displays as wild and hairy club-wielding brutes.

Figure 4.10 Sima de los Huesos In a cave beneath the hillside in Atapuerca, Spain, lies one of the most remarkable sites in all of paleoanthropology: the Sima de los Huesos ("Pit of Bones"). The bottom of the pit is crammed with animal bones, including cave bears, lions, foxes, and wolves. Even more remarkable, thousands of early human fossils dating back 400,000 years have been found here. The well-preserved remains come from about thirty individuals and comprise the greatest single cache of ancient *Homo* fossils in the world.

Based on abundant fossil evidence, we know that **Neandertals** were a distinct and extremely muscular group within the genus *Homo* that ranged through western Eurasia from about 30,000 to 200,000 years ago. Although they had brains on average somewhat larger than modern humans, their faces and skulls were quite different from those of later fossilized remains referred to as "anatomically modern humans." Their large noses and teeth projected forward more than is the case with modern people. They generally had a sloping forehead and prominent brow ridges over their eyes, and on the back of the skull, a bony mass provided for attachment of powerful neck muscles. These features, although not exactly in line with modern ideals of European beauty, are common in Norwegian and Danish skulls dating to about 1,000 years ago—the time of the Vikings (Ferrie, 1997). Nevertheless, these characteristics do little to negate the popular image of Neandertals as cave-dwelling brutes.

The rude reputation of Neandertals may also derive from the time of their discovery, as the first widely publicized Neandertal skull was found in 1856, well before scientific theories to account for human origins had gained acceptance. This odd-looking old skull, happened upon near Düsseldorf in Germany's Neander Valley ("valley" is *Tal* in German), took German scientists by surprise. Initially, they explained its extraordinary features as evidence of some disfiguring disease in an invading "barbarian" from the east who had crawled into a deep cave to die. Although it became evident that the skull belonged to an ancient human fossil, Neandertals are still a perplexing group surrounded by controversy.

We now understand that many aspects of the Neandertal's unique skull shape and body form represent

Neandertals An archaic human population that ranged through western Eurasia from about 30,000 to 200,000 years ago.

Figure 4.11 **Neandertal Skull and Face** Neandertals did not differ all that much from modern humans of European descent, as is evident in this artistic reconstruction of a Neandertal reindeer hunter who ranged the Dordogne Valley and surrounding hills in southwestern France about 50,000 years ago. French anthropological sculptor Elisabeth Daynès created this likeness using the cast of a skull excavated in a cave at La Ferrassie.

its biological adaptation to an extremely cold climate. We also know that its intellectual capacity for cultural adaptation was noticeably superior to that of earlier members of the genus *Homo*.

One of the most hotly debated arguments in paleoanthropology has been the genetic relationship of Neandertals to anatomically modern humans. Were they a separate species that became extinct less than 30,000 years ago? Or were they an archaic subspecies of *Homo sapiens*? And if they were not a dead end and inferior side branch in human evolution, did they actually contribute to our modern human gene pool? Recent genetic evidence demonstrates the latter (Orlando, et al., 2006, June 6; Hawks, 2006, July 21; Sankararaman et al, 2012) (**Figure 4.11**).

Meanwhile, other parts of the world were inhabited by variants of archaic *H. sapiens*, lacking the mid-facial projection and massive muscle attachments on the back of the skull common among the Neandertals. Human fossil skulls found near the Solo River in Java are a prime example. Dates for these specimens range between about 27,000 and 200,000 years ago. The fossils, with their modern-sized brains, display certain features of *H. erectus* combined with those of archaic as well as more modern *H. sapiens*. Human fossils from various parts of Africa, the most famous being a skull from Kabwe in Zambia, also show a combination of ancient and modern traits. Finally, similar remains have been found at several places in China.

Adaptations to a wide range of different natural environments by archaic *Homo sapiens* were, of course, both biological and cultural, but their capacity for cultural adaptation was predictably superior to what it had been

in earlier members of the genus *Homo*. Neandertals' extensive use of fire, for example, was essential to survival in a cold climate like that of Europe during the various glacial periods. They lived in small bands or single-family units, both in the open and in caves, probably communicating through language (see Chapter 5). Evidence of deliberate burials of the deceased among Neandertals reflects a measure of ritual behavior in their communities. Moreover, the fossil remains of an amputee discovered in Iraq and an arthritic man excavated in France imply that Neandertals took care of the disabled, something not seen previously in the human fossil record.

The toolmaking tradition of all but the latest Neandertals is called the **Mousterian tool tradition** after a site (Le Moustier) in the Dordogne region of southern France. We see this tradition among Neandertals in Eurasia and among their human contemporaries in northern Africa during the Middle Paleolithic, generally dating from about 40,000 to 125,000 years ago.

Although considerable variability exists, Mousterian tools are generally lighter and smaller than those of earlier traditions. Whereas previously only two or three flakes could be obtained from the entire stone core, Mousterian toolmakers obtained many smaller flakes, which they skillfully retouched and sharpened. Their tool kits also contained a greater variety of types than the earlier ones: hand axes, flakes, scrapers, borers, notched flakes for shaving wood, and many types of points that could be

Mousterian tool tradition The tool industry found among Neandertals in Eurasia, and their human contemporaries in northern Africa, during the Middle Paleolithic, generally dating from about 40,000 to 125,000 years ago.

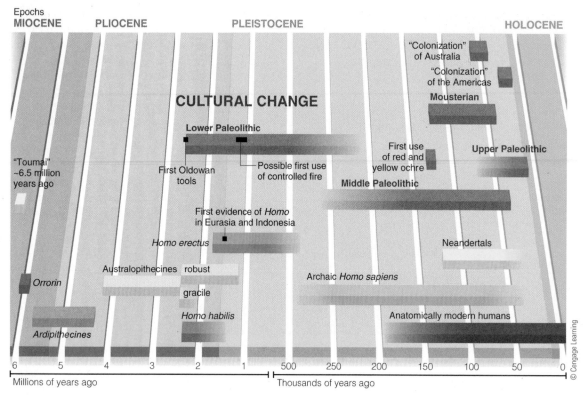

Figure 4.12 Human Evolutionary History Paleoanthropologists debate the exact relationship among the bipedal species along with the number of species that existed over the past 5 to 8 million years. The time spans for the Lower, Middle, and Upper Paleolithic vary tremendously by region. Note also that the time scale is expanded for the most recent 250,000 years.

attached to wooden shafts to make spears. This variety of tools facilitated more effective use of food resources and enhanced the quality of clothing and shelter. These types of stone tools were used by *all* people, Neandertals and their contemporaries elsewhere, including North Africa and Southwest Asia, during this time period.

For archaic *H. sapiens*, improved cultural adaptive abilities relate to the fact that the brain had achieved modern size. Such a brain made possible not only sophisticated technology but also conceptual thought of considerable intellectual complexity. Decorative pendants and objects with carved and engraved markings also appear in the archaeological record from this period. Objects were also commonly colored with pigments such as manganese dioxide and red or yellow ochre. The ceremonial burial of the dead and creation of nonutilitarian, decorative objects provide additional evidence supporting theoretical arguments in favor of symbolic thinking and language use in these ancient populations.

Establishing the relationship between anatomical change and cultural change over the course of human evolutionary history is complex (**Figure 4.12**). In the course

of the Middle Paleolithic (beginning around 200,000 years ago), individuals with a somewhat more anatomically modern human appearance began to appear in Africa and Southwest Asia. Although the earliest of these fossils are associated with the Mousterian tool industries used by Neandertals, over time new tool industries and other forms of cultural expression appeared. Whether these changes in skull shape are linked with superior cultural abilities is at the heart of the modern human origins debate. In Europe, the transition to the tools of the Upper Paleolithic occurred between 35,000 and 40,000 years ago. By this time, Neandertal technology was also comparable to the industries used by these anatomically modern *H. sapiens* (Mellars, 1989).

Anatomically Modern Peoples and the Upper Paleolithic

A veritable explosion of tool types and other forms of cultural expression beginning about 40,000 years ago constitutes what is known as the **Upper Paleolithic** transition. Upper Paleolithic tool kits include increased prominence of "blade" tools: long, thin, precisely shaped pieces of stone demonstrating the considerable skill of their creators. The Upper Paleolithic, lasting until about

Upper Paleolithic The last part (10,000 to 40,000 years ago) of the Old Stone Age, featuring tool industries characterized by long, slim blades and an explosion of creative symbolic forms.

10,000 years ago, is best known from archaeological evidence found in Europe, where numerous distinctive tool industries from successive time periods have been documented. In addition, the European archaeological record is rich with cave wall paintings, engravings, and bas-relief sculptures as well as many portable nonutilitarian artifacts from this period.

In Upper Paleolithic times, humans began to manufacture tools for more effective hunting and fishing, as well as gathering. Cultural adaptation also became more highly specific and regional, thus enhancing people's ability to survive under a wide variety of environmental conditions. Instead of manufacturing all-purpose tools, Upper Paleolithic populations inhabiting a wide range of environments—mountains, marshlands, tundra, forests, lake regions, river valleys, and seashores—all developed specialized devices suited to the resources of their particular habitat and to the different seasons. This versatility also permitted humans to spread out by crossing open water and Arctic regions to places never previously inhabited by humans, most notably Australia (between 40,000 and 60,000 years ago) and the Americas (about 15,000 to 20,000 years ago).

This degree of specialization required improved manufacturing techniques. The blade method of manufacture (**Figure 4.13**), invented by archaic *H. sapiens* and later used widely in Europe and western Asia, required less raw material than before and resulted in smaller and lighter tools with a better ratio between weight of flint and length of cutting edge (**Figures 4.14** and **4.15**).

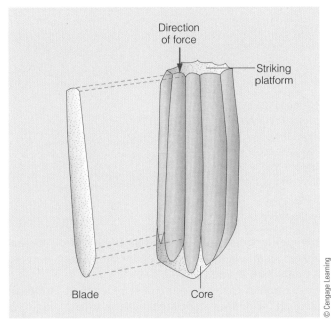

Figure 4.13 Core and Blade During the Upper Paleolithic, this new, more refined technique of manufacturing stone tools became common. The stone was broken to create a striking platform. Then, with another hard object, long, almost parallel-sided flakes were struck from the sides, resulting in sharp-edged blades to be used for a variety of cutting purposes.

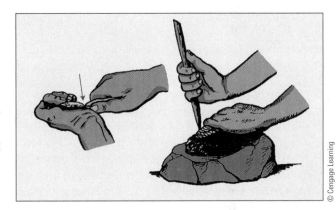

Figure 4.14 Pressure Flaking This tool manufacture technique—in which a bone, antler, or wooden tool is used to press rather than strike off small flakes—became widespread during the Upper Paleolithic. Here we see two pressure flaking methods.

Figure 4.15 Solutrean Biface The techniques of the Upper Paleolithic allowed for the manufacture of a variety of tool types. The finely wrought Solutrean bifaces of Europe, made using a pressure flaking method as illustrated in Figure 4.14, are shaped like plant leaves.

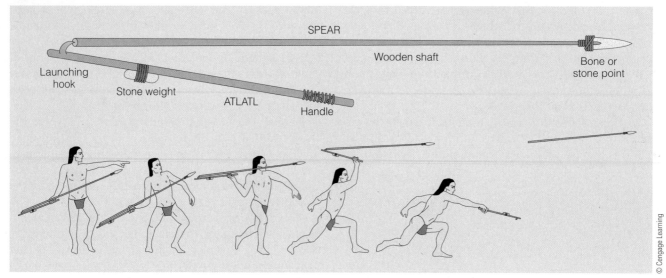

Figure 4.16 Spear Thrower Invented by early humans in the late Ice Age about 21,000 years ago, the atlatl or spear-thrower continued to be used by hunting peoples in many parts of the world until quite recently. Devised many thousands of years before the bow and arrow, this remarkable tool enhanced a hunter's success, making it possible to throw light spears much farther and with great force and accuracy. The entire atlatl would have been a foot or two long, with a handle on one end and a hook on the other that fitted into the blunt end of the spear. The hook was sometimes made of beautifully carved antler, bone, or stone.

Invented by Mousterian toolmakers, the *burin* (a stone tool with chisel-like edges) came into common use in the Upper Paleolithic. The burin provided an excellent means of working bone and antler used for tools such as fishhooks and harpoons. The spear-thrower, or *atlatl* (a Nahuatl word used by Aztec Indians in Mexico, referring to a wooden device, 1 to 2 feet long, with a hook on the end for throwing a spear), also appeared at this time. By effectively elongating the arm, the atlatl gave hunters increased force behind the spear throw (**Figure 4.16**).

Art was an important aspect of Upper Paleolithic cultures. As far as we know, humans had not produced representational artwork before. In some regions, tools and weapons were engraved with beautiful animal figures; pendants were made of bone and ivory, as were female figurines; and small sculptures were carved out of stone or modeled out of clay. Spectacular paintings and engravings depicting humans and animals of this period have been found on the walls of caves and rock shelters in Spain, France, Australia, and Africa (**Figure 4.17**). Because the southern African rock art tradition spans 27,000 years and lasted into historic times, documented accounts tell us that much of it depicts visions artists have when in altered states of consciousness related to spiritual practices. Along with the animals, the art also includes a variety of geometric motifs based on mental images spontaneously generated by the human nervous system when in trance.

Australian cave art, some of it older than European cave art and also associated with trancing, includes similar motifs. The occurrence of the same geometric designs in the cave art of Europe suggests trancing was a part of these prehistoric foraging cultures as well. The geometric motifs in Paleolithic art have also been interpreted as stylized human figures and patterns of descent. Given the great importance of kinship in all historically known communities of hunters, fishers, and gatherers, this should not be surprising. Whether or not a new kind of human—anatomically modern with correspondingly superior intellectual abilities—is responsible for this cultural explosion is hotly debated within paleoanthropology.

Hypotheses on the Origins of Modern Humans

On a biological level the great debate can be distilled to a question of whether one, some, or all populations of the archaic groups played a role in the evolution of modern *H. sapiens*. Those supporting the **multiregional hypothesis** argue that the fossil evidence suggests a simultaneous local transition from *H. erectus* to modern *H. sapiens* throughout the parts of the world inhabited by early members of the genus *Homo*.

multiregional hypothesis An evolutionary hypothesis that modern humans originated through a process of simultaneous local transition from *Homo erectus* to *Homo sapiens* throughout the inhabited world.

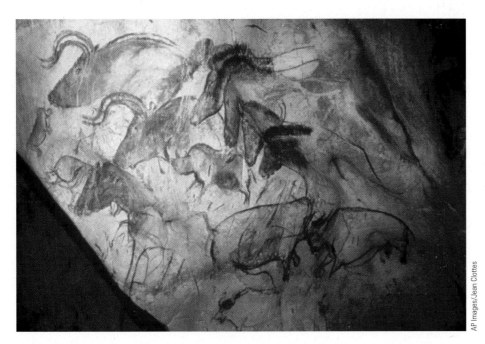

AP Images/Jean Clottes

Figure 4.17 Chauvet Cave Paintings These 31,000-year-old images, painted on a wall in the multichambered Chauvet Cave in the Ardèche region of southern France, provide spectacular evidence of early artistic creativity among our ancestors. In addition to the Ice Age animals depicted here—horses, wild ox, rhino, and bison—the chambers of Chauvet feature renderings of ten other species: bear, lion, mammoth, mountain goat, giant deer, owl, panther, red deer, and reindeer, as well as human handprints.

By contrast, those supporting the **recent African origins hypothesis** (also known as the *Eve* or *out of Africa* hypothesis) use genetic and other evidence to argue that all anatomically modern humans living today descend directly from one single population of archaic *H. sapiens* in Africa. Improved cultural capabilities then allowed members of this group to replace other archaic human forms as they began to spread out of Africa some time after 100,000 years ago. So although both models place human origins firmly in Africa, the first argues that our human ancestors began moving into Asia and Europe as early as 1.8 mya, whereas the second maintains that anatomically modern *H. sapiens* evolved only in Africa, completely replacing other members of the genus *Homo* as they spread throughout the world.

Though the recent African origins hypothesis is accepted by many paleoanthropologists, not every scholar supports it. Among those with opposing views, Chinese paleoanthropologists generally favor the multiregional hypothesis in part because it fits better with the fossil discoveries from Australia and Asia. The claim of ancient human roots in eastern Asia also resonates well with the region's traditional ethnocentric ideas about China as the place of human origins and the world's most ancient civilization. Traditionally, it is imagined as "the Middle Kingdom"—the center of humanity on earth.

Recent molecular research detecting ancient traces of gene flow between species and subspecies allows anthropologists to move beyond the opposition between the multiregional hypothesis and the recent African origins hypothesis (see Svante Pääbo in Anthropologists of Note, page 81). Both perspectives have become more nuanced due to new scientific data. And a new synthesis in human evolutionary theory is now emerging with

the **archaic admixture model**, which theorizes that *Homo sapiens* derives from limited interbreeding between anatomically modern humans as evolved in Africa and archaic human populations (Abi-Rached et al., 2011). Notably, this model, like the other two, places human origins firmly in Africa.

Despite such major breakthroughs, many details concerning human evolution remain unsolved. The issues continue to be embroiled in scientific debates over hominid lineages, fossil taxonomy, and prehistoric population migrations (Hawks & Wolpoff, 2001; Wolpoff, Hawks, & Caspari, 2000). What is known for certain is that all living people today are full-fledged members of the species *Homo sapiens*.

Human Biological Variation and the Problem of Race

The Neandertal debate raises fundamental questions about the complex relationship between biological and cultural human variation. As we reviewed the human fossil record

recent African origins hypothesis The hypothesis that all modern people are derived from one single population of archaic *Homo sapiens* from Africa who migrated out of Africa after 100,000 years ago, replacing all other archaic forms due to their superior cultural capabilities; also called the Eve or out of Africa hypothesis.

archaic admixture model Theoretical model of human evolution that modern *Homo sapiens* derive from limited interbreeding between anatomically modern humans, as evolved in Africa, and members of archaic human populations. Based on genetic evidence of introgression, it is a synthesis of the recent African origins hypothesis and the multiregional hypothesis.

throughout this chapter, inferences were made about the cultural capabilities of our ancestors partially based on biological features. Such questions are deeply embedded within a discipline that has a long history of studying cultural and biological variation within the human species and how it relates to the concept of **race** as a subspecies or discrete biological division within a species.

Today, anthropologists agree that no subspecies exist within currently surviving *Homo sapiens*. Consequently, as far as contemporary humanity is concerned, race is not a valid biological category. In fact, anthropologists work actively to expose the concept of race as scientifically inapplicable to humans. At the same time, they recognize the powerful symbolic significance of race as a social and political category in many countries, including the United States, Germany, Brazil, and South Africa.

Race as a Social Construct

To deal with the politically divisive aspects of racial symbolism, we must begin by understanding how the notion of distinct human races came to be. Earlier in this chapter, we discussed how European scholars struggled to make sense of the massive amounts of new information generated since the age of exploration, beginning about 500 years ago. Coming to them from the most remote corners of the world, this information forced them to critically rethink deeply rooted ideas about humanity and its relationship to other forms of life. In the quest for understanding, they reasoned not only on the basis of scientific facts but also from the perspective of their particular religious beliefs and cultural traditions. Looking back on their writings, we are now painfully aware of how ethnocentrism and other prejudices clouded their findings.

Among the most telling examples of this is the racial categorizing done by German anatomist Johann Blumenbach (1752–1840). Initially, Blumenbach adopted the classification system devised by the Swedish naturalist Linnaeus in 1758, which divided the human species into four major groups according to geographic area and classified all Europeans as "white," Africans as "black," American Indians as "red," and Asians as "yellow."

Later, in the 1795 edition of his book *On the Natural Variety of Mankind*, Blumenbach introduced some significant changes to this four-race scheme. Based on a comparative examination of his human skull collection, he judged as most beautiful the skull of a woman from the Caucasus Mountains between Russia and Turkey. It was more symmetrical than the others, and he thought it reflected nature's ideal form: the circle. Surely, Blumenbach reasoned, this perfect specimen resembled God's original creation. Moreover, he thought that the living inhabitants of the Caucasus region were the most

beautiful in the world. Based on these criteria, he concluded that this high mountain range not far from the lands mentioned in the Bible was near the place of human origins.

Building on his idea that the southeastern Europeans inhabiting the Caucasus looked most like the first humans, Blumenbach decided that all light-skinned peoples in Europe and adjacent parts of western Asia and northern Africa belonged to the same race. On this basis, he dropped the European race label and replaced it with "Caucasian." Although he continued to distinguish American Indians as a separate race, he regrouped dark-skinned Africans as "Ethiopian" and split those Asians not considered Caucasian into two separate races: "Mongolian" (referring to most inhabitants of Asia, including China and Japan) and "Malay" (indigenous Australians, Pacific Islanders, and others).

But Blumenbach did more than change labels: He also introduced a formal hierarchical ordering of the races he delineated. Convinced that Caucasians were closest to the original ideal humans created in God's image, he ranked them as superior. The other races, he argued, were the result of "degeneration." Moving away from their place of origin and adapting to different environments and climates, they had degenerated physically and morally into what many Europeans came to think of as inferior races (Gould, 1994).

Critically reviewing this and other early historical efforts to classify humanity in higher and lower forms, we now clearly recognize their factual errors and ethnocentric biases with respect to the concept of race. Especially disastrous is the notion of superior and inferior race because this has been used as justification for brutalities ranging from repression to slavery to mass murder and genocide. It has also been employed to justify stunning levels of mockery, as painfully illustrated in the following tragic story of Ota Benga, an Mbuti Pygmy man from Africa, who in the early 1900s was caged in a New York zoo with an orangutan.

Racism on Public Display: A Pygmy in the Bronx Zoo

Captured in a raid in Congo, Ota Benga somehow came into the possession of Samuel Verner, a North American missionary-explorer looking for exotic "savages" for exhibition in the United States. In 1904, Ota and a group of fellow Pygmies were shipped across the Atlantic and exhibited at a World's Fair in Saint Louis, Missouri. About twenty-three years old at the time, Ota was 4 feet 11 inches in height and weighed 103 pounds. Throngs of visitors came to see displays of dozens of indigenous peoples from around the globe, shown in their traditional dress and living in replica villages doing their customary things. The fair was a success for the organizers, and all the Pygmies survived to be shipped back to their homeland.

The enterprising Verner also returned to Congo and enlisted Ota to help him collect artifacts to be sold to the American Museum of Natural History in New York City. In the summer of 1906 Verner returned to the United States, along

---

race In biology, a subgroup within a species, not scientifically applicable to humans because there exist no subspecies within modern *Homo sapiens*.

with Ota. Soon thereafter, Verner went bankrupt and lost his entire collection to the bank. Left stranded in the big city, Ota was placed in the care of the museum and then taken to the Bronx Zoo, where he was put on exhibit in the monkey house, with an orangutan as company. Ota's sharpened teeth (a cultural practice among his own people) were seen as evidence of his supposedly cannibal nature.

After intensive protest, zoo officials released the unfortunate Pygmy from his cage and during the day let him roam free in the park, where he was often harassed by teasing visitors (**Figure 4.18**). Ota (often referred to as a "boy") was then turned over to an orphanage for African American children. In 1916, upon hearing that he would never return to his homeland, he took a revolver and shot himself through the heart (Bradford & Blume, 1992).

Challenging Racism

The racist display at the Bronx Zoo a century ago was by no means unique. Just a tip of the ethnocentric iceberg, it was the manifestation of a powerful ideology in which one small part of humanity sought to demonstrate and justify its claims of biological and cultural superiority. This had particular resonance in North America, where people of European descent were thrown together in a society with Native Americans, African slaves, and later Asians imported as a source of cheap

Wildlife Conservation Society

Figure 4.18 A Pygmy Man in the Bronx Zoo About twenty-five years old, Ota Benga is shown here holding a young chimpanzee in the Bronx Zoo in 1906. This Mbuti Pygmy had been captured in a raid in Congo and exhibited at the World's Fair in Saint Louis, Missouri.

labor. Indeed, such claims, based on false notions of race, have resulted in the oppression and genocide of millions of humans because of the color of their skin or the shape of their skulls.

Fortunately, by the early 20th century, some scholars began to challenge the concept of racial superiority. Among the strongest critics was Franz Boas (1858–1942), a Jewish scientist who immigrated to the United States because of rising anti-Semitism in his German homeland and who became the founder of North America's academic anthropology. As president of the American Association for the Advancement of Science, Boas criticized hierarchical notions of race in an important speech titled "Race and Progress," published in the prestigious journal *Science* in 1909.

Ashley Montagu (1905–1999), a British student of Boas's and one of the best-known anthropologists of his time, devoted much of his career to combating scientific racism. Like Boas, he was born into a Jewish family and personally felt the sting of anti-Semitism. Originally named Israel Ehrenberg, he changed his name in the 1920s and emigrated from England to the United States, where he fought racism in his writings and in academic and public lectures. Of all his works, none is more important than his book *Man's Most Dangerous Myth: The Fallacy of Race*. Published in 1942, it took the lead in exposing, on purely scientific grounds, the fallacy of human races as clearly bounded biological categories.

The dogma of "the inequality between humans and the races" (Métraux, 1953) provided ideological fodder to Nazi German politicians who capitalized on these ideas to dehumanize, enslave, and kill millions of Jews and Gypsies in Europe during the Second World War.

Although several leading anthropologists, including Ruth Benedict, publicly challenged racial segregation policies and a host of other discriminatory laws and practices in the United States and elsewhere, theories claiming an intellectual and genetic basis for "racial inferiority" of black Africans and their descendents in the Americas remained popular in the postwar period of the mid-20th century. In many parts of the United States, official racial segregation policies discriminating against African Americans were publicly defended and promoted by powerful political agents and news media.

Taught by well-established scholars at universities and medical schools on both sides of the Atlantic Ocean, theories justifying racial discrimination were also used in support of a regime based on white supremacy in South Africa. There, an apartheid system was officially established in 1948 by an ethnic minority of European descent.

Proclaiming racist discrimination a violation of universal human rights, the United Nations and its various agencies were instrumental in challenging race theories as obstructive to peaceful international coexistence. In its campaign to combat racial prejudice and discrimination, the UN secured the cooperation of an international group of anthropologists, biologists, geneticists, and other scholars demonstrating "the absurdity of the so-called 'scientific' bases of racial prejudice" (Métraux in Prins & Krebs, 2007, pp. 115–125).

Race as a Biological Construct

Social constructions of race are often tied up in the false but tenacious idea that there really is a biological foundation to the concept of human races. As already mentioned, in biology a *race* is defined as a subspecies: a population within a species that differs in terms of genetic variance from other populations of the same species. Simple and straightforward though such a definition may seem, there are three very important things to note about it.

First, it is arbitrary; there is no agreement on how many differences it takes to make a race. For some who are interested in the topic, different frequencies in the variants of one gene are sufficient; for others, different frequencies involving several genes are necessary. Ultimately, it has been impossible to reach agreement not just on the number of genes, but also on precisely which ones are the most important for defining races.

After arbitrariness, the second important thing to note about the biological definition of *race* is that it does not mean that any one so-called race has exclusive possession of any particular variant of any gene or genes. In human terms, the frequency of a trait like type O blood, for example, may be high in one racial population and low in another, but it is present in both. In other words, populations are genetically "open," meaning that genes flow between them. Because human populations are genetically open, no fixed racial groups have developed within our modern species (**Figure 4.19**).

The third important thing to note about the scientifically inappropriate use of the term *race* with respect to humans is that the differences among individuals within a particular population are generally greater than the differences among populations.

In sum, the biological concept of race does not apply to *Homo sapiens*. That said, to dismiss race as a biologically invalid category is not to deny the reality of human biological diversity. The task for anthropologists is to explain that diversity and the social meanings given to it rather than to try to falsely split our species into discrete categories called races.

Skin Color: A Case Study in Adaptation

The popular idea of race is commonly linked to skin color, a complex biological trait. Skin color is subject to great variation and is attributed to several key factors: the transparency or thickness of the skin; a copper-colored pigment called carotene; reflected color from the blood vessels (responsible for the rosy color of lightly pigmented people); and, most significantly, the amount of melanin (from *melas*, a Greek word meaning "black")—a dark

Figure 4.19 Descendants of Thomas Jefferson and Sally Hemings Many people have become accustomed to viewing so-called racial groups as natural and separate divisions within our species based on visible physical differences. However, these groups differ from one another in only 6 percent of their genes. For many thousands of years, individuals belonging to different human social groups have been in sexual contact. Exchanging their genes, they maintained the human species in all its colorful variety and prevented the development of distinctive subspecies (biologically defined races). This continued genetic mixing is effectively illustrated by the above photo of distant relatives, all of whom are descendents of Sally Hemings, an African American slave, and Thomas Jefferson, the Euramerican gentleman-farmer who had 150 slaves working for him at his Virginia plantation and served as third U.S. president (1801–1809).

pigment in the skin's outer layer. People with dark skin have more melanin-producing cells than those with light skin, but everyone (except those with albinism) has a measure of melanin.

Exposure to sunlight increases melanin production, causing skin color to deepen. Melanin is known to protect skin against damaging ultraviolet solar radiation; consequently, dark-skinned peoples are less susceptible to skin cancers and sunburn than are those with less melanin. Because the highest concentrations of dark-skinned people tend to be found in the tropical regions of the world, it appears that natural selection has favored heavily pigmented skin as a protection against exposure where ultraviolet radiation is most constant.

In northern latitudes, light skin has an adaptive advantage as the manufacturer of vitamin D through a chemical reaction dependent upon sunlight. Vitamin D is vital for maintaining the balance of calcium in the body. In northern climates with little sunshine, light skin allows enough sunlight to penetrate the skin and stimulate the formation of vitamin D, essential for healthy bones. Dark pigmentation interferes with this process. The severe consequences of vitamin D deficiency can be avoided through culture. Until recently, children in northern Europe and North America were regularly fed a spoonful of cod liver oil during the dark winter months. Today, pasteurized milk is often fortified with vitamin D.

Given what we know about the adaptive significance of human skin color, and the fact that, until 800,000 years ago, members of the genus *Homo* were exclusively creatures of the tropics, it is likely that lightly pigmented skins are a recent development in human history. Conversely, and consistent with humanity's African origins, darkly pigmented skins likely are quite ancient. The enzyme tyrosinase, which converts the amino acid tyrosine into the compound that forms melanin, is present in lightly pigmented peoples in sufficient quantity to make them very "black." The reason it does not is that they have genes that inactivate or inhibit it (Wills, 1994).

Human skin, more liberally endowed with sweat glands and lacking heavy body hair compared to other primates, effectively eliminates excess body heat in a hot climate. This would have been especially advantageous to our ancestors on the savannah, who could have avoided confrontations with large carnivorous animals by carrying out most of their activities in the heat of the day. For the most part, tropical predators rest during this period, hunting primarily from dusk until early morning. Without much hair to cover their bodies, selection would have favored dark skin in our human ancestors. In short, based on available scientific evidence, all humans appear to have a "black" ancestry, no matter how "white" some of them may appear to be today.

Obviously, one should not conclude that, because it may be a more recent development, lightly pigmented skin is better, or more highly evolved, than heavily pigmented skin. The latter is clearly better evolved to the conditions of life in the tropics or at high altitudes where exposure to ultraviolet light increases, although with cultural adaptations like protective clothing, hats, and more recently invented sunscreen lotions, lightly pigmented peoples can survive there. Conversely, the availability of supplementary sources of vitamin D allows more heavily pigmented peoples to do quite well far away from the tropics. In both cases, culture has rendered skin color differences largely irrelevant from a purely biological perspective. With time and with the efforts we see being made in many cultures today, skin color may lose its social significance as well.

Over the course of several million years, humans have gradually developed into a highly diverse and yet still unified single species inhabiting the entire earth. Biological adaptation to a wide geographic range of natural environments is responsible for some aspects of human variation. However, although evolution continues into the present, different cultures shape both the expression and the interpretation of human biological variation at every step. We humans do indeed stand with one foot in nature and another in culture.

CHAPTER CHECKLIST

What is evolution, when was this central biological theory formulated, and what is its molecular basis?

● Charles Darwin formulated a theory of evolution in 1859. His concept of evolution was descent with modification, which occurred as a population (a group of interbreeding individuals) adapted to its environment through natural selection.

● Through a series of experiments with pea plants in the late 19th century, Gregor Mendel discovered the nature of inheritance, upon which evolution depends, long before its molecular basis was known.

● Genes, the units of heredity, are segments of molecules of DNA (deoxyribonucleic acid), and the entire sequence of DNA is known as a genome.

● Mutation provides the ultimate source of genetic variation. These changes in DNA may be helpful or harmful to the individual organism, though most are neutral.

● Natural selection, the evolutionary force involved in adaptive change, reduces the frequency of alleles (gene variants) for harmful or maladaptive traits within a population and increases the frequency of alleles for adaptive traits.

One of the strengths of modern descriptive linguistics is the objectivity of its methods. For example, English-speaking anthropologists who specialize in this will not approach a language with the idea that it must have nouns, verbs, prepositions, or any other of the form classes identifiable in English. Instead, they see what turns up in the language and attempt to describe it in terms of its own inner workings. This allows for unanticipated discoveries. For instance, unlike many other languages, English does not distinguish between feminine and masculine nouns. English speakers use the definite article *the* in front of any noun, whereas Spanish varies with gender and numbers, requiring four types of such definite articles: *la* (singular feminine), *el* (singular masculine), *las* (plural feminine), and *los* (plural masculine)—as in *las casas* (the houses) and *los jardines* (the gardens).

German speakers go one step further, utilizing three gendered articles in singular, but only one in plural: *die* (singular feminine), *der* (singular masculine), *das* (singular neuter), and *die* (plural, regardless of gender). For cultural historical reasons, Germans consider the house neuter, so they say *das Haus*, but concur with Spaniards that the garden is masculine. Some nouns, however, reverse gender in German–Spanish translation: the feminine sun (*die Sonne*) transgenders into a masculine *el sol*, and the masculine moon (*der Mond*) turns into a feminine *la luna*.

However, these language gender issues are not relevant everywhere. In the Andean highlands in South America, Quechua-speaking Indians are not concerned about whether nouns are gendered or neutral, for their language has no definite articles at all.

Historical Linguistics

Although descriptive linguistics focuses on all features of a particular language at any one moment in time, historical linguistics deals with the fact that languages change. In addition to deciphering "dead" languages that are no longer spoken, specialists in this field investigate relationships between earlier and later forms of the same language, study older languages to track the processes of change into modern ones, and examine interrelationships among older languages. For example, they attempt to sort out the development of Latin (spoken almost 1,500 years ago in southern Europe) into the Romance languages of Italian, Spanish, Portuguese, French, and Romanian by identifying natural shifts in the original language and

tracking modifications brought on by centuries of direct contact with Germanic-speaking invaders from northern Europe.

When focusing on long-term processes of change, historical linguists depend on written records of languages. They have achieved considerable success in working out the relationships among different languages, and these are reflected in schemes of classification. For example, English is one of approximately 140 languages classified in the larger Indo-European language family (**Figure 5.2**). A **language family** is a group of languages descended from a single ancestral language. This family is subdivided into some eleven subgroups (Germanic, Romance, and so on), indicating that there has been a long period (6,000 years or so) of **linguistic divergence** from an ancient unified language (reconstructed as Proto-Indo-European) into separate "daughter" languages. English is one of several languages in the Germanic subgroup (**Figure 5.3**), all of which are more closely related to one another than they are to the languages of any other subgroup of the Indo-European family.

Despite the differences between them, the languages of one subgroup share certain features when compared to those of another. As an illustration, the word for father in the Germanic languages always starts with an *f* or closely related *v* sound (Dutch *vader*, German *Vater*, Gothic *Fadar*). Among the Romance languages, by contrast, the comparable word always starts with a *p*: French *père*, Spanish and Italian *padre*—all derived from the Latin *pater*. The original Indo-European word for father was *p'tēr*, so in this case, the Romance languages have retained the earlier pronunciation, whereas the Germanic languages have diverged.

Historical linguists are not limited to the faraway past, for even modern languages are constantly transforming—adding new words, dropping others, or changing meaning. Studying them in their specific cultural context can help us understand the processes of change that may have led to linguistic divergence in the past.

Processes of Linguistic Divergence

One force for change is selective borrowing between languages. This is evident in the many French words present in the English language—and in the growing number of English words cropping up in languages all around the world due to globalization. Technological breakthroughs resulting in new equipment and products prompt linguistic shifts. For instance, the electronic revolution that brought us radio, television, and computers has created entirely new vocabularies. Over the last decade or so, Internet use has widened the meaning of a host of already existing English words—from *hacking* and *surfing* to *spam*. Entirely new words such as *blogging*, *vlogging*, and

language family A group of languages descended from a single ancestral language.
linguistic divergence The development of different languages from a single ancestral language.

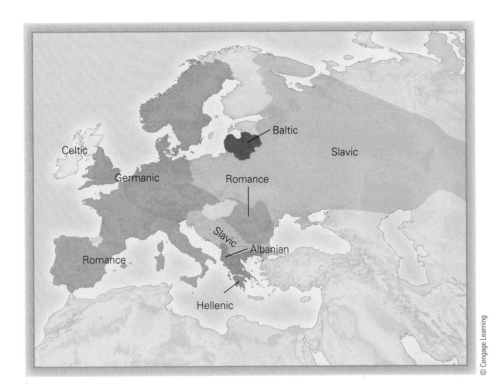

© Cengage Learning

Figure 5.2 European Language Subgroups in Europe Not all languages spoken in Europe are part of the Indo-European family. For example, Basque—an isolated language also known as Euskara—is still spoken in the French–Spanish borderland. Moreover, languages spoken by Hungarians, Estonians, Finns, Komi (in northeast Russia), and Saami (in northern Scandinavia) belong to the Uralic language family.

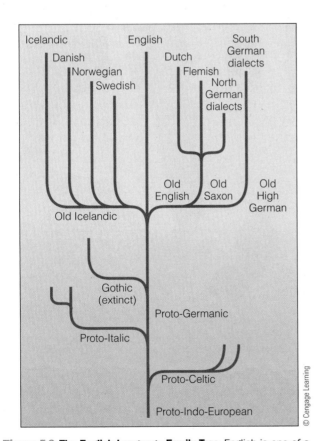

© Cengage Learning

Figure 5.3 The English Language Family Tree English is one of a group of languages in the Germanic subgroup of the Indo-European family. This diagram shows its relationship to languages in the same subgroup. The root is an ancestral language originally spoken by early farmers and herders who spread north and west over Europe, bringing with them both their customs and their language.

netiquette have been coined, leading to the creation of Internet dictionaries such as netlingo.com.

There is also a tendency for any group within a larger society to create its own unique vocabulary, whether it is a street gang, sorority, religious group, prison inmates, or platoon of soldiers. By changing the meaning of existing words or inventing new ones, members of the in-group can communicate with fellow members while effectively excluding outsiders who may be within hearing range. Increasing professional specialization also contributes to coining new words and greatly expanding vocabularies. Finally, there seems to be a human tendency to admire the person who comes up with a new and clever idiom, a useful word, or a particularly stylish pronunciation. In other words, no language stands still.

Language Loss and Revival

Perhaps the most powerful force for linguistic change is the domination of one society over another, as demonstrated during 500 years of European colonialism. Such dominations persist today in many parts of the world, such as Taiwan's indigenous peoples being governed by Mandarin-speaking Chinese, Tarascan Indians by Spanish-speaking Mexicans, or Bushmen by English-speaking Namibians. In many cases, foreign political control has resulted in linguistic erosion or even complete disappearance, sometimes leaving only a faint trace in old, indigenous names for geographic features such as hills and rivers.

Over the last 500 years about half of the world's 12,000 or so languages have become extinct as a direct result of warfare, epidemics, and forced assimilation brought on by colonial powers and other aggressive outsiders. Other than the dominant languages today, very few people speak the remaining 6,000 languages, and these languages are losing speakers rapidly due to globalization. In fact, half of the remaining languages have fewer than 10,000 speakers each, and the other half are spoken by less than 1,000 each. Put another way, half of the world's languages are spoken by just 2 percent of the world's population (Crystal, 2002; see also Knight, Studdert-Kennedy, & Hurford, 2000).

In North America, only 150 of the original 300 indigenous languages still exist, and many of these surviving tongues are moving toward extinction at an alarming rate. Thousands of indigenous languages elsewhere in the world are also threatened. For example, fewer than ten people still speak N|uu, a "click" language traditionally spoken in South Africa's Kalahari Desert. N|uu is the only surviving member of the !Ui branch of the Tuu language family (previously called Southern Khoisan) (**Figure 5.4**).

Anthropologists predict that the number of languages still spoken in the world today will be cut in half by the year 2100, in large part because children born into ethnic minority groups no longer use the ancestral language when they go to school, migrate to cities, join the larger workforce, and are exposed to printed and electronic media. The printing press, radio, satellite television, Internet, and text messaging are driving the need for a shared language, and increasingly that is English. In the past 500 years, this language—originally spoken by about 2.5 million people living only in part of the British Isles in northwestern Europe—has spread around the world. Today, some 375 million people (5.4 percent of the global population) claim English as their native tongue. About a billion others (about 15 percent of humanity) speak it as a second or foreign language.

Although a common language allows people from different ethnic backgrounds to communicate, there is the risk that a global spread of one language may contribute to the disappearance of others. And with the extinction

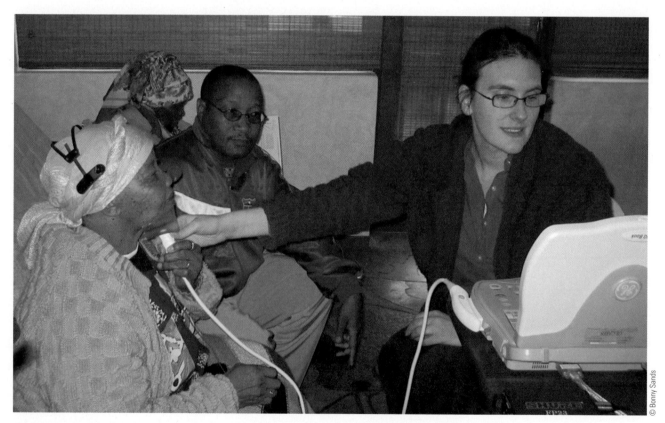

Figure 5.4 Modern Technology in Linguistic Analysis Several linguistic anthropologists are collaborating on field research with speakers of endangered Khoisan "click" languages such as N|uu in southern Africa. Using a portable ultrasound-imaging machine, they can capture the tongue movements of the click consonants. Here, U.S. linguist Johanna Brugman holds an ultrasound probe under the chin of one of the ten remaining N|uu speakers, Ouma Katrina Esau, who is helping to document how click sounds are made. Clicks are produced by creating suction within a cavity formed between the front and back parts of the tongue—except in the case of bilabial clicks in which the cavity is made between the lips and the back of the tongue. N|uu is one of only three languages remaining in the world that use bilabial clicks as consonants. The vertical bar in the word *N|uu* indicates a click sound.

of each language, we lose "hundreds of generations of traditional knowledge encoded in these ancestral tongues"—a vast repository of knowledge about the natural world, plants, animals, ecosystems, and cultural traditions (Living Tongues, 2012).

A key issue in language preservation efforts today is the impact of electronic media such as the Internet, where content still exists in relatively few languages, and 84 percent of Internet users are native speakers of just ten of the world's 6,000 languages. In 2001, UNESCO established Initiative B@ bel, which uses information and communication technologies to support linguistic and cultural diversity. Promoting multilingualism on the Internet, this initiative aims to bridge the digital divide—to make access to Internet content and services more equitable for users worldwide (**Figure 5.5**).

Sometimes, in reaction to a real or perceived threat of cultural dominance by powerful foreign societies, ethnic groups and even entire countries may seek to maintain or reclaim their unique identity by purging their vocabularies of "foreign" terms. Emerging as a significant force for linguistic change, such **linguistic nationalism** is particularly characteristic of the former colonial countries of Africa and Asia today. It is not limited to those countries, however, as one can see by periodic French attempts to purge their language of such Americanisms as *le hamburger*. Another example of this is France's decision to substitute the word *e-mail* with the government-approved term *couriel*.

For many ethnic minorities, efforts to counter the threat of linguistic extinction or to resurrect already extinct languages form part of their struggle to maintain a sense of cultural identity and dignity. A prime means by which powerful groups try to assert their dominance over minori-

ties living within their borders is to actively suppress their languages. Historically, examples of this include government-sanctioned efforts (1870s–1950s) to repress Native American cultures and fully absorb them into mainstream society. Government policies included taking Indian children away from their parents and putting them in boarding schools where only English was allowed, and students were often punished for speaking their traditional languages. Upon returning to their homes, many could no longer communicate with their own close relatives and neighbors.

Although now abolished, these institutions and the historical policies that shaped them did lasting damage to American Indian groups striving to maintain their cultural heritage. Especially over the past four decades, many of these besieged indigenous communities have been actively involved in language revitalization. Among numerous examples of this is the work of S. Neyooxet Greymorning, a Southern Arapaho, who developed ways to revive indigenous languages, including his own. Greymorning, a professor of anthropology and Native American studies at the University of Montana, tells his story in the Anthropology Applied feature.

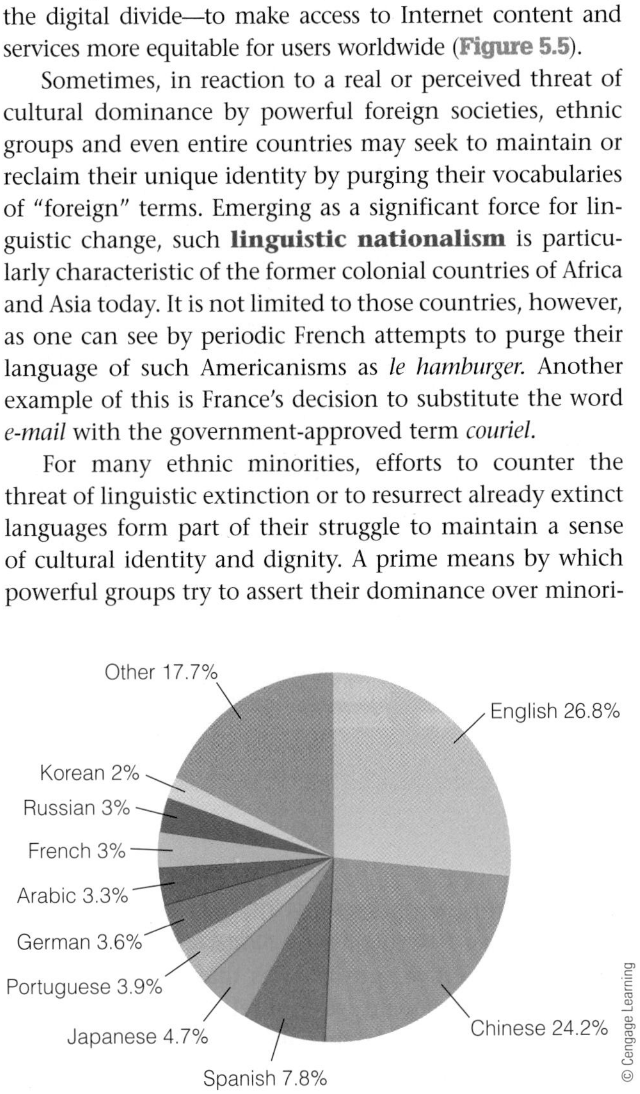

Language in Its Social and Cultural Settings

Language is not simply a matter of combining sounds according to certain rules to come up with meaningful utterances. Individuals communicate with one another constantly—in households, in the street, on the job, and so on. People often vary in the ways they perform speech based on social context and cultural factors such as gender, age, class, and ethnicity. Moreover, what people choose to speak about, whisper, or keep secret in silence often reflects what is socially important or culturally meaningful in their community. For that reason, linguistic anthropologists also focus on the actual use of language in relation to its various distinctive social and cultural settings. This third branch of linguistic study falls into two categories: sociolinguistics and ethnolinguistics.

Sociolinguistics

Sociolinguistics, the study of the relationship between language and society, examines how social categories—such as age, gender, ethnicity, religion, occupation, and

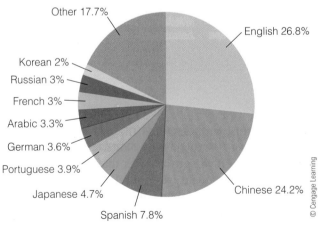

Figure 5.5 Language Use on the Internet Although the world's digital divide is diminishing, it is still dramatic.
As illustrated here, over 80 percent of today's 2 billion Internet users are native speakers of just ten of the world's 6,000 languages. Among the fastest-growing Internet language groups today are Arabic, Chinese, and Russian. (Figures shown in pie chart are rounded.)

Data from http://www.internetworldstats.com. Figure from Haviland/Prins/Walrath/McBride, *The Essence of Anthropology*, 3E, Fig. 2.5, p. 45. © 2013 Cengage Learning.

(Pie chart labels: Other 17.7%, English 26.8%, Korean 2%, Russian 3%, French 3%, Arabic 3.3%, German 3.6%, Portuguese 3.9%, Japanese 4.7%, Spanish 7.8%, Chinese 24.2%)

© Cengage Learning

linguistic nationalism The attempt by ethnic minorities and even countries to proclaim independence by purging their language of foreign terms.

sociolinguistics The study of the relationship between language and society through examining how social categories—such as age, gender, ethnicity, religion, occupation, and class—influence the use and significance of distinctive styles of speech.

Figure 5.6 Gendered Speech Howler Makers of the feature film *Dances with Wolves* aimed for cultural authenticity by casting Native American actors and hiring a female language coach to teach Lakota to those who did not know how to speak it. However, the lessons did not include the gendered speech aspect of Lakota—the fact that females and males follow different rules of syntax. So, when Native speakers of the language saw the film and realized that the actors portraying Lakota warriors were speaking like women, they snickered and then howled with laughter.

© Orion Pictures Corporation/Everett Collection

Such is the case in China, the world's most populous country with almost 1.4 billion inhabitants, almost all of whom speak Chinese. In fact, there are many Chinese languages, each consisting of many regional dialects. For instance, folk in Shanghai actually use a dialect of Wu Chinese spoken in the eastern region, whereas natives of Guangdong (Canton) speak a dialect of Yuehai, the major language of southwestern China. Migrants from the northern parts of the country, where numerous dialects of Mandarin Chinese are traditionally spoken, understand almost nothing of Wu or Yuehai because these Chinese languages are foreign to them. For this reason, almost all Chinese nationals today learn Standard Chinese, the country's official language, historically developed as a lingua franca based on a Mandarin dialect traditionally spoken in the country's capital city, Beijing.

Linguistic boundaries are not only geographic or territorial, but may also indicate or reflect social class, economic status, political rank, or ethnic identity. A classic example of the kind of dialect that may set one group apart from others within a single society is one spoken by many inner-city African Americans. Technically known as African American Vernacular English (AAVE), it has often been referred to as *black English* and *Ebonics*. Like any other dialect or language, AAVE is a highly structured mode of speech with patterned rules of sounds and sequences. Many of its distinctive features stem from the retention of sound patterns, grammatical rules concerning verbs, and even words of the West African languages spoken by the ancestors of present-day African Americans (Monaghan, Hinton, & Kephart, 1997).

In many societies where different dialects are spoken, individuals often become skilled at switching back and forth between them, depending on the situation in which they are speaking. Without being conscious of it, we all do the same thing when we switch from formality to informality in our speech, depending upon where we are and to whom we are talking. The process of changing from one language mode to another as the situation demands, whether from one language to another or from one dialect of a language to another, is known as **code switching**, the subject of several sociolinguistic studies. Fascinating new research on a distinct signing system known as Black ASL shows that code switching occurs even among those using sign language (McCaskill et al., 2012).

Ethnolinguistics

The study of the relationships between language and culture, and how they mutually influence and inform each other, is the domain of **ethnolinguistics**. In this type of research, anthropologists may investigate how a language reflects the culturally significant aspects of a people's traditional natural environment. For example, Aymara Indians living in the Bolivian highlands depend on the potato (or *luki*) as their major source of food, and their language has over 200 words for this vegetable, reflecting the many varieties they traditionally grow and the many different ways that they preserve and prepare it (**Figure 5.7**). Similarly, many people in the United States today possess a rich vocabulary allowing them to precisely

code switching The practice of changing from one mode of speech to another as the situation demands, whether from one language to another or from one dialect of a language to another.

ethnolinguistics A branch of linguistics that studies the relationships between language and culture and how they mutually influence and inform each other.

Figure 5.7

Linguistic Relativity
Aymara Indians living in the highlands of Bolivia and Peru in South America depend on the potato as their major source of food. Their language has over 200 words for this vegetable, reflecting the many varieties they traditionally grow and the many different ways they preserve and prepare it. This is an example of linguistic relativity.

distinguish between many different types of cars, categorized by model, year, and manufacturer.

Another example concerns cultural categories of color: languages have different ways of dividing and naming the range of light in the electromagnetic spectrum visible to the naked human eye. In modern English we speak of black, red, orange, yellow, green, blue, indigo, violet, and white, as well as "invisible" colors such as ultraviolet and infrared. Other languages mark out different groupings on this continuum of hues. For instance, Indians in Mexico's northwestern mountains speaking Tarahumara have just one word for both green and blue—*siyoname.*

In the Hanunóo language, as spoken by the Mangyan on the Philippine island of Mindoro, there is no word for color. Instead, these tropical forest-dwellers value objects like textiles, beads, animals, feathers, plants, and fruit based on levels of brightness and saturation. Their classification can be reduced to just four terms: lightness (*malagti*), corresponding to white and other lightly tinted colors; darkness (*mabiru*), referring to black and dark-shaded versions of gray, blue, and green; wetness (*malatuy*), akin to fresh greenness; and dryness (*marara*), associated with "dried-out" reddish colors (Conklin, 1955).

The idea that the words and grammar of a language are directly linked to culture and affect how speakers of the language perceive and think about the world is known as **linguistic relativity**. This theoretical concept is associated with the pioneering ethnolinguistic research carried out by anthropologist Edward Sapir and his student Benjamin Whorf during the 1930s. Focusing on the interplay of language, thought, and culture, their research resulted in what is now known as the *Sapir-Whorf hypothesis*: the idea that each language provides particular

grooves of linguistic expression that predispose speakers of that language to perceive the world in a certain way.

Whorf gained many of these insights while translating English into Hopi, a North American Indian language still spoken in Arizona. Doing this work, he discovered that Hopi differs from English not only in vocabulary but also in terms of its grammatical categories such as nouns and verbs. For instance, Hopi use numbers for counting and measuring things that have physical existence, but they do not apply numbers in the same way to abstractions like time. They would have no problem translating an English sentence such as "I see fifteen sheep grazing on three acres of grassland," but an equally simple sentence such as "Three weeks ago, I enjoyed my fifteen minutes of fame" would require a much more complex translation into Hopi.

It is also of note that Hopi verbs express tenses differently than English verbs. Rather than marking past, present, and future, with *-ed, -ing,* or *will,* Hopi requires additional words to indicate if an event is completed, is still ongoing, or is expected to take place. So instead of saying, "Three strangers stayed for fifteen days in our village," a Hopi would say something like, "We remember three strangers stay in our village until the sixteenth day."

In addition, Hopi verbs do not express tense by their forms. Unlike English verbs that change form to indicate past, present, and future, Hopi verbs distinguish among a statement of fact (if the speaker actually witnesses a certain event), a statement of expectation, and a statement that

linguistic relativity The theoretical concept directly linking language and culture, holding that the words and grammar of a language affect how its speakers perceive and think about the world.

expresses regularity. For instance, when you ask an English-speaking athlete "Do you run?" he may answer "yes," when in fact he may at that moment be sitting in an armchair watching TV. A Hopi athlete asked the same question in his own language might respond "no" because in Hopi the statement of fact "he runs" translates as *wari* ("running occurs"), whereas the statement that expresses regularity—"he runs," such as on the track team—translates as *warikngwe* ("running occurs characteristically").

This shows that the Hopi language structures thinking and behavior with a focus on the present—on getting ready and carrying out what needs to be done right now. Whorf summed it up like this: "A characteristic of Hopi behavior is the emphasis on preparation. This includes announcing and getting ready for events well beforehand, elaborate precautions to insure persistence of desired conditions, and stress on good will as the preparer of good results" (Carroll, 1956, p. 148). Based on his research on the Hopi language and culture, Whorf developed his important theoretical insight "that the structure of the language one habitually uses influences the manner in which one understands his environment. The picture of the universe shifts from tongue to tongue" (Carroll, 1956, p. vi).

In the 1990s linguistic anthropologists devised new research strategies to actually test Sapir and Whorf's original hypothesis. One study found that speakers of Swedish and Finnish (neighboring peoples who speak radically different languages) working at similar jobs in similar regions under similar laws and regulations show significantly different rates of on-the-job accidents. The rates are substantially lower among the Swedish speakers. What emerges from comparison of the two languages is that Swedish (one of the Indo-European languages) emphasizes information about movement in three-dimensional space. Finnish (a Ural-Altaic language unrelated to Indo-European languages) emphasizes more static relations among coherent temporal entities. As a consequence, it seems that Finns organize the workplace in a way that favors the individual person over the temporal organization in the overall production process. This in turn leads to frequent production disruptions, haste, and (ultimately) accidents.

If language does mirror cultural reality, it would follow that changes in a culture will sooner or later be reflected in changes in the language. We see this happening all around the world today, including in the English language (Wolff & Holmes, 2011).

Language Versatility

In most societies throughout the world, it is not unusual for individuals to be fluent in two, three, or more languages. They succeed in this in large part because they experience training in multiple languages as children—not as high school or college students, which is the educational norm in the United States.

In some regions where groups speaking different languages coexist and interact, people often understand one another but may choose not to speak the other's language. Such is the case in the borderlands of northern Bolivia and southern Peru where Quechua-speaking and Aymara-speaking Indians are neighbors. When an Aymara farmer speaks to a Quechua herder in Aymara, the Quechua will reply in Quechua, and vice versa, each knowing that the other understands both languages even if speaking just one. The ability to comprehend two languages but express oneself in only one is known as *receptive* or *passive bilingualism.*

In the United States, perhaps reflecting the country's enormous size and power, many citizens are not interested in learning a second or foreign language. This is especially significant—and troubling—because the United States is not only one of the world's most ethnically diverse countries, but also the world's largest economy and heavily dependent on international trade relations. In our globalized world, being bilingual or multilingual may open doors of communication not only for trade but for work, diplomacy, art, and friendship. Ironically, reluctance to learn another language prevails in the United States despite the fact that the majority language in the Americas is not English but Spanish; Spanish is not only the majority language of the hemisphere but also the fastest-growing language in the United States.

Beyond Words: The Gesture–Call System

As efficient as they are at naming and talking about ideas, actions, and things, all languages are to some degree inadequate at communicating certain kinds of information that people need to know in order to fully understand what is being said. For this reason, human speech is always embedded within a gesture–call system of a type that we share with nonhuman primates.

The various sounds and gestures of this system serve to "key" speech, providing listeners with the appropriate frame for interpreting what a speaker is saying. Messages about human emotions and intentions are effectively communicated by this gesture–call system: Is the speaker happy, sad, mad, enthusiastic, tired, or in some other emotional state? Is he or she requesting information, denying something, reporting factually, or lying? Very little of this information is conveyed by spoken language alone. In fact, research shows that humans convey far more information through nonverbal means (tone of voice, body language) than through verbal means in their interactions and communications with each other (Poyatos, 2002).

Nonverbal Communication

The **gesture** component of the gesture–call system consists of facial expressions and body postures and motions that convey intended as well as subconscious messages. The study of such nonverbal signals is known as **kinesics**.

Humanity's repertoire of body language is enormous. This is evident if you consider just one aspect of it: the fact that a human being has about fifty facial muscles and is thereby capable of making more than 7,000 facial expressions! Thus, it should not be surprising to hear that at least 60 percent of our total communication takes place nonverbally.

Often, gestural messages complement spoken messages—for instance, nodding the head while affirming something verbally, raising eyebrows when asking a question, or using hands and fingers to illustrate or emphasize what is being talked about. However, nonverbal signals are sometimes at odds with verbal ones, and they have the power to override or undercut them. For example, a person may say the words "I love you" a thousand times to another, but if it is not true, the nonverbal signals will likely communicate that falseness.

Anthropologists paid little attention to the analysis of nonverbal communication prior to the 1950s, but since then a great deal of research has been devoted to this intriguing subject. Cross-cultural studies in this field have shown that there are many similarities around the world in such basic facial expressions as smiling, laughing, crying, and displaying shock or anger. The smirks, frowns, and gasps that we have inherited from our primate ancestry require little learning and are harder to fake than conventional or socially obtained gestures that are shared by members of a group, albeit not always consciously so.

Routine greetings are also similar around the world. Europeans, Balinese, Papuans, Samoans, Bushmen, and at least some South American Indians all smile and nod, and if the individuals are especially friendly, they will raise their eyebrows with a rapid movement, keeping them raised for a fraction of a second. By doing so, they signal a readiness for contact. The Japanese, however, suppress the eyebrow flash, regarding it as indecent. This example illustrates that there are important cross-cultural differences as well as similarities.

Another example can be found in gestural expressions for yes and no. In North America, one nods the head down then up for yes or shakes it left and right for no. The people of Sri Lanka also nod to answer yes to a factual question, but if asked to do something, a slow sideways movement of the head means yes. In Greece, the nodded head means yes, but no is indicated by jerking the head back so as to lift the face, usually with the eyes closed and the eyebrows raised.

Another aspect of body language has to do with social space: how people position themselves physically in relation to others. **Proxemics**, the cross-cultural study of social space, came to the fore through the work of anthropologist Edward Hall (1914–2009), who coined the term (Hall, 1963, 1990). As a young man in the 1930s, Hall worked with construction crews of Hopi and Navajo Indians, building roads and dams. After earning his doctorate, he worked with the U.S. State Department to develop the new field of intercultural communication at the Foreign Service Institute, and while training some 2,000 Foreign Service workers, his ideas about nonverbal communication began to crystallize.

Hall's research showed that people from different cultures have different frameworks for defining and organizing social space—the personal space they establish around their bodies, as well as the macrolevel sensibilities that shape cultural expectations about how streets, neighborhoods, and cities should be arranged. Among other things, Hall's investigation of personal space revealed that every culture has distinctive norms for closeness (**Figure 5.8**). You can see this for yourself if you are watching a foreign film, visiting another country, or taking part in a multicultural group. How close to one another do people stand when talking in the street or riding in a subway or elevator? Does the pattern match the one you are accustomed to in your own cultural corner?

Hall identified the range of cultural variation in four categories of proxemically relevant social spaces: intimate (0–18 inches), personal-casual (1½–4 feet), social-consultive (4–12 feet), and public distance (12 feet and beyond). Hall warned that different cultural definitions of socially accepted use of space within these categories can lead to serious miscommunication and misunderstanding in cross-cultural settings (Hall, 1990). His research has been fundamental for the present-day training of international businesspeople, diplomats, and others involved in intercultural work.

Paralanguage

The second component of the gesture–call system is **paralanguage**—specific voice effects that accompany speech and contribute to communication. These include vocalizations such as giggling, groaning, or sighing, as well as voice qualities such as volume, intensity, pitch, and tempo.

The importance of paralanguage is suggested by the comment, "It's not so much *what* was said as *how* it was said." Obviously, whispering or shouting can make a big difference in meaning, even though the uttered words would be the same when written down. Minor differences in pitch, tempo, and phrasing may seem less obvious, but they still impact how words are perceived. Studies show, for example, that even subliminal messages communicated

gestures Facial expressions and body postures and motions that convey intended as well as subconscious messages.

kinesics The study of nonverbal signals in body language including facial expressions and bodily postures and motions.

proxemics The cross-cultural study of people's perception and use of space.

paralanguage Voice effects that accompany language and convey meaning. These include vocalizations such as giggling, groaning, or sighing, as well as voice qualities such as pitch and tempo.

Enculturation: The Self and Social Identity

From the moment of birth, a person faces multiple survival challenges. Obviously, newborns cannot take care of their own biological needs. Only in myths and romantic fantasies do we encounter stories about children successfully coming of age alone in the wilderness or accomplishing this feat having been raised by animals in the wild. Millions of children around the world have been fascinated by stories about Tarzan and the apes or the jungle boy Mowgli and the wolves. Moreover, young and old alike have been captivated by newspaper hoaxes about "wild" children, such as reports of a 10-year-old boy found running among gazelles in the Syrian Desert in 1946.

Fanciful imaginings aside, human children are biologically ill-equipped to survive without culture. This point has been driven home by several documented cases about feral children (*feral* comes from *fera*, which is Latin for "wild animal") who grew up deprived of human contact. None of them had a happy ending. For instance, there was nothing romantic about the girl Kamala, supposedly rescued from a wolf den in India in 1920: She moved about on all fours and could not feed herself. And everyone in Paris considered the naked "wild boy" captured in the woods outside Aveyron village in 1800 an incurable idiot.

Worse still is the true story of Genie, the "wild child" of Los Angeles, who spent her entire childhood in near total isolation. Imprisoned alone by her deranged father in a room with covered windows, she was infantile and emaciated when her nearly blind mother dragged the 13-year-old girl into a welfare office in 1970. Bounced back and forth between her mother, foster parents, and institutions, Genie never mastered the rudiments of language and now lives in a home for mentally disabled adults (Rymer, 1994). Clearly, the biological capacity for what we think of as human, which entails culture, must be nurtured to be realized.

Because culture is socially constructed and learned rather than biologically inherited, all societies must somehow ensure that culture is adequately transmitted from one generation to the next—a process we have already defined as *enculturation*. Because each group lives by a particular set of cultural rules, a child will have to learn the rules of his or her society in order to survive. Most of that learning takes place in the first few years when a child learns how to feel, think, speak, and ultimately act like an adult who embodies being Japanese, Kikuyu, Lakota, Norwegian, or whatever ethnic or national group into which the child is born.

The first agents of enculturation in all societies are the members of the infant's household, especially the child's mother. (In fact, cultural factors are at work even before birth through what a pregnant mother eats, drinks, and inhales, as well as the sounds, rhythms, and activity patterns of her daily life.) Who the other members are depends on how households are structured in each particular society.

As the young person matures, individuals outside the household are brought into the enculturation process. These usually include other relatives and certainly the individual's peers. In some societies, professionals are brought into the process to provide formal instruction. In many societies children are allowed to learn through observation and participation, at their own speed.

Self-Awareness

Enculturation begins with the development of **self-awareness**—the ability to identify oneself as an individual creature, to reflect on oneself, and to evaluate oneself (**Figure 6.1**). Humans do not have this cognitive ability at birth, even though it is essential for their successful social functioning. It is self-awareness that permits one to take social responsibility for one's conduct, to learn how to react to others, and to assume a variety of roles in society. An important aspect of self-awareness is the attachment of positive value to one's self. Without this, individuals cannot be motivated to act to their advantage.

Self-awareness does not come all at once. In modern industrial and postindustrial societies, for example, self and nonself are not clearly distinguished until a child is about 2 years of age, lagging somewhat behind other cultures (Rochat, 2001). Self-awareness develops in concert with neuromotor development, which is known to proceed at a slower rate in infants from industrial societies than in infants in many, perhaps even most, small-scale farming or foraging communities. The reasons for this slower rate are not yet clear, although the amount of human contact and stimulation that infants receive seems to play an important role.

As noted earlier in this text, infants in the United States, for example, generally do not sleep with their parents, most often being put in rooms of their own. This is seen as an important step in making them into individuals, "owners" of themselves and their capacities. As a consequence, they do not experience the steady stream of personal stimuli, including smell, movement, and warmth, that they would if co-sleeping. Private sleeping also takes away the opportunity for frequent nursing through the night.

self-awareness The ability to identify oneself as an individual, to reflect on oneself, and to evaluate oneself.

Figure 6.1 Self-Awareness Recognizing herself in the mirror, this young girl has developed the self-awareness necessary to understand that she is a distinct individual. In modern industrial and postindustrial societies, self-awareness is typically established by about age 2—later than in other societies.

© Laura Dwight/Corbis

In the majority of the world's societies, infants routinely sleep with their parents, or at least their mothers. Also, they are carried or held most other times, usually in an upright position, often in the company of other people and amid various activities. The mother typically responds to a cry or "fuss" within seconds, usually offering the infant her breast.

So it is among traditional Ju/'hoansi (pronounced "zhutwasi") people of southern Africa's Kalahari Desert, whose infants breastfeed on demand in short frequent bouts—commonly nursing about four times an hour, for 1 or 2 minutes at a time. Overall, a 15-week-old Ju/'hoansi infant is in close contact with his or her mother about 70 percent of the time (compared to 20 percent for home-reared infants in the United States). Moreover, Ju/'hoansi babies usually have considerable contact with numerous other adults and children of all ages.

This steady stream of varied stimuli is significant, for studies show that stimulation plays a key role in the hardwiring of the brain; it is necessary for development of the neural circuitry. Looking at breastfeeding in particular, the longer children are breastfed, the better their overall health, the higher they will score on cognitive tests, and the lower the risk of obesity, allergies, and attention deficit hyperactivity disorder (Dettwyler, 1997). Because our biological heritage as primates has programmed us to

develop in response to social stimuli, it is not surprising that self-awareness and a variety of other beneficial qualities develop more rapidly in response to close contact with other humans.

Social Identity Through Personal Naming

Personal names are important devices for self-definition in all cultures. It is through naming that a social group acknowledges a child's birthright and establishes his or her social identity. Among the many cultural rules that exist in each society, those having to do with naming are unique because they individualize a person and at the same time identify one as a group member. Names often express and represent multiple aspects of one's group identity—ethnic, gender, religious, political, or even rank, class, or caste. Without a name, an individual is anonymous, has no social identity. For this reason, many cultures consider name selection to be an important issue and mark the naming of a child with a special event or ritual known as a **naming ceremony**.

---

naming ceremony A special event or ritual to mark the naming of a child.

Naming Practices Across Cultures

Worldwide, there are countless contrasting approaches to naming. For example, Aymara Indians in the Bolivian highland village of Laymi do not consider an infant truly human until they have given the child a name—and naming does not happen until the child begins to speak the Aymara language, typically around the age of 2. Once the child shows the ability to speak like a human, he or she is considered fit to be recognized as such with a proper name. The naming ceremony marks the toddler's social transition from a state of nature to culture and consequently to full acceptance into the Laymi community.

Unlike the Aymara, Icelanders name babies at birth. Following ancient custom, Icelandic infants receive their father's personal given name as their last name. The suffix *sen* is added to a boy's name and *dottir* to a girl's name. Thus, a brother and sister whose father is named Sven Olafsen would have the last names Svensen and Svendottir, respectively.

Although *patronyms* are common in Iceland, sometimes the mother's first name is chosen for her child's surname. Such *matronyms* (surnames based on mother's names) may be preferred for a boy or girl whose mother remains unmarried, is divorced, or simply prefers her own name identifying family status. This is the case with an Icelandic woman named Eva having a daughter named Gudrun Evasdottir and son Gunnar Evason. Matronymic traditions occur in several other parts of the world, including the Indonesian island of Sumatra, homeland of the Minangkabau. In this ethic group of several million people, children are members of their mother's clan, inheriting her family name.

Among the Netsilik Inuit in Arctic Canada, a mother experiencing a difficult delivery would call out the names of deceased people of admirable character. The name being called at the moment of birth is thought to enter the infant's body and help the delivery, and the child would bear that name thereafter. Inuit parents may also name their children for deceased relatives in the belief that the spiritual identification will help shape their character (Balikci, 1970).

It is common in numerous cultures for a person to receive a name soon after birth and then acquire new names during subsequent life phases. Navajo Indians from the southwestern United States name a child at birth, but traditionalists often give the baby an additional ancestral clan name soon after the child laughs for the first time. Among the Navajo, laughter is seen as the earliest expression of human language, a signal that life as a social being has started. Thus, it is an occasion for celebration, and the person who prompted that very first laugh invites family and close friends to a First Laugh Ceremony. At the gathering, the party sponsor places rock salt in the baby's hand and helps slide the salt all over the little one's body. Representing tears—of both laughter and sadness—the salt is said to provide strength and protection, leading to a long, happy life. Then the ancestral name is given.[1]

In many cultures, a firstborn child's naming ceremony also marks a change in the parents' social status. This is reflected in what is known as *teknonymy* (from *teknon*, the Greek word for "child"), in which someone assumes an honorific name, usually derived from the oldest son, in place of (or alongside) his or her own given name. In Arab societies, such an honorific is known as *kunya*. For example, a young man who names his firstborn son Ishaq becomes known as Abu Ishaq ("Father of Isaac"), whereas his wife may assume the name Umm Ishaq ("Mother of Isaac"). Teknonymy occurs in societies in which only close relatives are permitted to address someone by his other personal name. If outsiders or inferiors do so, it may be regarded as inappropriate or disrespectful. Such a taboo exists among the Tuareg of the Sahara Desert in northern Africa, for example, where people prefer using the honorific name (**Figure 6.2**).

Naming and Identity Politics

Because names symbolically express and represent an individual's cultural self, they may gain particular significance in personal and collective identity politics. For instance, when an ethnic group or nation falls under the control of a more powerful and expanding neighboring group, its members may be forced to assimilate and give up their cultural identity. One early indicator may be that families belonging to the subjugated or overwhelmed group decide to abandon their own ancestral naming traditions. Such was the case when Russia expanded its empire into Siberia and colonized the Turkic-speaking Xakas. Within a few generations, most Xakas had Russian names (Butanayev, cited in Harrison, 2002).

The identity politics of personal naming practices can also be seen in North America. For example, American Indian families, whether they lived on or off their tribal reservations, came under pressure to forgo their cultural traditions, including their customary personal and family names. As part of the assimilation process, many agreed or were compelled to have their indigenous names translated into English. This was common practice in the 19th century, soon after the United States had annexed or conquered the Great Plains. An Osage named He-lo-ki-he, for instance, became Long Bow. Those who became Christian converts often adopted European names, at least for public identification and self-presentation. And so it was that No-pa-wal-la, another Osage tribesman, became known as Henry Pratt.

---

[1] Authors' participant observation at traditional Navajo First Laugh Ceremony of Wesley Bitsie-Baldwin; personal communication, LaVerne Bitsie-Baldwin and Anjanette Bitsie.

Brent Stirton/Reportage by Getty Images

Figure 6.2 Tuareg Naming Ceremony Tuareg women gather around bowls of macaroni for a newborn's naming ceremony inside a tented home typical of those long used by these Sahara Desert nomads in northern Niger. For this special occasion the women have smeared their hands and faces with indigo. Traditionally, Tuareg children are named on the eighth day after birth, and relatives come from near and far to participate and celebrate the arrival of a new member in their clan. The father and other male relatives gather outside for a Muslim religious ceremony, led by a *marabout*. This holy man offers a prayer and then ritually cuts the throat of a ram slaughtered for the feast. At that moment, the father publicly reveals his child's name, usually one taken from the Koran.

Name-change stories are also common among immigrants hoping to avoid racial discrimination or ethnic stigmatization. For instance, it was not uncommon for Jewish immigrants and their U.S.-born children trying to succeed in the entertainment industry to Americanize their names: Comedian Joan Molinsky became Joan Rivers and fashion designer Ralph Lifshitz became Ralph Lauren.

In identity politics, naming can also be a resistance strategy by a minority group asserting its cultural pride or even rights of self-determination against a dominant society. For instance, in the United States, African Americans with inherited Christian names that were imposed upon their enslaved ancestors have, in growing numbers, rejected those names. Many have also abandoned the faith tradition represented by those names to become members of the Nation of Islam (Black Muslims). An enduring example of this is champion boxer Cassius Clay, who converted to Islam in the mid-1960s. Rejecting his slave name, he became Muhammad Ali.

Self and the Behavioral Environment

The development of self-awareness requires basic orientations that structure the psychological fields in which the self acts. These include object orientation, spatial orientation, temporal orientation, and normative orientation.

Every individual must learn about a world of objects other than the self. Through this *object orientation*, each culture singles out for attention certain environmental features, while ignoring others or lumping them together into broad categories. A culture also explains the perceived environment. This is important, for a cultural explanation of one's surroundings imposes a measure of order and provides the individual with a sense of direction needed to act meaningfully and effectively.

Behind this lies a powerful psychological drive to reduce uncertainty—part of the common human need

VISUAL COUNTERPOINT

Figure 6.3 Spatial Orientation Traditionally, each culture provides its members with a comprehensive design for living, a master plan, to guide and instruct both individuals and the collective society for the environment they historically inhabit. Born and raised in the Arctic, Inuit and other Eskimos find many meaningful reference points in a region that appears endlessly empty and monotonous to outsiders. Without spatial orientation, one would soon be lost and surely perish. During the past few decades, the virtual environment of cyberspace has brought new challenges and opportunities to anyone with access to digital technology and the skills to navigate that electronic media world.

for a balanced and integrated perspective on the relevant universe. When confronted with ambiguity and uncertainty, people invariably strive to clarify and give structure to the situation; they do this in ways that their particular culture deems appropriate. Thus, our observations and explanations of the universe are largely culturally constructed and mediated symbolically through language. In fact, everything in the physical environment varies in the way it is perceived and experienced by humans. In short, we perceive the world around us through a cultural lens.

The behavioral environment in which the self acts also involves *spatial· orientation*, or the ability to get from one object or place to another. Notably, when we speak of trying to "orient" ourselves, we are using an ancient word for *rising* that refers to the east, where the sun comes up. Traditionally, place names commonly contain references to significant geographic features in the landscape.

Finding your way to class, remembering where you left your car keys, directing someone to the nearest bus stop, maneuvering through airports, and traveling through deep underground networks in subway tunnels are examples of highly complex cognitive tasks based on spatial orientation and memory. So is an Inuit hunter's ability to kayak or sled long distances across vast Arctic water, ice, or snow—determining the route by means of a mental map, gauging his location by the position of the

sun in daytime, the stars at night, and even by the winds and smell of the air (**Figure 6.3**).

Technological revolutions in the 20th century have led to the invention of a newly created media environment, where we learn to orient ourselves in cyberspace. Without our spatial orientations, whether in natural or virtual reality, navigating through daily life would be impossible.

Temporal orientation, which gives people a sense of their place in time, is also part of the behavioral environment. Connecting past actions with those of the present and future provides a sense of self-continuity. This is the function of a calendar. Derived from the Latin word *kalendae*, which originally referred to a public announcement at the first day of a new month, or moon, such a chart gives people a framework for organizing their days, weeks, months, and even years. Just as the perceived environment of objects is organized in cultural terms, so too are time and space.

A final aspect of the behavioral environment is the *normative orientation*. Moral values, ideals, and principles, which are purely cultural in origin, are as much a part of the individual's behavioral environment as are trees, rivers, and mountains. Without them people would have nothing by which to gauge their own actions or those of others. Normative orientation includes, but is not limited to, standards that indicate what ranges of behavior are acceptable for males, females, and whichever additional gender roles exist in a particular society.

Culture and Personality

In the process of enculturation, each individual is introduced to a society's natural and human-made environment along with a collective body of ideas about the self and others. The result is a kind of internalized cultural master plan of the cosmos in which the individual will feel, think, and act as a social being. It is each person's particular guide of how to run the maze of life. When we speak of someone's personality, we are generalizing about that person's internalized map over time. Thus, personalities are products of enculturation, as experienced by individuals, each with his or her distinctive genetic makeup.

Personality does not lend itself to a formal definition, but for our purposes we may take it as the distinctive way a person thinks, feels, and behaves. Derived from the Latin word *persona*, meaning "mask," the term relates to the idea of learning to play one's role on the stage of daily life. Gradually, the mask, as it is placed on the face of a child, begins to shape that person until there is little sense of the mask as something superimposed. Instead it feels natural, as if one were born with it. The individual has successfully internalized the culture.

Personality Development: A Cross-Cultural Perspective on Gender

Although *what* one learns is important to personality development, most anthropologists assume that *how* one learns is no less important. Along with psychological theorists, anthropologists view childhood experiences as strongly influencing adult personality, and they are most interested in analyses that seek to prove, modify, or at least shed light on the cultural differences in shaping personality.

For example, the traditional ideal in Western societies has been for men to be tough, aggressive, assertive, dominant, and self-reliant, whereas women have been expected to be gentle, pliable, and caring. To many, these personality contrasts between male and female seem so natural that they are thought to be biologically grounded and therefore fundamental, unchangeable, and universal. But are they? Have anthropologists identified any psychological or personality characteristics that universally differentiate men and women?

U.S. anthropologist Margaret Mead is well known as a pioneer in the cross-cultural study of both personality and gender. In the early 1930s she studied three ethnic groups in Papua New Guinea—the Arapesh, the Mundugamor, and the Tchambuli. This comparative research suggested that whatever biological differences exist between men and women, they are extremely malleable. In short, she concluded, biology is not destiny. Mead found that among the Arapesh, relations between men and women were expected to be equal, with both genders exhibiting what most North Americans traditionally consider feminine traits (cooperative, nurturing, and gentle). She also discovered gender equality among the Mundugamor (now generally called Biwat); however, in that community both genders displayed supposedly masculine traits (individualistic, assertive, volatile, aggressive). Among the Tchambuli (now called Chambri), however, Mead found that women dominated men (Mead, 1960).

More recent anthropological research suggests that some of Mead's interpretations of gender roles were incorrect—for instance, Chambri women neither dominate Chambri men nor vice versa. Yet, overall her research generated new insights into the human condition, showing that male dominance is not genetically fixed in our human "nature." Instead, it is socially constructed in the context of particular cultural adaptations, and, consequently, alternative gender arrangements can be created. (See the Anthropologist of Note feature on page 134 about Mead's teacher, colleague, and close friend Ruth Benedict for her pathbreaking work on personality as a cultural construct.) Although biological influence in male–female behavior cannot be ruled out, it has nonetheless become clear that each culture provides different opportunities and has different expectations for ideal or acceptable behavior (Errington & Gewertz, 2001).

Childrearing and Gender among the Ju/'hoansi

To understand the importance of childrearing practices for the development of gender-related personality characteristics, consider the Ju/'hoansi Bushmen, native to the Kalahari Desert in the borderlands of Namibia and Botswana in southern Africa. Traditionally subsisting as nomadic hunter-gatherers (foragers), in the latter 20th century many Ju/'hoansi were forced to settle down—tending small herds of goats, planting gardens for their livelihood, and engaging in occasional wage labor on white-owned farms (Wyckoff-Baird, 2010).

Ju/'hoansi who traditionally forage for a living stress equality and do not tolerate dominance and aggressiveness in either gender. Males are as mild-mannered as females, and females are as energetic and self-reliant as males. By contrast, among the Ju/'hoansi who have recently settled in permanent villages, males and

---

personality The distinctive way a person thinks, feels, and behaves.

is provided on demand and continues for several years. Children may interpret such indulgence as a reward, one that reinforces that the family is the main agent in providing for children's needs. Also on the supportive side, at a relatively young age children are assigned a number of child-care and domestic tasks, all of which make significant and obvious contributions to the family's welfare. Thus, children learn early on that it is normal for family members to share and actively help one another.

On the corrective side, adults actively discourage selfish or aggressive behavior. Moreover, they tend to be insistent on overall obedience, which commonly inclines the individual toward being subordinate to the group. This combination of encouragement and discouragement in the socialization process teaches individuals to put the group's needs above their own—to be obedient, supportive, noncompetitive, and generally responsible, to stay within the fold and not do anything potentially disruptive. Indeed, a person's very definition of self comes from the individual being a part of a larger social whole rather than from his or her individual existence.

Interdependence among the Beng of West Africa

Recognizing that dependence training comes in many unique cultural variations, we now briefly turn to the Beng, a group of about 20,000 Mande-speaking farmers living in twenty-two villages in the tropical woodlands of Côte d'Ivoire, West Africa. Each family forms a large household, which includes the spirits of deceased ancestors. These spirits, known as *wru*, spend nights with their living relatives but depart at dawn for their invisible spirit village called *wrugbe*.

Believing in reincarnation, the Beng look upon infants not as new creatures but as reincarnated spirit ancestors gradually emerging from *wrugbe* back into everyday life. For this reason, Beng babies are embraced as profoundly spiritual beings who at first are only tentatively attached to life on earth. Their cries are interpreted as a longing for something from *wrugbe*, and good parents do everything within their power to make earthly life so comfortable and appealing that the babies will not be tempted to return there. This includes extensive grooming

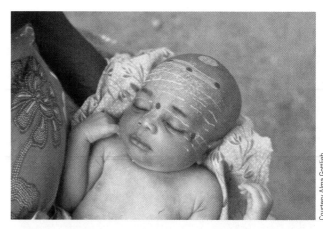

Figure 6.5 Beng Baby, Côte d'Ivoire, West Africa Beng people see babies as reincarnated ancestors with strong ties to the spirit world. To make sure these tiny "old souls" are not tempted to return to their *wrugbe*, or spirit village, they do everything possible to make earthly life appealing to them. This includes beautifying the child, as shown here, to help attract care from relatives and neighbors.

of the little ones to help attract additional care and love from relatives and neighbors (**Figure 6.5**). Held much of the day by an array of caregivers, Beng babies develop a broad variety of social ties and emotional attachments and appear generally free of stranger anxiety. Also, because they are thought to be living partly in the spirit world, these tiny "old souls" are allowed to determine their own sleeping and nursing schedules, and, notably, the biological mother is just one of many potential breastfeeders.

Having studied childrearing practices among these West African farmers, U.S. anthropologist Alma Gottlieb concludes that in Beng communities, the social goal is to promote *interdependence* rather than independence, in contrast to what is the normal practice in most North American families today. In short, Beng babies are made to feel "constantly cherished by as many people as possible," learning early on that individual security comes through the intertwining of lives, collectively sharing joys and burdens (Gottlieb, 2003, 2004, 2005).

Independence Training

Independence training fosters individual self-reliance and personal achievement. It is typically associated with societies in which a basic social unit consisting of parent(s) and offspring fends for itself. Independence training is particularly characteristic of mercantile (trading), industrial, and postindustrial societies where self-sufficiency and personal achievement are important traits for success, if not survival—especially for men, and increasingly for women.

This pattern also involves both encouragement and discouragement. On the negative side, a schedule, more than demand, dictates infant feeding. In North America, as noted previously, babies are rarely nursed for more

---

independence training Childrearing practices that foster independence, self-reliance, and personal achievement.

than a year. Many parents resort to an artificial nipple (pacifier) to satisfy the baby's sucking instincts—typically doing so to calm the child rather than out of an awareness that infants need sucking to strengthen and train coordination in the muscles used for feeding and speech.

North American parents are comparatively quick to start feeding infants baby food and even try to get them to feed themselves. Many are delighted if they can prop their infants up in the crib or playpen so that they can hold their own bottles. Moreover, as soon after birth as possible, children are commonly given their own private space, away from their parents. Collective responsibility is not pushed upon children; they are not usually given significant domestic tasks until later in childhood; and these are often carried out for personal benefit (such as to earn an allowance to spend as they wish) rather than as contributions to the family's welfare.

Displays of individual will, assertiveness, and even aggression are encouraged or at least tolerated to a greater degree than in cultures where dependence training is the rule. In schools, and even in the family, competition and winning are emphasized. Schools in the United States, for example, devote considerable resources to competitive sports. Competition is fostered within the classroom as well—overtly through practices such as spelling bees and awards and covertly through customs such as grading on a curve. In addition, there are various popularity contests, such as crowning a prom queen and king or holding an election to choose the classmate who is "best looking" or "most likely to succeed." Thus, by the time individuals have grown up in U.S. society, they have received a clear message: Life is about winning or losing, and losing is equal to failure (Turnbull, 1983b).

In sum, independence training is culturally adaptive in societies that emphasize individual achievement and in which members are expected to look out for their own interests. Its socialization patterns match cultural values and expectations increasingly prevalent in the spread of global capitalism.

One kind of training—independence, dependence, or a combination of both—is not inherently better or worse than any other. Compliant adults who are accepting of authority serve very well in a society that values cooperation and service toward the needs of the group. On the other hand, self-reliant, independent adults who are eager to explore new ways of doing things fit other societies that put a premium on individualism. Building on this basic cross-cultural comparison of childrearing practices, psychological anthropologists have greatly added to our increasingly sophisticated understanding of the complex relationship between culture and personality.

Group Personality

From the holistic perspective that anthropologists bring to the comparative study of childrearing, it is clear that these customary practices, personality development, and other aspects of culture are systemically interrelated. This insight has prompted research to explore whether whole societies might be analyzed in terms of particular personality types. Certainly, common sense suggests that personalities fitting for one culture may be less suitable for others. For example, an egocentric, aggressive personality would be out of place where modesty, self-denial, and sharing are the keys to success.

Unfortunately, common sense, like conventional wisdom in general, is not always the rule. Anthropologists asked themselves whether it would be possible to describe a group personality without falling into the trap of stereotyping. The answer is a qualified yes, especially with respect to traditional communities. The larger and more complex a society becomes, the greater its range in different personalities. In an abstract way, we may speak of a generalized *cultural personality* for a society, so long as we do not expect to find a uniformity of personalities within that society.

Consider, for example, the Yąnomami Indians, who subsist on foraging and horticulture in the tropical forests of the Amazon. Commonly, Yąnomami men strive to conform to a masculine ideal in their culture they call *waiteri*: being courageous, ferocious, humorous, and generous, all wrapped up into one heroic male personhood (Chagnon, 1990; Ramos, 1987). Yet, in their villages are men who are not so inclined and have quiet and somewhat retiring personalities. It is all too easy for an outsider to overlook these individuals when other, more "typical" Yąnomami are in the front row, pushing and demanding attention (**Figure 6.6**).

Modal Personality

Obviously, any productive approach to the problem of group personality must recognize that each individual is unique to a degree in both genetic inheritance and life experiences, and it must leave room for a range of different personality types in any society. In addition, personality traits that may be regarded as appropriate in men may not be so regarded in women, and vice versa. Given these qualifiers, we may focus our attention on the **modal personality**, defined as those character traits that occur with the highest frequency in a social group and are therefore the most representative of its culture.

Modal personality is a statistical concept rather than the personality of an average person in a particular society. As such, it raises other questions for investigation: How do more complex societies organize diversity? How does diversity relate to cultural change? Such questions are easily missed if one associates a certain type of personality with one particular culture, as did some earlier anthropologists (see Ruth Benedict in the Anthropologist of Note). At the same time, modal personalities of different groups can still be compared.

modal personality Those character traits that occur with the highest frequency in a social group and are therefore the most representative of its culture.

Rex Features via AP Images

Figure 6.9 Intersexuality in the Olympic Spotlight Caster Semenya is a South African middle-distance runner, born in 1991. At age 18, after winning the women's 800-meter race at the 2009 World Championships in Berlin, Semenya faced a global media storm with headlines such as "Gold Awarded amid Dispute over Runner's Sex." The International Association of Athletics Federations (IAAF) ordered biological testing that revealed that the runner has internal male sexual organs. After being withdrawn from international competitions, she was officially cleared by the IAAF in July 2010 and resumed her female athletic career. She ran in the 2011 World Championship and in the 2012 Summer Olympics, winning silver in both for the 800-meter event.

Such third-gender individuals are well known in Samoa, where males who take on the identity of females are referred to as *fa'afafines* ("the female way"). Becoming a *fa'afafine* is an accepted option for boys who prefer to dance, cook, clean house, and care for children and the elderly. In large families, it is not unusual to find two or three boys being raised as girls to take on domestic roles in their households (Holmes, 2000).

Transgenders cannot be simply lumped together as homosexuals. For example, the Tagalog-speaking people in the Philippines use the word *bakla* to refer to a man who views himself "as a male with a female heart." These individuals cross-dress on a daily basis, often becoming more "feminine" than Philippine women in their use of heavy makeup, in the clothing they wear, and in the way they walk. Like the Samoan *fa'afafines*, they are generally not sexually attracted to other *bakla* but are drawn to heterosexual men instead.

Another example is found among the Bugis, a Muslim ethnic group inhabiting Sulawesi Island in Indonesia and numbering more than 6 million. The Bugis acknowledge five genders: *oroané* (masculine male), *makunrai* (feminine female), *calabai* (feminine male), *calalai* (masculine female), and *bissu* (neither male nor female) (Davies, 2007). Representing and embodying all genders, *bissu* are traditionally high-ranking celibate intersexuals. Their name derives from the Bugis term for "clean" (*bessi*), and as such they serve as shamans, mediating between the human and the spirit world, inhabited by *dewata* (genderless spirits or gods). As one high-ranking Bugis, Angkong Petta Rala, explained in an interview, "*bissu* do not bleed, do not have breasts, and do not menstruate, therefore they are *clean* or *holy*" (Lathief, "Bissu: Imam-mam yang Menghibur," cited in Umar, 2008, pp. 7–8). Because traditional shamanism has no place in Islam theology, many Bugis view *bissu* as corrupted Muslims (Umar, 2008).

In addition, worldwide there are people who are gender variants: permanent or incidental transvestites (cross-dressers) without being homosexuals. Clearly, the cross-cultural sex and gender scheme is complex; the late 19th-century "homosexuality" and "heterosexuality" labels are inadequate to cover the full range of sex and gender diversity (Schilt & Westbrook, 2009).

Eunuchs

In addition to people who are intersexed or alternatively gendered, throughout history many boys and adult men have been subjected to neutering—crushing, cutting, or otherwise damaging their testicles. Commonly known as *castration*, this is an ancient and widespread cultural practice to transform someone's sexual status and thereby one's social identity.

Today, males sentenced as sex offenders in the United States and a growing number of European countries may request or be forced to undergo chemical castration, limiting or destroying their sex drive, not only as punishment but also as corrective treatment.

Historically, archaeological evidence from ancient Egypt, Iraq, Iran, and China suggests that castrating war captives may have begun several thousand years ago. Boys captured during war or slave-raiding expeditions were often castrated before being sold and shipped off to serve in foreign households, including royal courts. Castrated men were often put in charge of a ruler's harem, the women's quarters in a wealthy lord's household. In Europe, they became known as *eunuchs* (Greek for "guardian of the bed"), but in the Muslim world they were usually identified as *khādim*. In the 10th century, according to an early Kurdish historian, the caliph (ruler) of the Muslim empire in Baghdad had 11,000 *khādim*, 7,000 of whom were castrated black and 4,000 white slaves (Ayalon, 1999).

Eunuchs could rise to high status as priests and administrators, and some were even appointed to serve as military commanders as happened in the great Persian, Byzantine, and Chinese empires. Eunuchs served at the Chinese imperial court in Beijing for 2,000 years. During the Ming dynasty, the imperial household was said to include 20,000 of these castrated servants, some of whom achieved great prominence (Tsai, 1996). The last ruling emperor of China had about 1,500 eunuchs when he was forced to step down in 1912.

About the same time, the cultural institution of eunuchs also ended in Europe. Until then, a category of musical eunuchs, known as *castrati*, participated in operas and in Roman Catholic Church choirs, singing the female parts. Castrated before they reached puberty so as to retain their high voices, these selected boys were often orphaned or came from poor families. Without functioning testes to produce male sex hormones, physical development into manhood is aborted, so deeper voices—as well as body hair, semen production, and other usual male attributes—were not part of a castrati's biology.

In some cultures, there are also men who engage in self-castration or undergo voluntary castration. Early Christian monks in Egypt and neighboring regions voluntarily abstained from sexual relationships and sometimes castrated themselves for the sake of the kingdom of heaven. Such genital mutilation was also practiced among Coptic monks in Egypt and Ethiopia, until the early 20th century (Abbot, 2001).

One of the few places where there are still a substantial number of eunuchs—at least 500,000—is India. There, along with intersexuals and transgenders, they are known as *hijras*. Traditionally, *hijras* performed at important occasions such as births and marriages, but today many make a living, at least in part, as street performers (**Figure 6.10**).

Figure 6.10 Eunuchs in India These elegantly dressed street performers are eunuchs, part of a broad alternative gender category in India known as *hijras*. The exact number of eunuchs in India is unknown, but estimates range from 500,000 to 1 million. On the occasion pictured here, thousands of *hijras* from across the country gathered in the remote northern town of Rath—300 kilometers (185 miles) south of Lucknow, the capital of Uttar Pradesh state—for a convention to chart their collective agenda, including a more active role in politics.

Reuters

Collectively, these alternatively gendered individuals who are "neither man nor woman" are thought to number about 6 million in India alone (Nanda, 1999).

The Social Context of Sexual and Gender Identity

The cultural standards that define normal behavior for any society are determined by that society itself. Thus, what seems normal and acceptable (if not always popular) in one society is often considered abnormal and unacceptable—ridiculous, shameful, and sometimes even criminal—in another. For instance, according to a recent global report, state-sponsored homophobia (the irrational fear of humans with same-sex preferences) thrives in many countries, fueling aggressive intolerance. Worldwide, 78 out of 193 countries have laws criminalizing same-sex sexual acts between consenting adults. Most of these punish individuals found guilty with imprisonment, although five countries (Iran, Mauritania, Saudi Arabia, Sudan, Yemen—plus parts of Nigeria and Somalia) punish them with the death penalty (Itaborahy, 2012). Yet, as discussed earlier in this text, most countries do not have such laws and a growing number have passed legislation legalizing same-sex marriage.

The complexity, variability, and acceptability or unacceptability of sex and gender schemes across cultures is an important piece of the human puzzle—one that prods us to rethink social codes and the range of forces that shape personality as well as each society's definition of *normal* overall.

Normal and Abnormal Personality in Social Context

The boundaries that distinguish the normal from the abnormal vary across cultures and time, as do the standards of what is socially acceptable. In many cultures, individuals may stand out as "different" without being considered "abnormal" in the strictest sense of the word—and without suffering social rejection, ridicule, censure, condemnation, imprisonment, or some other penalty. Moreover, there are cultures that not only tolerate or accept a much wider range of diversity than others, but they may actually accord special status to the deviant or eccentric as unique, extraordinary, even sacred, as illustrated by the following example.

Sadhus: Holy Men in Hindu Culture

Ascetic Hindu monks in India and Nepal provide an ethnographic example of a culture in which abnormal individuals are socially accepted and even honored. These individuals, known as *sadhus*, illustrate the degree to which one's social identity and sense of personal self are cultural constructs. When a young Hindu man in India or Nepal decides to become a *sadhu*, he must transform his personal identity, change his sense of self, and leave his place in the social order. Detaching himself from the pursuit of earthly pleasures (*kama*) and power and wealth (*artha*), he makes a radical break with his family and friends and abandons the moral principles and rules of conduct prescribed for his caste (*dharma*). Symbolically expressing his death as a typical Hindu, he participates in his own funeral ceremony, followed by a ritual rebirth. As a born-again, he acquires a new identity as a *sadhu* and is initiated into a sect of religious mystics.

Surrendering all social, material, and even sexual attachments to normal human pleasures and delights, *sadhus* dedicate themselves to achieving spiritual union with the divine or universal soul. This is done through chanting sacred hymns or mystical prayer texts and yoga (an ascetic and mystic discipline involving prescribed postures and controlled breathing). The superhuman goal is to become liberated from the physical limits of the individual mortal self, including the cycle of life and death.

The life of suffering chosen by *sadhus* may even include self-torture as a form of extreme penance. Naked or near naked ("sky-clad"), they spend most of their time around cremation grounds. On a regular basis they apply ashes to their body, face, and long, matted hair. Some pierce their tongue or cheeks with a long iron rod, stab a knife through their arm or leg, or stick their head into a small hole in the ground for hours on end. One subsect, known as *Aghori*, drink and eat from human skull bowls as a daily reminder of human mortality (**Figure 6.11**).

Most Hindus revere and sometimes even fear *sadhus*. Sightings are not uncommon because an estimated 5 million *sadhus* live in India and Nepal (Heitzman & Wordem,

Normal and Abnormal Personality in Social Context

Figure 6.11 *Sadhu* **Holy Man, India** This Shaivite *sadhu* of the *Aghori* subsect drinks from a human skull bowl, symbolizing human mortality. He is a srict follower of the Hindu god Shiva, whose image can be seen behind him.

2006; Kelly, 2006). Of course, if one of these bearded, long-haired, and nearly naked Hindu monks decided to practice his extreme yoga exercises and other sacred devotions in western Europe or North America, observers would consider such a holy man to be severely mentally disturbed.

Mental Disorders Across Time and Cultures

As the Hindu mystic monks in South Asia illustrate, no matter how extreme or bizarre certain behaviors might seem in a particular place and time, the abnormal is not always socially rejected. Moreover, the standards that define normal behavior may shift over time.

Such is the case with manic depression (now more properly called *bipolar disorder*) and attention deficit hyperactivity disorder (ADHD), both previously regarded as dreaded liabilities. In western Europe and North America, the manic and hyperactivity aspects of these conditions have gradually become viewed as assets in the quest for success. More and more, they are

interpreted as indicative of "finely wired, exquisitely alert nervous systems" that make one highly sensitive to signs of change and able to fly from one thing to another, all the while exerting an intense energy and focused on the future. These are extolled as high virtues in the corporate world, where being considered "hyper" or "manic" is increasingly an expression of approval (Martin, 1999, 2009).

Just as social attitudes concerning a wide range of both psychological and physical differences change over time within a society, they also vary across cultures—as described in the Biocultural Connection on the next page.

Cultural Relativity and Abnormality

Does this suggest that normalcy is a meaningless concept when applied to personality? Within the context of a particular culture, the concept of normal personality is quite significant. Irving Hallowell, a major figure in the development of psychological anthropology, ironically observed that it is normal to share the delusions traditionally accepted by one's society. Abnormality involves

A Cross-Cultural Perspective on Psychosomatic Symptoms and Mental Health

Biomedicine, the dominant medical system of European and North American cultures, sometimes identifies physical ailments experienced by individuals as *psychosomatic*—a term derived from **psyche** ("mind") and *soma* ("body"). These ailments can be serious and painful, but because a precise physiological cause cannot be identified through scientific methods, the illness is viewed as something rooted in mental or emotional causes—and thus on some level not quite real.

Each culture possesses its own historically developed ideas about health, illness, and associated healing practices. Although biomedicine is based in modern Western traditions of science, it is also steeped in the cultural beliefs and practices of the societies within which it operates. Fundamentally informed by a dualistic mind–body model, biomedicine represents the human body as a complex machine with parts that can be manipulated by experts. This approach has resulted in spectacular treatments, such as antibiotics that have eradicated certain infectious diseases.

Today, the remarkable breakthroughs of biomedicine are spreading rapidly throughout the world, and people from cultures with different healing systems are moving into countries where biomedicine dominates. This makes treating illnesses defined by biomedicine as psychosomatic disorders all the more difficult.

Indicative of our biocultural complexity, psychological factors such as emotional stress, worry, and anxiety may stem from cultural contexts and result in increased physiological agitation like irregular heart pounding or palpitations, heightened blood pressure, headaches, stomach and intestinal problems, muscle pains and tensions, rashes, appetite loss, insomnia, fatigue, and a range of other troubles. Indeed, when individuals are unable to deal successfully with stressful situations in daily life and do not get the opportunity for adequate mental rest and relaxation, their natural immune systems may weaken, increasing their chances of getting a cold or some other infection. For people forced to adapt to a quickly changing way of life in their own country or immigrants adjusting to a foreign culture, these pressures may result in a range of disorders that are difficult to explain from the perspective of biomedicine.

Medical and psychological approaches developed in European and North American societies are often unsuccessful in dealing with these problems, for a number of reasons. For one, the various immigrant ethnic groups have different concepts of mind and body than do medical practitioners trained in biomedical Western medicine. Among many Caribbean peoples, for example, a widely held belief is that spiritual forces are active in the world and that they influence human identity and behavior. For someone with a psychosomatic problem, it is normal to seek help from a local *curandero* or *curandera* ("folk healer"), *a santiguadora* ("herbalist"), or even a *santéro* (a Santéria priest) rather than a medical doctor or psychiatrist. Not only does the client not understand the symbols of Western psychiatry, but a psychiatric visit is often too expensive and may imply that the person is *loco*.

During the past few decades, however, anthropologists have become increasingly involved in cross-cultural medical mediation, challenging negative biases and correcting misinformation about non-Western indigenous perceptions of mind–body connections. The inclusion of culturally appropriate healing approaches has gained acceptance among the Western medical and psychological establishment in Europe, North America, and many other parts of the world.

BIOCULTURAL QUESTION
Given the cross-cultural differences in concepts of mind and body, should authorities in a pluralistic society apply the same standards to faith healers as to medical doctors?

the development of a delusional system of which the culture does not approve. The individual, who is disturbed because he or she cannot adequately measure up to the norms of society and be happy, may be termed *neurotic*. When a person's delusional system is so different that it in no way reflects his or her society's norms, the individual may be termed *psychotic*.

If severe enough, culturally induced conflicts can produce psychosis and also determine its particular form. In a culture that encourages aggressiveness and suspicion, the insane person may be one who is passive and trusting. In a culture that encourages passivity and trust, the insane person may be the one who is aggressive and suspicious. Just as each society establishes its own norms, each individual is unique in his or her perceptions.

Although it is true that each particular culture defines what is and is not normal behavior, the situation is complicated by findings suggesting that major categories of mental disorders may be universal types of human affliction. Take, for example, schizophrenia—probably the most common of all psychoses and one that may be found in any culture, no matter how it is manifested. Individuals afflicted by schizophrenia experience distortions of reality that impair their ability to function adequately, so they often withdraw from the social world into their own psychological shell.

Although environmental factors play a role, evidence suggests that schizophrenia is caused by a biochemical disorder for which there is an inheritable tendency. One of its more severe forms is paranoid schizophrenia. Those suffering from it fear and mistrust nearly everyone. They hear voices that whisper dreadful things to them, and they are convinced that someone is "out to get them." Acting on this conviction, they engage in bizarre sorts of behaviors, which lead to their removal from society.

Culture-Bound Syndrome

A **culture-bound syndrome**, or *ethnic psychosis*, is a mental disorder specific to a particular cultural group (Simons & Hughes, 1985). A historical example is *windigo psychosis*, limited to northern Algonquian groups such as the Cree and Ojibwa. In their traditional belief systems, these Indians recognized the existence of cannibalistic monsters called windigos. Individuals afflicted by the psychosis developed the delusion that, falling under the control of these monsters, they were themselves transformed into windigos, with a craving for human flesh. As this happened, the psychotic individuals perceived people around them turning into edible animals—fat beavers, for instance. Although there are no known instances where sufferers of windigo psychosis actually devoured humans, they were acutely afraid of doing so, and people around them feared that they might.

Windigo psychosis may seem different from clinical cases of paranoid schizophrenia found in Euramerican cultures, but a closer look suggests otherwise. The disorder was merely being expressed in ways compatible with traditional northern Algonquian cultures. Ideas of persecution, instead of being directed toward other humans, were directed toward supernatural beings (the windigo monsters); cannibalistic panic replaced panic expressed in other forms.

Windigo behavior may seem exotic and dramatic, but psychotic individuals draw upon whatever imagery and symbolism their culture has to offer. For instance, the delusions of Irish schizophrenics draw upon the images and symbols of Irish Catholicism and feature Virgin and Savior motifs. In short, the underlying biomedical structure of the mental disorder may be the same in all cases, but its expression is culturally specific.

A Western example of a culture-bound syndrome is "hysteria," expressed by fainting spells, choking fits, and even seizures and blindness. Identified in industrializing societies of 19th-century Europe and North America, this disorder was particularly associated with young urban women in well-to-do social circles. In fact, the term invented for this "nervous disease" is derived from the Greek word meaning "uterus." Not only has the diagnosis of this disorder declined in the course of the 20th century, but the term itself was banished from the medical nomenclature (Gordon, 2000).

In more recent decades, we have seen the rise of two related culture-bound syndromes associated with consumer capitalism: *bulimia nervosa* and *anorexia nervosa.* Bulimia is characterized by frequent binge eating followed by vomiting or other frantic efforts to avoid gaining weight. Anorexia is an obsession to remain thin, evidenced in self-starvation that may result in death. This neurotic "fear of fatness" manifests itself in Western consumer societies where a growing percentage of the population is overweight or obese.

Bulimia and anorexia are primarily diagnosed in female adolescents who reside in a culture that exalts thinness, even as fast food and leisure snacking are more prevalent. With the globalization of consumer society's fat–thin contradiction, its associated psychological eating disorders are also crossing borders (Littlewood, 2004). Today, Japan is just behind the United States in deaths related to psychological eating disorders ("Eating disorders (most recent) by country," 2004).

Personal Identity and Mental Health in Globalizing Society

Anthropologists view childrearing, gender issues, social identity, and emotional and mental health issues in their cultural context; this perspective recognizes that each individual's unique personality, feelings of happiness, and overall sense of health are shaped or influenced by the particular culture within which the person is born and raised to function as a valued member of the community. These communities, however, are seldom stable.

As illustrated by the spread of consumer culture and its associated psychological disorders, people all across the world face sometimes bewildering challenges hurled at them by the forces of globalization. These forces impact how people raise their children, how their personalities are influenced, and how they maintain their individual and collective social, psychological, and mental health.

In the past few decades, medical and psychological anthropologists have made valuable contributions to improving health care, not only in so-called developing countries far away, but also in their own societies. However, mental health

culture-bound syndrome A mental disorder specific to a particular cultural group; also known as *ethnic psychosis*.

practices prevailing in Europe and North America remain ethnocentric when theorizing and treating psychological disorders—a problem reinforced by a reductionist biomedical mindset that largely ignores the role of cultural factors in the etiology, expression, course, and outcome of mental disorders. Furthermore, commercial pressures on the health-care establishment favor bioscience and pharmacotherapy, with drug companies providing a quick and cheap fix for the problem (Luhrmann, 2001).

Informed by cultural relativist views on normality and deviance, anthropological perspectives on identity, mental health, and psychiatric disorders are especially useful in pluralistic societies where people from different ethnic groups, each with a distinctive culture, coexist and interact. Intensified by globalization, this multi-ethnic convergence drives home the need for a medical pluralism providing multiple healing modalities suited for the cultural dynamics of the 21st century.

CHAPTER CHECKLIST

What is enculturation, and does it shape a person's personality and identity?

● Enculturation, the process by which individuals become members of their society, begins soon after birth. Its first agents are the members of an individual's household, and then it involves other members of society.

● For enculturation to proceed, a person must possess self-awareness, the ability to identify oneself as an individual, to reflect on oneself, and to evaluate oneself.

● A child's birthright and social identity are established through personal naming, a universal practice with numerous cross-cultural variations. A name is an important device for self-definition—without one, an individual has no identity, no self. Many cultures mark the naming of a child with a special ceremony.

● For self-awareness to emerge and function, four basic orientations are necessary to structure the behavioral environment in which the self acts: object orientation (learning about a world of objects other than the self), spatial orientation, temporal orientation, and normative orientation (an understanding of the values, ideals, and standards that constitute the behavioral environment).

How do a society's childrearing practices and concepts of sex and gender influence a person's behavior, personality, and identity?

● Gender behaviors and relations are malleable and vary cross-culturally. Each culture presents different opportunities and expectations concerning ideal or acceptable male–female behavior. In some cultures, male–female relations are based on equal status, with both genders expected to behave similarly. In others, male–female relations are based on inequality and are marked by different standards of expected behavior.

● Anthropological research demonstrates that gender dominance is a cultural construct and, consequently, that alternative male–female social arrangements can be created if so desired.

● Through cross-cultural studies psychological anthropologists have established the interrelation of personality, childrearing practices, and other aspects of culture.

● Dependence training, usually associated with traditional farming societies, stresses compliance in the performance of assigned tasks and dependence on the domestic group, rather than reliance on oneself.

● In contrast, independence training, typical of societies characterized by small, independent families, puts a premium on self-reliance, independent behavior, and personal achievement. Although a society may emphasize one sort of behavior over the other, it may not emphasize it to the same degree in both sexes.

● Some psychological anthropologists contend that childrearing practices have their roots in a society's customs for meeting the basic physical needs of its members and that these practices produce particular kinds of adult personalities.

● Intersexuals—individuals born with reproductive organs, genitalia, and/or sex chromosomes that are not exclusively male or female—do not fit neatly into either a male or female biological standard or into a binary gender standard. Numerous cultures have created social space for intersexuals, as well as transgenders—physically male or female persons who cross over or occupy an alternative social position in the binary male–female gender construction.

What determines cultural norms, and is there such a thing as group personality or national character?

● Early on, anthropologists worked on the problem of whether it is possible to delineate a group personality without falling into stereotyping. Each culture chooses, from the vast array of possibilities, those traits that it sees as normative or ideal. Individuals who conform to these traits are rewarded; the rest are not.

● The modal personality of a group is the body of character traits that occur with the highest frequency in a culturally bounded population. As a statistical concept, it opens up for investigation how societies organize the diverse personalities of their members, some of which conform more than others to the modal type.

● National character studies have focused on the modal characteristics of modern countries. Researchers have attempted to determine the childrearing practices and education that shape such a group personality.

● Many anthropologists believe national character theories are based on unscientific and overly generalized data; others focus on the core values promoted in particular societies, although recognizing that success in instilling these values in individuals may vary considerably.

● What is defined as *normal behavior* in any culture is determined by the culture itself; what may be acceptable or even admirable in one may not be so regarded in

another. Abnormality involves developing personality traits not accepted by a culture.

Does culture play a role in a person's mental health?

● Culturally induced conflicts not only can produce psychological disturbance but can also determine the form of the disturbance. Similarly, mental disorders that have a biological cause, like schizophrenia, will be expressed by symptoms specific to the culture of the afflicted individual. Culture-bound syndromes, or ethnic psychoses, are mental disorders specific to a particular ethnic group.

● Multi-ethnic convergence, intensified by globalization, drives home the need for a medical pluralism providing multiple healing modalities suited for the cultural dynamics of the 21st century.

QUESTIONS FOR REFLECTION

1. Considering the cultural significance of naming ceremonies in so many societies, including among the Khanty profiled in this chapter's opening photo and Challenge Issue, what do you think motivated your parents when they named you? Does that have any influence on your sense of self?

2. Do you think that the type of childhood training you received shaped your personality? If so, would you continue that approach with your own children?

3. Margaret Mead's cross-cultural research on gender relations suggests that male dominance is a cultural construct and, consequently, that alternative gender arrangements can be created. Looking at your grandparents, parents, and siblings, do you see any changes

in your own family? What about your own community? Do you think such changes are positive?

4. Given that over 70 million people in today's world are intersexed and that a very small fraction of these people have access to reconstructive surgery, what do you think of societies that have created cultural space for alternative gender options?

5. Do you know someone in your family, neighborhood, or school who is "abnormal"? What is the basis for that judgment, and do you think everyone shares that opinion? Can you imagine that personal habits you consider normal would be viewed as deviant in the past or in another country?

ONLINE STUDY RESOURCES

CourseMate

Access chapter-specific learning tools, including learning objectives, practice quizzes, videos, flash cards, glossaries, and more in your Anthropology CourseMate.

Log into **www.cengagebrain.com** to access the resources your instructor has assigned and to purchase materials.

Challenge Issue

Facing the challenge of getting food, fuel, shelter, and other necessities, humans must hunt, gather, produce, or otherwise obtain the means to satisfy such needs. During the span of human existence, this has been accomplished in a range of highly contrasting natural environments by different biological and cultural adaptations. Inventing and applying various technologies, humans have developed distinctive subsistence arrangements to harness energy and process required resources. Thus, we may find hunters in Namibia's desert, fishers in Norway, manioc planters in Brazil's rainforest, goat herders in Iran's mountains, steel-mill laborers in South Korea, computer techs in India's cities, and poultry farmers in rural Alabama. All human activities impact their environments, some radically transforming the landscape. Here we see peasant farmers practicing wet-rice cultivation on the mountainous slopes of southern China's Guangxi Province. They have carved out terraces to capture rainwater, prevent soil erosion, and increase food production.

Patterns of Subsistence

All living beings must satisfy certain basic needs to stay alive—including obtaining food, water, and shelter. Moreover, because these needs must be met on an ongoing basis, no creature could long survive if its relations with the environment were random and chaotic. People have a huge advantage over other animals in this regard. We have culture.

If the rains do not come and the hot sun turns grassland into desert, we may pump water from deep wells, quenching our thirst, irrigating the pastures, and feeding our grazing animals. Conversely, if the rains do not end and our pastures turn into marshlands, we may choose to build earth mounds for our villages or dig canals to drain flooded fields. And to keep our food supplies from rotting, we can preserve them by drying or roasting and keep them in safe storage places for protection and future use. When our tools fail or are inadequate, we may choose to replace them or invent better ones. And if our stomachs are incapable of digesting a particular food, we can prepare it by cooking.

We are, nonetheless, subject to similar basic needs and pressures as are all living creatures, and it is important to understand human survival from this point of view. The crucial concept that underlies such a perspective is adaptation: how humans adjust to and act upon the burdens and opportunities presented in daily life.

Adaptation

As discussed earlier in this book, *adaptation* is the process organisms undergo to achieve a beneficial adjustment to a particular environment. What makes human adaptation unique among all other species is our capacity to produce and reproduce culture, enabling us to creatively adapt to an extraordinary range of radically different environments. The biological underpinnings of this capacity include large brains and a long period of growth and development.

IN THIS CHAPTER YOU WILL LEARN TO

- Recognize the relationship between cultural adaptation and long-term cultural change.

- Distinguish between the different food-collecting and food-producing systems developed across the globe in the course of more than 40,000 years.

- Analyze the interrelationship of natural environment, technology, and social organization in cultures as systems of adaptation.

- Assess the significance of the Neolithic revolution in the context of cultural evolution.

- Explain the process of parallel evolution in contrast to convergent evolution.

- Critically discuss mass food production in the age of globalization.

Figure 7.1 Comanche Bison Hunt This depiction of a Comanche bison hunt was painted by artist George Catlin (1796–1872). Plains Indians such as the Comanche and Lakota developed similar cultures because they had to adapt to similar environmental conditions.

for every member of a society even in the short run. Complex, urban societies are not more highly evolved than those of food foragers. Rather, both are highly evolved but in quite different ways.

Cultural adaptation must also be understood from a long-term historical point of view. To fit into an ecosystem, humans (like all organisms) must have the potential to adjust to or become a part of it. A good example of this is the Comanche, whose known history begins in the highlands of southern Idaho (Wallace & Hoebel, 1952). Living in that harsh, arid region, these North American Indians traditionally subsisted on wild plants, small animals, and occasionally larger game. Their material equipment was simple and limited to what they (and their dogs) could carry or pull. The size of their groups was restricted, and what little social power could develop was in the hands of the shaman, who was a combination of healer and spiritual guide.

At some point in their nomadic history, the Comanche moved east onto the Great Plains, attracted by enormous bison herds. As much larger groups could be supported by the new and plentiful food supply, the Comanche needed a more complex political organization. Eventually, they acquired horses and guns from European and neighboring Indian traders. This enhanced their hunting capabilities

significantly and led to the emergence of powerful hunting chiefs (**Figure 7.1**).

The Comanche became raiders in order to get horses (which they did not breed for themselves), and their hunting chiefs evolved into war chiefs. The once materially unburdened and peaceful hunter-gatherers of the dry highlands became wealthy, and raiding became a way of life. In the late 18th and early 19th centuries, they dominated the southern Plains (now primarily Texas and Oklahoma). In moving from one regional environment to another and in adopting a new technology, the Comanche were able to take advantage of existing cultural capabilities to thrive in their new situation.

Sometimes societies that develop independently of one another find similar solutions to similar problems. For example, the Cheyenne Indians originally lived in the woodlands of the Great Lakes region where they cultivated crops and gathered wild rice, which fostered a distinct set of social, political, and religious practices. Then they moved to the Great Plains, where they became horse-riding bison hunters, taking up a form of Plains Indian culture resembling that of the Comanche, even though the cultural historical backgrounds of the two groups differed significantly. This is an example of **convergent evolution**—the development of similar cultural adaptations to similar environmental conditions by different peoples with different ancestral cultures.

Especially interesting is that the Cheyenne gave up crop cultivation completely and focused exclusively on hunting and gathering after their move into the vast grasslands of the northern High Plains. Contrary to the popular notion

convergent evolution In cultural evolution, the development of similar cultural adaptations to similar environmental conditions by different peoples with different ancestral cultures.

Figure 7.2 Stone Heads, Easter Island Few places have caused as much speculation as this tiny volcanic island, also known by the indigenous name of Rapa Nui. Isolated in the middle of the southern Pacific Ocean, it is one of the most remote and remarkable places on earth. Nearly 900 colossal stone statues, known as *moai*, punctuate the landscape. Towering up to 65 feet, they were made by the Rapanui people—Polynesian seafarers who settled there about 800 years ago. They greatly prospered and multiplied and then faced an ecosystemic collapse.

David Simchock/vagabondvistas.com

of evolution as a progressive movement toward increased manipulation of the environment, this ethnographic example shows that cultural historical changes in subsistence practices do not always shift from dependence on wild food to farming; changes may move in the other direction as well.

Related to the phenomenon of convergent evolution is **parallel evolution**, in which similar cultural adaptations to similar environmental conditions are achieved by peoples whose ancestral cultures were already somewhat alike. For example, the development of farming in Southwest Asia and Mesoamerica took place independently, as people in both regions, whose lifeways were already comparable, became dependent on a narrow range of plant foods that required human intervention for their protection and reproductive success. Both developed intensive forms of agriculture, built large cities, and created complex social and political organizations.

It is important to recognize that stability as well as change is involved in cultural adaptation and evolution; episodes of major adaptive change may be followed by long periods of relative stability in a cultural system. Moreover, not everybody benefits from change, especially if change is forced upon them. As history painfully demonstrates, all too often humans have made changes that have had disastrous results, leading to the deaths of countless people—not to mention other creatures—and to the destruction of the natural environment.

An Ecosystemic Collapse: The Tragic Case of Easter Island

Among the many examples of catastrophic environmental destruction is Easter Island in the southern Pacific, first settled about 800 years ago by Polynesian seafarers. Other

Polynesians referred to this remote 163-square-kilometer (63-square-mile) island as Rapa Nui, and its inhabitants became known as Rapanui.

When the Rapanui arrived, 75 percent of the island was densely forested, primarily with jubaea palms. Clearing the woods for food gardens of taros, yams, and sweet potatoes, the Rapanui also raised domesticated chickens, hunted wild birds, fished the ocean, and gathered nuts, fruits, and seeds. They prospered, producing surpluses, growing dramatically in number; and they formed into a few dozen clans under a paramount chief, a sacred king.

Trees, felled for fuel and to build homes and fishing canoes, were also used as rollers for transporting huge stone statues, which became an extraordinary hallmark of Rapanui culture (**Figure 7.2**). However, over time, success turned to failure—evidently due to a collapse of the fragile ecosystem brought about by a combination of natural and cultural factors (Alfonso-Durraty, 2012).

Rats, which had come to the island with the settlers, contributed to the demise. Feasting on palm seeds and reproducing rapidly, the rat population soared and hindered the reseeding of the slow-growing trees. By the mid-1600s, the palm groves had disappeared, apparently done in by rats and human deforestation. As the forests disappeared, rich topsoil eroded, other indigenous and endemic plants became extinct, crop yields diminished, springs dried up, and flocks of migrant birds stopped coming to the island to roost. Moreover, from about 1600 to 1640, El Niño—a warming of water surface temperatures—decreased

parallel evolution In cultural evolution, the development of similar cultural adaptations to similar environmental conditions by peoples whose ancestral cultures were already somewhat alike.

biomass production, diminishing fish and other marine resources (Stenseth & Voje, 2009).

All of this led to periodic famine and chronic warfare between Rapanui rival factions. With their nearest neighbors over 2,500 kilometers (1,500 miles) to their west, they were truly an isolated people who had nowhere to go. By the time Dutch seafarers arrived on Rapa Nui in 1722 (the name "Easter Island" was given by the Dutch explorers who landed there on Easter Sunday), its indigenous population had dropped to about 3,000. During the next two centuries, other foreigners added to the Rapanui's problems, bringing diseases and other miseries. These additional stressors nearly wiped the Rapanui from their treeless island, now covered by grass and volcanic rock (Métraux, 1957; Mieth & Bork, 2009).

Environmental destruction on a much more massive scale has occurred in many other parts of the world, especially in the course of the 20th century, ruining the lives of millions. Considering such collapses of ecosystems, we must avoid falling into the ethnocentric trap of equating change with progress or with seeing everything as adaptive.

Culture Areas

From early on, anthropologists recognized that ethnic groups living within the same broad habitat often share certain cultural traits. This reflects the fact that there is a fundamental relationship among their similar natural environment, available resources, and subsistence practices and that neighboring peoples are in contact and engage in exchange with one another.

Classifying groups according to their cultural traits, anthropologists have mapped geographic regions in which a number of societies have similar ways of life. Known as **culture areas**, such regions often correspond to ecological regions. In sub-Arctic North America, for example, migratory caribou herds graze across the vast tundra. For dozens of different groups that have made this area their home, these animals provide a major source of food as well as material for shelter and clothing. Adapting to more or less the same ecological resources in this sub-Arctic landscape, these groups have developed similar subsistence technologies and practices in the course of generations. Although they speak very different languages, they may all be said to form part of the same culture area.

Because of changes in the natural environment such as habitat destruction and the extinction of plant and animal species, culture areas are not always stable. Moreover, new species may be introduced, and technologies may be invented or adopted from more distant cultures. Such was the case with the indigenous culture area of the

culture area A geographic region in which a number of societies follow similar patterns of life.

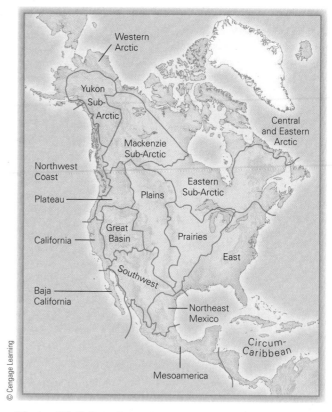

© Cengage Learning

Figure 7.3 Culture Areas This map shows the major culture areas that have been identified for North and Central America. Within each, there is an overall similarity of native cultures, as opposed to the differences that distinguish the cultures of one area from those of all others.

Great Plains in North America (**Figure 7.3**). For thousands of years, many indigenous groups with similar ways of life existed in this vast ecological area between the Mississippi River and the Rocky Mountains. Until the mid-1800s, when European immigrants invaded the region and almost completely annihilated the millions of free-ranging bison, these large grazing herds provided an obvious and practical source of food and materials for clothing and shelter.

The efficiency of indigenous groups in the southern grasslands increased greatly in the 1600s when they gained access to Spanish horses on the northern Mexican frontier and became mounted bison hunters. During the next century, the new horse complex spread northward to almost every indigenous group ranging in the Great Plains culture area. A total of thirty-one politically independent peoples, including the Cheyenne and Comanche just mentioned, reached a similar adaptation to this particular environment.

So it was that by the time Euramerican colonists invaded their vast hunting territories in the 19th century, the Indians of the Great Plains were all bison hunters, dependent on this animal for food, clothing, shelter, and bone tools. Each nation was organized into a number of warrior societies, and prestige came from hunting and fighting skills. Their villages were typically arranged in a distinctive circular pattern, and they shared many religious rituals, such as the Sun Dance.

During the 1870s and 1880s, railroads were built across the Great Plains, and mass slaughter of bison followed. More than 1 million of these animals were killed every year, mostly by non-Indians interested only in their hides and tongues (tongues were a luxury meat commodity, easily removed and compact to ship). With their herds almost exterminated, Indians of the Plains faced starvation, which made it impossible to effectively defend their homeland. This resulted in the near collapse of their traditional cultures from the 1890s onward.

Modes of Subsistence

Human societies all across the world have developed a cultural infrastructure that is compatible with the natural resources they have available to them and within the limitations of their various habitats. Each mode of subsistence involves not only resources but also the technology required to effectively capture and utilize them, as well as the kinds of work arrangements that are developed to best suit a society's needs. In the next few pages, we will discuss the major types of cultural infrastructure, beginning with the oldest and most universal mode of subsistence: food foraging.

Food-Foraging Societies

Before the domestication of food plants and animals, all people supported themselves through **food foraging**, a mode of subsistence involving some combination of hunting, fishing, and gathering wild plant foods. When food foragers had the earth to themselves, they had their pick of the best environments. But gradually, farming societies and, more recently, industrial and postindustrial societies (in which machines largely replaced human labor, hand tools, and animal power) appropriated the areas with rich soils and ample supplies of water. As a result, these expanding groups edged out the small foraging communities from their traditional habitats.

Today, at most a quarter of a million people—less than 0.004 percent of the world population of over 7 billion—still support themselves mainly as foragers. They are found only in the world's most marginal areas (frozen Arctic tundra, deserts, and inaccessible forests) and typically lead a migratory existence that makes it impractical to accumulate many material possessions. Because foraging cultures have nearly disappeared in areas having a natural abundance of food and fuel resources, anthropologists are necessarily cautious about making generalizations about the ancient human past based on in-depth studies of still-existing foraging groups that have adapted to more marginal habitats.

Present-day people who subsist by hunting, fishing, and wild plant collection are not following an ancient way of life because they do not know any better. Rather, they have been forced by circumstances into situations where foraging is the best means of survival or they simply prefer to live this way. In fact, foraging constitutes a rational response to particular ecological, economic, and sociopolitical realities. Moreover, for at least 2,000 years, hunters, fishers, and gatherers have met the demands for commodities such as furs, hides, feathers, ivory, pearls, fish, nuts, and honey within larger trading networks. Like everyone else, most food foragers are now part of a larger system with social, economic, and political relations extending far beyond regional, national, or even continental boundaries (**Figure 7.4**).

Characteristics of Food-Foraging Societies

Typically, foragers have ample and balanced diets and are less likely to experience severe famine than farmers. Their material possessions are limited, but so is their desire to amass things. Notably, they have plenty of leisure time for concentrating on family ties, social life, and spiritual development—apparently far more than people living in farming and industrial societies. Such findings clearly challenge the once widely held view that food foragers live a miserable existence. Among the few remaining food-foraging societies, there are some common features: mobility, small group size, flexible division of labor by gender, food sharing, egalitarianism, communal property, and rarity of warfare.

Mobility

Food foragers move as needed within a circumscribed region that is their home range to tap into naturally available food sources. Some groups, such as the Ju/'hoansi in the Kalahari Desert of southern Africa who depend on the reliable and highly drought-resistant mongongo nut, may keep to fairly fixed annual routes and cover only a restricted territory. Others, such as the traditional Shoshone in the western highlands of North America, had to cover a wider territory, their course determined by the local availability of the erratically productive pine nut.

A crucial factor in this mobility is availability of water. The distance between the food supply and the water must not be so great that more energy is required to fetch water than can be obtained from the food.

Small Group Size

Another characteristic of the food-foraging adaptation is the small size of local groups, typically fewer than a hundred people. No completely satisfactory explanation for this has been offered, but both ecological and social factors are involved. Among the ecological factors is the

---

food foraging A mode of subsistence involving some combination of hunting, fishing, and gathering of wild plant foods.

Figure 7.4 Remote but Not Isolated Peoples of the Kalahari Desert Human groups (including food foragers) do not exist in isolation except occasionally, and even then not for long. The bicycle this Bushman of southern Africa is riding is indicative of his links with the wider world, just as the wild tsama melons, bow, and quiver of arrows speak of his traditional hunter-gatherer life. For 2,000 years, Bushmen have been interacting regularly with neighboring farmers and pastoralists. Moreover, food foragers have supplied much of the commodities desired by the rest of the world, such as the elephant ivory used for keyboards on pianos so widely sought in 19th-century North America.

© Anthony Bannister; Gallo Images Corbis

carrying capacity of the land—the number of people that the available resources can support at a given level of food-getting techniques. This requires adjusting to seasonal and long-term changes in resource availability. Carrying capacity involves not only the immediate presence of food and water but also the tools and work necessary to secure them, as well as short- and long-term fluctuations in their availability.

In addition to seasonal or local adjustments, food foragers must make long-term adjustments to resources. Food-foraging populations usually stabilize at numbers well below the carrying capacity of their land. In fact, the home ranges of most food foragers can support from three to five times as many people as they typically do. In the long run, it may be more adaptive for a group to keep its numbers low rather than to expand indefinitely and risk destruction by a sudden and unexpected natural reduction in food resources. The population density of foraging groups surviving in marginal environments today rarely exceeds one person per square mile—a very low density.

How food-foraging peoples regulate population size relates to two things: how much body fat they accumulate and how they care for their children. Ovulation requires a certain minimum of body fat, and in traditional foraging societies this is not achieved until early adulthood. Hence, female reproductive maturity typically occurs between the early and mid-20s, and teenage pregnancies (at least successful ones) are virtually unknown (Frisch, 2002; Hrdy, 1999). Once a child is born, the mother nurses the child several

times each hour, even at night, and this continues over a period of four or five years. The constant stimulation of the mother's nipples suppresses the level of hormones that promote ovulation, making conception less likely, especially if work keeps the mother physically active, and she does not have a large store of body fat to draw on for energy (Konner & Worthman, 1980; Small, 1997). Continuing to nurse for several years, women give birth only at widely spaced intervals. Thus, the total number of offspring remains low but sufficient to maintain a stable population size (**Figure 7.5**).

Flexible Division of Labor by Gender

Division of labor exists in all human societies and is probably as old as human culture. Among food foragers, the hunting and butchering of large game as well as the processing of hard or tough raw materials are almost universally masculine occupations. By contrast, women's work in foraging societies usually focuses on collecting and processing a variety of plant foods, as well as other domestic chores that can be fit to the demands of breastfeeding and that are more compatible with pregnancy and childbirth.

Among food foragers today, the work of women is no less arduous than that of men. For example, Ju/'hoansi women may walk 12 miles a day to gather food, two or three times a week. They are carrying not only their children but also, on the return home, between 15 and 33 pounds of food. Still, they do not have to travel quite as far as do men on the hunt, and their work is usually less dangerous. Also, their tasks require less rapid mobility, do not need complete and undivided attention, and are readily resumed after interruption.

All of this is compatible with those biological differences that remain between the sexes. Certainly, women

---

carrying capacity The number of people that the available resources can support at a given level of food-getting techniques.

Although women in foraging societies commonly spend some time each day gathering plant foods, men rarely hunt on a daily basis (**Figure 7.6**). The amount of energy expended in hunting, especially in hot climates, is often greater than the energy return from the kill. Too much time spent searching out game might actually be counterproductive. Energy itself is derived primarily from plant carbohydrates, and it is usually the female gatherers who bring in the bulk of the calories. A certain amount of meat in the diet, though, guarantees high-quality protein that is less easily obtained from plant sources because meat contains exactly the right balance of all of the amino acids (the building blocks of protein) the human body requires. No one plant food does this, and in order to get by without meat people must hit on exactly the right combination of plants to provide the essential amino acids in the correct proportions.

Food Sharing

Another key feature of human social organization associated with food foraging is the sharing of food. Among the Ju/'hoansi, women have control over the food they collect and can share it with whomever they choose. Men, by contrast, are constrained by rules that specify how much meat is to be distributed and to whom. For the individual hunter, meat sharing is really a way of storing it for the future: His generosity, obligatory though it might be, gives him a claim on the future kills of other hunters. As a cultural trait, food sharing has the obvious survival value of distributing resources needed for subsistence.

Egalitarian Social Relations

A key characteristic of the food-foraging society is its egalitarianism. Because foragers are usually highly mobile and lack animal or mechanical transportation, they must be able to travel without many encumbrances, especially on food-getting expeditions. By necessity, the material goods they carry with them are limited to the barest essentials, which include implements for hunting, gathering, fishing, building, and cooking. (For example, the average weight of an individual's personal belongings among the Ju/'hoansi is just under 25 pounds.) In this context, it makes little sense for them to accumulate luxuries or surplus goods, and the fact that no one owns significantly more than another helps to limit status differences. Age and sex are usually the only sources of status differences.

It is important to realize that status differences by themselves do not constitute inequality, a point that is easily misunderstood especially when relations between men and women are concerned. In most traditional food-foraging societies, women did not and do not defer to men. To be sure, women may be excluded from some rituals in which men participate, but the reverse is also true.

Figure 7.5 Natural Birth Control Frequent nursing of children over four or five years acts to suppress ovulation among food foragers such as the Ju/'hoansi. As a consequence, women give birth to relatively few offspring at widely spaced intervals.

© Anthony Bannister; Gallo Images/Corbis

who are pregnant or who have infants to nurse cannot travel long distances in pursuit of game as easily as men can. By the same token, women may have preferred and been better at the less risky task of gathering.

But, saying that differing gender roles among food foragers is compatible with the biological differences between men and women is *not* saying that these roles are biologically determined. In fact, the division of labor by gender is often far less rigid among food foragers than it is in most other types of society. Thus, Ju/'hoansi males, when the occasion demands, willingly and without embarrassment gather wild plant foods, build huts, and collect water, even though all are regarded as women's work.

Notably, the food-gathering activities of women play a major role in the survival of their group: Research shows that contemporary food foragers may obtain up to 60 or 70 percent of their diet from plant foods, with perhaps some fish and shellfish also provided primarily by women (the exceptions tend to be food foragers living in Arctic regions, where plant foods are not available for much of the year).

VISUAL COUNTERPOINT

Figure 7.6 Ju/'hoansi Division of Labor Although food foragers such as the Ju/'hoansi Bushmen in southern African have a flexible division of labor, men usually do the hunting, whereas women prepare food. Both men and women gather wild foods such as ostrich eggs and edible plants—fruits, nuts, tubers. Here, Ju/'hoansi men return from a successful porcupine hunt, and women prepare a 3-pound ostrich egg omelet (equivalent to about two dozen chicken eggs). Traditionally, once the bird's large, hard shell has been emptied, it serves as a useful water container. If it shatters, pieces are fashioned into jewelry.

Moreover, the fruits of women's labor are controlled by them, not by men. Nor do women sacrifice their autonomy even in societies in which male hunting, rather than female gathering, brings in the bulk of the food.

Communal Property

Food foragers make no attempt to accumulate surplus foodstuffs, often an important source of status in agrarian societies. This does not mean that they live constantly on the verge of starvation because their environment is their natural storehouse. Except in the coldest climates (where a surplus must be set aside to see people through the long, lean winter season) or in times of acute ecological disaster, some food can almost always be found in a group's territory. Because food resources are typically shared and distributed equally throughout the group, no one achieves the wealth or status that hoarding might produce. In such a society, having more than others is a sign of deviance rather than a desirable characteristic.

The food forager's concept of territory contributes as much to social equality as it does to the equal distribution of resources. Most groups have home ranges within which access to resources is open to all members. What is available to one is available to all. If an Mbuti Pygmy hunter living in the forests of Central Africa discovers a honey tree, he has first rights; but when he has taken his share, others have a

turn. In the unlikely possibility that he does not take advantage of his discovery, others will. No individual within the community privately owns the tree; the system is first come, first served. Therefore, knowledge of the existence of food resources circulates quickly throughout the entire group.

Rarity of Warfare

Although much has been written on the theoretical importance of hunting for shaping the supposedly competitive and aggressive nature of the human species, most anthropologists are unconvinced by these arguments. To be sure, warlike behavior on the part of food-foraging peoples is known, but such behavior is a relatively recent phenomenon in response to pressure from expansionist states. In the absence of such pressures, food-foraging peoples are remarkably nonaggressive and place more emphasis on peacefulness and cooperation than they do on violent competition.

How Technology Impacts Cultural Adaptations among Foragers

Like habitat, technology plays an important role in shaping the characteristics of the foraging life discussed previously. The mobility of food-foraging groups may depend on the availability of water, as among the Ju/'hoansi, or of game animals and other seasonal resources, as among the Mbuti in the Democratic Republic of Congo in Central Africa. Different hunting technologies and techniques may also play a part in determining movement, as well as population size and division of labor by gender.

Consider, for example, the Mbuti Pygmies in the Ituri tropical forest. All Mbuti bands hunt elephants with spears. However, for other game some of the bands use bows, and others use large nets. Those equipped with nets have a cooperative division of labor in which men, women, and children collaborate in driving antelope and other game into the net for the kill. Usually, this involves very long hours and movement over great distances as participants surround the animals and beat the woods noisily to chase the game in one direction toward the great nets. Because this sort of "beat-hunt" requires the cooperation of seven to thirty families, those using this method have relatively large camps.

Among Mbuti bow hunters, on the other hand, only men go after the game. These archers tend to stay closer to the village for shorter periods of time and live in smaller groups, typically of no more than six families. Although there is no significant difference in overall population density between net- and bow-hunting areas, archers generally harvest a greater diversity of animal species, including monkeys (Bailey & Aunger, 1989; Terashima, 1983).

Food-Producing Societies

Habitat and technology do not tell the whole story of how we humans feed ourselves. After the emergence of tool making, which enabled humans to consume significant amounts of meat as well as plant foods, the next truly momentous event in human history was the domestication of plants and animals. Over time, this achievement transformed cultural systems, with humans developing new economic arrangements, social structures, and ideological patterns based on plant cultivation, breeding and raising animals, or a mixture of both.

The transition from food foraging to food production first took place about 10,000 years ago in Southwest Asia (the Fertile Crescent, including the Jordan River Valley and neighboring regions in the Middle East). This was the beginning of the **Neolithic** or New Stone Age (from the Greek *neo* meaning "new" and *lith* meaning "stone") in which people possessed stone-based technologies and depended on domesticated plants and/or animals. Within the next few thousand years, similar early transitions to agricultural economies took place independently in other parts of the world where human groups began to raise and (later) alter wild cereal plants such as wheat, maize (corn), and rice; legumes such as beans; gourds such as squash; and tubers such as potatoes. Doing the same with a number of wild animal species ranging in their hunting

territories, they began to domesticate goats, sheep, pigs, cattle, and llamas (**Figure 7.7**).

Because these activities brought about a radical transformation in almost every aspect of their cultural systems, Australian-born archaeologist Gordon Childe introduced the term **Neolithic revolution** to refer to the profound cultural change associated with the early domestication of plants and animals. As humans became increasingly dependent on domesticated crops, they mostly gave up their mobile way of life and settled down to till the soil, sow, weed, protect, harvest, and safely store their crops. No longer on the move, they could build more permanent dwellings and began to make pottery for storage of water, food, and so on.

Just why this change came about is one of the important questions in anthropology. Because food production requires more work than food foraging, is more monotonous, and is often a less secure means of subsistence, it is unlikely that people became food producers voluntarily.

Initially, it appears that food production arose as a largely unintended byproduct of existing food management practices. Among many examples, we may consider the Paiute Indians, whose desert habitat in the western highlands of North America includes some oasis-like marshlands. These foragers discovered how to irrigate wild crops in their otherwise very dry homeland, thus increasing the quantity of wild seeds and bulbs to be harvested. Although their ecological intervention was very limited, it allowed them to settle down for longer periods in greater numbers than otherwise would have been possible.

Unlike the Paiute, who stopped just short of a Neolithic revolution, other groups elsewhere in the world continued to transform their landscapes in ways that favored the appearance of new varieties of particular plants and animals, which came to take on increasing importance for people's subsistence. Although probably at first accidental, it became a matter of necessity as growth outstripped people's ability to sustain themselves through food foraging. For them, food production became a subsistence option of last resort.

Producing Food in Gardens: Horticulture

With the advent of plant domestication, some societies took up **horticulture** (from the Latin *hortus*, meaning "garden") in which small communities of gardeners cultivate crops with simple hand tools, using neither irrigation

---

Neolithic The New Stone Age; a prehistoric period beginning about 10,000 years ago in which peoples possessed stone-based technologies and depended on domesticated plants and/or animals for subsistence.

Neolithic revolution The domestication of plants and animals by peoples with stone-based technologies, beginning about 10,000 years ago and leading to radical transformations in cultural systems; sometimes referred to as the *Neolithic transition*.

horticulture The cultivation of crops in food gardens, carried out with simple hand tools such as digging sticks and hoes.

Figure 7.9 Bakhtiari Pastoralists In the Zagros Mountains region of Iran, pastoral nomads follow seasonal pastures, migrating vast distances with their huge herds of goats and sheep over rugged terrain that includes perilously steep, snowy passes and fast ice-cold rivers.

The Bakhtiari live in the political state of Iran but have their own traditional system of justice, including laws and a penal code. They are governed by tribal leaders, or *khans*, men who are elected or inherit their office. Most Bakhtiari *khans* grew wealthy when oil was discovered in their homeland around the start of the 20th century, and many of them are well educated, having attended Iranian or foreign universities.

Despite this, and although some of them own houses in cities, the *khans* spend much of their lives among their people in the mountains. Such prominence of men in both economic and political affairs is common among pastoral nomads; theirs is very much a man's world. That said, elderly Bakhtiari women eventually may gain a good deal of power. And some women of all ages today are gaining a measure of economic control by selling their beautiful handmade rugs to traders, which brings in cash to their households.

Although pastoral nomads like the Bakhtiari depend on their herds to meet their basic daily needs, they also trade surplus animals, leather, and wool (and various crafts such as woven rugs) with farmers or merchants. In exchange they receive crops and valued commodities such as flour, dried fruit, spices, tea, metal knives, pots and

kettles, cotton or linen textiles, guns, and (more recently) lightweight plastic containers, sheets, and so on. In other words, there are many ties that connect them to surrounding agricultural and industrial societies.

Intensive Agriculture: Urbanization and Peasantry

With the intensification of agriculture, some farming settlements grew into towns and even cities (**Figure 7.10**). Urbanization created greater complexity—labor specialization, the formation of elite groups, public management, taxation, and policing. For food and fuel, urbanized populations depended on what was produced or foraged in surrounding areas. Thus, the urban ruling class sought to widen its territorial power and political control over rural populations.

Once a powerful group managed to dominate a community of farmers, it also imposed its rules—forcing them to work harder and obliging them to make payments in farm produce or labor services as fees for land use and protection and/or as acknowledgment of submission. Burdened by taxes to feed those repressing them, these farmers were left with little for their own families and lost their independence. Subjected to an ever-more dominant group, they became **peasants**. These small-scale producers

peasant A small-scale producer of crops or livestock living on land self-owned or rented in exchange for labor, crops, or money and exploited by more powerful groups in a complex society.

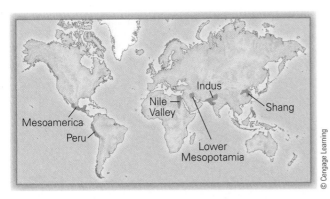

© Cengage Learning

Figure 7.10 Locations of Major Early Civilizations The Native civilizations of the western hemisphere developed wholly independently of those in Africa and Eurasia. Chinese civilizations may have developed independently of those that arose early in Mesopotamia, the Nile Valley, and the Indus Valley.

of crops or livestock live on land self-owned or rented in exchange for labor, crops, or money and are usually exploited by more powerful groups in a complex society (Wolf, 1966).

And so it continues in many parts of the world today. No matter how hard they work, peasants typically possess too little land of their own to go beyond meeting the most basic needs of their families. Unable to produce enough of a surplus to sell for cash, they rarely have capital to buy the laborsaving equipment that could increase their production. Most peasants remain stuck in poverty, struggling to make ends meet. Meanwhile, big landowners and wealthy merchants have the means to expand their holdings and to invest in new machinery that leads to increased productivity and profitability.

Industrial Food Production

Until about 200 years ago, human societies all across the world had developed cultural infrastructures based on foraging, horticulture, agriculture, or pastoralism. This changed with the invention of the steam engine in England, which brought about an industrial revolution that quickly spread to other parts of the globe. Replacing animal and human labor, as well as hand tools, new machines were invented, first powered by steam, then by biofuels (coal, gas, oil), sharply increasing factory production and boosting mass transportation. Throughout the 1800s and 1900s, this resulted in large-scale **industrial societies**. Technological inventions utilizing electricity and (since the 1940s) nuclear energy brought about more dramatic changes in social and economic organization on a worldwide scale.

Modern industrial technologies have transformed food production. In contrast to traditional farms and plantations, which historically depended on human labor (often forced) and on animal power in many places, modern agriculture depends on newly invented laborsaving

devices such as tractors, combines, milk machines, and so on. With large machines plowing, seeding, weeding, mowing, and harvesting crops, the need for farmhands and other rural workers is sharply diminished. This has also happened with livestock—in particular, hogs, cattle, and poultry.

Industrial food production may be defined as large-scale businesses involved in mass food production, processing, and marketing that primarily rely on laborsaving machines. It has had far-reaching economic, social, and political consequences, not all of which are readily recognized as related and intertwined. Today, large food-producing corporations own enormous tracts of land on which they mass-produce tons of mechanically harvested crops or raise huge numbers of meat animals. Crops and animals alike are harvested, processed, packed, and shipped with ever-greater efficiency to supermarkets to feed largely urban masses. Profits are considerable, especially for corporate owners and shareholders.

Although meat, poultry, and other agricultural products are relatively cheap and thus affordable, industrial food production by agribusiness has often been a disaster for millions of peasants and small farmers. Even medium-sized farms growing corn, wheat, or potatoes or raising cows, hogs, and chickens can rarely compete without government subsidies. For that reason, the number of family-owned farms in western Europe and North America has dramatically declined in the past few decades. This process has led to huge drops in many rural populations, decimating many farming communities.

For the family farms that have managed to survive, there is seldom enough income to cover the costs of a large household, including education, health care, farm and household insurance, and taxes. This situation forces individuals to seek money-earning opportunities elsewhere, often far away. Ironically, some hire on as cheap wage laborers in poultry- or meat-packing plants where working conditions are distasteful and often dangerous.

Maximizing profits, agribusinesses are constantly streamlining food production and seeking ways to reduce labor costs by trimming the number of workers, minimizing employee benefits, and driving down wages. Pushing for market expansion beyond regional or even national boundaries, the largest among them have gone global. In the United States, for example, the poultry industry, which requires vast quantities of corn and soy to feed the fast-growing roosters known as "broilers," now has

industrial society A society in which human labor, hand tools, and animal power are largely replaced by machines, with an economy primarily based on big factories.

industrial food production Large-scale businesses involved in mass food production, processing, and marketing, which primarily rely on labor-saving machines.

Challenge Issue

All humans face the challenge of securing resources needed for immediate and long-term survival. Whatever we lack, we may seek to get through exchange or trade. In today's capitalist societies, people can exchange almost anything of value without ever actually meeting in person. But the market in traditional societies is a real location where people personally meet to exchange goods at designated times. So it is at this market just outside Keren, a mountain city in Eritrea, a small country in northeastern Africa. Situated at a crossroads between the Red Sea and the vast desert in the interior, this strategically important city is an agricultural center surrounded by small farms. On Mondays, people gather here to purchase and peddle everything from spices and household utensils to fruits, vegetables, firewood, and roofing materials. On the outer edge of this sprawling market, turbaned farmers of the local Bilen tribe trade with nomadic herders of the region's Tigre tribe, buying or selling camels, cattle, sheep, goats, and mules. All around the world, at marketplaces like this one, people from different places forge and affirm social networks of friends, neighbors, and allies needed for their safety and well-being.

Economic Systems

An **economic system** is an organized arrangement for producing, distributing, and consuming goods. Because people, in pursuing a particular means of subsistence, necessarily produce, distribute, and consume things, our discussion of subsistence patterns in the previous chapter obviously involved economic matters. Yet economic systems encompass much more than we have covered so far.

Economic Anthropology

Although anthropologists have adopted theories and concepts from economists, theoretical principles derived from the study of capitalist market economies have limited applicability to economic systems in societies that are not industrialized and in which people do not produce and exchange goods for private profit. This is because, in these non-state societies, the economic sphere of behavior is not separate from the social, political, and religious spheres, and thus is not completely free to follow its own purely economic logic.

Although economic behavior and institutions can be analyzed in strictly economic terms, doing so ignores the crucial noneconomic considerations that impact the way things are in real life. To explain how the schedule of wants or demands of a given society is balanced against the supply of goods and services available, anthropologists introduce a noneconomic variable: culture. As a case in point, we may look briefly at yam production among the Trobriand Islanders, who inhabit a group of coral islands that lie in the southern Pacific Ocean off the eastern tip of New Guinea (Weiner, 1988).

Case Study: The Yam Complex in Trobriand Culture

Trobriand men spend a great deal of their time and energy raising yams—not for themselves or their own households, but to give to

economic system An organized arrangement for producing, distributing, and consuming goods.

IN THIS CHAPTER YOU WILL LEARN TO

- Explain why the anthropological variable of culture is important in understanding noncapitalist economies.

- Distinguish various economic arrangements for producing, distributing, and consuming goods.

- Compare forms of gift exchange, redistribution, and trade.

- Analyze how leveling mechanisms actually work in different cultures.

- Describe the role of money in market economies.

- Summarize the impact of global markets on local communities.

others, normally their sisters and married daughters. The purpose of cultivating these starchy edible roots is not to provision the households that receive them because most of what people eat they grow for themselves in gardens where they plant taro, sweet potatoes, tapioca, greens, beans, and squash, as well as breadfruit and banana trees. The reason a man gives yams to a woman is to show his support for her husband and to enhance his own influence.

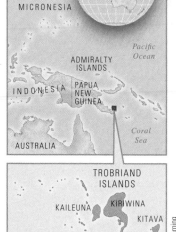

Once received by the woman, the gift yams are loaded into her husband's yam house, symbolizing his worth as a man of power and influence in his community (**Figure 8.1**). He may use some of these yams to purchase a variety of things, including arm shells, shell necklaces and earrings, betel nuts, pigs, chickens, and locally produced goods such as wooden bowls, combs, floor mats, lime pots, and even magic spells. He may use some yams to fulfill social obligations. For instance, a man is expected to present yams to the relatives of his daughter's husband when she marries and again when death befalls a member of the husband's family.

Finally, any man who aspires to high status and power is expected to show his worth by organizing a yam competition, during which he gives away huge quantities of yams to invited guests. As anthropologist Annette Weiner explains: "A yam house, then, is like a bank account; when full, a man is wealthy and powerful. Until yams are cooked or they rot, they may circulate as limited currency. That is why, once harvested, the usage of yams for daily food is avoided as much as possible" (Weiner, 1988, p. 86).

By giving yams to his sister or daughter, a man not only expresses his confidence in the woman's husband, but also makes the latter indebted to him. Although the recipient rewards the gardener and his helpers by throwing a feast, at which they are fed cooked yams, taro, and—what everyone especially looks forward to—ample pieces of pork, this in no way pays off the debt. The debt can be repaid only in women's wealth, which consists of bundles of banana leaves and skirts made of the same material dyed red.

Although the banana leaf bundles are of no utilitarian value, extensive labor is invested in their production, and large quantities of them, along with skirts, are regarded as essential for paying off all the members of other family

Figure 8.1 A Trobriand Yam Storage House Trobriand Island men devote a great deal of time and energy to raising yams, not for themselves but to give to others. These yams, which have been raised by men related through marriage to a chief, are about to be loaded into the chief's yam house.

groups who were close to a recently deceased relative in life and who assisted with the funeral. Also, the wealth and vitality of the dead person's family group are measured by the quality and quantity of the bundles and skirts so distributed.

Because a man has received yams from his wife's brother, he is obligated to provide his wife with yams for purchasing the necessary bundles and skirts, beyond those she has produced, to help with payments following the death of a member of her family. Because deaths are unpredictable and can occur at any time, a man must have yams available for his wife when she needs them. This, and the fact that she may require all of his yams, acts as an effective check on a man's wealth.

Like people the world over, the Trobriand Islanders assign meanings to objects that make those objects worth far more than their cost in labor or materials. Yams, for example, establish long-term relationships that lead to other advantages, such as access to land, protection, assistance, and other kinds of wealth.

Thus, yam exchanges are as much social and political transactions as they are economic ones. Banana leaf bundles and skirts, for their part, are symbolic of the political status of families and of their immortality. In their distribution, which is related to rituals associated with death, we see how men in Trobriand society are ultimately dependent on women and their valuables. Looked at in terms of modern capitalist economics, these activities appear meaningless, but viewed in terms of traditional Trobriand values and concerns, they make a great deal of sense.

Production and Its Resources

In every society, particular customs and rules govern the kinds of work done, who does the work, attitudes toward the work, how it is accomplished, and who controls the resources necessary to produce desired goods, knowledge, and services. The primary resources in any culture are raw materials, technology, and labor. The rules directing the use of these are embedded in a people's culture and determine the way the economy operates within any given natural environment.

Land and Water Resources

All societies regulate allocation of valuable natural resources—especially land and water. Food foragers must determine who will hunt game and gather plants in their home range and where these activities take place. Groups that rely on fishing or growing crops need to make similar decisions concerning who will carry out which task on which stretch of water or land. Farmers must have some means of determining title to land and access to water supplies for irrigation. Pastoralists require a system that determines rights to watering places and grazing land, as well as the right of access to land where they move their herds.

In Western capitalist societies, a system of private ownership of land and rights to natural resources generally prevails. Although elaborate laws have been enacted to regulate the buying, owning, and selling of land and water resources, if individuals wish to reallocate

© Cengage Learning

valuable farmland to some other purpose, for instance, they generally can.

In traditional nonindustrial societies, land is often controlled by kinship groups such as the family or band rather than by individuals. For example, among the Ju/'hoansi of the Kalahari Desert, each band of ten to thirty people lives on roughly 250 square miles of land, which they consider to be their territory—their own country. These territories are not defined by boundaries but in terms of waterholes that are located within them (**Figure 8.2**). The land is said to be owned by those who have lived the longest in the band, usually a group of brothers and sisters or cousins. Their concept of landholding, however, is not something easily translated into modern Western terms of private ownership. Within their traditional worldview, no part of their homeland can be sold for money or traded away for goods. Outsiders must ask permission to enter the territory, but denying the request would be unthinkable.

Territorial boundaries tend to be vaguely defined, and to avoid friction foragers may designate part of their territory as a buffer zone between them and their neighbors. The adaptive value of such a "no man's land" is obvious: The size of band territories, as well as the size of the bands, can adjust to keep in balance with availability of resources in any given place. Such adjustment would be more difficult under a system of individual ownership of clearly bounded land.

Among some African and Asian rural societies, a tributary system of land ownership prevails. All land is said to belong to the head chief, who allocates it to various subchiefs, who in turn distribute it to family groups. Then the family group leaders assign individual plots to each farmer. Just as in traditional Europe, these men owe allegiance to the subchiefs (or nobles) and the head chief (or king). The people who work the land must pay tribute (like rent or taxes) in the form of products or special services, such as fighting for the king when necessary.

These people do not really own the land; rather, it is a kind of lease. Yet, as long as the land is kept in use, rights to such use will pass to their heirs. No user, however, can give away, sell, or otherwise dispose of a plot of land without approval from the elder of the family group. When an individual no longer uses the allocated land, it reverts to the head of the large family group, who reallocates it to some other group member. The important operative principle here is that the system extends the individual's right to use land for an indefinite period, but the land is not "owned" outright. This serves to maintain the integrity of valuable farmland as such, preventing its loss through subdivision and conversion to other uses.

Technology Resources

All societies have some means of creating and allocating tools that are used to produce goods, as well as traditions for passing them on to succeeding generations. A society's

© Irven DeVore/Anthro-Photo

Figure 8.2 Core Features as Territory Markers Food foragers, like the Ju/'hoansi of the Kalahari Desert in southern Africa, define their territories on the basis of core features such as waterholes.

technology—the number and types of tools employed, combined with knowledge about how to make and use them—is directly related to the lifestyles of its members. Food foragers and pastoral nomads who are frequently on the move are apt to have fewer and more portable tools than more settled peoples such as sedentary farmers. Thus, the average weight of an individual's personal belongings among the Ju/'hoansi is just under 25 pounds, limited to the barest essentials such as implements for hunting, gathering, fishing, building, and cooking. Pastoral nomads, aided by pack animals, typically have more material possessions than foragers, but still fewer than people who live in permanent settlements.

Food foragers make and use a variety of tools, many ingenious in their effectiveness. Some of these they make for their individual use, but codes of generosity are such that a person may not refuse to give or loan what is requested. Tools may be given or loaned to others in exchange for the products resulting from their use. For

example, a Ju/'hoansi who gives his arrows to another hunter has a right to a share of any animals the hunter kills. Game is considered to belong to the man whose arrow killed it, even when he is not present on the hunt. In this context, it makes little sense for them to accumulate luxuries or surplus goods, and the fact that no one owns significantly more than another helps to limit status differences.

Among horticulturalists, the axe, digging stick, hoe, and containers are important tools. The person who makes a tool has first rights to it, but when he or she is not using it, any family member may ask to use it, and the request is rarely denied. Refusal would cause people to treat the tool owner with scorn for this singular lack of concern for others. If a relative helps raise the crop traded for a particular tool, that relative becomes part owner of the implement, and it may not be traded or given away without his or her permission.

In permanently settled agricultural communities, tools and other productive goods are more complex, heavier, and costlier to make. In such settings, individual ownership tends to be more absolute, as are the conditions under which people may borrow and use such equipment. It is

technology Tools and other material equipment, together with the knowledge of how to make and use them.

easy to replace a knife lost by a relative during palm cultivation but much more difficult to replace an iron plow or a diesel-fueled harvesting machine. Rights to the ownership of complex tools are more rigidly applied; generally, the person who has manufactured or purchased such equipment is considered the sole owner and decides who may use it and under which conditions, including compensation.

Labor Resources and Patterns

In addition to raw materials and technology, labor is a key resource in any economic system. A look around the world reveals many different labor patterns, but two features are almost always present in human cultures: a basic division of labor by gender and by age.

Division of Labor by Gender

Anthropologists have studied extensively the social division of labor by gender in cultures of all sorts. Whether men or women do a particular job varies from group to group, but typically work has been and often continues to be divided into the tasks of either one or the other. For example, the practices most commonly regarded as women's work have tended to be those that can be carried out near home and that are easily resumed after interruption. The tasks historically regarded as men's work have tended to be those requiring physical strength, rapid mobilization of high bursts of energy, frequent travel at some distance from home, and assumption of high levels of risk and danger.

Figure 8.3 Women's Work? These Hmong women in Vietnam are carrying heavy firewood, even though this work may be considered inappropriate for women in some cultures. For villagers living in the rural areas of developing countries all around the world, firewood is used as a source of energy for preparing meals—and women are usually the ones who collect and haul it.

Many exceptions occur, however, as in societies where women regularly carry burdensome loads or put in long hours of hard work cultivating crops in the fields (**Figure 8.3**). In some societies, women perform almost three-fourths of all work, and in several societies they have served as warriors. For example, in the 19th-century West African kingdom of Dahomey (now called Benin), thousands of women served in the armed forces of the Dahomean king, and some considered the women to be better fighters than their male counterparts. Also, there are references to female warriors in ancient Ireland, and archaeological evidence indicates their presence among Vikings.

During World War II in the early 1940s, some 58,000 Soviet Russian women engaged in frontline combat defending their homeland against German invaders, and during the Vietnam War in the 1960s and early 1970s, North Vietnamese women fought in mixed-gender communist army units. Today, women serve in the military of most countries, but only Canada, Denmark, France, Germany, and a few others permit them to join combat units.

Instead of looking for key biological factors to explain the social division of labor, a more useful strategy is to examine the kinds of work that men and women do in the context of specific societies to see how they relate to other cultural and historical factors. Researchers find a continuum of patterns, ranging from flexible integration of men and women to rigid segregation by gender (Sanday,1981).

The *flexible/integrated pattern* is exemplified by the Ju/'hoansi we just discussed and is seen most often among food foragers (as well as in communities in which crops are traditionally cultivated primarily for family consumption). In such societies, men and women perform up to 35 percent of activities with approximately equal participation, and tasks deemed especially appropriate for one gender may be performed by the other without loss of face, as the situation warrants. Where these practices prevail, boys and girls grow up in much the same way, learn to value cooperation over competition, and become equally habituated to adult men and women, who interact with one another on a relatively equal basis.

Societies following a *segregated pattern* define almost all work as either masculine or feminine, so men and women rarely engage in joint efforts of any kind. In such societies, it is inconceivable that someone would even think of doing something considered the work of the opposite sex. This pattern is frequently seen in pastoral nomadic, intensive agricultural, and industrial societies, where men's work keeps them outside the home for much of the time. Typically, men in such societies are expected to be tough, aggressive, and competitive—and this often involves assertions of male superiority, and hence authority, over women. Historically, societies segregated by gender often have imposed their control on societies featuring integration, upsetting the egalitarian nature of the latter.

In the third pattern of labor division by gender, sometimes called the *dual sex configuration*, men and women carry out their work separately, as in societies segregated by gender, but the relationship between them is one of balanced complementarity rather than inequality. Although each gender manages its own affairs, the interests of both men and women are represented at all levels. Thus, as in integrated societies, neither gender exerts dominance over the other. The pattern may be seen among certain American Indian peoples with economies based upon subsistence farming, as well as among several West African kingdoms, including that of the aforementioned Dahomeans.

In postindustrial societies, the division of labor by gender becomes blurred and even irrelevant, resembling the flexible/integrated pattern of traditional foragers briefly discussed previously. Although gender preferences and discrimination in the workplace exist in societies making the economic transition, cultural ideas more fitting agricultural or industrial societies predictably change in due time, adjusting to postindustrial challenges and opportunities.

Division of Labor by Age

Division of labor according to age is also typical of human societies. Among the Ju/'hoansi, for example, children are not expected to contribute significantly to subsistence until they reach their late teens. Indeed, until they possess adult levels of strength and endurance, many "bush" foods are tough for them to gather. Until that point, youngsters contribute primarily by taking care of their littlest siblings while grownups deal with subsistence needs.

Although elderly Ju/'hoansi will usually do some foraging for themselves, they are not expected to contribute much food. By virtue of their advanced age, they have memories of customary practices and events that happened far in the past. Thus, they are repositories of accumulated wisdom—the libraries of a nonliterate people—and are able to suggest solutions to problems younger adults have never before had to face. Considered useful for their knowledge, they are far from being unproductive members of society.

In some food-foraging societies, women do continue to make a significant contribution to provisioning in their later years. Among the Hadza of East Africa, the input of older women is critical to their daughters when they have new infants to nurse. The energy costs of lactation, along with the tasks of holding, carrying, and nursing an infant, all encumber the mother's foraging efficiency. Those most immediately affected by this are a woman's weaned children not yet old enough to forage effectively for themselves. The problem is solved by the foraging efforts of grandmothers (Hawkes, O'Connell, & Blurton Jones, 1997).

In many traditional farming societies, children as well as older people may make a greater contribution to the economy in terms of work and responsibility than is common in industrial or postindustrial societies. In most peasant communities across the globe, children not only look after their younger brothers and sisters but also help with housework, in the barn, or in the fields. By age 7 or so, boys begin to help out, weed the fields, bring in crops, care for small animals, or catch some fish and small game. By that same age, girls begin contributing to the work of the household. Soon, they are constantly busy with an array of chores—helping prepare food, fetching wood and water, sweeping, selling goods at local markets, and so forth (Vogt, 1990).

Children also work in many industrial societies, where poor and often large families depend on every possible contribution to the household. There, however, economic necessity may easily lead to the exploitation of children as cheap labor on farms, in mines, and in factories. Child

Bachpan Bachao Andolan

Figure 8.4 Child Labor in India Many of the soccer balls that children play with in the United States and Europe are handstitched by children in India, most working in factories under brutal conditions for pennies a day. After past scandals about soccer ball factories using child labor, many companies started adding labels stating that the balls were not made with child labor—but those labels are often sewn on the balls by children as young as 6 years old.

labor has become a matter of increasing concern as large capitalist corporations rely more and more on the low-cost production of food and goods in the world's poorer countries. Today, some 215 million child laborers (under age 14) are at work, almost all in developing economies where their families depend on the extra income they bring home. Many enter the labor force when they are only 6 or 7 years old, working full-time, from dawn to dusk, for extremely low wages ("New ILO global report on child labor," 2010) (Figure 8.4).

Many wealthy industrialized societies in Europe and North America long ago passed laws officially prohibiting institutionalized child labor. However, they still import vast quantities of goods available at bargain prices because they are made by poorly paid children—items ranging from rugs and carpets to clothing, toys, and soccer balls (Smith, 2008).

Cooperative Labor

Cooperative work groups can be found everywhere—in foraging as well as food-producing and in nonindustrial as well as industrial societies. Often, if the effort involves the whole community, a festive spirit permeates the work.

For example, in many rural parts of sub-Saharan Africa, work parties begin with the display of a pot of beer to be consumed after the tasks have been finished. Home-brewed from millet, their major cereal crop, the beer is not really payment for the work; indeed, the labor involved is worth far more than the beer consumed. Rather, together enjoying the low-alcohol but highly nutritious beverage is more of a symbolic activity to celebrate the spirit of friendship and mutual support. Recompense comes as individuals sooner or later participate in work parties for others. In areas all around the world, farmers traditionally help one another during harvest and haying seasons, often sharing major pieces of equipment.

In most human societies, the basic unit within which work takes place is the household. Traditionally—and still in many parts of the world—it is both a unit of production and consumption, where work as well as meals and domestic comfort are shared. In industrial societies these two economic spheres are now usually separated. This development is the result, in part, of task specialization.

Task Specialization

In contemporary industrial and postindustrial societies, there is a great diversity of specialized tasks to be performed, and no individual can even begin to know all of those customarily seen as fitting for his or her age and gender. However, although specialization continues to increase, modern technologies are making labor divisions based on gender less relevant. By contrast, in small-scale foraging and traditional crop-cultivating societies, in which division of labor typically occurs along lines of age and gender, each person has knowledge and competence in all aspects of work appropriate to his or her age and gender. Yet, even in these nonindustrial societies there is a measure of specialization.

An example of task specialization can be found among the Afar people of the Danakil Depression in the borderlands of Eritrea and Ethiopia, one of the lowest and hottest places on earth (Nesbitt, 1935). The desolate landscape features sulfur fields, smoking fissures, volcanic tremors, and vast salt plains. Since ancient times, groups of Afar men periodically mine the salt, hacking blocks from the plain's crust. The work is backbreaking, all the more so with temperatures soaring to 140 degrees Fahrenheit.

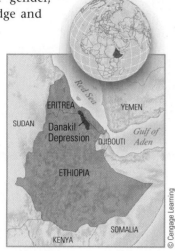

Along with the physical strength required for such work under the most trying conditions, successful mining demands specialized planning and organization skills for getting to and from the worksite. Pack camels have to be fed in advance because importing sufficient fodder for them interferes with their ability to carry out salt (**Figure 8.5**). Food and water, packed by Afar women at the desert's edge, must be carried in for the miners, typically numbering thirty to forty per group. Travel is arranged for nighttime to avoid the scorching sun (Mesghinna, 1966; O'Mahoney, 1970).

In the past few decades, we have seen the emergence of new forms of task specialization in an international division of labor and in response to global markets of supply and demand. Many of these specializations are linked to tourism, now one of the largest industries in the world. Estimates vary, but in 2011 the industry employed some 260 million people and generated about $6 trillion—9 percent of the total value of goods and services produced worldwide (World Travel & Tourism Council, 2012). Some communities that still hold onto a natural habitat with a wealth of plant and animal life are able to tap into a specialized niche known as *ecotourism*, as detailed in this chapter's Anthropology Applied feature.

Figure 8.5 Task Specialization: Mining Salt in Ethiopia Scorching hot and dry, the Danakil Desert in northeastern Africa lies some 370 feet below sea level—remains of what was once part of the Red Sea—with enormous salt flats. Afar nomads come here periodically to quarry this rock salt. Using camels, they haul the heavy slabs to the interior highlands for trade.

ANTHROPOLOGY APPLIED

Global Ecotourism and Local Indigenous Culture in Bolivia

By Amanda Stronza

We traveled in a small fleet of motorized canoes. As the sun dipped behind the trees one steamy afternoon in April 2002, we turned the last few bends of the Tuichi River and arrived at our destination, the Chalalán Ecolodge of northern Bolivia. Our group included eighteen indigenous leaders from various parts of the Amazon rainforest, a handful of regional tour operators, conservationists, environmental journalists, and me—an applied anthropologist studying the effects of ecotourism on local livelihoods, cultural traditions, and resource use. We had been navigating for nine hours through lowland rainforest to visit one of the first indigenous, community-run ecotourism lodges in the world.

As we wended our way, combing the riverbanks for caimans, capybaras, tapirs, and jaguars, our conversations meandered too. Mostly, the indigenous leaders shared stories of how ecotourism had affected their own forests and communities. They spoke of tourists who brought both opportunities and conflicts, and of their own efforts to balance conservation and development. They compared notes on wildlife in their regions, the kinds of visitors they had attracted, the profits they'd earned, the new skills they had gained, and the challenges they were facing as they sought to protect their lands and cultural traditions while

also engaging with the global tourism industry.

Having studied ecotourism in the Amazon since 1993, I felt honored to be on board participating in these discussions. With support from the Critical Ecosystem Partnership Fund, I had the opportunity that year—the International Year of Ecotourism—to assemble leaders from three indigenous ecotourism projects in South America. All three were partnerships between local communities and private tour companies or nongovernmental organizations. For example, the lodge we were visiting, Chalalán, came about through a partnership between the Quechua-Tacana community of San José de Uchupiamonas, Bolivia, and two global organizations, Conservation International and the Inter-American Development Bank. Much of the $1,450,000 invested in Chalalán went toward preparing community members to assume full ownership and management of the lodge within five years. After a successful transfer in 2001, the lodge now belonged to San José's 600-member Quechua-Tacana community.

The indigenous leaders who gathered for this trip had keen, firsthand knowledge about the costs and benefits ecotourism can bring. They were former hunters, now leading tourists as birding and wildlife guides; small farmers and artisans making traditional handicrafts to sell to visitors; river-savvy fishermen supplementing their incomes by driving tour boats; and local leaders whose intimate knowledge of their communities helped them manage their own tour companies. Among them was Chalalán's general manager Guido Mamani, who recounted the benefits Chalalán had brought to the Tacana of San José. "Ten years ago," he recalled, "people were leaving San José because there were few ways to make a living. Today, they are returning because of pride in the success of Chalalán. Now, they

see opportunity here." As a result of their renewed pride in their mix of Quechua and Tacana histories, the community has begun hosting tourists for cultural tours in San José. "We want to give tourists presentations about the community and our customs," Mamani explained, "including our legends, dances, traditional music, the coca leaves, the traditional meals. We want to show our culture through special walks focusing on medicinal and other useful plants."

Mamani and the other indigenous ecotourism leaders characterized the success of their lodges in three ways: economic, social, and environmental. Chalalán, for example, counted its economic success in terms of employment and new income. It directly employs eighteen to twenty-four people at a time, and additional families supply farm produce and native fruits to the lodge. With artisans selling handicrafts to tourists, the community has gained regional fame for its wooden carved masks. The social benefits of Chalalán include new resources for education, health care, and communication. With their profits from tourism, the community built a school, a clinic, and a potable water system. They also purchased an antenna, solar panels, and a satellite dish to connect with the world from their remote forests along the Tuichi River.

Beyond these sorts of material improvements, ecotourism has catalyzed symbolic changes for the people of San José. "We have new solidarity in our cultural traditions," one woman noted, "and now we want to show who we are to the outside world." These experiences of Chalalán and similar projects suggest that ecotourism may be more than just a conservation and development idea—it may also be a source of pride, empowerment, and strengthened cultural identity among indigenous peoples.

Written expressly for this text, 2011.

Distribution and Exchange

In societies without a money economy, the rewards for labor are usually direct. The workers in a family group consume what they harvest, eat what the hunter or gatherer brings home, and use the tools they themselves make. But even where no formal medium of exchange such as money exists, some distribution of goods takes place. Anthropologists often classify the cultural systems of distributing material goods into three modes: reciprocity, redistribution, and market exchange (Polanyi, 1968).

Reciprocity

Reciprocity refers to the exchange of goods and services, of roughly equal value, between two parties. This may involve gift giving. Notably, individuals or groups in most cultures like to think that the main point of the transaction is the gift itself, yet what actually matters are the social ties that are created or reinforced between givers and receivers. Because reciprocity is about a relationship between the self and others, gift giving is seldom really selfless. The overriding, if unconscious, motives of gift giving are to establish or reaffirm a social relationship, fulfill social obligations, and perhaps gain a bit of prestige in the process.

Cultural traditions dictate the specific manner and occasion of exchange. For example, when indigenous hunters in Australia kill a kangaroo, the meat is divided among the hunters' families and other relatives. Each person in the camp gets a particular share, the size and part depending on the nature of the person's kinship tie to the hunters.

Such obligatory sharing of food reinforces community bonds and ensures that everyone eats. By giving away part of a kill, the hunters get social credit for a similar amount of food in the future.

Reciprocity falls into several categories. The Australian food distribution example just noted constitutes an example of **generalized reciprocity**—exchange in which the value of what is given is not calculated, nor is the time of repayment specified (**Figure 8.6**). Gift giving, in the unselfish sense, also falls into this category. So, too, does the act of a kindhearted soul who stops to help a stranded motorist or someone else in distress and refuses payment with the admonition: "Pass it on to the next person in need."

Most generalized reciprocity, however, occurs among close kin or people who otherwise have very close ties with one another. Within such circles of intimacy, people give to others when they have the means and can count on receiving from others in time of need. Typically, participants will not consider such exchanges in economic terms but will couch them explicitly in terms of family and friendship social relations.

Exchanges that occur within a group of relatives or between friends generally take the form of generalized or balanced reciprocity. In **balanced reciprocity**, the giving and receiving, as well as the time involved, are quite specific: Someone has a direct obligation to reciprocate promptly in equal value in order for the social relationship to continue. Examples of balanced reciprocity in contemporary North American society include customary practices such as hosting a baby shower for young friends expecting their first baby, giving presents at birthdays and various other culturally prescribed special occasions,

Figure 8.6
Generalized Reciprocity among the Ju/'hoansi These Ju/'hoansi men are cutting up meat that will be shared by others in the camp. Food distribution practices of such food foragers are an example of generalized reciprocity.

© Stan Washburn/Anthro-Photo

and buying drinks when it is one's turn at a gathering of friends and associates.

Giving, receiving, and sharing as so far described constitute a form of social security or insurance. A family contributes to others when they have the means and can count on receiving from others in time of need.

Negative reciprocity is a third form of exchange, in which the aim is to get something for as little as possible. The parties involved have opposing interests and are not usually closely related; they may be strangers or even enemies. Often such exchanges are neither fair nor balanced, and they are not expected to be. This type of reciprocity may involve hard bargaining, manipulation, or outright cheating. An extreme form of negative reciprocity is to take something by force, although realizing that one's victim may seek compensation or retribution for losses.

Sometimes elements of negative as well as balanced reciprocity are present in an exchange. Such is often the case with political fundraising in the United States, in which big contributors expect their generosity will buy influence with a candidate, resulting in benefits of equal value. The politician may seek to do as little as possible in return, but not so little as to jeopardize future donations. Those who accept too much or who give too much in return risk legal repercussions.

Trade and Barter

Trade refers to a transaction in which two or more people are involved in an exchange of something—a quantity of food, fuel, clothing, jewelry, animals, or money, for example—for something else of equal value. In such a transaction, the value of the trade goods can be fixed by previous agreements or negotiated on the spot by the trading partners.

When there is no money involved and the parties negotiate a direct exchange of one trade good for another, the transaction is considered a *barter*. In barter, arguing about the price and terms of the deal may well be in the form of negative reciprocity, with each party aiming to get the better end of the deal. Relative value is calculated, and despite an outward show of indifference, sharp dealing is generally the rule, when compared to the more balanced nature of exchanges within a group.

One interesting mechanism for facilitating exchange between potentially adversarial groups is **silent trade** in which no verbal communication takes place. In fact, it may involve no actual face-to-face contact at all. Such cases have often characterized the dealings between food-foraging peoples and their food-producing neighbors—such as the Mbuti Pygmy of Congo's Ituri forest, who trade bushmeat for plantains and other crops grown by Bantu villagers on small farms. It works like this: People from the forest leave trade goods in a clearing, then retreat and wait. Agriculturalists come to the spot, survey the goods, leave what they think is a fair exchange of their own wares, and then leave. The forest people return, and if satisfied with the offer, take it with them. If not, they leave it untouched, signifying that they expect more. In this way, for 2,000 or so years, foragers have supplied various commodities in demand to a wider economy (Turnbull, 1961; Wilkie & Curran, 1993).

Silent trade may occur due to lack of a common language. A more probable explanation is that it helps control situations of distrust and potential conflict—maintaining peace by preventing direct contact. Another possibility that does not exclude the others is that it makes exchange possible when problems of status might make verbal communication unthinkable. In any event, silent trade provides for the exchange of goods between groups despite potential barriers.

Kula Ring: Gift Giving and Trading in the South Pacific

Balanced reciprocity can take more complicated forms, whereby mutual gift giving serves to facilitate social interaction, smoothing relations between traders wanting to do business. One classic ethnographic example of balanced reciprocity between trading partners seeking to be friends and do business at the same time is the **Kula ring** in the southwestern Pacific Ocean. This practice was first described by anthropologist Bronislaw Malinowski and involves thousands of seafarers going to great lengths to establish and maintain good trade relations; this centuries-old ceremonial exchange system continues to this day (Malinowski, 1961; Weiner, 1988).

Kula participants are men of influence who travel to islands within the Trobriand ring to exchange prestige items—red shell necklaces (*soulava*), which are circulated around the ring of islands in a clockwise direction, and white shell armbands (*mwali*), which are carried in the opposite direction (**Figure 8.7**). Each man in the Kula is linked to partners on the islands that neighbor his own. To a partner residing on an island in the clockwise direction, he offers a *soulava* and receives in return a *mwali*. He makes the reverse exchange of a *mwali* for a *soulava* to a partner living in the counterclockwise direction. Each of these trade partners eventually passes on the object to a Kula partner farther along the chain of islands.

---

reciprocity The exchange of goods and services, of approximately equal value, between two parties.

generalized reciprocity A mode of exchange in which the value of the gift is not calculated, nor is the time of repayment specified.

balanced reciprocity A mode of exchange in which the giving and the receiving are specific as to the value of the goods or services and the time of their delivery.

negative reciprocity A mode of exchange in which the aim is to get something for as little as possible. Neither fair nor balanced, it may involve hard bargaining, manipulation, outright cheating, or theft.

silent trade Exchange of goods between mutually distrusting ethnic groups so as to avoid direct personal contact.

Kula ring A mode of balanced reciprocity that reinforces trade and social relations among the seafaring Melanesians who inhabit a large ring of islands in the southwestern Pacific Ocean.

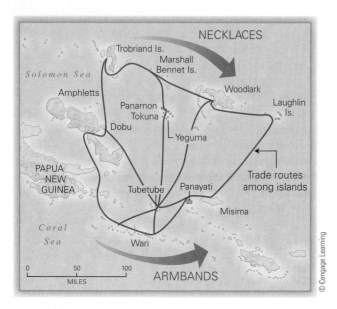

Figure 8.7 Kula Ring The ceremonial gift exchanges of shell necklaces and armbands in the Kula ring encourage trade and barter throughout the Melanesian islands.

Soulava and *mwali* are ranked according to their size, their color, how finely they are polished, and their particular histories. Some of them are so famous that they create a sensation when they appear in a village.

Traditionally, men make their Kula journeys in elaborately carved dugout canoes, sailing and paddling these boats, which are 6 to 7.5 meters (20 to 25 feet) long, across open waters to shores some 100 kilometers (about 60 miles) or more away (**Figure 8.8**). The adventure is often dangerous and may take men away from their homes for several weeks, sometimes even months. Although men on Kula voyages may use the opportunity to trade for practical goods, acquiring such items is not always the reason for these voyages—nor is Kula exchange a necessary part of regular trade expeditions.

Perhaps the best way to view the Kula is as an indigenous insurance policy in an economy fraught with danger and uncertainty. It establishes and reinforces social partnerships among traders doing business on distant shores, ensuring a welcome reception from people who have similar vested interests. This ceremonial exchange

Figure 8.8 Kula Boat In Melanesia, men of influence paddle and sail within a large ring of islands in the southwestern Pacific off the eastern coast of Papua New Guinea to participate in the ceremonial trading of Kula shells, which smoothes trade relations and builds personal prestige.

network does more than simply enhance the trade of foods and other goods essential for survival. Melanesians participating in the Kula ring have no doubt that their social position has to do with the company they keep, the circles in which they move. They derive their social prestige from the reputations of their partners and the valuables that they circulate. By giving and receiving armbands and necklaces that accumulate the histories of their travels and the names of those who have possessed them, men proclaim their individual fame and talent, gaining considerable influence for themselves in the process.

Like other forms of currency, *soulava* and *mwali* must flow from hand to hand; once they stop flowing, they may lose their value. A man who takes these valuables out of their interisland circuit invites criticism. Not only might he lose prestige or social capital as a man of influence, but he might become a target of sorcery for unraveling the cultural fabric that holds the islands together as a functioning social and economic order.

As this example from the South Pacific illustrates, the potential tension between trading partners may be resolved or lessened by participation in a ritual of balanced reciprocity. As an elaborate complex of ceremony, political relationships, economic exchange, travel, magic, and social integration, the Kula ring illustrates the inseparability of economic matters from the rest of culture. Although perhaps difficult to recognize, this is just as true in modern industrial societies as it is in traditional Trobriand society—as is evident when heads of state engage in ceremonial gift exchanges at official visits.

Redistribution

Redistribution is a form of exchange in which goods flow into a central place where they are sorted, counted, and reallocated. In societies with a sufficient surplus to support some sort of government, goods in the form of gifts, tribute, taxes, and the spoils of war are gathered into storehouses controlled by a chief or some other leader. From there they are handed out again. The leadership has three motives in redistributing this income: The first is to gain or maintain a position of power through a display of wealth and generosity; the second is to assure those who support the leadership an adequate standard of living by providing them with desired goods; and the third is to establish alliances with leaders of other groups by hosting them at lavish parties and giving them valuable goods.

The redistribution system of the ancient Inca empire in the Andean highlands of South America was one of the most efficient the world has ever known, both in the collection of tribute (obligatory contributions or gifts in the form of crops, goods, and services) and in its methods of administrative control (Mason, 1957). Administrators kept inventories of resources and a census of the population, which at its peak reached 6 million. Each craft specialist had to produce a specific quota of goods from materials supplied by overseers. Required labor was used for some agricultural and mining work. Unpaid labor was also used in a program of public works that included a remarkable system of roads and bridges throughout the mountainous terrain, aqueducts that guaranteed a supply of water, temples for worship, and storehouses that held surplus food for times of famine.

Careful accounts were kept of income and expenditures. A central administration, regulated by the Inca emperor and his relatives, had the responsibility for ensuring that production was maintained and that commodities were distributed. Holding power over this command economy, the ruling elite lived in great luxury, but sufficient goods were redistributed to the common people to ensure that no one would be left in dire need or face the indignity of pauperism.

Taxes imposed by central governments of countries all around the world today are one form of redistribution—required payments typically based on a percentage of one's income and property value. Typically, a portion of the taxes goes toward supporting the government itself whereas the rest is redistributed either in cash (such as welfare payments and government loans or subsidies to businesses) or in the form of services (such as military defense, law enforcement, food and drug inspection, schools, highway construction, and the like). Tax codes vary greatly among countries. In many European countries, wealthy citizens are taxed at a considerably higher percentage of their income than are U.S. citizens.

Spending Wealth to Gain Prestige

In societies where people devote most of their time to subsistence activities, gradations of wealth are small, kept that way through various cultural mechanisms and systems of reciprocity that serve to spread quite fairly what little wealth exists.

It is a different situation in ranked societies where substantial surpluses are produced, and the gap between the have-nots and the have-lots can be considerable. In these societies, showy display for social prestige—known as **conspicuous consumption**—is a strong motivator for the distribution of wealth. In industrial and postindustrial societies, excessive efforts to impress others with one's wealth or status play a prominent role. The display of symbolic prestige items particular to these societies—designer clothes, expensive jewelry, mansions, luxury cars, private planes—fits neatly into an economy based on consumer wants.

---

redistribution A mode of exchange in which goods flow into a central place, where they are sorted, counted, and reallocated.

conspicuous consumption A showy display of wealth for social prestige.

Figure 8.9 Potlatch Today Among Native Americans living along the Pacific Northwest coast of North America, one gains prestige by giving away valuables at the potlatch feast. Here we see Tlingit clan members dressed in traditional Chilkat and Raven's Tail robes during a recent potlatch in Sitka, Alaska.

A form of conspicuous consumption also occurs in some crop-cultivating and foraging societies. Various American Indian groups living along the Pacific Northwest coast—including the Tlingit, Haida, and Kwakwaka'wakw (Kwakiutl)—illustrate this through potlatches. A **potlatch** is a ceremonial event in which a village chief publicly gives away stockpiled food and other goods that signify wealth (**Figure 8.9**). (The term comes from the Chinook Indian word *patshatl*, which means "gift.")

Traditionally, a chief whose village had built up enough surplus to host such a feast for other villages in the region would give away large piles of sea otter furs, dried salmon, blankets, and other valuables while making boastful speeches about his generosity, greatness, and glorious ancestors. While other chiefs became indebted to him, he reaped the glory of successful and generous leadership and saw his prestige rise. In the future, his own

village might face shortages, and he would find himself on the receiving end of a potlatch. Should that happen, he would have to listen to the self-serving and pompous speeches of rival chiefs. Obliged to receive, he would temporarily lose prestige and status.

In extreme displays of wealth, chiefs even destroyed some of their precious possessions. This occurred with some frequency in the second half of the 19th century, after European contact triggered a process of cultural change that included new trade wealth. Outsiders might view such grandiose displays as wasteful to the extreme. However, these extravagant giveaway ceremonies have played an ecologically adaptive role in a coastal region where villages alternately faced periods of scarcity and abundance and relied upon alliances and trade relations with one another for long-term survival. The potlatch provided a ceremonial opportunity to strategically redistribute surplus food and goods among allied villages in response to periodic fluctuations in fortune.

A strategy that features this sort of accumulation of surplus goods for the express purpose of displaying wealth and giving it away to raise one's status is known

potlatch On the northwestern coast of North America, an indigenous ceremonial event in which a village chief publicly gives away stockpiled food and other goods that signify wealth.

as a **prestige economy.** In contrast to conspicuous consumption in industrial and postindustrial societies, the emphasis is not on amassing goods that then become unavailable to others. Instead, it is on gaining wealth in order to give it away for the sake of prestige and status.

Leveling Mechanisms

The potlatch is an example of a **leveling mechanism**— a cultural obligation compelling prosperous members of a community to give away goods, host public feasts, provide free service, or otherwise demonstrate generosity so that no one permanently accumulates significantly more wealth than anyone else. With leveling mechanisms at work, greater wealth brings greater social pressure to spend and give generously. In exchange for such demonstrated altruism, a person not only increases his or her social standing in the community, but may also keep disruptive envy at bay.

Underscoring the value of collective well-being over individual self-interest, leveling mechanisms are important for the long-term survival of traditional communities. The potlatch is just one example of many cultural varieties of leveling mechanism. By pressuring members into sharing their wealth in their own community rather than hoarding it or privately investing it elsewhere, leveling mechanisms do more than keep resources in circulation. They also reduce social tensions among relatives, neighbors, and others in the community, promoting a collective sense of togetherness. An added practical benefit is that they ensure that necessary services within the society are performed.

Market Exchange

To an economist, **market exchange** has to do with the buying and selling of goods and services, with prices set by rules of supply and demand. Personal loyalties and moral values are not supposed to play a role, but they often do. Because the actual location of the transaction is not always relevant in today's world, we must distinguish between the *marketplace* and *market exchange.*

Marketplace and Market Exchange

Typically, until well into the 20th century, market exchange was carried out in specific localities or *marketplaces.* This is still the case in much of the nonindustrial world and even in numerous centuries-old European and Asian towns and cities. In food-producing societies, marketplaces overseen by a centralized political authority provide the opportunity for farmers, pastoralists, or peasants in the surrounding rural territories to exchange some of their livestock and produce for needed items manufactured in factories or in the workshops of craft specialists

living (usually) in towns and cities. Thus, markets require some sort of complex division of labor as well as centralized political organization.

The traditional market is local, specific, and contained— like the one pictured at the beginning of this chapter. Prices are typically set on the basis of face-to-face bargaining rather than by unseen forces wholly removed from the transaction itself. Notably, sales do not necessarily involve money; instead, goods may be directly exchanged through some form of barter among the specific individuals involved.

In industrializing and industrial societies, many market transactions still take place in a specific identifiable location—including international trade fairs such as the mammoth semiannual Canton Trade Fair in Guangzhou, China. In the spring of 2012, 24,000 Chinese enterprises participated in the event, along with 520 companies from 44 foreign countries. Combined, they offered more than 150,000 products and generated more than $36 million in sales among 210,000 buyers from 213 countries ("111th Canton Fair," 2012).

It is increasingly common for people living in technologically wired parts of the world to buy and sell everything from cattle to cars without ever being in the same city, let alone the same space. For example, think of Internet companies such as eBay and Craigslist on which all buying and selling occur electronically and irrespective of geographic distance. When people talk about a market in today's industrial or postindustrial world, the particular geographic location where something is bought or sold is often not important at all.

The faceless market exchanges that take place in industrial and postindustrial societies stand in stark contrast to experiences in the marketplaces of nonindustrial societies, which involve much of the excitement of a fair. Traditional exchange centers are colorful places where a host of sights, sounds, and smells awaken the senses. Typically, vendors and/or their family members produced the goods they are selling, thereby personalizing the transactions. Dancers and musicians may perform, and feasting and fighting may mark the end of the day. In these markets social relationships and personal interactions are key elements, and noneconomic activities may overshadow economic ones. In short, such markets are gathering places where people renew friendships, see

prestige economy The creation of a surplus for the express purpose of displaying wealth and giving it away to raise one's status.

leveling mechanism A cultural obligation compelling prosperous members of a community to give away goods, host public feasts, provide free service, or otherwise demonstrate generosity so that no one permanently accumulates significantly more wealth than anyone else.

market exchange The buying and selling of goods and services, with prices set by rules of supply and demand.

VISUAL COUNTERPOINT

Figure 8.10 **Going to Market** In many societies, particularly in developing countries, the market is an important focus of social as well as economic activity, as shown in the photo on the right of a crowded outdoor marketplace in Aswan, Egypt. In contrast, the packer pictured on the left works at an Amazon.com distribution center in Fernley, Nevada, preparing orders purchased on the Internet. With online shopping, people buy and sell with no social interaction whatsoever.

relatives, gossip, and keep up with the world, while procuring needed goods they cannot produce for themselves (Plattner, 1989) (**Figure 8.10**).

Money as Means of Exchange

Although there have been marketplaces without money of any sort, money does facilitate trade. **Money** may be defined as something used to make payments for other goods and services as well as to measure their value. Its critical attributes are durability, transportability, divisibility, recognizability, and interchangeability. Items that have been used as money in various societies include salt, shells, precious stones, special beads, livestock, and valuable metals, such as iron, copper, silver, and gold. As revealed in this chapter's Biocultural Connection, cacao beans were also used as money—and more.

About 5,000 years ago, merchants and others in Mesopotamia (a vast area between the Tigris and Euphrates Rivers, encompassing much of present-day Iraq and neighboring border areas) began using pieces of precious metal such as silver in their transactions. Once they agreed on the value of these pieces as a means of exchange (money),

more complex commercial developments followed. As the means of exchange were standardized in terms of value, it became easier to accumulate, lend, or borrow money for specified amounts and periods of time against payment of interest. Gradually, some merchants began to do business with money itself, and they became bankers.

As the use of money became widespread, the metal units were adapted to long-term use, easy storage, and long-distance transportation. In many cultures, such pieces of iron, copper, or silver were cast as miniature models of especially valuable implements like sword blades, axes, or spades. But some 2,600 years ago in the ancient kingdom of Lydia (southwestern Turkey), they were molded into small, flat discs conforming to different sizes and weights (Davies, 2005). Over the next few centuries, metal coins were also standardized in terms of the metal's purity and value, such as 100 units of copper = 10 units of silver = 1 unit of gold.

By about 2,000 years ago, the commercial use of such coins was spreading throughout much of Europe and becoming increasingly common in parts of Asia and Africa, especially along trade routes and in urban centers. Thus, money set into motion radical economic changes in many traditional societies and introduced what has been called *merchant capitalism* in many parts of the world (Wolf, 1982).

---

money A means of exchange used to make payments for other goods and services as well as to measure their value.

BIOCULTURAL CONNECTION

Cacao: The Love Bean in the Money Tree

Several thousand years ago Indians in the tropical lowlands of southern Mexico discovered how to produce a hot brew from ground, roasted beans. They collected these beans from melon-shaped fruit pods growing in trees identified by today's scientists as *Theobroma cacao*. By adding honey, vanilla, and some flowers for flavoring, they produced a beverage that made them feel good and believed that these beans were gifts from their gods.

Soon, cacao beans became part of long-distance trade networks and appeared in the Mexican highlands, where the Aztec elite adopted this drink brewed from *cacahuatl*, calling it "*chocolatl*." In fact, these beans were so highly valued that Aztecs also used them as money. When Spanish invaders conquered Guatemala and Mexico in the 1520s, they adopted the region's practice of using cacao beans as currency inside their new colony. They also embraced the custom of drinking chocolate, which they introduced to Europe, where it became a luxury drink as well as a medicine.[a]

In the next 500 years, chocolate developed into a $14 billion global business, with the United States as the top importer of cacao beans or cacao products. Women buy 75 percent of the chocolate products, and on Valentine's Day more than $1 billion worth of chocolate is sold.

What is it about chocolate that makes it a natural love drug? Other than carbohydrates, minerals, and vitamins, it contains about 300 chemicals, including some with mood-altering effects. For instance, cacao beans contain several chemical components that trigger feelings of pleasure in the human brain. In addition to tryptophan, which increases serotonin levels, chocolate also contains phenylethylamine, an amphetamine-like substance that stimulates the body's own dopamine and has slight antidepressant effects. Chocolate contains anandamide (*anan* means "bliss" in Sanskrit), a messenger molecule that triggers the brain's pleasure center. Also naturally produced in the brain, anandamide's mood-enhancing effect is the same as that obtained from marijuana leaves.[b] Finally, chocolate also contains a mild stimulant called theobromine ("food of god"), which stimulates the brain's production of natural opiates, reducing pain and increasing feelings of satisfaction and even euphoria.

These chemicals help explain why the last Aztec ruler Montezuma drank so much chocolate. A Spanish eyewitness, who visited his royal palace in the Aztec capital in 1519, later reported that Montezuma's servants sometimes brought their powerful lord

in cups of pure gold a drink made from the cocoa-plant, which they said he took before visiting his wives. . . . I saw them bring in a good fifty large jugs of this chocolate, all frothed up, of which he would drink a little. They always served it with great reverence.[c]

BIOCULTURAL QUESTION

Viewed as a divine gift by Mexican Indians, chocolate stimulates our brain's pleasure center. Why would women buy this natural love drug in much greater quantities than men?

---

[a]For an excellent cultural history of chocolate, see Coe, S. D., & Coe, M. D. (1996). *The true history of chocolate*. New York: Thames and Hudson; Grivetti, L. E. (2005). From aphrodisiac to health food: A cultural history of chocolate. *Karger Gazette* (68).

[b]Personal communication, Lawrence C. Davis, Kansas State University.

[c]del Castillo, B. D. (1963). *The conquest of New Spain* (pp. 226–227) (translation and introduction by J. M. Cohen). New York: Penguin.

Local Economies and Global Capitalism

Imposing market production schemes on other societies and ignoring cultural differences can have unintended negative economic consequences, especially in this era of globalization. For example, it has led prosperous countries to impose inappropriate development schemes in parts of the world that they regard as economically underdeveloped. Typically, these schemes focus on increasing the target country's gross national product through large-scale production that all too often boosts the well-being of a few but results in poverty, poor health, discontent, and a host of other ills for many (**Figure 8.11**).

Among many examples of this scenario is the global production of soy, which has increased greatly in many parts of the world. Of particular note is Paraguay, where big landowners, in cooperation with large agribusinesses (most of which are owned by neighboring Brazilians), produce genetically modified seeds, developed and marketed by foreign companies, especially the U.S.-based multinational

Figure 8.11 Protesting the World Trade Organization Founded in 1995 to regulate international trade, the World Trade Organization (WTO) has often been accused of favoring rich countries over poor ones. Public gatherings to protest its policies have been and continue to be common worldwide—particularly in developing countries with large numbers of subsistence farmers struggling to hold onto their livelihoods in the face of globalizing agribusiness. This crowd of protesters gathered during an informal meeting of trade officials from thirty-five countries hosted by India in its capital city, New Delhi, in 2009. Headquartered in Geneva, the WTO has 155 member countries.

corporation Monsanto. Although these landowners and agribusinesses possess just 1 percent of the total number of Paraguayan farms, they own almost 80 percent of the country's agricultural land. Exporting the soy, they make hefty profits because production costs are low, and international demand is high for cattle feed and biofuel.

But the victims of progress are the poor—hundreds of thousands of small farmers, landless peasants, rural laborers, and their families. Traditionally growing much of their own food (plus a bit extra for the local market) on small plots, many of them have been edged out and forced to work for hunger wages or to migrate to the city, or even abroad, in order to survive. Those who stay face malnutrition and other hardships because they lack enough fertile land to feed their families and do not earn enough to buy basic foodstuffs (Fogel & Riquelme, 2005).

Because every culture is an integrated system (as illustrated by the barrel model presented in the chapter on

culture), a shift in the infrastructure, or economic base, impacts interlinked elements of the society's social structure and superstructure. As the ethnographic examples of the potlatch and the Kula ring show, economic activities in traditional cultures are intricately intertwined with social and political relations, and may even involve spiritual elements. Agribusinesses and other large-scale economic operations or development schemes that do not take such structural complexities into consideration may have unforeseen harmful consequences for a society.

Fortunately, there is now a growing awareness on the part of development officials that future projects are unlikely to succeed without the expertise that anthropologists can bring to bear. And, in some parts of the world anthropologists with indigenous roots are leading the way in shaping development agendas that build on rather than destroy tradition—as relayed in this chapter's Anthropologist of Note about Rosita Worl, a Tlingit from Juneau, Alaska.

ANTHROPOLOGIST OF NOTE

Rosita Worl

Alaskan anthropologist **Rosita Worl,** whose Tlingit names are Yeidiklats'akw and Kaa hani, belongs to the Thunderbird Clan from the ancient village of Klukwan in southeastern Alaska. During her growing-up years by the Chilkat River, elders taught her to speak loudly so her words could be heard above the sound of crashing water. And her mother, a cannery union organizer, took her along to meetings.

As a university student, Worl led a public protest for the first time—successfully challenging a development scheme in Juneau detrimental to local Tlingit. When she decided to

Tlingit anthropologist Rosita Worl is president of the Sealaska Heritage Institute and a board member of the Alaska Federation of Natives.

pursue her anthropology doctorate at Harvard, she did so with a strong sense of purpose: "You have to be analytical about your culture," she says. "At one time, before coming into contact with other societies, we were just able to live our culture, but now we have to be able to keep it intact while integrating it into modern institutions. We have to be able to communicate our cultural values to others and understand how those modern institutions impact those values."

Worl's graduate studies included fieldwork among the Inupiat of Alaska's North Slope region—research that resulted in her becoming a spokesperson at state, national, and international levels for the protection of whaling practices and the indigenous subsistence lifestyle. For over three decades now, she has fought to safeguard traditional rights to natural resources essential for survival, for current and future generations, including her own children and grandchildren.

A recognized leader in sustainable, culturally informed economic development, Worl has held several major positions at the Sealaska Corporation, a large Native-owned business enterprise with almost 18,000 shareholders primarily of Tlingit and neighboring Haida and Tsimshian descent. Created under the 1971 Alaska Native Claims Settlement Act, Sealaska is now the largest private landholder in southeastern Alaska. Its subsidiaries collectively employ over a thousand people and include timber harvesting,

marketing wood products, land and forest resource management, construction, and information technology. Putting the holistic perspective and analytical tools of anthropology into practice, Worl has spearheaded efforts to incorporate the cultural values of southeast Alaska Natives into Sealaska—including shareholding opportunities for employees.

Currently, Worl serves as president of Sealaska Heritage Institute, a Native nonprofit organization that seeks to perpetuate and enhance Tlingit, Haida, and Tsimshian cultures, including language preservation and revitalization. Also on the faculty of the University of Alaska Southeast, she has written extensively about indigenous Alaska for academic and general audiences. She founded the journal *Alaska Native News* to educate Native Alaskans on a range of issues and is deeply involved in the implementation of the 1990 Native American Graves Protection and Repatriation Act.

Sought for her knowledge and expertise, Worl has served on the board of directors of the Smithsonian Institution's National Museum of the American Indian, as well as Cultural Survival, Inc. She has earned many honors for her work, including the American Anthropological Association's Solon T. Kimball Award for Public and Applied Anthropology, received in 2008 in recognition of her exemplary career in applying anthropology to public life in Alaska and beyond.

Informal Economy and the Escape from State Bureaucracy

Powerful business corporations promote their profit-making agendas through slogans such as "free trade," "free markets," and "free enterprise." But the commercial

success of such enterprises, foreign or domestic, does not come without a price, and all too often that price is paid by still-surviving indigenous foragers, small farmers, herders, fishermen, local artisans such as weavers and carpenters, and so on. From their viewpoint, such slogans of freedom have the ring of "savage capitalism," a term now commonly used in Latin America to describe a world order in which the powerless are often condemned to poverty and misery.

© Hideo Haga/HAGA/The Image Works

Figure 9.1 Sex Appeal among the Trobrianders To attract lovers, young Trobriand women and men must look as attractive and seductive as possible. This young woman's beauty has been enhanced by face painting and adornments given to her by her father.

modern industrialized world have converged toward those of the Trobrianders, even though the traditional ideal of premarital sexual abstinence has not been abandoned entirely and is upheld in many traditional Christian, Muslim, and similarly conservative families.

Control of Sexual Relations

In the absence of effective birth control, the usual outcome of sexual activity between fertile individuals of the opposite sex is that, sooner or later, the woman becomes pregnant. Given the intricate array of social responsibilities involved in rearing the children that are born of sexual relations—and the potential for conflict resulting from unregulated sexual competition—it is not surprising

that all societies have cultural rules that seek to regulate those relations, although those rules vary considerably across cultures.

For instance, in some societies, sexual intercourse during pregnancy is taboo, whereas in others it is looked upon positively as something that promotes the growth of the fetus. And although some cultures sharply condemn same-sex acts or relations, many others are indifferent and do not even have a special term to distinguish homosexuality as significant in its own right. In several cultures same-sex acts are not only accepted but even prescribed.

Such is the case in some Papua societies in New Guinea, for example, where certain prescribed male-to-male sexual acts are part of initiation rituals required of all boys to become respected adult men (Kirkpatrick, 2000). In those cultures, people traditionally see the transmission of semen from sexually mature males to younger boys, through oral sex, as vital for building up the strength needed to protect against the supposedly debilitating effects of adult heterosexual intercourse (Herdt, 1993).

Despite longstanding culture-based opposition to homosexuality in many areas of the world, this sexual orientation exists within the wider range of human sexual relations, emotional attractions, and social identities, and it is far from uncommon (**Figure 9.2**). Homosexuality is found in diverse contexts—from lifelong loving relationships to casual sexual encounters, and from being fully open to being utterly private and secretive. During the past few decades, public denigration and condemnation of homosexuality have diminished in numerous countries, and same-sex relationships have become a publicly accepted part of the cosmopolitan lifestyle in metropolitan centers from Amsterdam to Paris and Rio de Janeiro to San Francisco. As recently as 2009, India decriminalized homosexuality, followed by several other countries (Timmons & Kumar, 2009). Clearly, the social rules and cultural meanings of all sexual behavior are subject to great variability not only across cultures but also across time.

Marriage and the Regulation of Sexual Relations

As noted previously, in much of Europe and North America the traditional ideal was (and in some communities still is) that all sexual activities outside of marriage were disapproved or even forbidden. Individuals were expected to establish a family through marriage, by which one gains an exclusive right of sexual access to another person. The main purpose of sexual intercourse was not erotic pleasure but reproduction.

Recognizing the potential risks of unregulated sexual relations, including unplanned pregnancies by a man other than the lawful husband, these societies often criminalized extramarital affairs as adultery. Reinforcing public awareness of the moral rules, authorities could turn sexual

VISUAL COUNTERPOINT

Figure 9.2 **Expressions of Same-Sex Affection** Although same-sex relationships have existed for thousands of years and are permitted in many parts of the world, homosexuals in sexually restrictive societies are shamed and shunned, and may be beaten, flogged, banished, imprisoned, or even murdered. Even in societies that have become less restrictive, public displays of same-sex affection (between men in particular) are often looked upon as distasteful or even disgusting. One nationwide exception in the United States is the sports arena where athletes freely hug each other, and may even pat each other on the behind or leap into each other's arms without bringing their sexual orientation into question. Attitudes are shifting all around the globe, however, as evident in this photo of two just-wed Argentinean men kissing after receiving their official marriage license on November 16, 2009—the first in Latin America. This Buenos Aires couple sought a license not only because they love each other, but also because they wanted the shared health insurance policy, inheritance rights, and other privileges married couples in their country traditionally enjoy.

transgressions into a public spectacle of shame, torture, or even death. According to strict religious law—historically shared by Jews, Christians, and Muslims alike—adultery was punishable by death. The Bible demands that both wrongdoers, having placed themselves outside the moral community, be stoned to death outside the town entrance (Deuteronomy 22:24 and Leviticus 20:10).

Many centuries later, among European Christian colonists in 17th- and 18th-century New England, a woman's participation in adultery remained a serious crime. Although it did not lead to stoning, women so accused were shunned by the community and could be imprisoned.

Such restrictions remain (or are sometimes reinstated) in those traditional Muslim societies in northern Africa and western Asia where age-old Shariah law regulates social behavior in strict accordance with religious standards of morality.

For example, in a Taliban-controlled village in northern Afghanistan, conservative mullahs (priests) found a young couple guilty of adultery, proclaiming it an offense prohibited by God. Buried waist-deep in holes outside the village, the 23-year-old married woman and her 28-year-old lover were stoned to death in the summer of 2010,

a brutal spectacle attended by hundreds of villagers and filmed on a mobile phone (Amnesty International, 2010). Turning legal transgressions into a public display, authorities reinforce awareness of the rules of social conduct, even if a sentence is ultimately dropped or changed.

A side effect of such restrictive rules of sexual behavior is that they may contribute to limiting the spread of sexually transmitted diseases. For instance, the global epidemic of HIV/AIDS has had dramatically less impact in northern Africa's Muslim countries than in the non-Muslim states of sub-Saharan Africa. Statistics vividly illustrate the impact of religious and cultural prohibitions (although other factors may also be involved): The reported percentage of adults infected by the virus is 0.1 percent in Algeria, Morocco, and Tunisia, in contrast to some 17 percent in South Africa, 25 percent in Botswana, and 26 percent in Swaziland (Gray, 2004; UNAIDS, 2009).

Notably, because sexuality is a taboo topic in Muslim societies, many may not seek appropriate counseling, testing, and treatment for HIV/AIDS. For this reason, the actual infection rate may be somewhat higher than reported in these figures (Hasnain, 2005). Communities devastated by this sexually transmitted disease not only confront a serious public health problem but also face a cultural challenge in that they must create a new public awareness and adjust attitudes about sexual pleasure so that they do not endanger their collective well-being.

Yet most cultures in the world do not sharply regulate an individual's sexual practices. Indeed, a majority of all cultures are considered sexually permissive or semipermissive (the former having few or no restrictions on sexual experimentation before marriage, the latter allowing some experimentation but less openly). A minority of known societies—about 15 percent—have rules requiring that sexual involvement take place only within marriage.

This brings us to an anthropological definition of **marriage**—a culturally sanctioned union between two or more people that establishes certain rights and obligations between the people, between them and their children, and between them and their in-laws. Such marriage rights and obligations most often include, but are not limited to, sex, labor, property, childrearing, exchange, and status. Thus defined, marriage is universal. Notably, our definition of *marriage* refers to "people" rather than "a man and a woman" because in some countries same-sex marriages are socially acceptable and allowed by law, even though opposite-sex marriages are far more common. We will return to this point later in the chapter.

In many cultures, marriage is considered the central and most important social institution. In such cultures, people will spend considerable time and energy on maintaining marriage as an institution. They may do so in various ways, including highlighting the ritual moment when the wedding takes place, festively memorializing the event at designated times such as anniversaries, and making it difficult to divorce.

In some societies, however, marriage is a relatively marginal institution and is not considered central to the establishment and maintenance of family life and society. For instance, marriage has lost much of its traditional significance in wealthy northwestern European nations, in part due to changes in the political economy, more balanced gender relations, and shared public benefits of these capitalist welfare states.

Sexual and Marriage Practices among the Nayar

The relative unimportance of marriage as the major defining institution for establishing a family is not unique to wealthy European nations. For instance, historically, marriage has been of marginal significance in the family life of the Nayar of Kerala in southwestern India. A landowning

warrior caste, corporations made up of kinsmen related in the female line traditionally hold their estates. These blood relatives live together in a large household, with the eldest male serving as manager.

Like Trobriand Islanders, the Nayar are a sexually permissive culture. A classic anthropological study describes three transactions related to traditional Nayar sexual and marriage practices, many of which have changed since the mid-1900s (Goodenough, 1970; Gough, 1959). The first, occurring shortly before a girl experiences her first menstruation, involves a ceremony that joins her with a "ritual husband." This union does not necessarily involve sexual relations and lasts only a few days. Neither individual has any further obligation, but when the girl becomes a woman, she and her children typically participate in ritual mourning for the man when he dies. This temporary union establishes the girl as an adult ready for motherhood and eligible for sexual activity with men approved by her household.

The second transaction takes place when a young Nayar woman enters into a continuing sexual liaison with a man approved by her family. This is a formal relationship that requires the man to present her with gifts three times each year until the relationship is terminated. In return, the man can spend nights with her. Despite ongoing sexual privileges, however, this "visiting husband" has no economic obligations to her, nor is her home regarded as his home. In fact, she may have the same arrangement with more than one man at the same time. Regardless of the number of men with whom she is involved, this second transaction, the Nayar version of marriage, clearly specifies who has sexual rights to whom and includes rules that deter conflicts between the men.

If a Nayar woman becomes pregnant, one of the men with whom she has a relationship (who may or may not be the biological father) must formally acknowledge paternity by presenting gifts to the woman and the midwife. This establishes the child's birthrights—as does birth registration in Western societies. Once a man has ritually acknowledged fatherhood by gift giving, he may continue to take interest in the child, but he has no further obligations. Support and education for the child are the responsibility of the mother and her brothers, with whom she and her offspring live.

Indeed, unlike most other cultural groups in the world, the traditional Nayar household includes only the mother,

marriage A culturally sanctioned union between two or more people that establishes certain rights and obligations between the people, between them and their children, and between them and their in-laws. Such marriage rights and obligations most often include, but are not limited to, sex, labor, property, childrearing, exchange, and status.

Figure 9.3 Charles Darwin and His First-Cousin Wife, Emma Wedgewood Before proposing, Charles made a "pros and cons" list about marrying Emma. It said nothing about their close familial relationship. Rather, the concerns of this famous English naturalist centered on the question of whether supporting a wife and children would compromise his scientific career. Ultimately, the idea of a "constant companion (& friend in old age)" won out. During their three-month engagement he wrote to her: "I think you will humanize me, & soon teach me there is greater happiness, than building theories, & accumulating facts in silence & solitude." Bonds of real affection linked the couple throughout their long lives.

her children, and her other biological or blood relatives, technically known as **consanguineal kin**. It does not include any of the "husbands" or other people related through marriage—technically known as **affinal kin**. In other words, sisters and their offspring all live together with their brothers and their mother and her brothers. Historically, this arrangement addressed the need for security in a cultural group in which warfare was common.

Among the Nayar, sexual relations are forbidden between consanguineal relatives and thus are permitted only with individuals who live in other households. This brings us to another human universal: the incest taboo.

Incest Taboo

Just as marriage in its various forms is found in all cultures, so is the **incest taboo**—the prohibition of sexual contact between certain close relatives. But what is defined as "close" is not the same in all cultures. Moreover, such definitions may be subject to change over time. Although the scope and details of the taboo vary across cultures and time, almost all societies past and present strongly forbid sexual relations at least between parents and children and nearly always between siblings. In some societies the taboo

extends to other close relatives, such as cousins, and even some relatives linked through marriage (**Figure 9.3**).

Anthropologists have long been fascinated by the incest taboo and have proposed several explanations for its cross-cultural existence and variation. The simplest explanation is that our species has an "instinctive" repulsion for incest. It has been documented that human beings raised together have less sexual attraction for one another. However, by itself this "familiarity breeds contempt" argument may simply substitute the result for the cause. The incest taboo ensures that children and their parents, who are constantly in close contact, avoid regarding one another as sexual objects. Besides this, if an instinctive horror of incest exists, how do we account for the far from rare violations of the incest taboo? In the United States, for instance, over 10 percent of children under 18 years of age have been involved in incestuous relations (U.S. Dept. of Health and Human Services, 2005; Whelehan, 1985).

---

consanguineal kin Biologically related relatives, commonly referred to as blood relatives.

affinal kin People related through marriage.

incest taboo The prohibition of sexual relations between closely related individuals.

Moreover, so-called instinctive repulsion does not explain institutionalized incest, such as a requirement that the divine ruler of the Inca empire in ancient Peru be married to his own (half) sister. Sharing the same father, both siblings belonged to the political dynasty that derived its sacred right to rule the empire from Inti, its ancestral Sun God. And by virtue of this royal lineage's godly origin, their children could claim the same sacred political status as their human-divine father and mother. Ancient emperors in Egypt also practiced such religiously prescribed incest based on a similar claim to godly status.

Early students of genetics argued that the incest taboo prevents the harmful effects of inbreeding. Although this is so, it is also true that, as with domestic animals, inbreeding can increase desired characteristics as well as detrimental ones. Furthermore, undesirable effects will show up sooner with inbreeding, so whatever genes are responsible for them are quickly eliminated from the population. That said, a preference for a genetically different mate does tend to maintain a higher level of genetic diversity within a population, and in evolution this variation works to a species' advantage. Without genetic diversity a species cannot adapt biologically to environmental change.

The inbreeding or biological-avoidance theory of incest can be challenged on several fronts. For instance, detailed census records made in Roman Egypt about 2,000 years ago show that brother–sister marriages were not uncommon among ordinary members of the farming class, and we have no evidence for linking this cultural practice to any biological imperatives (Leavitt, 1990). To the contrary, some anthropologists have argued that the incest taboo exists as a cultural means to preserve the stability and integrity of the family, which is essential to maintaining social order. Sexual relations between family members other than the husband and wife would introduce competition, destroying the harmony of a social unit fundamental to societal order.

Endogamy and Exogamy

Whatever its cause, the utility of the incest taboo can be seen by examining its effects on social structure. Closely related to prohibitions against incest are cultural rules against **endogamy** (from Greek *endon*, "within," and *gamos*, "marriage"), or marriage within a particular group of individuals (cousins and in-laws, for example). If the group is defined as one's immediate family alone, then societies generally prohibit or at least discourage endogamy, thereby promoting **exogamy** (*exo* is Greek for "outside"), or marriage outside the group. Yet, a

society that practices exogamy at one level may practice endogamy at another. Among the Trobriand Islanders, for example, each individual has to marry outside of his or her own clan and lineage (exogamy). However, because eligible sex partners are to be found within one's own community, village endogamy is commonly practiced.

Since the early 20th century, restrictions on close-kin marriages have increased in Europe and other parts of the world. Because of this, worldwide migrations by peoples from countries in which such marriages remain customary may lead to cross-cultural problems. British anthropologist Adam Kuper recently discussed this issue based on research with Muslim immigrant families from Pakistan. (Notably, Kuper's own paternal grandparents, Baltic Jews who immigrated to South Africa, were first cousins.) According to Kuper,

> In Pakistan, and in the Pakistani diaspora, a preference is commonly expressed for marriage within the extended family or *birādarī*. . . . Perhaps unexpectedly, the rate of cousin marriage among Pakistani immigrants to Britain is higher than the rate in rural Pakistan. And the rate of cousin marriage is particularly high among younger British Pakistanis. Around a third of the marriages of the immigrant generation were with first cousins, but well over half the marriages of the British-born generation are with first cousins. This is a consequence of British immigration regulations. . . . It is very difficult to enter Britain unless one is married to a British citizen. In most cousin marriages, one partner immigrates to Britain from Pakistan. Alison Shaw found that 90 per cent of the first-cousin marriages in her sample of British Pakistanis in Oxford involved one spouse who came directly from Pakistan. . . . (Kuper, 2008, p. 731)

Kuper notes that although health risks to offspring of such close-kin marriages are "rather low," and generally "within the limits of acceptability," research by geneticists does indicate that "the risk of birth defects or infant mortality is roughly doubled for the children of first cousins." However, he adds, in western Europe this debate is not just about medical risks, but also about immigration and cultural friction: "Father's brother's daughter marriage is taken to be a defining feature of Islamic culture, and it is blamed not only for overloading the health service but also for resistance to integration and cultural stagnation. It is also associated with patriarchy, the suppression of women, and forced marriages" (Kuper 2008, p. 731).

In the United States, laws against first-cousin marriages exist in thirty-one states, and there is a general assumption nationwide that these laws are rooted in genetics (Ottenheimer, 1996). (See a discussion of U.S. marriage prohibitions in the Biocultural Connection.)

endogamy Marriage within a particular group or category of individuals.

exogamy Marriage outside a particular group or category of individuals.

BIOCULTURAL CONNECTION

Marriage Prohibitions in the United States

By Martin Ottenheimer

In the United States, every state has laws prohibiting the marriage of some relatives. Every state forbids parent–child and sibling marriages, but there is considerable variation in prohibitions concerning more distant relatives. For example, although the majority of states ban marriage between first cousins, nineteen states allow it and others permit it under certain conditions. Notably, the United States is the only country in the Western world that has prohibitions against first-cousin marriage.

Many people in the United States believe that laws forbidding marriage between family members exist because parents who are too close biologically run the risk of producing children with mental and physical defects. Convinced that first cousins fall within this "too close" category, they believe laws against first-cousin marriage were established to protect families from the effects of harmful genes.

There are two major problems with this belief: First, cousin prohibitions were enacted in the United States long before the discovery of the genetic mechanisms of disease. Second, genetic research has shown that offspring of first-cousin couples do not have any significantly greater risk of

negative results than offspring of very distantly related parents.

Why, then, do some North Americans maintain this belief? To answer this question, it helps to know that laws against first-cousin marriage first appeared in the United States right after the mid-1800s when evolutionary models of human behavior became fashionable. In particular, a pre-Darwinian model that explained social evolution as dependent upon biological factors gained popularity. It supposed that "progress from savagery to civilization" was possible when humans ceased inbreeding. Cousin marriage was thought to be characteristic of savagery, the lowest form of human social life, and it was believed to inhibit the intellectual and social development of humans. It became associated with "primitive" behavior and dreaded as a threat to a civilized America.

Thus, a powerful myth emerged in American popular culture, which has since become embedded in law. That myth is held and defended to this day, sometimes with great emotion despite being based on a discredited social evolutionary theory and contradicted by the results of modern genetic research.

Recently, a group of geneticists published the result of a study of consanguineous unions, estimating that there is "about a 1.7–2.8% increased risk for congenital defects above the population background risk."[a] Not only is this a high estimate, it is also well within the bounds of the margin of statistical error. But even so, it is a lower risk than that associated with offspring from women over the age of 40—who are not forbidden by the government to marry or bear children.

BIOCULTURAL QUESTION

What do you think is the underlying cultural logic that makes some societies traditionally forbid first cousins from marrying each other, whereas others, equally unfamiliar with genetics, accept or even prefer such marriages?

Written expressly for this text, 2005; revised and updated, 2011.

---

[a]Bennett, R. L., et al. (2002, April). Genetic counseling and screening of consanguineous couples and their offspring: Recommendations of the National Society of Genetic Counselors. *Journal of Genetic Counseling 11* (2), 97–119.

Early anthropologists suggested that our ancestors discovered the advantage of intermarriage as a means of creating bonds of friendship. French anthropologist Claude Lévi-Strauss (see the Anthropologist of Note) elaborated on this idea. He saw exogamy as a form of intergroup social exchange in which "wife-giving" and "wife-taking" (or, as happens in communities with female-headed households, husband-giving and husband-taking) created alliances between distinct communities. By extending the social network, potential enemies turn into relatives who may provide support in times of hardship or violent conflict.

Building on the theory advanced by Lévi-Strauss, other anthropologists have proposed that exogamy is an

important means of creating and maintaining political alliances and promoting trade between groups, thereby ensuring mutual protection and access to needed goods and resources not otherwise available. Forging wider kinship networks, exogamy also functions to integrate distinctive groups and thus potentially reduces violent conflict.

Distinction Between Marriage and Mating

In contrast to mating, which occurs when individuals join for purposes of sexual relations, marriage is a socially

ANTHROPOLOGIST OF NOTE

Claude Lévi-Strauss (1908–2009)

Claude Lévi-Strauss lived to be 100. When he died, he was the most celebrated anthropologist in the world. Born in Belgium, where his father briefly worked as a portrait painter, he grew up in Paris. As a boy during World War I, Claude lived with his grandfather, a rabbi of Versailles.

He studied law and philosophy at the Sorbonne, married a young anthropologist named Dina Dreyfus, and became a philosophy teacher. In 1935, the couple ventured across the ocean to Brazil's University of São Paulo, where his wife taught anthropology and he sociology. Influenced by 18th-century romantic philosopher Rousseau and fascinated by historical accounts of Brazilian Indians, he preferred ethno graphic research and lectured on tribal social organizations.

In 1937, he and Dina organized an expedition into the Amazon forest, visiting Bororo and other tribal villages and collecting artifacts for museums. In 1938, they made another journey and researched recently contacted Nambikwara Indians. Back in Paris together in 1939, their marriage dissolved. That same year, the Second World War erupted, and the French army mobilized its soldiers, including Lévi-Strauss.

A year after Nazi Germany conquered France in 1940, Lévi-Strauss escaped to New York City, where he became an anthropology professor at the New School for Social Research. Teaching courses on South American Indians during the war years, he befriended other European exiles, including the linguist Roman Jakobson, who pioneered the structural analysis of language.

Renowned French anthropologist Claude Lévi-Strauss at age 100 in his home library.

After the war, Lévi-Strauss became French cultural consul in the United States, based in New York. Maintaining ties with the academic community, including anthropologist Margaret Mead, he completed his two-part doctoral thesis: *The Elementary Structures of Kinship and The Family and Social Life of the Nambikwara Indians*. Theoretically influenced by Jakobson's structural linguistics, his thesis analyzed the logical structures underlying the social relations of kin-ordered societies.

Building on Marcel Mauss's 1925 study of gift exchange as a means to build or maintain a social relationship, he applied the concept of reciprocity to kinship, arguing that marriage is based on the exchange relationship between kin-groups of "wife-givers" and "wife-takers." Returning to France in late 1947, he became associate director of the ethnographic museum in Paris and successfully defended his thesis at the Sorbonne. His structural analysis was recognized as a pioneering study in kinship and marriage.

In 1949, Lévi-Strauss joined an international body of experts invited by UNESCO to discuss and define the *race concept*, a disputed term associated with discrimination and genocide. Three years later, he authored *Race and History*, a book that became instrumental in UNESCO's worldwide campaign against racism and ethnocentrism. By then, he had become an anthropology professor at the École Pratique des Hautes Études in Paris. Continuing his prolific writing, he published *Tristes Tropiques* (1955). This memoir about his ethnographic adventures among Amazonian Indians won him international fame. His next book, *Structural Anthropology* (1963), also became a classic. It presented his theoretical perspective that the human mind produces logical structures, classifying reality in terms of binary oppositions (such as light–dark, good–evil, nature–culture, and male–female) and that all humans share a mental demand for order expressed in a drive toward classification.

In 1959, Lévi-Strauss was appointed to a chair in social anthropology at the Collège de France and founded his own institute there. Specializing in the comparative study of religion, he undertook a massive comparative study and structural analysis of myths, resulting in a series of instantaneously classic books. In 1973, he was elected to the centuries-old Académie Française, a prestigious institution with just forty members known as "immortals." Countless other honors from around the world followed.

Now, survived by his wife, Monique, and two sons, he lies in a small rural cemetery in Burgundy, near his old mansion, where he liked to reflect on the human condition.

binding and culturally recognized relationship. Only marriage is backed by social, political, and ideological factors that regulate sexual relations as well as reproductive rights

and obligations. Even among the Nayar in India, discussed previously, where traditionally marriage seems to have involved little other than a sexual relationship, a woman's husband is legally obligated to provide her with gifts at specified intervals. Additionally, Nayar woman may not legally have sex with a man to whom she is not married.

Thus, although mating is biological, marriage is cultural. This is evident when we consider the various forms of marriage around the world.

Forms of Marriage

Within societies, and all the more so across cultures, we see contrasts in the constructs and contracts of marriage. Indeed, as is evident in the definition of *marriage* given previously, this institution comes in various forms—and these forms are distinct in terms of the number and gender of spouses involved.

Monogamy

Monogamy—marriage in which both partners have just one spouse—is the most common form of marriage worldwide. In North America and most of Europe, it is the only legally recognized form of marriage. In these places, not only are other forms prohibited, but systems of inheritance, whereby property and wealth are transferred from one generation to the next, are based on the institution of monogamous marriage. In some parts of the world (including Europe and North America) where divorce rates are high and people who have been divorced remarry, an increasingly common form of marriage is **serial monogamy**, whereby an individual marries a series of partners in succession.

Polygamy

Monogamy is the most common marriage form worldwide, but it is not the most culturally preferred. That distinction goes to **polygamy** (one individual having multiple spouses) and specifically to **polygyny**, in which a man is married to more than one woman (*gyne* is Greek for "woman" and "wife"). Favored in about 80 to 85 percent of the world's cultures, polygyny is commonly practiced in parts of Asia and much of sub-Saharan Africa (Lloyd, 2005).

Although polygyny is the favored marriage form in these places, monogamy exceeds it, but for economic rather than moral or legal reasons. In many polygynous societies, in which a groom is usually expected to compensate a bride's family in cash or kind, a man must be fairly wealthy to be able to afford more than one wife. Multiple surveys of twenty-five sub-Saharan African countries where polygyny is common show that it declined by about half between the 1970s and 2001. This dramatic decline has many reasons, one of which is related to families making an economic transition from traditional farming and herding to wage labor in cities. Nonetheless, polygyny remains highly significant with an overall average of 25 percent of married women in such unions (Lloyd, 2005).

Polygyny is particularly common in traditional food-producing societies that support themselves by herding grazing animals or growing crops and in which women do the bulk of cultivation. Under these conditions, women are valued both as workers and as childbearers. Because the labor of wives in polygynous households generates wealth and little support is required from husbands, the wives have a strong bargaining position within the household. Often, they have considerable freedom of movement and some economic independence through the sale of crafts or crops. Wealth-generating polygyny is found in its fullest elaboration in parts of sub-Saharan Africa and southwestern Asia, though it is known elsewhere as well (White, 1988).

In societies practicing wealth-generating polygyny, most men and women do enter into polygynous marriages, although some are able to do so earlier in life than others. This is made possible by a female-biased sex ratio and/or a mean age at marriage for females that is significantly below that for males. In fact, this marriage pattern is frequently found in societies in which violence, including war, is common and many young males lose their lives in fighting. Their high combat mortality results in a population in which women outnumber men.

By contrast, in societies in which men are more heavily involved in productive work, generally only a small minority of marriages are polygynous. Under these circumstances, women are more dependent on men for support, so they are valued as childbearers more than for the work they do. This is commonly the case in pastoral nomadic societies in which men are the primary owners and tenders of livestock. This makes women especially vulnerable if they prove incapable of bearing children, which is one reason a man may seek another wife.

Another reason for a man to take on secondary wives is to demonstrate his high position in society. But where men do most of the productive work, they must work extremely hard to support more than one wife, and few actually do so. Usually, it is the exceptional hunter or male shaman ("medicine man") in a food-foraging society or a particularly wealthy man in a horticultural, agricultural, or pastoral society who is most apt to practice polygyny. When he does, it is usually of the *sororal* type, with the co-wives being sisters. Having lived their lives together before marriage, the sisters continue to do so with their husband, instead of occupying separate dwellings of their own.

Polygyny also occurs in a few places in Europe. For example, English laws concerning marriage changed in 1972 to accommodate immigrants who traditionally practiced

---

monogamy A marriage form in which both partners have just one spouse.

serial monogamy A marriage form in which a man or a woman marries or lives with a series of partners in succession.

polygamy A marriage form in which one individual has multiple spouses at the same time; from the Greek words *poly* ("many") and *gamos* ("marriage").

polygyny A marriage form in which a man is married to two or more women at the same time; a form of polygamy.

polygyny. Since that time polygamous marriages have been legal in England for some specific religious minorities, including Muslims and Sephardic Jews. According to one family law specialist, the real impetus behind this law change was a growing concern that "destitute immigrant wives, abandoned by their husbands, [were] overburdening the welfare state" (Cretney, 2003, pp. 72–73).

It is estimated that about 100,000 people currently live in polygamous households in the United States. Of these, about 20,000 are Mormons belonging to the Fundamentalist Church of Jesus Christ of Latter-Day Saints, many of whom reside in the Utah–Arizona border towns of Hildale and Colorado City (**Figure 9.4**). They hold on to a 19th-century Mormon doctrine that plural marriage brings exaltation in heaven—even though the practice was officially declared illegal in the United States in 1862 and was renounced in 1890 by the Church of Jesus Christ of Latter-Day Saints, the mainstream Mormon church headquartered in Salt Lake City.

A small but growing number of other Christian fundamentalists groups in the United States also practice polygamy, but most polygamists in the country are immigrants (both Muslim and non-Muslim) originating from Asian and African countries in which the practice is traditionally embedded and legal. Polygamous households are also growing among Black Muslim orthodox households in several major U.S. cities (McDermott, 2011; Schilling, 2012).

Despite its illegality and concerns that the practice can jeopardize the rights and well-being of young women, regional law enforcement officials have adopted a "live and let live" attitude toward religious-based polygyny in their region. Women involved in the practice are sometimes outspoken in defending it. One woman—a lawyer and one of nine co-wives—expresses her attitude toward polygyny as follows:

> I see it as the ideal way for a woman to have a career and children. In our family, the women can help each other care for the children. Women in monogamous relationships don't have that luxury. As I see it, if this lifestyle didn't already exist, it would have to be invented to accommodate career women. (Johnson, 1991, p. A22)

In some societies, if a man dies, leaving behind a wife and children, it is customary that one of his brothers marries the widowed sister-in-law. But this obligation does not preclude the brother having another wife then or in the future. This custom, called the *levirate* (from the Latin *levir*, which means "husband's brother"), provides security for the widow (and her children). A related marriage tradition is the *sororate* (Latin *soror* means "sister"), in which a man has the right to marry a sister (usually younger) of his deceased wife. In some societies, the sororate also applies to a man who has married a woman who is unable to bear children. This practice entitles a man to a replacement wife from his in-laws. In societies that have the levirate and sororate—customary in many traditional foraging, farming, and herding cultures—the in-law relationship between the two families is maintained even after the spouse's death and secures an established alliance between two groups.

VISUAL COUNTERPOINT

Figure 9.4 Polygamous Marriages An American Christian polygamist with his three wives and children stand in front of their dormitory-style home in Utah (*left*), and a Baranarana man of Upper Guinea poses with his two wives and children (*right*). Although this marriage form is legally prohibited in the United States, perhaps as many as 100,000 Americans live in polygamous households today.

Although monogamy and polygyny are the most common forms of marriage in the world today, other forms do occur. **Polyandry**, the marriage of one woman to two or more men simultaneously, is known in only a few societies. The rarity of polyandry could be due to longer life expectancy for women or to slightly lower female infant mortality, either of which might produce a society with a surplus of women.

Fewer than a dozen societies are known to have favored this form of marriage, but they involve people as widely separated from one another as the Marquesan Islanders of Polynesia and Tibetans in Asia (**Figure 9.5**). In Tibet, where inheritance is in the male line and arable land is limited, the marriage of brothers to a single woman (*fraternal polyandry*) keeps the land together by preventing it from being repeatedly subdivided among sons from one generation to the next. Unlike monogamy, it also holds down population growth, thereby avoiding increased pressures on resources. Finally, among Tibetans who practice a mixed economy of farming, herding, and trading in the Trans Himalayas, fraternal polyandry provides the household with an adequate pool of male labor for all three subsistence activities (Levine & Silk, 1997).

Figure 9.5 Polyandrous Marriage Polyandry—marriage between one woman and two or more men—occurs in fewer than a dozen societies, including among the Nyinba people living in northwest Nepal's Nyinba Valley in the Humla district near Tibet. Pictured here, from right: the older husband Chhonchanab with first daughter Dralma, the wife Shilangma, the younger husband KaliBahadur, and the second daughter Tsering.

Other Forms of Marriage

Notable among several other marriage forms is **group marriage**. Also known as *co-marriage*, this is a rare arrangement in which several men and women have sexual access to one another. Until a few decades ago, Inupiat Eskimos in northern Alaska, for instance, engaged in "spouse exchange" (*nuliaqatigiit*) between non-kin, with two conjugal husband–wife couples being united by shared sexual access. Highly institutionalized arrangements, these intimate relationships implied ties of mutual aid and support across territorial boundaries and were expected to last throughout the lifetime of the participants (Chance, 1990). The ties between the couples were so strong that their children retained a recognized relationship to one another (Spencer, 1984).

There are also arrangements anthropologists categorize as **fictive marriage**—marriage by proxy to the symbols of someone not physically present in order to establish a social status for a spouse and heirs. One major reason for such a marriage is to control rights to property in the next generation.

Various types of fictive marriages exist in different parts of the world. In the United States, for example, proxy marriage ceremonies accommodate physically separated partners, such as seafarers, prisoners, and military personnel deployed abroad.

In several traditional African societies—most famously among Nuer cattle herders of southern Sudan—a woman may marry a man who has died without heirs. In such situations the deceased man's brother may become his stand-in, or proxy, and marry a woman on his behalf. As in the case of the marriage custom of the sororate discussed previously, the biological offspring will be considered as having been fathered by the dead man's spirit. Recognized as his legitimate children, they are his rightful heirs. Because such spouses are absent in the flesh yet believed to exist in spirit form, anthropologists refer to these fictive unions as *ghost marriages* (Evans-Pritchard, 1951).

Choice of Spouse

The Western romantic ideal that an individual should be free to marry whomever he or she chooses is certainly not universally embraced. In many societies, marriage and the establishment of a family are considered far too important to be left to the desires of young people. The individual relationship of two people who are expected to spend their lives together and raise their children together is viewed as incidental to the more serious matter of allying two families through the marriage bond. Marriage involves a transfer of rights between families, including rights to property and rights over children, as well as sexual rights. Thus, marriages tend to be arranged for the economic and political advantage of the family unit.

Although arranged marriages are rare in North American society, they do occur. Among ethnic minorities, they may

polyandry A marriage form in which a woman is married to two or more men at one time; a form of polygamy.

group marriage A marriage form in which several men and women have sexual access to one another; also called *co-marriage*.

fictive marriage A marriage form in which a proxy is used as a symbol of someone not physically present to establish the social status of a spouse and heirs.

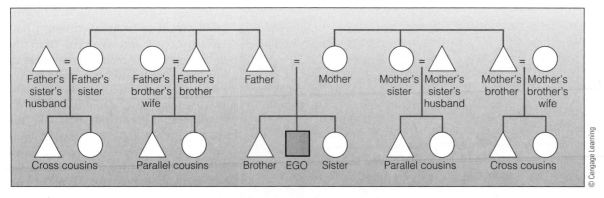

Figure 9.6 Kinship Relationships Anthropologists use diagrams of this sort to illustrate kinship relationships. This one shows the distinction between cross cousins and parallel cousins. In such diagrams, males are always shown with triangles, females with circles, marital ties with an equal sign (=), sibling relationships with a horizontal line, and parent–child relationships with a vertical line. Terms are given from the perspective of the individual labeled EGO, who can be male or female.

Cousin Marriage

Although cousin marriage is prohibited in some societies, certain cousins are the preferred marriage partners in others. A **parallel cousin** is the child of a father's brother or a mother's sister (**Figure 9.6**). In some societies, the preferred spouse for a man is his father's brother's daughter (or, from the woman's point of view, her father's brother's son). This is known as *patrilateral parallel-cousin marriage*.

Although not obligatory, such marriages have been favored historically among Arabs, the ancient Israelites, and the ancient Greeks. All of these societies are (or were) hierarchical in nature—that is, some people are ranked higher than others because they have more power and property—and although male dominance and descent are emphasized, daughters as well as sons inherit property of value. Thus, when a man marries his father's brother's daughter (or a woman marries her father's brother's son), property is retained within the single male line of descent. Generally, in these societies the greater the property, the more this form of parallel-cousin marriage is apt to occur.

A **cross cousin** is the child of a mother's brother or a father's sister (see Figure 9.6). Some societies favor *matrilateral cross-cousin marriage*—marriage of a man to his mother's brother's daughter or a woman to her father's sister's son. This preference exists among food foragers (such as the Aborigines of Australia) and some farming cultures (including various peoples of southern India). Among food foragers, who inherit relatively little in the way of property, such marriages help establish and maintain ties of solidarity between social groups. In agricultural societies, however, the transmission of property is an important determinant. In societies that trace descent

exclusively in the female line, for instance, property and other important rights usually pass from a man to his sister's son; under cross-cousin marriage, the sister's son is also the man's daughter's husband.

Same-Sex Marriage

As noted earlier in this chapter, our definition of *marriage* refers to a union between "people" rather than "a man and a woman" because in some societies same-sex marriages are socially acceptable and officially allowed by law. Marriages between individuals of the same sex may provide a way of dealing with problems for which opposite-sex marriage offers no satisfactory solution. This is the case with woman–woman marriage, a practice permitted in many societies of sub-Saharan Africa, although in none does it involve more than a small minority of all women.

Details differ from one society to another, but woman–woman marriages among the Nandi of western Kenya may be taken as representative of such practices in Africa (Oboler, 1980). The Nandi are a pastoral people who also do considerable farming. Control of most significant property and the primary means of production—livestock and land—is exclusively in the hands of men and may be transmitted only to their male heirs, usually their sons. Because polygyny is the preferred form of marriage, a man's property is

---

parallel cousin The child of a father's brother or a mother's sister.

cross cousin The child of a mother's brother or a father's sister.

Figure 9.7 Same-Sex Marriage in the United States Tory receives a celebratory kiss from her father alongside her new spouse, Monica, at their wedding in Connecticut, where same-sex marriage became legal in 2008.

normally divided equally among his wives for their sons to inherit. Within the household, each wife has her own home in which she lives with her children, but all are under the authority of the husband, who is a remote and aloof figure within the family. In such situations, the position of a woman who bears no sons is difficult; not only does she not help perpetuate her husband's male line—a major concern among the Nandi—but also she has no one to inherit the proper share of her husband's property.

To get around these problems, a woman of advanced age who bore no sons may become a female husband by marrying a young woman. The purpose of this arrangement is for the young wife to provide the male heirs her female husband could not. To accomplish this, the woman's wife enters into a sexual relationship with a man other than her female husband's male husband; usually it is one of his male relatives. No other obligations exist between this woman and her male sex partner, and her female husband is recognized as the social and legal father of any children born under these conditions.

In keeping with her role as female husband, this woman is expected to abandon her female gender identity and, ideally, dress and behave as a man. In practice, the ideal is not completely achieved, for the habits of a lifetime are difficult to reverse. Generally, it is in the context of domestic activities, which are most highly symbolic of female identity, that female husbands most completely assume a male identity.

The individuals in woman–woman marriages enjoy several advantages. By assuming male identity, a barren or sonless woman raises her status considerably and even achieves near equality with men, who otherwise occupy a far more favored position in Nandi society than women. A woman who marries a female husband is usually one who is unable to make a good marriage, often because she (the female husband's wife) has lost face as a consequence of premarital pregnancy. By marrying a female husband, she too raises her status and also secures legitimacy for her children. Moreover, a female husband is usually less harsh and demanding, spends more time with her, and allows her a greater say in decision making than a male husband does. The one thing she may not do is engage in sexual activity with her marriage partner. In fact, female husbands are expected to abandon sexual activity altogether, including with their male husbands to whom they remain married even though the women now have their own wives.

In contrast to woman–woman marriages among the Nandi are same-sex marriages that include sexual activity between partners. Over the past decade, the legal recognition of such unions has become a matter of vigorous debate in some parts of the world. Nearly a dozen countries—Argentina, Belgium, Canada, Denmark, Iceland, the Netherlands, Norway, Portugal, South Africa, Spain, and Sweden—have legalized same-sex marriages. In the United States, such marriages are now legal in nine states, as well as the District of Columbia (**Figure 9.7**).

The issue of same-sex marriage remains unsettled in many parts of the world, with official policies sometimes swinging back and forth—evidence of the fact that cultures are dynamic and capable of change. In addition, close to a dozen U.S. states and about two dozen countries around the world recognize *civil unions* (also known as *civil* or *domestic partnerships*), which offer a varying range of marriage benefits.

Among the arguments most commonly marshaled by opponents of same-sex unions is the claim that marriage has always been between males and females—but as we have just seen, this is not true. Same-sex marriages have been documented not only for a number of societies in Africa but in other parts of the world as well (Kuefler, 2007). As among the Nandi, they provide acceptable positions in society for individuals who might otherwise be marginalized.

Marriage and Economic Exchange

Marriages in many human societies are formalized by some sort of economic exchange. This may take the form of a gift exchange known as **bridewealth** (sometimes called *bride-price*), which involves payments of money or valuable goods to a bride's parents or other close kin.

This usually happens in patrilineal societies in which the bride will become a member of the household in which her husband grew up; this household will benefit from her labor as well as from the offspring she produces. Thus, her family must be compensated for their loss.

Bride-price not a simple buying and selling of women; rather, it can contribute to the bride's household (through purchases of jewelry or furnishings) or can help finance an elaborate and costly wedding celebration. It also enhances the stability of the marriage because it usually must be refunded if the couple separates. Other forms of compensation are an exchange of women between families—"My son will marry your daughter if your son will marry my daughter." Yet another is **bride service**, a period of time during which the groom works for the bride's family.

In a number of societies, especially those with an agriculturally based economy, women often bring a dowry with them at marriage. A **dowry** is a woman's share of parental property that, instead of passing to her upon her parents' death, is given to her at the time of her marriage (**Figure 9.8**). This does not mean that she retains control of this property after marriage. In some European and Asian countries, for example, a woman's property traditionally falls exclusively under her husband's control. Having benefited by what she has brought to the marriage, however, he is obligated to look out for her future

© John Eastcott/Yva Momatiuk/Woodfin Camp & Associates

Figure 9.8 Dowries in Traditional Farming Societies In some societies, when a woman marries she receives her share of the family inheritance (her dowry), which she brings to her new family (unlike bride-price, which passes from the groom's family to the bride's family). Shown here are Slovakian women in a traditional farming village each carrying a trousseau (*výbava nevesty*)—consisting of the bride's clothes, linen, bedding, and other objects of her dowry—in a festive procession to her new home. Traditionally, the bride keeps her finer linen in a beautifully carved or painted dowry chest. In addition, her birth family contributes some livestock, land, or other form of wealth, which Slovaks call *veno*, to the new household. Held in her name, this property provides the woman with a measure of independence from her husband.

well-being, including her security after his death. In the United States today, a form of dowry persists with the custom of the bride's family paying the wedding expenses.

One of the functions of dowry is to ensure a woman's support in widowhood (or after divorce), an important consideration for societies in which men carry out the bulk of productive work, and women are valued for their reproductive potential rather than for the work they do. In such societies, women incapable of bearing children are especially vulnerable, but the dowry they bring with them at marriage helps protect them against desertion. Another function of dowry is to reflect the economic status of the woman in societies in which differences in wealth are important. It also permits women, with the aid of their parents and kin, to compete through dowry for desirable (that is, wealthy) husbands.

Divorce

Like marriage, divorce in most societies is a matter of great concern to the couple's families because it impacts not only the individuals dissolving their marital relationship but also offspring, in-laws, other relatives, and sometimes entire communities. Indeed, divorce may have social, political, and economic consequences far beyond the breakup of a couple and their household.

Across cultures, divorce arrangements can be made for a variety of reasons and with varying degrees of difficulty. Among the Gusii farmers of western Kenya, for instance, sterility and impotence are grounds for a divorce. Among certain aboriginal peoples in northern Canada and Chenchu foragers in central India, divorce is traditionally discouraged after children are born; couples usually are urged by their families to accept their differences. By contrast, in the southwestern United States, a traditional Hopi Indian woman in Arizona could divorce her husband at any time merely by placing his belongings outside the door to indicate he is no longer welcome. Among the most common reasons for divorce across cultures are infidelity, sterility, cruelty, and desertion (Betzig, 1989; Goodwin, 1999).

In most non-Western societies, a divorced woman quickly remarries, thus adult unmarried women are rare. In many societies, economic considerations are often the strongest motivation to wed. On the island of New Guinea, a man does not marry because of sexual needs, which he can readily satisfy out of wedlock, but because there it is important to have a female partner to carry out tasks that traditionally fall to women—making pots and cooking his meals, fabricating nets, and weeding his plantings. Likewise, women in communities that depend on males for their fighting abilities need husbands who are raised to be able warriors as well as good hunters.

Although divorce rates may be high in various parts of the world, they have become so high in Western industrial and postindustrial societies that many worry about the future of what they view as traditional and familiar forms of marriage and the family. It is interesting to note that although divorce was next to impossible in Western societies between 1000 and 1800, in those centuries few marriages lasted more than about ten or twenty years, due to high mortality rates caused in part by inadequate health care and poor medical expertise (Stone, 2005). For instance, women dying in childbirth ended many marriages. With increased longevity, separation by death has diminished, and separation by legal action has grown. In the United States divorce rates have leveled off since peaking in the 1980s, but over 40 percent of marriages still do not survive (Morello, 2011).

Family and Household

Dependence on group living for survival is a basic human characteristic. We have inherited this from primate ancestors, although we have developed it in our own distinctly human way—through culture. No matter how each culture defines what constitutes a family, this social unit forms the basic cooperative structure that ensures an individual's primary needs and provides the necessary care for children to develop as healthy and productive members of the group and thereby ensure its future.

Comparative historical and cross-cultural studies reveal a wide variety of family patterns, and these patterns may change over time. Thus, the definition of **family** is necessarily broad: two or more people related by blood, marriage, or adoption. The family may take many forms, ranging from a single parent with one or more children, to a married couple or polygamous spouses with offspring, to several generations of parents and their children.

In all known cultures, past and present, gender plays at least some role in determining the division of labor. An effective way to facilitate economic cooperation between men and women and simultaneously provide for a close bond between mother and child is by establishing residential groups that include adults of both sexes. The differing nature of male and female roles, as defined by different cultures, makes it advantageous in many cultures for a child to have an adult of the same sex available to serve as a proper model for the appropriate adult role. The presence of adult men and women in the same residential group provides for this. The men, however, need not be the women's

---

bridewealth The money or valuable goods paid by the groom or his family to the bride's family upon marriage; also called *bride-price*.

bride service A designated period of time when the groom works for the bride's family.

dowry A payment at the time of a woman's marriage that comes from her inheritance, made to either her or her husband.

family Two or more people related by blood, marriage, or adoption. The family may take many forms, ranging from a single parent with one or more children, to a married couple or polygamous spouses with or without offspring, to several generations of parents and their children.

Figure 9.9 Household Versus Family Households can include many individuals not related to one another biologically or through marriage, as is seen in this royal household celebration at the Yoruba palace in Oyo, Nigeria. Commonly in societies with nobility, the royal family lives with many others not related to the ruler.

husbands. In some societies they are the women's brothers—as in the case of the Nayar, discussed earlier in this chapter, among whom sisters and their children live together with their brothers and their mother and her brothers.

For purposes of cross-cultural comparison, anthropologists define the **household** as a domestic unit of one or more persons living in one residence. In the vast majority of human societies, most households are made up of family members, but they may also include nonrelatives, such as servants. However, there are many other arrangements.

For instance, among the Mundurucu Indians, a horticultural people living in the center of Brazil's Amazon rainforest, married men and women are members of separate households, meeting periodically for sexual activity. At age 13, boys join their fathers in the men's house. Meanwhile, their sisters continue to live with their mothers and the younger boys in two or three houses grouped around the men's house. Thus, the men's house constitutes one household inhabited by adult males and their sexually mature sons, and the women's houses are inhabited by adult women and prepubescent boys and girls.

An array of other domestic arrangements can be found in other parts of the world, including situations in which coresidents of a household are not related biologically or by marriage—such as the service personnel in an elaborate royal household, apprentices in the household of craft specialists, low-status clients in the household of rich and powerful patrons, or groups of children being raised by paired teams of adult male and female community members in an Israeli kibbutz (a collectively owned and operated agricultural settlement). So it is that *family* and *household* are not always synonymous (**Figure 9.9**).

Forms of the Family

To discuss the various forms families take in response to particular social, historical, and ecological circumstances, we must first distinguish between a **conjugal family** (in Latin *conjugere* means "to join together"), which is formed on the basis of marital ties, and a **consanguineal family** (based on the Latin word *consanguineus*, literally meaning "of the same blood"), which consists of related women, their brothers, and the women's offspring.

Consanguineal families are not common, but there are more examples than the classic case of the Nayar described earlier in the chapter. Among these are the Musuo of southwestern China and the Tory Islanders—a Roman Catholic, Gaelic-speaking fishing people living off the coast of Ireland. Typically, Tory Islanders do not marry until they are in their late 20s or early 30s. By then, commented one local woman,

> It's too late to break up arrangements that you
> have already known for a long time. . . . You
> know, I have my sisters and brothers to look
> after, why should I leave home to go live with
> a husband? After all, he's got his sisters and his
> brothers looking after him. (Fox, 1981)

Notably, because the community numbers but a few hundred people, husbands and wives are within easy commuting distance of each other.

According to a cross-cultural survey of family types in 192 cultures around the world, the extended family is most common, present in nearly half of those cultures, compared

household A domestic unit of one or more persons living in one residence. Other than family members, a household may include nonrelatives, such as servants.
conjugal family A family established through marriage.
consanguineal family A family of blood relatives, consisting of related women, their brothers, and the women's offspring.
nuclear family A group consisting of one or two parents and dependent offspring, which may include a stepparent, stepsiblings, and adopted children. Until recently this term referred only to the mother, father, and child(ren) unit.

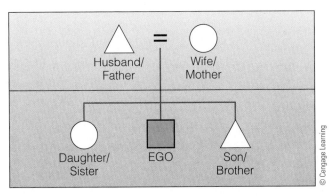

© Cengage Learning

Figure 9.10 The Nuclear Family This diagram shows the relationships in a traditional nuclear family, a form that is common but declining in North America and much of Europe.

to the nuclear family at 25 percent, and polygamy at 22 percent (Winick, 1970). Each of these is discussed next.

The Nuclear Family

The smallest family unit is the **nuclear family**, made up of one or two parents and dependent offspring, which may include a stepparent, stepsiblings, and adopted children (**Figure 9.10**). Until recently, the term *nuclear family* referred solely to the mother, father, and child(ren) unit—the family form that most North Americans, Europeans, and many others regard as the normal or natural nucleus of larger family units. In the United States, traditional mother, father, child(ren) nuclear family households reached their highest frequency around 1950, when 60 percent of all households conformed to this model (Stacey, 1990). Today, such families make up about 20 percent of U.S. households, and the term *nuclear family* is used to cover the social reality of several types of small parent–child units, including single parents with children and same-sex couples with children (Irvine, 1999; U.S. Census Bureau, 2010).

Industrialization and market capitalism have played a historical role in shaping the nuclear family most of us are familiar with today. One reason for this is that factories, mining and transportation companies, warehouses, shops, and other businesses generally pay individual wage earners

only for the jobs they are hired to do. Whether these workers are single, married, divorced, or have siblings or children is really not a concern to the profit-seeking companies. Because jobs may come and go, individual wage earners must remain mobile to adapt to the labor markets. And because few wage earners have the financial resources to support large numbers of relatives without incomes of their own, industrial or postindustrial societies do not favor the continuance of larger extended families (discussed below), which are standard in most societies traditionally dependent on pastoral nomadism, agriculture, or horticulture.

Interestingly, the nuclear family is also likely to be prominent in traditional foraging societies such as that of the Eskimo people who live in the barren Arctic environments of eastern Siberia (Russia), Alaska, Greenland, and Canada (where Eskimos are now known as Inuit) (**Figure 9.11**). In the winter the traditional Inuit husband and wife, with their children, roam the vast Arctic Canadian snowscape in their quest for food. The husband hunts and makes shelters. The wife cooks, is responsible for the children, and makes the clothing and keeps it in good repair. One of a wife's traditional chores is to chew her husband's boots to soften the leather for the next day so that he can resume his quest for game. The wife and her children could not survive without the husband, and life for a man is unimaginable without a wife.

© Cengage Learning

Similar to nuclear families in industrial societies, those living under especially harsh environmental conditions must be prepared to fend for themselves. Such isolation comes with its own set of challenges, including the difficulties of rearing children without multigenerational support

© Eastcott-Momatiuk/The Image Works

Figure 9.11 Nuclear Families in the Canadian Arctic Among Inuit people in Canada who still hunt for much of their food, nuclear families, such as the one shown here, are typical. Their isolation from other relatives is usually temporary. Much of the time they are found in groups of at least a few related families.

Figure 9.12 Extended Family Households In many Maya communities, sons bring their wives to live in houses built on the edges of a small open plaza, on one edge of which their father's house already stands. Numerous household activities are carried out on this plaza—children play while adults do some productive work or socialize with guests. The head of the family is the sons' father, who makes most of the important decisions. All members of the family work together for the common good and deal with outsiders as a single unit.

© Joe Cavanaugh/DDB Stock

and a lack of familial care for the elderly. Nonetheless, this form of family is well adapted to a mode of subsistence that requires a high degree of geographic mobility. For the Inuit in Canada, this mobility permits the hunt for food; for other North Americans, the hunt for jobs and improved social status require a mobile form of family unit.

The Extended Family

When two or more closely related nuclear families cluster together in a large domestic group, they form a unit known as the **extended family**. This larger family unit, common in traditional horticultural, agricultural, and pastoral societies around the world, typically consists of siblings with their spouses and offspring, and often their parents. All of these kin, some related by blood and some by marriage, live and work together for the common good and deal with outsiders as a single unit. Extended family households exist in many parts of the world, including among the Maya of Central America and Mexico (Vogt, 1990) **(Figure 9.12)**.

Because members of the younger generation bring their husbands or wives to live in the family, extended families have continuity through time. As older members die off, new members are born into the family. Extended families have built into them particular challenges. Among these are difficulties that the in-marrying individual is likely to have in adjusting to the spouse's family.

Nontraditional Families and Nonfamily Households

In North America and parts of Europe, increasing numbers of people live in nonfamily households, either alone or with people who are not relatives. In fact, about one-third

of households in the United States fall into this category **(Figure 9.13)**. Many others live as members of what are often called *nontraditional families*.

Increasingly common are *cohabitation* households, made up of unmarried couples. Since 1960, such households have increased dramatically in number especially among young couples in their 20s and early 30s in North America and parts of Europe. In Norway, for example, over half of all live births now occur outside marriage. One reason for this is that Norwegian couples who have lived together for at least two years and who have children have many of the same rights and obligations as their married counterparts (Noack, 2001). For many, however, cohabitation represents a relatively short-term domestic arrangement because most cohabiting couples either marry or separate within two years (Forste, 2008).

Cohabitation breakup has contributed to the growing number of *single-parent* households—as have increases in divorce, sexual activity outside marriage, declining marriage rates among women of childbearing age, and the number of women preferring single motherhood. In the United States, more than a third of all births occur outside of marriage (Stein & St. George, 2009). The percentage of U.S. single-parent households has grown to nearly 10 percent, whereas the number composed of married couples with children has dropped to about 20 percent. Although single-parent households account for about 10 percent of all U.S. households, they are home to 30 percent of all children (under 18 years of age) in the country (U.S. Census Bureau, 2010).

In the vast majority of cases, a child in a single-parent household lives with the mother. Single-parent households headed by women are neither new nor restricted to industrial or postindustrial societies. They have been studied for a long time in Caribbean countries, where men historically have been exploited as a cheap source of labor for sugar, coffee, or banana plantations. In more recent decades, many of these men are now also working as temporary migrant laborers in foreign countries, primarily in the United States—often living in temporary households composed of fellow laborers.

extended family Two or more closely related nuclear families clustered together in a large domestic group.

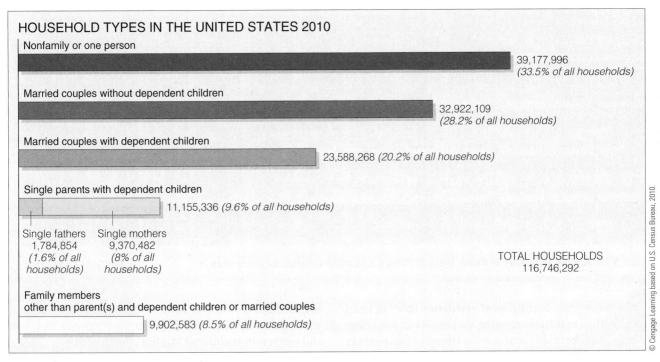

HOUSEHOLD TYPES IN THE UNITED STATES 2010

Nonfamily or one person
39,177,996
(33.5% of all households)

Married couples without dependent children
32,922,109
(28.2% of all households)

Married couples with dependent children
23,588,268 *(20.2% of all households)*

Single parents with dependent children
11,155,336 *(9.6% of all households)*

Single fathers
1,784,854
(1.6% of all households)

Single mothers
9,370,482
(8% of all households)

TOTAL HOUSEHOLDS
116,746,292

Family members
other than parent(s) and dependent children or married couples
9,902,583 *(8.5% of all households)*

© Cengage Learning based on U.S. Census Bureau, 2010.

Figure 9.13 Various Kinds of U.S. Households What has been traditionally considered the most prevalent household type, married couples with dependent children, is now only about 20 percent of the total number of households.

Also significant today are the high numbers of *blended families*. These are families composed of a married couple together raising children from previous unions.

Residence Patterns

When some form of conjugal or extended family is the norm, family exogamy requires that either the husband or wife, if not both, must move to a new household upon marriage. There are several common patterns of residence that a newly married couple may adopt—the prime determinant being ecological circumstances, although other factors enter in as well. Thus, postmarital residence arrangements, far from being arbitrary, are adaptive in character.

Patrilocal residence is a pattern in which a married couple lives in the husband's father's place of residence. This arrangement is most often found in cultural situations in which men play a predominant role in subsistence, particularly if they own property that can be accumulated; when polygyny is customary; when warfare is prominent enough to make cooperation among men especially important; and when an elaborate political organization exists in which men wield authority. These conditions are most often found together in societies that rely on animal husbandry and/or intensive agriculture for subsistence. Where patrilocal residence is customary, the bride often must move to a different band or community. In such cases, her parents' family is not only losing the services of a useful family member, but they are losing her potential offspring as well. Hence, usually there is some kind of compensation to her family, most commonly bride-price.

Matrilocal residence, in which a married couple lives in the wife's mother's place of residence, is likely if cultural ecological circumstances make the role of the woman predominant for subsistence. It is found most often in horticultural societies in which political organization is relatively uncentralized and cooperation among women is important. The Hopi Indians provide one example. Although it is the Hopi men who do the farming, the women control access to land and "own" the harvest. Men are not even allowed in the granaries. Under matrilocal residence, men usually do not move very far from the family in which they were raised, so they are available to help out there from time to time. Therefore, marriage usually does not involve compensation to the groom's family. Less common, but also found in matrilineal societies, is *avunculocal residence*, in which the couple lives with the husband's mother's brother.

In **neolocal residence**, a married couple forms a household in a separate location. This occurs when the independence of the nuclear family is emphasized. In industrial societies such as the United States—in which most economic activity occurs outside rather than inside the family, and it is important for individuals to be able to move where jobs can be found—neolocal residence is better suited than any of the other patterns.

patrilocal residence A residence pattern in which a married couple lives in the husband's father's place of residence.

matrilocal residence A residence pattern in which a married couple lives in the wife's mother's place of residence.

neolocal residence A residence pattern in which a married couple establishes its household in a location apart from either the husband's or the wife's relatives.

© Harald E. L. Prins

Challenge Issue

All humans face the challenge of creating and maintaining a social network that reaches beyond the capabilities of close relatives or a single household to provide security and support. On a basic level that network is arranged by kinship, extending to more distantly related individuals who claim descent from the same ancestor. For many traditional peoples around the world, including Scottish highlanders, large kin-groups called clans have been important. There are several dozen Scottish clans, with members often sharing the same surname. Pictured here is the opening parade of the international Clan Grant summer games in Spey Valley, Scotland. Like members of other clans, the Grants publicly show their collective identity by wearing kilts and shawls with the distinct tartan (plaid) of their clan. Over several centuries, thousands of Scots were deported, fled, or emigrated from their homelands, settling overseas, especially in Australia, Canada, and the United States. Many, including people from Clan Grant, married into North American Indian tribes. Today, their widely scattered offspring can be found across the globe, including among Cherokee, Cree, or Muskogee Indians. Aided by the Internet, many seek to reestablish social ties of shared descent, traveling long distances to clan gatherings to celebrate their cultural heritage with traditional dancing, piping, games, and food. Cherokees attended the Clan Grant gathering shown here.

Kinship and Descent

10

All societies rely on some form of family and household organization to meet basic human needs: securing food, fuel, and shelter; protecting against danger; coordinating work; regulating sexual activities; and organizing childrearing. Although they may be efficient and flexible, the family and household organizations of many societies may not be sufficient to handle all the challenges they confront. For example, members of one independent local group often need some means of interacting with people outside their immediate circle for defense against natural disasters or outside aggressors. A wider circle may also be necessary in forming a cooperative workforce for tasks that require more participants than close relatives alone can provide.

Humans have come up with many ways to widen their circles of support to meet such challenges. One is through a formal political system, with personnel to make and enforce laws, keep the peace, allocate scarce resources, and perform other regulatory and societal functions. But the predominant way to build this support in societies that are not organized as political states—especially foraging, crop-growing, and herding societies—is by means of **kinship**, a network of relatives into which individuals are born and married, and with whom they cooperate based on customarily prescribed rights and obligations. The more that individuals become enmeshed in larger networks, as happens in political states, the less they depend on kinship for survival. Still, as explained in this chapter, kinship is fundamental in the organization of any society, past and present.

Descent Groups

A common way of organizing a society along kinship lines is by creating what anthropologists call descent groups. Found in many societies, a **descent group** is any kin-group whose members share a direct line of descent from a real (historical) or fictional common ancestor. Members of such a group trace their shared connections back to such an

kinship A network of relatives into which individuals are born and married, and with whom they cooperate based on customarily prescribed rights and obligations.

descent group Any kin-group whose members share a direct line of descent from a real (historical) or fictional common ancestor.

IN THIS CHAPTER
YOU WILL LEARN TO

- Explain how kinship is the basis of social organization in every culture.

- Apply kinship terminology as a cross-cultural code for analyzing social networks.

- Contrast cultures in which ancestry is traced through foremothers, forefathers, or both.

- Distinguish the characteristics of lineages and clans from those of kindreds.

- Identify three kinship terminology systems and the significance of their distinct classifications of close relatives for family attitudes and behavior.

- Interpret totemism as a cultural phenomenon.

- Discuss the significance of kinship in the contexts of adoption and new reproductive technologies.

BIOCULTURAL CONNECTION

Maori Origins: Ancestral Genes and Mythical Canoes

Anthropologists have been fascinated to find that the oral traditions of Maori people in New Zealand fit quite well with scientific findings. New Zealand, an island country whose dramatic geography served as the setting for the *Lord of the Rings* film trilogy, lies in a remote corner of the Pacific Ocean about 1,900 kilometers (1,200 miles) southeast of Australia. Named by Dutch seafarers who landed on its shores in 1642, it was claimed by the British as a colony about 150 years later. Maori, the country's indigenous people, fought back but were outgunned, outnumbered, and forced to lay down their arms in the early 1870s. Today, nearly 600,000 of New Zealand's 4.1 million citizens claim some Maori ancestry.

Maori have an age-old legend about how they came to Aotearoa ("Land of the Long White Cloud"), their name for New Zealand: More than twenty-five generations ago,

their Polynesian ancestors arrived in a great fleet of sailing canoes from Hawaiki, their mythical homeland sometimes identified with Tahiti where the native language closely resembles their own. According to chants and genealogies passed down through the ages, this fleet consisted of at least seven (perhaps up to thirteen) seafaring canoes. Estimated to weigh about 5 tons, each of these large dugouts had a single claw-shaped sail and carried 50 to 120 people, plus food supplies, plants, and animals.

As described by Maori anthropologist Te Rangi Hiroa (Peter Buck), the seafaring skills of these voyagers enabled them to navigate by currents, winds, and stars across vast ocean expanses.[a] Perhaps escaping warfare and tribute payments in Hawaiki, they probably made the 5-week-long voyage around 1350 AD, although there were earlier and later canoes as well.

Traditional Maori society is organized into about thirty different *iwis* ("tribes"), grouped into thirteen *wakas* ("canoes"), each with its own traditional territory. Today, prior to giving a formal talk, Maori still introduce themselves by identifying their *iwi*, their *waka,* and the major sacred places of their ancestral territory. Their genealogy connects them to their tribe's founding ancestor who was a crewmember or perhaps even a chief in one of the giant canoes mentioned in the legend of the Great Fleet.[b]

Maori oral traditions about their origins mesh with scientific data based on anthropological and more recent genetic research. Study by outsiders can be controversial because Maori equate an individual's genes to his or her genealogy, which belongs to one's *iwi* or ancestral community. Considered sacred and entrusted to the tribal elders, genealogy is traditionally surrounded by *tapu* ("sacred prohibitions").[c] The Maori term for genealogy is *whakapapa* ("to set layer upon layer"), which is also a word for gene. This Maori term captures something of the original *genous,* the Greek word for "begetting offspring." Another Maori word for *gene* is *ira tangata* ("life spirit of mortals"), and for them, a gene has *mauri* (a "life force"). Given these spiritual associations, genetic investigations of Maori human DNA could not proceed until the Maori themselves became actively involved in the research.

Together with other researchers, Maori geneticist Adele Whyte has examined sex-linked genetic markers, namely mitochondrial DNA in women and Y chromosomes in men.[d] She recently calculated that the number of Polynesian females required to found New Zealand's Maori population ranged between 170 and 230 women. If the original fleet sailing to Aotearoa consisted of seven large canoes, it probably carried a total of about 600 people (men, women, and children).

ancestor through a chain of parent–child links. The addition of a few culturally meaningful obligations and taboos helps hold the structured social group together.

Although many important functions of the descent group are taken over by other institutions when a society becomes politically organized as a state, elements of such kin-ordered groups (kin-groups) may continue. We see this with many traditional indigenous societies that have become part of larger state societies yet endure as distinctive kin-ordered communities. So it is with the Maori of New Zealand, featured in this chapter's Biocultural

Connection. Retaining key elements of their traditional social structure, they are still organized in about thirty large descent groups known as *iwi* ("tribes"), which form part of larger social and territorial units known as *waka* ("canoes").

Descent group membership must be sharply defined in order to operate effectively in a kin-ordered society. If membership is allowed to overlap, it is unclear where someone's primary loyalty belongs, especially when different descent groups have conflicting interests. Membership can be determined in a number of ways. The most common way is what anthropologists refer to as *unilineal descent.*

The canoes the ancient Maori used probably looked similar to this contemporary Maori sea canoe.

A comparison of the DNA of Maori with that of Polynesians across the Pacific Ocean and peoples from Southeast Asia reveals a genetic map of ancient Maori migration routes. Mitochondrial DNA, which is passed along virtually unchanged from mothers to their children, provides a genetic clock linking today's Polynesians to southern Taiwan's indigenous coastal peoples, showing that female ancestors originally set out from that island off the southeastern coast of China about 6,000 years ago.[e] In the next few thousand years, they migrated by way of the Philippines and then hopped south and east from island to island. Adding to their gene pool in the course of later generations, Melanesian males from New Guinea and elsewhere joined the migrating bands before arriving in Aotearoa.

In short, Maori cultural traditions in New Zealand are generally substantiated by anthropological as well as molecular biological data.

BIOCULTURAL QUESTION

Why do you think the Maori view genealogy as sacred and attach certain prohibitions to it?

[a]Buck, P. H. (1938). *Vikings of the Pacific.* Chicago: University Press of Chicago.

[b]Hanson, A. (1989). The making of the Maori: Culture invention and its logic. *American Anthropologist 91* (4), 890–902.

[c]Mead, A. T. P. (1996). Genealogy, sacredness, and the commodities market. *Cultural Survival Quarterly 20* (2).

[d]Whyte, A. L. H. (2005). Human evolution in Polynesia. *Human Biology 77* (2), 157–177.

[e]"Gene study suggests Polynesians came from Taiwan." (2005, July 4). Reuters.

Unilineal Descent

Unilineal descent (sometimes called *unilateral descent*) establishes group membership based on descent traced exclusively through either the male *or* the female line of ancestry.

Traditionally, unilineal descent groups are common in many parts of the world. Each newborn becomes part of a specific descent group, traced through the female line (by **matrilineal descent**) or through the male line (by **patrilineal descent**). In matrilineal societies females are culturally recognized as socially significant because they are considered responsible for the descent group's continued existence. In patrilineal societies, this responsibility falls on the male members

---

unilineal descent Descent traced exclusively through either the male or the female line of ancestry to establish group membership.

matrilineal descent Descent traced exclusively through the female line of ancestry to establish group membership.

patrilineal descent Descent traced exclusively through the male line of ancestry to establish group membership.

of the descent group, thereby enhancing their social importance.

The two major forms of a unilineal descent group (be it patrilineal or matrilineal) are the lineage and the clan. A **lineage** is a unilineal kin-group descended from a common ancestor or founder who lived four to six generations ago and in which relationships among members can be exactly stated in genealogical terms. A **clan** is an extended unilineal kin-group, often consisting of several lineages, whose members claim common descent from a remote ancestor, usually legendary or mythological.

Patrilineal Descent and Organization

Patrilineal descent is the more widespread of the two unilineal descent systems. Through forefathers, members of a patrilineal group trace their descent from a common ancestor (**Figure 10.1**). Brothers and sisters belong to the descent group of their father's father, their father, their father's siblings, and their father's brother's children. A man's son and daughter also trace their descent back through the male line to their common ancestor. In the typical patrilineal group, authority over the children rests with the father or his elder brother. A woman belongs to the same descent group as her father and his brothers, but her children do not because they are born into her husband's descent group.

Patrilineal kinship organization is traditionally embedded in many cultures worldwide and often endures despite radical political and economic changes. So it is among the Han, China's ethnic majority. Even after the 1949 communist revolution that radically changed Chinese society, remnants of the old patrilineal clan system persist—especially in rural areas.

Patrilineal Descent among Han Chinese

For a few thousand years the basic unit for economic cooperation among the Han Chinese was the large extended family, typically including aged parents and their sons, their sons' wives, and their sons' children (Hsiaotung, 1939). With patrilocal residence, Han children grew up in a

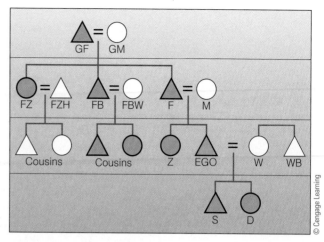

Figure 10.1 **Tracing Patrilineal Descent** Only the individuals symbolized by a filled-in circle or triangle are in the same descent group as EGO (the central person from whom the degree of each kinship relationship is traced). The abbreviation F stands for father, B for brother, H for husband, S for son, M for mother, Z for sister, W for wife, D for daughter, and G for grand.

household dominated by their father and his male relatives. The father was a source of discipline, and children customarily maintained a respectful social distance.

With brothers and their sons being part of the same household, a Han boy's paternal uncle was like a second father. He was treated with the same obedience and respect as the father, and his sons were like brothers. Accordingly, the Han kinship term for one's own father is also used for the father's brother, and the term for a brother is used for the father's brother's sons. When extended families became too large and unwieldy, one or more sons established separate households—but the tie to their household of birth remained strong.

Although family membership was and is important for each Han individual, the traditional primary social unit is the lineage, or in Han terms, the *tsu*. Each *tsu* is a corporate kin-group whose members trace their ancestry back about five generations exclusively through the male line to a common ancestor. A woman belongs to her father's *tsu*, but traditionally, for all practical purposes, she was absorbed by the *tsu* of her husband, with whom she lived after marriage.

The *tsu* could be counted on to help its members economically, and it functioned as a legal body, passing judgment on misbehaving members. People affiliated with the same *tsu* came together on ceremonial occasions, including weddings, funerals, and rituals honoring their ancestors. Recently deceased ancestors, up to about three generations back, were given offerings of food and paper money on the anniversaries of their births and deaths, whereas more distant ancestors were collectively worshiped five times a year. Each *tsu*

lineage A unilineal kin-group descended from a common ancestor or founder who lived four to six generations ago and in which relationships among members can be exactly stated in genealogical terms.

clan An extended unilineal kin-group, often consisting of several lineages, whose members claim common descent from a remote ancestor, usually legendary or mythological.

Figure 10.2 An Ancestral Temple in Zhejiang Province, China Among the Han, the ethnic majority in China, almost all ancestral temples, or clan houses, are dedicated to male fore-bears, reflecting the country's long-established patrilineal rules of descent and cultural values. Clan members affirm their place in the kin-group by making offerings to the ancestors in special temples such as the one pictured here, located in a family home.

maintained its own shrine for storage of ancestral tablets on which the names of all members were recorded (**Figure 10.2**).

Just as families periodically split up into new ones, larger descent groups periodically splintered along the lines of their main family branches. Causes for splits included disputes among brothers over management of landholdings and suspicion of unfair division of profits. Even after such fissions, a new *tsu* continued to recognize and honor its lineage tie to the old *tsu*. Thus, over many generations, a whole hierarchy of descent groups came into being, with all persons having the same surname considering themselves to be members of a great patrilineal clan. With this came the rule that individuals bearing the same clan surname could not marry each other. This marriage rule is still widely practiced today.

Traditionally, owing obedience and respect to their fathers and older patrilineal relatives, Han children had to marry whomever their parents chose for them. Sons were required to care for their elderly parents and to fulfill ceremonial obligations to them after their death. In turn, inheritance passed from fathers to sons, with an extra share going to the eldest because he ordinarily made the greatest contribution to the household.

Han women, by contrast, had no claims on their families' heritable property. Once married, a woman was in effect cast off by her own *tsu* in order to produce children for her husband's family and *tsu*. Yet, members of her birth *tsu* retained some interest in her after her departure. For example, her mother would assist her in the birth of her children, and her brothers or some other male relative might intervene if her husband or other members of his family treated her badly.

Although *tsu* bonds have weakened in communist China, some of the obligations and attitudes of the traditional corporate kin-group persist today. At a minimum, contemporary Han Chinese maintain the traditions of children obeying and respecting their fathers and older patrilineal relatives.

As the Han example suggests, a patrilineal society is very much a man's world. No matter how needed and valued women may be, they find themselves in a difficult position. Far from resigning themselves to a subordinate position, however, they actively work the system to their own advantage as best they can.

From Lineage to Clan

In the course of time, as generation succeeds generation and new members are born into the lineage, the kin-group's membership may become too large to manage or may outgrow the lineage's resources. When this happens, as we have seen with the Chinese *tsu*, **fission** occurs; that is, the original lineage splits into new, smaller lineages. Usually, the members of the new lineages continue to recognize their original relationship to one another. The result of this process is the appearance of a larger kind of descent group: the clan.

As already noted, a *clan*—typically consisting of several lineages—is an extended unilineal descent group whose members claim common descent from a distant ancestor (usually legendary or mythological) but are unable to trace the precise genealogical links back to that ancestor. This stems from the great genealogical depth of the clan, whose founding ancestor lived so far in the past that the links must be assumed rather than known in detail. A clan differs from a lineage in another respect: It lacks the residential unity that is generally (although not always) characteristic of a lineage's core members.

As with the lineage, descent may be patrilineal, matrilineal, or ambilineal. Hopi Indians are an example of matrilineal clans (*matriclans*), whereas Han Chinese and Scottish highlanders, pictured in this chapter's opening, provide examples of patrilineal clans (*patriclans*). Tracing descent exclusively through men from a founding paternal ancestor, Scottish highland clans are often identified with the prefix "Mac" or "Mc" (from an old Celtic word meaning "son of"), such as MacDonald, McGregor, and Maclean.

Because clan membership is often dispersed rather than localized, it usually does not involve a shared holding of tangible property. Instead, it involves collective participation in ceremonial and political matters. Only on special occasions will the membership gather together for specific purposes.

However, clans may handle important integrative functions. Like lineages, they may regulate marriage through exogamy. Because of their dispersed membership, clans give individuals the right of entry into associated local groups no matter where they are. Members usually are expected to give protection and hospitality to others in the clan. Traditionally, this more encompassing kinship construct facilitated free travel of clan members to multiple member villages.

Lacking the residential unity of lineages, clans frequently depend on symbols—of animals, plants, natural forces, colors, and special objects—to provide members with solidarity and a ready means of identification. These symbols, called *totems*, often are associated with the clan's mythical origin and reinforce for clan members an awareness of common descent.

The word *totem* comes from the Ojibwa American Indian word *ototeman*, meaning "he is a relative of mine." **Totemism** was defined by British anthropologist A. R. Radcliffe-Brown (1931) as a set of customary beliefs and practices that set up a special system of relations between the society and important plants, animals, and other natural objects. Totemism varies among cultures. For example, Aborigines in central Australia such as the Arunta believe that each clan descends from a mythological spirit animal. Native Americans in northwest Canada such as the Tsimshian on the Pacific Coast also use totemic animals to designate their exogamous matrilineal clans but do not claim these creatures are mythological clan ancestors.

Among these coastal Indians, individuals inherit their lineage affiliations from their mothers. As such, every Tsimshian forms part of a matrilineal "house group," a corporate kin-group known as a *waap* (the plural is *wuwaap*). Typically, each village consists of about twenty such houses, ranked according to importance. Each Tsimshian house group forms part of a larger exogamous matrilineal clan, of which there are four. An animal symbolically represents these clans: Blackfish (Killer Whale), Wolf, Eagle, and Raven. Carvings of these crest animals, coupled with several other animal and human images symbolically marking the mythology and history of the lineage and validating its claims and privileges, are displayed on monumental red-cedar *totem poles* standing upright in front of the large wooden dwellings inhabited by the *wuwaap* (Anderson, 2006) (**Figure 10.6**).

We can see a reductive variation of totemism in contemporary industrial and postindustrial societies in which sports teams are often given the names of such powerful wild animals as bears, lions, and wildcats. In the United States, this extends to the Democratic Party's donkey and the Republican Party's elephant, and to the Elks, the Lions, and other fraternal and social organizations. These animal emblems, or mascots, however, do not involve the notion of biological descent and the strong sense of kinship that they symbolize for clans, nor are they linked with the traditional ritual observances associated with clan totems.

Phratries and Moieties

Larger kinds of descent groups are phratries and moieties (**Figure 10.7**). A **phratry** (after the Greek word for "brotherhood") is a unilineal descent group composed of at least two clans that supposedly share a common ancestry, whether or not they really do. Like individuals in the clan, phratry members cannot trace precisely their descent links to a common ancestor, although they firmly believe such an ancestor existed. For example, there are nine phratries in Hopi society, and within each phratry member clans are expected to support one another and observe strict exogamy. Because people from all nine phratries can be found living in any given Hopi village,

---

fission In kinship studies, the splitting of a descent group into two or more new descent groups.

totemism The belief that people are related to particular animals, plants, or natural objects by virtue of descent from common ancestral spirits.

phratry A unilineal descent group composed of at least two clans that supposedly share a common ancestry, whether or not they really do.

Figure 10.6 Tshimshian People Raising a Totem Pole The tradition of erecting totem poles to commemorate special events endures in several Native American communities in the Pacific Northwest. Carved from tall cedar trees, these spectacular monuments display a clan or lineage's ceremonial property and are prominently positioned as posts in the front of a house, as markers at gravesites, and at other places of significance. Often depicting legendary ancestors and mythological animals, the painted carvings symbolically represent a descent group's cultural status and associated privileges in the community. Noted carver David Boxley, a member of the Eagle clan, gifted this pole to the community.

marriage partners can usually be found in one's home community. This same dispersal of membership provides individuals with rights of entry into villages other than their own.

If the entire society is divided into only two major descent groups, whether they are equivalent to clans or phratries, each group is called a **moiety** (after the French word *moitié*, for "half"). Members of the moiety believe themselves to share a common ancestor but cannot prove it through definitive genealogical links. As a rule, the feelings of kinship among members of lineages and clans are stronger than those of members of phratries and moieties.

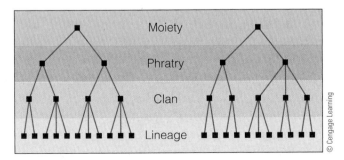

Figure 10.7 Descent Groups This diagram shows the organizational hierarchy of moieties, phratries, clans, and lineages. Each moiety is subdivided into phratries, each phratry is subdivided into clans, and each clan is subdivided into lineages.

This may be due to the much larger size and more diffuse nature of the latter groups.

Because feelings of kinship are often weaker between people from different clans, the moiety system is a cultural invention that binds clan-based communities into a social network of obligatory giving and receiving. By institutionalizing reciprocity between groups of clans, the moiety system joins together families who otherwise would not be sufficiently invested in maintaining the commonwealth.

Like lineages and clans, phratries and moieties are often exogamous, and so are bound together by marriages between their members. And like clans, they provide members rights of access to other communities. In a community that does not include one's clan members, one's phratry members are still there to turn to for hospitality. Finally, moieties may perform reciprocal services for one another. Among them, individuals look to members of the opposite "half" in their community for the necessary mourning rituals when a member of their own moiety dies. Such interdependence between moieties serves to maintain the cohesion of the entire society.

The principle of institutionalized reciprocity between groups of matrilineal clans organized into two equal

moiety Each group, usually consisting of several clans, that results from a division of a society into two halves on the basis of descent.

Figure 10.8 Village Life in Moieties Many Amazonian Indians in South America's tropical woodlands traditionally live in circular villages socially divided into moieties. Here we see the Canela Indians' Escalvado village as it was in 1970. The village is 300 meters (165 feet) wide. The community's "upper" moiety meets in the western part. Nearly all of the 1,800 members of the Canela tribe reside in the village during festival seasons, but otherwise they are largely dispersed into their smaller, farm-centered circular villages. (Behind the larger-circle village is a smaller abandoned village where part of the tribe lived before uniting under one chief. Missionaries built the landing strip that runs through it.)

© Ray Roberts Brown/Smithsonian Institution

halves, or moieties, is beautifully illustrated in the circular settlement pattern of many traditional Indian villages in the tropical forest of South America's Amazon region (**Figure 10.8**). Dwellings located in half of the village are those of clans belonging to one exogamous moiety, and those on the opposite side are the dwellings of clans belonging to the other. Because their clans are often matrilineal, the institutionalized rules of reciprocity in this kin-ordered community traditionally require that a woman marry a man from a clan house on the opposite side of the village, who then moves into her ancestral clan house. Their son, however, will one day have to find a wife from his father's original moiety and will have to move to his father's mother's side of the village. In this way, the moiety system of institutionalized reciprocity functions like a social "zipper" between clans engaged in a repetitive cycle of exchange relations.

Bilateral Kinship and the Kindred

Important as patrilineal or matrilineal descent groups are in many cultures, such kin-groups do not exist in every society. In some, we encounter another type of extended family group known as the **kindred**—a grouping of blood relatives based on bilateral descent. The kindred includes

all relatives with whom **EGO** shares at least one grandparent, great-grandparent, or even great-great-grandparent, on his or her father's *and* mother's side. Thus, depending on how many generations back one reckons, someone's kindred may include the entire direct-line offspring of his or her eight great-grandparents, or sometimes even sixteen great-great-grandparents (**Figure 10.9**).

In societies in which small domestic units (nuclear families or single-parent households) are of primary importance, bilateral kinship and kindred organization are likely to result. This can be seen in modern industrial and postindustrial societies, in emerging market economies in the developing world, and in still-existing food-foraging societies throughout the world.

Most Europeans and peoples of European descent in other parts of the world are familiar with the kindred: Those who belong to it are simply referred to as "relatives." It typically includes those blood relatives on both sides of the family who are seen on important occasions, such as family weddings, reunions, and funerals. In Ireland, Puerto Rico, or the United States, for example, nearly everyone can identify the members of their kindred up to grandparents (or even great-grandparents) and to their first cousins, nephews, and nieces. Some can even identify second cousins in their kindred, but few can go beyond that.

In traditional societies with bilateral descent, kindreds play a significant role in a variety of situations. Kindred members ("next of kin") may be called upon to seek justice or revenge for harm done to someone in the group. They might raise bail, serve as witnesses, or help compensate a victim's family. If blood money (financial reparation for the loss of a murdered relative) is involved, kindred members would be entitled to a share of it. In such societies, a trading or raiding party may be composed of a kindred, with the

kindred A grouping of blood relatives based on bilateral descent. Includes all relatives with whom EGO shares at least one grandparent, great-grandparent, or even great-great-grandparent, on his or her father's *and* mother's side.

EGO In kinship studies, the central person from whom the degree of each kinship relationship is traced.

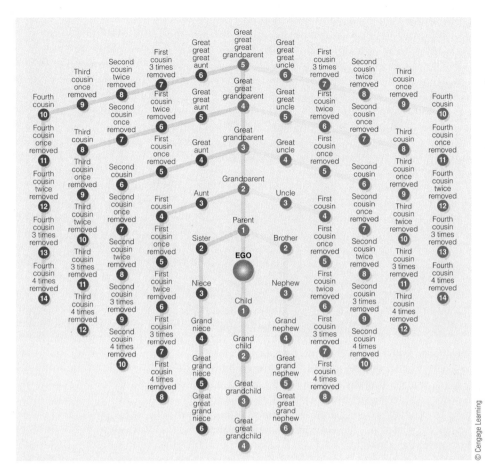

Figure 10.9 EGO and His or Her Kindred The kindred designates a person's exact degree of blood relatedness to other members of the family. This determines not only one's social obligations toward relatives, but also one's rights. For instance, when a wealthy widowed great-aunt without children dies without a will, specific surviving members of her kindred will be legally entitled to inherit from her.

© Cengage Learning

group coming together to perform a particular function, share in the results, and then disband. The kindred may also act as a ceremonial group for initiations and other rites of passage. Finally, kindreds may play a role in regulating marriage through exogamy.

Because kindreds are EGO-centered, each is unique, except among full siblings. Beyond being in the middle of one's own kindred, a person belongs to several kindreds centered on other individuals with memberships that overlap to various degrees. Thus, each person can turn to his or her own kindred for aid, or may be called upon by others, by virtue of being a member of their kindreds.

Kinship Terminology and Kinship Groups

A system of organizing people who are relatives into different kinds of groups—whether kindreds, lineages, or clans—influences how relatives are labeled. Kinship terminology systems vary considerably across cultures, reflecting the positions individuals occupy within their respective societies and helping to differentiate one relative from another. Distinguishing factors include gender, generational differences, or genealogical differences. In the various systems of kinship terminology, any one of these factors may be emphasized at the expense of others.

By looking at the terms a particular society uses for their relatives, an anthropologist can determine the structure of kin-groups, discern the most important relationships, and sometimes interpret the prevailing attitudes concerning various relationships. For instance, a number of languages use the same term to identify a brother and a cousin, and others have a single word for cousin, niece, and nephew. Some cultures find it useful to distinguish the eldest brother from his younger brothers and have different words for them. And unlike English, many languages distinguish between an aunt who is a mother's sister and one who is a father's sister.

Regardless of the factors emphasized, all kinship terminologies accomplish two important tasks. First, they classify similar kinds of individuals into single specific categories; second, they separate different kinds of individuals into distinct categories. Generally, two or more kin are merged under the same term when the individuals have more or less the same rights and obligations with respect to the person referring to them as such. This is the case among most English-speaking North Americans, for instance, when someone refers to a mother's sister and a father's sister both as an aunt. As far as the speaker is concerned, both relatives possess a similar status.

Several different systems of kinship terminology result from the application of the previously discussed principles—including the Eskimo, Hawaiian, Iroquois, Crow, Omaha, Sudanese, Kariera, and Aranda systems, each named after the ethnographic example first or best described by anthropologists. The last five of these

Figure 10.10 **Inuit Family at Outpost Camp Home, Baffin Island, Nunavut, Canada** The Inuit in Canada are one of several large Eskimo groups inhabiting Arctic regions from Greenland to Alaska and eastern Siberia. Although they speak different languages and dialects, they share a traditional way of life primarily based on hunting and fishing in which the nuclear family is the primary social unit. As such, their kinship terminology system specifically identifies EGO's mother, father, brother, and sister and lumps all other relatives into a few broad categories that do not distinguish the side of the family from which they derive.

systems are fascinating in their complexity and are found among only a few of the world's societies. However, to illustrate some of the basic principles involved, we will focus our attention on the first three systems.

The Eskimo System

The Eskimo system, which is comparatively rare among all the world's systems, is the one used by most contemporary Europeans, Australians, and North Americans. It is also used by a number of indigenous food-foraging peoples, including

Arctic peoples such as the Inuit and other Eskimos—hence the name (**Figure 10.10**).

Sometimes referred to as the *lineal system*, the **Eskimo system** emphasizes the nuclear family by specifically identifying mother, father, brother, and sister while lumping together all other relatives into a few large categories (**Figure 10.11**). For example, the father is distinguished from the father's brother (uncle), but the father's brother is not distinguished from the mother's brother (both are called uncle). The mother's sister and father's sister are treated similarly, both called aunt. In addition, all the sons

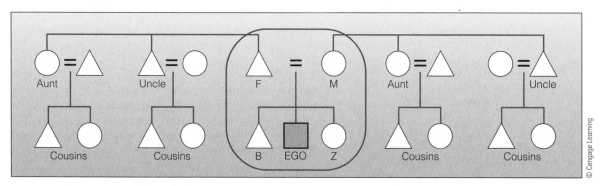

Figure 10.11 **The Eskimo Kinship System** Kinship terminology in this system emphasizes the nuclear family (circled). EGO's father and mother are distinguished from EGO's aunts and uncles, and siblings are distinguished from cousins.

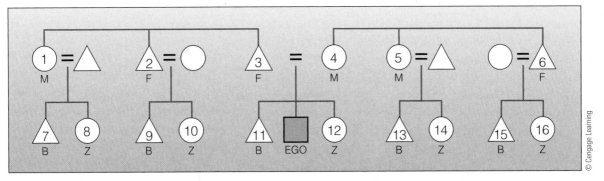

Figure 10.12 The Hawaiian Kinship System In this kinship system the men numbered 2 and 6 are called by the same term as father (3); the women numbered 1 and 5 are called by the same term as mother (4). All cousins of EGO's own generation (7 through 16) are considered brothers (B) and sisters (Z).

and daughters of aunts and uncles are called cousin, thereby making a generational distinction but without indicating the side of the family to which they belong or even their gender.

Unlike other terminologies, the Eskimo system provides separate and distinct terms for nuclear family members. This is probably because the Eskimo system is generally found in bilateral societies where the dominant kin-group is the kindred, in which only immediate family members are important in day-to-day affairs. This is especially true of modern European and North American societies, in which many families are independent—living apart from and not directly involved with other relatives except on special occasions. Thus, most North Americans (and others) generally distinguish between their closest kin (parents and siblings) but lump together (as aunts, uncles, cousins) other kin on both sides of the family.

The Hawaiian System

The **Hawaiian system** of kinship terminology, common (as its name implies) in Hawaii and other islands in the central Pacific Ocean but found elsewhere as well, is the least complex system in that it uses only a few terms. The Hawaiian system is also called the *generational system* because all relatives of the same generation and sex are referred to by the same term (**Figure 10.12**). For example, in one's parents' generation, the term used to refer to one's father is used as well for the father's brother and mother's brother. Similarly, one's mother, mother's sister, and father's sister are all grouped together under a single term. In EGO's generation, male and female cousins are distinguished by gender and are equated with brothers and sisters.

The Hawaiian system reflects the absence of strong unilineal descent, and members on both the father's and the mother's sides are viewed as more or less equal. The siblings of EGO's father and mother are all recognized as being similar relations and are merged under a single term appropriate for their gender. In like manner, the children belonging to

the siblings of EGO's parents are related to EGO in the same way as are the brother and sister. Falling under the incest taboo, they are ruled out as potential marriage partners.

The Iroquois System

In the **Iroquois system** of kinship terminology, the father and father's brother are referred to by a single term, as are the mother and mother's sister; however, the father's sister and mother's brother are given separate terms (**Figure 10.13**). In one's own generation, brothers, sisters, and parallel cousins (offspring of parental siblings of the same sex—that is, the children of the mother's sister or father's brother) of the same sex are referred to by the same terms, which is logical enough considering that they are the offspring of people who are classified in the same category as EGO's actual mother and father. Cross cousins (offspring of parental siblings of opposite sex—that is, the children of the mother's brother or father's sister) are distinguished by terms that set them apart from all other kin. In fact, cross cousins are often preferred as spouses, for marriage to them reaffirms alliances between related lineages or clans.

Iroquois terminology, named for the Iroquois Indians of North America's woodlands, is in fact very widespread and is usually found with unilineal descent groups. It was, for example, the terminology in use until recently in rural Chinese society.

Eskimo system Kinship reckoning in which the nuclear family is emphasized by specifically identifying the mother, father, brother, and sister, while lumping together all other relatives into broad categories such as uncle, aunt, and cousin; also known as a *lineal system*.

Hawaiian system Kinship reckoning in which all relatives of the same sex and generation are referred to by the same term: also known as the *generational system*.

Iroquois system Kinship reckoning in which a father and father's brother are referred to by a single term, as are a mother and mother's sister, but a father's sister and mother's brother are given separate terms. Parallel cousins are classified with brothers and sisters, whereas cross cousins are classified separately but not equated with relatives of some other generation.

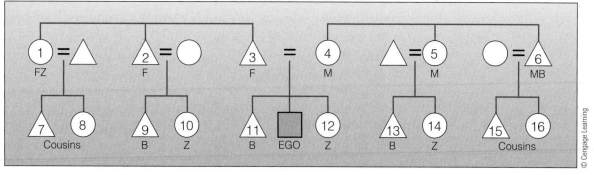

Figure 10.13 The Iroquois Kinship System According to the Iroquois system of kinship terminology, EGO's father's brother (2) is called by the same term as the father (3); the mother's sister (5) is called by the same term as the mother (4); but the people numbered 1 and 6 are each referred to by a distinct term. Those people numbered 9 through 14 are all considered siblings, but 7, 8, 15, and 16 are considered cousins.

Making Relatives

In every culture—from kin-ordered foraging, herding, or farming communities to state-organized capitalist societies—people have developed ideas about the status of relatives. These ideas concern how someone becomes one of "us"—whether by birth, paternal recognition, or some other means. And although many languages may stress the biological, as the English term *blood relative* demonstrates, what ultimately matters is the culturally defined social status of a person who is recognized as kin, with all the specific rights and obligations that come with being a daughter, son, brother, or sister to someone else in that kin-group. That is what "being related" is all about and what gives it symbolic meaning with practical consequences. Each kin term marks out a specific set of rights and obligations for individuals socially identified by such a cultural label. In state societies governed by law, these rights may even be legally spelled out in detail.

Fictive Kin by Ritual Adoption

One example of making relatives of individuals who are not biologically related is adoption—as discussed in the previous chapter's Globalscape on the transnational adoption of children. Adoption is a longstanding and widespread cultural practice in many societies all across the world.

Historically, families and clans facing exceptional challenges to their survival sometimes went to war to obtain human captives from other societies—sometimes young men, but usually women and children. These captives would then be adopted. This occurred among Iroquois Indians in northeastern America. In the 17th and 18th centuries, they often incorporated specially selected war captives and other valued strangers, including European colonists, into their kin-groups in order to make up for population losses due to warfare and disease. As soon as these newcomers were ceremonially naturalized, they acquired essentially the same birthright status as those actually born into one of the families and were henceforth identified by the same kin term as the member being replaced.

Today, it is still not uncommon in traditional societies, especially in kin-ordered communities, for the head of a clan or family to adopt an outsider, especially when such an individual is valued as a contributing member because of unique skills or contacts with the outside world. Anthropologists may be adopted in this way, as noted in our fieldwork chapter, when they are conducting long-term participant observation in a culture in which such ritual incorporation into a kin-group is customary. As outsiders committed to learning the language and culture, anthropologists may also offer valuable services in return, bringing useful gifts such as steel axes or machetes. As adopted members of a family or clan, such out/insiders provide a useful link with powerful external forces, including international organizations with a mission to protect human rights.

Becoming a godparent is a form of ritual adoption traditionally practiced in many parts of Europe—and spreading to other parts of the world through European colonization or settlement. Generally, this involves the parent(s) of a newborn child inviting another adult, whether already a relative or not, to sponsor their child when he or she is baptized and formally named. This creates a spiritual relationship in which the godfather and godmother assume co-responsibility for the child's wellbeing. (**Figure 10.14**).

One of the many variations of this institution is *compadrazgo*, or "coparenthood." Especially common in Latin America, *compadrazgo* involves a child's father and/or mother and godfather and/or godmother becoming linked to each other through the ritual of a Roman

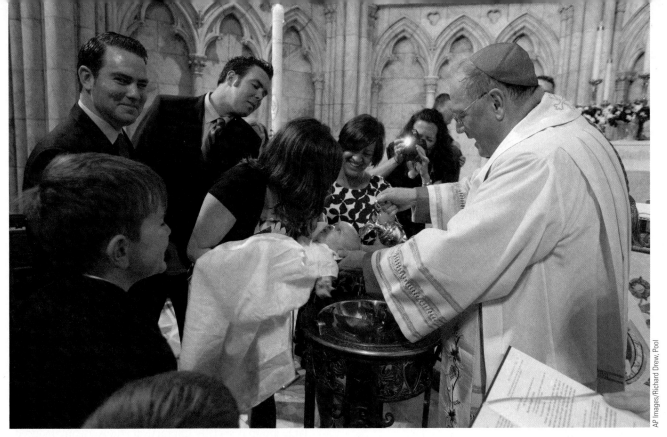

Figure 10.14 Godparents at Baby's Baptism In addition to being born into a family, people may gain relatives through adoption. Godparenting is a form of ritual adoption in which a person accepts certain lasting obligations toward someone else's child. Typically, it includes sponsoring the child's baptism ceremony, indicating a spiritual relationship. Here we see Cardinal Timothy Dolan, Archbishop of New York, baptizing a little girl held by her mother. Standing behind her, the baby's father smiles proudly while Father Dolan sprinkles blessed water on the child's head, symbolizing spiritual purification and admission into the Roman Catholic Church. Also looking on with joy are the father's brother and mother's sister. As the designated godfather and godmother, they assume responsibility for their godchild's faith and upbringing. Although the child's parents each chose a sibling for this important role, they could have selected anyone in good standing with the church.

Catholic baptism; they thereby agree to certain mutual rights and obligations. In *compadrazgo*, the main emphasis is placed not on the child–godparent relationship but on the fictive kinship between the child's parents and the sponsor who becomes a ritual coparent, or *compadre*. Historically common in South Europe and Latin America, such quasi-kinship is

> a pact for mutual support between the two *compadres*, co-parents, involved. Such a pact can be entered into between two *compadres* who are each other's equals in social and economic standing. Very often, however, it is formed between people, of whom one is wealthier, of higher social standing and more powerful politically than the other. (Wolf & Hansen, 1972, pp. 131–132)

Kinship and New Reproductive Technologies

Today's advances in reproductive technologies also pose new opportunities for kin-making. As defined in the previous chapter, *new reproductive technologies (NRTs)* are alternative means of reproduction such as surrogate motherhood and in vitro fertilization. Since 1978, when the world's first test-tube baby was created, thousands of babies have been created outside the womb, without sexual intercourse—and all kinds of new technologies have become part of the reproductive repertoire.

These technologies have opened up a mind-boggling array of reproductive possibilities and social relations. For example, if a child is conceived from a donor egg, implanted in another woman's womb, to be raised by yet another woman, who is the child's mother? To complicate matters even further, the egg may have been fertilized by sperm from a donor not married to, or in a sexual relationship with, any of these women. Indeed, it has been suggested that about a dozen different modern kin-type categories are embraced in the concepts of mother and father in today's changing societies (Stone, 2005).

Clearly, NRTs challenge previously held notions of parenthood and kinship. They force us to rethink what being biologically related to others really means. Moreover, they drive home the point that the human capacity for securing relatives is not only impressive and ingenious but also fascinating.

Challenge Issue

Beyond ties of kinship and household, people extend their social networks to cope with multiple challenges of human survival. They form groups based on shared identities, interests, or objectives, with memberships that may be compulsory or voluntary. Together, individuals interact, collaborate, and overcome obstacles. Collective action strengthens ties that bind but also reduces tensions that divide. In playing games, including sports, people show off superior mental or physical skills within and between groups but also reveal or act out some of their culture's core values. Many sports have their origins in warfare, with rivals demonstrating skills and endurance. Here we see Afghan horsemen playing a traditional sport, in which sometimes up to 200 riders fiercely compete for possession of a headless body of a goat. For this reason, the region's Tajik and Pashtun refer to their national sport as *buzkashi* ("goat-grabbing"). Players from rival teams pick up and carry the carcass around a marker at one end of the field and then throw it into the scoring circle at the opposite end. Competing for glory and prize money on special holidays, all the players—and spectators— in these gender-segregated cultures are male.

Grouping by Gender, Age, Common Interest, and Social Status

**IN THIS CHAPTER
YOU WILL LEARN TO**

- Explain how social groups are formed based on age and gender, with anthropological examples of each.

- Identify different types of common-interest groups, noting their function in expanding an individual's social network beyond relatives, friends, and neighbors.

- Distinguish between egalitarian and stratified societies, with examples of each.

- Compare open-class and closed-class societies, with cultural anthropological details of each.

- Evaluate the structural similarities and differences between class, caste, and race in a stratified society.

- Recognize the challenges and opportunities of social mobility in different types of societies.

Anthropologists have given considerable attention to kinship and marriage, which operate as organizing principles in all societies and are usually the prime basis of social order in stateless societies. Yet, because ties of kinship and household are not always sufficient to handle all the challenges of human survival, people also form groups based on gender, age, common interest, and social status.

Grouping by Gender

As shown in preceding chapters, division of labor along gender lines occurs in all human societies. In some cultures, many tasks that men and women undertake may be shared, or people may perform work normally assigned to the opposite sex without loss of face. In others, however, men and women are rigidly segregated in what they do. Such is the case in many maritime cultures, where seafarers aboard fishing, whaling, and trading ships are usually men. For instance, we find temporary all-male communities aboard ships of coastal Basque fishermen in northwestern Spain, Yupik Eskimo whalers in Alaska, and Swahili merchants sailing along the East African coast. These seafarers commonly leave their wives, mothers, and daughters behind in their home ports, sometimes for months at a time.

Clearly demarcated grouping by gender also occurs in many traditional horticultural societies. For instance, among the Mundurucu Indians of Brazil's Amazon rainforest, men and women work, eat, and sleep separately. From age 13 onward, males live together in one large house, whereas women, girls, and preteen boys occupy two or three houses grouped around the men's house: Men associate with men, and women with women.

Figure 11.1 Sacred Trumpets of the Amazon Gender-based groups are common among the Mundurucu and numerous other Amazonian Indian nations such as the Yawalapiti pictured here, who live on the Tuatuari River in Brazil's upper Xingu region. Gender issues are symbolically worked out in their mythologies and ceremonial dances. One common theme concerns ownership of the sacred trumpets, which represent spiritual power. The tribesmen zealously guard these trumpets, and only men are allowed to play them. Traditionally, women were even forbidden to see them.

© Reuters/Corbis

Among the Mundurucu, relations between the sexes are not harmonious but rather are in opposition. According to their belief, sex roles were once reversed. Women ruled over men and controlled the sacred trumpets that are the symbols of power and represent the reproductive capacities of women. But because women could not hunt, they could not supply the meat demanded by the ancient spirits that possessed the trumpets. This enabled the men to take the trumpets from the women, establishing their dominance in the process. Ever since, the trumpets have been carefully guarded and hidden in the men's house, and traditionally women were prohibited from even seeing them (**Figure 11.1**).

Thus, Mundurucu men express fear and envy toward women and seek to control them by force. For their part, the women neither like nor accept a submissive status, and even though men occupy all formal positions of political and religious leadership, women are autonomous in the economic realm.

Alongside notable differences, there are also interesting similarities between the Mundurucu beliefs and those of traditional European and North American cultures. For example, many 19th-century European and U.S. intellectuals held to the idea that patriarchy (rule by men) had replaced an earlier state of matriarchy (rule by women). Moreover, the idea that men may use force to control women is deeply embedded in Judaic, Christian, and Muslim traditions. Although gender inequality has largely been erased in many parts of the world, gender-based groups persist for purposes of mutual support, religious worship, sports, and entertainment.

Grouping by Age

Like gender, grouping by age is based on human biology and as such is a cultural universal. All human societies recognize a number of life stages. The demarcation and duration of these stages vary across cultures, but each one provides distinctive social roles and comes with certain cultural features such as specific patterns of activity, attitudes, obligations, and prohibitions.

In many cultures, the social position of an individual in a specific life stage is also marked by a distinctive outward appearance in terms of dress, hairstyle, body paint, tattoos, insignia, or some other symbolic distinction. Typically, these stages are designed to help the transition from one age to another, to teach needed skills, or to lend economic assistance. Often they are taken as the basis for the formation of organized groups.

In North America today, for instance, a child's first friends are usually children of his or her own age. Starting preschool or kindergarten with age-mates, children typically move through a dozen or more years in the educational system together. At specified ages they are allowed to see certain movies, drive cars, and do things reserved for adults, such as voting, drinking alcoholic beverages, and serving in the military. Ultimately, North Americans retire from their paid jobs at a specified age and, increasingly, spend the final years of their lives in retirement communities, segregated from the rest of society. In the course of their life cycle, they are referred to by a series of labels, including "babies," "teenagers," "adults," "middle-agers," and "senior citizens"—whether they like it or not and for no other reason than the number of years they have lived.

Age classification also plays a significant role in non-Western societies that, at a minimum, mark distinctions among immature, mature, and older people whose physical powers are waning. In these societies old age often has profound significance, bringing with it the period of greatest respect (for women it may mean the first social equality with men). Rarely are the elderly shunted aside or abandoned. Even the Inuit of the Canadian Arctic, who are often cited as a migratory people who literally abandon their old and infirm relatives, do so only in truly desperate circumstances, when the traveling group's physical survival is at stake. In all oral tradition societies, elders are the repositories of accumulated wisdom for their people. Recognized as such and no longer expected to carry out many subsistence activities, they play a major role in passing on cultural knowledge to their grandchildren.

As a result of improvements in health care, medical technology, and other factors reducing mortality, more and more people live longer today than in previous generations, especially in wealthy societies. In the United States, for example, the average life expectancy rose from about 49 in 1900 to 68 in 1950 and reached just above 77 in 2000. Generally, women live longer than men, but the gap has widened from less than two years a century ago to more than five today, with American women now enjoying an average life expectancy of about 80 years. Japanese women hold the record for the world's longest life expectancy, with an average life span of about 86.5, whereas Japanese men average about six years less.

With the rise in average life expectancy, people not only grow older but also grow in numbers. For instance, the number of U.S. senior citizens 65 years and older is expected to swell from about 40 million to 70 million (20 percent of the overall U.S. population) within the next two decades. Consequently, health and welfare costs for the elderly will continue to rise, a social and financial burden shared with Japan and many other rapidly aging societies (U.S. Census Bureau, Statistical Abstract, 2012).

Institutions of Age Grouping

An organized category of people with membership on the basis of age is known as an **age grade**. Entry into and transfer out of age grades may be accomplished individually, either by a biological distinction, such as puberty, or by a socially recognized status, such as marriage or childbirth.

Members of an age grade may have much in common—engaging in similar activities and sharing the same orientation and aspirations. In many cultures, a specific time is established for ritually moving from a younger to an older grade. An example of this is the traditional Jewish ceremony of the *bar mitzvah* (a Hebrew term meaning "son of the commandment"), marking that a 13-year-old boy has reached the age of religious duty and responsibility.

Bat mitzvah, "daughter of the commandment," is the term for the equivalent ritual for a girl.

Although members of senior groups commonly expect deference from and acknowledge certain responsibilities to their juniors, this does not necessarily mean that one grade is seen as better, or worse, or even more important than another. There can be standardized competition (opposition) between age grades, such as that traditionally between first-year and second-year students on U.S. college campuses.

In addition to age grades, some societies feature age sets (sometimes referred to as *age classes*). An **age set** is a formally established group of people born during a certain time span who move together through the series of age-grade categories. Members of an age set usually remain closely associated throughout their lives. This is akin to but distinct from the broad and informal North American practice of identifying generation clusters composed of all individuals born within a particular time frame—such as baby boomers (1946–1964), Gen-Xers (1961–1981), and the Millennial or Internet generation (1982–2000) (year spans approximate).

The notion of an age set implies strong feelings of loyalty and mutual support. Because such groups may possess property, songs, shield designs, and rituals and are internally organized for collective decision making and leadership, age sets are distinct from simple age grades.

Age Grouping in East Africa

Although age is a criterion for group membership in many parts of the world, its most varied and elaborate use is found in several pastoral groups in East Africa, such as the Maasai, Samburu, and Tiriki in Kenya (Sangree, 1965). In Tiriki society, each boy born within a fifteen-year period joins a particular age set. Seven named age sets exist, but only one is open for membership at a time. When it closes, the next one opens. And so it continues until the passage of 105 years (7 times 15), when the first set's membership is gone due to death, and it opens once again to take in new recruits.

Members of Tiriki age sets remain together for life as they move through four successive age grades. Advancement in age grades occurs at fifteen-year intervals, coinciding with the closing of the oldest age set and the opening of a new one. Each age group has its own particular duties and responsibilities. Traditionally, the first age grade, the Warriors, served as guardians of the country, and members

---

age grade An organized category of people based on age; every individual passes through a series of such categories over his or her lifetime.

age set A formally established group of people born during a certain time span who move together through the series of age-grade categories; sometimes called *age class*.

Figure 11.2 Maasai Warrior Age-Grade Ceremony Like the Tiriki and some other pastoralists in East Africa, the Maasai form age sets—established groups of people born during a similar time span who move together through the series of age-grade categories. The opening parade, shown here, of the elaborate *eunoto* ceremony begins the coming of age of *morans* ("Warriors") for Maasai subclans of western Kenya. At the end of the ceremony, these men will be in the next age grade—junior adults—ready to marry and start families. Members of the same age set, they were initiated together into the Warrior age grade as teenagers. They spent their Warrior years raiding cattle (an old tradition that is now illegal but nonetheless still practiced) and protecting their community homes and animal enclosures (from wild animals and other cattle raiders). The *eunoto* ceremony includes a ritual in which mothers shave the heads of the Warriors, marking the end of many freedoms and the passage to manhood.

gained renown through fighting (**Figure 11.2**). Under British colonial rule, however, this traditional function largely fell by the wayside with the decline of intergroup raiding and warfare; individual members of this age grade may now find excitement and adventure by leaving their community for extended employment or study elsewhere.

The next age grade, the Elder Warriors, had few specialized tasks in earlier days beyond learning skills they would need later on by assuming an increasing share of administrative activities. For example, they would chair the postfuneral gatherings held to settle property claims after someone's death. Traditionally, Elder Warriors also served as envoys between elders of different communities. Nowadays, they hold nearly all of the administrative and executive roles opened up by the creation and growth of a centralized Tiriki administrative bureaucracy.

Judicial Elders, the third age grade, traditionally handled most tasks connected with the administration and settlement of local disputes. Today, they still serve as the local judiciary body.

Members of the Ritual Elders, the senior age grade, used to preside over the priestly functions of ancestral shrine observances on the household level, at subclan meetings, at semiannual community appeals, and at rites of initiation into the various age grades. They also were credited with access to special magical powers. With the decline of ancestor worship over the past several decades, many of these traditional functions have been lost, and no new ones have arisen to take their places. Nonetheless, Ritual Elders continue to hold the most important positions in the initiation ceremonies, and their power as sorcerers and expungers of witchcraft is still recognized.

Grouping by Common Interest

The rise of urban, industrialized societies in which individuals are often separated from their kin has led to a proliferation of **common-interest associations**—associations that result from an act of joining and are

© Louise Gubb/Corbis

VISUAL COUNTERPOINT

Figure 11.3 Common-Interest Associations The range of common-interest associations is astounding, as suggested by these photos of Shriners and Yakuza gang members. The Shriners (*left*), capped in tasseled red fezzes, are a secret fraternal order of middle-class males committed to "fun, fellowship, and service." Founded in the United States in 1870, the group was named after the Ancient Arabic Order of Nobles of the Mystic Shrine. Today, it is an international organization with 200 chapters across North and South America, Europe, and Southeast Asia. Much older than the Shriners, the Yakuza is a Japanese crime syndicate, whose members sport elaborate and visually specific tattoos with samurai images. Its 100,000 or so members, organized in three major associations, refer to their groups as "chivalrous organizations" (*ninkyō dantai*), claiming to be redistributing wealth through crime. Operating in the Japanese underworld as well as abroad, the Yakuza resembles the mafia historically based in Sicily.

based on sharing particular activities, objectives, values, or beliefs (**Figure 11.3**). Some are rooted in common ethnic, religious, or regional background. Such associations help people meet a range of needs from companionship to safe work conditions to learning a new language and customs upon moving from one country to another.

Common-interest associations are also found in many traditional societies, and there is some evidence that they arose with the emergence of the first horticultural villages. Notably, associations in traditional societies may be just as complex and highly organized as those found in industrialized countries.

Kinds of Common-Interest Associations

The variety of common-interest associations is astonishing. In the United States, they include sport, hobby, and civic service clubs; religious and spiritual organizations; political parties; labor unions; environmental

organizations; urban gangs; private militias; immigrant groups; academic organizations such as the American Anthropological Association; women's and men's clubs of all sorts—the list goes on and on. Their goals may include the pursuit of friendship, recreation, and the promotion of certain values, as well as governing, seeking peace on a local or global scale, and defending economic interests.

Some associations aim to preserve traditional songs, history, language, moral beliefs, and other customs among members of various ethnic minorities. So it is among many immigrant groups from Africa who live in major cities around the world, including in the United States. Today, some 250,000 African-born immigrants live in the New York metropolitan area. The city's largest African group hails from Ghana, a former British colony in West

common-interest association An association that results from an act of joining based on sharing particular activities, objectives, values, or beliefs, sometimes rooted in common ethnic, religious, or regional background.

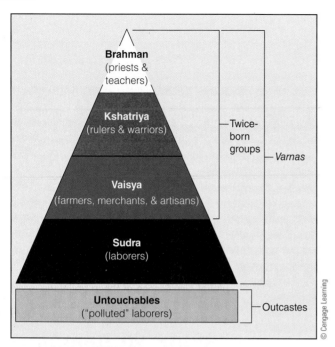

Figure 11.7 The Hindu Caste System Hindu castes are organized into four "grades of being" called *varnas* ("colors") that determine what members are permitted to do, touch, or eat; where they live; how they dress; and who they can marry. The highest-ranking order Brahman is associated with the color white, below which are Kshatriya (red) and Vaisya (brown). Below these three are Sudra (black), who make a living as laborers. Lower still are the "polluted" laborers, the Untouchables, who are charged with cleaning the streets and with the collection and disposal of garbage, animal carcasses, and sewage.

Falling outside the *varna* system is a fifth category of degraded individuals. These outcastes, known as Untouchables or as *Dalits* (a Sanskrit name meaning "crushed" or "suppressed"), are tasked with doing the dirty work in society—collecting garbage, removing animal carcasses, cleaning streets, and disposing of dung, sewage, and other refuse (**Figure 11.8**). Brahmans and members of other *varnas* avoid direct contact with Untouchables, believing that touching or accepting food from them would result in ritual pollution. Commonly associated with filth, outcastes constitute a large pool of cheap labor at the beck and call of those controlling economic and political affairs. In an effort to bestow some dignity on these poverty-stricken victims of the caste system, Hindu nationalist leader Mahatma Gandhi renamed them *harijan* or "children of God."

Although India's national constitution of 1950 sought to abolish the caste system, the traditional hierarchy remains deeply entrenched in Hindu culture and is still widespread throughout southern Asia, especially in rural India. In what has been called India's hidden apartheid, entire villages in many Indian states remain completely segregated by caste.

Untouchables represent about 15 percent of India's population—nearly 170 million people—and must endure social isolation, humiliation, and discrimination based exclusively on their birth status. Even their shadows are seen as polluting. They may not cross the line dividing their part of the village from that occupied by higher castes, may not drink water from public wells, and may not visit the same temples as the higher castes. Their children are still often made to sit at the back of classrooms, and in rural areas some are denied access to education altogether. However, over the past half century, Untouchables, in concert with the lowest-ranking Sudra castes, have built a civil rights movement—described later in this chapter (Office of the United Nations Higher Commissioner for Human Rights, 2007).

Similar castelike situations are found in other places in the world. In Bolivia, Ecuador, and several other South and Central American countries, for example, the wealthy upper class remains almost exclusively white and rarely intermarries with people of American Indian or African descent. In contrast, the lower class of working poor in those countries is primarily made up of American Indian, black, or mixed-race laborers and peasants.

Likewise, most European stratified societies were historically organized in closed social classes known as *estates*—ranked as clergy, nobility, and citizens—each with distinctive political rights (privileges). Titles and forms of address hierarchically identified these estates, and they were publicly distinguished by dress and codes of behavior. Not unlike the lowest castes in the Hindu caste system, a large underclass of millions of serfs ranked at the bottom of the European hierarchy. Prohibited from owning land or a business, *serfs* could not vote and did not enjoy the rights of free citizens. Often dirt poor, they worked on large farms and houses owned by the elite. Unlike slaves, they could not be traded as personal property of their masters, but they were restricted in their right to free movement and required their master's consent to marry.

Serfdom existed for many centuries in much of Europe. Russia was that continent's last country to abolish this system in 1861—just two years before slavery was abolished in the United States. It was several more decades before the slave system officially ended in Brazil, China, and other countries.

Historical Racial Segregation in South Africa and the United States

Other than social class, caste, and estate, the hierarchy in a stratified society may be based on ethnic origin or skin color. For instance, dark-skinned individuals culturally classified as colored or black may encounter social rules excluding them from certain jobs or neighborhoods and making it difficult if not impossible to befriend or marry someone with a lighter skin color. (As discussed earlier in

Figure 11.8 Doing the Dirty Work Rubbish picking is a task traditionally performed by Dalits (Untouchables) in the hierarchical caste system of Indian society. These pickers in Mysore, Karnataka, India, may sometimes be joined by a roaming holy cow.

our text, the terms *race, black,* and *white* are purely social constructions, with no basis in biology. For simplicity, we use them here without quotation marks.)

One of the best-known historical examples of a pluralistic country with social stratification based on the notion of race is South Africa. From 1948 to 1992, a minority of 4.5 million people of European descent sought to protect its power and "racial purity" by means of a repressive regime of racial segregation and discrimination against 25 million indigenous black Africans. Known as *apartheid* (an Afrikaans-Dutch term meaning "segregation" or "separation"), this white superiority ideology officially relegated indigenous dark-skinned Africans to a low-ranking stratum. Similar to the Hindu caste system with its concepts of ritual purity and pollution, South African whites feared pollution of their purity through direct personal contact with blacks (**Figure 11.9**).

Until the mid-20th century, institutionalized racial segregation officially prevailed in the United States, where the country's ruling upper class was historically comprised exclusively of individuals of European (Caucasian or white) descent. For generations, it was against the law for whites to marry blacks or American Indians. Even after black slavery was abolished in the United States in 1863, such interracial mixing prohibitions remained in force in many states from Maine to Florida. Today, despite significant steps toward equality since enactment of civil rights laws in the 1960s that officially prohibited race-based segregation and race-based discrimination, American blacks

as a racial minority (with notable individual exceptions) still rank lower in terms of wealth and health (Boshara, 2003; Kennickell, 2003).

Indicators of Social Status

Social classes are manifested in various ways, including *symbolic indicators*. For example, in the United States certain activities and possessions are indicative of class: occupation (a garbage collector has a different class status than a medical specialist); wealth (rich people are generally in a higher social class than poor people); dress ("white collar" versus "blue collar"); form of recreation (people in the upper class are expected to play golf rather than shoot pool down at the pool hall—but they can shoot pool at home or in a club); residential location (people in the upper class do not ordinarily live in slums); kind of car; and so on. All sorts of status symbols are indicative of class position, including measures such as the number of bathrooms in a person's house. That said, class rankings do not fully correlate with economic status or pay scales. The local garbage collector or unionized car-factory laborer typically makes more money than an average college professor with a doctorate.

Symbolic indicators involve factors of lifestyle, but differences in life chances may also signal differences in class standing. Life is apt to be easier for members of an upper class as opposed to a lower class. This shows up in a tendency for lower infant mortality and longer life

© Nigel Dickinson

Challenge Issue

Maintaining peace and order is a daily challenge in every society, especially when different ethnic and religious communities coexist under the same political umbrella. Such is the case in Kano territory situated in the savannahs of northern Nigeria. For hundreds of years an independent domain occupied by Hausa and Fulani peoples, Kano is historically ruled by an emir who now governs according to Shariah, a moral and legal code based on what traditional Muslims accept as God's infallible law. The emirate endured under British colonial rule and has continued as a state in Nigeria, a multi-ethnic and religiously diverse republic since 1960. Here we see Kano's emir, Alhaji Ado Bayero (dressed in white), in a *durbar*, which is a military parade held annually in a festival ending the Muslim holy month of Ramadan. Regional chiefs who head cavalry regiments surround the emir, showcasing their horsemanship in a public display of loyalty. Pious and wealthy, this emir has promoted modern economic development and embraced Western education. In recent years, however, an extremist sect has broken the peace in his emirate, asserting that pure Islam has been corrupted by Westernization. Calling themselves *Boko Haram* ("Western education is sinful"), these militants have launched *jihad* ("holy war") to create a Muslim fundamentalist state.

Politics, Power, War, and Peace

**IN THIS CHAPTER
YOU WILL LEARN TO**

- Analyze how the issue of power is crucially important in every society.

- Recognize the difference between authority and coercion.

- Distinguish and discuss types of political organization and leadership.

- Determine how politics, economics, and maintenance of (in)equality are linked.

- Contrast systems of justice and conflict resolution across cultures.

- Recognize causes of warfare past and present.

- Identify the role of ideology in justifying aggression versus nonviolent resistance.

- Evaluate the importance of diplomacy and treaties in restoring and maintaining peace.

In all societies, from the largest to the smallest, people face the challenge of maintaining social order, securing safety, protecting property, resolving conflicts, and much more. This involves mobilizing, contesting, and controlling power. All human relations entail a degree of **power**, which refers to the ability of individuals or groups to impose their will upon others and make them do things even against their own wants or wishes.

Ranging from persuasion to violence, power drives politics—a term that derives from the Greek word *polis*, referring to a self-governing "city." Many definitions have been proposed, but one of the most famous is that **politics** is the process determining who gets what, when, and how (Lasswell, 1990). In the political process, coalitions of individuals and groups defend or dispute an established economic, social, or ideological order as they fight or negotiate with rival factions and foreign neighbors. Political organization takes many forms, of which the state is just one.

Ironically, the political ties that facilitate much-needed human coexistence and cooperation also create the dynamics that may lead to social tension and sometimes to violent conflict within and between groups. We see this in a wide range of situations, from riots to rebellions to revolutions. Therefore, every society must have ways and means for resolving internal conflicts and preventing a breakdown of its social order. Moreover, each society must possess the capacity to deal with neighboring societies in peaceful or troubled times.

Today, state governments and international political coalitions play a central role in maintaining social order across the globe. Despite the predominance of state societies, there are many groups in which political organization consists of flexible and informal kinship systems. Between these two polarities of kin-ordered and state-organized political systems lies a world of variety.

power The ability of individuals or groups to impose their will upon others and make them do things even against their own wants or wishes.
politics The process determining who gets what, when, and how.

Systems of Political Organization

The term **political organization** refers to the way power is accumulated, arranged, executed, and structurally embedded in society, whether in organizing a whale hunt, managing irrigated farmlands, collecting taxes, or raising a military force. In short, it is the means through which a society creates and maintains social order. It assumes a variety of forms among the peoples of the world, but anthropologists have simplified this complex subject by identifying four basic kinds of political systems: bands, tribes, chiefdoms, and states (**Figure 12.1**). The first two are uncentralized systems; the latter two are centralized.

Uncentralized Political Systems

Until recently, many non-Western peoples have had neither chiefs with established rights and duties nor any fixed form of government, as those who live in modern states understand the term. Instead, marriage and kinship have formed their principal means of social organization. The economies of these societies are primarily of a subsistence type, and populations are typically small.

Leaders do not have real power to force compliance with the society's customs or rules, but if individuals do not conform, they may become targets of scorn and gossip or even be banished. Important decisions are usually made in a collective manner by agreement among adults. Dissenting members may decide to act with

TYPES OF POLITICAL ORGANIZATION
The symbol → indicates that the attribute varies between less and more complex societies of that type.

	BAND	TRIBE	CHIEFDOM	STATE
MEMBERSHIP				
Number of people	Dozens and up	Hundreds and up	Thousands and up	Tens of thousands and up
Settlement pattern	Mobile	Mobile or fixed: 1 or more villages	Fixed: 2 or more villages	Fixed: Many villages and cities
Basis of relationships	Kin	Kin, descent groups	Kin, rank, and residence	Class and residence
Ethnicities and languages	1	1	1	1 or more
GOVERNMENT				
Decision making, leadership	Egalitarian	Egalitarian or Big Man	Centralized, hereditary	Centralized
Bureaucracy	None	None	None, or 1 or 2 levels	Many levels
Monopoly of force and information	No	No	No → Yes	Yes
Conflict resolution	Informal	Informal	Centralized	Laws, judges
Hierarchy of settlement	No	No	No → Paramount village or head town	Capital
ECONOMY				
Food production	No	No → Yes	Yes → Intensive	Intensive
Labor specialization	No	No	No → Yes	Yes
Exchanges	Reciprocal	Reciprocal	Redistributive (tribute)	Redistributive (taxes)
Control of land	Band	Descent group	Chief	Various
SOCIETY				
Stratified	No	No	Yes, ranked by kin	Yes, by class or caste
Slavery	No	No	Some, small-scale	Some, large-scale
Luxury goods for elite	No	No	Yes	Yes
Public architecture	No	No	No → Yes	Yes
Indigenous literacy	No	No	No → Some	Often

© Cengage Learning

Figure 12.1 Four Types of Political Systems This figure outlines the four basic types of political systems: bands, tribes, chiefdoms, and states. Bands and tribes are uncentralized political organizations; chiefdoms and states are centralized.

the majority, or they may choose to adopt some other course of action, including leaving the group.

This egalitarian form of political organization provides great flexibility, which in many situations offers an adaptive advantage. Because power in these kin-ordered communities is shared, with nobody exercising exclusive control over collective resources or public affairs, individuals typically enjoy much more freedom than those who are part of larger and more complex political systems.

Bands

The **band** is a relatively small and loosely organized kin-ordered group that inhabits a common territory and that may split periodically into smaller family groups that are politically and economically independent. Typically, bands are found among food foragers and other small-scale migratory communities in which people organize into politically autonomous extended family groups that usually camp together as long as environmental and subsistence circumstances are favorable. Bands periodically break up into smaller groups to forage for food or visit other relatives. The band is the oldest form of political organization because all humans were once food foragers and remained so until the development of farming and pastoralism over the past 10,000 years.

Given their foraging mode of subsistence, band population densities are usually less than one person per square mile. Because bands are egalitarian and small, numbering at most a few hundred people, there is no real need for formal, centralized political systems. Everyone is related to—and knows on a personal basis—everyone else with whom dealings are required, so there is high value placed on getting along. Conflicts that do arise are usually settled informally through gossip, ridicule, direct negotiation, or mediation. When negotiation or mediation is used, the focus is on reaching a solution considered fair by all concerned parties, rather than on conforming to some abstract law or rule.

Decisions affecting a band are made with the participation of all its adult members, with an emphasis on achieving consensus—a collective agreement—rather than a simple majority. Individuals become leaders by virtue of their abilities and serve in that capacity only as long as they retain the confidence of the community. They cannot coerce others to abide by their decisions. A leader who exceeds what people are willing to accept quickly loses followers.

An example of the informal nature of band leadership is found among the Ju/'hoansi Bushmen of the Kalahari Desert, mentioned in earlier chapters. Each Ju/'hoansi band is composed of a group of families that live together, linked through kinship ties to one another and to the headman (or, less often, headwoman). The head, called the *kxau*, or "owner," is the focal point for the band's claims on the territory through which it traditionally

Figure 12.2 Band Leadership Toma Tsamkxao was the headman of a Ju/'hoansi band. Lightly armed, he led his migratory community of hunters and gatherers in the Kalahari Desert. They ranged the region freely much as their ancestors did for almost 40,000 years. About half a century ago, outsiders imposed radical changes on Bushmen bands. Some, guided by wise leaders like Tsamkxao, survived the upheaval and now subsist on a mix of livestock and crop farming, crafts and tourism, and some traditional foraging.

ranges as a migratory community (**Figure 12.2**). He or she does not personally own the land and natural resources but symbolically represents the ancestral rights of band members to them. If the head leaves the area to live elsewhere, people turn to someone else to lead them.

When local resources are no longer adequate to sustain a band, the leader coordinates and leads the move, selecting the new campsite. Except for the privilege of having first choice of a spot for his or her own fire, the leader of the band has few unique rewards or duties. For example, a Ju/'hoansi head is not a judge and does not punish other band members. Troublemakers and wrongdoers are judged and held accountable by public opinion, usually expressed by gossip, which can play an important role in curbing socially unacceptable behavior.

Through gossip—talking behind someone's back and spreading rumors about behavior considered disruptive, shameful, or ridiculous—people accomplish several

political organization The way power, as the capacity to do something, is accumulated, arranged, executed, and structurally embedded in society; the means through which a society creates and maintains social order and reduces social disorder.

band A relatively small and loosely organized kin-ordered group that inhabits a specific territory and that may split periodically into smaller extended family groups that are politically and economically independent.

objectives while avoiding the potential disruption of open confrontation. First, gossip underscores and reinforces the cultural standards of those who abide by the unwritten rules of proper conduct. At the same time, the gossip discredits those who violate standards of socially acceptable behavior. Furthermore, because gossip can damage a person's reputation and is often fueled by hidden jealousy or a secret desire to retaliate against someone considered too accomplished or successful, it may function as a leveling mechanism to reduce a real or perceived threat of an individual becoming too dominant.

Another prime technique in small-scale societies for resolving disputes, or even avoiding them in the first place, is mobility. Those unable to get along with others of their group may feel pressured to move to a different group in which existing kinship ties give them rights of entry.

Tribes

The second type of uncentralized authority system is the tribe. In anthropology, the term **tribe** refers to a wide range of kin-ordered groups that are politically integrated by some unifying factor and whose members share a common ancestry, identity, culture, language, and territory.

Typically, a tribe has an economy based on some form of crop cultivation or livestock raising. Tribes develop when a number of culturally related bands come together, peacefully settle disputes, participate in periodic visiting and communal feasting, and intermarry for purposes of economic exchange and/or collective self-defense against common enemies. For this reason, tribal membership is usually larger than band membership. Moreover, tribal population densities generally far exceed that of migratory bands and may be as high as 250 people per square mile. Greater population density introduces a new set of problems, as opportunities for bickering, begging, adultery, and theft increase markedly, especially among people living in permanent villages.

Each tribe consists of one or more self-supporting and self-governing local community (including smaller kin-groups earlier discussed as bands) that may then form alliances with others for various purposes. As in the band, political organization in the tribe is informal and temporary. Whenever a situation requiring political integration of all or several groups within the tribe arises—perhaps for defense, to carry out a raid, to pool resources in times of scarcity, or to capitalize on a windfall that must be distributed quickly before it spoils—groups come together to deal with the situation in a cooperative manner. When the problem is satisfactorily solved, each group then resumes autonomy.

In many tribal societies, the organizing unit and seat of political authority is the clan, composed of people who consider themselves descended from a common ancestor. Within the clan, elders or headmen and/or headwomen regulate members' affairs and represent their clan in interactions with other clans. As a group, the elders of all the clans may form a council that acts within the community or for the community in dealings with outsiders. Because clan members usually do not all live together in a single community, clan organization facilitates joint action with members of related communities when necessary.

Leadership in tribal societies is also relatively informal, as is evident in a wide array of past and present examples. Among these is the Big Man common in Melanesia, including New Guinea and other islands in the South Pacific. Heading up localized descent groups or a territorial group, the Big Man combines a measure of interest in his community's welfare with a great deal of cunning and calculation for his own personal gain. His power is personal, for he holds no political office in any formal sense, nor is he elected. His prestige as a political leader is the result of strategic acts that raise him above most other tribe members and that attract loyal followers who benefit from or depend on his success.

The Kapauku in the west central highlands of New Guinea typify this form of political organization. Among these Papua, the Big Man is called the *tonowi* ("rich one"). To achieve this status, one must be male, wealthy, generous, and eloquent. Physical bravery and an ability to deal with the supernatural are also common *tonowi* characteristics, but they are not essential (**Figure 12.3**).

A Kapauku Big Man functions as the headman of the village unit in a wide variety of situations within and beyond the community. He represents his group in dealing with outsiders and other villages and acts as negotiator and/or judge when disputes break out among his followers. As a *tonowi*, he acquires political power through giving loans. Villagers comply with his requests because they are in his debt (often interest-free), and they do not want to have to repay their loans. Those who have not yet borrowed from him may wish to do so in the future, so they, too, want to keep his goodwill. A *tonowi* who refuses to lend money to fellow villagers may be shunned, ridiculed, and, in extreme cases, even killed by a group of warriors. Such unfavorable reactions ensure that individual economic wealth is dispersed throughout the community.

A Big Man gains further support from his relatives and from taking into his household young male apprentices

---

tribe In anthropology, the term for a range of kin-ordered groups that are politically integrated by some unifying factor and whose members share a common ancestry, identity, culture, language, and territory.

Figure 12.3 Big Man from West Papua, New Guinea Wearing his official regalia, the *tonowi* is recognizable among fellow Kapauku and neighboring Papua highlanders as a man of wealth and power.

who receive business training along with food and shelter. He also gives them a loan that enables them to marry when the apprenticeship ends. In return, they act as messengers and bodyguards. After leaving, they remain tied to the *tonowi* by bonds of affection and gratitude.

Because a Big Man's wealth comes from his success at breeding pigs (the focus of the entire Kapauku economy, as described in the chapter on patterns of subsistence), it is not uncommon for a *tonowi* to lose his fortune rapidly due to poor management or simple bad luck with his pigs. Thus, the Kapauku political structure shifts frequently: As one man loses wealth and consequently power, another gains it and becomes a *tonowi*. These changes prevent any single Big Man from holding political power for too long.

Political Integration Beyond the Kin-Group

Age sets, age grades, and common-interest groups discussed in the previous chapter are among the political integration mechanisms used by tribal societies. Cutting across territorial and kin-groupings, these organizations link members from different lineages and clans. For example, among the Tiriki

of East Africa (discussed in the previous chapter), the Warrior age grade guards the village and grazing lands, whereas Judicial Elders resolve disputes. The oldest age grade, the Ritual Elders, advise on matters involving the well-being of all the Tiriki people. With the tribe's political affairs in the hands of the various age grades and their officers, this type of organization enables the largely independent kin-groups to solve conflicts and sometimes avoid feuding between the lineages.

The Pashtun, a large ethnic group with tribes on both sides of the border between Afghanistan and Pakistan, provide another example of decentralized political organization. Periodically, groups of male elders, each representing their kinfolk, gather to deal with collective challenges. In such a political assembly, known as a *jirga*, these Pashtun tribal leaders make joint decisions by consensus—from settling disputes, working out treaties, and resolving trade issues to establishing law and order in their war-torn homelands (**Figure 12.4**).

Centralized Political Systems

Political authority is not centralized in bands and tribes, but this changes when populations grow, individuals specialize, division of labor increases, and surplus is exchanged in expanding trade networks. This process creates opportunities for some enterprising individuals or groups to gain control at the expense of others. In such increasingly complex societies, political authority and power are concentrated in a single individual (the chief) or in a body of individuals (the state). In centralized systems, political organization relies more heavily on institutionalized power, authority, and even coercion.

Chiefdoms

A **chiefdom** is a politically organized territory centrally ruled by a chief heading a kin-based society with prestige ranking and a redistributive economy. Rank in such a hierarchical political system is determined by the closeness of one's relationship to the chief. Those closest are officially superior and receive deferential treatment from those of lower status. The office of the chief is usually for life and often hereditary. Typically, it passes from a man to his younger brother, a son, or his sister's son, depending on whether descent is traced patrilineally or matrilineally.

Unlike the headman or headwoman in bands and tribes, the leader of a chiefdom is generally a true authority figure with the power to command, settle disputes, punish, and reward. This chief serves to maintain peace and order within and between allied communities.

Chiefdoms have a recognized hierarchy consisting of major and minor authorities that control major and

chiefdom A politically organized society in which several neighboring communities inhabiting a territory are united under a single ruler.

Figure 12.4 Gathering of Tribal Leaders In traditional kin-ordered societies such as tribes, political power is neither centralized nor monopolized. Instead, social networks of extended families, lineages, or clans share political power. As shown in this photo of tribal elders attending a *Loya Jirga* ("Grand Assembly") in Afghanistan's capital city of Kabul, Pashtun leaders gather periodically to discuss and resolve conflicts and other collective challenges.

minor subdivisions. Such an arrangement is a chain of command, linking leaders at every level, with each owing personal loyalty to the chief. It serves to bind groups in the heartland to the chief's headquarters, whether it is a large tent, wood house, or stone hall. Although leaders of chiefdoms are almost always male, in some cultures a politically astute wife, sister, or single daughter of a deceased chief could inherit this powerful position as well.

Chiefs usually control the economic activities of those who fall under their political rule. Typically, chiefdoms involve redistributive systems, and the chief has control over surplus goods and perhaps even over the community's labor force. Thus, he (and sometimes she) may demand a share of the harvested crop from farmers, which may then be redistributed throughout the domain. Similarly, manpower may be periodically drafted to form battle groups, build fortifications, dig irrigation works, or construct ceremonial sites.

The chief may also amass a great amount of personal wealth and pass it on to offspring. Land, cattle, and luxury goods produced by specialists can be collected by the chief and become part of the power base. Moreover, high-ranking families of the chiefdom may engage in the same practice and use their possessions as evidence of superior social status.

Traditionally, chiefdoms have been unstable, with lesser chiefs trying to take power from higher-ranking chiefs, or rival chiefs vying for supreme power as paramount chiefs. In precolonial Hawaii, for example, where war was the way to gain territory and maintain power, great chiefs set out to conquer each other in an effort to become paramount chief of all the islands. When one chief defeated another, the loser and all his nobles were dispossessed of their property and lucky to escape alive. The new paramount chief then appointed his own supporters to positions of political power.

Among the many symbols indicating their supreme political rank, paramount chiefs carry a title of renown not only recognized in their own domain but beyond. In English, the title *paramount chief* is often translated as "king." This covers a range of political authority figures— from the high-ranking ruler elected by an alliance of chiefs to the leader of a politically centralized society historically divided in chiefdoms. As such, indigenous royal titles— *malku* in Aymara for rulers in the Andean highlands of Bolivia; *raja* in Hindi for those in India; *gyalpo* in Tibetan for Himalayan rulers in Sikkim and Bhutan; *emir* or *sultan*, both Arabic, for rulers throughout Islamic Asia and North Africa; and *vorst* or *fürst* in Germanic Europe—are all translated as "king." Historically, the Indian subcontinent alone numbered 565 princely states, both large and small.

The political distinction between a paramount chiefdom, princely state, or kingdom by whatever name cannot be sharply drawn. As an intermediary form of political organization between tribes and states, most chiefdoms, paramount chiefdoms, and kingdoms have disappeared in the course of time. However, many hundreds still exist in parts of Asia and Africa, for example—albeit no longer as politically independent or sovereign domains. Subordinated to the state as a more powerful political system, those that endure do so as an enclosed territorial division such as a district or province, with its traditional rulers and their successors remaining in office, although with reduced authority.

Due to their wealth and prestige, and holding onto traditional titles and other high-status symbols, high-ranking chiefs and kings (or queens) are often well positioned to successfully adapt to the new order. Especially in pluralistic states with an ineffective or otherwise challenged centralized government, regional political rulers such as traditional paramount chiefs, emirs, and kings may (re)gain power and claim greater independence.

Such is the case with chiefs among the Kpelle, the largest ethnic group in Liberia, a pluralistic West African country

Figure 12.5 Paramount Chiefs and International Diplomacy In a special diplomatic ceremony commemorating the bilateral relationship between Liberia and China and expressing appreciation for China's economic investment and financial aid in his domain, Paramount Chief Moses Galakrumah of the Kpelle chiefdom of Panta, Bong County, appointed the Chinese ambassador Zhou Yuxiao as honorary paramount chief. Together with Chief Elder Togba Gbonpelee, he briefed his high-ranking Chinese guest on the history of the Panta chiefdom and dressed China's senior envoy in a traditional Kpelle robe, along with a wooden sword and staff— symbols of power and bravery.

inhabited by about 30 ethnic groups. Traditionally, the Kpelle are politically divided in several independent paramount chiefdoms, each comprising an alliance of smaller chiefdoms. Whereas the Kpelle inhabit territories in Liberia's eastern interior, African Americans from the United States, including former slaves, colonized its coastal region. Aided by the American Colonization Society, these black settlers founded the Republic of Liberia in 1847, naming its capital Monrovia in honor of U.S. president James Monroe. Since then, these Americo-Liberians have dominated the country's political economy. However, they never fully succeeded in centralizing political power. This left traditional paramount chiefs among the Kpelle and their neighbors largely in control of regional affairs as salaried state officials, mediating between the inhabitants in their districts (traditional chiefdoms) and the central government.

Today, many Kpelle are rice farmers, but they also engage in wage labor. Their paramount chief, like those of other ethnic groups, receives government commissions on taxes and court fees collected within his district, plus a commission for providing laborers for Liberia's numerous foreign-owned mines and rubber plantations. He also gets a stipulated amount of rice from each farming household and gifts from people who approach him for favors. Moreover, he has the authority to settle disputes, and people compensate him for that as well.

In keeping with his high social status, a Kpelle chief has at his disposal uniformed messengers, a literate clerk, and the symbols of wealth: several wives, embroidered gowns, and freedom from manual labor. After a devastating civil war (1989–2003), Liberia's government has tried to rebuild the pluralistic country's economy by decentralizing some of its governing power, granting the traditional chiefs more political, legal, and administrative control. Some now even participate in international diplomacy for their country (**Figure 12.5**).

States

The **state** is a politically organized territory occupied by a class-stratified society with a centralized government and definite boundaries. The most formal of political systems, it is organized and directed by a government that has the capacity and authority to manage and tax its subjects, make laws and maintain order, and use military force to defend or expand its territories. Two of the smallest states today measure less than 2.5 square kilometers (1 square mile), whereas the largest covers about 17 million square kilometers (6.6 million square miles).

state A political institution established to manage and defend a complex, socially stratified society occupying a defined territory.

The fact that the president of the United States takes the oath of office by swearing on a Bible is another instance of the use of religion to legitimize political power, as is the phrase "one nation, under God" in the Pledge of Allegiance. U.S. coins are etched with the phrase "In God We Trust," many governmental meetings begin with a prayer or an invocation, and the expression "so help me God" is routinely used in legal proceedings. Despite an official separation of church and state, religious legitimization of government lingers. Similarly, for her coronation in 1953, Queen Elizabeth II placed her right hand on a Bible and kissed the sacred book when she signed the oath.

Politics and Gender

Historically, irrespective of cultural configuration or type of political organization, women have held important positions of political leadership far less often than men. But there have been many significant exceptions, including some female chiefs *heading* Algonquian Indian communities in southern New England in the 17th century and among the Taino, Timucua, Caddo, and other early American Indian chiefdoms in the Caribbean and southeastern United States. Traditionally, there were also female rulers of Polynesian chiefdoms and kingdoms in the Pacific, including Tonga, Samoa, and Hawaii. Moreover, there were numerous powerful queens heading monarchies and even empires in Asia, Africa, and Europe during the past few thousand years (Linnekin, 1990; Ralston & Thomas, 1987; Trocolli, 2005).

Perhaps the most notable example among historical female rulers is Queen Victoria, the long-reigning queen of England, Scotland, Wales, and Ireland. Also recognized as monarch in a host of colonies all over the world, Victoria even acquired the title Empress of India. Ruling the British empire from 1837 until 1901, she was perhaps the world's wealthiest and most powerful leader. Her great-great-granddaughter Queen Elizabeth II has ruled nearly as long. Elizabeth ascended to the royal throne as sovereign head of Great Britain upon the death of her father, King George VI. With her coronation the following year, she became the symbolic head of the Commonwealth, an intergovernmental organization of fifty-four independent states (almost all former British colonies), collectively promoting free trade, rule of law, human rights, and world peace.

High-profile female leadership is becoming more common, and in most contemporary societies women have gained the same political rights and opportunities as men. In recent years, a growing number of women have been elected as presidents, chancellors, or prime ministers. Countries with elected female heads of state now or in recent years include Argentina, Australia, Brazil, Chile, Costa Rica, Germany, India, Indonesia, Ireland, Liberia, Norway, Pakistan, the Philippines, Sri Lanka, and Thailand. Others lead political opposition parties, sometimes heading mass movements. Among the latter is Aung San Suu Kyi in Myanmar (Burma), profiled toward the end of this chapter.

Although there have been and continue to be many societies in which women have lower visibility in the political arena, that does not necessarily indicate that they lack power in political affairs. For example, among the six allied Iroquois Indian nations in northeastern America, only men were appointed to serve as high-ranking chiefs on the confederacy's great council; however, they were completely beholden to women, for only their "clan mothers" could select candidates to this high political office. Moreover, women actively lobbied the men on the councils, and the clan mothers had the right to depose a chief representing their clan whenever it suited them.

As for women having more visible roles in traditional societies, one example is the dual-sex government system of the Igbo in Nigeria, West Africa. Among the Igbo, each political unit traditionally had separate political institutions for men and women, so that both genders had an autonomous sphere of authority as well as an area of shared responsibility (Okonjo, 1976). At the head of each political unit was a male *obi*, considered the head of government although he presided over only the male community, and a female *omu*, the acknowledged mother of the whole community but in practice concerned with the female section. Unlike a queen (though both she and the *obi* were crowned), the *omu* was neither the *obi*'s wife nor the previous *obi*'s daughter.

Just as the *obi* had a council of dignitaries to advise him and act as a check against any arbitrary exercise of power, a council of women served the *omu*. The duties of the *omu* and her advisors involved tasks such as establishing rules and regulations for the community market (marketing was a woman's activity) and hearing cases involving women brought to her from throughout the town or village. If such cases also involved men, then she and her council would cooperate with the *obi* and his council.

In the Igbo system, women managed their own affairs. They had the right to enforce their decisions and rules with sanctions similar to those employed by men, including strikes, boycotts, and "sitting on" someone, including a man:

> To "sit on" or "make war on" a man involved gathering at his compound, sometimes late at night, dancing, singing scurrilous songs which detailed the women's grievances against him and often called his manhood into question, banging on his hut with the pestles women used for pounding yams, and perhaps . . . roughing him up a bit. A man might be sanctioned in this way for mistreating his wife, for violating the women's market rules, or for letting his cows eat the women's crops. The women would stay at his hut throughout the day, and late into the night if necessary, until he repented and promised to mend his ways. (Van Allen, 1997, p. 450)

When the British imposed colonial rule on the Igbo in the late 1800s, they failed to recognize the autonomy and power of the women. This is ironic because, as noted earlier, the long-reigning and powerful head of the British empire at the time was Queen Victoria. Nevertheless, British colonial administrators introduced reforms that destroyed traditional arrangements of female autonomy and power. As a result, Igbo women lost much of their traditional equality and became politically subordinate to men.

Cultural Controls in Maintaining Order

Every culture has various forms of **cultural control** to ensure that individuals or groups conduct themselves in ways that support the social order. People who challenge or disturb the order face negative consequences. We may distinguish between internal and external forms of cultural control.

As discussed in an earlier chapter, individuals born and raised in a particular society undergo a process of enculturation during which ideas, values, and associated structures of emotion are internalized, impacting their thoughts, feelings, and behavior. The internalization of cultural control leads to what we know as **self-control**—a person's capacity to manage his or her spontaneous feelings and to restrain impulsive behavior.

The second form of cultural control is external, as it is based on historically developed or politically imposed rules of order enforced by others in society. This external form is **social control**, which authorities in ranked or stratified societies such as chiefdoms and states maintain by various means of persuasion and coercion, including intimidation, threats, and financial or physical punishment.

Internalized Control

Developed during the enculturation process and deeply embedded in our consciousness, self-control may be motivated by ideas or emotions associated with positive cultural values such as self-denial for the common good. For example, many cultures honor traditions of charity, self-sacrifice, or other good deeds. Performed out of a desire to help those in need, such acts of kindness or generosity may spring from a spiritual or religious worldview.

Self-control may also be motivated by negative ideas and associated emotions such as a fear of misfortune or bad luck—concepts that are culturally relative and variable. As an example, we may look at Wape hunters in Papua New Guinea. Traditionally, Wape hunters believe that the spirits of their deceased ancestors roam the woods claimed by their lineage, protect them from enemy invaders, and assist them in the hunt by driving wild game their way (Mitchell, 1973). Moreover, they believe that ancestral spirits punish anyone who has wronged them or their descendants by preventing wrongdoers from finding game or hitting their mark. Like the devout Christian who avoids sinning for fear of hell, the Wape hunter fears some sort of supernatural punishment for wrongdoing, even though no one in his village may be aware of his bad deed. For the Wape, then, successful hunting depends upon avoiding quarrels and maintaining tranquility within the community so as not to antagonize anybody's deceased ancestor.

Externalized Control: Sanctions

Because internalized controls are not wholly sufficient even in bands and tribes, every society develops externalized social controls, known as **sanctions**, designed to

---

cultural control Control through beliefs and values deeply internalized in the minds of individuals.

self-control A person's capacity to manage her or his spontaneous feelings, restraining impulsive behavior.

social control External control through open coercion.

sanction An externalized social control designed to encourage conformity to social norms.

encourage conformity to social standards of acceptable behavior. Operating within social groups of all sizes and involving a mix of cultural and social controls, sanctions may vary significantly within a given society, but they fall into one of two categories: positive or negative.

Positive sanctions consist of incentives to conform, such as awards, titles, promotions, and other demonstrations of recognized approval. Negative sanctions consist of threats such as shaming, fining, flogging, branding, banishing, jailing, and even killing for violating the standards.

For sanctions to be effective, they must be applied consistently, and they must be generally known among members of the society. Even if some individuals are not convinced of the advantages of social conformity, they are still more likely to obey society's rules than to accept the consequences of not doing so.

Sanctions may be formal or informal, depending on whether a legal statute is involved. In the United States, the man who goes shirtless in shorts to a church service may be subject to a variety of informal sanctions, ranging from disapproving glances from the clergy to the chuckling of other parishioners. If, however, he were to show up without any clothing at all, he would be subject to the formal negative sanction of arrest for indecent exposure. Only in the second instance would he have been guilty of breaking the **law**—formal rules of conduct that, when violated, effectuate negative sanctions.

Cultural Control: Witchcraft

In societies with or without centralized political systems, witchcraft sometimes functions as an agent of cultural control and involves both self-control and social controls. An individual will think twice before offending a neighbor if convinced that the neighbor could retaliate by resorting to black magic. Similarly, individuals may not wish to be accused of practicing witchcraft, and so they behave with greater circumspection.

Among the Azande of South Sudan, people who think they have been bewitched may consult an oracle, who, after performing the appropriate mystical rites, may establish or confirm the identity of the offending witch (Evans-Pritchard, 1937). Confronted with this evidence, the witch will usually agree to cooperate in order to avoid any additional trouble. Should the victim die, the relatives of the deceased may choose to make magic against the witch, ultimately accepting the death of some villager as evidence of both guilt and the efficacy of their magic.

For the Azande, witchcraft provides not only a sanction against antisocial behavior but also a means of dealing with natural hostilities and death. No one wishes to be thought of as a witch, and surely no one wishes to be victimized by one. By institutionalizing their emotional responses, the Azande successfully maintain social order.

Holding Trials, Settling Disputes, and Punishing Crimes

Among traditional Inuit in northern Canada, the customary way of settling a dispute is through a *song duel* in which the individuals insult each other through songs specially composed for the occasion. Although society does not intervene, spectators represent its interests, and their applause determines the outcome. If, however, social harmony cannot be restored—and that is the goal, rather than assigning and punishing guilt—one or the other disputant may move to another band. Ultimately, there is no binding legal authority (**Figure 12.9**).

By contrast, in Western societies someone who commits an offense against another person may become subject to a series of complex legal proceedings. In criminal cases the primary concern is to assign and punish guilt rather than to help out the victim. The offender will be arrested by the police; tried before a judge and perhaps a jury; and, depending on the severity of the crime, may be fined, imprisoned, or even executed. Rarely does the victim receive restitution or compensation. Throughout this chain of events, the accused party is dealt with by police, judges, jurors, and jailers, who may have no personal acquaintance whatsoever with the plaintiff or the defendant.

The judge's work is difficult and complex. In addition to sifting through evidence presented in a courtroom trial, he or she must consider a wide range of norms, values, and earlier rulings to arrive at a decision that is considered just, not only by the disputing parties but by the public and other judges as well.

Traditionally, in numerous politically centralized societies, incorruptible supernatural, or at least nonhuman, powers are thought to make judgments through a *trial by ordeal*. For example, among the Kpelle of Liberia discussed earlier in this chapter, when guilt is in doubt a licensed "ordeal operator" may apply a hot knife to a suspect's leg. If the leg is burned, the suspect is guilty; if not, innocence is assumed. But the operator does not merely heat the knife and apply it. After massaging the suspect's legs and determining the knife is hot enough, the operator then strokes his own leg with it without being burned, demonstrating

---

law Formal rules of conduct that, when violated, effectuate negative sanctions.

Figure 12.9 **Inuit Song Duel** Among Inuit of northern Canada, the traditional way of settling a dispute in the community is through a song duel, in which the individuals insult each other in songs composed for the occasion. The applause of onlookers determines the winner, and the affair is considered closed; no further action is expected.

that the innocent will escape injury. The knife is then applied to the suspect.

Up to this point—consciously or unconsciously—the operator has read the suspect's nonverbal cues: gestures, the degree of muscular tension, amount of perspiration, and so forth. From this the operator can judge whether the anxiety the accused exhibits indicates probable guilt; in effect, a psychological stress evaluation has been made. As the knife is applied, it is manipulated to either burn or not burn the suspect, once this judgment has been made. The operator does this manipulation easily by controlling how long the knife is in the fire, as well as the pressure and angle at which it is pressed against the leg (Gibbs, 1983).

The use of the lie detector (polygraph) in the United States is a similar example of assessing guilt, although the guiding ideology is scientific rather than metaphysical. This nonhuman agency is thought to establish objectively who is lying and who is not, but in reality the polygraph operator cannot just "read" the needles of the machine. He or she must judge whether they are registering a high level of anxiety brought on by the testing situation, as opposed to the stress of guilt. Thus, the polygraph operator has much in common with the Kpelle ordeal operator.

Although state societies make a clear distinction between offenses against an individual and those against the state, in non-state societies such as bands and tribes all offenses are viewed as transgressions against individuals or kin-groups (families, lineages, clans, and so on). Disputes between individuals or kin-groups may seriously disrupt the social order, especially in small groups where the disputants, though small in absolute numbers, may be a large percentage of the total population. For example, although the Inuit traditionally have no effective domestic or economic unit

beyond the family, a dispute between two people will interfere with the ability of members of separate families to come to one another's aid when necessary and is consequently a matter of wider social concern. Through collectively evaluating the situation and determining who is right or wrong, community members focus on restoring social harmony rather than punishing an offender.

Punitive justice, such as imprisonment, may be the most common approach to justice in state societies, but it has not proven to be an effective way of changing criminal behavior. As a result, indigenous communities in Canada have successfully urged their federal government to reform justice services to make them more consistent with indigenous values and traditions (Criminal Code of Canada, §718.2e). In particular, they have pressed for restorative justice techniques such as the Talking Circle, traditionally used in various forms by several Native American groups. For this, parties involved in a conflict come together in a circle with equal opportunity to express their views—one at a time, free of interruption. Usually, a "talking stick" (or an eagle feather or some other symbolic object) is held by whoever is speaking to signal that she or he has the right to talk at that moment, and others have the responsibility to listen.

In North America over the past four decades there has been significant movement away from the courts in favor of outside negotiation and mediation to resolve a wide variety of disputes. Many jurists see this as a means to clear overloaded court dockets so as to concentrate on more important cases. Leaders in the field of dispute resolution today are finding effective ways to bring about balanced resolutions to conflict. An example of this approach is examined in the Anthropology Applied feature.

For illustration purposes, consider three famous battles: In the 1815 Battle of Waterloo that ended Napoleon's rule of the French empire, some 150,000 soldiers and 45,000 horses engaged in combat south of Brussels on a battlefield under 8 square kilometers (3 square miles in size). Within just nine hours, 45,000 men and 34,000 horses lay dead or wounded. During World War II, the Battle of Stalingrad, fought from the fall of 1942 into January 1943, claimed about 1.5 million casualties. At the end of the war, only 5,000 out of 300,000 German soldiers returned from Russia alive. In the Battle of Hsupeng (also known as the Huaihai Campaign) ending the Chinese civil war in early 1949, more than 2 million troops fought on a flat plain of 7,600 square miles, with almost 700,000 casualties (including captives).

The evolution of warfare is also driven by new inventions in military technology, with weapons becoming increasingly complex and effective—from slings, clubs, spears, and arrows to machine guns, supersonic jet fighters, atomic bombs, high-energy laser beams, computer viruses, and pilotless drones (**Figure 12.10**). In modern warfare, casualties are not just civilians but also *children*, and they far outnumber the casualty rate of soldiers.

Almost a century ago, tens of thousands of soldiers on the French-German frontline in World War I experienced chemical warfare for the first time in human history. Although other poison gases had been used a few years earlier, troops in the trenches in 1917 were attacked by mustard gas—a chemical poison that causes blindness, large blisters on exposed skin, and (if inhaled)

Heather Ainsworth/The New York Times/Redux

Figure 12.10 Drone Pilot Operator From his computer console at a military command post in New York State, this U.S. Attack Wing airman remotely operates a drone aircraft in support of American ground troops battling enemies in tribal territories of Afghanistan and neighboring Pakistan. Equipped with Hellfire missiles, his drone surveys the terrain with powerful cameras beaming live video via satellite. Drones can be thought of as modern versions of dangerous spirits magically directed by invisible warlords. U.S. forces have used Predator drones since 1995, targeting enemies primarily in Muslim insurgencies across western Asia and North Africa. During that same period, the entertainment industry has provided opportunities for "child soldiers" across the globe to play telewarfare video games in arcades or at home.

bleeding and blistering in the mouth, throat, and lungs. The development of weapons of mass destruction has been horrendously effective.

Today, the chemical, biological, and nuclear weapon arsenals stockpiled by many states are sufficient to wipe out all life on the planet, many times over. Because dangerous poisons, such as the anthrax bacterium or the nerve gas Sarin, are cheap and easy to produce, non-state groups, including terrorists, also seek to acquire to them, if only to threaten to use them against more powerful opponents.

Ideologies of Aggression

Whatever may be possible in terms of military technology, it takes ideas and motivation to turn humans into killers, and that stems from culture. Justifications for war are embedded in a society's *worldview*—the collective body of ideas that members of a culture generally share concerning the ultimate shape and substance of their reality. It is said that war is dehumanizing; that ideological process usually begins with degrading opponents to a lower status as barbaric, evil, ugly, worthless, or otherwise inferior. Having thus dehumanized their opponents, humans conjure justifications for slaughter and pillage, often raping vanquished women, mutilating enemy bodies for trophies, and turning captives into slaves.

Ultimately, war also dehumanizes the aggressor. Recalling his experiences in trench warfare in which he was wounded in the summer of 1917, a German combat veteran wrote: "We have become wild beasts. . . . We have lost all feeling for one another [and] plunge again into the horror . . . madly savage and raging; we will kill, for they are still our mortal enemies [and] if we don't destroy them, they will destroy us" (Remarque, 1929, pp. 113–116).

No matter how extreme and negative the emotions may be when confronting the enemy, warriors are usually physically and mentally trained for combat. In preparing and conditioning young men (and sometimes women) for the battlefield, they are indoctrinated by an ideology justifying war, which may come wrapped in magic and other metaphysics.

There are all too many examples of how religious and ideological justifications for war are embedded in a society's worldview. They range from the Christian Crusades directed against Muslims in Palestine and surrounding Islamic territories about 700 to 900 years ago to the more recent *jihad* waged by Islamic fundamentalists in southwestern Asia and North Africa. The latter include militant extremists, such as Al-Qaeda and Jemaah Islamiyah, aiming to restore "pure" Islam, topple regimes that promote or tolerate religious corruption, and expel all infidels (nonbelievers) from ancestral

soil. The following example from East Africa provides a more detailed look.

A Crusade in Uganda: The Rise and Fall of a Militant Christian Cult

Once described as the Pearl of Africa, Uganda is a pluralistic country with about 34 million inhabitants divided into more than a dozen ethnic groups, including the Acholi. During the colonial period, British missionaries converted a large majority of Ugandans to Christianity.

Since gaining independence in 1962, Uganda has suffered numerous regional insurgencies, civil wars, and interethnic clashes, resulting in death or displacement for millions. During the 1981–1986 Ugandan Bush War, Acholi soldiers fought with the losing faction, suffering huge losses and humiliation.

By 1986, many Acholi Christians believed the apocalypse described in the Bible's Book of Revelation was upon them. One such Acholi was Alice Auma, a 30-year-old woman who had been married and divorced twice for being barren. Alice found inspiration in the biblical promise of a "new earth" free of suffering and death. Through a vision she believed was divine, she learned that a holy messenger had chosen her as his spirit-medium. Sometimes this powerful spirit took possession of Alice. She named him *Lakwena*—the Acholi word for "apostle" or "messenger from God"—and claimed that he commanded the heavenly force of 144,000 redeemed men described in Revelation.

In 1986, spiritually empowered by Lakwena, Alice became a *nebi* (Acholi translation for a "biblical prophet"). At séances, she gave herself over to *malaika* (Swahili for "angels"), who filled her with power to heal people diagnosed as victims of evil spirits. Gaining a reputation as a witchdoctor, she became known as Alice Lakwena. Her patients included many Acholi soldiers who believed they were possessed by *cen*—the polluting spirits of killed enemies seeking revenge. To keep their soul and body clean, Alice ordered them to abstain from alcohol and sex.

Feeling divinely directed to liberate her homeland from evil and found a Christian theocracy based on the Ten Commandments, Alice recruited 8,000 Acholi and other northern warriors for a crusade to free Uganda from all enemies of God. She called her militant cult the Holy

Spirit Mobile Force. In late 1987, supernaturally aided by Lakwena and his phantom army of 144,000, Alice led 7,000 of her warriors southward, aiming to capture Uganda's capital city, Kampala.

Filled with *malaika*, Alice's troops marched in cross-shaped battle formations, carrying Bibles and singing hymns. They had smeared their bodies with holy oil extracted from wild shea nuts, assured it would shield them from bullets. They were armed with rifles, plus magic sticks and stones blessed to explode when hurled at the enemy. In the first few battles, they scored victories when terrified government troops ran away. But 80 kilometers east of Kampala, the Holy Spirit Mobile Force was massacred, mowed down in a barrage of mortar attacks and machine-gun fire. Convinced that bullets could not pierce the purified, Alice interpreted this defeat as evidence that evil spirits had gained control over many in her own army. Abandoning the battlefield, she escaped into Kenya where she died in a refugee camp twenty years later.

Hundreds of Holy Spirit warriors who survived the ordeal joined other rebel groups, including the Lord's Resistance Army (LRA) formed by Joseph Kony, an Acholi witchdoctor. A former Roman Catholic altar boy related to Alice, Kony adopted some of her spiritual repertoire in founding a militant cult based on a mixture of indigenized Christian and Muslim beliefs and practices. After growing to a force of 4,000 warriors, his insurgency degenerated into a murderous campaign based on terror tactics. The LRA also kidnapped many thousands of children, indoctrinating them to become merciless fighters (**Figure 12.11**).

By 2006, LRA troops had dwindled to about 600, and the Uganda army had forced them across the border into the Democratic Republic of Congo. The rebels hid out in Garamba National Park—a vast wilderness inhabited by elephants, giraffes, hippos, rare white rhinoceroses, and many other animals.

Since then, despite peace talk efforts, Kony's soldiers continue to carry out periodic raids. For instance, in a June 2008 foray into South Sudan, they forcibly added some 1,000 new recruits, including hundreds of abducted children. In air and ground military offensives throughout the following six months, Ugandan soldiers attacked rebel camps in the Garamba forest, killing more than 150 LRA troops, capturing another 50 (including several low-level commanders), and rescuing many of the kidnapped children and other forced recruits. The LRA retaliated with killing raids, capturing replacement recruits, including more children.

In the past few years, nearly half a million people have fled their villages for fear of attack—not only in the Democratic Republic of Congo, but also in neighboring

Figure 12.11 Young Acholi Soldier in the Lord's Resistance Army After Alice Lakwena's crusade ended in a bloodbath, her relative Joseph Kony adopted some of her ideas, forming the Lord's Resistance Army (LRA). Unlike Alice, he often forced children into service. In 2006 he and his fighters, including the armed teenager pictured here, retreated into the Democratic Republic of Congo's vast Garamba National Park and staged raids from there. Wanted for war crimes and accused of being a demon, Kony remains in hiding.

Sudan and the Central African Republic. Kony, the rebel army's charismatic Christian cult leader, remains at large, still believing in his divinely guided insurgency (Allen, 2006; Behrend, 1999; Finnström, 2008).

Genocide

As these cross-cultural examples of violent conflict indicate, warfare often involves a complex dynamic of economic, political, and ideological interests. Such is especially the case when violence escalates into **genocide**—the physical extermination of one people by another, either as a deliberate act or as the accidental outcome of activities

---

genocide The physical extermination of one people by another, either as a deliberate act or as the accidental outcome of activities carried out by one people with little regard for their impact on others.

carried out by one people with little regard for their impact on others.

The most widely known act of genocide in recent history was the attempt of the Nazis during World War II to wipe out European Jews and Roma (Gypsies) in the name of racial superiority and improvement of the human species. Reference to this mass extermination as *the* Holocaust—as if it were unique—tends to blind us to the fact that genocide is an age-old and ongoing phenomenon, with many examples from across the globe and throughout human history. In North America, for example, European settlers massacred numerous indigenous communities from the 1500s up until the late 1800s in California.

One of the most infamous 19th-century acts of genocide was the systematic killing of the indigenous inhabitants of Tasmania, a large island about the size of Ireland and located just south of Australia. Collectively known as Palawa, they subsisted as hunter-gatherers probably not unlike their ancestors who migrated there almost 40,000 years ago. European seafarers first came ashore in 1642 but made no contact.

About 160 years later, the British claimed the remote island and designated it as a penal colony for exiled prisoners. Then numbering about 5,000, the Palawa were divided into several regional ethnic groups speaking different languages. Armed with spears, Palawa warriors defending their families and hunting territories were no match for the invaders equipped with firearms. On December 1, 1826, the island newspaper *Colonial Times* declared:

> SELF DEFENSE IS THE FIRST LAW OF NATURE. THE GOVERNMENT MUST REMOVE THE NATIVES—IF NOT, THEY WILL BE HUNTED DOWN LIKE WILD BEASTS, AND DESTROYED!

Soon, slaughter and newly introduced diseases led to Palawa extinction, and the island was fully secured for British sheep farmers and the commercial wool industry. In 1876, the last full-blooded Tasmanian was carried to her grave. A similar tragedy unfolded in Tierra del Fuego, a large island on the tip of the South American continent, where British sheep farmers drove off the indigenous Selk'nam, who are also extinct.

Among numerous more contemporary examples of genocide, Khmer Rouge soldiers in Cambodia killed 1.7 million fellow citizens, or 20 percent of that country's population, between 1975 and 1979. During the next decade, government-sponsored terrorism against indigenous communities in Guatemala reached its height, and Saddam Hussein's government used poison gas against the Kurdish ethnic minority in northern Iraq. In 1994, Hutus in the African country of Rwanda slaughtered about 800,000 of their Tutsi neighbors ("Leave none to tell the story: Genocide in Rwanda," 2004). Estimates vary,

but during the 20th century as many as 83 million people died of genocide (White, 2001). The horrors continue in the current century with, among others, the genocidal campaign against the non-Arab black peoples in the Darfur desert region of western Sudan.

Armed Conflicts Today

Currently, there are several dozen wars raging around the globe. They occur not only *between* states but also *within* pluralistic countries where interethnic conflicts abound and/or where the political leadership and government bureaucracy are corrupt, repressive, ineffective, or without popular support (**Figure 12.12**).

Notably, many armies around the world recruit not only adult men but also women and children. Experts estimate that some 250,000 child soldiers, many as young as 12, are participating in armed conflicts around the world, especially in Africa. Among the notorious examples is the Lord's Resistance Army mentioned previously, which reportedly kidnapped over 60,000 children to train as fierce fighters ("Child soldiers global report 2008," 2009; UN Dispatch, 2006).

The following examples offer some specific data on wars from the last decade of the 20th century to today. In the 1990s, about 2.5 million people died, and many millions more became refugees due to fighting in South Sudan, leading to that region's secession and political independence as a new state in 2011. And since warfare erupted in the eastern region of the Democratic Republic of Congo in 1998, almost 6 million people have died, and millions more have been forced to flee their home villages. Involving eight African states and about twenty-five armed forces, this gruesome war with mass murder and mass rape is known as Africa's World War.

Foreign military intervention is also a hallmark of long-lasting wars in regions that are strategically important or that are rich in natural resources, including Afghanistan and Iraq. In addition to many hundreds of thousands of fatalities in these countries, primarily among noncombatants (children, women, elderly), there has been massive destruction of roads, bridges, buildings, and livelihoods. Without a political leadership capable of effectively governing these pluralistic countries, providing security, and maintaining law and order, both war-torn countries seem doomed to be failed states.

Beyond these wars, there are numerous so-called low-intensity wars involving guerrilla organizations, rebel armies, resistance movements, terrorist cells, and a host of other armed groups engaged in violent conflict with official state-controlled armed forces. Every year, confrontations result in hundreds of hot spots and violent flashpoints, most of which are never reported in Western news media.

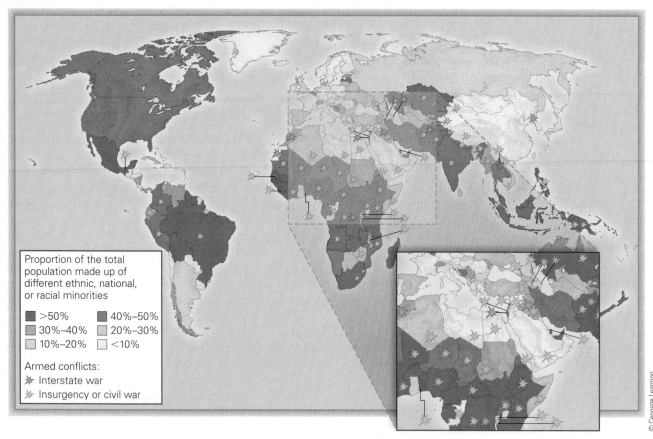

Figure 12.12 Ethnic Groups and Violent Conflict In pluralistic societies in which two or more ethnic groups or nationalities form part of the same political state, violent conflict between neighboring groups is not uncommon.

Peace Through Diplomacy

The resolution of conflicts within and between groups by nonviolent means is a vital part of this chapter's discussion. Throughout history, people have tried to prevent conflicts from escalating into violence, just as they have endeavored to end existing violence and restore peaceful relations. For this to succeed, politically organized groups designate high-ranking trusted individuals to discuss a mutually acceptable agreement to secure peace. Authorized as representatives acting on behalf of their tribal elders, chief, king, or other sovereign head, these envoys usually carry evidence of their official status and mission as envoys or diplomats (from the Greek *diploma*, originally meaning "folded paper").

Diplomatic evidence may be in the form of a written document, marked by a signature, seal, or some other sign representing the authorizing government. In different cultures across the globe, a wide range of ceremonial artifacts have been used in diplomatic protocol—such as special shell-beaded belts (*wampum*) presented by Iroquois chiefs and long-stemmed tobacco pipes smoked by Lakota leaders and numerous other Plains Indian peoples.

Thus equipped, delegates participate in formal rituals brokering terms of agreement, including mutually binding rules to prevent or end conflict and live in friendship and peace. These terms so negotiated may secure rights of access or claims to tracts of disputed land, water, other natural resources, safe passage across territorial boundaries for trade or pilgrimages to sacred sites, and a host of other issues setting rules to maintain order and avoid conflict.

A formally binding agreement between two or more groups that are independent and politically self-governing (such as tribes, chiefdoms, and states) is a contract known as a **treaty**. Determining issues of war and peace and influencing the survival and well-being of multitudes, treatymaking is ritually concluded with a ceremonial performance. When the rules as formulated in a treaty are ignored or violated, the pact of friendship is broken. With relations chilling or turning hostile, war may follow.

treaty A contract or formally binding agreement between two or more groups that are independent and self-governing political groups such as tribes, chiefdoms, and states.

Figure 12.13 West Papua Independence Movement Lani tribal leader Benny Wenda (center in red shirt) became a political prisoner in Indonesia due to his role in West Papua's struggle for independence from Indonesia. He escaped while awaiting trial. Fearing for his life and expecting no justice from a legal system that denied Papua indigenous rights, he went into exile and was granted asylum by the British government in 2002. Lobbying for his country's peaceful transition to independence, Wenda launched the International Parliamentarians for West Papua (IPWP) at the British Parliament in London, on October 15, 2008. Here we see Wenda and other West Papuans with several British Parliamentarians in the House of Commons. Standing next to Wenda is IPWP's chairman, Andrew Smith, a Member of Parliament (MP) from Oxford. This cross-party group of politicians supporting self-determination for the people of West Papua has grown to almost 100 parliamentarians. A former Labour Party cabinet minister, Smith also chairs Britain's All Party Parliamentary Group for West Papua, which meets regularly.

Treaties between two sovereign parties are known as *bilateral* treaties, and these have been made for many thousands of years. International treaties are more recent, involving many neighboring states on a continent or, since the past century, across the globe. Today, many indigenous nations who could not resist more powerful states claiming political control or ownership over their ancestral lands are appealing to international organizations for support in their struggle against repression, respect for their human rights and cultural freedom, and restoration of their political rights of self-determination in their homeland.

Throughout the world today, there are politically repressed ethnic and religious groups as well as indigenous peoples who struggle for freedom and self-determination. Among them are tribal peoples of West Papua, New Guinea, many of whom remained isolated from the outside world until half a century ago. Those living in remote highland villages had little knowledge of the expansionist strategy guiding neighboring Indonesia into politically annexing their homeland in 1963. Soon thereafter, frustrated in their political desire for independence, indigenous activists founded the Free Papua Movement. Since then, Indonesian military and police have brutally repressed Papua freedom fighters, threatening, imprisoning, and killing thousands; thousands more have been driven into hiding in the forested mountains or into exile abroad. One exiled West Papua leader, Benny Wenda, now lives in England; from there he continues the struggle for his country's independence through international organizations and diplomatic channels (**Figure 12.13**).

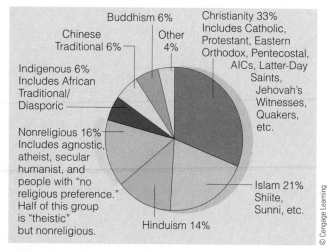

Buddhism 6%

Chinese Traditional 6%

Other 4%

Christianity 33% Includes Catholic, Protestant, Eastern Orthodox, Pentecostal, AICs, Latter-Day Saints, Jehovah's Witnesses, Quakers, etc.

Indigenous 6% Includes African Traditional/ Diasporic

Nonreligious 16% Includes agnostic, atheist, secular humanist, and people with "no religious preference." Half of this group is "theistic" but nonreligious.

Islam 21% Shiite, Sunni, etc.

Hinduism 14%

© Cengage Learning

Figure 13.1 Major Religions of the World This chart shows the world's major religions with percentages of their adherents. The total adds up to more than 100 percent due to rounding. Two have enormous followings: Christianity, with almost 2.2 billion adherents (half of whom are Roman Catholic), and Islam, with about 1.7 billion (an overwhelming majority of whom are Sunnis). Within both religions are numerous major and minor divisions, splits, and sects.

Sources: adherents.com; Pew Research Center, 2011.

Roles of Spirituality and Religion

Among people in all societies, particular spiritual or religious beliefs and practices fulfill individual and collective psychological and emotional needs. They reduce anxiety by providing an orderly view of the universe and answers to existential questions, including those concerning suffering and death. They provide a path by which people transcend the burdens of mortal existence and attain, if only momentarily, hope and relief.

Spiritual or religious beliefs and practices also serve numerous cultural purposes. For instance, a religion held in common by a group of people reinforces community values and provides moral guidelines for personal conduct. It also offers narratives and rituals used to confirm a social hierarchy and sanction political power; conversely, it may allow for narratives *countering* the legitimacy of powerholders, even providing justifications and rituals to resist and challenge them. Last but not least, people often turn to religion or spirituality in the hope of reaching a specific goal, such as restoring health, securing a harvest, ending violence, or being rescued from danger (**Figure 13.2**).

AP Images/Ed Way

Figure 13.2 Bugi Sailors Praying, Indonesia The Bugi of Sulawesi (Celebes) are famous for their oceangoing schooners. For generations, these Indonesian seafarers have plied the waters between Malaysia and Australia, transporting spices and other freight. Life at sea is risky—sudden storms, piracy, and other mishaps—and sailors pray for safety. This prayerful Bugi gathering in Jakarta on Java Island took place on a holiday ending Ramadan, the Islamic month of fasting. During that time Muslims refrain from eating, drinking liquids, smoking, and sexual activities, from sunrise to sunset. This taboo serves to purify thought and build restraint for Allah's sake.

Anthropologists recognize that not everyone believes in a supernatural force or entity, but they also agree that there is no known culture that does not provide some set of ideas about existence beyond ordinary and empirically verifiable reality, or—for lack of a better word—ideas concerning the supernatural or metaphysical. Because such ideas serve cultural purposes and fulfill emotional and psychological needs, it makes sense that spirituality and religion developed tens of thousands of years ago and spread across the globe.

In the wake of major technological inventions and new discoveries since the 1600s, European intellectuals predicted that magic, myth, and religion would be replaced by empirical research, proven facts, and scientific theories. They expected that as science progressed, beliefs and rituals based on what they argued to be ignorance and superstition would gradually disappear. Some even forecasted the end of religion altogether. But to date, and despite tremendous scientific achievements, that has not occurred. In many places, the opposite trend seems to prevail, in particular where radical technological, social, and economic transformations destabilize the long-established cultural order, challenge deeply embedded worldviews, and leave people feeling insecure and threatened. Confronted by sweeping changes over which people have little or no control, many turn to religion and spirituality.

Anthropological Approach to Spirituality and Religion

Worldwide, people are inspired and guided by strongly held ideas about the supernatural, putting into practice what they deeply believe to be true or right. It is not the responsibility of anthropologists to pass judgment on the metaphysical truth of any particular faith system, but it is their challenge to show how each embodies a number of revealing facts about humanity and the particular cultural superstructure, or worldview, within which these religious or spiritual beliefs are ideologically embedded.

Based on a cross-cultural and comparative historical perspective on worldviews, we define **religion** as an organized system of ideas about the spiritual sphere or the supernatural, along with associated ceremonial practices by which people try to interpret and/or influence aspects of the universe otherwise beyond their access or control. Similar to religion, **spirituality** is concerned with the sacred, as distinguished from ordinary reality, but it is often individual rather than collective and

does not require a formal institution. Both indicate that many aspects of the human experience are thought to be beyond natural or scientific explanation.

Because no culture, including those of modern industrial and postindustrial societies, has achieved complete certainty in controlling existing or future conditions and circumstances of human life, spirituality and/or religion continue to play a role in all known cultures. However, considerable variability exists globally (**Figure 13.3**).

At one end of the anthropological spectrum are food-foraging peoples, whose technological ability to control their natural environment is limited. Broadly speaking, they hold that nature is pregnant with the spiritual. Embedded and manifested in all aspects of their culture, spirituality permeates their daily activities—from food hunting or gathering to making fires, building homes, and conversations about life before or after death. It also mirrors and confirms the egalitarian nature of social relations in their societies, in that individuals do not plead with high-ranking deities for aid the way members of stratified societies more typically do. Their holistic worldview is often referred to as *naturalistic*, an imprecise but workable term.

At the other end of our spectrum are state societies with commercial or industrial economies, sophisticated technologies, and social stratification based on a complex division of labor. There, high-ranking social groups typically seek to control and manage the construction of a society's worldview as an ideological means of legitimizing and reinforcing their vested interests in its hierarchical structure. Usually featuring a ranked order of supernatural beings—for instance, God and (in some religions) the angels, saints, or other holy figures—it simultaneously reflects and reinforces the stratified system in which it is embedded. In such societies, religion tends to be less integrated into everyday activities, and its practice is usually confined to specific times, occasions, and locations.

Religions provide a powerful ideology justifying inequality in a state society, but may also inspire subordinated peoples to envision an alternative social order freeing them from exploitation, repression, and humiliation. Thus, religiously motivated social movements have challenged political establishments.

---

religion An organized system of ideas about the spiritual sphere or the supernatural, along with associated ceremonial practices by which people try to interpret and/or influence aspects of the universe otherwise beyond their control.

spirituality Concern with the sacred, as distinguished from material matters. In contrast to religion, spirituality is often individual rather than collective and does not require a distinctive format or traditional organization.

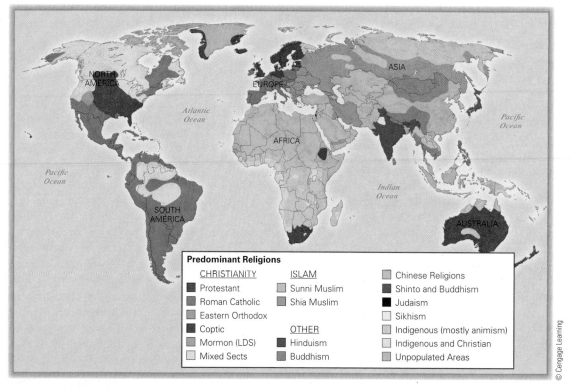

Figure 13.3 Global Distribution of Predominant Religions This map depicts only the global distribution of major religions, indicating where they predominate. In some areas, the mixture of different religions is such that no single faith is shared by most of that region's inhabitants. Not detailed enough to show pockets with significant numbers of a particular faith, it also omits many religions that are dispersed or eclipsed by others—including several worldwide ones such as Ahmadiyya (a Muslim sect, with 10 million adherents); Jehovah's Witnesses (a Christian sect with 7 million adherents); and Bahá'í (with 6 million adherents, emphasizing the spiritual unity of all mankind and recognizing divine messengers from various religions).

Myth and the Mapping of a Sacred Worldview

Because much remains beyond human capacity to actually observe and explain based on obvious or empirical evidence alone, people have creatively worked out narratives explaining the fundamentals of human existence—where we and everything in our world came from, why we are here, and where we are going. Describing a worldview, these narratives are referred to as **myths** (*mythos*, Greek for "word," "speech") and play a fundamental role in religious and spiritual beliefs. Mapping a people's *cosmology*—their understanding of the universe, its form and working—myths are believed to be true, even sacred, by those subscribing to the particular worldview engendering such narratives.

Typically, a myth features supernatural forces or beings engaged in extraordinary or miraculous performances. It

may offer a morality play, providing an ethical code for its audience and guidelines for human behavior. For example, the Puranas (a body of religious texts, including cosmological myths, considered sacred by Buddhists and Hindus) are rich in such material. So are the Bible, Koran, and Torah, each held sacred in distinct but historically related religions originating in Southwest Asia. We will discuss myths further within the context of art in the next chapter, but here it is important to underscore that these stories, whether orally transmitted or in writing, have been passed on from generation to generation and inform believers with a sacred map of the cosmos or universe and their place in it.

Supernatural Beings and Spiritual Forces

A hallmark of religion is belief in spiritual forces and supernatural beings. Attempting to control by religious means what cannot be controlled in other ways, humans turn to prayer, sacrifice, and other religious or spiritual rituals. Their actions presuppose the existence of spiritual forces that can

---

myth A sacred narrative that explains the fundamentals of human existence—where we and everything in our world came from, why we are here, and where we are going.

Figure 13.4 Judeo-Christian God Giving Life to Adam The patriarchal nature of traditional Euramerican society is depicted on the ceiling of the Sistine Chapel in Rome, Italy. The image of a supreme male diety creating the first man, named Adam ("human being"), is culturally articulated and ideologically justified by its Judeo-Christian theology. Afterward, according to this biblical story, the first woman, named Eve, is formed from Adam's rib.

be tapped into, or supernatural beings interested in human affairs and available for aid. In many cultures, these supernatural forces or spiritual beings are associated with unique geographic locations valued as sacred sites—extraordinary rocks, lakes, wells, waterfalls, mountains, and so forth.

Supernatural beings can be divided into three categories: deities (gods and goddesses), ancestral spirits, and other sorts of spirit beings. Although the variety of deities and spirits recognized by the world's cultures is tremendous, it is possible to make certain generalizations about them.

Gods and Goddesses

Not all religions *anthropomorphize* the divine, but many do. Symbolically constructing a divine order that mirrors a society's gender structure, many religions recognize male and female deities. Gods and goddesses, or divinities, are the great and more remote supernatural beings. Generally speaking, cultures that subordinate women to men attribute masculine gender to the more powerful gods or supreme deity. For instance, in traditional Christian religions believers speak of God as a father who had a divine son born from a human mother but do not entertain thoughts of God as a mother or as a divine daughter (**Figure 13.4**). Such male-privileging religions developed in many societies traditionally based on the herding of animals or intensive agriculture, frequent warfare, and politics controlled by men.

Goddesses, by contrast, are likely to be prominent in societies where women play a significant role in the economy and enjoy relative equality with men. Such societies are most often those that depend on crop cultivation traditionally carried out solely or mostly by women. Typically, these may feature fertility and earth goddesses.

Some religions recognize deities represented as male–female combinations. For example, one of the Greek gods, also recognized in the Roman empire, was Hermaphroditus, the beautiful two-sexed son of Hermes (alias Mercury) and Venus (alias Aphrodite). A similar third-gender divinity is recognized by Hindus worshiping Ardhanarishvara ("the Lord who is half woman").

If a religion recognizes only one supremely powerful divinity as creator and master of the universe, we speak of **monotheism**. If it acknowledges more than one divinity, each governing a particular domain, we label it **polytheism**. Gods and goddesses of ancient Greece illustrate the latter: Zeus ruled the sky, Poseidon the sea, and Hades the underworld and the dead. In addition to these three brothers, Greek mythology features a host of other deities, both male and female, each similarly concerned with specific aspects of life and the universe. Athena and Nike, for instance, were goddesses of war and victory, respectively. A **pantheon**, or the collection of gods and goddesses such as those of the Greeks, is common in many religions, today most famously in Hinduism.

Because states typically have grown through conquest, often their pantheons have expanded, with local deities of conquered peoples being incorporated into the official state pantheon. A frequent feature of pantheons is the presence of a supreme deity, who may be all but totally ignored by humans. Aztecs of the Mexican highlands, for instance, recognized a supreme duo to whom they paid little attention. Assuming this divine pair was unlikely to be interested in ordinary humans, they devoted themselves to lesser deities thought to be more directly concerned with human affairs.

Ancestral Spirits

Beliefs in ancestral spirits support the concept that human beings consist of intertwined components: body/matter (physical) and mind/soul (spiritual). This dualistic concept carries with it the possibility of a spirit being freed from the body—through dream, trance, or death—and even having a separate existence. Frequently, where a belief in

---

monotheism The belief in only one supremely powerful divinity as creator and master of the universe.

polytheism The belief in multiple gods and/or goddesses, as contrasted with monotheism—the belief in one god or goddess.

pantheon All the gods and goddesses of a people.

ancestral spirits exists, these nonphysical beings are seen as retaining an active interest and membership in society.

Beliefs in ancestral spirits are found in many parts of the world, especially among people having unilineal descent systems with their associated ancestor orientation. In several African cultures, the concept is highly elaborate, and people believe ancestral spirits behave much like humans. They are able to feel hot, cold, and pain and may even die a second death by drowning or burning. Because spirits sometimes participate in family and lineage events, seats will be provided for them, even though they are invisible. If spirits are annoyed, they may send sickness or death. Eventually, they are reborn as new members of their lineage, so adults need to observe infants closely to determine just who has been reborn.

Ancestor spirits also play an important role in the patrilineal society of traditional China. Giving birth to sons is historically regarded as an obligation to the ancestors because boys inherit their father's ancestral duties. For the gift of life, a boy is forever indebted to his parents, owing them obedience, deference, and a comfortable old age. Even after their death, he has to provide for them in the spirit world, placing food, money, and incense on ancestral altars on the anniversaries of their births and deaths.

Other Types of Supernatural Beings and Spiritual Forces

Animism

One widespread concept concerning supernatural beings is **animism**, a belief that nature is enlivened or energized by distinct personalized spirit beings separable from physical bodies or the material substance they inhabit. Spirits such as souls and ghosts are thought to dwell in humans, animals, and plants, as well as human-made artifacts and natural features such as stones, mountains, and wells; for animists, the world is filled with particular spirits.

These spirit beings are a highly diverse lot. Less remote than gods and goddesses, they may be benevolent, malevolent, or just plain neutral. Involved in people's daily affairs, they also may be awesome, terrifying, lovable, or mischievous. Because they may be pleased or irritated by human actions, people are obliged to be concerned about them.

Animism is typical of those who see themselves as being a part of nature rather than superior to it (**Figure 13.5**). This includes most food foragers and food gardeners, among others. Deities, if they are believed to exist at all in such societies, may be seen as having created the world and perhaps making it fit to live in; but in animism, spirits are the ones to beseech when ill, the ones to help or hinder the shaman, and the ones whom the ordinary hunter may meet when off in the wilderness.

Animatism

Although supernatural power is often thought of as being vested in spirit beings, it does not have to be. Such is the case with **animatism**—the belief that nature is enlivened or energized by an impersonal force or supernatural energy, which may make itself manifest in any special place, thing, or living creature. This basic concept, which probably developed well before the first transition from food foraging to food production 10,000 years ago, is still present in many societies around the

Figure 13.5 Inuit Food Ritual Inuit of Arctic Canada refer to spirit beings as *anirniit* (singular *anirniq*, meaning "breath") and still obey certain taboos and perform rituals when killing game animals and dividing the meat. This is to avoid offending the animal's spirit (which remains alive and may take revenge on the hunter). Today, most Inuit are Christians, and their concept of *anirniq* is akin to "soul." But traditional food rituals continue. In this photo, Inuit at Baffin Island pray before a shared Easter feast of fish and seal meat.

world today. For example, in China it appears in the form of a concept known as *qi* (or *ch'i*), which may be translated as "vital energy." Inuit people in Arctic Canada think of this force in terms of a "cosmic breath-soul" they call *sila*. In northeastern America, Algonquian-speaking indigenous peoples refer to impersonal spirit power as *manitou*.

One of the best-studied examples of animatism can be found in the Pacific where Oceanic peoples inhabiting hundreds of islands share a concept they refer to as *mana*. Not unlike the idea of a cosmic energy passing into and through everything, affecting living and nonliving matter alike, *mana* is probably best defined as "supernaturally conferred potency" (Keesing, 1992, p. 236)—similar to "the force" in the *Star Wars* films. Traditional Maori, Tahitians, Tongans, and other Oceanic peoples typically attribute success (identified by actual achievements such as triumph in combat, bountiful harvest, abundant fish or game, and so on) to *mana*—and see it as proof of *mana*. In short, this metaphysical concept rests on pragmatic evidence.

Animism (a belief in distinct spirit beings) and animatism (which lacks particular substance or individual form) are not mutually exclusive and are often found in the same culture. This is the case among the Inuit pictured in Figure 13.5, who believe in spirit beings known as *anirniit* as well as in the impersonal spirit power they call *sila* (Merkur, 1983).

In many religious traditions, certain geographic places are thought to be spiritually significant or are held sacred for various reasons, including ideas here discussed in terms of animism and animatism. Typically, such sites are rivers, lakes, waterfalls, islands, forests, caves, and—especially—mountains. We revisit the topic of sacred sites later in the chapter.

Religious Specialists

Most cultures include individuals who guide others in their spiritual search and ritual practices. Thought to be inspired, enlightened, or even holy, they command respect for their skills in contacting and influencing spiritual beings and manipulating or connecting to supernatural forces. Often, they display unique personality traits that make them particularly well suited to perform these tasks for which they have undergone special training.

Priests and Priestesses

In societies with resources to support a full-time religious specialist, a **priest or priestess** will be authorized to perform sacred rituals and mediate between fellow humans and supernatural powers, divine spirits, or deities. In many societies, they are familiar figures known by official titles such as *lama, kahuna, imam, priest, minister, rabbi, swami*, or *copa pitào*. How they dress, what they eat, where they live, and numerous other indicators may distinguish them from others in society and symbolically indicate their special status.

Reserving exclusive rights to exercise spiritual power, groups of priests and/or priestesses bond together in an effort to monopolize the means of sacred practice. This includes controlling holy sites of worship, supervising prescribed rituals, and maintaining possession of regalia, relics, statues, images, texts, and other representations of holiness. In so doing, they also create, promote, and maintain the ideological sources needed to symbolically construct the religious authority from which they derive their legitimacy.

When deities are identified in masculine terms, it is not surprising that the most important religious leadership positions are reserved for men. Such is the case in Judaism, Islam, as well as the Roman Catholic Church, the latter of which has always been headed by a male pope and his all-male council, the College of Cardinals.

Female religious specialists are likely to be found only in societies in which women are acknowledged to significantly contribute to the economy, and gods and goddesses are both recognized (Lehman, 2002). Also, all around the world women fully devoted to a religious life have formed their own gender-segregated institutions such as all-female convents headed by an abbess. Such nunneries not only exist in countries with longstanding Christian traditions, but were also founded in the Himalayas and many other Buddhist regions in southern and eastern Asia, including Taiwan, as described by American anthropologist Hillary Crane in the Biocultural Connection on the next page.

Spiritual Lineages: Legitimizing Religious Leadership

As with political institutions discussed in the previous chapter, religious organizations are maintained by rules that define ideological boundaries, establish membership criteria, and regulate continuity of legitimate leadership in the faith community. And, like other institutions, religions have always been challenged by changes. Even in a highly stable cultural system, every generation must deal with natural transitions in the life cycle, including death

animism The belief that nature is enlivened or energized by distinct personalized spirit beings separable from bodies.

animatism The belief that nature is enlivened or energized by an impersonal spiritual force or supernatural energy, which may make itself manifest in any special place, thing, or living creature.

priest or priestess A full-time religious specialist formally recognized for his or her role in guiding the religious practices of others and for contacting and influencing supernatural powers.

BIOCULTURAL CONNECTION

Change Your Karma and Change Your Sex?

By Hillary Crane

As Mahayana Buddhists, Taiwanese Chan (Zen) monastics believe that all humans are able to reach enlightenment and be released from reincarnation. But they believe it is easier for some because of the situation into which they are born—for example, if one is born in a country where Buddhism is practiced, in a family that teaches proper behavior, or with exceptional mental or physical gifts.

Chan monastics view contrasting human circumstances as the result of the karma accrued in previous lives. They believe certain behavior—such as diligently practicing Buddhism—improves karma and the chances of attaining spiritual goals in this lifetime or coming back

in a better birth. Other behavior—such as killing a living being, eating meat, desiring or becoming attached to things or people—accrues bad karma.

One way karma manifests itself is in one's sex. Taiwanese Buddhists believe that being born female makes it harder to attain spiritual goals. This idea comes, in part, from the inferior status of women in Taiwan and the belief that their "complicated bodies" and monthly menstruation cycles can distract them. Moreover, they believe, women are more enmeshed in their families than men, and their emotional ties keep them focused on worldly rather than spiritual tasks.

Taiwanese Buddhists who decide to become monks and nuns must break from their families to enter a monastery. Because women are thought to be more attached to their families than are men, leaving home is seen as a particularly big step for nuns and a sign that they are more like men than most women. In fact, a nun's character is considered masculine, unlike the frightened, indecisive, and emotional traits usually associated with women in Taiwan. When they leave home nuns even stop referring to themselves as women and call one another *shixiong* ("dharma brother"). They use this linguistic change to signal that they identify themselves as men and to remind one another to behave like men, particularly like the monks at the temple.

Monastics also reduce their attachments to worldly things like music and food. Nuns usually emphasize forsaking food and eat as little as possible. Their appearance, already quite masculine because they shave their heads and wear loose, gray clothing, becomes even more so when they lose weight—particularly in their hips, breasts, and thighs. Also, after becoming monastics, they often experience a slowing or stopping of their menses. Although these physical changes can be attributed to change in diet and lifestyle, the nuns point to them as signs they are becoming men, making progress toward their spiritual goals, and improving their karma.

BIOCULTURAL QUESTION
The Zen Buddhist ideal of enlightenment, realized when the soul is released from reincarnation, prescribes an extreme ascetic lifestyle for nuns that makes them physically incapable of biological reproduction. Do you think that their infertility allows these female monastics to emotionally adapt to a way of life that denies them motherhood?

Written expressly for this text, 2008. For a more detailed treatment of this topic, see Crane, H. (2001). Men in spirit: The masculinization of Taiwanese Buddhist nuns. *Ph.D dissertation, Brown University.*

of religious leaders. In many religions, spiritual leadership is thought to be vested in divine authority, representing or even embodying the divine itself. How do religions secure legitimate successors and avoid disruption and confusion?

Several major religions follow a principle of leadership in which divine authority is passed down from a spiritual founding figure, such as a prophet or saint, to a chain of successors who derive legitimacy as religious leaders from their status in such a lineage. Here identified as **spiritual lineage**, this principle has been worked out in numerous cross-cultural variations over the course of thousands of years. It not only applies to leadership of entire religions but to segmental divisions of religions, such as sects and orders.

spiritual lineage A principle of leadership in which divine authority is passed down from a spiritual founding figure, such as a prophet or saint, to a chain of successors.

Whereas kings in traditional political dynasties derive legitimacy from their ancestral blood lineage, religious leaders obtain it from their spiritual line of descent as specified in each particular religious tradition. The longer these lineages have existed, the greater their opportunities for building up a fund of symbolic capital—ideas and rituals, including sacred gestures, dances, songs, and texts. This fund also includes regalia, paintings, statues, and sacred architecture such as shrines, tombs, and temples, along with the land on which they stand. Thus, some religious leaders and their followers have accumulated a considerable amount of material wealth utilized in the exercise of religious authority, in addition to the immaterial holdings of traditional knowledge and sacred rituals.

Here, to illustrate the cross-cultural range of spiritual lineages, we distinguish four major forms. First, in some religions, spiritual leaders or high-ranking priests claim divine authority based on recognized biological descent from a common ancestor believed to have been a prophet, saint, or otherwise sacred, holy, or even divine being. Such is the case with *kohanim*, high-ranking Israelite priests, claiming patrilineal descent from the legendary high priest Aaron believed to have lived about 3,500 years ago.

In other religions, leaders personally groom, train, and appoint a spiritual heir, a successor tasked with guarding and continuing the spiritual legacy of the order or sect as established by its founder. For example, a sect of Muslim mystics known as Sufi is widely dispersed across Asia and North Africa and historically divided into many dozens of orders, or brotherhoods. Each brotherhood is headed by a master teacher, known by an honorific title such as *sheikh*. The sheikh derives his spiritual authority from his position in a *silsila* (Arabic, meaning "chain"), named after a founding saint who originally laid down a particular method of prayer and ritual practiced by followers seeking oneness with God (Abun-Nasr, 2007; Anjum, 2006).

A third form of legitimizing the authority of a religious leader is by election. In such cases, a group of leading elders comes together in a ritual gathering at a traditionally designated location and chooses one of their own to succeed the deceased leader. One of the best-known examples in world history is the election of a pope by a group of cardinals—"princes" of the Roman Catholic Church who proclaim the new pope to be the divinely ordained spiritual heir of St. Peter, Vicar of Christ. Believed by 1.2 billion Christians to hold the sacred key to heaven, the pope is traditionally addressed as "Holy Father." The current Pope Benedict XVI is the 265th holder of this nearly 2,000-year-old religious office.

A fourth and final example of spiritual lineage is found in Tibetan Buddhism, divided into four major orders or schools. Each has its own monasteries, monks of various ranks from novice to lama, and a wealth of ancient texts, ritual practices, meditations, and other sacred knowledge passed on largely by oral tradition. Highest in rank among the monks are reincarnated saints. These are individuals who, fully emanating the divine Buddha spirit, achieved enlightenment during their lifetime; led by compassion, they chose to give up *nirvana* ("eternal bliss") after death to return to life on earth. To fulfill this role, such a saintly person must be recognized. Toward this end, a select group of high-ranking lamas guided by omens seeks out a newborn boy believed to be a *tulku* ("emanated incarnation") of a recently deceased saintly lama in their spiritual lineage. Once they find the little boy, they ritually induct and enthrone him and begin grooming him for his designated spiritual leadership position in the Buddhist order (**Figure 13.6**).

Of about 500 *tulku* lineages in Tibetan Buddhism, the most famous is the Dalai Lama ("teacher who is spiritually as deep as the ocean"). This illustrious lineage traces its origins to a high-ranking monk named Gendun Drup (1391–1474), thought to have embodied the Buddha spirit of compassion. A few years after the death of the thirteenth Dalai Lama in 1933, high-ranking monks from his order identified a 2-year-old boy in a small farming village as his reincarnated "wisdom mind." Renaming him Tenzin Gyatso, they later enthroned the little *tulku* as His Holiness, the fourteenth Dalai Lama— the highest-ranking political and spiritual position among Tibetan Buddhists for centuries.

Shamans

Societies without religious professionals have existed far longer than those that have them. Although lacking full-time specialists, they have always included individuals considered capable of connecting with supernatural beings and forces—individuals such as shamans. That capacity, partially based on learned techniques, is also based on personality and particular emotional experiences that could be described as "mystical." Supplied with spiritual knowledge in the form of a vision or some other extraordinary revelation, they are believed to be supernaturally empowered to heal the sick, change the weather, control the movements of animals, and foretell the future. As they perfect these and related skills, they may combine the role of a diviner and a healer, becoming a shaman.

Originally, the word *shaman* referred to medical-religious specialists, or spiritual guides, among the Tungus and other Siberian pastoral nomads with animist beliefs. By means of various techniques such as fasting, drumming, chanting, or dancing, as well as hallucinogenic mushrooms (*fly agaric*), these shamans enter into a trance. In this waking dream state, they experience visions of an alternate reality inhabited by spirit beings such as guardian animal spirits who may assist with healing. Similar spiritual practices exist in many indigenous cultures outside Siberia, especially in the Americas. For that reason, the term *shaman* is frequently applied to a variety of part-time spiritual leaders, diviners, and traditional healers active in many other parts of the world (Kehoe, 2000).

VISUAL COUNTERPOINT

© Matthieu Ricard

© Matthieu Ricard

Figure 13.6 Buddhist Lama Dilgo Khyentsé Rinpoche and His Reincarnation Dilgo Khyentsé Yangsi Rinpoche There are many spiritual lineages in Tibetan Buddhism not as well known as that of the Dalai Lama. The monk on the left is a reincarnation of a Buddhist master identified as the first Khyentsé ("Compassionate Wisdom"). In 1832 at age 12, the first Khyentsé was recognized as the combined incarnation of an 8th-century Tibetan religious king and a profoundly learned Buddhist master. Renamed Jamyang Khyentsé Wangpo and receiving intensive training, he was ordained throne-holder of a major Tibetan monastery and became a living saint. Dying in 1892, he reincarnated in 1910 as a little boy—a *tulku* renamed Dilgo Khyentsé Rinpoche (*Rinpoche*, a title given to *tulkus*, means "Precious One"). Before Dilgo Khyentsé passed away at the Shechen Monastery in Nepal at age 81, he gave subtle indications concerning how and where his "wisdom mind" would be reincarnated. After his death, another high-ranking lama in his order, who had been his close friend and disciple, had visions and dreams. Guided by these instructions, a search party identified a boy born in Nepal in the summer of 1993 as his reincarnation. The boy (*right*) was renamed Dilgo Khyentsé Yangsi in 1996. With his legitimate status in this *tulku* lineage confirmed by the Dalai Lama, the young monk was enthroned at his predecessor's monastery the following year.

Anthropologist Michael Harner (see Anthropologist of Note feature), a modern-day shamanic practitioner famous for his participant observation among Shuar (or Jivaro) Indian shamans in the Amazon rainforest, defined a **shaman** as someone who at will enters an altered state of consciousness "to contact and utilize an ordinarily hidden reality in order to acquire knowledge, power, and to help other persons. The shaman has at least one, and usually more, 'spirits' in his or her personal service" (Harner, 1980, p. 20).

shaman A person who at will enters an altered state of consciousness to contact and utilize an ordinarily hidden reality in order to acquire knowledge, power, and to help others.

Shamanic Experience

Someone may become a shaman by passing through stages of learning and practical experience, often involving psychological and emotional ordeals brought about by isolation, fasting, physical torture, sensory deprivation, and/or *hallucination* (Latin, for "mental wandering"). Hallucinations may occur when one is in a trance state; they can come about spontaneously, but they can also be induced by drumming or consuming mind-altering drugs such as psychoactive vines or mushrooms.

Because shamanism is rooted in altered states of consciousness and the human nervous system universally produces these trance states, individuals experience

ANTHROPOLOGIST OF NOTE

Michael J. Harner (b. 1929)

A world-renowned expert on shamanism, American anthropologist **Michael Harner** studied at the University of California, Berkeley. Starting out in archaeology and collaborating with Alfred Kroeber on Mohave pottery research, he later switched to ethnography. Intrigued by the Jívaro, legendary for shrinking human heads, he ventured into eastern Ecuador's tropical forest in 1956, at age 27. For nearly a year, he lived among these Amazonian Indians, now better known as Shuar. They still subsisted on food gardens and by hunting and gathering; they fiercely guarded their freedom and launched raids on enemy tribes.

Holding an animistic worldview, the Shuar distinguish between what Harner has identified as ordinary and non-ordinary realities. They believe that supernatural forces govern daily life and that spirit beings can be perceived and engaged only by shamans capable of entering non-ordinary reality. They access this reality by drinking *natema*, a bitter brew made from a jungle vine known as *ayahuasca* ("vine of the soul"). As they told Harner, drinking this hallucinogenic potion, shamans enter an altered state of consciousness in which they perceive and engage what they believe are the "true" forces governing sickness and health, life and death.

Harner returned to the Upper Amazon in 1960 for more ethnographic fieldwork, this time among the Conibo in eastern Peru. Seeking greater insight on *ayahuasca's* psychological impact on the native cosmology, he drank the magic brew. Passing through the door of perception into the shamanic view of reality, he found himself in a world beyond his "wildest dreams": a supernatural landscape inhabited by spirit beings. Singing incredibly beautiful music, they began to carry his soul away and he felt he was dying. Coming out of this experience, and later ones with Conibo shamans, Harner realized that anthropologists had seriously underestimated the powerful influence hallucinogenic drugs had on Amazonian Indian ideologies and practices.

In 1963, Harner earned his doctorate at UC Berkeley, and the next year went back to Shuar country for additional shamanic experience. In 1966, having taught at UC Berkeley and served as associate director of the Lowie Museum of Anthropology, he became a visiting professor at Yale and Columbia Universities. In 1969, he did fieldwork among a neighboring Jivaroan-speaking tribe, the Achuara, and the following year joined the graduate faculty of the New School for Social Research in New York City. Over the next few years he published his monograph, *The Jívaro: People of the Sacred Waterfalls*, an edited volume titled *Hallucinogens and Shamanism*, and numerous academic articles.

Continuing cross-cultural research on shamanism, Harner became interested in drumming as an alternative means of achieving what he now identifies as SSC (shamanic state of consciousness). Learning and using this method of monotonous percussive sound ("sonic driving"), he began offering training workshops and in 1979 founded the Center for Shamanic Studies. A year later, he published *The Way of the Shaman*, a groundbreaking book now translated into a dozen languages.

Collaborating with his wife, clinical psychologist Sandra Harner, he established the Foundation for Shamanic Studies, a nonprofit charitable and educational organization dedicated to the preservation, study, and transmission of shamanic knowledge. Its Urgent Assistance program supports the survival of shamanic healing knowledge among such indigenous peoples as the Canadian Inuit, Scandinavian Sámi, and Tuvans of central Asia and Siberia.

Since resigning from his university professorship in 1987, this anthropologist has been fully devoted to shamanic studies and healing practice, training others, including physicians, psychotherapists, and other health care professionals. The Foundation's faculty assists him in this work.

In his most recent book, *Cave and Cosmos: Shamanic Encounters with Spirits and Heavens* (2013), Harner recounts and compares experiences of shamanic "ascension" and offers instructions on his core-shamanism techniques.

© 2011 France Viana

Michael Harner—anthropologist, shaman, and founder of the Foundation for Shamanic Studies in Mill Valley, California.

Figure 13.7 Traditional Shaman in Mongolia This female shaman in Mongolia, bordering Siberia, uses a drum crafted from the wood of a tree struck by lightning and covered with leather made from a female red deer. It is believed that when the shaman goes into a trance, her drum transforms into a magical steed that carries her into the dark sky of her ancestors.

similarly structured visual, auditory, somatic (touch), olfactory (smell), and gustatory (taste) hallucinations. The widespread occurrence of shamanism and the remarkable similarities among shamanic traditions everywhere are consequences of this universal neurological inheritance. But the meanings ascribed to sensations experienced in altered states and made of their content are culturally determined; hence, despite their overall similarities, indigenous traditions typically vary in particular details (**Figure 13.7**).

Shamans can be contrasted with priests and priestesses in that the latter serve dieties of the society. As agents of divine beings, priests and priestesses order believers what to think and do, whereas shamans may challenge or negotiate with the spirits. In return for services rendered, shamans may collect a fee—money, fresh meat, or some other valuable. In some cases, shamans are rewarded by the prestige that comes as a result of a healing or some other extraordinary feat.

Shamanic Healing

Shamans are essentially spiritual go-betweens who acts on behalf of some human client, often to bring about healing or to foretell a future event. Typically, they enter a trance state, experience the sensation of traveling to the alternate world, and see and interact with spirit beings. Shamans try to impose their will upon these spirits, an inherently dangerous contest, considering the superhuman powers that spirits are thought to possess.

An example of this can be seen in the trance dances of the Ju/'hoansi Bushmen of Africa's Kalahari Desert. Traditional Ju/'hoansi belief holds that illness and misfortune are caused by invisible arrows shot by spirits.

The arrows can be removed by healers, those who possess the powerful healing force called *n/um* (the Ju/'hoansi equivalent of *mana*). Some healers can activate *n/um* by solo singing or instrument playing, but more often this is accomplished through the medicinal curing ceremony or trance dance (**Figure 13.8**).

Acting on behalf of a client or patient, a shaman may put on a dramatic performance; such an artful

Figure 13.8 Ju/'hoansi Shaman Healer and Helper in Trance Dance Ju/'hoansi shamans may find their way into a trance by dancing around a fire to the pulsating sound of melodies sung by women. Eventually, sometimes after several hours, "the music, the strenuous dancing, the smoke, the heat of the fire, and the healers' intense concentration cause their *n/um* to heat up. When it comes to a boil, trance is achieved. At that moment, the *n/um* becomes available as a powerful healing force to serve the entire community. In trance, a healer lays hands on and ritually cures everyone sitting around the fire" (Shostak, 2000, pp. 259–260).

demonstration of spiritual power assures members of the community that prevailing upon supernatural powers and spirits otherwise beyond human control can bring about invulnerability from attack, success at love, or the return of health.

The precise effects of the shamanic treatment are not known, but its psychological and emotional impact is thought to contribute to the patient's recovery. For healing to occur, the shaman needs to be convinced of the effectiveness of his or her spiritual powers and techniques. Likewise, the patient must see the shaman as a genuine healing master using appropriate techniques. Finally, to close the triangle's "magic field," the community within which the shaman operates on the patient must view the healing ceremony and its practitioner as potentially effective and beneficial. From an anthropological perspective, shamanic healings can be understood by means of a three-cornered model: the *shamanic complex* (**Figure 13.9**). This triangle is created by the interrelationship of the shaman, the patient, and the community to which both belong.

Shamanic healing ceremonies involve social-psychological dynamics also present in Western medical treatments. Consider, for example, the *placebo effect*—the beneficial result a patient experiences after a particular treatment, due to the person's expectations concerning the treatment rather than from the treatment itself. Notably, some people involved in modern medicine work collaboratively with practitioners of traditional belief systems toward the healing of various illnesses (Harner & Harner, 2000; Offiong, 1999).

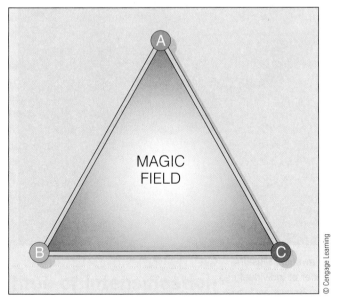

Figure 13.9 The Shamanic Complex Shamanic healing takes place within a "magic field" created when the shaman (A) and patient (B), as well as their community (C), are all convinced that the shaman is a genuine healing master using appropriate techniques that are effective and beneficial. Similar psychological processes are involved in Western medical treatments.

Ritual Performances

Rituals are culturally prescribed symbolic acts or procedures designed to guide members of a community in an orderly way through personal and collective transitions. Relieving anxiety and tensions in crises, rituals provide symbolic means of reinforcing a group's social bonds. Not all of them concern the sacred (consider, for example, college graduation ceremonies in North America). But those that do are ideologically linked to beliefs in the supernatural, playing a crucial role as spirituality or religion in action.

Anthropologists have classified several different types of ritual. These include rituals of purification, rites of passage, rites of intensification, and magical rituals, including witchcraft.

Rites of Purification: Taboo and Cleansing Ceremonies

In many religious and spiritual traditions, rituals have been developed to symbolically restore one's place in the cosmic order, removing "dirt," washing "impurity," and making "clean" in body, mind, and soul. Anthropologists specializing in comparative religion have been intrigued by the cross-cultural variation in cultural categories classifying certain animals, plants, objects, or acts as unclean or dirty and others as dangerous.

In every society, people follow certain culturally prescribed rules about what is dirty or filthy, or whichever term symbolically represents pollution—rules that say what they cannot eat, drink, touch, talk, or even think about. For instance, many millions of Hindus eat pork but avoid beef because they regard the cow as a sacred animal. On the other hand, many millions of Muslims consume beef but avoid pork because in Islam swine is considered unclean. In the words of British anthropologist Mary Douglas, "Dirt offends against order. Eliminating it is not a negative movement, but a positive effort to organise the environment" (1966, pp. 2–3).

Culturally prescribed avoidances involving ritual prohibitions are known as **taboo**, a term derived from the Polynesian word *tabu* (or *tapu*). Among Pacific Islanders it refers to something that has supernatural power and is to be avoided. It can apply to an object (such as food), a person (such as a high-ranking noble), or a place (a shrine or temple). Especially applied to blood and anything associated with sickness and death, taboos are

ritual A culturally prescribed symbolic act or procedure designed to guide members of a community in an orderly way through personal and collective transitions.

taboo Culturally prescribed avoidances involving ritual prohibitions, which, if not observed, lead to supernatural punishment.

Rites of intensification do not have to be limited to times of overt crisis. In regions where human activities change in accordance with seasonal climatic shifts, these rites take the form of annual ceremonies. They are particularly common among horticultural and agricultural peoples. Ritually articulating traditional ideas about the role of the supernatural in the cyclical return of rain, the light and warmth of the sun, and other factors of nature vital to healthy and bountiful crops, these ceremonies are staged to correspond with the crucially important planting and harvesting seasons. A similar cultural linkage between the annual subsistence cycle and the ceremonial calendar with its rites of intensification can be found in societies based on seasonal fishing and herding or hunting of migratory animals.

Magical Rituals

People in many cultures believe that supernatural powers can be compelled to act in certain ways for good or evil purposes by recourse to specified formulas. In short, they believe in **magic** and carry out magical rituals to ensure positive ends such as good crops, fertility of livestock, replenishment of hunted game, prevention of accidents, healing of illness, protection against injury, promise of victory, and the defeat of enemies, real or imagined. In traditional societies many of these rituals rely on *fetishes*—objects believed to possess magical powers (**Figure 13.12**).

Magical rituals are also popular in wealthy industrialized societies. Individuals commonly seek "good luck" when the outcome is in doubt or beyond one's influence—from lighting a votive candle for someone going through a hard time, to wearing lucky boxers on a hot date, to the curious gesturing baseball pitchers perform on the mound.

Anthropologists distinguish between two fundamental principles of magic. The first principle—that like produces like—is identified as **imitative magic** or *sympathetic magic*. In Myanmar (Burma) in Southeast Asia, for example, a rejected lover might engage a sorcerer to make an image of his would-be love. If this image were tossed into water, to the accompaniment of certain charms, it was expected that the girl would go mad and suffer a fate similar to that of her image.

The second principle is that of **contagious magic**—the idea that things or persons once in contact can influence each other after the contact is broken. The most

© SSPL/The Image Works

Figure 13.12 Congolese Fetish This 100-year-old carving from the Democratic Republic of Congo is a *nkondi*, with supernatural power coming in part from magic herbs hidden inside by a diviner. Such fetishes are traditionally used to identify wrongdoers, including thieves and witches responsible for mishaps, diseases, or death. A *nkondi* is activated by provocations (such as hammering nails into it) or invocations urging magic punishment of the suspects.

common example of contagious magic is the permanent relationship between an individual and any part of his or her body, such as hair, fingernails, or teeth. For instance, the Basutos of Lesotho in southern Africa were careful to conceal their extracted teeth to make sure they did not fall into the hands of certain mythical beings who could harm the owners of the teeth by working magic on them. Related to this is the custom in Western societies of treasuring things that have been touched by special people. Such items range from a saint's relics to possessions of other admired or idolized individuals, from rock stars to sports heroes to spiritual gurus.

magic Specific formulas and actions used to compel supernatural powers to act in certain ways for good or evil purposes.

imitative magic Magic based on the principle that like produces like; sometimes called *sympathetic magic*.

contagious magic Magic based on the principle that things or persons once in contact can influence each other after the contact is broken.

Figure 13.13 Assessing Ch'i Energy Feng shui master R. D. Chin determines the *ch'i* of a new office space in a Manhattan skyscraper, one side of which faces the city's central *ch'i* point—the Empire State Building. The consultant is planning the space, with the location of stairways and the CEO's office to be determined.

© Ann Bingley Gallops, Open Spaces Feng Shui

Divination: Omens and Oracles

Designed to access or influence supernatural powers, magical rituals have also been developed to prepare for the uncertain future—for the unseen and for the not yet present. Fears of pending dangers—for example, storms, attacks, betrayals, diseases, and death—call for precautionary measures, such as what to avoid and where to go. How does one find and interpret the signs, or *omens*, foretelling the future? The answer, as developed in many cultures, is through **divination**, a magical ritual designed to discover what is unknowable by ordinary means, in particular signs predicting fate or destiny.

Various ancient methods of divination exist, including *geomancy* (from Greek, *geo* for "earth" and *manteia* for "divination"), a technique traditionally considered sacred and practiced by shamans, prophets, fortunetellers, or other oracles in communication with supernatural forces. Skilled to interpret omens, a diviner practicing geomancy may toss a handful of sand or pebbles, for example, and then analyze its random patterns, searching for information hidden to ordinary people. Other divination methods include decoding flame or smoke patterns in a fire (*pyromancy*), wind and cloud formation in the air (*aeromancy*), or colors, ripples, and whirls in water (*hydromancy*).

Whereas Mongolian and Chinese shamans traditionally use an animal shoulder blade (*scapulamancy*) for divination purposes, Aymara *yachajs* ("possessors of knowledge") in the Andean highlands may probe sacred coca leaves or the convoluted pile of intestines of a slaughtered guinea pig for omens. Much better known, of course, is the divination technique involving palm reading (*chiromancy*), perhaps most famously practiced by female Gypsy fortunetellers. So-called mediums are popular, too, also in the United States, where many people believe them to be capable of contacting spirits of deceased relatives ready to pass on messages from beyond by means of an ancient ritual method known as *necromancy*.

Believed to possess knowledge hidden from ordinary people, diviners are feared in many cultures. However, they are also in high demand among those who believe in diviners' capacity to predict the future, and those believers may seek consultation before undertaking something important or risky. An example of this is *feng shui*, an ancient Chinese divination technique. Literally translated as "wind-water," its traditional Chinese characters signify "tao of heaven and earth." In the past few decades, this method has grown in popularity in North America as well, in particular in California, where homebuilders and buyers frequently hire feng shui consultants to help them design or redesign homes and offices to conform to the principle of *qi* or *ch'i* ("vital energy") **(Figure 13.13)**.

In some religious traditions, including Christianity, fortunetelling and other divination rituals have long been viewed with suspicion, and in many places these practices have been prohibited. Especially when performed by individuals functioning in other religious or spiritual traditions believed to be false or worse, divination is condemned as evil magic, sorcery, or witchcraft.

Witchcraft: Anxiety and Fears of Evil Magic

Magical rituals intended to cause misfortune or inflict harm are often referred to as sorcery, or **witchcraft**, believed to be practiced by individuals embodying evil

divination A magical procedure or spiritual ritual designed to discern what is not knowable by ordinary means, such as foretelling the future by interpreting omens.

witchcraft Magical rituals intended to cause misfortune or inflict harm.

power or those collaborating with malevolent supernatural beings. In contrast to magic-working experts inclined to do good, these individuals inspire awe, or even fear. Historically, such dangerous magic-working individuals are known in English under a variety of names such as *wizard, sorcerer,* or simply *witch*—imprecise terms often used interchangeably. This is also true for other languages using a variety of terms like *brujo* (Spanish), *uwisin* (Shuar), *umthakathi* (Zulu), *mchawi* (Swahili), and *wu* (Chinese).

Fear of witches is especially prevalent during periods of uncertainty and transition. When mysterious illnesses, devastating droughts, accidental deaths, economic uncertainties, and other upheavals disturb the cultural order, confusion may result in a surge of suspicion and a focus on disliked, unsociable, isolated individuals. Especially in patrilineal or patrilocal communities, the accused is often an older woman, typically single or widowed and without children. For instance, about 80 percent of the estimated 50,000 "witches" tried, tortured, and killed in Europe in the 16th and 17th centuries were female. Among matrilineal and matrilocal groups, however, people tend to think of witches as male.

Not all people suspected of mysterious malevolence are prosecuted, let alone executed, but witchcraft accusations clearly function as a social control mechanism, horribly reinforcing the moral code. Fear of being accused of being a witch encourages individuals to suppress as best they can those personality traits that are looked upon with disapproval. A belief in witchcraft thus serves as a broad control on what is believed to be antisocial behavior (Behringer, 2004).

Navajo Skin-Walkers

Beliefs in evil magic are widespread and take many forms. One interesting example comes from the Navajo, Native Americans historically surviving as sheepherders and small-scale irrigation farmers in the vast deserts of Arizona and New Mexico. The Navajo have a substantial repertoire of sacred rituals for healing victims of sorcery, all related to accusations of evil magic.

Among Navajos, who live in a residence group organized around a head woman, traditional belief holds that a person suffering from severe anxiety disorder, repetitive nightmares, or delusions is a victim of sorcery. The idea is that a ghost or some other evil spirit, traveling under cover of darkness, is responsible. And

© Cengage Learning

according to the Navajo, the suspect is a powerful sorcerer, almost always a man, probably someone who has killed a relative and committed incest.

These dangerous Navajo sorcerers, resembling the werewolf of European folklore and the *nagual* in rural Mexico, are believed to be able to change themselves into animal form. Referred to as a *'ánt'įįhnii* ("skin-walker"), such a sorcerer stealthily goes to a secluded spot, such as a cave at night. There, he transforms into a coyote or wolf. Disguised in animal form, he emerges and runs fast toward his victim, bringing on *'ánt'į* ("the curse"). Having completed his accursed mission, the skin-walker swiftly returns to his hideaway, transforms again into human form, and slips back into his home before dawn (Kluckhohn, 1944; Selinger, 2007).

Sacred Sites: Saints, Shrines, and Miracles

Sacred sites are typically positioned in a transitional, or *liminary*, zone between the natural and supernatural, the secular and spiritual, earth and heaven. Reaching high into the sky, mountaintops are often considered to be magical places, shrouded in mystery. For instance, the Japanese view the snowcapped perfect volcanic cone of Mount Fuji ("Ever-Lasting Life") as a sacred place. Ancient Greeks considered Mount Olympus to be the mythological abode of Zeus, the king of all their gods. Likewise, Kikuyu view Mount Kenya as the earthly dwelling place of their creator god Ngai.

Some sites become sacred because they are places where ordinary human beings experienced something extraordinary—heard a divine voice or saw a guardian spirit, patron saint, or archangel. Often a site is declared sacred because believers associate it with a miracle-working mystic, saint, prophet, or other holy person. The tombs of such individuals often turn into shrines (*scrinium*, Latin for "round box" or "container," holding relics). For example, stories of miraculous events and special powers emanating from Muslim tombs are common wherever Sufism, a far-reaching mystical branch of Islam, is popular (Gladney, 2004).

Based on the principle of contagious magic, any material substance physically linked to a miraculous event or individual may itself become revered as holy or sacred. This may include bones, fingernails, hair, or any other body part believed to have belonged to a saint, or something the person wore, possessed, or simply touched. All these things may be treasured as holy relics and safeguarded in a shrine, inspiring the faithful.

Burial sites of saints often gain such importance that people feel inspired to construct a very large shrine for the saint's entombment; termed a *mausoleum*, some of these are large enough for the interment of lesser saints and pious individuals desiring proximity to the sacred saint after death. However large or small, shrines are religious focal points for prayer, meditation, and sacrifice.

Figure 13.14 **Pilgrims at Mount Kailash in Tibet** Rising 6,700 meters (over 22,000 feet), this mountain has been sacred for many generations to Buddhists and Hindus, as well as Jains and followers of Bön (Tibet's indigenous religion). Every year a few thousand pilgrims make the tortuous 52-kilometer (32-mile) trek around it, some of them by crawling the entire distance.

© Alexander van der Made

Pilgrimages: Devotion in Motion

Every year, many millions of devotees of many religions—including Buddhism, Christianity, Hinduism, Islam, and their many branches—walk, climb, or even crawl to a sacred or holy site. Whether it is a saint's tomb, a mountain, lake, river, waterfall, or some other particular place believed to be metaphysically significant, *pilgrims* (from Latin *peregrinus*, meaning "wanderer") travel there seeking enlightenment, proving their devotion, and/or hoping to experience a miracle.

On their sacred journey, pilgrims participate in a religious drama, performing ritually prescribed acts such as prayers, chants, or prostrations. A devotion in motion, the **pilgrimage** demands personal sacrifices from the travelers. Enjoying little comfort, they may suffer from thirst and hunger, heat and cold, pain and fear while on the road, sometimes for many days or even months. Pilgrims often travel through unfamiliar territories where they may run into problems, including robbery, kidnapping, starvation, and even death. To identify their status as spiritually inspired travelers, some wear special clothes, shave their heads, carry amulets, chant prayers, or perform other prescribed rituals along the way.

One of the most challenging pilgrimages is the climb up the slopes of a mountain range in the Himalayas where Mount Kailash rises 6,700 meters (over 22,000

feet). Located in western Tibet, this black, snowcapped mountain stands out boldly in a dramatic landscape sacred to Hindus and Buddhists, as well as Jains and Bönpos (**Figure 13.14**). The latter, who practice an ancient Tibetan shamanic religion, refer to this hallowed mountain as Tisé ("Water Peak") because it is the source of four sacred rivers. For Hindus, it is the holy abode of Lord Shiva, the destroyer of ignorance and illusion and the divine source of yoga. Jains view Kailash as the sacred place where their divine cultural hero Rishabha ("Bull")—an incarnation of Lord Vishnu—first achieved full enlightenment. Finally, Tibetan Buddhists revere it as Gangs Rinpoche ("Snow Lord") and believe it to be the abode of Khorlo Demchok ("Circle of Bliss")—a wrathful deity who uses his power to destroy the three major obstacles to enlightenment: anger, greed, and ignorance.

For all four of these religious traditions, climbing to the summit of this holy mountain is taboo. So, pilgrims demonstrate their devotion by means of a ritual encirclement, or circumambulation—clockwise by Buddhists and Hindus, and in reverse by Jains and Bönpos. The rugged, 52-kilometer (32-mile) trek is seen

---

pilgrimage A devotion in motion. Traveling, often on foot, to a sacred or holy site to reach for enlightenment, prove devotion, and/or experience a miracle.

as a sacred ritual that removes sins and brings good fortune. Each year thousands follow the ancient tradition of encircling the mountain on foot. The most devout pilgrims turn their circumambulation into a sacrificial ordeal: Prostrating their bodies full length, they extend their hands forward and make a mark on the ground with their fingers; then they rise, pray, crawl ahead on hands and knees to the mark, and then repeat the process again and again.

One of the world's largest pilgrimages is the *hajj*—a performance of piety now made by 1.8 million Muslims traveling to Mecca in Saudi Arabia each year from all across the globe. The largest contingent of hajjis—about 300,000 a year—comes from Indonesia. One of the five pillars of Islam, the hajj brings all of these pilgrims together for collective prayers and other sacred rituals at the Kaaba in Mecca, their religion's holiest site.

Christianity, originating in what was an eastern province of the Roman empire about 2,000 years ago, has created a sacred landscape dotted with dozens of major pilgrimage sites in Southwest Asia and Europe. As in other ancient religions, these sites are symbolically associated with miracles and legendary holy men and women. For example, for nearly a millennium Christian pilgrims from all over Europe have made the long and difficult journey to Santiago de Compostela. Tens of thousands travel to this Spanish seaport each year—most by foot, some by bicycle, and a few on horseback like their medieval counterparts. About 180,000 pilgrims walk the final 100 kilometers to the old cathedral with the shrine containing the sacred remains of the apostle Saint James venerated as Santiago (Santo-Iago) since the Middle Ages and recognized as the official patron saint of Spain. Many more Roman Catholics make pilgrimages to shrines devoted to Saint Mary, as described following.

Female Saints: Divine Protection for the Weak

Many religions consider the divine order primarily or exclusively as masculine, as noted earlier. Ideologically reproducing the hierarchical social order dominated by men, this arrangement reflects the worldview of traditional cultures that revere male deities, prophets, and saints in officially sponsored cults and devotions. But religions are not monolithic, and some provide flexible spiritual space for alternatives, such as Christian cults devoted to female saints such as Mary, the virgin mother of Jesus Christ, the son of God.

More powerful than the pope in Rome, Mary has been loved and adored as a holy mother residing in heaven. Worldwide, Roman Catholic multitudes look up to her for divine protection. Like other Christian saints, she is

thought to perform miracles and to be capable of physically manifesting herself at places and times of her choosing. Through the centuries, many believers claim to have witnessed such holy moments, some officially reporting the miracle. Typically, these believers are young members of the underclass—herders, peasants, or fishermen, for example. Beyond stories about the female saint manifesting herself to such low-status rural folk, the discovery of sacred relics (such as a drowned or buried statue representing Mary) may also generate excitement and hope in difficult times.

Stories and relics religiously associated with miracles performed by saints such as the Virgin Mary quickly attract popular attention and turn into myths. Inspired or led by individuals claiming divine authority based on immediate revelation, devotees typically build a shrine to commemorate the encounter or to safeguard the sacred relic. Developing outside the power structure of established religious institutions, these local devotions may turn into popular cults. Difficult if not impossible to stop, these cults may spawn mass movements, leading church authorities to consider whether to formally approve of the cult and take control of the Marian (Saint Mary) devotion. Sanctioned by the church or not, these shrines attract pilgrims in search of divine forgiveness, protection, healing, and compassionate love.

Among the best known Marian pilgrimage sites are the ones in Lourdes (France) and Fatima (Portugal), along with the Mexican shrine dedicated to the brown-skinned Virgin of Guadalupe detailed in the next section.

Black Madonnas and Brown-Skinned Virgin Mothers

As folk-based popular religious movements, Saint Mary cults not only developed across Europe, but also in Latin America, the Philippines, and other parts of the world historically colonized and dominated by Roman Catholics originating from Europe. The religious ideas and rituals of Catholicism changed many indigenous cultures—and were also changed by them. Of particular interest in this shifting religious landscape are Black Madonnas: brown or dark-colored clay or wooden statues, or painted images, representing the virgin mother. One of the many Black Madonna statues is enshrined in Aparecida, Brazil, where a popular cult emerged in her honor in the mid-18th century and now attracts over 10 million pilgrims annually.

Another popular devotion involving brown-skinned Saint Mary concerns the Virgin of Guadalupe, highlighted in this chapter's opening photo. As mentioned there, this Mexican cult originated in 1531, a decade after the Aztec Indian empire had been conquered by a Spanish army. That year, a recently converted young

Figure 13.15 Virgin of Guadalupe Pilgrim, Mexico City On December 9, 1531, Saint Mary appeared to Mexican Indian Juan Diego, a recent Christian convert, as he passed by Tepeyac Hill in what is now Mexico City. At the site of this encounter, the Basilica of Our Lady of Guadalupe was built with a shrine containing sacred evidence of this miraculous apparition. Pictured here is a weary pilgrim, sleeping alongside images of the virgin outside the basilica.

Aztec Christian named Juan Diego proclaimed a remarkable encounter with a holy woman who appeared to him in a blaze of light. Speaking his native Nahuatl tongue, she identified herself as the virgin mother and asked that a shrine be built in her honor. After their miraculous meeting, he discovered her image mysteriously imprinted on the inside of his simple white-hemp *tilma* ("cloak"). Seen as divine proof of Mary's manifestation, this sacred relic was soon enshrined in the chapel built in her honor at the foot of the hill where she appeared—now part of Mexico City.

A few decades later, a powerful Spanish bishop imposing religious order in the Mexican colony became aware of the emerging brown-virgin cult and saw it as an ideological means of unifying and controlling a racially divided population. Eventually, in 1780 church authorities officially declared her patron saint of Mexico, even promoting her to the title of Empress of the Americas in 1945. In 2002, nearly 500 years after Juan Diego's mystical encounter started this Marian devotion, Pope John Paul II canonized him before a crowd of 12 million. Diego became the first Native American to be declared a Roman Catholic saint. Today, most of the 6 million pilgrims who visit the Virgin of Guadalupe's shrine each year to see the sacred *tilma* relic discovered by Diego are mestizo or indigenous Mexicans (**Figure 13.15**).

Desecration: Ruining Sacred Sites

Although popular shrines are destinations for believers from near and far, they are also potential targets of **desecration**. By means of such ideologically inspired violation of a sacred site, enemies aim to inflict harm, if only symbolically, on people judged to have impure, false, or evil beliefs and ritual practices. Desecrations have occurred across the globe for thousands of years, as evidenced in archaeological sites and recorded in oral traditions or historical documents.

For example, during the Protestant Reformation in the 16th and 17th centuries, Christian Protestant iconoclasts campaigning against idolatry in the Netherlands and England destroyed untold numbers of ancient Roman Catholic statues and other treasures kept in sacred shrines. More recently, in Afghanistan, Taliban religious authorities shattered two huge 1,500-year-old statues they considered to be idols. Carved into the side of a sandstone cliff in the high mountain valley of Bamiyan, one of them, representing a celestial wisdom Buddha ("the enlightened one") stood 55 meters (180 feet) high; the other, representing Siddhartha Gautama, the founder of Buddhism himself, rose to 37 meters (121 feet). In 2001, the Taliban obliterated both monuments with artillery and dynamite.

Destruction in the name of religion is not unique to Christian or Muslim puritans, as militant Hindus and others also engage in similar desecrations. All of this pales in comparison with China's Cultural Revolution in the 1960s, when masses of activists, swept up in state-sponsored antireligious fervor, went on a rampage destroying religious monuments, sculptures, carvings, and paintings, as well as a large number of age-old sacred shrines.

---

desecration Ideologically inspired violation of a sacred site intended to inflict harm, if only symbolically, on people judged to have impure, false, or even evil beliefs and ritual practices.

Cultural Dynamics in the Superstructure: Religious and Spiritual Change

New technologies, improved means of transportation, internationalization of production and labor markets, and worldwide movements of ideas and practices all contribute to challenging and even destabilizing long-established cultural systems and associated worldviews. Reacting to these challenges and radical upheavals, people often turn to the supernatural to allay the anxiety of a world going awry.

The need to find deeper meaning in life and to make sense of an increasingly complex, uncharted, confusing, and sometimes frightening existence drives humans to continue their explorations—religious and spiritual, as well as scientific. Some people bundle or devise their own spiritual beliefs and rituals. Others form or join new spiritual movements.

Reactionary religious movements are also on the rise in culturally destabilized societies. Typically, these call for a radical return to traditional foundations prescribed in sacred texts and narrowly interpreted by conservative spiritual leaders. Examples include Islamic fundamentalism in countries such as Afghanistan, Egypt, and Iran; Jewish fundamentalism in Israel and the United States; and Hindu fundamentalism in India. Christian fundamentalism is represented in the dramatic growth of evangelical denominations in the United States, Latin America, and sub-Saharan Africa.

Revitalization Movements

No anthropological consideration of religion is complete without some mention of **revitalization movements**—movements for radical cultural reform in response to widespread social disruption and collective feelings of great stress and despair.

As deliberate efforts to construct a more satisfying culture, revitalization movements aim to reform not just the religious sphere of activity but may also impact an entire cultural system. Many such movements developed in indigenous societies where European colonial exploitation caused enormous upheaval. They also occurred in 16th-century Europe—as evidenced in the emergence of Puritans, Mennonites, and other Protestant groups when traditional societies faced radical transformations triggered by early capitalism and other

forces. Likewise, revitalization movements emerged in response to the industrial revolution triggering similar radical transformations in agrarian societies in the 19th century, not only in Europe but also in the northeastern United States, where Mormonism, Jehovah's Witnesses, Seventh-Day Adventists, and others began as Christian revitalization movements.

Revitalization movements can be found in many religions. One of the best known among Muslims is Ahmadiyya, founded in South Asia during British colonial rule in the late 19th century when Christian missionaries were actively proselytizing in predominantly Hindu, Muslim, or Sikh communities. Known as Ahmadis, followers of this Muslim sect number about 10 million across the globe. They believe that Allah (God) sent Mirza Ghulam Ahmad (1835–1908) as a prophet, a divinely ordained reformer (*mujjaddid*) like Muhammad. As the long-awaited Messiah, he embodied the second coming of the Christ, sent to bring about, by peaceful means, the final triumph of Islam as the only true religion for humanity, end all religious strife, and restore divinely guided morality, justice, and peace.

Recent U.S. revitalization movements also include the revival or introduction of traditional American Indian ceremonies such as the sweat lodge now common on many tribal reservations in North America, as well as the spectacular Sun Dance ceremony held each summer at various reservations in the Great Plains. Similar cultural revivals of "spiritual neo-traditions" are on the rise in many parts of the world, including Europe (Prins, 1994). Tens of thousands of people in Great Britain, attracted to a naturalistic worldview, now practice forms of "ecospiritualism" (Prins, 1996, p. 206), which often involves a revival of the ancient pre-Christian Celtic tradition of Druidry (**Figure 13.16**).

A similar nature-centered revival of pre-Christian beliefs and rituals is under way in Germanic-speaking parts of northern Europe, such as among Asatru in Scandinavia. Seeking a sacred relationship with nature, they worship the earth, elements of the sky, and forces such as thunder, as well as spirits they believe arise from sacred places like mountains and rivers. Similar tradition-based ecospiritual movements are developing throughout the industrialized world, including the United States.

Syncretic Religions

In Africa, during and following the period of foreign colonization and missionization, indigenous groups resisted or creatively revised Christian teachings and formed culturally appropriate religious movements. During the past century, thousands of indigenous Christian churches have been founded in Africa. These churches are often born of alternative theological interpretations and new divinely inspired revelations. They also originate from disapproval

---

revitalization movements Social movements for radical cultural reform in response to widespread social disruption and collective feelings of great stress and despair.

Figure 13.16 Stonehenge, Wiltshire County, England In 2010, the neo-tradition of Druidry was officially recognized as a religion in Great Britain. Stonehenge, a 4,500-year-old Neolithic site, is one of its sacred centers. With 10,000 followers, modern Druidry is rooted in the pre-Christian tradition of the Celtic peoples indigenous to the British Isles.

by foreign missionaries concerning the preservation of traditional beliefs and rituals culturally associated with animism, ancestor worship, and spirit possession, as well as kinship and marriage.

Today, the African continent is as religiously and spiritually diverse as ever. Although at least 40 percent of the population is Christian, and more than another 40 percent is Muslim, myriad African indigenous religions persist and are often merged with Christianity or Islam.

Syncretic Religions Across the Atlantic: Vodou in Haiti

In almost four centuries of trans-Atlantic slave trading, African captives stolen from hundreds of towns and villages from Mauretania south to Angola and beyond were shipped without material belongings to labor on cotton, sugar, coffee, and tobacco plantations from Virginia to Brazil. Ripped from family and community, individual slaves clung to some of their ancestral beliefs and knowledge of rituals.

Sharing a life of forced labor, slaves from different ethnic, linguistic, and religious backgrounds formed small communities, pooled remembered religious ideas and rituals, and creatively forged a spiritual repertoire of their own. Founded on a mix of Yoruba and other African beliefs and practices, their emerging religions also incorporated Christian features, including terminology from the languages of slave-owning colonists. In some cases,

elements from a region's indigenous American cultures were also included.

Such creative blending of indigenous and foreign beliefs and practices into new cultural forms illustrates what anthropologists define as **syncretism**. Especially after slavery was abolished in the course of the 1800s, these syncretic spiritual repertoires developed into Afro-Caribbean religions such as Vodou in Haiti and Santería in Cuba, which resemble Candomblé in Brazil. All of these religions are spreading as adherents freely migrate across borders (Fernández Olmos & Paravisini-Gebert, 2003).

Vodou emerged in Haiti in the early 1800s after this small tropical country in the Caribbean Sea won its independence from France in a decade-long slave revolt. The name means "divine spirit" in the language of the Fon, a large ethnic group in Benin and southwestern Nigeria. Providing an escape from the indignities of poverty and hopelessness, Vodou was developed by ex-slaves speaking French-based Creole. Now mostly poor black peasants, they are nominal Roman Catholics who, like their African ancestors across the Atlantic, believe in spirit possession.

Vodou rituals center on the worship of what Haitians refer to as *loas*—also known by Creole terms such as *anges* ("angels"), *saints* ("saints"), or simply as *mystères* ("mysteries"). This tradition is essentially based on a belief in

---

syncretism The creative blending of indigenous and foreign beliefs and practices into new cultural forms.

AP Images/Andre Penner

a reciproc
and those
the divine
can be su
Dancing
is when a
body, rep
possessior

Religi
and S

Although
of Islam's
to **secula**
population
ing or reje
als. Over t
Europeans

Secular
capitalist c

secularizat
toward a non
spiritual belie

Challenge Issue

Humans in all cultures face the challenge of creatively articulating ideas and emotions concerning themselves and the world around them. Across the globe, people have developed art forms—musical, visual, verbal, movement, and so on—that symbolically express meanings and messages. Art may be individual and personal. It may also communicate, stimulate, and reinforce experiences and feelings of collective cultural identity. So it is with this group of Amazonian Indians in traditional ceremonial paint and dress. Their heads are crowned with colorful radiating feathers that represent the universe. Their faces and bodies are painted with black and red designs that convey strength—the black dye made of charcoal and *genipap* fruit juice, the red of crushed *urucu* seeds. And they carry age-old tribal weapons—clubs, spears, bows, and arrows. What is not traditional is their transportation. These Kayapo warriors are riding in a rented Brazilian bus to a town on the lower Xingu River to stage a political protest. With dance, song, oratory, and body ornamentation, they are demonstrating against a $17 billion hydropower project, the third largest in the world. For two decades they have held artful protests to halt the building of a dam that threatens the health and cultural traditions of the Kayapo, along with those of other Xingu River tribes.

The Arts

14

Humans in all cultures throughout time have expressed feelings and ideas about themselves and the world around them through **art**—the creative use of the human imagination to aesthetically interpret, express, and engage life, modifying experienced reality in the process. Art comes in many forms, including visual, verbal, musical, and motion—sometimes in combination and in an ever-expanding array of formats made possible by the continual emergence of new technologies. Most societies, past and present, have used art to symbolically express almost every part of their culture, including ideas about religion, kinship, and ethnic identity.

From an anthropological perspective, the photo that opens this chapter is far more than a curious image of traditionally painted, feathered, and armed Kayapo Indians traveling to a protest rally in a modern bus. Their intended event is an illustration of **performance art**—a creatively expressed promotion of ideas by artful means dramatically staged to challenge opinion and/or provoke purposeful action. In Kayapo culture, dancing combined with the singing of warrior chants is a traditional variation of this art form—as it is in many societies all across the globe. Through this particular performance, dramatically and artfully staged as a public spectacle in an electronic media environment, they expected to reach a global audience of millions and win widespread support for their political struggle against an overpowering opponent (Conklin, 1997; Prins, 2002). Although demonstrations by Kayapo and neighboring tribes of the Xingu River have drawn international attention, the dam is now being built and will soon flood 400 square kilometers (150 square miles) of tropical forest and destroy their habitat.

Despite daily evidence of political (and commercial) uses of art, most people living in the industrialized corners of the world think of the arts almost exclusively as an aesthetic pleasure for personal or shared enjoyment. From this "art for art's sake" perspective, art appears to be confined to a distinctive cultural domain, quite apart from political, economic, religious, and otherwise pragmatic or ideological activities. But in most traditional cultures, art is almost always deeply embedded, so much so that many of these cultures do not have a distinctive term for it.

art The creative use of the human imagination to aesthetically interpret, express, and engage life, modifying experienced reality in the process.

performance art A creatively expressed promotion of ideas by artful means dramatically staged to challenge opinion and/or provoke purposeful action.

IN THIS CHAPTER YOU WILL LEARN TO

Define *art* and examine how it is intertwined with other parts of a cultural system.

Summarize anthropology's cross-cultural and comparative historical perspective on art.

Identify different types of art, each with specific anthropological examples.

Recognize how art expresses worldview and analyze its functions in the context of religion and shamanism.

Explain and give examples of the relationship between art and cultural identity.

Analyze how art has become a commodity in a market economy, and critically evaluate what that means in a globalized environment of rapid change.

For instance, commenting on beautiful ivory figurines carved by Aivilik Inuit (Eskimo hunters in Arctic Canada), anthropologist Edmund Carpenter observes: "No word meaning 'art' occurs in Aivilik, nor does 'artist.' . . . Art to the Aivilik is an act, not an object; a ritual, not a possession. . . . They are more interested in the creative activity than in the product of that activity [and do not differentiate between] works of art and utilitarian objects: but the two are usually one (Carpenter, 1959, n.p.). Carpenter elaborates:

> When we look at [Eskimo] art & see the particular shape of it, we are only looking at its after-life. Its real life is the movement by which it got to be that shape. Eskimo often discard carvings immediately after making them. (Carpenter, 1968, pp. 69–74; see also Prins & McBride, 2012)

In many cultures, the "real life" of some artful objects begins with death because they are made not to please or be admired by the living, but to accompany people who have passed on to an afterlife. We see an example of this in exquisite objects discovered in the ancient tomb of the young Egyptian Tutankhamen. Museumgoers in today's world have flocked to King Tut exhibitions. Yet, the objects on display were not created for human eyes, but rather to guarantee the eternal life of the divine pharaoh and to protect him from evil forces that might enter his body and gain control over it. Symbols of worldview, they were deeply embedded in the culture.

Similarly, we may listen to the singing of a sea chantey purely for aesthetic pleasure, as a form of entertainment. But, in the era of sailing by wind power alone, sea chanteys served very useful and practical purposes. They set the appropriate rhythm for the performance of specific shipboard tasks such as hoisting or reefing sails, and the same qualities that make them pleasurable to listen to today served to coordinate these tasks and to relieve boredom.

Such intricate links between art and other aspects of life are common in human societies around the world. This can also be seen in the way that art has been incorporated into everyday, functional objects—from utensils, pottery, and baskets used to serve, carry, or store food to carpets and mats woven by nomadic herders to cover the ground inside their portable tent dwellings. Designs painted on or woven or carved into such objects typically express ideas, values, and objects that have meaning to an entire community (**Figure 14.1**).

All of this goes to show that artful expression is as basic to human beings as talking and is by no means limited to a unique category of individuals specialized as artists. For example, all human beings adorn their

VISUAL COUNTERPOINT

Figure 14.1 Functional and Aesthetic Art On the left is a wooden spoon used by the Dan people of Côte d'Ivoire in West Africa, carver unknown. On the right is a bronze sculpture, *Spoon Woman*, created by the Italian artist Alberto Giacometti in 1926. Both may be beautiful, but one is functional and the other purely aesthetic. Usually, traditional utilitarian objects, no matter how exquisite, are identified only in terms of the "primitive" or "tribal" cultures in which they were made. In contrast, "works of art," created for the sake of art itself, are typically tied to the name of the person who made them. How curious it is that this great modern piece credited to the famous Giacometti was inspired by an elegant functional object made by a now-nameless West African.

Dan peoples, Liberia, Cote d'Ivoire, Ceremonial Ladle, Wood, Height 20-1/2 × Width 4-3/4 × Depth 3-1/4 inches. Indiana University Art Museum, Bloomington,63.221. Photograph by: Michael Cavanagh and Kevin Montague

Giraudon/Art Resource, N.Y. © 2012 Alberto Giacometti Estate/Licensed VAGA and Artists Rights Society (ARS), New York, NY

bodies in certain ways and by doing so make a statement about who they are, both as individuals and as members of society. Similarly, people in all cultures tell stories in which they express their values, hopes, and concerns and in the process reveal much about themselves and the nature of the world as they see it.

In short, all peoples engage in artistic expression. And, they have been doing this in countless ways for more than 40,000 years—from carving mammoth ivory figures, to fashioning and playing vulture wing bone flutes, to painting animals on ancient rock walls, to digital music jamming on iPhones. Far from being a luxury to be afforded or appreciated by a minority of sophisticated experts or frivolous lovers of art, creativity is a necessary activity in which everyone participates in one way or another.

Whether a particular work of art is intended to be appreciated purely for beauty or to serve some practical purpose, it requires the same special combination of symbolic representation of form and expression of feeling that constitute the creative imagination. Because human creativity and the ability to symbolize are universal, art is an important subject for anthropological study.

The Anthropological Study of Art

Anthropologists have found that art often reflects a society's collective ideas, values, and concerns. Indeed, through the cross-cultural study of art, we may discover much about different worldviews and religious beliefs, as well as political ideas, social values, kinship structures, economic relations, and historical memory.

In approaching art as a cultural phenomenon, anthropologists have the pleasant task of cataloguing, photographing, recording, describing, and analyzing all possible forms of imaginative activity in any particular culture. An enormous variety of forms and modes of artistic expression exists in the world. Because people everywhere continue to create and develop in ever-new ways, there is no end to the interesting process of collecting and describing the world's ornaments, ceremonial masks, body decorations, clothing variations, blanket and rug designs, pottery and basket styles, monuments, architectural embellishments, legends, work songs, dances, and other art forms—many of them rich with religious symbolism.

To study and analyze art, anthropologists employ a combination of aesthetic, narrative, and interpretive approaches. The distinctions among these methods can be illustrated through a famous work of Western art, Leonardo da Vinci's painting *The Last Supper*, showing Jesus Christ and his apostles on their last night together

before his arrest and crucifixion. A non-Christian viewing this late 15th-century mural in Italy will see thirteen people at a table, apparently enjoying a meal. Although one of the men clutches a bag of money and appears to have knocked over a dish of salt, nothing else in the scene seems out of the ordinary.

Aesthetically, our non-Christian observer may admire the way the composition fits the space available, how the attitudes of the men are depicted, and the means by which the artist conveys a sense of movement. As narrative, the painting may be seen as a record of customs, table manners, dress, and architecture. But to interpret this picture—to perceive its real meaning—the viewer must be aware that in Christian symbolic culture money traditionally represents the root of all evil, and spilling the salt suggests impending disaster. But even this is not enough; to fully understand this work of art, one must know something of the beliefs of Christianity. And if one wishes to understand other renditions of the Last Supper made by artists in other corners of the world, it is necessary to bring insights about those cultures into the equation as well (**Figure 14.2**). In other words, moving to the interpretive level of studying art requires knowledge of the symbols and beliefs of the people responsible for the art (Lewis-Williams, 1990).

A good way to deepen our insight into the relationship between art and the rest of culture is to examine critically some of the generalizations that have already been made about specific art forms. Because it is impossible to cover all art forms in the space of a single chapter, we will concentrate on just a few—visual, verbal, and musical—in that order.

Visual Art

For many people, the first thing that springs to mind in connection with the word *art* is some sort of visual image, be it a painting, drawing, sketch, or whatever. Created primarily for visual perception, **visual art** ranges from etchings and paintings on various surfaces (including the human body) to sculptures and weavings made with an array of materials.

In many parts of the world, people have been making pictures in one way or another for a very long time—etching in bone; engraving in rock; painting on cave walls and rock surfaces; carving and painting on wood, gourds, and clay pots; or painting on textiles, bark cloth, animal hide, or even their own bodies. Some form of visual art is a part of every historically known human culture, and extraordinary examples have been found at prehistoric sites dating back almost 45,000 years.

visual art Art created primarily for visual perception, ranging from etchings and paintings on various surfaces (including the human body) to sculptures and weavings made with an array of materials.

Courtesy of Erin Erkun

Figure 14.2 *The Last Supper* **by Marcos Zapata (c. 1710–1773)** To interpret this painting, one must know about Christianity and the artist's cultural background. It depicts the final meal shared by a spiritual leader and his twelve followers the eve before his execution, an event commemorated by Christians for nearly 2,000 years. For centuries, artists in many societies have imagined this event in paintings, often copying from others before them. This artist was an indigenous painter living in Cuzco, once capital of the Inca empire and long colonized by Spaniards. Baptized as a Christian, he was influenced by European imagery but made cultural adjustments so fellow Andean Indians coming to the church would understand its significance. Directly looking at us is St. Peter, showing his sacred key to heaven. At the center of the table sits Jesus, foretelling his death as a sacrifice, promising he will resurrect and return as the Messiah. However, instead of a sheep lamb, Zapata painted a roasted *cui* (*Cavia porcellus*) on the platter. Traditionally eaten by Andean highlanders, this domesticated guinea pig has long been used for sacrificial and divining purposes; it is a culturally relevant substitute for the sacrificial lamb, a traditional Israelite symbol representing their divine rescue from slavery in Egypt. He also substituted red wine with *chicha*, an indigenous beer made of fermented maize.

Symbolism in Visual Art

As a type of symbolic expression, visual art may be representational (imitating closely the forms of nature) or abstract (drawing from natural forms but representing only their basic patterns or arrangements). In some of the Indian art of North America's northwest coast, for example, animal figures may be so highly stylized as to be difficult for an outsider to identify. Although the art appears abstract, the artist has created it based on nature, even though he or she has exaggerated and deliberately transformed various shapes to express a particular feeling toward the animals. Because artists do these exaggerations and transformations according to the aesthetic principles of their Indian culture, their meanings are understood not just by the artist but by other members of the community as well.

This collective understanding of symbols is a hallmark in traditional art. Unlike modern Western art, which is judged in large part on its creative originality and the unique vision of an individual artist, traditional art is all about community and shared symbolism. Consider, for example, symbols related to kinship. As discussed in earlier chapters, small-scale traditional societies—hunter-gatherers, nomadic herders, slash-and-burn horticulturists—are profoundly interested in kinship relations. In such societies, kinship may be symbolically expressed in stylized motifs and colorful designs etched or painted on human skin, animal hides or bones, pottery, wood, rocks, or almost any other surface imaginable. To cultural outsiders these designs appear to be purely decorative, ornamental, or

VISUAL COUNTERPOINT

Figure 14.3 **Kinship Symbolism in Art** In the figure at left, the top row shows the stylized human figures that are the basic bricks used in the construction of genealogical patterns. The bottom row shows how these basic figures are linked arm-and-leg with diagonally adjacent figures to depict descent. For thousands of years people all over the world have linked such figures together, creating the familiar geometric patterns that we see in countless art forms—from pottery to sculpture to weavings—patterns that informed eyes recognize as genealogical. Pictured in the figure on the right are traditional wooden shields with kinship designs made by Asmat people in West Papua.

abstract, but they can actually be decoded in terms of genealogical iconography primarily illustrating social relations of marriage and descent (Prins, 1998; Schuster & Carpenter, 1996) **(Figure 14.3)**.

Shared symbolism has also been fundamental to the traditional visual art of tattooing—although that is changing in some parts of the world, as discussed in the following Original Study.

ORIGINAL STUDY

The Modern Tattoo Community *BY MARGO DEMELLO*

As an anthropology graduate student in the early 1990s, I had no idea what (or, more accurately, whom) to study for my field research. Working as an animal advocate, I had a house full of creatures to care for, which left me in no position for long-term travel to a far-off field site.

Then one of my professors suggested a topic that was literally under my nose—tattooing. I myself had several tattoos and spent quite a bit of time with other tattooed people, including my husband, who had just become a professional tattooist.

Early on in my research, I, along with my husband, strove to find a way to "join" what is known as the "tattoo community," finding that it was not as friendly and open as we had imagined it to be. As an anthropologist, I came to see that the sense of exclusion we felt reflected the fact that we were on the lower rungs of a highly stratified social group in which an artist's status is based on such features as class, geography, and professional and artistic credentials,

and a "fan" might be judged on the type and extent of his or her tattoos, the artist(s) who created them, the level of media coverage achieved, and more. This awareness led to one of the major focuses of my work: how class and status increasingly came to define this once working-class art form.

Ultimately, I spent almost five years studying and writing about tattooing, finding my "community" wherever tattooed people talked about themselves and each other—within the pages of tattoo magazines and mainstream newspapers, on Internet newsgroups, and at tattoo-oriented events across the country. I spent countless hours in tattoo shops watching the artists work; I collected what I call "tattoo narratives," which are often elaborate, sometimes spiritual, stories that people tell about their tattoos; and I followed the careers of seminal artists. I even learned to tattoo a bit myself, placing a few particularly ugly images on my patient husband's body.

Tattoos are created by inserting ink or some other pigment through the epidermis (outer skin) into the dermis (the second layer of skin) through the use of needles. They

Generally, the narratives that make up the verbal arts have been divided into several basic and recurring categories, including myth, legend, and tale.

Myth

As discussed in the previous chapter, the term **myth** comes from the Greek word *mythos*, meaning "speech" or "story." It is a narrative that explains the fundamentals of human existence—where we and everything in our world came from, why we are here, and where we are going. A myth provides a rationale for religious beliefs and practices and sets cultural standards for proper behavior. A typical creation or origin myth, traditional with the western Abenaki Indians of northwestern New England and southern Quebec, is as follows:

In the beginning, *Tabaldak*, "The Owner," created all living things but one—the spirit being who was to accomplish the final transformation of the earth. *Tabaldak* made man and woman out of a piece of stone, but he didn't like the result, their hearts being cold and hard. So, he broke them up, and their remains today can be seen in the many stones that litter the landscape of the Abenaki homeland. Then *Tabaldak* tried again, this time using living wood, and from this came all later Abenakis. Like the trees from which the wood came, these people were rooted in the earth and could dance as gracefully as trees swaying in the wind.

The one living thing not created by *Tabaldak* was *Odzihózo*, "He Makes Himself from Something." This transformer created himself out of dust, but he wasn't able to accomplish it all at once. At first, he managed only his head, body, and arms; the legs came later, growing slowly as legs do on a tadpole. Not waiting until his legs were grown, he set out to transform the shape of the earth. He dragged his body about with his hands, gouging channels that became the rivers. To make the mountains, he piled dirt up with his hands. Once his legs grew, *Odzihózo's* task was made easier; by merely extending his legs, he made the tributaries of the main stream. . . .

The last work he made was Lake Champlain and liked it so well that he climbed onto a rock in Burlington Bay and changed himself into stone so he could sit there and enjoy his masterpiece through the ages. He is still there and he is still given offerings of tobacco as Abenakis pass this way. The Abenaki call the rock *Odzihózo*, since it is the Transformer himself. (Haviland & Power, 1994)

Such a myth, insofar as it is believed, accepted, and perpetuated in a culture, expresses part of a people's traditional worldview. This Abenaki myth accounts for the existence of rivers, mountains, lakes, and other features of the landscape (such as Odzihózo Rock pictured in **Figure 14.5**), as well as of humans and all other living things. It also sanctions particular attitudes and behaviors. The myth is a product of creative imagination and is a work of art, as well as potentially a religious statement.

Extrapolating from the details of this particular Abenaki myth, we may conclude that these people recognize a kinship among all living things; after all, they were all part of the same creation, and even humans were made from living wood. This idea of closeness among all living things led the Abenaki to show special respect to the animals they hunted in order to sustain their own lives. For example, before eating meat, they placed an offering of grease on the fire to thank Tabaldak.

A characteristic of myths, including this one, is that they simplify and explain the unknown in terms of the known. The analysis of myths has been carried to great lengths, becoming a field of study almost unto itself. Myth making is an extremely significant kind of human creativity, and studying the myth-making process and its results can offer valuable insight into the way people perceive and think about their world.

Legend

A **legend** is a story about a memorable event or figure handed down by tradition and told as true but without historical evidence. Legends commonly consist of pseudo-historical narratives that account for the deeds of heroes, the movements of peoples, and the establishment of local customs, typically with a mixture of realism and the supernatural or extraordinary. As stories, they are not necessarily believed or disbelieved, but they usually serve to entertain as well as to instruct and to inspire or bolster pride in family, community, or nation. Legends all around the world tell us something about the cultures in which they are found.

A noteworthy example of a popular legend is that American Indians at Cape Cod welcomed the English Pilgrims who came to the "New World" seeking religious freedom—generously sharing their food and helping the newcomers survive their first winter. Gaining acceptance in the 19th century, this romantic first-arrival story is often told during Thanksgiving, an important national holiday in the United States. For Native Americans, it is a false representation of what actually happened almost 400 years ago—the beginning of a foreign invasion and violent dispossession of their ancestral homeland. Thus, many Native Americans do not celebrate Thanksgiving Day.

To a degree, in literate societies the function of legends has been taken over by history. The trouble is that history does not always tell people what they want to hear about

---

myth A sacred narrative that explains the fundamentals of human existence—where we and everything in our world came from, why we are here, and where we are going.

legend A story about a memorable event or figure handed down by tradition and told as true but without historical evidence.

© Ray Brown

Figure 14.5 Odzihózo Rock, Lake Champlain, Burlington, Vermont This small granite island is featured in the creation myth of Abenaki Indians, the original inhabitants of this region. For untold generations, they have referred to it as Odzihózo after the mythical transformer who laid out the river channels and lake basins in northeastern North America.

themselves, or, conversely, it tells them things that they would prefer not to hear. By projecting their culture's hopes and expectations onto the record of the past, they seize upon and even exaggerate some past events while ignoring or giving scant attention to others. Although this often takes place unconsciously, so strong is the motivation to transform history into legend that states have even gone so far as to deliberately rewrite it.

An **epic** is a long, dramatic narrative, recounting the celebrated deeds of a historic or legendary hero, often sung or recited in poetic language. In parts of western and Central Africa, people hold remarkably elaborate and formalized recitations of extremely long legends, lasting several hours and even days. These long narratives have been described as veritable encyclopedias of a culture's most diverse aspects, with direct and indirect statements about history, institutions, relationships, values, and ideas. Epics are typically found in nonliterate societies with some form of state political organization; they serve to transmit and preserve a culture's legal and political precedents and practices.

Legends may incorporate mythological details, especially when they make an appeal to the supernatural, and are therefore not always clearly distinct from myth. Legends may also incorporate proverbs and

incidental tales and thus be related to other forms of verbal art as well.

For the anthropologist, the secular and apparently realistic portions of legends, whether long or short, carry particular significance because of the clues they provide as to what constitutes a culture's approved or ideal ethical behavior. The subject matter of legends is essentially problem solving and mentoring, and the content is likely to include physical and psychological trials of many kinds. Certain questions may be answered explicitly or implicitly: In what circumstances, if any, does the culture permit homicide? What kinds of behavior are considered heroic or cowardly? Does the culture stress forgiveness over retaliation as an admirable trait?

Tale

A third type of creative narrative, the **tale**, is recognized as fiction that is for entertainment but may also draw a moral or teach a practical lesson. Consider this brief

---

epic A long, dramatic narrative, recounting the celebrated deeds of a historic or legendary hero, often sung or recited in poetic language.

tale A creative narrative that is recognized as fiction for entertainment but may also draw a moral or teach a practical lesson.

Figure 14.6 Father, Son, and Donkey in China A Uyghur father prepares his donkey cart together with his son to transport fruits to the market. A scene such as this may bring to mind the internationally popular "Father, Son, and Donkey" tale. Told in different versions, this tale conveys a basic motif or story situation—father and son trying in vain to please everyone. (The cart, basket, and saddle blanket are examples of functional art.)

summary of a tale from Ghana in West Africa, known as "Father, Son, and Donkey" (**Figure 14.6**):

A father and his son farmed their corn, sold it, and spent part of the profit on a donkey. When the hot season came, they harvested their yams and prepared to take them to storage, using their donkey. The father mounted the donkey and they all three proceeded on their way until they met some people. "What? You lazy man!" the people said to the father. "You let your young son walk barefoot on this hot ground while you ride on a donkey? For shame!" The father yielded his place to the son, and they proceeded until they came to an old woman. "What? You useless boy!" said the old woman. "You ride on the donkey and let your poor father walk barefoot on this hot ground? For shame!" The son dismounted, and both father and son walked on the road, leading the donkey behind them until they came to an old man. "What? You foolish people!" said the old man. "You have a donkey and you walk barefoot on the hot ground instead of riding?" And so it goes. Listen: When you are doing something and other people come along, just keep on doing what you like.

This is precisely the kind of tale that is of special interest in traditional folklore studies. It is an internationally popular "numbskull" tale. Versions of it have

been recorded in India, Southwest Asia, southern and western Europe, and North America, as well as in West Africa. It is classified or catalogued as exhibiting a basic **motif** or story situation—father and son trying to please everyone—one of the many thousands that have been found to recur in tales around the world. Despite variations in detail, every version follows the same basic structure in the sequence of events, sometimes called the syntax of the tale: A peasant father and son work together, a beast of burden is purchased, the three set out on a short excursion, the father rides and is criticized, the son rides and is criticized, both walk and are criticized, and a conclusion is drawn.

Tales of this sort (not to mention myths and legends) that are found to have wide geographic distribution raise some questions: Where did they originate? Did the story arise only once and then pass from one culture to another (diffusion)? Or did the stories arise independently (independent invention) in response to like causes in similar settings, or perhaps as a consequence of inherited mental preferences and images deeply embedded in the evolutionary construction of the human brain? Or is it merely that there are logical limits to the structure of stories, so that, by coincidence, different cultures are bound to come up with similar motifs and syntax (Gould, 2000)?

A surprisingly large number of motifs in European and African tales are traceable to ancient sources in India, evidence of diffusion of tales. Of course, purely local tales also exist. Within any particular culture, anthropologists usually can categorize local types of tales: animal, human experience, trickster, dilemma, ghost, moral, scatological, nonsense tales, and so on. In West Africa, for example, there is a remarkable prevalence of stories with animal protagonists. Many were carried to the slaveholding areas of the Americas; the Uncle Remus stories about Brer Rabbit and Brer Fox may be part of this tradition.

The significance of tales for the anthropologist rests partly in this matter of their distribution. They provide evidence of either cultural contacts or cultural isolation and of limits of influence and cultural cohesion.

Anthropologists are interested, however, in more than these questions of distribution. Like legends, tales very often illustrate local solutions to universal human ethical problems, and in some sense they state a moral philosophy. Anthropologists recognize that regardless of where the tale of the father, the son, and the donkey originated, the fact that it is told in West Africa suggests that it states something valid for that culture. The tale's lesson of a necessary degree of self-confidence in the face of arbitrary social criticism is therefore something that can be found in the culture's values and beliefs.

motif A story situation in a tale.

Figure 14.7 Bedouin Women Singing and Making Bread The *ghinnawas* or "little songs" of the Awlad 'Ali Bedouins in Egypt punctuate conversations carried out while the people perform everyday chores. Through these songs, they can express what otherwise are taboo subjects.

Other Verbal Art

Myths, legends, and tales, prominent as they are in anthropological studies, in many cultures turn out to be no more important than many other verbal arts. In the culture of the Awlad 'Ali Bedouins of Egypt's western desert, for example, poetry is a lively and active verbal art, especially as a vehicle for personal expression and private communication. These Bedouins use two forms of poetry. One is the elaborately structured and heroic poems men chant or recite only on ceremonial occasions and in specific public contexts. The other is the *ghinnawas* or "little songs" that punctuate everyday conversations, especially of women. Simple in structure, these deal with personal matters and feelings more appropriate to informal social situations, and older men regard them as the unimportant productions of women and youths (**Figure 14.7**).

Despite this official devaluation in the male-dominated Bedouin society, "little songs" play a vital part in people's daily lives. In these poems individuals are shielded from the consequences of making statements and expressing sentiments that contravene the moral system. Paradoxically, by sharing these "immoral" sentiments only with intimates and veiling them in impersonal traditional formulas, those who recite them demonstrate

that they have a certain control, which actually enhances their moral standing. As is often true of folklore in general, the "little songs" of the Awlad 'Ali provide a culturally appropriate outlet for otherwise taboo thoughts or opinions (Abu-Lughod, 1986). The same is true for disaster jokes or comedic satire in numerous contemporary societies.

In all cultures the words of songs constitute a kind of poetry. Poetry and stories recited with gesture, movement, and props become drama. Drama combined with dance, music, and spectacle becomes a public celebration. The more we look at the individual arts, the clearer it becomes that they often are interrelated and interdependent. The verbal arts are, in fact, simply differing manifestations of the same creative imagination that produces music and the other arts.

Musical Art

Evidence of humans making music reaches far back in time. Archaeologists have found flutes and whistles (resembling today's recorders) made from the bones of mammoths and birds and dating back at least 42,000 years (Higham et al., 2012). And historically known food-foraging peoples were not without music. In the Kalahari Desert, for example, a Ju/'hoansi hunter off by himself would play a tune on his bow simply to help pass the time. (Long before anyone thought of beating swords into plowshares, some genius discovered that bows could be used not just to kill but to make music as well.) In northern New England, Abenaki shamans used cedar flutes to call game, lure enemies, and attract women. In addition, shamans would use a drum—over which two rawhide strings were stretched to produce a buzzing sound, representing singing—to allow communication with the spirit world.

The study of music in specific cultural settings, or **ethnomusicology**, began in the 19th century with the collection of folk songs and has developed into a specialized subfield of anthropological study. Ethnomusicologists look at music within its cultural context and from a comparative and relativistic perspective (Nettl, 2005). Early ethnomusicologists focused primarily on non-Western musical traditions in tribal cultures. Today, some also study folk music or music played and enjoyed in different ethnic communities within industrialized modern states.

Music is a form of communication that includes a nonverbal auditory component. The information it transmits is often abstract and emotional rather than concrete and objective, and different listeners experience it in a variety of ways. Such factors make it difficult to construct a definition that satisfies across cultures. Broadly speaking, **music** may be defined as an art form whose medium is sound and silence; a form of communication that includes a nonverbal auditory component with elements of tonality, rhythm, pitch, and timbre.

In general, human music is said to differ from natural sounds—the songs of birds, wolves, and whales, for example—by being almost everywhere perceived in terms of a repertoire of tones at fixed or regular intervals: in other words, a scale. Scale systems and their modifications make up what is known as *tonality* in music. These vary cross-culturally, so it is not surprising that something that sounds musical to one group of people may come across as noise to another.

Humans make closed systems out of a formless range of possible sounds by dividing the distance between a tone and its first overtone or sympathetic vibration (which always has exactly twice as many vibrations as the basic tone) into a series of measured steps. In the Western or European system, the distance between the basic tone and the first overtone is called

the *octave*; it consists of seven steps—five whole tones and two semitones. The whole tones are further divided into semitones, collectively resulting in a twelve-tone musical scale. Interestingly, some birds pitch their songs to the same scale as Western music (Gray et al., 2001), perhaps influencing the way these people developed their scale.

One of the most common alternatives to the semitonal system is the *pentatonic* (five-tone) system, which divides the octave into five nearly equidistant tones. Such scales may be found all over the world, including in much European folk music. Arabic and Persian music have smaller units of a third of a tone with seventeen and twenty-four steps in the octave. Even quarter-tone scales are used in large parts of South Asia, North Africa, and the Middle East with subtleties of shading that are nearly indistinguishable to most Western ears. Thus, even when Westerners can hear what sounds like melody and rhythm in these systems, for many the total result may sound peculiar or "out of tune."

Pitch is the quality of a sound governed by the rate of vibrations producing it—in other words, the degree of highness or lowness of a tone. *Timbre*, another element of music, is the characteristic quality of sound produced by a particular instrument or voice—also known as *tone color*. It is what distinguishes one musical sound from another, even when they have the same pitch and loudness. For example, a violin and a flute playing the same note equally loud have a different timbre.

Another organizing factor in music is *rhythm*. Involving tempo, stress, and measured repetition, it may be more important than tonality. One reason for this may be our constant exposure to natural pulses, such as our own heartbeat and patterns of breathing and walking. Even before we are born, we are exposed to our mother's heartbeat and to the rhythms of her movements, and as infants we experience rhythmic touching, petting, stroking, and rocking (Dissanayake, 2000).

The rhythms of traditional European music are most often measured into recurrent patterns of two, three, and four beats, with combinations of weak and strong beats to mark the division and form patterns. Non-European music is likely to move in patterns of five, seven, or eleven beats, with complex arrangements of internal beats and sometimes *polyrhythms*: one instrument or singer using a pattern of three beats, for example, whereas another uses a pattern of five or seven. Polyrhythms are frequent in the drum music of West Africa, which shows remarkable precision in the overlapping of rhythmic lines (**Figure 14.8**). Non-European music also may contain *shifting rhythms*: a pattern of three beats, for example, followed by a pattern of two or five beats with little or no regular

ethnomusicology The study of a society's music in terms of its cultural setting.

music Broadly speaking, an art form whose medium is sound and silence; a form of communication that includes a nonverbal auditory component with elements of tonality, pitch, rhythm, and timbre.

worldview, giving clues about everything from gender and kinship relations to religious beliefs, political ideas, and historical memory.

For those within a society, art may serve to display social status, spiritual identity, and political power. An example of this can be seen in the totem poles of Indians living along North America's northwest coast. Erected in front of the homes of chiefs, these poles are inscribed with symbols that are visual reminders of the social hierarchy. Similarly, art is used to mark kinship ties, as seen in Scottish tartans designed to identify clan affiliation. It can also affirm group solidarity and identity beyond kinship lines, as evidenced in national emblems such as the dragon (Bhutan), bald eagle (United States), maple leaf (Canada), crescent moon (Turkey), and cedar tree (Lebanon) that typically appear on coins and government buildings.

Sometimes art is employed to express political themes and influence events, as in the counter-culture rock and folk music of the 1960s in the United States. Other times it is used to transmit traditional culture and ancestral ties, as in epic poems passed down from generation to generation. Myths, another verbal art form, may offer basic explanations about the world and set cultural standards for right behavior.

As an activity or behavior that contributes to human well-being and that helps give shape and significance to life, art is often intricately intertwined with religion and spirituality. In fact, in elaborate ceremonies involving ornamentation, masks, costumes, songs, dances, and effigies, it is not easy to say precisely where art stops and religion begins. Shamans drum to help create a trance state, Buddhist monks chant to focus their meditation, Christians sing hymns to praise God. Also, since ancient times, rituals and symbols concerning death have been infused with artistry—from evocative funereal music and beautiful sacred objects buried with a body to detailed mummy portraits in ancient Egypt. Today, in some parts of the world, artisans create coffins that are so creative that they find their way into museums as art (see the Globalscape feature, next page).

Furthermore, music, dance, and other arts may be used, like magic, to "enchant"—to take advantage of the emotional or psychological predispositions of another person or group so as to cause them to perceive reality in a way favorable to the interests of the enchanter. Often art is created to honor or beseech the aid of a deity, an ancestral spirit, or an animal spirit. Indeed, the arts may be used to manipulate a seemingly inexhaustible list of human passions, including desire, terror, wonder, love, fantasy, and vanity. Marketing specialists are well aware of this, which is why they routinely employ certain music and images in their advertising—as do promoters of political, ideological, charitable, or other causes.

Art in all its varied forms is used in a vast number of ways for a great array of purposes. To simplify our discussion of its numerous functions, we will consider a particular art form as embedded in a cultural system: music.

Figure 14.8 Senegalese Musician Zale Seck Like so many other cultural elements, musical instruments and styles of playing and singing now circulate around the globe, as do the artists themselves. One such example is West African musician Saliou "Zale" Seck, known for his "funky crisscrossing rhythms." A member of the Lébou tribe, *Zale* was born in the old fishing town of Yoff, just north of Senegal's capital city of Dakar. He performs Wolof percussive music on a traditional skin-covered *djembe* (hand drum) and *sabar* (played with one hand and a stick). Coming from a long line of *griots* (oral historians-traditional storytellers), he transmits his people's memory through lyrics of love and humanity. Fluent in French (his country was a French colony for many years), Zale has toured Europe and played on radio and television in France. Recently, Zale relocated to the French-speaking Canadian city of Quebec to further pursue his musical career.

recurrence or repetition of any one pattern, although the patterns are fixed and identifiable as units.

Melody involves both tonality and rhythm. It is a rhythmical succession of musical tones organized as a distinct phrase or sequence of phrases.

The Functions of Art

Art in all its many forms has countless functions beyond adding beauty and entertainment to everyday life. For anthropologists and others seeking to understand cultures beyond their own, art offers insights into a culture's

Figure 15.1 Bagpipers, Royal Army Marching Band of Bhutan Unlike neighboring India, Bhutan remained independent from British colonial rule. This small Himalayan kingdom, known to the Bhutanese as Drukyul ("land of the dragons"), is generally averse to foreign cultural influences. However, the Drukpa ("dragon people") have selectively embraced a few innovations, including the Scottish bagpipes, which found their way here via India during the colonial era. Wearing traditional dress, bagpipers in the royal band play imported instruments, producing a droning sound similar to age-old sacred trumpets played by Buddhist monks in this region. They and other Drukpa musicians lead the way for singing the national anthem Druk Tsendhen ("the thunder dragon kingdom"), honoring the fifth traditional Druk Gyalpo ("dragon king"), who serves as head of this Buddhist state.

firmly based on a *geocentric* worldview as revealed in sacred texts. Facing a death sentence, Galileo recanted and was condemned to life under house arrest. In 1758, after numerous additional scientific breakthroughs challenged Catholic dogma, heliocentric books were removed from the forbidden list of that powerful international institution.

Diffusion

The spread of certain ideas, customs, or practices from one culture to another is known as **diffusion**. So common is cross-cultural borrowing that U.S. anthropologist Ralph Linton suggested that it accounts for as much as 90 percent of any culture's content.

People are creative about their borrowing, however, picking and choosing from multiple possibilities and sources. Usually, their selections are limited to those compatible with the existing culture. An example is the inclusion of bagpipes in the marching band of the royal army of Bhutan. Traditionally played by Scottish Highland regiments when marching into combat and in official ceremonies, this musical instrument features one double-reed pipe operated by finger stops and three drone pipes. All the pipes are sounded by air forced with the left arm from a leather bag kept filled by the player's breath. The bagpipe's drone sounds resemble those of Bhutan's traditional sacred trumpets played in ancient Buddhist religious ceremonies in this small Himalayan kingdom (**Figure 15.1**).

The extent of cultural borrowing can be surprising. Consider, for example, paper, the compass, and gunpowder. All three of these innovations were invented in China long before Europeans became aware of them about 700 years ago. Accepting these foreign artifacts, Europeans

diffusion The spread of certain ideas, customs, or practices from one culture to another.

Figure 15.2 Making Corn Mush in Italy Having spread from the tropics of the Mexican highlands to much of the rest of North and South America, corn diffused rapidly to the rest of the world after Italian explorer Christopher Columbus first crossed the Atlantic in 1492. A long-time favorite dish in Italy is polenta (a thick mush made of cornmeal). Here we see it being made the traditional way: boiled in a big copper cauldron over a fire of hot coals and then spread out and cooled to firmness on a wooden or stone slab. In recent years, polenta has become a favored menu item in many chic American restaurants.

© Hubert Stadler/Corbis

and others analyzed and improved them where needed. Such is the case with the mixture of sulfur, charcoal, and potassium nitrate the Chinese used for fireworks and portable hand cannons. Soon after learning about it, Europeans, Koreans, and Arabs adopted and adapted this primitive artillery and gunpowder, triggering a revolution in traditional warfare from the 1300s onward. Two centuries later, Europeans introduced firearms to the Americas. Within decades, indigenous groups such as the Mi'kmaq in the Gulf of Maine began using them in their raids, transforming warfare as they had known it for generations.

America's indigenous peoples not only adopted weapons and other foreign trade goods, but also shared numerous inventions and discoveries their ancestors had made in the course of many centuries. Of special note is the range of domestic plants developed ("invented") by the Indians—potatoes, beans, tomatoes, peanuts, avocados, manioc, chili peppers, squash, chocolate, sweet potatoes, and corn ("maize"), to name a few—all of which now furnish a major portion of the world's food supply. In fact, American Indians are recognized as primary contributors to the world's varied cuisine and credited with developing the largest array of nutritious foods (Weatherford, 1988).

Diffusion of a Global Staple Food: Maize

Particularly significant among the domesticated plants diffusing from the Americas is corn, also known as *maize* (derived from a Caribbean Indian word *maíz*). The English originally referred to this Native American cereal plant as "Indian corn." First cultivated by indigenous peoples in the Mexican highlands over 7,000 years ago, this food crop diffused to much of the rest of North, Central, and South America over the next few millennia.

In 1493, the explorer Columbus returned from America to Spain with a sampling of maize. First planted in kitchen gardens in Andalusia, in the course of several decades maize spread to other parts of Spain and Portugal. From there it diffused southwest, reaching France and northern Italy by the late 1530s. Producing more calories per acre than traditional European crops, it was initially grown as green fodder to feed pigs and other livestock. However, forced by poverty and famine, peasants and other poor folk in southern Europe accepted this new food as cornmeal cakes or thick porridge (**Figure 15.2**). Portuguese traders introduced maize to western Africa and across the Indian Ocean to South Asia from where it spread to China before the mid-1500s.

Diffusing across the globe, maize has become one of the world's major staple foods and has been culturally incorporated under many different names. This dietary revolution not only altered people's lives but is also responsible for enormous population growth, especially since the 18th century (Braudel, 1979). Today, a greater weight of maize is produced each year than rice, wheat, or any other grain—about 800 million tons, with over half of the global production taking place in the United States and China.

In recent years, an enormous quantity of maize has been grown for biomass fuel, such as ethanol, as an alternative to nonrenewable fossil fuels such as oil. Moreover, the production of genetically engineered maize (manipulated with herbicide or drought-resistant genes) has been gaining ground, especially in the United States and many developing countries, but this practice is resisted by European farmers and consumers.

Diffusion of a Global Measurement System: Metrics

Another remarkable example of diffusion—breaking through multiple language barriers and long-held local traditions—is the metric system used for measuring length, weight, capacity, currency, and temperature. Based on a classification in

Figure 15.3 Camel Mobile Library Providing books and reading materials to the Somali-speaking nomads in the remote Garissa and the Wajir areas in its northeastern districts, Kenya's National Library Association challenges the region's 85 percent illiteracy rate. The program consists of three teams, each with three male camels capable of traveling routes impassable even for 4-wheel drive vehicles. One camel is loaded with two boxes containing 200 books, one transports the library tent, and a third carries miscellaneous items needed for the program.

which standard units of measurement are multiplied or divided by 10 in order to produce larger or smaller units, this rational system has simplified calculations and is practical on many levels of accounting and management.

A Dutch engineer first proposed the use of decimal fractions for measures, weights, and currency in everyday life. Three centuries later, in 1795, soon after the revolution that toppled the royal regime, the French First Republic adopted the metric system as its official system of measurement. Then, with French military expansion under Napoleon in the early 19th century, the system was forced upon conquered neighboring countries—standardizing a bewildering array of regional and local measurement systems on the European continent.

By 1900, about forty countries had adopted the metric system. It continued to spread during the 20th century, despite initial reluctance or even resistance in some countries, such as Great Britain. Since the early 1970s, that country and most of its former colonies have fully transitioned to metric. British law now defines each "Imperial unit" in terms of the metric equivalent (although many older Britons still hold on to traditional measurements such as inches, feet, and miles in daily life). Today, at least officially, the metric system is almost universal, with the exception of just seven countries including Myanmar (Burma), Liberia, and, most notably, the United States (Cardarelli, 2003; Vera, 2011).

Cultural Loss

Most often people look at cultural change as an accumulation of innovations. Frequently, however, the acceptance of a new innovation results in **cultural loss**—the

cultural loss The abandonment of an existing practice or trait.

abandonment of an existing practice or trait. For example, in ancient times chariots and carts were used widely in northern Africa and southwestern Asia, but wheeled vehicles virtually disappeared from Morocco to Afghanistan about 1,500 years ago. Camels replaced them, not because of some reversion to the past but because camels used as pack animals worked better. The old Roman empire roads had deteriorated, and these sturdy animals traveled well with or without roads. Their endurance, longevity, and ability to ford rivers and traverse rough ground made pack camels admirably suited for the region. Plus, they were economical in terms of labor: A wagon required a man for every two draft animals, but a single person could manage up to six pack camels.

Reflecting on Westerners' surprise over this rejection of a cultural innovation, U.S. paleontologist Stephen Jay Gould commented that

> Wheels have come to symbolize in our culture . . . intelligent exploitation and technological progress. . . . The success of camels reemphasizes a fundamental theme. . . . Adaptation, be it biological or cultural, represents a better fit to specific, local environments, not an inevitable stage in a ladder of progress. Wheels were a formidable invention, and their uses are manifold. . . . But camels may work better in some circumstances. Wheels, like wings, fins, and brains, are exquisite devices for certain purposes, not signs of intrinsic superiority. (Gould, 1983, p. 159)

Gould's point remains relevant in many remote and hot desert regions, where camels are still the favored and most reliable form of transportation for many purposes (**Figure 15.3**).

Often overlooked is another facet of losing apparently useful traits: loss without replacement. An example of this is the historical absence of boats among the indigenous

Figure 15.4 Protesting Acculturation Until a few decades ago, these Aché Indians survived as traditional hunters and gatherers in the deep tropical forest of eastern Paraguay. Not unlike the Ju/'hoansi of southern Africa, they were organized in small migratory bands and rarely had contact with outsiders. Armed with spears and bows and arrows, they could not defend their homeland against large numbers of foreign invaders equipped with chainsaws, bulldozers, and firearms. Massacres and foreign diseases, coupled with massive deforestation of their hunting territories, almost annihilated these people in the 1950s and 1960s. Since then, they have been exposed to intensive acculturation. Here we see the breakup of an Aché encampment in the middle of Asunción, Paraguay's capital city, where they lived during many weeks of protest against government policies.

inhabitants of the Canary Islands, a group of small islands isolated off North Africa's Atlantic coastline. The ancestors of these people must have had boats because without them they could never have transported themselves and their domestic livestock to the islands in the first place. Later, without boats, they had no way to communicate with other islands or with the mainland. This loss of something useful came about due to the islands' lack of stone suitable for making polished stone axes, which in turn limited the islanders' carpentry (Coon, 1954).

Repressive Change

Innovation, diffusion, and cultural loss all may take place among peoples who are free to decide for themselves what changes they will or will not accept. However, people do not always have the liberty to make their own choices. Frequently, they are forced to make changes they would not willingly make, usually in the course of conquest and colonialism. A direct outcome in many cases is repressive change to a culture, which anthropologists call *acculturation*. The most radical form of repressive change is ethnocide.

Acculturation and Ethnocide

Acculturation is the massive cultural change that occurs in a society when it experiences intensive firsthand contact with a more powerful society. It always involves an element of force—either directly, as in conquests, or indirectly, as in the implicit or explicit threat that force will be used if people refuse to make the demanded changes. Other variables include degree of cultural difference; circumstances, intensity, frequency, and hostility of contact; relative status of the agents of contact; who is dominant and who is submissive; and whether the nature of the flow is reciprocal or nonreciprocal. *Acculturation* and *diffusion* are not equivalent terms; one culture can borrow from another without being in the least forced into change (**Figure 15.4**).

In the course of cultural contact, any number of things may happen. Merger or fusion occurs when two cultures lose their separate identities and form a single culture, as historically expressed by the melting pot ideology of English-speaking, Protestant Euramerican culture in the United States. Sometimes, though, one of the cultures loses its autonomy

acculturation The massive cultural change that occurs in a society when it experiences intensive firsthand contact with a more powerful society.

but retains its identity as a subculture in the form of a caste, class, or ethnic group. This is typical of conquest or slavery situations. The United States provides examples of these phenomena, despite its melting pot ideology; we need look no further than the nearest American Indian reservation.

Acculturation may occur as a result of military conquest, political and economic expansion, or massive invasion and breaking up of cultural structures by dominant newcomers who know or care little about the traditional beliefs and practices of the people they seek to control. Under the sway of powerful outsiders—and unable to effectively resist imposed changes and obstructed in carrying out many of their own social, religious, and economic activities—subordinated groups are forced into new social and cultural practices that tend to isolate individuals and destroy the integrity of their traditional communities. In virtually all parts of the world today, people are faced with the tragedy of forced removal from their traditional homelands, as entire communities are uprooted to make way for hydroelectric projects, grazing lands for cattle, mining operations, or highway construction.

Ethnocide, the violent eradication of an ethnic group's collective cultural identity as a distinctive people, occurs when a dominant society deliberately sets out to destroy another society's cultural heritage. This may take place when a powerful nation aggressively expands its territorial control by annexing neighboring peoples and their territories, incorporating the conquered groups as subjects. A policy of ethnocide typically includes forbidding a subjugated nation's ancestral language, criminalizing their traditional customs, destroying their religion and demolishing sacred places and practices, breaking up their social organizations, and dispossessing or removing the survivors from their homelands—in essence, stopping short of physical extermination while removing all traces of their unique culture.

Tibet provides one tragic example of ethnocide. The Chinese communist army in 1950 invaded Tibet and subsequently initiated ethnocidal policies by means of systematic attacks against traditional Tibetan culture. Seeking to stamp out deeply rooted religious beliefs and practices, the communists ordered the demolition of most Buddhist temples and monasteries. Following a mass uprising, hundreds of thousands of Tibetans were killed or forced into exile abroad. Trying to annihilate Tibetan identity, China sought to turn the surviving Tibetans into political subjects who would culturally identify themselves as Chinese nationals (Smith, 2009). There have been dramatic demonstrations against Chinese rule. In 2011 and 2012, at least fifty Tibetans protested by setting themselves on fire (Gladstone, 2012).

Ethnocide may also take place when so many carriers of a culture die that those who manage to survive become refugees, living among peoples of different cultures. Examples of this may be seen in many parts of the world today.

Ethnocide in Amazonia: Yąnomami

A particularly well-documented case of ethnocide occurred in South America's Amazon rainforest in 1968, when developers hired killers to wipe out several Indian groups, using arsenic, dynamite, and machine guns from light planes. To this day, violence continues to haunt indigenous peoples inhabiting this vast tropical forest. Most of these groups are besieged by outsiders aggressively penetrating their homelands in search of precious resources and, in the process, destroying their way of life.

Ethnocide in the Amazon is especially well documented for the Yąnomami Indians of the Upper Orinoco drainage. With a current population of about 24,000 (9,000 living in Brazil and 15,000 across the border in Venezuela), these hunters and food gardeners occupy about 18 million hectares. They reside in about 125 autonomous villages, each inhabited by 30 to 300 people living collectively in large circular dwellings known as *shabonos*.

Almost completely isolated from the outside world until the mid-1900s, the Yąnomami did experience cultural change prior to first contact with foreign traders and Christian missionaries. Evidence for this was in their gardens, where they planted nonindigenous food crops—plantains and bananas, both originating in Africa—acquired through exchange. This adoption increased gardening productivity, triggering population growth and, so it seems, more raids in intervillage conflicts.

Through trading and raiding, the Yąnomami also acquired iron tools, especially machetes and axes. Having these, along with newly introduced firearms, their internal conflicts became increasingly violent. According to some anthropologists, a condition of endemic warfare ensued, with violence becoming the cause of death for perhaps nearly a third of adult men.

Cultural change accelerated when foreign missionaries and traders became a permanent presence on their frontiers beginning in the 1950s. Despite their fierce reputation, the Yąnomami soon became victims of repeated assaults by gold miners, cattle ranchers, and other foreigners seeking to capitalize on their natural resources.

In the late 1960s, a measles epidemic killed hundreds of Yąnomami. Without microbiological knowledge of bacteria and viruses, these Amazonian Indians traditionally attribute illness and death to evil magic, or sorcery, and this demands that surviving relatives seek revenge.

ethnocide The violent eradication of an ethnic group's collective cultural identity as a distinctive people; occurs when a dominant society deliberately sets out to destroy another society's cultural heritage.

Threats to Yąnomami survival multiplied in the 1980s, when many thousands of Brazilian loggers and *garimpeiros* ("gold miners") invaded their lands, attacking villagers defending their territories (Turner, 1991). Miners also illegally crossed into Venezuela, spreading the violence. The Brazilian state, considering legalizing large-scale logging and mining in indigenous territories, stepped up its military presence in these borderlands, sending troops, building barracks, and expanding airstrips in the Yąnomami heartland. Huge stretches of forest were torched to build mining camps. Dozens of planes flew in daily, transporting personnel, equipment, and fuel.

Miners, loggers, and soldiers lured Yąnomami women with commodities, infecting them with sexually transmitted diseases that spread quickly into the indigenous communities. On top of prostitution, the invaders introduced alcoholism. Processing the ore, miners also polluted the rivers with mercury, poisoning fish and other creatures, including the Yąnomami. Within the decade, 20 percent of the Yąnomami died, and 70 percent of their ancestral lands in Brazil were illegally expropriated.

A campaign against this ethnocide, led by the Committee for the Creation of Yąnomami Park and Survival International, forced the Brazilian government to protect indigenous territories and expel the miners. Creating a Yąnomami Park (in fact, a reservation) in 1992, the Brazilian state slowed but failed to stop the ethnocide and *ecocide* (environmental destruction) because *garimpeiros* crossed the border into Venezuela where they continued massacring Yąnomami men, women, and children.

In the mid-1990s, after years of pressure by the Inter-American Commission on Human Rights, Venezuelan state authorities finally agreed to protect the Yąnomami in the remote borderlands and to provide some basic health care to reduce alarming mortality rates. To this day, Amazonian Indians such as the Yąnomami are forced to live in a climate of fear, with violent intimidation, physical threats, and occasional killings, aggravated by poor health, low life expectancy, and discrimination, challenging their survival as an indigenous people.

In such difficult times, spiritual leaders are especially important. Among these is Davi Kopenawa, a shaman from the Yąnomami village of Watoriketheri (**Figure 15.5**). He and other shamans—traditionally skilled in contacting dangerous spirits in order to cure the sick and seek revenge against enemies—now confront the deadly forces of ethnocide and ecocide. Recognized as a spokesperson for the Yąnomami in Brazil, Kopenawa has gained an international reputation as a political activist. He uses his extraordinary powers in defense of his Amazonian homeland, negotiating with powerful foreign institutions, corporations, and nongovernmental organizations in a heroic effort to stop the relentless destruction of Brazil's indigenous peoples, cultures, and environment (Conklin, 2002; Kopenawa & Albert, 2010).

Directed Change

Although the process of acculturation often unfolds without planning, powerful elites may devise and enforce programs of cultural change, directing immigrant or subordinated groups into learning and accepting dominant society's cultural beliefs and practices. So it was with the Ju/'hoansi of southern Africa. Rounded up by government officials in the early 1960s, these Bushmen were confined to a reservation in Tsumkwe where they could not possibly provide for their own needs. The government supplied them with rations, but these were insufficient to meet basic nutritional needs.

Figure 15.5 Yąnomami Shaman and Political Activist Davi Kopenawa Traditionally, Yąnomami shamans such as Davi Kopenawa, seen here surrounded by women and children standing in front of their *shabono*, cure the sick by contacting the spirit world. Known as *shabori*, they apply their skills in negotiating extraordinary challenges with *hekura* ("dangerous spirits"). Today, those challenges include ethnocide and ecocide. Yąnomami rely on shamans such as Kopenawa to use their remarkable powers when negotiating with strangers representing powerful foreign institutions, corporations, and nongovernmental organizations in an effort to prevent further harm to their communities.

© Fiona Watson/Survival

In poor health and prevented from developing meaningful alternatives to traditional activities, the Ju/'hoansi became embittered and depressed, and their death rate came to exceed the birthrate. Within the next few years, however, surviving Ju/'hoansi began to take matters into their own hands. They returned to waterholes in their traditional homeland, where, assisted by anthropologists and others concerned with their welfare, they are trying to sustain themselves by raising livestock. Whether this will succeed remains to be seen because there are still many obstacles to overcome.

One byproduct of colonial dealings with indigenous peoples has been the growth of applied anthropology, which was originally focused on advising government programs of directed cultural change and solving practical problems through anthropological techniques and knowledge. For example, in the United States, the Bureau of American Ethnology was founded in 1876 to gather reliable data the government might use to formulate Indian policies. At the time, anthropologists were convinced of the practicality of their discipline, and many who did ethnographic work among Indians devoted a great deal of time, energy, and money to assisting their informants, whose interests were frequently at risk.

In the 20th century, the scope and intent of applied anthropology expanded. In the first part of that century, the applied work of Franz Boas—who almost singlehandedly trained an entire generation of anthropologists in the United States—proved instrumental in reforming the country's immigration policies. With impressive statistical data based on comparative skull measurements and related physical anthropological studies, this German Jewish immigrant challenged popular race theories of the day. He demonstrated that theories privileging non-Jewish immigrants from western Europe and discrimination against Jews and others deemed undesirable were based not on fact but on deeply rooted racial prejudice.

In the 1930s, anthropologists with clearly pragmatic objectives did a number of studies in industrial and other institutional settings in the United States. With World War II came increased involvement in colonial administration beyond U.S. borders, especially in the Pacific, by American officers trained in anthropology. The rapid postwar recovery of Japan was due in no small measure to the influence of anthropologists in structuring the U.S. occupation. Anthropologists continue to play an active role today in administering U.S. trust territories in the Pacific.

All too often, however, states and other powerful institutions directly intervening in the affairs of different ethnic groups or foreign societies fail to seek professional advice from anthropologists who possess relevant cross-cultural expertise and deeper insights. Such failures have contributed to a host of avoidable errors in planning and executing nation-building programs in ethnically divided countries such as Iraq and Afghanistan, both of which are now devastated by war and violence.

Today, applied anthropologists are in growing demand in the field of international development because of their specialized knowledge of social structure, value systems, and the functional interrelatedness of cultures targeted for development. Those working in this arena face a particular challenge: As anthropologists, they are bound to respect other peoples' dignity and cultural integrity, yet they are asked for advice on how to change certain aspects of those cultures. If the people themselves request the change, there is no difficulty, but typically the change is requested from outsiders. Supposedly, the proposed change is for the good of the targeted population, yet members of that community do not always see it that way. The extent to which applied anthropologists should go in advising outsiders how to manipulate people to embrace the changes proposed for them is a serious ethical question, especially when it concerns people without the power to resist.

In direct response to such critical questions concerning the application and benefits of anthropological research, an alternative type of practical anthropology has emerged during the last half century. Known by a variety of names—including action anthropology and committed, engaged, involved, and advocacy anthropology—this involves community-based research and action in collaboration and solidarity with indigenous societies, ethnic minorities, and other besieged or repressed groups. In sum, not only are the practical applications of anthropology necessary, but there is a growing demand for anthropologically informed pragmatic solutions.

Reactions to Change

The reactions of indigenous peoples to the changes outsiders have thrust upon them have varied considerably. Some have responded by moving to the nearest available forest, desert, or other remote place in hopes of being left alone. In Brazil, a number of communities once located near the coast took this option a few hundred years ago and were successful until the great push to develop the Amazon forest began in the 1960s. Others, like many Indians of North America, took up arms to fight back but were ultimately forced to sign treaties and surrender much of their ancestral land, after which they were reduced to an impoverished underclass in their own territories. Today, they continue to fight through nonviolent means to retain their identities as distinct peoples and to regain control over natural resources on their lands.

Resisting **assimilation**, a process of cultural absorption of an ethnic minority by a dominant society, people often seek emotional comfort from **tradition**—customary ideas

---

assimilation Cultural absorption of an ethnic minority by a dominant society.

tradition Customary ideas and practices passed on from generation to generation, which in a modernizing society may form an obstacle to new ways of doing things.

and practices passed on from generation to generation, which in a modernizing society may form an obstacle to new ways of doing things. Traditions play an important role in a cultural process identified as **accommodation**. In anthropology, this refers to an adaptation process by which a people modifies its traditional culture in response to pressures by a dominant society so as to preserve its distinctive ethnic identity and resist assimilation (Prins, 1996). In pursuit of such an accommodation strategy, ethnic groups may try to retain their distinctive identities by maintaining cultural boundaries such as holding onto traditional language, festive ceremonies, customary dress, ritual songs and dances, unique food, and so on. Later in this chapter we discuss two ethnographic examples of accommodation.

Syncretism

When people are able to hold on to some of their traditions in the face of powerful outside domination, the result may be *syncretism*—defined in an earlier chapter as the creative blending of indigenous and foreign beliefs or practices into new cultural forms. Not unlike hybrids in the animal or plant worlds, these new forms take shape in a dynamic process of cultural adaptation in which groups gradually negotiate a collective response to new challenges in their social environment. Vodou, practiced in Haiti and described in a previous chapter, is one of many examples of religious syncretism. But syncretism also occurs in other cultural domains, including art and fashion, architecture, marriage rituals, warfare, and even sports.

An intriguing illustration of this can be found among the Trobriand Islanders of the southern Pacific, whose cultural practices we looked at in earlier chapters. Yams are to Trobrianders what reindeer are for the Nenets—the staple of their subsistence, the wealth of their economy, and the core of their culture. These edible tubers (*Dioscorea batatas*, often confused with sweet potatoes) may grow longer than 1.5 meters (5 feet) and weigh over 65 kilograms (150 pounds). After women harvest the crop, everyone celebrates. The major event in their traditional July and August harvest festivals is a *kayasa*, a ritual competition in which rival village chiefs show off their *kuvi*—colossal yams over 3.5 meters (12 feet) long. Centered on these huge tubers, the *kayasa* ceremony involves dancing and ritual fighting between neighboring communities. The chief hosting the event is always declared the winner.

When Trobrianders were under colonial rule, British administrators as well as Christian protestant missionaries and teachers took notice of the *kayasa* ceremony. They found it scandalous for its erotic displays of "wild" dancing, accompanied by chanting and shouting—suggestive of sexual intercourse, body parts, and so on. A Methodist

missionary set about "civilizing" these tropical islanders by teaching cricket at the mission school. He hoped this gentlemanly sport would replace Trobriand rivalry and fighting, encouraging comportment in dress, sportsmanship, and ultimately religion.

But that is not what happened. Although the Trobrianders took to the sport, they "rubbished" the British rules. Making cricket their own, they played in traditional battle dress and incorporated battle magic and erotic dancing into the game. They modified the British style of pitching, making it resemble the old Trobriand way of throwing a spear. And following the game, they held massive feasts, where wealth was displayed to enhance their prestige (**Figure 15.6**).

Cricket, in its altered form, has been made to serve traditional systems of prestige and exchange. Exuberance and pride are displayed by everyone associated with the sport, and the players are as much concerned with conveying the full meaning of who they are as with scoring runs. From the sensual dressing in preparation for the game to the team chanting songs full of sexual metaphors to the erotic dancing between the innings, it is clear that each participant is playing for his own importance, for the fame of his team, and for the hundreds who watch the playful spectacle.

Revitalization Movements

In contrast to cultural changes that are invited or initiated by peoples themselves, those that are imposed or experienced as disruptive may be resisted or rejected. Such a reaction may lead to a *reform* movement or take on a more extreme character as a *revitalization movement*. As noted in the chapter on religion and spirituality, such radical movements develop in response to widespread social disruption and collective feelings of anxiety and despair. They are often, but not always, religiously or spiritually based. Some revitalization movements take on an armed revolutionary character, as did the Taliban in Afghanistan. When primary ties of culture, social relationships, and activities are broken, and meaningless activity is imposed by outside forces, individuals and groups characteristically react by rejecting newly introduced cultural elements and reclaiming historical roots and traditional identity, along with a measure of spiritual imagination.

Anthropologists recognize a sequence common to the revitalization process. First is the normal state of society, in which stress is not too great, and sufficient cultural means exist to satisfy needs. Next comes a phase

accommodation In anthropology, refers to an adaptation process by which a people resists assimilation by modifying its traditional culture in response to pressures by a dominant society in order to preserve its distinctive ethnic identity.

Figure 15.6 **Syncretism: Trobriand Cricket** Indigenous peoples have reacted to colonialism in many different ways. When British missionaries pressed Trobriand Islanders of Melanesia to celebrate their regular yam harvests with a game of "civilized" cricket rather than traditional "wild" erotic dances, Trobrianders responded by transforming the staid British sport into an exuberant event that featured sexual chants and dances between innings. This is an example of syncretism—the creative blending of indigenous and foreign beliefs and practices into new cultural forms.

© Wolfgang Kaehler/Corbis

of cultural upheaval, triggered by foreign invasion, domination, and exploitation, leading to growing frustration and stress brought about by cultural upheaval. The third phase is marked by a deepening of the crisis in which normal means of resolving social and psychological tensions are inadequate or fail. The decline may trigger a radical response in the form of a collective effort to restore, or revitalize, the culture. During this phase, a prophet or some other spiritual leader inspired by supernatural visions or guidance attracts a following, leading to a cult sometimes spiraling into a religious movement (Wallace, 1970).

Cargo Cults

One particular historical example of a revitalization movement is the **cargo cult**—a spiritual movement (especially noted in Melanesia in the Southwest Pacific) in reaction to disruptive contact with Western capitalism; the cult promises resurrection of deceased relatives, destruction or enslavement of white foreigners, and the magical arrival of utopian riches.

Indigenous Melanesians referred to the white man's wealth as "cargo" (pidgin English for European trade goods transported by ships or airplanes). In times of great social stress, native prophets emerged, predicting that the time of suffering would come to an end and a new paradise on earth would soon arrive. Their deceased

ancestors would return to life, and the rich white man would magically disappear—swallowed by an earthquake or swept away by a huge wave. However, the valued Western trade goods would be left for the prophets and their cult followers, who performed rituals to hasten this supernatural redistribution of wealth (see Lindstrom, 1993; Worsley, 1957).

A Contemporary Indigenous Revitalization Movement: Qullasuyu

In contrast to Melanesia's cargo cults, which were intensive and passing, a revitalization movement may also gain political state support and change a society's cultural institutions. One example of this is now taking place in Bolivia. In this pluralistic South American country, most citizens are of indigenous descent and still speak an ancestral home language other than Spanish. The two most common are Aymara and Quechua, spoken by people inhabiting what was historically known as Qullasuyu, the southeastern district of Tawantinsuyu (*Quechua* means "union of four districts"), the indigenous name for the ancient Inca empire.

Following the December 2005 election of President Evo Morales, Bolivia's indigenous revitalization movement has enjoyed that country's government support. The son of an Aymara father and Quechua mother, this socialist head of state was previously a militant peasant leader representing masses of migrant farmers growing coca in the subtropical lowlands. Since the 1980s, he had risen to prominence as an agrarian trade union leader promoting indigenous farmers' rights. The day before his presidential inauguration in January 2006, his unique

---

cargo cult A spiritual movement (especially noted in Melanesia) in reaction to disruptive contact with Western capitalism, promising resurrection of deceased relatives, destruction or enslavement of white foreigners, and the magical arrival of utopian riches.

Figure 15.7 Celebrating Aymara New Year Aymara Indians mark the new year by participating in a sunrise ceremony at the sacred ruins of Tiwanaku near the shore of Lake Titicaca. Signifying the beginning of 5515 (on the Aymara calendar) at dawn in mid-June 2007, they celebrated the event at the northern solstice—an astronomical event when the sun reaches its lowest excursion relative to the equator on the celestial sphere. Their hands raised to catch the first morning rays, these Bolivians participate in a Qullasuyu revitalization movement that for many includes a return to precolonial indigenous beliefs and rituals, such as worship of the sun as the supreme reigning sky deity.

stance as the country's first indigenous president was publicly recognized at a special ceremony held at the famous archaeological site of Tiwanaku. Standing there, flanked by *amautas* ("spiritual leaders"), Morales was vested with the neotraditional indigenous royal title of *apu mallku* ("condor king") of Qullasuyu.

Situated between La Paz and Lake Titicaca, Tiwanaku is unequaled in cultural significance as the ceremonial center of Bolivia's indigenous revitalization movement. Long abandoned, its enormous temple complex with its large pyramid, Akapana, was the capital of an ancient civilization that endured for many centuries before mysteriously collapsing about a thousand years ago. Because its inhabitants left no written records, their language remains unknown, which means Aymara and Quechua peoples can share this archaeological site symbolically representing their proud cultural heritages. Vesting these ruins with political and spiritual meaning as a sacred monument, they feel inspired to reclaim indigenous autonomy and to reject the foreign culture imposed on them during almost 500 years of colonial domination and capitalist exploitation.

In 2007, pursuing his revitalization agenda, President Morales chose Tiwanaku for an official event celebrating the adoption of the United Nations Declaration for the Rights of Indigenous Peoples. Two years later, the seven-colored *wiphala* representing Qullasuyu became Bolivia's

official co-flag. It now flies alongside the country's long-established red, yellow, and green national banner (Van Cott, 2008; Yates, 2011).

After four years in office, doubling as *apu mallku* and president, Morales was reelected. Again, his 2010 indigenous head-of-state celebration was conducted on top of Tiwanaku's pyramid ruin mound, Akapana. As before, spiritual leaders in spectacular neotraditional dress stood at his side while multitudes of Aymara and Quechua watched with a spirit of admiration and celebration.

Beyond restoring, preserving, and protecting indigenous cultural sites, customs, and so on, the revitalization movement in Bolivia involves a reclamation of precolonial sacred rituals, such as the worship of indigenous earth and sky deities, in particular the sun and moon (**Figure 15.7**). Informed by an animistic worldview, the movement seeks to restore a more harmonious relationship among communities of humans, animals, and plants, as well as the rest of the natural environment—recognizing all as part of one large ecosystem, a living "Mother Earth," traditionally held sacred as Pachamama. Formalizing this, in 2010 Bolivia's Plurinational Legislative Assembly passed the *Ley de Derechos de la Madre Tierra* ("The Law of the Rights of Mother Earth"), granting all of nature equal rights to humans (Estado Plurinacional de Bolivia, 2010).

Rebellion and Revolution

As briefly noted with respect to the Taliban in Afghanistan, when the scale of discontent within a society reaches a critical level, the possibilities are high for a violent reaction such as a rebellion or **insurgency**—organized armed resistance by a group of rebels to an established government or authority in power. For instance, there have been many peasant insurgencies around the world in the course of history. Historically, such uprisings are triggered by repressive regimes that impose new taxes on already struggling small farmers unable to feed their families under such levels of exploitation (Wolf, 1999b).

One recent example is the Zapatista Maya Indian insurgency in southern Mexico, which began in the mid-1990s and has not yet been resolved. This uprising involves thousands of poor Indian farmers whose livelihoods have been threatened by disruptive changes imposed on them; their human rights under the Mexican constitution have never been fully implemented (**Figure 15.8**).

In contrast to insurgencies, which have rather limited objectives, a **revolution**—a radical change in a society or culture—involves a more dramatic transformation. Revolutions occur when the level of discontent in a society is very high. In the political arena, revolution involves the forced overthrow of the existing government and the establishment of a completely new one.

Such was the case when Muslim fundamentalists in Iran toppled the imperial regime of the shah in 1979 and replaced him with Ayatollah Khomeini, a high-ranking Shiite Muslim religious leader. Returning to his homeland from exile and becoming Iran's new leader, he instituted a new social and political order based on Islamic fundamentalist principles.

The question of why revolutions erupt, as well as why they frequently fail to live up to the expectations of the people initiating them, is uncertain. It is clear, however, that the colonial policies of countries such as Britain, France, Spain, Portugal, and the United States during the 19th and early 20th centuries have created a worldwide situation in which revolution is nearly inevitable. Despite the political independence most colonies have gained since World War II, powerful countries continue to exploit many of these "underdeveloped" countries for their natural resources and cheap labor, causing a deep resentment of rulers beholden to foreign

powers. Further discontent has been caused as governing elites in newly independent states try to assert their control over peoples living within their boundaries. By virtue of a common ancestry, possession of distinct cultures, persistent occupation of their own territories, and traditions of self-determination, the peoples they aim to control identify themselves as distinct nations and refuse to recognize the legitimacy of what they regard as a foreign government.

Thus, in many former colonies, large numbers of people have taken up arms to resist annexation and absorption by imposed state governments run by people of other nationalities. As they attempt to make their multi-ethnic states into unified countries, ruling elites of one nationality set about stripping the peoples of other nations within their states of their lands, resources, and particular cultural identities. The phenomenon is so common that Belgian sociologist Pierre van den Berghe has renamed what modern states refer to as "nation building" as, in fact, "nation killing" (Van den Berghe, 1992).

One of the most important facts of our time is that the vast majority of the distinct peoples of the world have never consented to rule by the governments of states within which they find themselves living (Nietschmann, 1987). In many newly emerging countries, such peoples feel they have no other option than to take up weapons in armed protest and fight.

Apart from rebellions against authoritarian regimes, such as in the Chinese, French, and Russian revolutions, many uprisings in modern times have been insurgencies against political rule imposed by foreign powers. Such resistance usually takes the form of national independence movements that wage campaigns of armed defiance against colonial or imperial dominance. The Mexican war of liberation against Spain in the early 1800s and the Algerian struggle for independence from France in the 1950s are relevant examples.

Of the hundreds of armed conflicts in the world today, almost all are in the economically poor countries of Africa, Asia, and Latin America, many of which were at one time under European colonial domination. Of these wars, the majority are between the state and one or more nations or ethnic groups within the state's borders. These groups are seeking to maintain or regain control of their personal lives, communities, lands, and resources in the face of what they regard as repression or subjugation by a foreign power.

Revolutions do not always accomplish what they set out to do. One of the stated goals of the 1949 Chinese communist revolution, for example, was to liberate women from the oppression of a strongly patriarchal society in which a woman owed lifelong obedience to a male relative—first her father, later her husband, and, after his death, her oldest son. Although changes were

---

insurgency An organized armed resistance or violent uprising to an established government or authority in power; also known as *rebellion*.
revolution Radical change in a society or culture. In the political arena, it involves the forced overthrow of the existing government and establishment of a completely new one.

Matias Recart/AFP/Getty Images

Figure 15.8 Zapatista Revolutionary Movement On New Year's Day 1994, when the North American Free Trade Agreement (NAFTA) went into effect, 3,000 armed peasants belonging to the Zapatista revolutionary movement invaded towns in southern Mexico. Mostly Maya Indians, they declared war on the Mexican government, claiming that globalization was destroying their rural communities. Strong Internet presence helped them build an international network of political support. Now committed to nonviolent resistance to Mexican state control, Zapatistas have created thirty-two self-governing municipalities and established their own local health, justice, and education services. These municipalities are grouped in five regional zones, called *caracoles* (conch shell), referring to Maya sacred cosmology as mythological upholders of the sky. The *caracoles* consist of various Maya ethnic groups—Cho'l, Mam, Tojolabal, Tzeltal, Tzotzil, and Zoque—each headed by a representative council.

and continue to be made, the transformation overall has been frustrated by the cultural lens through which the revolutionaries viewed their work. A tradition of deeply rooted patriarchy extending back at least 2,200 years is not easily overcome and has influenced many of the decisions made by communist China's leaders since the revolution.

Despite the current rapid changes taking place in China's expanding urban areas, in many rural parts of the country a woman's life is still largely determined by her relationship to a man—be it her father, husband, or son—rather than by her own efforts or failures. Moreover, many rural women face official local policies that identify their primary roles as wives and mothers. When they do work outside the house, it is generally at jobs with low pay, low status, and no benefits (**Figure 15.9**).

Women's no-wage home labor (and low-wage outside labor) for their husbands' households have been essential to China's economic expansion, which relies on the allocation of labor by the heads of patrilineal households (Liu, 2007).

In part due to China's one-child rule resulting in a shortage of marriage partners for men, rural women face the threat of being abducted for wives and workers. In 2000, after an outbreak of "bride-napping" during the previous decade, government authorities cracked down on the practice. Tens of thousands of women and girls were freed, but the practice continues ("Bartered brides," 2009; "China to execute bride traffickers," 2000; U.S. Department of State, 2007).

Facing obstacles that many rural Chinese women feel are insurmountable, more than 1 million of them

Figure 15.9 Rural Women Removing Chips From Computer Boards, Guiyu, China Since the late 1980s, e-waste from developed countries has been imported to China and broken down at Guiyu. The city comprises 21 villages with 5,500 family workshops handling e-waste and being exposed to carcinogens.

attempt suicide each year—typically by swallowing pesticides or fertilizer. Of these, 150,000 die. Rural China is the only place on earth where more women kill themselves than men (Pearson et al., 2002).

The situation of rural women in China shows that the undermining of revolutionary goals, if it occurs, is not necessarily by political opponents. Rather, it may be a consequence of the revolutionaries' own traditional cultural background. In rural China, that includes patrilineal exogamy, patrilocality, and a patriarchal conservatism in which female labor is controlled by male heads of families. As long as these traditional views continue to hold sway, women will be seen as commodities.

Revolution is a relatively recent phenomenon, occurring only during the past 5,000 years or so. The reason is that rebellion requires a centralized political authority to rebel against, and states did not exist before 5,000 years ago. In kin-ordered societies organized as tribes and bands, without a centralized government, there could be no rebellion or political revolution.

Modernization

One of the most frequently used terms to describe social and cultural changes as they are occurring today is **modernization**. This is most clearly defined as an all-encompassing and global process of political and socioeconomic change, whereby developing societies acquire some of the cultural characteristics common to Western industrial societies.

Derived from the Latin word *modo* ("just now"), modernization literally refers to something "in the present time." The dominant idea behind this concept is that "becoming modern" is becoming like European, North American, and other wealthy industrial or postindustrial societies, with the clear implication that not to do so is to be stuck in the past—backward, inferior, and needing to be improved. It is unfortunate that the term *modernization* continues to be so widely used, but because it is, we need to recognize its problematic one-sidedness, even as we continue to use it.

The process of modernization may be best understood as consisting of five subprocesses, all interrelated and with no fixed order of appearance:

- *Technological development*: In the course of modernization, traditional knowledge and techniques give way to the application of scientific knowledge and techniques borrowed mainly from the industrialized West.
- *Agricultural development*: This is represented by a shift in emphasis from subsistence farming to commercial farming. Instead of raising crops and livestock for their own use, people turn with growing frequency to the production of cash crops, with increased reliance on a cash economy and on global markets for selling farm products and purchasing goods.
- *Urbanization*: This subprocess is marked particularly by population movements from rural settlements into cities.

modernization The process of political and socioeconomic change, whereby developing societies acquire some of the cultural characteristics of Western industrial societies.

- *Industrialization*: Here human and animal power become less important, and greater emphasis is placed on material forms of energy—especially fossil fuels—to drive machines.
- *Telecommunication*: The fifth and most recent subprocess involves electronic and digital media processing and sharing of news, commodity prices, fashions, and entertainment, as well as political and religious opinions. Information is widely dispersed to a mass audience, far across national borders.

As modernization proceeds, other changes are likely to follow. In the political realm, political parties and some sort of electoral apparatus frequently appear, along with the development of an administrative bureaucracy. In formal education, institutional learning opportunities expand, literacy increases, and an indigenous educated elite develops. Many long-held rights and duties connected with kinship are altered, if not eliminated, especially when distant relatives are concerned. If social stratification is a factor, social mobility increases as ascribed status becomes less important and personal achievement counts for more.

Finally, as traditional beliefs and practices are undermined, formalized religion becomes less important in many areas of thought and behavior. As discussed in the chapter on religion, this may turn into a growing trend toward a nonreligious worldview with people ignoring or rejecting institutionalized spiritual beliefs and rituals. Known as *secularization*, this process is especially noteworthy in highly organized capitalist states like Germany, for many centuries predominantly Lutheran and Roman Catholic. Now, almost 40 percent of Germans identify themselves as nonreligious, an increase from less than 4 percent just forty years ago.

Secularization is also taking place in other western European countries, as well as in other parts of the world. However, in places in which the state is weak and unbridled capitalism has dramatically increased insecurity among the exploited and impoverished masses, the opposite may result, with a reactionary trend toward a more spiritual or even religious worldview. This phenomenon is evident in many eastern European, Asian, and African countries—discussed in the chapter on religion.

Indigenous Accommodation to Modernization

A closer examination of traditional cultures that have felt the impact of modernization will help to illustrate some of the problems such cultures have encountered. Earlier in this chapter, we noted that ethnic groups, unable to resist changes but unwilling to surrender their distinctive cultural heritage and identity, may pursue a strategy of accommodation. Many have done so, but with variable success. Here we offer two ethnographic examples: the Sámi people living in the Arctic and sub-Arctic tundra of northwest Russia and Scandinavia and the Shuar Indians of Ecuador.

Sámi Herders: The Snowmobile Revolution and Its Unintended Consequences

Until about half a century ago, Sámi reindeer herders in Scandinavia's Arctic tundra lived much like the Nenets featured in this chapter's opening photo. In the 1960s, however, they purchased snowmobiles, expecting motorized transportation to make herding physically easier and economically more advantageous. But that is not what happened.

Given the high cost of buying, maintaining, and fueling the machines, Sámi herders faced a sharp rise in their need for money. To obtain cash, men began going outside their communities for wage labor more than just occasionally, as had previously been the case. Moreover, once snowmobiles were introduced, the familiar, prolonged, and largely peaceful relationship between herder and beast changed into a noisy, traumatic one. The humans that reindeer encountered came speeding out of the woods on noisy, smelly machines that invariably chased the animals, often for long distances. Instead of helping the reindeer in their winter food quest, aiding does with their calves, and protecting the herd from predators, the men appeared only periodically, either to slaughter or to castrate the animals (**Figure 15.10**).

The reindeer became wary of people, resulting in de-domestication, with reindeer scattering and running off to less accessible areas. In addition, snowmobile harassment seemed to adversely affect birthing and the survival of calves. For example, within a decade the average size of the family herd among the Sámi in Finland had dropped from fifty to twelve—a number that is not economically viable. The financial cost of mechanized herding and the decline in domesticated herd size have led many Sámi to abandon herding altogether (Pelto, 1973). Today, only about 10 percent of Sámi in Finland are full-time herders, and they vie with outside economic institutions such as forestry and tourism for access to and use of land (Williams, 2003). Their situation is echoed among Sámi across Scandinavia (Wheelersburg, 1987).

hamburger, it has become emblematic of what is often perceived as the homogenization of the world's different cultures in the age of globalization, sometimes referred to as the "McDonaldization" of societies (Ritzer, 1983).

Yet, as we look at reactionary movements—including the rise of religious fundamentalism, nationalism, and ethnic identity politics around the world—the forecast of a single global culture appears unrealistic. If a single homogenous global culture is not in the making, what is?

Global Integration Processes

For more than a century now, integration processes have been pursued on a worldwide scale, albeit with mixed success. One of the first international organizations was the Red Cross, followed by the International Olympic Games (**Figure 16.3**). The need for global integration became all the more urgent in the wake of the Second World War, which ended with atomic bombs and resulted in the ruination

of hundreds of cities and the deaths of 55 million people. Recognizing the urgency of international cooperation, the world's most powerful states instituted the World Bank and the International Monetary Fund in 1944. To prevent perpetual war, they also formed the United Nations (UN) in 1945, soon followed by a number of global nongovernmental organizations (NGOs) such as the UN Education and Science Organization (UNESCO), World Health Organization (WHO), and later the World Trade Organization (WTO). Likewise, global humanitarian aid organizations formed, such as Amnesty International and Doctors Without Borders.

In addition, countries all around the world have developed mass tourism industries that connect people in other ways. Tourism is a $1.1 trillion industry in which an estimated 900 million international tourists travel per year. The industry generates over $3 billion in receipts daily.

Such global integration mechanisms connect people all around the world, and they play a constructive role in maintaining a world system. Notably, however, they do not produce a global transnational culture.

Figure 16.3 2012 Olympics, London, England The Olympics are unique among the many strands in today's global web. Inspired by the ancient Greek sporting event held at Olympia 2,000 years ago, the games have become a global spectacle, with thousands of athletes from all around the world competing in a different country every four years. In today's world—where powerful states have conquered and destroyed many smaller nations and tens of millions have been killed in warfare worldwide—this global sports gathering is a crucial ritual, celebrating international peace in a friendly rivalry for medals and prestige.

Pluralistic Societies and Multiculturalism

As described in the chapter on politics, ethnic groups or nations have organized as independent states for about 5,000 years. Many expanded—often by means of military conquest—and as republics, kingdoms, or empires engaged in nation-building projects, pressing subject or allied peoples into cultural assimilation. Other neighboring ethnic groups joined together, confederating into one political union or territorial state. In such *pluralistic societies*, each member group maintains its distinctive language and cultural heritage.

Today, there are a number of other forms of political integration among neighboring ethnic groups, such as the twenty-seven countries that collectively established the European Union. These countries achieved this unification despite the hindrances of linguistic differences, distinctive cultural traditions, bureaucratic red tape, and (most recently) a sovereign debt crisis.

One way of curbing divisive pressures inherent in pluralistic societies is to officially adopt a public policy of **multiculturalism** based on mutual respect and tolerance for cultural differences. In contrast to state policies of assimilation in which a dominant ethnic group uses its power to impose its own culture as the standard, policies of multiculturalism assert the value of different cultures coexisting within a country, stressing reciprocal responsibility of all citizens to accept the rights of others to freely express their views and values. An example of long-established multiculturalism may be seen in states such as Switzerland, where peoples speaking German, French, Italian, and Romansh coexist under the same government.

Cultural pluralism is more common than multiculturalism, but several multi-ethnic countries have recently changed their cultural assimilation policies. One example of a country moving toward multiculturalism is the United States, which now has over 120 different ethnic groups within its borders, in addition to hundreds of federally recognized American Indian groups. Another is Australia with over a hundred ethnic groups and eighty languages spoken within its territorial boundaries. Many European countries are seeing similar shifts, as millions of foreign immigrants have settled there during the past few decades.

Such changes are never easy and often spark protests. As a consequence of swings of majority opinion in the political electorate, some governments stop pursuing multiculturalism, focusing instead on cultural assimilation and social integration of immigrant minorities.

Pluralistic Societies and Fragmentation

Pluralistic societies, in virtually all parts of the world, show a tendency to fragment, usually along major linguistic, religious, or ethno-nationalist divisions. Because of this trend, some predict a world in which ethnic groups will become increasingly nationalistic rather than united in response to globalization, each group stressing its unique cultural heritage and emphasizing differences with neighboring groups. This *devolution* inclination is evident in numerous nationalist movements today—including separatist movements of the Scots in the United Kingdom (Britain), the Kurds in Turkey and Iraq, and the Karen in Myanmar (Burma). In the United States, indigenous nations, such as the Mohawk of Akwesasne, continue to seek greater political self-determination on their tribal territories.

When states with extensive territories lack adequate transportation and communication networks or major unifying cultural forces (such as a common religion or national language), it is more likely that separatist intentions will be realized. One recent example is the political breakup of the Soviet Union in 1991 into about a dozen independent republics—Russia, Armenia, Belarus, Estonia, Ukraine, Moldova, and Georgia, among others. A year after Moldova's independence, this pluralistic society fragmented even further when its border region, Transnistria, broke away and formed a sovereign republic with limited recognition. And in 2008, about seventeen years after Georgia gained its own independence as an internationally recognized state, this multi-ethnic republic diminished in size when two of its ethnically distinct regions, South Ossetia and Abkhazia, officially split after years of separatist pressure. More recently, in July 2011 Sudan in northeastern Africa officially split along an ethnic, religious, and geographic fault line, producing international recognition of the Republic of South Sudan as the 193rd member state of the United Nations.

Global Migrations: Refugees, Migrants, and Diasporic Communities

Throughout history, challenges such as famine, poverty, and violent threats by dangerous neighbors have forced people to move—often scattering members of an ethnic group. People also move for other reasons, including economic opportunity and political or religious freedom. Whether forced or free, **migration**—mobility in geographic space, involving temporary or permanent change in usual place of residence—has always had a significant effect on world social geography, contributing to cultural change and development, to the diffusion of ideas and innovations, and to the complex mixture of peoples and cultures found in the world today.

multiculturalism The public policy for managing cultural diversity in a multi-ethnic society, officially stressing mutual respect and tolerance for cultural differences within a country's borders.

migration Mobility in geographic space, involving temporary or permanent change in usual place of residence. Internal migration is movement within countries; external migration is movement to a foreign country.

Internal migration occurs when people move within the boundaries of their country, shifting their usual residence from one civil division to another. Typically, migrants leave their farms, villages, and small towns in the rural backlands and move to cities to find greater economic opportunity, escape from poverty and starvation, and possibly avoid armed conflict in their home region. *External migration* is movement from one country to another (**Figure 16.4**). Such migration may be voluntary (people seeking better conditions and opportunities abroad), but all too often it may be involuntary. People who are taken as slaves or prisoners, or who have been driven from their homelands by war, political unrest, religious persecution, or environmental disasters, are involuntary migrants.

Every year, a few million people migrate to wealthy countries in search of wage labor and a better future for themselves and their offspring. Although most cross international borders as legal immigrants, seeking work permits and ultimately citizenship in their new homeland, many migrants are illegal and do not enjoy crucial rights and benefits. Beyond the masses of migrants, nearly 45 million refugees can be found in almost half of the world's countries. Some 15 million refugees have been forced outside their countries, most of them suffering in

makeshift camps where they cannot make a living (UN Refugee Agency, 2011).

Migrants and refugees often face great challenges as poor newcomers in host societies—all the more so because they may encounter racism and discrimination. As a consequence, many newcomers form or join communities of people who have come from the same part of the world. Modern transportation and telecommunication technology make it possible for these *diasporic communities*, which exist all across the globe, to remain in contact with relatives and friends who have settled elsewhere, as well as with their country of origin. Indicative of this aspect of globalization is that today about 200 million people (almost 3 percent of the world's population) live outside their countries of birth—not as refugees or immigrants but as *transnationals* who earn their living in one country as they remain citizens of another.

Over the past few decades, mass migration across international borders has dramatically changed the ethnic composition of affluent societies in Australia, western Europe, and North America. For example, today, the number of foreign-born people residing in the United States far exceeds that of the 38 million native-born African Americans. Most of these immigrants come from Latin

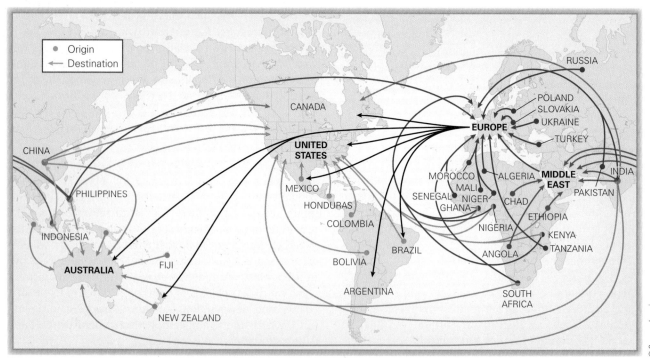

Figure 16.4 Migrating for Work In our globalized world, nearly 215 million people have moved across international borders for better income-earning opportunities. They include farm and meat plant laborers, cleaners, cab drivers, construction workers, servers in the tourism industry, as well as shopkeepers, nurses, doctors, engineers, and computer specialists. Not shown here is the international flow of 15 million refugees, over half from Asian and African countries. Unlike migrants who choose to move in hopes of improving their lives, refugees are forced to flee to save their lives or preserve their freedom.

America, including 13 million from Mexico alone. As the largest and fastest-growing group of immigrants in the United States, these immigrants are settled primarily in California and Texas, where many form Spanish-speaking ethnic enclaves.

In addition, the United States is now home to over 25 million immigrants from Asian countries (such as China and India) and sub-Saharan African countries (such as Nigeria and Ethiopia). Over the past three decades, the number of African immigrants self-identifying as "black" has rapidly increased from 65,000 to more than 1.1 million—and that figure continues to grow. Black immigrants from the Caribbean now number 1.7 million, but their rate of increase is slowing down. Collectively, these many millions of new immigrants contribute to the ever-changing multicultural fabric of U.S. society (Capps, McCabe, & Fix, 2012).

Meanwhile, on the other side of the Atlantic, millions of foreign migrants are radically changing European societies and cultures. For instance, almost 20 percent (about 12 million) of the people living in France today are foreign-born immigrants and their offspring, primarily originating from former colonial territories in West Africa and Southeast Asia. Islam is now the second-largest religion in France with about 6 million adherents. Likewise, England is now home to over 1.5 million South Asians, plus another 1.3 million people of African descent, also hailing predominantly from the former British colonies.

About 3.5 million people of Turkish origin now reside in western Germany, not counting a few million other foreign-born immigrants and their offspring. Initially needed as cheap unskilled laborers, Turks were hired as "guest workers" in highly industrialized urban areas. Because most of them remained, the authorities instituted a family reunification policy, which resulted in hundreds of thousands of Turkish relatives entering the country. Even after several decades in Germany, most German Turks do not possess citizenship and have not become culturally integrated into German society. Turkish, spoken by Germany's largest ethnic minority, has become that country's second language.

As a consequence of millions of foreign immigrants, Europe's native-born or *autochtonous* (from the Greek *auto*, "self," and *khton*, "soil") populations are currently wrestling with their national identities in a period of rapid change. With their concerns compounded by economic insecurity, social tensions are on the rise, and so are racism and xenophobia, directed especially against foreign-born Muslims who do not assimilate.

Although migrants frequently experience hostility, hardship, disappointment, and sometimes failure in their new countries, those who remain trapped in their troubled lands of origin often face worse challenges: malnutrition, hunger, chronic disease, and violence. By means of telecommunications technology, including the Internet and mobile phones, millions of foreign migrants today remain in touch with relatives and friends in their homeland communities, not only to gain news but also for emotional and financial support. Worldwide, electronic transfers to developing countries total some $351 billion per year (World Bank, 2012). Remittances, however, have declined due to the global recession, causing real hardship in the impoverished communities that have come to depend on the support.

Migrants and Xenophobia: Violent Conflict in Assam

Migrants moving to areas traditionally inhabited by other ethnic groups may run into hostile opposition, especially when they compete for scarce resources, pose a threat to security, or are otherwise unwelcome as newcomers. As such, they may be targeted for a hate-mongering campaign. Such **xenophobia**—fear or hatred of strangers or anything foreign—is especially inflammatory when social tensions rise in times of economic insecurity, challenging collective health and well-being. Under such circumstances, space for intercultural tolerance narrows; instead of blurring social boundaries, these divisions become more sharply defined, emphasizing ethnic differences over human commonalities.

This situation is evident when attitudes toward foreign laborers and recent immigrants grow so intensely negative that it does not take much to ignite brutal violence. In the summer of 2012, for example, xenophobia erupted into interethnic violence in Assam, northeast India, as the Bodos, an indigenous Buddhist mountain people, clashed with Bengali-speaking Muslim immigrants over scarce farmland. Within a few weeks, dozens of people from both sides had been killed, and many more were wounded. Nearly 400 settlements in disputed areas were abandoned, as about 400,000 Bengalis packed up what they could carry and fled. This population is now dispersed in 270 refugee camps (**Figure 16.5**).

Migrants, Urbanization, and Slums

Most migrants are poor and begin their new lives in expanding urban areas. During the past fifty years, the world's urban population has more than tripled. Today, for the first time in world history, a majority of our species now resides in urban areas—over 3.5 billion people. Just two centuries ago, at the start of the industrial revolution, only about 3 percent of the world's population lived in cities.

Until 1950, the largest city in the world was London. Although briefly overtaken by New York, the current urban frontrunner has long been Tokyo, now counting 37 million inhabitants. Cities have not only grown in size but also in number. Today, there are almost 500 cities with populations exceeding 1 million. Of these more than

xenophobia Fear or hatred of strangers or anything foreign.

Figure 16.5 Migrants on the Run Bengali Muslims—newcomers to villages in India's northeast state of Assam—leave their homes following ethnic clashes with the indigenous Bodos in which many people were killed and dozens of homes were burned to the ground. Government troops sent to quell communal clashes over land rights were ordered to shoot suspected rioters on sight.

twenty-five are megacities, each with populations over 10 million. Urban areas are gaining about 67 million people per year—about 1.3 million every week. As the global population grows, the number of big cities will increase substantially, with the majority located in coastal areas of developing countries.

Historically, cities grow primarily as a result of migration by masses of people escaping rural poverty or seeking economic opportunity. Many of these migrants have little or no education, lack technical skills, and have little or nothing to offer other than selling their labor power. Girls and young women, in particular, may be forced into sexual labor as prostitutes, risking their health, safety, and general well-being. Their expectations crushed by harsh reality, and far away from their home regions, migrants often find themselves condemned to a life in squalor in crowded shanty towns or slums, with limited access to clean water, waste disposal, and electricity.

One of the main concentrations of urban poor on the planet today can be found in Lagos, Nigeria's commercial capital and Africa's largest city. In just four decades, its population has exploded from less than 1.4 million in 1970 to perhaps 21 million today. Unable to manage the enormous influx of migrants and their offspring, the city now features huge overcrowded slums where two-thirds of the city's inhabitants reside.

Lagos is not unique: Unplanned, makeshift, urban squatter settlements are burgeoning around the globe. For instance, about half of the 11 million inhabitants of Manila, capital of the Philippines, now live in slums (**Figure 16.6**).

Worldwide, about 1 billion people currently reside in slums, and the number is rapidly growing. They face similar challenges as they struggle to survive in places of urban squalor variously known as *villas miserias, ghettos, barrios, favelas, bidons, chalis, kampungs, aashwa'i,* or *mabanda*. About 60 percent of these slum-dwellers live in Asia, 20 percent in Africa, 13 percent in Latin America and the Caribbean, and only 6 percent in Europe. Remarkably, in sub-Saharan Africa, 72 percent of the urban population lives in slums—a higher proportion than anywhere else in the world (Birch & Wachter, 2011; United Nations Human Settlements Program, 2003).

Figure 16.6 Slum in Manila Half of the inhabitants of Manila, the capital of the Philippines, live in slums such as this.

Structural Power in the Age of Globalization

How did our species manage to construct such a world—so interconnected and so unfairly arranged between millions of have-lots and billions of have-nots? A simple question, but difficult to answer. Part of the explanation, most scholars will agree, lies in a new form of expansive international capitalism as it emerged since the mid-1900s. Operating under the banner of globalization, it builds on earlier cultural structures of worldwide trade networks, and it is the successor to a system of colonialism in which a handful of powerful, mainly European, capitalist states ruled and exploited foreign nations inhabiting distant territories.

Enormously complex and turbulent, globalization is a dynamically structured process in which individuals, business corporations, and political institutions actively rearrange and restructure the political field to their own competitive advantage, vying for increasingly scarce natural resources, cheap labor, new commercial markets, and ever-larger profits. This restructuring occurs in a vast arena spanning the entire globe. Doing this requires a great deal of power.

As discussed in the chapter on politics, *power* refers to the ability of individuals or groups to impose their will upon others and make them do things even against their own wants or wishes. Power plays a major role in coordinating and regulating the collective behavior toward law and order within and beyond a particular community or society.

There are different levels of power within societies, as well as among societies. Anthropologist Eric Wolf pointed out the importance of understanding a macro level of power that he referred to as **structural power**—power that organizes and orchestrates the systemic interaction within and among societies, directing economic and political forces on the one hand and ideological forces that shape public ideas, values, and beliefs on the other (Wolf, 1999a). The concept of structural power applies not only to regional political organizations such as chiefdoms or states, but also captures the complex new cultural formations currently restructuring and transfiguring societies and environments everywhere on earth.

Joseph Nye—a Harvard University political scientist and former assistant secretary of defense in the U.S. government—refers to these two major interacting forces in the worldwide arena as "hard power" and "soft power" (Nye, 2002).

structural power Power that organizes and orchestrates the systemic interaction within and among societies, directing economic and political forces on the one hand and ideological forces that shape public ideas, values, and beliefs on the other.

Figure 16.7 Global Military Spending by Country In 2011, world military spending reached $1.55 trillion, with the United States accounting for more than 44 percent of the total. (Expenditures are rounded to the nearest billion.)

Source: Stockholm International Peace Research Institute, 2012.

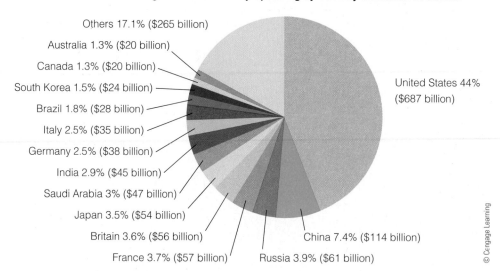

Percentage of Global Military Spending by Country in *Billions* of Dollars

Others 17.1% ($265 billion)
Australia 1.3% ($20 billion)
Canada 1.3% ($20 billion)
South Korea 1.5% ($24 billion)
Brazil 1.8% ($28 billion)
Italy 2.5% ($35 billion)
Germany 2.5% ($38 billion)
India 2.9% ($45 billion)
Saudi Arabia 3% ($47 billion)
Japan 3.5% ($54 billion)
Britain 3.6% ($56 billion)
France 3.7% ($57 billion)
United States 44% ($687 billion)
China 7.4% ($114 billion)
Russia 3.9% ($61 billion)

© Cengage Learning

Hard power is the kind of coercive power that is backed up by economic and military force. **Soft power** coopts rather than coerces, pressing others through attraction and persuasion to change their ideas, beliefs, values, and behaviors. Propaganda is a form of soft power, although the exercise of ideological influence (the global struggle for hearts and minds) also operates through more subtle means, such as foreign aid, international diplomacy, news media, sports, entertainment, museum exhibits, and academic exchanges.

Military Hard Power

Today, the United States has more hard power at its disposal than any of its allies or rivals worldwide. It is the global leader in military expenditure, spending $687 billion in 2011, followed by China ($114 billion). As the world's still dominant superpower, the United States is responsible for about 44 percent of the $1.55 trillion spent on arms worldwide (**Figure 16.7**).

Moreover, although there are seven other states with nuclear-weapon capability (Britain, France, and China, as well as Israel, India, Pakistan, and North Korea, collectively possessing about 900 active nuclear warheads), Russia and the United States have by far the largest nuclear arsenals at their disposal. Russia has about 4,500 operational warheads, plus several thousand nonoperational warheads. The United States possesses about 5,100 warheads and 3,500 that are retired and awaiting dismantlement (Arms Control Association, 2012).

In addition to military might, hard power involves using economic strength as a political instrument of coercion or intimidation in the global structuring process. Among other things, this means that economic size and

productivity, technological capability, and finance capital may be brought to bear on the global market, forcing less powerful states to weaken the systems protecting their workers, natural resources, and local markets.

As the world's largest economy and leading exporter, the United States has long pushed for free trade for its corporations doing business on a global scale. Sometimes it uses military power to impose changes on a foreign political landscape by means of armed interventions or full-scale invasions.

In the past century, the world's wealthiest and most powerful countries—including the United States, Germany, Russia, China, Japan, Britain, and France—have engaged in such belligerence. For this reason, many others view these heavily armed behemoths with suspicion, even as potential threats, apt to use overwhelming military force in order to benefit their own interests, from fruit to fuel, microchips to automobiles, and phones to satellites.

Home to more global corporations than any other country, the United States endeavors to protect its interests by investing in what it refers to as a "global security environment." However, through maneuvering toward this strategic objective, the nuclear-armed superpower often confronts opposition from (potentially) hostile rivals such as Russia and China, contesting its ambitions for worldwide supremacy. Moreover, numerous other countries, unable to afford expensive weapons systems or blocked from developing or acquiring them, have invested in biological or chemical weaponry. Still others, including relatively powerless political groups, have resorted to insurgencies, guerrilla tactics, or terrorism.

Economic Hard Power

Global corporations, rare before the latter half of the 20th century, now are a far-reaching economic and political force in the world. Modern-day business giants such as Shell, Toyota, and General Electric are actually clusters of several corporations joined by ties of common ownership and responsive to a common management strategy. Usually tightly controlled by a head office in one country, megacorporations organize

hard power Power that coerces others and that is backed up by economic and military force.

soft power Power that coopts rather than coerces, pressing others through attraction and persuasion to change their ideas, beliefs, values, and behaviors.

and integrate production across the international boundaries of different countries for interests formulated in corporate boardrooms, regardless of whether these are consistent with the interests of people in the countries in which they operate. Megacorporations are the products of the technological revolution, for without mass transportation, sophisticated data processing equipment, and telecommunication they could not conduct or manage their transnational capitalist operations.

Although typically thought of as responding impersonally to outside market forces, megacorporations are in fact controlled by an ever-shrinking number of wealthy capitalists who benefit directly from their operations. Unlike political leaders, the world's largest individual stockholders and most powerful corporate directors are virtually unknown to the general public. For that matter,

most people cannot even name the world's ten leading global corporations, which include Walmart, Shell, and Toyota. Each of the top ten business giants currently generates annual revenues well over $200 billion, and three of them top the $400 billion mark (**Figure 16.8**).

So great is the power of large businesses operating all across the globe that they increasingly thwart the wishes of national governments or international organizations such as the United Nations, Red Cross, and the International Court of Justice. Because megacorporations restrict information about their operations, it can be difficult for governments to make informed policy decisions. It took years for the U.S. Congress to extract information from tobacco companies so that it could make decisions about tobacco legislation, and it is nearly as slow-going today getting energy and media companies to provide data needed for regulatory purposes.

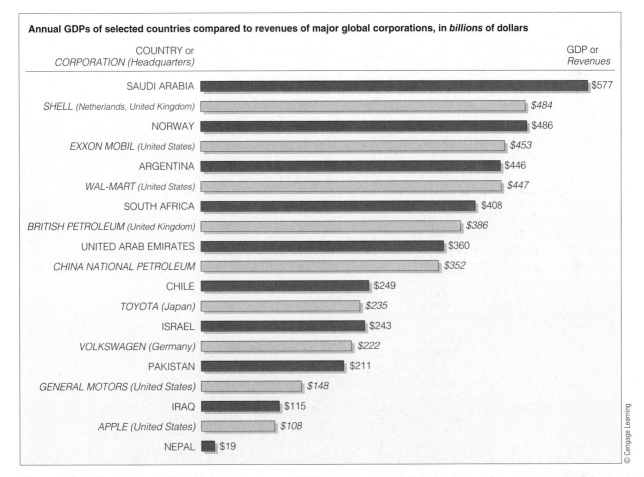

Annual GDPs of selected countries compared to revenues of major global corporations, in *billions* of dollars

COUNTRY or CORPORATION (Headquarters) / GDP or Revenues

- SAUDI ARABIA — $577
- SHELL (Netherlands, United Kingdom) — $484
- NORWAY — $486
- EXXON MOBIL (United States) — $453
- ARGENTINA — $446
- WAL-MART (United States) — $447
- SOUTH AFRICA — $408
- BRITISH PETROLEUM (United Kingdom) — $386
- UNITED ARAB EMIRATES — $360
- CHINA NATIONAL PETROLEUM — $352
- CHILE — $249
- TOYOTA (Japan) — $235
- ISRAEL — $243
- VOLKSWAGEN (Germany) — $222
- PAKISTAN — $211
- GENERAL MOTORS (United States) — $148
- IRAQ — $115
- APPLE (United States) — $108
- NEPAL — $19

© Cengage Learning

Figure 16.8 GDPs of Selected Countries and Revenues of Global Corporations In today's consumer-driven world, it is not uncommon for the yearly revenues of large multinational corporations to equal and even exceed the total value of all goods and services produced within many countries per year, known as a country's gross domestic product (GDP). This graph shows the annual GDPs of selected countries alongside the annual revenues of leading global corporations. Notably, revenues of each of the top three corporations exceeded the GDPs of 171 of the world's 195 countries. Not shown here are the countries with the highest and lowest GDPs. Half have GDPs below $30 billion, a third below $10 billion, and about a quarter below $5 billion. Only 15 countries surpass $1 trillion, including the United States at just over $15 trillion, with China in second place at about $7 trillion. Note that GDP says nothing about the unequal distribution of wealth within a country.

Source: Based on the Global 500 list of corporate revenues and the World Development Indicators database, 2012.

Beyond this information problem, global corporations have repeatedly shown they can overrule foreign policy decisions. Although some might see this as a hopeful trend for getting beyond ethnocentric motivations, it raises the unsettling issue of whether the global arena should be controlled by immense powerful private corporations interested only in financial profits. According to a recent study that diagrammed the interrelationships of more than 43,000 corporations, 147 companies control nearly 40 percent of the monetary value of all transnational corporations. Of the top fifty of these companies, most are involved in banking, financial services, and insurance (Ehrenberg, 2011; Vitali, Glattfelder, & Battiston, 2011).

Global corporations are changing the shape of the world and the lives of individuals everywhere, including those they employ. In the never-ending search for cheap labor, these megacorporations have returned to a practice once common in the textile mills of 19th-century Britain and New England but now on a much larger scale. More than ever before, they have come to favor women for low-skilled assembly jobs. In so-called underdeveloped countries, as subsistence farming gives way to mechanized agriculture for production of crops for export, women are less able to contribute to their families' survival. Along with the devaluation of domestic work, this pressures women to seek jobs outside the household to contribute to its support. Because most women in these countries do not have the time or resources to get an education or to develop special job skills, only low-paying jobs are open to them.

Faceless relations between producers and consumers, which are characterized by a grossly unequal distribution of power, have exacted a high cost: a terrible sense of indifference, apathy, even a loss of faith in the dehumanized system itself. When workers do not trust their bosses and bosses do not trust one another, production and trade relations on every level are damaged. This alienation may ultimately lead to a systemic breakdown (Blacksmith & Harter, 2011; Gurchiek, 2012).

With production, trading, and banking operations on a global scale, the breakdown in one part of the system may trigger a worldwide chain reaction of failures. This is what occurred with the global financial crisis in 2008, sparked by the bankruptcy of a handful of mismanaged Wall Street firms—a crisis with worldwide ramifications not yet resolved (Ribeiro, 2009).

Globalization does more than create a worldwide arena in which megacorporations reap megaprofits. It also wreaks havoc in many traditional cultures, destroying their natural habitats and disrupting their long-established social organization. Consider, for example, how international investors have turned to precious metals like gold and silver in response to current financial crises and economic uncertainty. In recent years, a sharply growing international demand for silver bullion sent prices skyrocketing from an average of $4.60 per ounce in 2002 to over $35.00 per ounce in 2011—the highest price in over two decades.

Capitalizing on this trend, the U.S.-based General Minerals Corporation (GMC) bought the rights to the Mallku Khota concession in Bolivia in 2003. One of the world's largest undeveloped silver and indium deposits, this concession in the Andean highlands is named after the local Quechua Indian peasant community. In 2004, GMC began exploring the area under its Bolivian subsidiary, Compañía Minera Mallku Khota (CMMK).

In 2006, the same year political activist and leftist leader Evo Morales became the first indigenous person to be elected president of Bolivia, GMC formed the South American Silver Corporation (SAC). Based in Vancouver, Canada, SAC took over CMMK and began operating in Mallku Khota. Exploration showed that the area contains

Figure 16.9 Indigenous Protest Against Global Mining Company In the summer of 2012, members of indigenous communities from Bolivia's Mallku Khota region traveled nearly 300 kilometers to the capital city of La Paz for a political demonstration. Their protest concerned foreign mining operations on their lands. Several Quechua activists were killed during the protest.

AP Images/Juan Karita

over 370 million ounces of silver (plus some 1,600 tons of indium and more than 2,000 tons of gallium), with an estimated (after-tax) net value of $1.54 billion. Expecting to produce more than 13 million ounces of silver per year, as well as 80 tons of indium and 15 tons of gallium, the corporation projected a 15-year mine-life.

Plans began to unravel when Mallku Khota began protesting that the company would ruin their land. After local Quechua activists took five miners hostage, clashes with police followed, and several Quechua were killed during a protest demonstration in La Paz in the summer of 2012 (**Figure 16.9**). A few weeks later, before actual mining operations had started, Bolivia's government expropriated the Mallku Khota project.

Now that the concession has been nationalized, the state-owned mining company may seek an Asian investment partner, several of which are already active in Bolivia (but are based on China, Japan, and South Korea). Will the Bolivian government make sure its indigenous population reaps some benefits from this company developed on their lands? Or will this be another example of the global trend of economic inequality in which the poor become poorer and the rich richer?

Soft Power: A Global Media Environment

In addition to reliance on military and economic hard power in the global quest for dominance and profit, competing states and corporations utilize the ideological persuasion of soft power as transmitted through electronic and digital media, communication satellites, and other information technology. One of the major tasks of soft power is to sell the general idea of globalization as something positive and progressive (as "freedom," "free trade," "free market") and to frame or brand anything that opposes capitalism in negative terms.

Global mass media corporations like Cable News Network (CNN) possess enormous soft power. This U.S.-based private company produces and distributes news and other information through transnational cable and satellite networks, as well as websites. With bureaus in over thirty countries, its twenty-four-hour news coverage is available to more than 1.5 billion people all over the world. Like other media giants, such as BBC and Al Jazeera, CNN not only reports news but also selects the visual imagery and determines what to stress or repress. By means of their tremendous soft power, these corporations influence public perception and action ("hearts and minds").

The far-reaching capabilities of modern electronic and digital technologies have led to the creation of a global media environment that plays a major role in how individuals and even societies view themselves and their place in the world. Together with radio and television, the Internet is now the dominant means of mass communication around the world. The global flow of information made possible by fiber-optic cables, cell towers, and communication satellites orbiting the earth is almost entirely digital-electronic, taking place in a new boundless cultural space that has been called a "global mediascape"(Appadurai, 1990).

In recent years, the power of corporations has become all the greater through media expansion. Over the past two decades, a global commercial media system has developed, dominated by a few megacorporations (such as General Electric, Time Warner, and Disney), most based in the United States. Control of television, Internet, and other media, as well as the advertising industry, gives global corporations enormous influence on the ideas and behavior of hundreds of millions of ordinary people across the world (**Figure 16.10**).

Social Media: Parties with Cookies

Social media, spawned by the Internet, is used for multiple purposes—from popular entertainment to political action. Among countless examples is the *flash mob* in which individuals, responding to a signal, briefly come together at a designated spot in a public space for a joint performance and then disperse.

Figure 16.10 Global Branding The poorest people in the world often wear clothing discarded by those who are better off—and people from all walks of life can be found wearing clothes with corporate logos, as demonstrated by this Maká Indian woman in Paraguay. The power wielded by big business (such as the Disney media corporation) is illustrated by the fact that corporations influence consumers to pay for clothing and countless other goods that advertise corporate products.

© Harald E. L. Prins

Overpopulation

In 1750, 1 billion people lived on earth. Over the next two centuries our numbers climbed to nearly 2.5 billion. And between 1950 and 2000, the world population soared above 6 billion. Today, the world's population is over 7 billion, with one-third of our species residing in just two countries: China and India. Such staggering increases are highly significant because population growth increases the scale of hunger and pollution—and the many troubles tied to them. Although controlling population growth does not eliminate the other difficulties, we are unlikely to be able to solve them unless population growth is stopped or even reversed.

Despite progress in population control, the number of humans on earth continues to grow overall. Projections are extremely tricky, given variables such as war, famine, and infectious diseases, but current estimates suggest that global population will surge to 9 billion by 2050 (Kaiser, 2011). The severity of the situation becomes clear with the realization that the present world population can be sustained only by using up nonrenewable resources such as oil.

Hunger, Obesity, and Malnutrition

As frequently dramatized in media reports, hundreds of millions of people face hunger on a regular basis, leading to a variety of health problems, premature death, and other forms of suffering. Today, over a quarter of the world's countries do not produce enough food to feed their populations, and they cannot afford to import what is needed.

Hunger is caused not only by drought and pests, but also by violent ethnic, religious, or political conflicts that displace families. During the 20th century, 44 million people died due to human-made famine (The Hunger Project, 2011; White, 2001). For example, in several sub-Saharan African countries plagued by chronic civil strife, it has been almost impossible to raise and harvest crops because hordes of hungry refugees, roaming militias, and underpaid soldiers constantly raid the fields (**Figure 16.11**).

Beyond violent political, ethnic, or religious conflicts that uproot families from their traditional food sources,

Figure 16.11 World's Largest Refugee Camp In Somalia, Africa, extended drought and years of civil war have caused chronic famine and chased huge numbers of people out of the country. Nearly 500,000 are stuck in this vast camp in Dadaab, Kenya, near the Somalia border. It was established in 1991 to provide food and shelter for up to 90,000 refugees fleeing the war, but two decades of ongoing conflict and natural disasters in Somalia have generated a continuous flow of Somalis into the camp. Housing more than five times the number for which it was originally built, the camp is jammed and resources are inadequate. Moreover, situated on a flood plain, it is inaccessible for extended periods during the rainy season, making the delivery of life-saving food, water, and health care unreliable.

famine is fueled by a global food production and distribution system geared to satisfy the demands of the world's most powerful countries. For example, in Africa, Asia, and Latin America, millions of acres once devoted to subsistence farming have been given over to the raising of cash crops for export. This has enriched members of elite social classes in these parts of the world, while satisfying the appetites of people in developed countries for coffee, tea, chocolate, bananas, and beef. Small-scale farmers who used to till the land for their own food needs have been relocated—either to urban areas, where all too often there is no employment for them, or to areas ecologically unsuited for farming.

Also of note, governments of the wealthiest capitalist states in North America and western Europe spend between $100 billion and $300 billion annually on agricultural subsidies given primarily to large farmers and agricultural corporations. Small farmers in poor countries cannot compete with subsidized agribusinesses that are selling mass-produced and often genetically engineered crops. Many small farmers have been forced to quit farming, leave their villages, and seek work in cities or as migrant workers abroad.

Today, about 1 billion people in the world experience chronic hunger. A majority (almost 650 million) of these people live in Asia and the Pacific islands. Next comes sub-Saharan Africa with about 265 million, followed by the Middle East and North Africa with 53 million, and another 15 million in the world's wealthy countries (Food and Agriculture Organization of the United Nations, 2009). Of particular note, every year famine claims the lives of some 6 million children ages 5 and under, and those who survive it often suffer physical and mental impairment (The Hunger Project, 2011; Swaminathan, 2000).

Most of the world's hungry are victims of structural violence. This is because the increasing rate of starvation is due not only to environmental calamities, but to human actions ranging from warfare to massive job cuts, growing poverty rates, and the collapse of local markets caused by foreign imports.

Ironically, although many millions are starving in some parts of the world, many millions of others are overeating—literally eating themselves to death. In fact, the number of overfed people now exceeds those who are underfed. According to the World Watch Institute in Washington, DC, more than 1.1 billion people worldwide are now overweight. Over 350 million of these are obese, but still often malnourished in that their diets lack certain nutrients. Evaluating the mortality risk associated with obesity, health-care workers use a body mass index (BMI), indicating human body fat based on a person's weight and height. A BMI of 18.5 to 25 indicates optimal weight, whereas moderately obese individuals measure between 30 and 35, severely obese from 35 to 40, and morbidly obese even higher than that.

Seriously concerned about the sharp rise in associated health problems (including stroke, diabetes, cancer, and heart disease), the World Health Organization classifies obesity as a global epidemic. Overeating is particularly unhealthy for individuals living in societies where machines have eased the physical burdens of work and other human activities, which helps explain why more than half of the people in some industrial and post-industrial countries are overweight.

However, the obesity epidemic is not due solely to excessive eating and lack of physical activity. A key ingredient is the high sugar and fat content of mass-marketed foods. Thus, in Japan, where food habits differ significantly from those in the United States, obesity plagues just over 3 percent of the population, compared to the U.S. rate of 36 percent among adults and 17 percent among those ages 2 to 19. In fact, U.S. obesity figures have doubled over the past three decades, placing it at the top of the obesity chart among wealthy industrialized countries. Obesity rates differ between men and women, higher and lower income groups, and various ethnic groups. The highest U.S. rate is among African American women, half of whom suffer from obesity. Due to the high rates of childhood obesity, current U.S. youth are the first generation not expected to outlive their parents (Centers for Disease Control and Prevention, 2012).

The problem has become a serious concern even in some developing countries, especially where people have switched to a diet based on processed or canned fast food. The highest rates of obesity in the world can now be found among island nations in the Pacific Ocean, such as Nauru, Fiji, Samoa, and Tonga. Nauru, formerly known as Pleasant Island, tops the list.

Traditionally, Nauruans valued food as a symbol of well-being and social pride, considered fat to be a sign of beauty, and associated large body size with strength and prosperity (Pollock, 1995). In the days when Nauruans still depended largely on fishing and gathering for most of their food, obesity was not a medical problem. So, what happened?

Only 21 square kilometers (8 square miles) in size, Nauru is composed of sedimentary rock that contains vast deposits of phosphates—raw material used to make fertilizer. In the early 1900s, foreign companies descended upon this lush tropical island and over the next six decades mined more than 34 million tons of rock. Most of it was shipped to Australia, where it was processed and used to enrich vast stretches of farmland. Nauru, stripped of fertile soil and vegetation, became a cratered wasteland (Nazzal-Batayneh, 2005).

Compensating the indigenous inhabitants for the destruction of their small paradise, mining companies provided families with royalties. With cash in hand, and increasingly less access to traditional foods such as coconut, pandanus fruit, and fish, islanders purchased imported processed foods high in sugar and fat. Today, phosphate wealth has disappeared, but the junk food diet remains, and 80 percent of the indigenous population of this small island republic in Micronesia has become obese; almost half of Nauruans ages 55 to 64 now have diabetes, and large numbers are ill and dying from diseases once rare among Pacific Islanders (**Figure 16.12**).

Pollution and Global Warming

Pollution is another key aspect of structural violence brought on by the world's most powerful countries, which are also the greatest producers and consumers of energy. During the past 200 years, global cultural development has relied on burning increasing quantities of fossil fuels (coal, oil, and gas), with dire results: Massive deforestation and desertification, along with severe air, water, and soil pollution, now threaten all life on earth.

In addition, fossil fuel use has dramatically increased carbon dioxide levels, trapping more heat in the earth's atmosphere. Most atmospheric scientists believe that the efficiency of the atmosphere in retaining heat—the greenhouse effect—is being enhanced by increased carbon dioxide, methane, and other gases produced by industrial and agricultural activities. The result, global warming, threatens to dramatically alter climates in all parts of the world.

Rising temperatures are causing more and greater storms, droughts, and heat waves, devastating populations in vulnerable areas. And if the massive meltdown of Arctic ice continues, rising sea levels will inundate low coastal

Figure 16.12 Structural Violence and Obesity On the South Pacific island of Nauru, the world's smallest independent republic, about 80 percent of the 14,000 inhabitants are now classified as obese. Averaging 35 BMI, this island nation in Micronesia also has the world's highest rate of diabetes. Their small tropical paradise stripped bare by phosphate mining companies, these indigenous peoples have become dependent on junk food. Many are now ill and dying from diseases historically uncommon among Oceanic peoples.

areas worldwide. Entire islands may soon disappear, including thousands of villages and even large cities. Experts also predict that global warming will lead to an expansion of the geographic ranges of tropical diseases and increase the incidence of respiratory illnesses due to additional smog caused by warmer temperatures. Also, they expect an increase in deaths due to heat waves, as witnessed in Europe (70,000 deaths in 2003) and Russia (55,000 deaths in 2010) (Parry, 2011).

Especially since the industrial revolution about two centuries ago, societies have experienced the negative effects of environmental degradation. Much of this ruin is caused by ever-increasing amounts of non-biodegradable waste and toxic emissions into the soil, water, and air. Until very recently, this pollution was officially tolerated for the sake of maximizing profits that primarily benefit select individuals, groups, and societies. Today, industries in many parts of the world are producing highly toxic waste at unprecedented rates. Pollutants such as various oxides of nitrogen or sulfur cause the development of acid precipitation, which damages soil, vegetation, and wildlife. Air pollution in the form of smog is often dangerous for human health.

Moreover, poisonous smokestack gases are clearly implicated in acid rain, which is damaging lakes and forests all over northeastern North America. Air containing water vapor with a high acid content is, of course, harmful to the lungs, but there is a greater health hazard involved. As groundwater and surface water become more acidic, the solubility of lead, cadmium, mercury, and aluminum, all of them toxic, rises sharply. For instance, for 17 percent of the world's farmland, the aluminum contamination is high enough to be toxic to plants—and has been linked to senile dementia, Alzheimer's, and Parkinson's disease, three major health problems in industrial countries.

Finding their way into the world's oceans, toxic substances also create hazards for seafood consumers. For instance, Canadian Inuit face health problems related to eating fish and sea mammals that feed in waters contaminated by industrial chemical waste such as polychlorinated biphenyls (PCBs) (see the Biocultural Connection). Also of great concern are harmful chemicals in plastics used for water bottles, baby bottles, and can linings. Environmental poisoning affects peoples all across the globe.

Structural violence also manifests itself in the shifting of manufacturing and hazardous waste disposal from developed to developing countries. In the late 1980s, a tightening of environmental regulations in industrialized countries led to a dramatic rise in the cost of hazardous waste disposal. Seeking cheaper ways to get rid of the wastes, "toxic traders" began shipping hazardous waste to eastern Europe and especially to poor and underdeveloped countries in western Africa—thereby passing on the health risks of poisonous cargo to the world's poorest people (see the Globalscape).

Toxic Breast Milk Threatens Arctic Culture

Asked to picture the Inuit people inhabiting the Arctic coasts of Canada, Greenland, and Labrador, you are likely to envision them dressed in fur parkas and moving across a pristine, snow-covered landscape on dogsleds—perhaps coming home from hunting seal, walrus, or whale.

Such imaginings are still true—except for the pristine part. Although Inuit live nearer to the North Pole than to any city, factory, or farm, they are not isolated from the pollutants of modern society. Chemicals originating in the cities and farms of North America, Europe, and Asia travel thousands of miles to Inuit territories via winds, rivers, and ocean currents. These toxins have a long life in the Arctic, breaking down very slowly due to icy temperatures and low sunlight. Ingested by zooplankton, the chemicals spread through the seafood chain as one species consumes another. The result is alarming levels of pesticides, mercury, and industrial chemicals in Arctic animals—and in the Inuit people who rely on fishing and hunting for food.

Of particular note are toxic chemicals known as PCBs (polychlorinated biphenyls), used widely over several decades for numerous purposes, such as industrial lubricants, insulating materials, and paint stabilizers. Research shows a widespread presence of PCBs in the breast milk of women around the globe. But nowhere on earth is the concentration higher than among the Inuit—on average seven times that of nursing mothers in Canada's biggest cities.[a]

PCBs have been linked to a wide range of health problems—from liver damage to weakened immune systems to cancer. Studies of children exposed to PCBs in the womb and through breast milk show impaired learning and memory functions.

Beyond having a destructive impact on the health of humans (and other animal species), PCBs are impacting the economy, social organization, and psychological well-being of Arctic peoples. Nowhere is this truer than among the 450 Inuit living on Broughton Island, near Canada's Baffin Island. Here, word of skyrocketing PCB levels cost the community its valuable market for Arctic char fish. Other Inuits refer to them as "PCB people," and it is said that Inuit men now avoid marrying women from the island.[b]

Inuit people, who have no real alternatives for affordable food, soundly reject the suggestion that the answer to these problems is a change of diet. Abandoning the consumption of traditional seafood would destroy a 4,000-year-old culture based on hunting and fishing. Countless aspects of traditional Inuit culture—from worldview and social arrangements to vocabularies and myths—are linked to Arctic animals and the skills it takes to rely on them for food and so many other things. As one Inuit put it: "Our foods do more than nourish our bodies. They feed our souls. When I eat Inuit foods, I know who I am."[c]

The manufacture of PCBs is now banned in many Western countries (including the United States), and PCB levels are gradually declining worldwide. However, because of their persistence (and widespread presence in remnant industrial goods such as fluorescent lighting fixtures and electrical appliances), they are still the highest-concentration toxins in breast milk, even among mothers born after the ban.

Furthermore, even as PCBs decline, other commercial chemicals are finding their way northward. To date, about 200 hazardous compounds originating in industrialized regions have been detected in the bodies of Arctic peoples.[d] Global warming is fueling the problem, because as glaciers and snow melt, long-stored toxins are released.

BIOCULTURAL QUESTION

Because corporations are able to profit from large-scale and long-distance commercial activities, we should not be surprised that their operations may also cause serious damage to fellow humans in remote natural environments. What do you think of the profiteering of structural violence?

[a]Colborn, T., Dumanoski, D., & Myers, J. P. (1997). *Our stolen future* (pp. 107–108). New York: Plume/Penguin.

[b]Arctic Monitoring Assessment Project (AMAP). (2003). *AMAP assessment 2002: Human health in the Arctic* (pp. xii–xiii, 22–23). Oslo: AMAP.

[c]Ingmar Egede, quoted in Cone, M. (2005). *Silent snow: The slow poisoning of the Arctic* (p. 1). New York: Grove.

[d]Additional sources: Johansen, B. E. (2002). The Inuit's struggle with dioxins and other organic pollutants. *American Indian Quarterly* 26 (3), 479–490; Natural Resources Defense Council. (2005, March 25). Healthy milk, healthy baby: Chemical pollution and mother's milk. www.NRDC.org; Williams, F. (2005, January 9). Toxic breast milk? *New York Times Magazine*.

Can this Inuit woman trust her breast milk?

© B & C Alexander/Photo Researchers, Inc.

ANTHROPOLOGIST OF NOTE

Paul Farmer (b. 1959)

Medical anthropologist Paul Farmer with patients in Haiti.

Medical anthropologist **Paul Farmer**—doctor, Harvard professor, world-renowned infectious disease specialist, and recipient of a MacArthur "genius" grant—grew up in a trailer park in Florida without running water.[a] Admitted to Duke University on scholarship, he majored in anthropology and labored alongside poor Haitian farmworkers in North Carolina's tobacco fields. After getting his BA in 1982, he spent a year in Haiti and found his life's calling: to diagnose and cure infectious diseases and transform health care on a global scale by focusing on the world's poorest communities. Returning to the United States, Farmer earned both an MD and a PhD in anthropology from Harvard in 1990.

While still a graduate student, Farmer returned frequently to Haiti and became increasingly involved in health issues in the area of Cange, a remote village in the destitute Central Plateau region. There, he formed a group called Zanmi Lasante (Haitian Kreyol for "Partners in Health"). A handful of other American activists joined him in the endeavor, including his fellow anthropologist and Harvard Medical School friend, Jim Yong Kim, who became president of the World Bank three decades later.

In 1985, the Zanmi Lasante group established a clinic with financial support from a Boston philanthropist. Two years later they founded the Boston-based Partners in Health (PIH) foundation to support their growing endeavor to help the poorest of the poor deal with infectious diseases, especially AIDS and tuberculosis.

The endeavor includes research (ethnographic as well as medical) needed to carry the work forward with a clear vision. As an applied anthropologist aiming to ease human suffering, Farmer bases his activism on holistic and interpretive ethnographic analysis that includes "a historical understanding of the large-scale social and economic structures in which affliction is embedded."[b] Issues of structural violence are fundamental in his research and practice. Noting that social and economic inequalities "have powerfully sculpted not only the [demographic] distribution of infectious diseases but also the course of health outcomes among the afflicted," he concludes, "inequality itself constitutes our modern plague."[c]

Since its founding, Zanmi Lasante has expanded its one-room clinic to a multiservice health complex that includes a primary school, an infirmary, a surgery wing, a training program for health outreach workers, a 104-bed hospital, a women's clinic, and a pediatric care facility. Moreover, it has pioneered the treatment of multidrug-resistant tuberculosis and HIV in Haiti. Partners in Health, now funded by a wide range of organizations, has expanded its reach to include Lesotho, Malawi, and Rwanda in Africa, as well as Peru, Mexico, Russia, and the United States. The foundation's reach continues to grow, fueled by Farmer's passionate conviction that health is a human right.

In concert with his active and extensive work with PIH around the globe, Farmer is a professor of medical anthropology in Harvard University's Department of Social Medicine. He also maintains an active practice in infectious diseases and is chief of the Division of Social Medicine and Health Inequalities at Brigham and Women's Hospital in Boston. Among numerous honors, he has received the Margaret Mead Award from the American Anthropological Association and is the subject of the Pulitzer Prize–winning book by Tracy Kidder (see footnote below).

---

[a]This profile draws from numerous sources, including: Kidder, T. (2003). *Mountains beyond mountains: The quest of Dr. Paul Farmer, a man who would cure the world.* New York: Random House.

[b]Farmer, P. (2004, June). An anthropology of structural violence. *Current Anthropology 45,* 3, 305–325; see also Farmer, P. (1996). On suffering and structural violence: A view from below. *Daedalus 125* (1), 261–283.

[c]Farmer, P. (2001). *Infections and inequalities: The modern plagues* (p. 15). Berkeley: University of California Press.

Mark Rosenberg 8-2001

did or did not change. Moreover, they try to identify the particular knowledge and insights that each culture holds concerning the human condition—including contrasting views about the place of human beings in the world, how natural resources are used and treated, and how one relates to fellow humans and other species.

Anthropologists are trained to understand and explain economic, social, political, ideological, biological, and environmental features and processes as parts of interrelated dynamic systems. Theoretical concepts, such as structural power and structural violence, reveal the complex and significant interconnections between remote and seemingly unrelated factors and processes.

A holistic and integrative perspective, as developed and tested by several generations of anthropologists in the course of more than a century of cross-cultural research in all parts of the world, has become essential to our understanding of such troubling problems as ethnocide, overpopulation, poverty, food shortages, environmental destruction, and disease in the age of globalization. The value of this perspective has been confirmed by international organizations that now employ anthropologists for their professional insights. For example, after a series of ill-conceived and mismanaged development projects that harmed more than helped local populations, the World Bank contracted dozens of anthropologists for projects all around the world. In fact, Jim Yong Kim, a Korean American physician with a doctorate in anthropology, now heads this powerful global institution. Other international organizations—as well as some global corporations, news media, and state government and intelligence agencies—also employ anthropologists.

There have always been anthropologists who reach beyond studying different cultures to assist besieged groups struggling to survive in today's rapidly changing world. In so doing, they put into practice their own knowledge about humankind—knowledge deepened through the comparative perspective of anthropology, which is cross-culturally, historically, and biologically informed. Counted among these applied anthropologists are Ann Dunham, profiled earlier in this chapter, and Paul Farmer, a world-renowned medical doctor, anthropologist, and human rights activist (see the Anthropologist of Note).

An interdisciplinary profession straddling the arts, sciences, and humanities, anthropology has a remarkable record of contributing important knowledge about our own species and all its stunning complexity and amazing variety. Anthropology's distinct holistic approach has helped to solve practical problems on local and global levels—and continues to do so today. More relevant than ever, it offers vital insight toward a cross-cultural understanding of globalization and its highly diverse local impact.

Most of the unique individuals drawn to this discipline are inspired by the old but still valid idea that anthropology must aim to live up to its longstanding ideal as the most liberating of the sciences. As stated by the famous anthropologist Margaret Mead, "Never doubt that a small group of committed people can change the world; indeed it is the only thing that ever has."

CHAPTER CHECKLIST

What does our world look like today?

● Since the industrial revolution began 200 years ago, modern technology has radically increased production, transportation, and communication worldwide, and the human population has grown to more than 7 billion—half living and working in urban areas.

● With the launching of the first telecommunication satellites in the mid-1950s, followed by the Internet in the 1960s, personal computers in the 1970s, and the World Wide Web in the 1990s, the digital revolution has accelerated the globalization process. Using social media, a few billion humans weave in and out of cyberspace on a daily basis.

● The growing interconnectedness of our species is evident in the global flow of humans, their products, and their ideas—made possible by modern mass transportation and telecommunications media. This has resulted in many external similarities across cultures, spawning speculation that humanity's future will feature a single homogenous global culture. This is sometimes referred to as the "McDonaldization" of societies.

● Beyond fashion, food, film, and other cultural overlaps, global integrative processes include the Olympic Games, the United Nations, the World Health Organization, as well as humanitarian aid organizations such as the Red Cross and Amnesty International.

● Anthropologists are skeptical that a global culture or political system is emerging; comparative historical and cross-cultural research shows the persistence of distinctive worldviews and the tendency of large multi-ethnic states to come apart.

What are pluralistic societies and multiculturalism?

● In pluralistic societies two or more ethnic groups or nationalities are politically organized into one territorial state. Ethnic tension is common in such states and sometimes turns violent, which can lead to formal separation.

● To manage cultural diversity within such societies, some countries have adopted multiculturalism, which is an official public policy of mutual respect and tolerance for cultural differences.

● An example of long-established multiculturalism may be seen in states such as Switzerland, where people speaking German, French, Italian, and Romansh coexist under the same government.

Is fragmentation common in pluralistic societies?

● Pluralistic societies, in virtually all parts of the world, show a tendency to fragment, usually along major linguistic, religious, or ethno-nationalist divisions.

● Especially when state territories are extensive and lack adequate transportation and communication networks, as well as major unifying cultural forces such as a common religion or national language, separatist intentions may be realized.

● Throughout history, challenges such as famine, poverty, and violent threats by dangerous neighbors have forced people to move—often scattering members of an ethnic group.

● Migration—voluntary or involuntary—is mobility in geographic space, involving temporary or permanent change in usual place of residence. It may be internal (within the boundaries of one's country) or external (from one country to another).

● Every year several million people migrate to wealthy countries in search of wage labor and a better future. In addition 45 million refugees can be found in almost half of the world's countries.

● Migrants moving to areas traditionally inhabited by other ethnic groups may face xenophobia—fear or hatred of strangers.

● Most migrants begin their new lives in expanding urban areas. Today, 1 billion people live in slums.

What is structural power?

● *Structural power* refers to the global forces that direct economic and political institutions and shape public ideas and values. It comes in two forms: hard power, which is coercive and is backed up by economic and military force, and soft power, which coopts through ideological persuasion.

● The most powerful country in the world today remains the United States, home to more global corporations than any other state. Responsible for 44 percent of the world's $1.55 trillion military expenditures, it engages in military interventions around the world to defend or benefit its corporate interests.

● Cutting across international boundaries, global corporations are a powerful force for worldwide integration despite the political, linguistic, religious, and other cultural differences that separate people. Their power and wealth often exceeds that of national governments.

● Major players in the globalization process, these megacorporations influence the ideas and behavior of people worldwide. In pursuit of wealth and power, states and corporations now compete for increasingly scarce natural resources, cheap labor, new commercial markets, and ever-larger profits in a huge political arena spanning the entire globe.

● Competing states and corporations utilize the ideological persuasion of soft power (as transmitted through electronic and digital media, communication satellites, and other information technology) to sell the general idea of globalization as something positive and to frame or brand anything that opposes capitalism in negative terms.

● The far-reaching capabilities of modern communication technologies have led to the creation of a new global media environment that plays a major role in how individuals and even societies view themselves and their place in the world.

● Although providing megaprofits for large corporations, globalization often wreaks havoc in many traditional cultures and disrupts long-established social organization. This engenders worldwide resistance against superpower domination—and with that an emerging world system that is inherently unstable, vulnerable, and unpredictable.

How has the globalization of structural power led to an increase in structural violence?

● One result of globalization is the expansion and intensification of structural violence—physical and/or psychological harm (including repression, cultural and environmental destruction, poverty, hunger and obesity, illness, and premature death) caused by impersonal, exploitative, and unjust social, political, and economic systems.

● Structural violence is a systemic violation of the human rights of individuals and communities to a healthy, peaceful, and dignified life as defined by the Universal Declaration of Human Rights adopted by members of the United Nations in 1948.

● Reactions against the structural violence of globalization include the rise of traditionalism and revitalization movements—efforts to return to life as it was (or how people think it was) before the familiar order became unhinged and people became unsettled. These may take the form of resurgent ethno-nationalism or religious fundamentalist movements.

How might anthropological know-how help counter structural violence?

● Some dramatic changes in cultural values and motivations, as well as in social institutions and the types of technologies we employ, are required if humans are going to realize a sustainable future for generations to come. The shortsighted emphasis on consumerism and individual self-interest characteristic of the world's affluent countries needs to be abandoned in favor of a more balanced social and environmental ethic.

● Anthropologists have a contribution to make in bringing about this shift. They are well versed in the dangers of culture-bound thinking, and they bring a holistic biocultural and comparative historical perspective to the challenge of understanding and balancing the needs and desires of local communities in the age of globalization.

● Inspired by human rights ideals, there have always been "applied" anthropologists who reach beyond studying different cultures to assist besieged groups struggling to survive in today's rapidly changing world.

QUESTIONS FOR REFLECTION

1. Since the launching of the first satellites into orbit and the start of the Internet, the telecommunications revolution has changed how humans interact, entertain, work, and even make and maintain friendships. Can you imagine a world in which cyberspace is militarized and social media are suppressed and dismantled? How would you and your friends adjust to that new reality?

2. Reflecting on the human condition past and present, and the challenges facing your own family in the age of globalization, do you imagine the future in terms of continued progress? How do you measure that, and by which cultural standard?

3. Considering the relationship between structural power and structural violence, does your own lifestyle—in terms of buying clothes and food, driving cars, and so on—reflect or have an effect on the globalization process?

4. In the global mediascape, television viewers and Internet users are not only consumers of news and entertainment but are also exposed to soft power. Can you think of an example of soft power in your daily life? And at which point does such influence turn into propaganda or manipulation?

5. When you hear or read about Muslim religious fundamentalists in western Asia or northern Africa strongly defending their traditional beliefs and practices, or even aggressively rejecting modern changes imported from the United States or Europe, do you recognize similar reactionary movements in your own country? What fuels such reactions?

ONLINE STUDY RESOURCES

CourseMate

Access chapter-specific learning tools, including learning objectives, practice quizzes, videos, flash cards, glossaries, and more in your Anthropology CourseMate.

Log into **www.cengagebrain.com** to access the resources your instructor has assigned and to purchase materials.

Glossary

accommodation In anthropology, refers to an adaptation process by which a people resists assimilation by modifying its traditional culture in response to pressures by a dominant society in order to preserve its distinctive ethnic identity.

acculturation The massive cultural change that occurs in a society when it experiences intensive firsthand contact with a more powerful society.

adaptation A series of beneficial adjustments of organisms to their environment.

advocacy anthropology Research that is community based and politically involved.

affinal kin People related through marriage.

age grade An organized category of people based on age; every individual passes through a series of such categories over his or her lifetime.

age set A formally established group of people born during a certain time span who move together through the series of age-grade categories; sometimes called *age class*.

agriculture Intensive crop cultivation, employing plows, fertilizers, and/or irrigation.

alphabet A series of symbols representing the sounds of a language arranged in a traditional order.

ambilocal residence A residence pattern in which a married couple may choose either matrilocal or patrilocal residence.

animatism The belief that nature is enlivened or energized by an impersonal spiritual force or supernatural energy, which may make itself manifest in any special place, thing, or living creature.

animism The belief that nature is enlivened or energized by distinct personalized spirit beings separable from bodies.

anthropology The study of humankind in all times and places.

applied anthropology The use of anthropological knowledge and methods to solve practical problems, often for a specific client.

archaeology The study of cultures through the recovery and analysis of material remains and environmental data.

archaic admixture model Theoretical model of human evolution that modern *Homo sapiens* derive from limited interbreeding between anatomically modern humans, as evolved in Africa, and members of archaic human populations. Based on genetic evidence of introgression, it is a synthesis of the recent African origins hypothesis and the multiregional hypothesis.

art The creative use of the human imagination to aesthetically interpret, express, and engage life, modifying experienced reality in the process.

assimilation Cultural absorption of an ethnic minority by a dominant society.

Australopithecus The genus including several species of early bipeds from Africa living between about 1 and 4.2 million years ago, one of whom was directly ancestral to humans.

authority Claiming and exercising power as justified by law or custom of tradition.

balanced reciprocity A mode of exchange in which the giving and the receiving are specific as to the value of the goods or services and the time of their delivery.

band A relatively small and loosely organized kin-ordered group that inhabits a specific territory and that may split periodically into smaller extended family groups that are politically and economically independent.

bilateral descent Descent traced equally through father and mother's ancestors; associating each individual with blood relatives on both sides of the family.

bioarchaeology The archaeological study of human remains—bones, skulls, teeth, and sometimes hair, dried skin, or other tissue—to determine the influences of culture and environment on human biological variation.

biocultural An approach that focuses on the interaction of biology and culture.

biological anthropology The systematic study of humans as biological organisms; also known as *physical anthropology*.

bipedalism "Two-footed"—walking upright on both hind legs—a characteristic of humans and their ancestors.

bride-price The money or valuable goods paid by the groom or his family to the bride's family upon marriage; also called *bridewealth*.

bride service A designated period of time when the groom works for the bride's family.

bridewealth The money or valuable goods paid by the groom or his family to the bride's family upon marriage; also called *bride-price*.

cargo cult A spiritual movement (especially noted in Melanesia) in reaction to disruptive contact with Western capitalism, promising resurrection of deceased relatives, destruction or enslavement of white foreigners, and the magical arrival of utopian riches.

carrying capacity The number of people that the available resources can support at a given level of food-getting techniques.

cartography The craft of making maps of remote regions.

caste A closed social class in a stratified society in which membership is determined by birth and fixed for life.

chiefdom A politically organized society in which several neighboring communities inhabiting a territory are united under a single ruler.

civil disobedience Refusal to obey civil laws in an effort to induce change in governmental policy or legislation, characterized by the use of passive resistance or other nonviolent means.

clan An extended unilineal kin-group, often consisting of several lineages, whose members claim common descent from a remote ancestor, usually legendary or mythological.

code switching The practice of changing from one mode of speech to another as the situation demands, whether from one language to another or from one dialect of a language to another.

coercion Imposition of obedience or submission by force or intimidation.

co-marriage A marriage form in which several men and women have sexual access to one another; also called *group marriage*.

common-interest association An association that results from the act of joining, based on sharing particular activities, objectives, values, or beliefs, sometimes rooted in common ethnic, religious, or regional background.

conjugal family A family established through marriage.

consanguineal family A family of blood relatives, consisting of related women, their brothers, and the women's offspring.

consanguineal kin Biologically related relatives, commonly referred to as blood relatives.

conspicuous consumption A showy display of wealth for social prestige.

contagious magic Magic based on the principle that things or persons once in contact can influence each other after the contact is broken.

convergent evolution In cultural evolution, the development of similar cultural adaptations to similar environmental conditions by different peoples with different ancestral cultures.

core values Those values especially promoted by a particular culture.

cross cousin The child of a mother's brother or a father's sister.

cultural adaptation A complex of ideas, technologies, and activities that enables people to survive and even thrive in their environment.

cultural anthropology The study of patterns in human behavior, thought, and emotions, focusing on humans as culture-producing and culture-reproducing creatures. Also known as *social* or *sociocultural anthropology.*

cultural control Control through beliefs and values deeply internalized in the minds of individuals.

cultural evolution Cultural change over time—not to be confused with progress.

cultural loss The abandonment of an existing practice or trait.

cultural relativism The idea that one must suspend judgment of other people's practices in order to understand them in their own cultural terms.

cultural resource management A branch of archaeology concerned with survey and/or excavation of archaeological and historical remains that might be threatened by construction or development; also involved with policy surrounding protection of cultural resources.

culture A society's shared and socially transmitted ideas, values, emotions, and perceptions, which are used to make sense of experience and generate behavior and are reflected in that behavior.

culture area A geographic region in which a number of societies follow similar patterns of life.

culture-bound A perspective that produces theories about the world and reality that are based on the assumptions and values from the researcher's own culture.

culture-bound syndrome A mental disorder specific to a particular ethnic group; also known as *ethnic psychosis.*

culture shock In fieldwork, the anthropologist's personal disorientation and anxiety that may result in depression.

Denisovans A recently discovered archaic human sister group of Neandertals in eastern Eurasia, dating to about 30,000 to 200,000 years ago.

dependence training Childrearing practices that foster compliance in the performance of assigned tasks and dependence on the domestic group, rather than reliance on oneself.

desecration Ideologically inspired violation of a sacred site intended to inflict harm, if only symbolically, on people judged to have impure, false, or even evil beliefs and ritual practices.

descent group Any kin-group whose members share a direct line of descent from a real (historical) or fictional common ancestor.

dialects The varying forms of a language that reflect particular regions, occupations, or social classes and that are similar enough to be mutually intelligible.

diffusion The spread of certain ideas, customs, or practices from one culture to another.

digital ethnography An ethnographic study of social networks, communicative practices, and other cultural expressions in cyberspace by means of digital visual and audio technologies; also called *cyberethnography* or *netnography.*

displacement Referring to things and events removed in time and space.

divination A magical procedure or spiritual ritual designed to discern what is not knowable by ordinary means, such as foretelling the future by interpreting omens.

DNA (deoxyribonucleic acid) The store of genetic information used in the development and functioning of all living organisms, including our own species.

dowry A payment at the time of a woman's marriage that comes from her inheritance, made to either her or her husband.

economic system An organized arrangement for producing, distributing, and consuming goods.

ecosystem A system, or a functioning whole, composed of both the natural environment and all the organisms living within it.

egalitarian societies Societies in which people have about the same rank and share equally in the basic resources that support income, status, and power.

EGO In kinship studies, the central person from whom the degree of each kinship relationship is traced.

eliciting devices Activities and objects used to draw out individuals and encourage them to recall and share information.

empirical Research based on observations of the world rather than on intuition or faith.

enculturation The process by which a society's culture is passed on from one generation to the next and individuals become members of their society.

endogamy Marriage within a particular group or category of individuals.

epic A long, dramatic narrative, recounting the celebrated deeds of a historic or legendary hero, often sung or recited in poetic language.

Eskimo system Kinship reckoning in which the nuclear family is emphasized by specifically identifying the mother, father, brother, and sister, while lumping together all other relatives into broad categories such as uncle, aunt, and cousin; also known as a *lineal system.*

ethnic group People who collectively and publicly identify themselves as a distinct group based on shared cultural features such as common origin, language, customs, and traditional beliefs.

ethnicity This term, rooted in the Greek word *ethnikos* ("nation") and related to *ethnos* ("custom"), is the expression for the set of cultural ideas held by an ethnic group.

ethnic psychosis A mental disorder specific to a particular ethnic group; also known as *culture-bound syndrome.*

ethnocentrism The belief that the ways of one's own culture are the only proper ones.

ethnocide The violent eradication of an ethnic group's collective cultural identity as a distinctive people; occurs when a dominant society deliberately sets out to destroy another society's cultural heritage.

ethnographic fieldwork Extended on-location research to gather detailed and in-depth information on a society's customary ideas, values, and practices through participation in its collective social life.

ethnography A detailed description of a particular culture primarily based on fieldwork.

ethnolinguistics A branch of linguistics that studies the relationships between language and culture and how they mutually influence and inform each other.

ethnology The study and analysis of different cultures from a comparative or historical point of view, utilizing ethnographic accounts and developing anthropological theories that help explain why certain important differences or similarities occur among groups.

ethnomusicology The study of a society's music in terms of its cultural setting.

Eve hypothesis An evolutionary hypothesis that modern humans are all derived from one single population of archaic *Homo sapiens* who migrated out of Africa after 100,000 years ago, replacing all other archaic forms due to their superior cultural capabilities; also known as the *recent African origins hypothesis* or the *out of Africa hypothesis.*

evolution Changes in the genetic makeup of a population over generations.

exogamy Marriage outside the group.

extended family Two or more closely related nuclear families clustered together into a large domestic group.

family Two or more people related by blood, marriage, or adoption. The family may take many forms, ranging from a single parent with one or more children, to a married couple or polygamous spouses with or without offspring, to several generations of parents and their children.

fictive marriage A marriage form in which a proxy is used as a symbol of someone not physically present to establish the social status of a spouse and heirs.

fieldwork The term anthropologists use for on-location research.

fission In kinship studies, the splitting of a descent group into two or more new descent groups.

folklore A term coined by 19th-century scholars studying the unwritten stories and other artistic traditions of rural peoples to distinguish between "folk art" and the "fine art" of the literate elite.

food foraging A mode of subsistence involving some combination of hunting, fishing, and gathering of wild plant foods.

forensic anthropology The identification of human skeletal remains for legal purposes.

formal interview A structured question/answer session, carefully notated as it occurs and based on prepared questions.

gender The cultural elaborations and meanings assigned to the biological differentiation between the sexes.

gendered speech Distinct male and female speech patterns that vary across social and cultural settings.

gene flow The movement of the genes from one population to another.

generalized reciprocity A mode of exchange in which the value of the gift is not calculated, nor is the time of repayment specified.

genes The basic physical units of heredity that specify the biological traits and characteristics of each organism.

genetic drift Chance fluctuations of allele (gene variant) frequencies in the gene pool of a population.

genocide The physical extermination of one people by another, either as a deliberate act or as the accidental outcome of activities carried out by one people with little regard for their impact on others.

genome The genetic design of a species with its complete set of DNA.

gestures Facial expressions and body postures and motions that convey intended as well as subconscious messages.

globalization Worldwide interconnectedness, evidenced in rapid global movement of natural resources, trade goods, human labor, finance capital, information, and infectious diseases.

grammar The entire formal structure of a language, including morphology and syntax.

group marriage A marriage form in which several men and women have sexual access to one another; also called *co-marriage*.

hard power Power that coerces others and that is backed up by economic or military force.

Hawaiian system Kinship reckoning in which all relatives of the same sex and generation are referred to by the same term; also known as the *generational system*.

historical archaeology The archaeological study of places for which written records exist.

holistic perspective A fundamental principle of anthropology: The various parts of human culture and biology must be viewed in the broadest possible context in order to understand their interconnections and interdependence.

hominoid The broad-shouldered tailless group of primates that includes all living and extinct apes and humans.

Homo erectus "Upright human." A species within the genus *Homo* first appearing just after 2 million years ago in Africa and ultimately spreading throughout the Old World.

Homo habilis "Handy human." The earliest members of the genus *Homo* appearing about 2.5 million years ago, with larger brains and smaller faces than australopithecines.

horticulture The cultivation of crops in food gardens, carried out with simple hand tools such as digging sticks and hoes.

household A domestic unit of one or more persons living in one residence. Other than family members, a household may include nonrelatives, such as servants.

Human Relations Area Files (HRAF) A vast collection of cross-indexed ethnographic, biocultural, and archaeological data catalogued by cultural characteristics and geographic location; archived in about 300 libraries on microfiche and/or online.

hypothesis A tentative explanation of the relationships between certain phenomena.

idealist perspective A theoretical approach stressing the primacy of superstructure in cultural research and analysis.

imitative magic Magic based on the principle that like produces like; sometimes called *sympathetic magic*.

incest taboo The prohibition of sexual relations between closely related individuals.

incorporation In a rite of passage, reincorporation of a temporarily removed individual into society in his or her new status.

independence training Childrearing practices that promote independence, self-reliance, and personal achievement.

industrial food production Large-scale businesses involved in mass food production, processing, and marketing, which primarily rely on labor-saving machines.

industrial society A society in which human labor, hand tools, and animal power are largely replaced by machines, with an economy primarily based on big factories.

informal economy A network of producing and circulating marketable commodities, labor, and services that for various reasons escape government control.

informal interview An unstructured, open-ended conversation in everyday life.

informed consent A formal recorded agreement between the subject and the researcher to participate in the research.

infrastructure The economic foundation of a society, including its subsistence practices and the tools and other material equipment used to make a living.

insurgency An organized armed resistance or violent uprising to an established government or authority in power; also known as *rebellion*.

intersexuals People born with reproductive organs, genitalia, and/or sex chromosomes that are not exclusively male or female.

irrigation theory The theory that explains civilization's emergence as the result of the construction of elaborate irrigation systems, the functioning of which required full-time managers whose control blossomed into the first governing body and elite social class; also known as *hydraulic theory*.

Iroquois system Kinship reckoning in which a father and a father's brother are referred to by a single term, as are a mother and mother's sister, but a father's sister and mother's brother are given separate terms. Parallel cousins are classified with brothers and sisters, while cross cousins are classified separately but not equated with relatives of some other generation.

key consultant A member of the society being studied who provides information that helps researchers understand the meaning of what they observe. Early anthropologists referred to such individuals as *informants*.

kindred A grouping of blood relatives based on bilateral descent. Includes all relatives with whom EGO shares at least one grandparent, great-grandparent, or even great-great-grandparent on his or her father's *and* mother's side.

kinesics The study of nonverbal signals in body language including facial expressions and bodily postures and motions.

kinship A network of relatives into which individuals are born and married, and with whom they cooperate based on customarily prescribed rights and obligations.

Kula ring A mode of balanced reciprocity that reinforces trade and social relations among the seafaring Melanesians who inhabit a large ring of islands in the southwestern Pacific Ocean.

language A system of communication using sounds, gestures, or marks that are put together according to certain rules, resulting in meanings that are intelligible to all who share that language.

language family A group of languages descended from a single ancestral language.

law Formal rules of conduct that, when violated, effectuate negative sanctions.

legend A story about a memorable event or figure handed down by tradition and told as true but without historical evidence.

legitimacy In politics, the right of political leaders to govern—to hold, use, and allocate power—based on the values a particular society embraces.

leveling mechanism A cultural obligation compelling prosperous members of a community to give away goods, host public feasts, provide free service, or otherwise demonstrate generosity so that no one permanently accumulates significantly more wealth than anyone else.

lineage A unilineal kin-group descended from a common ancestor or founder who lived four to six generations ago, and in which relationships among members can be exactly stated in genealogical terms.

linguistic anthropology The study of human languages—looking at their structure, history, and relation to social and cultural contexts.

linguistic divergence The development of different languages from a single ancestral language.

linguistic nationalism The attempt by ethnic minorities and even countries to proclaim independence by purging their language of foreign terms.

linguistic relativity The theoretical concept directly linking language and culture, holding that the words and grammar of a language affect how its speakers perceive and think about the world.

linguistics The modern scientific study of all aspects of language.

Lower Paleolithic The first part of the Old Stone Age, spanning from about 200,000 to 2.6 million years ago.

magic Specific formulas and actions used to compel supernatural powers to act in certain ways for good or evil purposes.

market exchange The buying and selling of goods and services, with prices set by rules of supply and demand.

marriage A culturally sanctioned union between two or more people that establishes certain rights and obligations between the people, between them and their children, and between them and their in-laws. Such marriage rights and obligations most often include, but are not limited to, sex, labor, property, childrearing, exchange, and status.

material culture The durable aspects of culture such as tools, structures, and art.

materialist perspective A theoretical approach stressing the primacy of infrastructure (material conditions) in cultural research and analysis.

matrilineal descent Descent traced exclusively through the female line of ancestry to establish group membership.

matrilocal residence A residence pattern in which a married couple lives in the wife's mother's place of residence.

mediation The settlement of a dispute through negotiation assisted by an unbiased third party.

medical anthropology A specialization in anthropology that brings theoretical and applied approaches from cultural and biological anthropology to the study of human health and disease.

migration Mobility in geographic space, involving temporary or permanent change in usual place of residence; internal migration is movement within countries; external migration is movement to a foreign country.

modal personality Those character traits that occur with the highest frequency in a social group and are therefore the most representative of its culture.

modernization The process of political and socioeconomic change, whereby developing societies acquire some of the cultural characteristics of Western industrial societies.

moiety Each group, usually consisting of several clans, that results from a division of a society into two halves on the basis of descent.

molecular anthropology The anthropological study of genes and genetic relationships, which contributes significantly to our understanding of human evolution, adaptation, and diversity.

molecular clock The hypothesis that dates of divergences among related species can be calculated through an examination of the genetic mutations that have accrued since the divergence.

money A means of exchange used to make payments for other goods and services as well as to measure their value.

monogamy A marriage form in which both partners have just one spouse.

monotheism The belief in only one supremely powerful divinity as creator and master of the universe.

morphemes The smallest units of sound that carry a meaning in language. They are distinct from phonemes, which can alter meaning but have no meaning by themselves.

morphology The study of the patterns or rules of word formation in a language, including the guidelines for verb tense, pluralization, and compound words.

motif A story situation in a tale.

Mousterian tool tradition The tool industry found among Neandertals in Eurasia, and their human contemporaries in northern Africa, during the Middle Paleolithic, generally dating from about 40,000 to 125,000 years ago.

multiculturalism The public policy for managing cultural diversity in a multi-ethnic society, officially stressing mutual respect and tolerance for cultural differences within a country's borders.

multiregional hypothesis An evolutionary hypothesis that modern humans originated through a process of simultaneous local transition from *Homo erectus* to *Homo sapiens* throughout the inhabited world.

multi-sited ethnography The investigation and documentation of peoples and cultures embedded in the larger structures of a globalizing world, utilizing a range of methods in various locations of time and space.

music Broadly speaking, an art form whose medium is sound and silence; a form of communication that includes a nonverbal auditory component with elements of pitch, rhythm, and timbre.

mutations Abrupt changes in the DNA that alter the genetic message carried by that cell.

myth A sacred narrative that explains the fundamentals of human existence—where we and everything in our world came from, why we are here, and where we are going.

naming ceremony A special event or ritual to mark the naming of a child.

nation A people who share a collective identity based on a common culture, language, territorial base, and history.

natural selection The principle or mechanism by which individuals having biological characteristics best suited to a particular environment survive and reproduce with greater frequency than individuals without those characteristics.

Neandertals An archaic human population that ranged through western Eurasia from about 30,000 to 200,000 years ago.

negative reciprocity A mode of exchange in which the aim is to get something for as little as possible. Neither fair nor balanced, it may involve hard bargaining, manipulation, outright cheating, or theft.

negotiation The use of direct argument and compromise by the parties to a dispute to arrive voluntarily at a mutually satisfactory agreement.

Neolithic revolution The domestication of plants and animals by peoples with stone-based technologies, beginning about 10,000 years ago and leading to radical transformations in cultural systems; sometimes referred to as the *Neolithic transition.*

neolocal residence A residence pattern in which a married couple establishes its household in a location apart from either the husband's or the wife's relatives.

new reproductive technologies (NRTs) Alternative means of reproduction such as surrogate motherhood and in vitro fertilization.

nuclear family A group consisting of one or two parents and dependent offspring, which may include a stepparent, stepsiblings, and adopted children. Until recently, this term referred only to the mother, father, and child(ren) unit.

Oldowan tool tradition The first stone tool industry, beginning between 2.5 and 2.6 million years ago at the start of the Lower Paleolithic.

out of Africa hypothesis An evolutionary hypothesis that modern humans are all derived from one single population of archaic *Homo sapiens* who migrated out of Africa after 100,000 years ago, replacing all other archaic forms due to their superior cultural capabilities; also known as the *recent African origins hypothesis* or the *Eve hypothesis.*

paleoanthropology The anthropological study of biological changes through time (evolution) to understand the origins and predecessors of the present human species.

pantheon All the gods and goddesses of a people.

paralanguage Voice effects that accompany language and convey meaning. These include vocalizations such as giggling, groaning, or sighing, as well as voice qualities such as pitch and tempo.

parallel cousin The child of a father's brother or a mother's sister.

parallel evolution In cultural evolution, the development of similar cultural adaptations to similar environmental conditions by peoples whose ancestral cultures are already somewhat alike.

participant observation In ethnography, the technique of learning a people's culture through social participation and personal observation within the community being studied, as well as interviews and discussion with individual members of the group over an extended period of time.

pastoralism The breeding and managing of migratory herds of domesticated grazing animals, such as goats, sheep, cattle, llamas, and camels.

patrilineal descent Descent traced exclusively through the male line of ancestry to establish group membership.

patrilocal residence A residence pattern in which a married couple lives in the husband's father's place of residence.

peasant A small-scale producer of crops or livestock living on land self-owned or rented in exchange for labor, crops, or money and exploited by more powerful groups in a complex society.

performance art A creatively expressed promotion of ideas by artful means dramatically staged to challenge opinion and/or provoke purposeful action.

personality The distinctive way a person thinks, feels, and behaves.

phonemes The smallest units of sound that make a difference in meaning in a language.

phonetics The systematic identification and description of distinctive speech sounds in a language.

phonology The study of language sounds.

phratry A unilineal descent group composed of at least two clans that supposedly share a common ancestry, whether or not they really do.

physical anthropology The systematic study of humans as biological organisms; also known as *biological anthropology.*

pilgrimage A devotion in motion. Traveling, often on foot, to a sacred or holy site to reach for enlightenment, prove devotion, and/or experience a miracle.

pluralistic society A society in which two or more ethnic groups or nationalities are politically organized into one territorial state but maintain their cultural differences.

political organization The way power, as the capacity to do something, is accumulated, arranged, executed, and structurally embedded in society; the means through which a society creates and maintains social order and reduces social disorder.

politics The process determining who gets what, when, and how.

polyandry A marriage form in which a woman is married to two or more men at one time; a form of polygamy.

polygamy A marriage form in which one individual has multiple spouses at the same time; from the Greek words *poly* ("many") and *gamos* ("marriage").

polygyny A marriage form in which a man is married to two or more women at the same time; a form of polygamy.

polytheism The belief in multiple gods and/or goddesses, as contrasted with monotheism—the belief in one god or goddess.

postindustrial society A society with an economy based on research and development of new knowledge and technologies, as well as providing information, services, and finance capital on a global scale.

potlatch On the northwestern coast of North America, an indigenous ceremonial event in which a village chief publicly gives away stockpiled food and other goods that signify wealth.

power The ability of individuals or groups to impose their will upon others and make them do things even against their own wants or wishes.

prehistory A conventional term used to refer to the period of time before the appearance of written records; does not deny the existence of history, merely of *written* history.

prestige economy The creation of a surplus for the express purpose of displaying wealth and giving it away to raise one's status.

priest or priestess A full-time religious specialist formally recognized for his or her role in guiding the religious practices of others and for contacting and influencing supernatural powers.

primary innovation The creation, invention, or chance discovery of a completely new idea, method, or device.

primates A subgroup of mammals that includes humans, apes, monkeys, tarsiers, lorises, and lemurs.

primatology The study of living and fossil primates.

progress In anthropology, a relative concept signifying that a society or country is moving forward to a better, more advanced stage in its cultural development toward greater perfection.

projection In cartography, refers to the system of intersecting lines (of longitude and latitude) by which part or all of the globe is represented on a flat surface.

proxemics The cross-cultural study of people's perception and use of space.

qualitative data Nonstatistical information such as personal life stories and customary beliefs and practices.

quantitative data Statistical or measurable information, such as demographic composition, the types and quantities of crops grown, or the ratio of spouses born and raised within or outside the community.

race In biology, the taxonomic category of subspecies that is not applicable to humans because the division of humans into discrete types does not represent the true nature of human biological variation. In some societies race is an important social category.

rebellion Organized armed resistance to an established government or authority in power; also known as *insurgency.*

recent African origins hypothesis An evolutionary hypothesis that modern humans are all derived from one single population of archaic *Homo sapiens* who migrated out of Africa after 100,000 years ago, replacing all other archaic forms due to their superior cultural capabilities; also known as the *Eve hypothesis* or the *out of Africa hypothesis.*

reciprocity The exchange of goods and services, of approximately equal value, between two parties.

redistribution A mode of exchange in which goods flow into a central place, where they are sorted, counted, and real-located.

religion An organized system of ideas about the spiritual sphere or the supernatural, along with associated ceremonial practices by which people try to interpret and/or influence aspects of the universe otherwise beyond their control.

revitalization movements Social movements for radical cultural reform in response to widespread social disruption and collective feelings of great stress and despair.

revolution Radical change in a society or culture. In the political arena, it involves the forced overthrow of an existing government and establishment of a completely new one.

rite of intensification A ritual that takes place during a crisis in the life of the group and serves to bind individuals together.

rite of passage A ritual that marks an important ceremonial moment when members of a society move from one distinctive social stage in life to another, such as birth, marriage, and death. It features three phases: separation, transition, and incorporation.

rite of purification A symbolic act carried out by an individual or a group to establish or restore purity when someone has violated a taboo or is otherwise metaphorically unclean.

ritual A culturally prescribed symbolic act or procedure designed to guide members of a community in an orderly way through personal and collective transitions.

sanction An externalized social control designed to encourage conformity to social norms.

secondary innovation The deliberate application or modification of an existing idea, method, or device.

secularization A process of cultural change in which a population tends toward a nonreligious worldview, ignoring or rejecting institutionalized spiritual beliefs and rituals.

self-awareness The ability to identify oneself as an individual, to reflect on oneself, and to evaluate oneself.

self-control A person's capacity to manage her or his spontaneous feelings, restraining impulsive behavior.

separation In a rite of passage, the temporary ritual removal of the individual from society.

serial monogamy A marriage form in which a man or a woman marries or lives with a series of partners in succession.

shaman A person who at will enters an altered state of consciousness to contact and utilize an ordinarily hidden reality in order to acquire knowledge, power, and to help others.

signals Instinctive sounds and gestures that have a natural or self-evident meaning.

silent trade A process for the exchange of goods between mutually distrusting ethnic groups so as to avoid direct personal contact.

slash-and-burn cultivation An extensive form of horticulture in which the natural vegetation is cut, the slash is subsequently burned, and crops are then planted among the ashes; also known as *swidden farming*.

social class A category of individuals in a stratified society who enjoy equal or nearly equal prestige according to the hierarchical system of evaluation.

social control External control through open coercion.

social mobility An upward or downward change in one's social class position in a stratified society.

social structure The rule-governed relationships—with all their rights and obligations—that hold members of a society together. This includes households, families, associations, and power relations, including politics.

society An organized group or groups of interdependent people who generally share a common territory, language, and culture and who act together for collective survival and well-being.

sociolinguistics The study of the relationship between language and society through examining how social categories—such as age, gender, ethnicity, religion, occupation, and class—influence the use and significance of distinctive styles of speech.

soft power Power that coopts rather than coerces, pressing others through attraction and persuasion to change their ideas, beliefs, values, and behaviors.

species The smallest working units in biological classificatory systems; reproductively isolated populations or groups of populations capable of interbreeding to produce fertile offspring.

spirituality Concern with the sacred, as distinguished from material matters. In contrast to religion, spirituality is often individual rather than collective and does not require a distinctive format or traditional organization.

spiritual lineage A principle of leadership in which divine authority is passed down from a spiritual founding figure, such as a prophet or saint, to a chain of successors.

state A political institution established to manage and defend a complex, socially stratified society occupying a defined territory.

stratified societies Societies in which people are hierarchically divided and ranked into social strata, or layers, and do not share equally in basic resources that support income, status, and power.

structural power Power that organizes and orchestrates the systemic interaction within and among societies, directing economic and political forces on the one hand and ideological forces that shape public ideas, values, and beliefs on the other.

structural violence Physical and/or psychological harm (including repression, environmental destruction, poverty, hunger, illness, and premature death) caused by impersonal, exploitative, and unjust social, political, and economic systems.

subculture A distinctive set of ideas, values, and behavior patterns by which a group within a larger society operates, while still sharing common standards with that larger society.

superstructure A society's shared sense of identity and worldview. The collective body of ideas, beliefs, and values by which members of a society make sense of the world—its shape, challenges, and opportunities—and understand their place in it. This includes religion and national ideology.

swidden farming An extensive form of horticulture in which the natural vegetation is cut, the slash is subsequently burned, and crops are then planted among the ashes; also known as *slash-and-burn cultivation*.

symbol A sound, gesture, mark, or other sign that is arbitrarily linked to something else and represents it in a meaningful way.

sympathetic magic Magic based on the principle that like produces like; also known as *imitative magic*.

syncretism The creative blending of indigenous and foreign beliefs and practices into new cultural forms.

syntax The patterns or rules by which words are arranged into phrases and sentences.

taboo Culturally prescribed avoidances involving ritual prohibitions, which, if not observed, lead to supernatural punishment.

tale A creative narrative that is recognized as fiction for entertainment but may also draw a moral or teach a practical lesson.

technology Tools and other material equipment, together with the knowledge of how to make and use them.

theory A coherent statement that provides an explanatory framework for understanding; an explanation or interpretation supported by a reliable body of data.

tonal language A language in which the sound pitch of a spoken word is an essential part of its pronunciation and meaning.

totemism The belief that people are related to particular animals, plants, or natural objects by virtue of descent from common ancestral spirits.

tradition Customary ideas and practices passed on from generation to generation, which in a modernizing society may form an obstacle to new ways of doing things.

transgenders People who cross over or occupy an intermediate position in the binary male–female gender construction.

transition In a rite of passage, temporary isolation of the individual following separation and prior to incorporation into society.

treaty A contract or formally binding agreement between two or more groups that are independent and self-governing political groups such as tribes, chiefdoms, and states.

tribe In anthropology, the term for a range of kin-ordered groups that are politically integrated by some unifying factor and whose members share a common ancestry, identity, culture, language, and territory.

unilineal descent Descent traced exclusively through either the male or the female line of ancestry to establish group membership.

Upper Paleolithic The last part (10,000 to 40,000 years ago) of the Old Stone Age, featuring tool industries characterized by long, slim blades and an explosion of creative symbolic forms.

urgent anthropology Ethnographic research that documents endangered cultures; also known as *salvage ethnography*.

verbal art Creative word use on display that includes stories, myths, legends, tales, poetry, metaphor, rhyme, chants, drama, cant, proverbs, jokes, puns, riddles, and tongue twisters.

visual art Art created primarily for visual perception, ranging from etchings and paintings on various surfaces (including the human body) to sculptures and weavings made with an array of materials.

whistled speech An exchange of whistled words using a phonetic emulation of the sounds produced in spoken voice; also known as *whistled language*.

witchcraft Magical rituals intended to cause misfortune or inflict harm.

worldview The collective body of ideas that members of a culture generally share concerning the ultimate shape and substance of their reality.

writing system A set of visible or tactile signs used to represent units of language in a systematic way.

xenophobia Fear or hatred of strangers or anything foreign.

References

Abbot, E. (2001). *A history of celibacy.* Cambridge, MA: Da Capo Press.

Abi-Rached, L., et al. (2011). The shaping of modern human immune systems by multiregional admixture with archaic humans. *Science* 334 (6052), 89–94.

Abu-Lughod, L. (1986). *Veiled sentiments: Honor and poetry in a Bedouin society.* Berkeley: University of California Press.

Abun-Nasr, J. M. (2007). *Muslim communities of grace: The Sufi brotherhoods in Islamic religious life.* New York: Columbia University Press.

adherents.com.

Aguirre Beltrán, G. (1974). Applied anthropology in Mexico. *Human Organization 33* (1), 1–6.

Alemseged, Z., et al. (2006, September 21). A juvenile early hominin skeleton from Dikika, Ethiopia. *Nature 443,* 296–301.

Alfonso-Durraty, M. (2012). Personal communication.

Allen, T. (2006). *Trial justice: The International Criminal Court and the Lord's Resistance Army.* London & New York: Zed Books/International African Institute.

American Anthropological Association. (2007). Executive board statement on the Human Terrain System Project. www.aaanet.org/about/policies/statements/human-terrain-system-statement.cfm

Amnesty International. (2010, August 16). Afghan couple stoned to death by Taleban. www.amnesty.org/en/news-and-updates/afghan-couple-stoned-death-taleban-2010-08-16 (retrieved October 6, 2012)

Amnesty International. (2012). Death penalty in 2011. www.amnesty.org/en/death-penalty (retrieved September 5, 2012)

Anderson, M. S. (2006). *The Allied Tribes Tsimshian of north coastal British Columbia: Social organization, economy and trade.* Unpublished PhD dissertation. http://faculty.arts.ubc.ca/menzies/documents/anderson.pdf

Anjum, T. (2006). Sufism in history and its relationship with power. *Islamic Studies 45* (2), 221–268.

Antón, S. C. (2003). A natural history of *H. erectus. Yearbook of Physical Anthropology 46,* 126–170.

Appadurai, A. (1990). Disjuncture and difference in the global cultural economy. *Public Culture 2,* 1–24.

Appadurai, A. (1996). *Modernity at large: Cultural dimensions of globalization.* Minneapolis: University of Minnesota Press.

Arctic Monitoring Assessment Project. (2003). *AMAP assessment 2002: Human health in the Arctic* (pp. xii–xiii, 22–23). Oslo: AMAP.

Aristotle. (350 BC). *The history of animals* (Book II, Part 8). http://classics.mit.edu/Aristotle/history_anim.html (retrieved December 4, 2012)

Arms Control Association. (2012). Nuclear weapons: Who has what at a glance. www.armscontrol.org/factsheets/Nuclearweaponswhohaswhat (retrieved October 1, 2012)

Arsuaga, J. L., et al. (2000). The Atapuerca human fossils. *Human Evolution 15,* 1–2.

Aureli, F., & de Waal, F. B. M. (2000). *Natural conflict resolution.* Berkeley: University of California Press.

Ayalon, D. (1999). *Eunuchs, caliphs, and sultans: A study in power relationships.* Jerusalem: Mangess Press.

Bailey, R. C., & Aunger, R. (1989). Net hunters vs. archers: Variations in women's subsistence strategies in the Ituri forest. *Human Ecology 17,* 273–297.

Baker, P. (Ed.). (1978). *The biology of high altitude peoples.* London: Cambridge University Press.

Balikci, A. (1970). *The Netsilik Eskimo.* Garden City, NY: Natural History Press

Balzer, M. M. (1981). Rituals of gender identity: Markers of Siberian Khanty ethnicity, status, and belief. *American Anthropologist 83* (4), 850–867.

Barnard, A. (1995). Monboddo's *Orang outang* and the definition of man. In B. Corbey & B. Theunissen (Eds.), *Ape, man, apeman: Changing views since 1600* (pp. 71–85). Leiden: Department of Prehistory, Leiden University.

Barnouw, V. (1985). *Culture and personality* (4th ed.). Homewood, IL: Dorsey Press.

Barr, R. G. (1997, October). The crying game. *Natural History,* 47.

"Bartered brides." (2009, March 12). *Economist.* www.economist.com/node/13278577 (retrieved October 31, 2012)

Barth, F. (1960). *Nomadism in the mountain and plateau areas of South West Asia. The problems of the arid zone* (pp. 341–355). Paris: UNESCO.

Basel Action Network. (2010). Country status: Waste trade ban agreements. http://ban.org/country_status/ country_status_chart.html (retrieved November 3, 2012)

Bates, D. G. (2001). *Human adaptive strategies: Ecology, culture, and politics* (2nd ed.). Boston: Allen & Bacon.

Bateson, G., & Mead, M. (1942). *Balinese character: A photographic analysis.* New York: New York Academy of Sciences.

Becker, J. (2004, March). China's growing pains. *National Geographic,* 68–95.

Beeman, W. O. (2000). Introduction: Margaret Mead, cultural studies, and international understanding. In M. Mead & R. Métraux (Eds.), *The study of culture at a distance* (pp. xiv–xxxi). New York & Oxford, UK: Berghahn Books.

Behrend, H. (1999). *Alice Lakwena and the Holy Spirits: War in northern Uganda 1986–97.* Oxford, UK: James Currey.

Behringer, W. (2004). *Witches and witch-hunts: A global history.* Cambridge, UK: Polity Press.

Bekoff, M., et al. (Eds.). (2002). *The cognitive animal: Empirical and theoretical perspectives on animal cognition.* Cambridge, MA: MIT Press.

Bendyshe, T. (Ed.) (1865). *The anthropological treatises of Johann Friedrich Blumenbach.* London: Anthropological Society.

Benedict, R. (1934). *Patterns of culture.* Boston: Houghton Mifflin.

Bennett, R. L., et al. (2002, April). Genetic counseling and screening of consanguineous couples and their offspring: Recommendations of the National Society of Genetic Counselors. *Journal of Genetic Counseling 11* (2), 97–119.

Bermúdez de Castro, J. M., Martinón-Torres, M., Carbonell, E., Sarmiento, S., Rosas, A., van der Made, J., & Lozano, M. (2004). The Atapuerca sites and their contribution to the knowledge of human evolution in Europe. *Evolutionary Anthropology 13,* 25–41.

Bermúdez de Castro, J. M., Martinón-Torres, M., Gómez-Robles, A., Prado-Simón, L., Martín-Francés, L., Lapresa, M., Olejniczak, A., & Carbonell, E. (2011). Early Pleistocene human mandible from Sima del Elefante (TE) cave site in Sierra de Atapuerca (Spain): A comparative morphological study. *Journal of Human Evolution 61* (1), 12–25.

Berna, F., Goldberg, P., Horwitz, L. K, Brink, J., Holt, S., Bamford, M., & Chazan, M. (2012). Microstratigraphic evidence of in situ fire in the Acheulean strata of Wonderwerk Cave, Northern Cape province, South Africa. *Proceedings*

of the National Academy of Sciences 109 (20), 1215–1220.

Bernard, H. R. (2006). *Research methods in anthropology: Qualitative and quantitative approaches* (4th ed.). Walnut Creek, CA: AltaMira Press.

Betzig, L. (1989). Causes of conjugal dissolution: A cross-cultural study. *Current Anthropology* 30, 654–676.

Birch, E. L., & Wachter, S. M. (Eds.). (2011). *Global urbanization.* Philadelphia: University of Pennsylvania Press.

Blackless, M., et al. (2000). How sexually dimorphic are we? Review and synthesis. *American Journal of Human Biology* 12, 151–166.

Blacksmith, N., & Harter, J. (2011, October 28). Majority of American workers not engaged in their jobs. *Gallup Wellbeing.* www.gallup.com/poll/150383/Majority-American-Workers-Not-Engaged-Jobs.aspx (retrieved October 1, 2012)

Blakey, M. (2003, October 29). Personal communication. *African Burial Ground Project.* Department of Anthropology, College of William & Mary.

Blakey, M. (2010, May). African Burial Ground Project: Paradigm for cooperation? *Museum International* 62 (1–2), 61–68.

Blok, A. (1974). *The mafia of a Sicilian village 1860–1960.* New York: Harper & Row.

Blok, A. (1981). Rams and billy-goats: A key to the Mediterranean code of honour. *Man, New Series* 16 (3), 427–440.

Blumberg, R. L. (1991). *Gender, family, and the economy: The triple overlap.* Newbury Park, CA: Sage.

Blumenbach, J. F. (1795). *On the natural variety of mankind* (rev. ed.) Germany: University of Göttingen.

Boas, F. (1909, May 28). Race problems in America. *Science* 29 (752), 839–849. www.jstor.org/stable/1634659 (retrieved December 13, 2012)

Boas, F. (1931). Race and progress. *Science* 79 (1905), 1–8.

Bodley, J. H. (2007). *Anthropology and contemporary human problems* (5th ed.). Lanham, MD: AltaMira Press.

Bodley, J. H. (2008). *Victims of progress* (5th ed.). Lanham, MD: AltaMira Press.

Boehm, C. (1987). *Blood revenge.* Philadelphia: University of Pennsylvania Press.

Bogucki, P. (1999). *The origins of human society.* Oxford, UK: Blackwell Press.

Boshara, R. (2003, January/February). Wealth inequality: The $6,000 solution. *Atlantic Monthly.*

Bošković, A. (Ed.). (2009). *Other people's anthropologies: Ethnographic practice on the margins.* Oxford, UK: Berghahn Books.

Bradford, P. V., & Blume, H. (1992). *Ota Benga: The Pygmy in the zoo.* New York: St. Martin's Press.

Braudel, F. (1979). *The structures of everyday life: Civilization and capitalism 15th–18th century* (vol. 1, pp. 163–167). New York: Harper & Row.

Brettell, C. B., & Sargent, C. F. (Eds.). (2000). *Gender in cross-cultural perspective* (3rd ed.). Upper Saddle River, NJ: Prentice-Hall.

Brody, H. (1981). *Maps and dreams.* New York: Pantheon.

Broecker, W. S. (1992, April). Global warming on trial. *Natural History,* 14.

Brunet, M., et al. (2002). A new hominid from the Upper Miocene of Chad, Central Africa. *Nature* 418, 145–151.

Buck, P. H. (1938). *Vikings of the Pacific.* Chicago: University Press of Chicago.

Bermúdez de Castro, J. M., Martinón-Torres, M., Gómez-Robles, A., Prado-Simón, L., Martín-Francés, L., Lapresa, M., Olejniczak, A., & Carbonell, E. (2011). Early Pleistocene human mandible from Sima del Elefante (TE) cave site in Sierra de Atapuerca (Spain): A comparative morphological study. *Journal of Human Evolution* 61 (1), 12–25.

Caichang, T. (1968). *Juedianmingzhai neiyan* (Essays on political and historical matters) Taipei: Wenhai Chubanshe.

Capps, R., McCabe, K., & Fix, M. (2012). *Diverse streams: Black African migration to the United States.* Washington, DC: Migration Policy Institute. www.migrationpolicy.org/pubs/CBI-AfricanMigration.pdf (retrieved September 30, 2012)

Cardarelli, F. (2003). *Encyclopedia of scientific units, weights, and measures. Their SI equivalences and origins.* London: Springer.

Carneiro, R. L. (2003). *Evolutionism in cultural anthropology: A critical history.* Boulder, CO: Westview Press.

Caroulis, J. (1996). Food for thought. *Pennsylvania Gazette* 95 (3), 16.

Carpenter, E. S. (1959). *Eskimo.* Toronto: University of Toronto Press.

Carpenter, E. S. (1968). We wed ourselves to the mystery: A study of tribal art. *Explorations* 22, 66–74.

Carroll, J. B. (Ed.). (1956). *Language, thought and reality: Selected writings of Benjamin Lee Whorf.* Cambridge, MA: MIT Press.

Cartmill, E. A., & Byrne, R. W. (2010) Semantics of orangutan gesture: Determining structure and meaning through form and use. *Animal Cognition.* doi: 10.1007/s10071-010-0328-7

Cartmill, M. (1998). The gift of gab. *Discover* 19 (11), 64.

Catford, J. C. (1988). *A practical introduction to phonetics.* Oxford, UK: Clarendon Press.

Centers for Disease Control and Prevention. (2012). Overweight and obesity. www.cdc.gov/obesity/index.html (retrieved November 8, 2012)

Chagnon, N. A. (1988a). Life histories, blood revenge, and warfare in a tribal population. *Science* 239, 935–992.

Chagnon, N. A. (1988b). *Yanomamö: The fierce people* (3rd ed.). New York: Holt, Rinehart & Winston.

Chagnon, N. A. (1990). On Yanomamö violence: Reply to Albert. *Current Anthropology* 31 (2), 49–53.

Chambers, R. (1995). *Rural development: Putting the last first.* Englewood Cliffs, NJ: Prentice-Hall.

Chance, N. A. (1990). *The Iñupiat and Arctic Alaska: An ethnography of development.* New York: Harcourt.

Chang, L. (2005, June 9). A migrant worker sees rural home in new light. *Wall Street Journal.*

Chase, C. (1998). Hermaphrodites with attitude. *Gay and Lesbian Quarterly* 4 (2), 189–211.

Chatty, D. (1996). *Mobile pastoralists: Development planning and social change in Oman.* New York: Columbia University Press.

"Child soldiers global report 2008." (2009). Despite progress, efforts to end the recruitment and use of child soldiers are too little and too late for many children. www.childsoldiersglobalreport.org/ (retrieved August 28, 2012)

"China to execute bride traffickers." (2000, October 20). *BBC News.* http://news.bbc.co.uk/2/hi/asia-pacific/981675.stm (retrieved October 31, 2012)

Claeson, B. (1994). The privatization of justice: An ethnography of control. In L. Nader (Ed.), *Essays on controlling processes* (pp. 32–64). *Kroeber Anthropological Society Papers* (no. 77). Berkeley: University of California Press.

Clay, J. W. (1996). What's a nation? In W. A. Haviland & R. J. Gordon (Eds.), *Talking about people* (2nd ed., pp. 188–189). Mountain View, CA: Mayfield.

Coco, L. E. (1994). Silicone breast implants in America: A choice of the official breast? In L. Nader (Ed.), *Essays on controlling processes* (pp. 103–132). *Kroeber Anthropological Society Papers* (no. 77). Berkeley: University of California Press.

Coe, S. D., & Coe, M. D. (1996). *The true history of chocolate.* New York: Thames & Hudson.

Cohen, J. (1997). Is an old virus up to new tricks? *Science* 277, 312–313.

Cohen, M. N., & Armelagos, G. J. (Eds.). (1984). *Paleopathology at the origins of agriculture.* Orlando: Academic Press.

Colborn, T., Dumanoski, D., & Myers, J. P. (1997). *Our stolen future.* New York: Plume/Penguin Books.

Cole, J. W., & Wolf, E. R. (1999). *The hidden frontier: Ecology and ethnicity in an alpine valley* (with a new introduction). Berkeley: University of California Press.

Collier, J., & Collier, M. (1986). *Visual anthropology: Photography as a research method.* Albuquerque: University of New Mexico Press.

Cone, M. (2005). *Silent snow: The slow poisoning of the Arctic.* New York: Grove Press.

Conklin, B. (1997). Body paint, feathers, and VCRs: Aesthetics and authenticity in Amazonian activism. *American Ethnologist* 24 (4), 711–737.

Conklin, B. A. (2002). Shamans versus pirates in the Amazonian treasure chest. *American Anthropologist* 104 (4), 1050–1061.

Conklin, H. C. (1955). Hanunóo color categories. *Southwestern Journal of Anthropology* 11, 339–344.

Connelly, J. C. (1979). Hopi social organization. In A. Ortiz (Ed.), *Handbook of North American Indians: Southwest* (vol. 9, pp. 539–553). Washington, DC: Smithsonian Institution Press.

Conroy, G. C. (1997). *Reconstructing human origins: A modern synthesis.* New York: Norton.

Coon, C. S. (1954). *The story of man.* New York: Knopf.

Coon, C. S. (1958). *Caravan: The story of the Middle East.* New York: Holt, Rinehart & Winston.

Corbey, R. (1995). Introduction: Missing links, or the ape's place in nature. In R. Corbey & B. Theunissen (Eds.), *Ape, man, apeman: Changing views since 1600* (p. 1). Leiden: Departement of Prehistory, Leiden University.

Crane, H. (2001). *Men in spirit: The masculinization of Taiwanese Buddhist nuns.* PhD dissertation, Brown University.

Cretney, S. (2003). *Family law in the twentieth century: A history.* New York: Oxford University Press.

Criminal Code of Canada, § 718.2(e).

Crocker, W. A., & Crocker, J. (2004). *The Canela: Kinship, ritual, and sex in an Amazonian tribe.* Belmont, CA: Wadsworth.

Crystal, D. (2002). *Language death.* Cambridge, UK: Cambridge University Press.

Cuzange, M.-T., et al. (2007) Analyses comparatives au radiocarbone pour la Grotte Chauvet. *International Radiocarbon Conference 49* (2), 339–347.

Darwin, C. (1859). *On the origin of species by means of natural selection, or the preservation of favoured races in the struggle for life.* New York: Atheneum.

Darwin, C. (1871). *The descent of man, and selection in relation to sex.* New York: Random House (Modern Library).

Darwin, C. (2007). *On the origin of species by means of natural selection, or the preservation of favoured races in the struggle for life* (p. 53). New York: Cosimo. (orig. 1859)

Davies, G. (2005). *A history of money from the earliest times to present day* (3rd ed.). Cardiff, UK: University of Wales Press.

Davies, S. G. (2007). *Challenging gender norms: Five genders among the Bugis in Indonesia.* Belmont, CA: Thomson Wadsworth.

Deetz, J. (1977). *In small things forgotten: The archaeology of early American life.* Garden City, NY: Doubleday/Anchor.

Defleur, A., White, T., Valensi, P., Slimak, L., & Crégut-Bonnoure, É. (1999). Neandertal cannibalism at Moula-Guercy, Ardèche, France. *Science 286* (5437), 128–131.

Delagnes, A. (2012). Inland human settlement in southern Arabia 55,000 years ago. New Evidence from the Wadi Surdud Middle Paleolithic site complex, Western Yemen. *Journal of Human Evolution 63* (3), 452–474.

del Carmen Rodríguez Martínez, M., et al. (2006). Oldest writing in the New World. *Science 313* (5793), 1610–1614.

del Castillo, B. D. (1963). *The conquest of New Spain* (translation and introduction by J. M. Cohen). New York: Penguin Books.

Delio, M. (2004). Global chaos, just for fun. *Wired.* www.wired.com/culture/lifestyle/news/2004/06/63872 (retrieved October 1, 2012)

Demay, L., Péan, S., & Matou-Mathis, M. (2012). Mammoths used as food and building resources by Neanderthals: Zooarchaeological study applied to layer 4,

Molodova I (Ukraine). *Quaternary International 276–277,* 212–226.

DeMello, M. (2000). *Bodies of inscription: A cultural history of the modern tattoo community.* Durham, NC: Duke University Press.

Dettwyler, K. A. (1997, October). When to wean. *Natural History,* 49.

de Waal, F. B. M. (1998). Comment. *Current Anthropology 39,* 407.

de Waal, F. B. M. (2000). Primates—A natural heritage of conflict resolution. *Science 28,* 586–590.

de Waal, F. B. M. (2001). *The ape and the sushi master.* New York: Basic Books.

de Waal, F. B. M., & Johanowicz, D. L. (1993). Modification of reconciliation behavior through social experience: An experiment with two macaque species. *Child Development 64,* 897–908.

de Waal, F. B. M., Kano, T., & Parish, A. R. (1998). Comments. *Current Anthropology 39,* 408, 413.

Diamond, J. (1996). Empire of uniformity. *Discover 17* (3), 83–84.

Diamond, J. (1998). Ants, crops, and history. *Science 281,* 1974–1975.

Diamond, J. (2005). *Collapse: How societies choose to fail or succeed.* New York: Viking/Penguin Books.

Dikötter, F. (1997). *The construction of racial identities in China and Japan.* Honolulu: University of Hawai'i Press.

Dikötter, F. (2010). Forging national unity: Ideas of race in China. *Global Dialogue 12* (2), 23–35.

Dillehay, T. D., Ramirez, C., Pino, M., Collins, M. B., Rossen, J., & Pina-Navarro, J. D. (2008). Monte Verde: Seaweed, food, medicine, and the peopling of South America. *Science 320* (5877), 784–786.

Dissanayake, E. (2000). Birth of the arts. *Natural History 109* (10), 89.

Douglas, M. (1966). *Purity and danger: An analysis of concepts of pollution and taboo.* London: Routledge & Kegan Paul.

Dreger, A. D. (1998, May/June). "Ambiguous sex" or ambivalent medicine? *Hastings Center Report 28* (3), 2435. http://alicedreger.com/ambivalent_medicine_files/Dreger%20HCR%201998%20Ambiguous%20Sex.pdf

Dunbar, P. (2008, January 19). The pink vigilantes: The Indian women fighting for women's rights. *Mail Online.* www.dailymail.co.uk/news/article-509318/The-pink-vigilantes-The-Indian-women-fighting-womens-rights.html (retrieved August 26, 2012)

Dunham, S. A. (2009). *Surviving against the odds: Village industry in Indonesia.* Durham, NC: Duke University Press.

"Eating disorders (most recent) by country." (2004). *Nationmaster.com.* www.nationmaster.com/graph/mor_eat_dis-mortality-eating-disorders (retrieved August 1, 2012)

Eaton, S. B., Konner, M., & Shostak, M. (1988). Stone-agers in the fast lane: Chronic degenerative diseases in evolutionary perspective. *American Journal of Medicine 84* (4), 739–749.

Egan, T. (1999, February 28). The persistence of polygamy. *New York Times Magazine,* 52.

Ehrenberg, R. (2011, September 24). Financial world dominated by a few deep pockets. *Science News 180* (7). 13.

www.sciencenews.org (retrieved October 1, 2012)

El Guindi, F. (2004). *Visual anthropology: Essential method and theory.* Walnut Creek, CA: AltaMira Press.

Embree, J. F. (1951). Raymond Kennedy, 1906–50. *Far Eastern Quarterly 10* (2), 170–172.

Erickson, P. A., & Murphy, L. D. (2003). *A history of anthropological theory* (2nd ed.). Peterborough, Ontario: Broadview Press.

Errington, F. K., & Gewertz, D. B. (2001). *Cultural alternatives and a feminist anthropology: An analysis of culturally constructed gender interests in Papua New Guinea.* Cambridge, UK, & New York: Cambridge University Press.

Esber, G. S., Jr. (1987). Designing Apache houses with Apaches. In R. M. Wulff & S. J. Fiske (Eds.), *Anthropological praxis: Translating knowledge into action* (pp. 187–196). Boulder, CO: Westview Press.

Estado Plurinacional de Bolivia. (2010). *Anteproyecto de Ley de la Madre Tierra por las Organizaciones Sociales del Pacto de Unidad.* www.redunitas.org/NINA_Anteproyectode%20ley%20madre%20tierra.pdf (retrieved September 23, 2012)

Evans-Pritchard, E. E. (1937). *Witchcraft, oracles, and magic among the Azande.* London: Oxford University Press.

Evans-Pritchard, E. E. (1951). *Kinship and marriage among the Nuer.* New York: Oxford University Press.

Fagan, B. M. (1995). *People of the earth* (8th ed., p. 19). New York: HarperCollins.

Fagan, B. M. (2000). *Ancient lives: An introduction to archaeology.* Englewood Cliffs, NJ: Prentice-Hall.

Farmer, P. (1996). On suffering and structural violence: A view from below. *Daedalus 125* (1), 261–283.

Farmer, P. (2001). *Infections and inequalities: The modern plagues.* Berkeley: University of California Press.

Farmer, P. (2004, June). An anthropology of structural violence. *Current Anthropology 45,* 3.

Fausto-Sterling, A. (1993, March/April). The five sexes: Why male and female are not enough. *The Sciences 33* (2), 20–24.

Fausto-Sterling, A. (2003, August 2). Personal e-mail communication.

Fausto-Sterling, A., et al. (2000). How sexually dimorphic are we? Review and synthesis. *American Journal of Human Biology 12,* 151–166.

Fedigan, L. M. (1986). The changing role of women in models of human evolution. *Annual Review of Anthropology 15,* 25–56.

Fernández Olmos, M., & Paravisini-Gebert, L. (2003). *Creole religion of the Caribbean: An introduction from Vodou and Santería to Obeah and Espiritismo.* New York: New York University Press.

Ferrie, H. (1997). An interview with C. Loring Brace. *Current Anthropology 38,* 851–869.

Field, L. W. (2004). Beyond "applied" anthropology. In T. Biolsi (Ed.), *A companion to the anthropology of American Indians* (pp. 472–479). Oxford, UK: Blackwell Press.

Finnström, S. (2008). *Living with bad surroundings: War, history, and everyday moments in northern Uganda.* Durham, NC: Duke University Press.

Fisher, R., & Ury, W. L. (1991). *Getting to yes: Negotiating agreement without giving in* (2nd ed.). Boston: Houghton Mifflin.

Fogel, R., & Riquelme, M. A. (2005). *Enclave sojero. Merma de soberania y pobreza.* Asuncion: Centro de Estudios Rurales Interdisciplinarias.

Food and Agriculture Organization of the United Nations. (2009, June 19). 1.02 billion people hungry: One sixth of humanity undernourished—more than ever before. www.fao.org/news/story/en/item/20568/icode/ (retrieved October 3, 2012)

Forde, C. D. (1968). Double descent among the Yakö. In P. Bohannan & J. Middleton (Eds.), *Kinship and social organization* (pp. 179–191). Garden City, NY: Natural History Press.

Forste, R. (2008). *Prelude to marriage, or alternative to marriage? A social demographic look at cohabitation in the U.S.* Working paper. Social Science Electronic Publishing. http://papers.ssrn.com/sol3/papers.cfm?abstract_id=269172 (retrieved August 18, 2012)

Fouts, R. S., & Waters, G. (2001). Chimpanzee sign language and Darwinian continuity: Evidence for a neurology continuity of language. *Neurological Research 23,* 787–794.

Fox, R. (1968). *Encounter with anthropology.* New York: Dell.

Fox, R. (1981, December 3). [Interview]. Coast Telecourses, Inc., Los Angeles.

Freeman, L. G. (1992). *Ambrona and Torralba: New evidence and interpretation.* Paper presented at the 91st annual meeting, American Anthropological Association.

Frisch, R. (2002). *Female fertility and the body fat connection.* Chicago: University of Chicago Press.

Frost, P. (2012). Vitamin D deficiency among northern Native Peoples: A real or apparent problem? *International Journal of Circumpolar Health 71,* 18001. www.circumpolarhealthjournal.net/index.php/ijch/article/view/18001 (retrieved December 5, 2012)

Frye, D. P. (2000). Conflict management in cross-cultural perspective. In F. Aureli & F. B. M. de Waal, *Natural conflict resolution* (pp. 334–351). Berkeley: University of California Press.

Fu, Q., Rudan, P., Pääbo, S., & Krause, J. (2012). Complete mitochondrial genomes reveal Neolithic expansion into Europe. *PLoS One 7* (3), e32473.

Gandhi, M. K. (Ed.). (1999). *The collected works of Mahatma Gandhi* (vols. 8 & 19). New Delhi: Publications Division, Government of India.

Garrigan, D., Mobasher, Z., Severson, T., Wilder, J. A., & Hammer, M. F. (2005). Evidence for archaic Asian ancestry on the human X chromosome. *Molecular Biology and Evolution 22* (2), 189–192.

Geertz, C. (1973). *The interpretation of culture.* London: Hutchinson.

"Gene study suggests Polynesians came from Taiwan." (2005, July 4). Reuters.

Gibbons, A. (1993). Where are new diseases born? *Science 261,* 680–681.

Gibbons, A. (2011). Who were the Denisovans? *Science 333,* 1084–1087.

Gibbs, J. L., Jr. (1983). [Interview]. *Faces of culture: Program 18.* Fountain Valley, CA: Coast Telecourses.

Gillespie, R. (2002). Dating the first Australians. *Radiocarbon 44* (2), 455–472.

Ginsburg, F. D., Abu-Lughod, L., & Larkin, B. (Eds.). (2009). *Media worlds: Anthropology on new terrain.* Berkeley: University of California Press.

Gladney, D. C. (2004). *Dislocating China: Muslims, minorities and other subaltern subjects.* London: Hurst.

Gladstone, R. (2012, August 27). China: 2 Tibetan teenagers set themselves on fire. *nytimes.com.* www.nytimes.com/2012/08/28/world/asia/2-tibetan-teenagers-set-themselves-on-fire-in-china.html (retrieved September 21, 2012)

"Global 500: Our annual ranking of the world's largest corporations." (2012). *CNN Money.* http://money.cnn.com/magazines/fortune/global500/2012/full_list/index.html (retrieved October 1, 2012)

González, R. J. (2009). *American counterinsurgency: Human science and the human terrain.* Chicago: University of Chicago Press.

Goodenough, W. H. (1970). *Description and comparison in cultural anthropology.* Chicago: Aldine.

Goodwin, R. (1999). *Personal relationships across cultures.* New York: Routledge.

Gould, S. J. (1994). The geometer of race. *Discover 15* (11), 65–69.

Gordon, R. (2000). *Eating disorders: Anatomy of a social epidemic* (2nd ed.). New York: Wiley-Blackwell.

Gordon, R., Lyons, H., & Lyons, A. (Eds.). (2010). *Fifty key anthropologists.* New York: Routledge.

Gottlieb, A. (2003). *The afterlife is where we come from: The culture of infancy in West Africa.* Chicago: University of Chicago Press.

Gottlieb, A. (2004). Babies as ancestors, babies as spirits: The culture of infancy in West Africa. *Expedition 46* (3), 13–21.

Gottlieb, A. (2005). Non-Western approaches to spiritual development among infants and young children: A case study from West Africa. In P. L. Benson et al. (Eds.), *The handbook of spiritual development in childhood and adolescence* (pp. 150–162). Thousand Oaks, CA: Sage.

Gough, K. (1959). The Nayars and the definition of marriage. *Journal of the Royal Anthropological Institute of Great Britain and Ireland 89,* 23–34.

Gould, S. J. (1983). *Hen's teeth and horses' toes.* New York: Norton.

Gould, S. J. (1989). *Wonderful life.* New York: Norton.

Gould, S. J. (1991). *The flamingo's smile: Reflections in natural history.* New York: Norton.

Gould, S. J. (2000). The narthex of San Marco and the pangenetic paradigm. *Natural History 109* (6), 29.

Grant, M. (1916). *The passing of the great race; or, The racial basis of European history.* New York: Scribner.

Gray, P. B. (2004, May). HIV and Islam: Is HIV prevalence lower among Muslims? *Social Science & Medicine 58* (9), 1751–1756.

Gray, P. M., et al. (2001). The music of nature and the nature of music. *Science 291,* 52.

Green, R. E., et al. (2010, May 7). A draft sequence of the Neandertal genome. *Science 328* (5979), 710–722.

Greymorning, S. N. (2001). Reflections on the Arapaho Language Project or, when Bambi spoke Arapaho and other tales of Arapaho language revitalization efforts. In K. Hale & L. Hinton, *The green book of language revitalization in practice* (pp. 287–297). New York: Academic Press.

Griffin, D., & Fitzpatrick, D. (2009, September 1). Donor says he got thousands for his kidney. *CNNWorld.com.* http://articles.cnn.com/2009-09-01/world/blackmarket.organs_1_kidney-transplants-kidney-donor-kidney-specialist?_s=PM:WORLD (retrieved June 10, 2012)

Grivetti, L. E. (2005). From aphrodisiac to health food: A cultural history of chocolate. *Karger Gazette* (68).

Gurchiek, K. (2012). Survey finds significant erosion in engagement around the world. *Society for Human Resource Management.* www.weknownext.com/workforce/survey-finds-significant-erosion-in-engagement-around-globe (retrieved October 1, 2012)

Haglund, W. D., Conner, M., & Scott, D. D. (2001). The archaeology of contemporary mass graves. *Historical Archaeology 35* (1), 57–69.

Hall, E. T. (1963). A system for the notation of proxemic behavior. *American Anthropologist 65,* 1003–1026.

Hall, E. T. (1990). *The hidden dimension.* New York: Anchor.

Hammer M. F., et al. (2012). Genetic evidence for archaic admixture in Africa. *Proceedings of the American Academy of Sciences 108* (37), 15123–15128.

Hanson, A. (1989). The making of the Maori: Culture invention and its logic. *American Anthropologist 91* (4), 890–902.

Harding, S. F. (2001). *The book of Jerry Falwell: Fundamentalist language and politics.* Princeton, NJ: Princeton University Press.

Hardy, K., et al. (2012). Neanderthal medics? Evidence for food, cooking, and medicinal plants entrapped in dental calculus. *Naturwissenschaften 99* (8), 617–626.

Harner, M. J. (Ed.). (1973). *Hallucinogens and shamanism.* New York: Oxford University Press.

Harner, M. J. (1980). *The way of the shaman: A guide to power and healing.* San Francisco: Harper & Row.

Harner, M. J. (1984). *The Jivaro: People of the sacred waterfalls.* Berkeley: University of California Press.

Harner, M. J. (2013). *Cave and cosmos: Shamanic encounters with spirits and heavens.* Berkeley: North Atlantic Books.

Harner, M. J., & Harner, S. (2000). Core practices in the shamanic treatment of illness. *Shamanism 13* (1&2), 19–30.

Harpending, H., & Cochran, G. (2002). In our genes. *Proceedings of the National Academy of Sciences, USA 99* (1), 10–12.

Harris, M. (1979). *Cultural materialism: The struggle for a science of culture.* New York: Random House.

Harris, M. (1989). *Cows, pigs, wars, and witches: The riddles of culture.* New York: Vintage/Random House.

Harrison, K. D. (2002). Naming practices and ethnic identity in Tuva. *Proceedings of the Chicago Linguistics Society 35* (2).

Harvati, K., Frost, S. R., & McNulty, K. P. (Eds.). (2008). Neandertals revisited: New approaches and perspectives. Dordrecht (Netherlands): Springer.

Harvey, F. (2012, September 24). Trafigura lessons have not been learned, report warns. *The Guardian.* www.guardian.co.uk/environment/2012/sep/25/trafigura-lessons-toxic-waste-dumping (retrieved October 3, 2012)

Hasnain, M. (2005, October 27). Cultural approach to HIV/AIDS harm reduction in Muslim countries. *Harm Reduction Journal 2,* 23.

Hatton, T. J., & Bray, B. E. (2010). Long run trends in the heights of European men, 19th-20th centuries. *Economics and Human Biology 8* (3), 405–413.

Haviland, W. A., & Power, M. W. (1994). *The original Vermonters: Native inhabitants, past and present* (2nd ed.). Hanover, NH: University Press of New England.

Hawkes, K., O'Connell, J. F., & Blurton Jones, N. G. (1997). Hadza women's time allocation, offspring, provisioning, and the evolution of long postmenopausal life spans. *Current Anthropology 38,* 551–577.

Hawks, J. (2006, July 21). Neandertal Genome Project. http://johnhawks.net/weblog

Hawks, J. (2012). Dynamics of genetic and morphological varieties with Neandertals. *Journal of Anthropological Sciences 90,* 1–17.

Hawks, J. (n.d.). Weblog: Paleoanthropology, genetics, and evolution. http://johnhawks.net/taxonomy/term/376 (retrieved December 6, 2012)

Hawks, J. D., & Wolpoff, M. H. (2001). The accretion model of Neandertal evolution. *Evolution 55* (7), 1474–1485.

Heitzman, J., & Wordem, R. L. (Eds.). (2006). *India: A country study* (sect. 2, 5th ed.). Washington, DC: Federal Research Division, Library of Congress.

Helmuth, H. (1983). Anthropometry and the secular trend in growth of Canadians. *Zeitschrift für Morphologie und Anthropologie 74* (1), 75–90.

Henry, A. G., Brooks, A. S., & Piperno, D. R. (2011). Microfossils in calculus demonstrate consumption of plants and cooked foods in Neanderthal diets (Shanidar III, Iraq; Spy I and II, Belgium). *Proceedings of the National Academy of Sciences 108* (2), 486–491.

Henry, S., & Porter, D. (2011, October 27). Levy Izhak Rosenbaum pleads guilty to selling black market kidneys. *Huffingtonpost.com.* www.huffingtonpost.com/2011/10/27/levy-izhak-rosenbaum-plea_n_1035624.html (retrieved June 10, 2012)

Herdt, G. H. (1993). Semen transactions in Sambia culture. In D. N. Suggs & A. W. Mirade (Eds.), *Culture and human sexuality* (pp. 298–327). Pacific Grove, CA: Brooks/Cole.

Higham, T., et al. (2012). Testing models for the beginnings of the Aurignacian and the advent of figurative art and music: The radiocarbon chronology of Geißenklösterle. *Journal of Human Evolution 62* (6), 664–676.

Himmelfarb, E. J. (2000, January/February). First alphabet found in Egypt. Newsbrief. *Archaeology 53* (1).

Hitchcock, R. K., & Enghoff, M. (2004). *Capacity-building of first people of the Kalahari, Botswana: An evaluation.* Copenhagen: International Work Group for Indigenous Affairs.

"HIV & AIDS information from avert.org." www.avert.org.

Hodgson, A. (2012). Special report: Income inequality rising across the globe. *Euromonitor International.* http://blog.euromonitor.com/2012/03/special-report-income-inequality-rising-across-the-globe.html (retrieved October 1, 2012)

Holmes, L. D. (2000). "Paradise Bent" (film review). *American Anthropologist 102* (3), 604–605.

Hopkin, M. (2007, February 22). Chimps make spears to catch dinner. *Nature.* doi:10.1038/news070219–11

Hoquet, T. (2007). Buffon: From natural history to the history of nature? *Biological Theory: Integrating Development, Evolution, and Cognition 2* (4), 413–419.

Horst, H., & Miller, D. (2006). *The cell phone: An anthropology of communication.* New York: Berg.

Hostetler, J. A., & Huntington, G. E. (1992). *Amish children: Education in the family, school, and community* (2nd ed.). New York: Harcourt, Brace & Jovanovich.

Hrdy, S. B. (1999). Body fat and birth control. *Natural History 108* (8), 88.

Hsiaotung, F. (1939). *Peasant life in China.* London: Kegan Paul.

Hublin, J.-J. (2009). The origin of Neandertals. *Proceedings of the National Academy of Sciences 106* (38), 16022–16027.

The Hunger Project. (2011). www.thp.org (retrieved October 1, 2012)

Huxley, J. (1942). *Evolution: The modern synthesis.* London: Allen & Unwin.

Huxley, T. H. (1863). *Evidence as to man's place in nature.* London: Williams & Norgate.

Indriati, E., Swisher C. C., Lepre, C., Quinn, R. L., Surivanto R. A. (2011). The age of the 20 meter Solo River Terrace, Java, Indonesia and the Survival of Homo erectus in Asia. PLoS One 6 (6), e21562.

Ingmanson, E. J. (1998). Comment. *Current Anthropology 39,* 409.

International Telecommunication Union. (2012). 2011 ICT facts and figures. www.itu.int/ITU-D/ict/facts/2011/material/ICTFactsFigures2011.pdf (retrieved June 4, 2012)

Internet World Stats: Usage and Population Statistics. www.internetworldstats.com (retrieved June 4, 2012)

"Interview with Laura Nader." (2000, November). *California Monthly.*

Irvine, M. (1999, November 24). Mom-and-pop stores grow rare. *Burlington Free Press.*

Itaborahy, P. L. (2012). State-sponsored homophobia: A world survey of laws criminalising same-sex sexual activity between consenting adults. Brussels: International Lesbian, Gay, Bisexual, Trans and Intersex Association. http://old.ilga.org/Statehomophobia/ILGA_State_Sponsored_Homophobia_2012.pdf

"Italy–German verbal war hots up." (2003, July 9). Reuters. *Deccan Herald.* http://archive.deccanherald.com/deccanherald/july09/f4.asp (retrieved July 31, 2012)

Jablonski, N. G., & Chaplin. G. (2002). Skin deep. *Scientific American 287* (4), 74–81.

Jablonski, N. G., & Chaplin. G. (2012). Human skin pigmentation as an adaptation to UV radiation. *Proceedings of the National Academy of Sciences 107* (suppl. 2), 8962–8968.

Jacobs, S. E. (1994). Native American two-spirits. *Anthropology Newsletter 35* (8), 7.

Johansen, B. E. (2002). The Inuit's struggle with dioxins and other organic pollutants. *American Indian Quarterly 26* (3), 479–490.

Johnson, D. (1991, April 9). Polygamists emerge from secrecy, seeking not just peace but respect. *New York Times,* A22.

Johnson, N. B. (1984). Sex, color, and rites of passage in ethnographic research. *Human Organization 43* (2), 108–120.

Jolly, A. (1991). Thinking like a vervet. *Science 251,* 574.

Jones, S. (2005). Transhumance re-examined. *Journal of the Royal Anthropological Institute 11* (4), 841–842.

Kaiser, J. (2011, May 4). 10 billion plus: Why world population projections were too low. *Science Insider.* http://news.sciencemag.org/scienceinsider/2011/05/10-billion-plus-why-world-population.html (retrieved October 1, 2012)

Karkanas, P., et al. (2007). Evidence for habitual use of fire at the end of the Lower Paleolithic: Site-formation processes at Qesem Cave, Israel. *Journal of Human Evolution 53,* 197–212.

Keesing. R. M. (1992). Some problems in the study of Oceanic religion. *Anthropologica 34* (2), 231–246.

Kehoe, A. (2000). *Shamans and religion: An anthropological exploration in critical thinking.* Prospect Heights, IL: Waveland Press.

Keiser, L. (1991). *Friend by day, enemy by night: Organized vengeance in a Kohistani community.* Fort Worth: Holt, Rinehart & Winston.

Kelly, T. L. (2006). *Sadhus, the great renouncers.* Photography exhibit, Indigo Gallery, Naxal, Kathmandu, Nepal. www.asianart.com/exhibitions/sadhus/index.html (retrieved August 1, 2012)

Kennickell, A. B. (2003, November). *A rolling tide: Changes in the distribution of wealth in the U.S. 1989–2001.* Washington, DC: Federal Reserve Board/Levy Economics Institute.

Kidder, T. (2003). *Mountains beyond mountains: The quest of Dr. Paul Farmer, a man who would cure the world.* New York: Random House.

Kilcullen, D. (2007, May 12). Religion and insurgency. *Small Wars Journal.* http://smallwarsjournal.com/blog/religion-and-insurgency (retrieved August 1, 2012)

Kirkpatrick, R. C. (2000). The evolution of human homosexual behavior. *Current Anthropology 41*, 384.

Kluckhohn, C. (1944). Navajo witchcraft. *Papers of the Peabody Museum of American Archaeology and Ethnology 22* (2).

Knauft, B. (1991). Violence and sociality in human evolution. *Current Anthropology 32*, 391–409.

Knight, C., Studdert-Kennedy, M., & Hurford, J. (Eds.). (2000). *The evolutionary emergence of language: Social function and the origins of linguistic form.* Cambridge, UK: Cambridge University Press.

Koch, G. (1997). Songs, land rights, and archives in Australia. *Cultural Survival Quarterly 20* (4).

Konner, M., & Worthman, C. (1980). Nursing frequency, gonadal function, and birth spacing among !Kung hunter-gatherers. *Science 207*, 788–791.

Kopenawa, D., & Albert, B. (2010). *La chute du ciel: Paroles d'un chaman Yanomami.* Paris: Terre Humaine, Plon.

Krajick, K. (1998). Greenfarming by the Incas? *Science 281*, 323.

Krause, J., et al. (2007). Neanderthals in Central Asia and Siberia. *Nature 449*, 902–904.

Kraybill, D. B. (2001). *The riddle of Amish culture.* Baltimore: Johns Hopkins University Press.

Kruger, J., et al. (2005, December). Egocentrism over e-mail: Can people communicate as well as they think? *Journal of Personality and Social Psychology 89* (6), 925–936.

Kuefler, M. (2007). The marriage revolution in late antiquity: The Theodosian Code and later Roman marriage law. *Journal of Family History 32* (4), 343–370.

Kumar, S. (2005). Molecular clocks: Four decades of evolution. *Nature Reviews Genetics 6*, 654–662.

Kuper, A. (2008). Changing the subject—about cousin marriage, among other things. *Journal of the Royal Anthropological Institute 14* (4), 717–735.

LaFont, S. (Ed.). (2003). *Constructing sexualities: Readings in sexuality, gender, and culture.* Upper Saddle River, NJ: Prentice-Hall.

Lakoff, R. T. (2004). *Language and woman's place.* M. Bucholtz (Ed.). New York: Oxford University Press.

Laluela-Fox, C., et al. (2007). A melanocortin 1 receptor allele suggests varying pigmentation among Neanderthals. *Science 318* (5855), 1453–1455.

Lasswell, H. D. (1990). *Politics: Who gets what, when, how.* Gloucester, MA: Peter Smith.

Leach, E. (1982). *Social anthropology.* Glasgow: Fontana Paperbacks.

"Leave none to tell the story: Genocide in Rwanda." (2004). www.hrw.org/legacy/reports/1999/rwanda/ (retrieved August 28, 2012)

Leavitt, G. C. (1990). Sociobiological explanations of incest avoidance: A critical review of evidential claims. *American Anthropologist 92*, 982.

Leclerc-Madlala, S. (2002). Bodies and politics: Healing rituals in the democratic South Africa. In V. Faure (Ed.), *Les cahiers de l'IFAS,* no. 2. Johannesburg: The French Institute.

Lee, R. B., & Daly, R. H. (1999). *The Cambridge encyclopedia of hunters and gatherers.* New York: Cambridge University Press.

Lehman, E. C., Jr. (2002, Fall). Women's path into the ministry. *Pulpit & Pew Research Reports 1*, 4.

Lemelle, A. J. (2007). One drop rule. In G. Ritzer (Ed.), *Blackwell encyclopedia of sociology* (pp. 3265–3266). Malden, MA: Blackwell Press.

Lenhart, A. (2012, March 19). Teens, smartphones & texting. *Pew Internet & American Life Project.* http://pewinternet.org/Reports/2012/Teens-and-smartphones.aspx (retrieved August 23, 2012)

Levine, N. E., & Silk, J. B. (1997). Why polyandry fails. *Current Anthropology 38*, 375–398.

Levine, R. A. (2007). Ethnographic studies of childhood: A historical overview. *American Anthropologist 109* (2), 247–260.

Lévi-Strauss, C. (1952). *Race and history.* Paris: UNESCO.

Lévi-Strauss, C. (1955). *Tristes tropiques.* Paris: Librarie Plon.

Lévi-Strauss, C. (1963). The sorcerer and his magic. In *Structural anthropology.* New York: Basic Books. (orig. 1958)

Lewin, R. (1987). Four legs bad, two legs good. *Science 235*, 969.

Lewis-Williams, J. D. (1990). *Discovering southern African rock art.* Cape Town & Johannesburg: David Philip.

Li, X., Harbottle, G., Zhang, J., & Wang, C. (2003). The earliest writing? Sign use in the seventh millennium BC at Jiahu, Henan Province, China. *Antiquity 77*, 31–44.

Lindenbaum, S. (2004). Thinking about cannibalism. *Annual Review of Anthropology 33*, 475–498.

Lindstrom, L. (1993). *Cargo cult: Strange stories of desire from Melanesia and beyond.* Honolulu: University of Hawaii Press.

Linnaeus, C. (1735). *The system of nature.* www.linnaeus.uu.se/online/animal/1_1.html

Linnaeus, C. (1758). *Systema naturae per regna tria naturae, secundum classes, ordines, genera, species, cum characteribus, differentiis, synonymis, locis* (10th rev. ed.). Stockholm: Laurentii Salvii.

Linnekin, J. (1990). *Sacred queens and women of consequence: Rank, gender, and colonialism in the Hawaiian Islands.* Ann Arbor: University of Michigan Press.

Little, K. L. (1973). *African women in town: An aspect of Africa's social revolution* (pp. 58–62). New York: Cambridge University Press.

Littlewood, R. (2004). Commentary: Globalization, culture, body image, and eating disorders. *Culture, Medicine, and Psychiatry 28* (4), 597–602.

Liu, J. (2007). *Gender and work in urban China: Women workers of the unlucky generation.* London: Routledge.

Living Tongues. www.livingtongues.org (retrieved June 4, 2012)

Lloyd, C. B. (Ed.). (2005). *Growing up global: The changing transitions to adulthood in developing countries.* Washington, DC: National Academies Press.

Lock, A. (1980). *The guided reinvention of language.* New York: Academic Press.

Lock, M. (2001). *Twice dead: Organ transplants and the reinvention of death.* Berkeley: University of California Press.

Louie, A. (2004). *Chineseness across borders: Renegotiating Chinese identities in China and the United States.* Durham & London: Duke University Press.

Luhrmann, T. M. (2001). *Of two minds: An anthropologist looks at American psychiatry.* New York: Vintage.

Lurie, N. O. (1973). Action anthropology and the American Indian. In *Anthropology and the American Indian: A symposium.* San Francisco: Indian Historical Press.

Mair, L. (1957). *An introduction to social anthropology.* London: Oxford University Press.

Malinowski, B. (1945). *The dynamics of culture change.* New Haven, CT: Yale University Press.

Malinowski, B. (1961). *Argonauts of the western Pacific.* New York: Dutton.

Marcus, G. (1995). Ethnography in/of the world system: The emergence of multi-sited ethnography. *Annual Review of Anthropology 24*, 95–117.

Martin, E. (1999). Flexible survivors. *Anthropology News 40* (6), 5–7.

Martin, E. (2009). *Bipolar expeditions: Mania and depression in American culture.* Princeton, NJ: Princeton University Press.

Mason, J. A. (1957). *The ancient civilizations of Peru.* Baltimore: Penguin Books.

Mathieu, C. (2003). *A history and anthropological study of the ancient kingdoms of the Sino-Tibetan borderland—Naxi and Mosuo.* New York: Mellen.

McCaskill, C., Lucas, C., Bayley, R., & Hill, J. (2012). *The hidden treasure of Black ASL: Its history and structure* (with contributions from J. C. Hill, R. Dummet-King, P. Baldwin, & R. Hogue). Washington, DC: Gallaudet University Press.

McDermott, R. (2011, April 1). Polygamy: More common than you think. *Wall Street Journal.* http://online.wsj.com/article/SB10001424052748703806304576234551596322690.html (retrieved October 7, 2012)

McDonald's. (2012). www.aboutmcdonalds.com (retrieved September 29, 2012)

McFate, M. (2007). *Role and effectiveness of socio-cultural knowledge for counterinsurgency.* Alexandria, VA: Institute for Defense Analysis.

McGrew, W. C. (2000). Dental care in chimps. *Science 288*, 1747.

McKenna, J. J., & McDade, T. (2005, June). Why babies should never sleep alone: A review of the co-sleeping controversy in relation to SIDS, bedsharing, and breastfeeding. *Pediatric Respiratory Reviews 6* (2), 134–152.

Mead, A. T. P. (1996). Genealogy, sacredness, and the commodities market. *Cultural Survival Quarterly 20* (2).

Mead, M. (1960). Anthropology among the sciences. *American Anthropologist 63*, 475–482.

Mead, M. (1963). *Sex and temperament in three primitive societies* (3rd ed). New York: Morrow. (orig. 1935)

Mead, M., & Métraux, R. (Eds.). (1953). *The study of culture at a distance.* Chicago: University of Chicago Press.

Medicine, B. (1994). Gender. In M. B. Davis (Ed.), *Native America in the twentieth century.* New York: Garland.

Mendel, G. (1866). Versuche über Pflanzen-Hybriden. *Verh. Naturforsch. Ver. Brünn* 4: 3–47 (in English in 1901, *Journal of the Royal Horticultural Society 26*, 1–32)

Mellars, P. (1989). Major issues in the emergence of modern humans. *Current Anthropology 30*, 356–357.

Merkur, D. (1983). Breath-soul and wind owner: The many and the one in Inuit religion. *American Indian Quarterly 7* (3), 23–39.

Mesghinna, H. M. (1966). Salt mining in Enderta. *Journal of Ethiopian Studies 4* (2).

Métraux, A. (1953). Applied anthropology in government: United Nations. In A. A. Kroeber (Ed.), *Anthropology today: An encyclopedic inventory* (pp. 880–894). Chicago: University of Chicago Press.

Métraux, A. (1957). *Easter Island: A stone-age civilization of the Pacific.* New York: Oxford University Press.

Meyer, J. (2008). Typology and acoustic strategies of whistled languages: Phonetic comparison and perceptual cues of whistled vowels. *Journal of the International Phonetic Association 38*, 69–94.

Meyer, J., & Gautheron, B. (2006). Whistled spech and whistled languages. In K. Brown (Ed.), *Encyclopedia of language & linguistics* (2nd ed., vol. 13, pp. 573–576). Oxford, UK: Elsevier.

Meyer, J., Meunier, F., & Dentel, L. (2007). Identification of natural whistled vowels by non-whistlers. *Proceedings of Interspeech 2007.* Antwerp, Belgium.

Meyer, M., et al. (2012). A high-coverage genome sequence from an archaic Denisovan individual. *Science 338* (6104), 222–226.

Mieth, A., & Bork, H.-R. (2009). Humans, climate or introduced rats—which is to blame for the woodland destruction on prehistoric Rapa Nui (Easter Island)? *Journal of Archaeological Science.* doi:10.1016/j.jas.2009.10.006

Miles, H. (1990). The cognitive foundations for reference in a signing orangutan. In S. Parker & K. Gibson (Eds.), *"Language" and intelligence in monkeys and apes: Comparative developmental perspectives* (pp. 511–539). Cambridge, UK: Cambridge University Press.

Miles, H. (1993). Language and the orangutan: The "old person" of the forest. In P. Cavalieri & P. Singer (Eds.), *The great ape project* (pp. 45–50). New York: St. Martin's Press.

Miles, H. (1999). Symbolic communication with and by great apes. In S. Parker, R. Mitchell, & H. Miles (Eds.), *The mentality of gorillas and orangutans: Comparative perspectives* (pp. 197–210). Cambridge, UK: Cambridge University Press.

Mitchell, W. E. (1973, December). A new weapon stirs up old ghosts. *Natural History Magazine*, 77–84.

Monaghan, L., Hinton, L., & Kephart, R. (1997). Can't teach a dog to be a cat? The dialogue on Ebonics. *Anthropology Newsletter 38* (3), 1, 8, 9.

Montagu, A. (1964). *Man's most dangerous myth: The fallacy of race* (4th ed.). New York: World Publishing.

Morello, C. (2011, May 18). Number of long-lasting marriages in U.S. has risen, Census Bureau reports. *Washington Post.*

Murthy, D. (2011). Emergent digital ethnographic methods for social research. In S. N. Hesse-Biber (Ed.), *The handbook of emergent technologies in social research* (pp. 158–179). New York: Oxford University Press.

Nader, L. (Ed.). (1996). *Naked science: Anthropological inquiry into boundaries, power, and knowledge.* New York: Routledge.

Nader, L. (1997). Controlling processes: Tracing the dynamics of power. Current Anthropology 38, 715–717.

Nader, L. (2002). *The life of the law: Anthropological projects.* Berkeley: University of California Press.

Nanda, S. (1992). Arranging a marriage in India. In P. R. DeVita (Ed.), *The naked anthropologist* (pp. 139–143). Belmont, CA: Wadsworth.

Nanda, S. (1999). *Neither man nor woman: The hijras of India.* Belmont, CA: Wadsworth.

Nash, J. (1976). Ethnology in a revolutionary setting. In M. A. Rynkiewich & J. P. Spradley (Eds.), *Ethics and anthropology: Dilemmas in fieldwork.* New York: Wiley.

Nast, H. J. (2005). *Concubines and power: Five hundred years in a northern Nigerian palace.* Minneapolis: University of Minnesota Press.

Natadecha-Sponsal, P. (1993). The young, the rich and the famous: Individualism as an American cultural value. In P. R. DeVita & J. D. Armstrong (Eds.), *Distant mirrors: America as a foreign culture* (pp. 46–53). Belmont, CA: Wadsworth.

Natural Resources Defense Council. (2005, March 25). Healthy milk, healthy baby: Chemical pollution and mother's milk. www.nrdc.org/breastmilk/ (retrieved October 3, 2012)

Nazzal-Batayneh, M. (2005). Nauru: An environment destroyed and international law. www.lawanddevelopment .org/articles/nauru.html (retrieved October 3, 2012)

Nesbitt, L. M. (1935). *Hell-hole of creation.* New York: Knopf.

Nettle, B. (2005). *The study of ethnomusicology: Thirty-one issues and concepts.* Chicago: University of Illinois Press.

"New ILO global report on child labor." (2010, May 8). International Labour Organization. www.ilocarib.org.tt/ index.php?option=com_content&view= article&id=1363:new-ilo-global-report-on -child-labour&catid=214:2010-news& Itemid=1209 (retrieved August 7, 2012)

Newport, F. (2012). In U.S., 46% hold creationist view of human origins. Highly religious Americans most likely to believe in creationism. *Gallup.* www. gallup.com/poll/155003/hold-creation- ist-view-human-origins.aspx (retrieved December 5, 2012)

Nietschmann, B. (1987). The third world war. *Cultural Survival Quarterly 11* (3), 1–16.

Noack, T. (2001). Cohabitation in Norway: An accepted and gradually more regulated way of living. *International Journal of Law, Policy, and the Family 15* (1), 102–117.

Nye, J. (2002). *The paradox of American power: Why the world's only superpower can't go it alone.* New York: Oxford University Press.

O'Barr, W. M., & Conley, J. M. (1993). When a juror watches a lawyer. In W. A. Haviland & R. J. Gordon (Eds.), *Talking about people* (2nd. ed., pp. 42–45). Mountain View, CA: Mayfield.

Oboler, R. S. (1980). Is the female husband a man? Woman/woman marriage among the Nandi of Kenya. *Ethnology 19*, 69–88.

O'Carroll, E. (2008, June 27). Spain to grant some human rights to apes. *Christian Science Monitor.*

Office of the United Nations Higher Commissioner for Human Rights, Committee on the Elimination of Racial Discrimination, India. (2007, March). Consideration of state reports. www2.ohchr.org/english/bod- ies/cerd/cerds70.htm (retrieved August 25, 2012)

Offiong, D. A. (1999). Traditional healers in the Nigerian health care delivery system and the debate over integrating traditional and scientific medicine. *Anthropological Quarterly 72* (3), 118–130.

Okonjo, K. (1976). The dual-sex political system in operation: Igbo women and community politics in midwestern Nigeria. In N. Hafkin & E. Bay (Eds.), *Women in Africa.* Stanford, CA: Stanford University Press.

Olivier, J. G. L., Janssens-Maenhout, G., & Peters, J. A. H. W. (2012). *Trends in global CO₂ emissions.* The Hague: PBL Netherlands Environmental Assessment Agency. http://edgar.jrc. ec.europa.eu/CO2REPORT2012.pdf (retrieved November 7, 2012)

O'Mahoney, K. (1970). The salt trade. *Journal of Ethiopian Studies 8* (2).

One Earth Future Foundation. (2012). *The economic cost of Somali piracy 2011.* http://oceansbeyondpiracy.org/ sites/default/files/economic_cost_of_ piracy_2011_summary.pdf (retrieved August 28)

"111th Canton Fair." (2012). *Live Trading News.* www.livetradingnews. com/111th-canton-fair-74669.htm#. UCKSrcgsAch (retrieved August 8, 2012)

Orlando, L., et al. (6 June 2006). Correspondence: Revisiting Neandertal diversity with a 100,000 year old mtDNA sequence. *Current Biology 16*, 400–402.

Ortiz, I., & Cummins, M. (2011). Global inequality: Beyond the bottom billion—A rapid review of income distribution in 141 countries. *UNICEF.* www.unicef.org/ socialpolicy/index_58230.html (retrieved October 1, 2012)

Ottenheimer, M. (1996). *Forbidden relatives: The American myth of cousin marriage.* Champaign: University of Illinois Press.

Paredes, J. A., & Purdum, E. D. (1990). "Bye, bye Ted. . .". *Anthropology Today 6* (2), 9.

Parés, J. M., et al. (2000). On the age of hominid fossils at the Sima de los Huesos, Sierra de Atapuerca, Spain: Paleomagnetic evidence. *American Journal of Physical Anthropology 111*, 451–461.

Parry, W. (2011, March 17). Recent heat waves likely warmest since 1500 in Europe. www.livescience.com/13296- european-russia-heat-waves-climate- change.html (retrieved November 8, 2012)

Patterson, F. G. P., & Gordon, W. (2002). Twenty-seven years of Project Koko and Michael. In B. Galdikas et al. (Eds.), *All apes great and small: Chimpanzees, bonobos, and gorillas* (vol. 1, pp. 165–176). New York: Kluwer Academic.

Pearson, V., Phillips, M. R., He, F., & Ji, H. (2002). Attempted suicide among young rural women in the People's Republic of China: Possibilities for prevention. *Suicide and Life-Threatening Behavior 32* (4), 359–369.

Pease, T. (2000, Spring). Taking the third side. *Andover Bulletin*.

Pelto, P. J. (1973). *The snowmobile revolution: Technology and social change in the Arctic*. Menlo Park, CA: Cummings.

Pew Research Center, Pew Forum on Religion & Public Life. (2011). The future of the global Muslim population: Projections for 2010–2030. www.pewforum.org/The-Future-of-the-Global-Muslim-Population.aspx (retrieved September 17, 2012)

Pew Research Center, Pew Forum on Religion & Public Life. (2011a). Global survey of evangelical Protestant leaders. www.pewforum.org/Christian/Evangelical-Protestant-Churches/Global-Survey-of-Evangelical-Protestant-Leaders.aspx#evangelical (retrieved December 5, 2012)

Pew Research Center, Pew Forum on Religion & Public Life. (2012, October 9). "Nones" on the rise: One-in-five adults have no religious affiliation. www.pewforum.org/Unaffiliated/nones-on-the-rise.aspx#_ftn3 (retrieved October 23, 2012)

Pike, A. W. G., et al. (2012). U-series dating of Paleolithic art in 11 caves in Spain. Science 336, 1409–1413.

Pink, S. (2001). *Doing visual ethnography: Images, media, and representation in research*. Thousand Oaks, CA: Sage.

Plattner, S. (1989). Markets and market places. In S. Plattner (Ed.), *Economic anthropology*. Stanford, CA: Stanford University Press.

Polanyi, K. (1968). The economy as instituted process. In E. E. LeClair Jr. & H. K. Schneider (Eds.), *Economic anthropology: Readings in theory and analysis* (pp. 127–138). New York: Holt, Rinehart & Winston.

Pollan, M. (2008). *In defense of food: An eater's manifesto*. New York: Penguin Books.

Pollock, N. J. (1995). Social fattening patterns in the Pacific—the positive side of obesity. A Nauru case study. In I. DeGarine & N. J. Pollock (Eds.), *Social aspects of obesity* (pp. 87–109). London: Routledge.

Pospisil, L. (1963). *The Kapauku Papuans of West New Guinea*. New York: Holt, Rinehart & Winston.

Powdermaker, H. (1939). *After freedom: A cultural study in the Deep South*. New York: Viking.

Poyatos, F. (2002). *Nonverbal communication across disciplines* (3 vols.). Amsterdam: John Benjamins.

Price, D. H. (2011). How the CIA and Pentagon harnessed anthropological research during the Second World War and Cold War with little critical notice. *Journal of Anthropological Research 67* (3), 333–356.

Prins, H. E. L. (1994). Neo-traditions in Native communities: Sweat lodge and Sun Dance among the Micmac today. In W. Cowan (Ed.), *Proceedings of the 25th Algonquian conference* (pp. 383–394). Ottawa: Carleton University Press.

Prins, H. E. L. (1996). *The Mi'kmaq: Resistance, accommodation, and cultural survival*. New York: Harcourt Brace.

Prins, H. E. L. (1998). Book review of Schuster, C., & Carpenter, E. *American Anthropologist 100* (3), 841.

Prins, H. E. L. (2002). Visual media and the primitivist perplex: Colonial fantasies and indigenous imagination in North America. In F. Ginsburg, L. Abu-Lughod, & B. Larkin (Eds.), *Media worlds: Anthropology on new terrain* (pp. 58–74). Berkeley: University of California Press.

Prins, H. E. L. (2010). The atlatl as combat weapon in 17th-century Amazonia: Tapuya Indian warriors in Dutch colonial Brazil. *The Atlatl 23* (2), 1–3.

Prins, H. E. L., & Krebs, E. (2006). Toward a land without evil: Alfred Métraux as UNESCO anthropologist 1948–1962. In *60 years of UNESCO history. Proceedings of the international symposium in Paris, 16–18 November 2005*. Paris: UNESCO.

Prins, H. E. L., & McBride, B. (2012). Upside down: Arctic realities & indigenous art (museum review essay). *American Anthropologist 114* (2), 359–364.

Pruetz, J. D., & Bertolani, P. (2007, March 6). Savanna chimpanzees, *Pan troglodytes verus*, hunt with tools. *Current Biology 17*, 412–417.

Quinn, N. (2005). Universals of child rearing. *Anthropological Theory 5*, 475–514.

Radcliffe-Brown, A. R. (1931). Social organization of Australian tribes. *Oceana Monographs 1*, 29.

Radelet, M. L., & Lacock, T. L. (2009). Do executions lower homicide rates? The views of leading criminologists. *Journal of Criminal Law and Criminology 99* (2), 489.

Ralston, C., & Thomas, N. (Eds.). (1987). Sanctity and power: Gender in Polynesian history. *Journal of Pacific History* (special issue) *22* (3–4).

Ramos, A. R. (1987). Reflecting on the Yanomami: Ethnographic images and the pursuit of the exotic. *Current Anthropology 2* (3), 284–304.

Rappaport, R. A. (1969). Ritual regulation of environmental relations among a New Guinea people. In A. P. Vayda (Ed.), *Environment and cultural behavior* (pp. 181–201). Garden City, NY: Natural History Press.

Rathje, W., & Murphy, C. (2001). *Rubbish!: The archaeology of garbage*. Tucson: University of Arizona Press.

Rathke, L. (1989). To Maine for apples. *Salt Magazine 9* (4), 24–47.

Reich, D., et al. (2010). Genetic history of an archaic hominin group from Denisova Cave in Siberia. *Nature 468*, 1053–1060.

Remarque, E. M. (1929). *All quiet on the western front*. Boston: Little, Brown.

Reynolds, V. (1994). Primates in the field, primates in the lab. *Anthropology Today 10* (2), 4.

Ribeiro, G. L. (2009). Non-hegemonic globalizations: Alternative transnational processes and agents. *Anthropological Theory 9* (3), 297–329.

Richards, P. (1995). Local understandings of primates and evolution: Some Mende beliefs concerning chimpanzees. In R. Corbey & B. Theunissen (Eds.), *Ape, man, apeman: Changing views since 1600* (pp. 265–273). Leiden: Department of Prehistory, Leiden University.

Rideout, V. J., Foehr, U. G., & Roberts, D. F. (2010, January). *Generation M²: Media in the lives of 8- to18-year-olds*. A Kaiser Family Foundation Study. Menlo Park, CA: Henry J. Kaiser Family Foundation. www.kff.org/entmedia/upload/8010.pdf (retrieved August 25, 2012)

Ritzer, G. (1983). The McDonaldization of society, *Journal of American Culture 6* (1), 100–107.

Ritzer, G. (2007). *The coming of post-industrial society* (2nd ed.). New York: McGraw-Hill.

Robben, A. C. G. M. (2007). Fieldwork identity: Introduction. In A. C. G. M. Robben & J. A. Sluka (Eds.), *Ethnographic fieldwork: An anthropological reader*. Malden, MA: Blackwell Press.

Robben, A. C. G. M., & Sluka, J. A. (Eds.). (2007). *Ethnographic fieldwork: An anthropological reader*. Malden, MA: Blackwell Press.

Rochat, P. (2001). Origins of self-concept. In G. Bremner & A. Fogel (Eds.), *Blackwell handbook of infant development* (pp. 191–212). Malden, MA: Blackwell Press.

Roebroeks, W., & Villa, P. (2011). On the earliest evidence for habitual use of fire in Europe. *Proceedings of the National Academy of Sciences, USA 108*, 5210–5014.

Rogers, A. R., Iltis, D., & Wooding, S. (2004). Genetic variation at the MC1R locus and the time since loss of human body hair. *Current Anthropology 45* (1), 105–108.

Rosaldo, M. Z. (1980). *Knowledge and passion: Ilongot notions of self & social life* (Cambridge Studies in Cultural Systems). New York: Cambridge University Press.

Roscoe, W. (1991). *Zuni man-woman*. Albuquerque: University of New Mexico Press.

Rudel, T. K., Bates, D., & Machinguiashi, R. (2002). Ecologically noble Amerindians? Cattle ranching and cash cropping among Shuar and colonists in Ecuador. *Latin American Research Review 37* (1), 144–159.

Rupert, J. L., & Hochachka, P. W. (2001). The evidence for hereditary factors contributing to high altitude adaptation in Andean natives: A review. *High Altitude Medicine & Biology 2* (2), 235–256.

Rymer, R. (1994). *Genie: A scientific tragedy*. New York: HarperCollins.

Salzman, P. C. (1967). Political organization among nomadic peoples. *Proceedings of the American Philosophical Society 111*, 115–131.

Sanday, P. R. (1981). *Female power and male dominance: On the origins of sexual inequality*. Cambridge, UK: Cambridge University Press.

Sangree, W. H. (1965). The Bantu Tiriki of western Kenya. In J. L. Gibbs Jr. (Ed.), *Peoples of Africa* (pp. 69–72). New York: Holt, Rinehart & Winston.

Sanjek, R. (1990). On ethnographic validity. In R. Sanjek (Ed.), *Field notes*. Ithaca, NY: Cornell University Press.

Sankararaman, S., Patterson, N., Li, H., Pääbo, S., & Reich, D. (2012). The date of interbreeding between Neandertals and modern humans. *PLoS Genetics 8* (10), e1002947. doi:10.1371/journal.pgen.1002947

Schaeffer, S. B., & Furst, P. T. (Eds.). (1996). *People of the peyote: Huichol Indian history, religion, and survival.* Albuquerque: University of New Mexico Press.

Schilling, C. (2012, August 20). Love, American style: Polygamy gets sizzle. *WorldNetDaily.* www.wnd.com/2012/08/love-american-style-polygamy-gets-sizzle/ (retrieved October 7, 2012)

Schilt, K., & Westbrook, L. (2009, August). Doing gender, doing heteronormativity: "Gender normals," transgender people, and the social maintenance of heterosexuality. *Gender & Society 23* (4), 440–464.

Schoepfle, M. (2001). Ethnographic resource inventory and the National Park Service. *Cultural Resource Management 5*, 1–7.

Schuster, C., & Carpenter, E. (1996). *Patterns that connect: Social symbolism in ancient and tribal art.* New York: Abrams.

Selinger, B. (2007). The Navajo, psychosis, Lacan, and Derrida. *Texas Studies in Literature and Language 49* (1), 64–100.

Senut, B. et al. (2001). First hominid from the Miocene (Lukeino formation, Kenya). *Comptes Rendus de l'Académie de Sciences, Paris 332*, 137–144.

Seyfarth, R. M., et al. (1980). Monkey responses to three different alarm calls: Evidence for predator classification and semantic communication. *Science 210*, 801–803.

Sharp, G. (1973). *The politics of nonviolent action.* Boston: Extending Horizons Books, Porter Sargent Publishers.

Sharp, G. (2010). *From dictatorship to democracy: A conceptual framework for liberation* (4th ed.). East Boston: Einstein Institution.

Shea, P. J. (2007). Excellent legacies of Abo Bayero. In A. U. Adamu (Ed.), *Chieftaincy and security in Nigeria: Past, present, and future* (pp. i–vi). http://ibrahimshekarau.com/downloads/videos1/books/12.pdf (retrieved August 26, 2012)

Shook, J. R., et al. (Eds.). (2004). *Dictionary of modern American philosophers, 1860–1960.* Bristol, UK: Thoemmes Press.

Shostak, M. (2000). *Nisa: The life and words of a !Kung woman.* Cambridge, MA: Harvard University Press.

Simons, R. C., & Hughes, C. C. (Eds.). (1985). *The culture-bound syndromes: Folk illnesses of psychiatric and anthropological interest.* New York: Springer.

Sivak, M., & Schoettle, B. (2012). Accounting for climate in ranking countries' carbon dioxide emissions. *American Scientist.* www.americanscientist.org/issues/id.15839,y.0,no.,content.true,page.3,css.print/issue.aspx (retrieved November 7, 2012)

Skoglund, P., & Jakobsson, M. (2011, October 31). Archaic human ancestry in East Asia. *Proceedings of the National Academy of Sciences, USA.* www.pnas.org/content/early/2011/10/24/1108181108.full.pdf+html

Skoglund, P., Malström, H., Raghavan, M., Storå, J., Hall, P., Willersley, E., Gilbert, M. T., Götherström, A., & Jakobsson, M. (2012). Origins and genetic legacy of Neolithic farmers and hunter-gatherers in Europe. *Science 336* (6080), 466–469.

Sluka, J. A. (2007). Fieldwork relations and rapport: Introduction. In A. C. G. M. Robben & J. A. Sluka (Eds.), *Ethnographic fieldwork: An anthropological reader.* Malden, MA: Blackwell Press.

Small, M. F. (1997). Making connections. *American Scientist 85*, 503.

Smith, M. D. (2008, September 16). Indian child labor exploited in production of soccer balls. *Huffington Post.* www.aolnews.com/2008/09/16/indian-child-labor-exploited-in-production-of-soccer-balls/ (retrieved August 7, 2012)

Smith, W. W. (2009). *China's Tibet: Autonomy or assimilation?* Lanham, MD: Rowman & Littlefield.

Solecki, R. S. (1977). The implications of the Shanidar Cave Neandertal flower burial. *Annals of the New York Academy of Sciences 293*, 114–124.

Speck, F. G. (1997). *Penobscot man.* Orono: University of Maine Press.

Spencer, R. F. (1984). North Alaska Coast Eskimo. In D. Damas (Ed.), *Arctic: Handbook of North American Indians* (vol. 5, pp. 320–337). Washington, DC: Smithsonian Institution Press.

Stacey, J. (1990). *Brave new families.* New York: Basic Books.

Stanford, C. B. (2001). *Chimpanzee and red colobus: The ecology of predator and prey.* Cambridge, MA: Harvard University Press.

Steady, F. C. (2001). *Women and the Amistad connection, Sierra Leone Krio Society.* Rochester, VT: Schenkman.

Stein, R., & St. George, D. (2009, May 13). Babies increasingly born to unwed mothers. *Washington Post.*

Stenseth, N. C., & Voje, K. L. (2009). Easter Island: Climate change might have contributed to past cultural and societal changes. *Climate Research 39*, 111–114.

Stockholm International Peace Research Institute. (2012). www.sipri.org/ (retrieved November 8, 2012)

Stolberg, S. G. (2011, February 16). Shy U.S. intellectual created playbook used in a revolution. *New York Times.* www.nytimes.com/2011/02/17/world/middleeast/17sharp.html?pagewanted=all (retrieved August 28, 2012)

Stone, L. (2005). *Kinship and gender: An introduction* (3rd ed.). Boulder, CO: Westview Press.

Stringer, C. (2012). The status of *Homo heidelbergensis* (Schoetensack 1908). *Evolutionary Anthropology: Issues, News, and Reviews 21* (3), 101–107.

Sturm, R. A. (2009). Molecular genetics of human pigmentation diversity. *Human Molecular Genetics 18*, 9–17.

Suárez-Orozoco, M. M., Spindler, G., & Spindler, L. (1994). *The making of psychological anthropology, II.* Fort Worth: Harcourt Brace.

Swaminathan, M. S. (2000). Science in response to basic human needs. *Science 287*, 425.

Tattersall, I., & Schwartz, J. H. (1999). Hominids and hybrids: The place of Neanderthals in human evolution. *Proceedings of the National Academy of Science 96* (13), 7117–7119.

Teenstra, M. D. (1836). *De Nederlandsche West-Indische Eilanden.* Amsterdam: C. G. Sulpke.

Terashima, H. (1983). Mota and other hunting activities of the Mbuti archers: A socio-ecological study of subsistence technology. *African Studies Monograph* (Kyoto), 71–85.

Than, K. (2010, June 14). World's oldest cave art found—made by Neanderthals? *National Geographic News 6.* http://news.nationalgeographic.com/news/2012/06/120614-neanderthal-cave-paintings-spain-science-pike/

Thomas, E. M. (1994). *The tribe of the tiger: Cats and their culture.* New York: Simon & Schuster.

Timmons, H., & Kumar, H. (2009, July 3). Indian court overturns gay sex ban. *New York Times.*

Trocolli, R. (2005). *Elite status and gender: Women leaders in chiefdom societies of the Southeastern U.S.* PhD dissertation, University of Florida.

Tsai, S.-S. H. (1996). *The eunuchs in the Ming dynasty.* Albany: SUNY Press.

Turnbull, C. M. (1961). *The forest people.* New York: Simon & Schuster.

Turnbull, C. M. (1983a). *Mbuti Pygmies: Change and adaptation.* New York: Holt, Rinehart & Winston.

Turnbull, C. M. (1983b). *The human cycle.* New York: Simon & Schuster.

Turner, T. (1991). Major shift in Brazilian Yanomami policy. *Anthropology Newsletter 32* (5), 1, 46.

"Two Americans are found slain on Jeep journey in Central Java." (1950, April 29). *New York Times.*

Tylor, E. B. (1871). *Primitive culture: Researches into the development of mythology, philosophy, religion, language, art and customs.* London: Murray.

Umar, U. (2008). *Dancing with spirits: Negotiating bissu subjectivity through Adat.* MA thesis, Department of Religious Studies. University of Colorado, Boulder. Ann Arbor, MI: ProQuest.

UNAIDS. (2009). *2009 AIDS epidemic update.* www.unaids.org/en/dataanalysis/epidemiology/2009aidsepidemicupdate/ (retrieved June 28, 2012)

UN Dispatch. (2006, July 26). Study estimates 250,000 active child soldiers. www.undispatch.com/study-estimates-250000-active-child-soldiers (retrieved August 28, 2012)

UNESCO. (1952) The race concept: Results of an inquiry. In *The race question in modern science.* Paris: UNESCO. http://unesdoc.unesco.org/images/0007/000733/073351eo.pdf (retrieved December 13, 2012)

UNESCO Decade for Literacy. www.unesco.org/new/en/education/themes/education-building-blocks/literacy/un-literacy-decade/

UNESCO Institute for Statistics. The official source of literacy data. www.uis.unesco.org/literacy/Pages/default.aspx?SPSLanguage=EN (retrieved June 4, 2012)

United Nations Declaration on the Rights of Indigenous Peoples. (2007). www.un.org/esa/socdev/unpfii/documents/DRIPS_en.pdf (retrieved November 8, 2012)

United Nations Human Settlements Programme. (2003). *The challenge of slums: Global report on human settlement.* London: Earthscan Publications.

United Nations Literacy Decade (2003–2012). UNESCO. www.unesco.org/new/en/education/themes/education-building-blocks/literacy/un-literacy-decade (retrieved June 4, 2012)

United Nations, Universal Declaration of Human Rights. www.un.org/en/documents/udhr/index.shtml (retrieved October 1, 2012)

UN Refugee Agency. (2011, June 20). World Refugee Day: UNHCR report finds 80 per cent of world's refugees in developing countries. www.unhcr.org/4dfb66ef9.html (retrieved September 30, 2012)

Ury, W. L. (1982). *Talk out or walk out: The role and control of conflict in a Kentucky coal mine.* PhD dissertation, Harvard University Press.

Ury, W. L. (1993). *Getting past no: Negotiating your way from confrontation.* New York: Bantam.

Ury, W. L. (1999). *Getting to peace: Transforming conflict at home, at work, and in the world.* New York: Viking.

Ury, W. L. (2002, Winter). A global immune system. *Andover Bulletin.*

Ury, W. L. (2007). *The power of a positive no.* New York: Bantam.

U.S. Census Bureau. (2010). Families and living arrangements. www.census.gov/hhes/families/ (retrieved August 19, 2012)

U.S. Census Bureau, Statistical Abstract. (2012). Births, deaths, marriages, and divorces: Life expectancy. www.census.gov/compendia/statab/cats/births_deaths_marriages_divorces/life_expectancy.html (retrieved August 23, 2012)

U.S. Department of Health and Human Services, Administration on Children, Youth, and Families. (2005). *Child maltreatment 2003.* Washington, DC: U.S. Government Printing Office.

U.S. Department of State, Diplomacy in Action. (2007). China. www.state.gov/j/drl/rls/hrrpt/2007/100518.htm (retrieved October 31, 2012)

Van Allen, J. (1997). Sitting on a man: Colonialism and the lost political institutions of Igbo women. In R. Grinker & C. Steiner (Eds.), *Perspectives on Africa.* Boston: Blackwell Press.

Vance, A. (2012, October 4). Facebook: The making of 1 billion users. *Businessweek.com.* www.businessweek.com/articles/2012-10-04/facebook-the-making-of-1-billion-users (retrieved November 8, 2012)

Van Cott, D. L. (2008). *Radical democracy in the Andes.* Cambridge, UK: Cambridge University Press.

Van den Berghe, P. (1992). The modern state: Nation builder or nation killer? *International Journal of Group Tensions 22* (3), 191–208.

Van Eck, C. (2003). *Purified by blood: Honour killings amongst Turks in the Netherlands.* Amsterdam: Amsterdam University Press.

Van Gennep, A. (1960). *The rites of passage.* Translated by M. Vizedom & G. L. Caffee. Chicago: University of Chicago Press. (orig. 1909)

Van Willigen, J. (1986). *Applied anthropology.* South Hadley, MA: Bergin & Garvey.

Van Willigen, J. (2002). *Applied anthropology: An Introduction.* Westport, CT: Bergin & Garvey.

Venter, J. C. (2007, May 3). The *Time* 100: Scientists and thinkers: Svante Pääbo. *Time.com.* www.time.com/time/specials/2007/time100/article/0,28804,1595326_1595329_1616144,00.html (retrieved December 14, 2012)

Vera, H. (2011). *The social life of measures: Metrication in the United States and Mexico, 1789–2004,* PhD dissertation, Sociology and Historical Studies, New School for Social Research.

Vidya, R. (2002). Karnataka's unabating kidney trade. *Frontline.* www.frontlineonnet.com/fl1907/19070610.htm (retrieved June 10, 2012)

Vitali, S., Glattfelder, J. B., & Battiston, S. (2011). The network of global corporate control. *PloS One 6* (10), e25995. doi:10.1371/journal.pone.0025995

Vogt, E. Z. (1990). *The Zinacantecos of Mexico: A modern Maya way of life* (2nd ed.). Fort Worth: Holt, Rinehart & Winston.

Wallace, A. F. C. (1970). *Culture and personality* (2nd ed.). New York: Random House.

Wallace, E., & Hoebel, E. A. (1952). *The Comanches.* Norman: University of Oklahoma Press.

Weatherford, J. (1988). *Indian givers: How the Indians of the Americas transformed the world.* New York: Ballantine.

Weaver, T. (2002). Gonzalo Aguirre Beltrán: Applied anthropology and indigenous policy. In *The dynamics of applied anthropology in the twentieth century: The Malinowski award papers* (pp. 34–37). Oklahoma City: Society for Applied Anthropology.

Weiner, A. B. (1988). *The Trobrianders of Papua New Guinea.* New York: Holt, Rinehart & Winston.

Wenzel, G. W., & McCartney, A. P. (1996, September). Richard Guy Condon (1952–1995). *Arctic 49* (3), 319–320.

Werner, D. (1990). *Amazon journey.* Englewood Cliffs, NJ: Prentice-Hall.

Wheelersburg, R. P. (1987). New transportation technology among Swedish Sámi reindeer herders. *Arctic Anthropology 24* (2), 99–116.

Whelehan, P. (1985). Review of incest, a biosocial view. *American Anthropologist 87,* 678.

White, D. R. (1988). Rethinking polygyny: Co-wives, codes, and cultural systems. *Current Anthropology 29,* 529–572.

White, M. (2001). *Historical atlas of the twentieth century.* http://users.erols.com/mwhite28/20centry.htm (retrieved August 28, 2012)

White, T., Asfaw, B., Degusta, D., Gilbert, H., Richards, G., Suwa, G., & Howell, F. C. (2003). Pleistocene *Homo sapiens* from the Middle Awash, Ethiopia. *Nature 423,* 742–747.

White, T. D., et al. (2009, October). *Ardipithecus ramidus* and the paleobiology of early hominoids. *Science 326* (5949), 64, 75–86.

Whiting, J. W. M., & Child, I. L. (1953). *Child training and personality: A cross-cultural study.* New Haven, CT: Yale University Press.

Whittaker, J. C. (2010). Weapon trials: The atlatl and experiments in hunting technology. In J. R. Ferguson (Ed.), *Designing experimental research in archaeology: Examining technology through production and use* (pp.195–224). Boulder: University Press of Colorado.

Whyte, A. L. H. (2005). Human evolution in Polynesia. *Human Biology 77* (2), 157–177.

Wilkie, D. S., & Curran, B. (1993). Historical trends in forager and farmer exchange in the Ituri rainforest of northeastern Zaire. *Human Ecology 21* (4), 389–417.

Williams, F. (2005, January 9). Toxic breast milk? *New York Times Magazine.*

Williams, S. (2003). Tradition and change in the sub-Arctic: Sámi reindeer herding in the modern era. *Scandinavian Studies 75* (2), 228–256.

Williamson, R. K. (1995). The blessed curse: Spirituality and sexual difference as viewed by Euramerican and Native American cultures. *The College News 18* (4).

Wills, C. (1994). The skin we're in. *Discover 15* (11), 79.

Winick, C. (Ed.). (1970). *Dictionary of anthropology.* Totowa, NJ: Littlefield, Adams.

Wolf, E. R. (1966). *Peasants.* Englewood Cliffs, NJ: Prentice-Hall.

Wolf, E. R. (1982). *Europe and the people without history.* Berkeley: University of California Press.

Wolf, E. R. (1999a). *Envisioning power: Ideologies of dominance and crisis.* Berkeley: University of California Press.

Wolf, E. R. (1999b). *Peasant wars of the twentieth century* (2nd ed.). Norman: University of Oklahoma Press.

Wolf, E. R., & Hansen, E. C. (1972). *The human condition in Latin America.* New York: Oxford University Press.

Wolf, E. R., & Trager, G. I. (1971). Hortense Powdermaker: 1900–1970. *American Anthropologist 73* (3), 784.

Wolff, P., & Holmes, K. J. (2011). Linguistic relativity. *WIRE's Cognitive Science 2,* 253–265.

Wolpoff, M. (1996). *Australopithecus:* A new look at an old ancestor. *General Anthropology 3* (1), 2.

Wolpoff, M., & Caspari, R. (1997). *Race and human evolution.* New York: Simon & Schuster.

Wolpoff, M. H., Hawks, J., & Caspari, R. (2000). Multiregional, not multiple origins. *American Journal of Physical Anthropology 112,* 129–136.

Wolpoff, M. H., Mannheim, B., Mann, A., Hawks, J., Caspari, R., Rosenberg, K. R., Frayer, D. W., Gill, G. W., & Clark, G. C. (2004). Why not the Neandertals? *World Archaeology 36* (4), 527–546.

Wong, K. (2010). Did Neandertals think like us? *Scientific American 302* (2), 72–75. www.bristol.ac.uk/archanth/staff/zilhao/scientificamericanjune2010.pdf

World Bank. (2012). Migration and remittances. *WorldBank.org.* http://web.worldbank.org/WBSITE/EXTERNAL/NEWS/0,,contentMDK:20648762~pagePK:64257043~piPK:437376~theSitePK:4607,00.html (retrieved October 1, 2012)

World Bank. (2012a). Poverty. www.worldbank.org/en/topic/poverty (retrieved October 1, 2012)

World Commission on Environment & Development. (1987). Our common future. A/42/427. www.un-documents.net/ocf-ov.htm (retrieved September 29, 2012)

World Development Indicators Database. (2012, September 18). Gross domestic product, 2011. *Worldbank.org.* http://databank.worldbank.org/databank/download/GDP.pdf (retrieved October 1, 2012)

World Travel & Tourism Council. (2012). Annual report, 2011. www.wttc.org

World Watch Institute. www.worldwatch.org/

Worsley, P. (1957). *The trumpet shall sound: A study of "cargo" cults in Melanesia.* London: Macgibbon & Kee.

Wrangham, R., & Peterson, D. (1996). *Demonic males.* Boston: Houghton Mifflin.

Wyckoff-Baird, B. (2010, March 19). Indicators from Ju/'hoan Bushmen in Namibia. *Cultural Survival.* www.culturalsurvival.org/ourpublications/csq/article/indicators-juhoan-bushmen-namibia (retrieved October 2, 2012)

Yates, D. (2011). *Archaeological practice and political change: Transitions and transformations in the use of the past in nationalist, neoliberal and indigenous Bolivia.* PhD dissertation, Department of Archaeology, Cambridge, UK: University of Cambridge.

Young, W. C. (2000). Kimball award winner. *Anthropology News 41* (8), 29.

Zilhão, J., et al. (2010). Symbolic use of marine shells and mineral pigments by Iberian Neandertals. *Proceedings of the National Academy of Sciences 107* (3), 1023–1028.